Social Justice and Its Enemies

Social Justice and Its Enemies

Written and Edited by

Thomas Ford Hoult

Schenkman Publishing Company Inc.

HALSTED PRESS DIVISION
JOHN WILEY AND SONS
New York — London — Sydney — Toronto

Photo Credits: Page 50, SANE (Society for a Sane Nuclear Policy)
                  Page 152, from "Poverty and Economic Development in
                  New York City," published by First National City Bank,
                  December, 1968.
                  Page 192, Photo by Bruce Davidson
                  Page 332, Art Young, *The Best of Art Young* (NY: The
                  Vanguard Press, 1936), p. 158, "Robots."
                  Page 441, Art Young, *The Best of Art Young* (NY: The
                  Vanguard Press, 1936), p. 177, "Twas Ever Thus."
                  Page 502, Art Young, *The Best of Art Young* (NY:
                  Vanguard Press, 1936), p. 38, "The Minister"

Distributed solely by Halsted Press, A Division
   of John Wiley & Sons, Inc. New York.

Library of Congress Cataloging in Publication Data

Hoult, Thomas Ford, comp.
   Social justice and its enemies.

   1. United States—Social conditions—Addresses,
essays, lectures.   2. Social problems—Addresses,
essays, lectures.   I. Title.
HN65.H595   1975   309.1'73   74-17373
ISBN 0-470-41530-4
ISBN 0-470-41531-2 (pbk.)

Dedicated to

Gunnar Myrdal

whose life and work
is an inspiring mix
of fine scholarship
and concern for the
human condition

Contents

Contents

ILLUSTRATIONS

A Point of View

This volume has been compiled to illustrate systematically the idea that *social problems are created to the degree that injustice prevails.* This is not a theory of problems; it is too diffuse to qualify as such. But it *is* a broad postulate the systematic illustration of which may help to generate testable theory.

Two questions arise immediately: What is injustice? And what are social problems? Such questions bring us legitimately into the realm of theory since there are a number of important theoretical conceptions of both justice (and its mirror opposite, injustice) and social problems. Among the several provocative theories of justice, that devised by Ginsberg has been adopted for present purposes.*

Professor Ginsberg, a British social anthropologist, asserts that social justice has three critical components:

1. a minimum of arbitrariness, especially of power used arbitrarily.
2. an equitable distribution of the means to well-being.
3. adequate methods to rectify wrong.

Thus, it may be said that justice has three main "enemies" which together constitute injustice: 1) arbitrariness, especially power used arbitrarily, 2) an inequitable distribution of the means to well-being, and 3) inadequate ways of rectifying wrong. These three major aspects of injustice, with particular regard to their relationship to social problems, are illustratively examined in the first three parts of this book.

*Morris Ginsberg, *On Justice in Society* (New York: Cornell University Press, 1965).

But what is a social problem? A standard definition gives us this: A social problem is any collectively remediable situation regarded by a significant number of group members as a threat to one or more of their basic values. However "standard," we depart from such definitions in favor of the following:

> A social problem is any sociocultural phenomenon which prevents a significant number of societal participants from effectively developing and utilizing their full potential.

This definition is derived from the humanistic belief that *every* human has at least latent merit and should have the opportunity to develop to the greatest extent possible consistent with the well-being of others. Humanistically speaking, therefore, the worst social problems are those massive conditions—such as racism, war, poverty, disease, and official indifference to suffering—which repress and destroy countless multitudes.

The suggested definition of social problems, based as it is on the humanistic faith, is an expression of what may be termed sociology in the prophetic mode. It is *sociology* in that it stresses systematic study of social interaction and structure; but, as with prophecy, it also evaluates and, where appropriate, approves or disapproves. It is thus "normative" in the purely sociological sense—i.e., it incorporates a particular standard and makes judgments in terms of that standard.

Sociology in the prophetic mode is often termed "new" or "radical"; when it is humanistic in orientation, it is quite appropriately called *humanistic sociology*. The fundamental role of this type of social science is to provide social analyses such that those striving to create a more humane social order will have enhanced chances of success.

Humanistic sociology's frank ideological commitment stands in sharp contrast to the value-neutrality advocated by "old" sociology. The commitment of new, humanistic sociologists is prompted by two things that seem compelling. First, such sociologists know that a sociology worthy of the name cannot exist in a politically repressive environment, hence they feel a *professional* obligation to participate in building and safeguarding democratic institutions and procedures. Second, they feel that repressive regimes are strengthened when indigenous intellectuals assume a "neutral" political posture; "value neutrality" is thus inadvertent ideological commitment.

The open ideological stance of humanistic sociologists does not imply that they are non-scientific. Indeed, scientific method is here regarded as a primary means for ascertaining what is really going on in the world in contrast to the myths that the powerful like to have the masses believe. But since science can be used for evil as well as good, the humanistic sociologist is characteristically concerned about the nature of research clients. Again, this is unlike the "old" sociology whose practitioners so often assert that their professional role is solely to provide accurate information, not to cast judgment on the uses or users of the information.

The terms "new" and "old" to describe types of sociologists imply an unfortunate degree of invidiousness, especially in connection with the study of social problems. So-called old sociologists, as well as the so-called new, have made many notable contributions to the study of problems. This is particularly the case in recent years when startling technological innovations and growing populations have combined to generate massive problems that threaten the very *existence* of humankind. Such threats have seemed so pressing to some sociologists of late that they have asserted a sociology relevant to the needs of the age is a discipline which concentrates almost solely on social problem situations and conditions such as those depicted in the pages of this volume. These pages imply that human life is in many respects in a sorry state—perhaps even more so than when Samuel Taylor Coleridge observed, in his *Ode to Tranquility*:

Aloof with hermit-eye I scan
The present work of present man—
A wild and dream-like trade of blood and guile,
Too foolish for a tear, too wicked for a smile.

PART 1

Arbitrariness

The word arbitrary *has many related meanings, a number of which are encompassed by the way the word is used in this work. That way is suggested by the following lists:*

<u>Arbitrary</u>

<u>Synonyms</u>	<u>Antonyms</u>
irrational	*fit*
unreasonable	*proper*
random	*applicable*
despotic	*apropos*
capricious	*germane*
lawless	*relevant*
unrelated	*pertinent*
extraneous	*apposite*
alien	*apt*
outlandish	*congruous*

In short, arbitrariness is not in evidence when any phenomenon, relative to some other, is pertinent, relevant, fit or proper. But when any phenomenon is irrational, despotic, capricious, unrelated, and so on, it is arbitrary. And such arbitrariness, whether in the form of despotism, irrationality, or what have you, is very often closely associated with social problems, as indicated in the selections which follow. These selections describe various aspects of four major phenomena in connection with which arbitrariness is particularly evident: war and imperialism, racism, the stigmatized, and red tape.

5

War and Imperialism

Undoubtedly war is the most spectacular example of power used arbitrarily. Even when humane considerations make participation in war a sad necessity, as in the battle against the Nazi legions, there are numerous examples of overreaction, atrocities, and gross maltreatment of innocent civilians. Such deplorable actions are not confined to the enemy; they seem to be an inevitable part of war and militarism everywhere and at all times. This generalization is illustrated by the selections which follow.

We begin with a brief reference to American imperialism. This is followed by Pierre Van Paassen's conclusion that World War I was prolonged by profit considerations. World War II also was marked by deception and horror, as illustrated by American duplicity about Pearl Harbor and the atomic bombing of a Japanese city that had no war industries. In the cold war period following W,W,II the United States and the U.S.S.R. engaged in eyeball-to-eyeball confrontations that frequently threatened to end in an atomic war that would destroy the world.

After the French failed to subdue the Vietnamese in spite of 90 percent financing by the United States, the United States stepped in to help a series of South Vietnam dictators preserve the special privileges which the French had accorded the Mandarin class. This war, America's longest and in many ways most costly, engendered a number of atrocities. It also undermined American relations with long-term allies; and it eroded almost all belief that the American experiment in democracy is the hope of the world.

And now that we are in the post-cold-war/post-VN period, what have we as a nation learned? Apparently little, as suggested by the articles describing our current armaments and plans for future wars.

The World War I Period

AMERICAN IMPERIALISM*

Woodrow Wilson, who opposed extracontinental expansion prior to the Spanish-American War, later explained why it was necessary. "Since trade

*From Sidney Lens, *The Forging of the American Empire* (New York: Thomas Y. Crowell Company, 1971), p. 195.

ignores national boundaries," he wrote in 1907, "and the manufacturer insists on having the world as a market, the flag of his nation must follow him, and the doors of the nations which are closed against him must be battered down. Concessions obtained by financiers must be safeguarded by ministers of state, even if the sovereignty of unwilling nations be outraged in the process. Colonies must be obtained or planted, in order that no useful corner of the world may be overlooked or unused."

THE PEOPLE AWAKE*

In this portion of one of his well-known books, Pierre Van Paassen indicates that at the height of World War I, the Russian revolution raised once again the spectre of defeat for the privileged classes of Europe. So that more widespread revolution could be prevented, and—as subsequent events suggest—only for that reason, the two major opponents, Germany and the Allies, agreed to halt the war.

...In 1917, millions of weary hearts thrilled with a new hope. The infinite patience of the martyred peoples, Rolland announced, had reached the point of exhaustion. The kettle was boiling at last. To prevent an explosion, the governments had closed up all the cracks beforehand and seated themselves on top. Despite these precautionary measures, the pent-up steam was beginning to escape with a snarling hiss. The conviction that the nations had been the victim of a colossal bloody swindle was gaining ground. Here and there the free spirit of human beings who had been imprisoned in the iron-bound cells of nationality during the four years of collective hysteria ventured to look across the borders again. In the suffering eyes of their neighbors they recognized their own features, distorted by the same murderous illusion. "Amongst the masses indignation was deepening over the incalculable treasure which had proved easily available for the frenzied game of war, whereas financial support for the measures aiming at their own social amelioration had never been forthcoming without bitter struggle."

A vague, inarticulate movement, as that of a giant stirring in his sleep, became discernible. The peoples were waking up. The chains that bound them began to rattle. There was still talk in the press and in the propaganda bureaus about baby-murdering Huns and cannibalistic Senegalese, but

*Adapted from Pierre Van Paassen, *Days of Our Years*. Rev. ed. (Garden City, N.Y.: Garden City Publishing Co., 1940), pp. 71–79.

not a few of those in the trenches clearly saw through the mystification. The four years of "righteous war had piled up more ruins and folly than had the feudal lords and the Church in the ten centuries of their undisputed almightiness."

From the distance came "the dull thud of Lenin's heavy ax-blows." The pamphlets of Romain Rolland, the only man who had kept himself free of hatred, were finding their way into the trenches. Rolland spoke the words of human pity and brotherly love which the Church should have spoken. He sought to pierce the icy crust of hatred which covered the European Continent, and called on the adversaries to stretch out their hands to each other in the name of their common humanity. . . .

The poilus of France began to debate whether or not to return to their firesides before Clemenceau's "war to the bitter end" should have reached that dismal climax. In the spring of 1918, André Maginot admitted[1] in a secret session of the Chamber that there remained but one single division between Paris and the battle line on which the government could place absolute reliance. The red flag had been hoisted on the ruined sugar refinery of Souchez. In response, a German regiment had intoned the "Marseillaise" and had walked across no man's land to fraternize. Letters tied to clods of earth were being thrown from the one trench to the other. Messages were exchanged. It became necessary to forbid British troops to converse with German prisoners of war. The press curtailed publication of casualty lists. Divisions had to be shifted to break up secret contacts established with the enemy across the line of death.

Tens of thousands of men were still dying each day. But in the chateaux, far from the crash of high explosives, and protected from aerial raiders by an agreement with the German high command not to bombard each other's headquarters,[2] the Allied generals and politicians kept up their quarrels about precedence and prestige. Joffre, who had suggested putting Foch in an old ladies' home after the Somme, was himself pushed out by Nivelle. Pétain took up the succession for a time until Castelnau stepped into his shoes. The lack of accord amongst the gold-braided chiefs threatened to prolong the war eternally. A heavy subterranean rumble of discontent shook the army zones. Mutinies broke out. At one time, eighty-seven French regiments were affected, at another time, one hundred and fifteen. Courts-martial functioned night and day. For a mere whisper of discontent in a regiment, a company was decimated. Divisions were purposely sent into battle to be massacred, to kill the spirit of defeatism.

Strikes were being called in Paris and Lyons. In December, 1917, the metalworkers folded their arms and demonstrated on the boulevards. The sons of the Communards had recognized the futility of the blood bath into which the united front with the ruling class had tricked them. The repression increased. The bitter disillusion over "millions of lives sacrificed for a resulting zero turned the wrath of those morally responsible for the disaster against the men who had foreseen it." Spy hunts were organized. The censors redoubled their efforts to prevent the people from learning the extent of the horror. The billboards in the big cities were placarded with flaming posters, warning against the sinister intrigues of pacifists, against enemy agents and foreign gold, against emissaries from the dead International of labor. Crowds were enjoined to silence in public. Shut up— fight! Do not reason—kill! Since one lie which raises the morale of the troops and of the civilian population is worth a thousand truths in wartime, lie factories were set in operation. They supplanted the universities. Savants and intellectuals, authors and pulpiteers, those who prided themselves on stating the truth for its own sake, began howling with the pack. Men gave up their convictions as easily as their lives. Free investigation, independence of judgment, human pity—all were put in moth balls and laid in the storage room till after the war. Criticism was abolished, conscience proscribed. Christendom repudiated its name by adopting Mars. The Deity was split into a number of tribal Jehovahs. From a hundred thousand pulpits the voice of Antichrist roared hatred.

Every new retreat of the armies was interpreted as the result of defeatist propaganda; never were the quarreling old generals held responsible. Every diplomatic blunder was attributed to spies; not a single statesman would ever admit that a ghastly error had been made. Civil and military courts were working overtime. The medieval system of *lettres de cachet* was revived in France. Secret denunciation filled the jails. Men who showed too much zeal in laying bare the machinations of the international cannon trust and its press in seeking to prolong the war were enjoined to keep silent or railroaded to jail. One of the most outspoken pacifists, Almereyda, whose testimony on the witness stand would have revealed the extent of the corruption in high places, was found garroted in his cell. Seeing an opportunity to dispose of his political opponents, the old "Tiger of France" seized upon the frenzy against defeatism to try Joseph Caillaux for high treason. Malvy was banished. Briand escaped by a hairsbreadth. . . .

Nor was the end in sight! Men were not yet tired of hatred. The battlefields were turning into abattoirs. At Verdun, on the Chemin des Dames, in Flanders, the holocaust to Moloch, the dance of death, was reaching an obscene climax. The armies had received new weapons from the laboratories. Poison gas had been used freely. Now experiments were being made with disease germs. Even if this diabolic device was not utilized in 1918, it will remain the eternal mark of shame of a dehumanized, debased generation which seriously pondered its employment. Boys who could scarcely support the weight of a rifle were being drafted and thrown into the gaping jaws of death as sacrifice units. The new German levies holding the Hindenburg line had hunger stamped on their face. Sanatoria and jail, venereal hospitals and insane asylums—all were being combed for more cannon fodder. The monster was insatiable. The Europe of Christianity and humanism was sinking into a miasma of gore and lies.

Then word came from Italy about factory occupations. There had been trouble amongst the submarine crews at the German naval base at Kiel. The "Kaiser's coolies" were refusing to go down below the waves to meet a certain death. Alsatians serving in the German army were flocking into France. French conscripts ran into Switzerland and Spain for safety. Bosnians deserted the double eagle of Habsburg to join their Serbian brothers. A Czech army was wandering aimlessly over the Muscovite plain. A famine was raging in Bulgaria, the black plague had broken out in Salonika, typhus was decimating the Turkish army. Over in France the imperial Russian troops who had been brought from Odessa to bolster up the Allied morale, and who had covered themselves with glory at Verdun, refused to fight the moment Russia was out of the war. They were disarmed and massacred, ten thousand of them, by order of Foch, to preserve the French army from the virus of revolutionism.[3] Then, soviets sprang from the ground in Hungary. Standing on foreign soil, the Belgian army was so torn by dissension over the growth of the movement for Flemish autonomy at home, that its best divisions were disarmed and consigned to the lumber camps in southern France. Here they were presently joined by the Russian volunteers in the Canadian army who had downed arms the moment Trotsky signed the peace of Brest-Litovsk. From Italy came word of regiments constituting themselves into a Division of Peace. Signs were multiplying on every hand that the peoples were growing tired of the dance that imperialism had called. The prospect of glory and victory had long since receded from view. It now appeared certain that the war, from whatever angle one looked at it, was going to be a bad bargain for everyone concerned. Neither ideals, ambitions, nor national interests were going to be satisfied. Only blood and tears. . . .

Germany had based all her calculations on a swiftly conducted war and an early victory. At the outset she had a supply of war stocks which could scarcely have carried her through a year of warfare on two fronts. The Allies, therefore, could have brought the Kaiser to his knees before the end of 1915, by instituting an economic blockade.[4] But that would have meant giving up the choicest profits of war: the contraband commerce. Throughout the first three years of the war the Reich received an uninterrupted stream of supplies through Holland, Switzerland, and the Scandinavian countries, especially cotton, without which she could not have continued to fight for a day. This went on until America angrily protested that England, Germany's chief adversary, was crowding her out of the European market.[5] German capitalism had not neglected its opportunities either: right up to the beginning of 1917, the Krupp Works of Essen shipped a quarter of a million tons of steel a month through Switzerland to the Comité des Forges in France.[6] In addition to payment in gold, one of the conditions in this deal was that French aviation was to refrain from bombarding the iron-ore mines, the blast furnaces and the rolling mills of the Longwy district which had been occupied by Germany early in the war.[7] Ships loaded with nickel from New Caledonia, destined for Germany, seized by French destroyers in open sea and brought to port at Brest and Cherbourg and there declared prizes of war by the maritime court, were ordered released by the French government and reached Bremen safely.[8] Representatives of the German chemical trust, of the Swiss copper interests, and of Vickers, Krupp, Schneider-Creusot, and the Comité des Forges met in Vienna at the moment when the armies were locked in a death struggle in the mud of Flanders. Their sole purpose was to devise ways and means of keeping the war going profitably. "*On croyait mourir pour la patrie, on mourait pour les industriels,*" said Anatole France when he learned the answer of Senator Bérenger as to why the metallurgical district of Thionville was not taken back at the outbreak of the war, when it was undefended by the Germans and the French army was within a stone's throw. The reason no attempt had been made to recapture Thionville was that it would have brought the war to a premature termination. "For the occupation of Thionville," declared the Senator, "would have reduced Germany to seven million tons of poor steel per year; all production would have been stopped. Seizure of Thionville would have put an end to the war immediately." The stoppage of the war was to be prevented at all costs. General Sarrail, commanding in Lorraine, worked out a plan of strategy in 1915 to capture, or else destroy, the Briey district where Germany exploited the captured blast furnaces of the Comité des Forges. When the Commander in Chief, Joffre, got wind of the projected offensive, Sarrail was called to Paris, had an interview with Poincaré, President of the Republic, and the plan was shelved. Thanks to French ore, made available by the initial order to the French armies to withdraw twenty-two kilometers from the border before a single blow had been struck, Germany was able during four years to inundate the East and the West, on land and the high seas, with a torrent of steel. In return for magnetos for airplane motors, shipped by Germany, France gave bauxite, an indispensable ingredient in the manufacture of aluminum for Zeppelins. The dreadful barbed wire strung out by the British at Ypres and on the Somme, which became a deathtrap for the Prussian Guard, was manufactured by the

Drahtwerke of Opel and Company, and had found its way through Holland to England. Australia shipped fat to Germany via Norway and Denmark; the Straits Settlements copra; Ceylon tea; Wales coke and coal, tar, ammoniac and glycerine for high explosives, all of it in British ships. The Allied high command tranquilly figured on finishing the war with the fresh forces from America in the fall or winter of 1919. When Lenin repeated his call for peace over and over again, the Entente maintained an obstinate silence. The Allies were more than ever determined to gain the victory without jeopardizing the interests of the ruling classes. On the other hand, strikes increased, and the peasants who had once set chateaux aflame were growing restless. In alarm, the French government proposed to replace the men employed in munition plants with workers to be imported from America. They desired to send the entire French male population to the front. A violent wave of protest was the answer to this proposal. The Council of Labor threatened to call a general strike and the scheme was dropped. But now the government began to look for ways and means to disband the labor unions. Time was growing short. America's participation in the war had made a final victory in the field a virtual certainty. A new danger loomed on the horizon, and it was growing more and more precise: a further postponement of peace threatened to bring on a social revolution. Only when the upper classes recognized the imminence of what would have been a major disaster to the ruling cliques of bankers and merchants of death was a single high command for all fronts finally instituted, and, upon the urging of America, the economic blockade at last applied in earnest. Germany immediately realized that the end had come. She launched a last desperate offensive and collapsed.

. . . .

In Berlin the banners of the people were marching in the Sieges Allee. Crowds ripped the epaulets from the *Junkers'* shoulders. Bismarck's statue was crowned with a Phrygian bonnet. Bavaria abolished parliament and set up a council of people's commissars. Munich sang the "Carmagnole." In Berlin the Philharmonic Orchestra struck up the "Marseillaise" under the statue of Frederick the Great. At the front the butts of rifles went up in the air, cannons were spiked, machine guns beaten to smithereens. One hundred and thirty French regiments were on the point of leaving the line and marching on Paris.

Then the Armistice was signed!

It came not a day too early. Another three months and Soviet France would have been exchanging greetings with the liberated German people. The ruling classes of Europe had recognized the common danger. No tediously prolonged negotiations had been necessary to bring the war to a close. Instinct had spoken. Immediately after the meeting in the forests of Rethondes, Foch and Hindenburg agreed to leave a gap of fifty miles between the retreating Germans and the allied victors to prevent contact and fraternization. Prussia's Iron Division, entirely made up of *Junkers*, was summoned from the Baltic front to maintain order in Berlin. Clemenceau suggested distributing the American Expeditionary Force over the length and breadth of France "to hold a revolution in check." Before the retreating German army had quite crossed the Rhine, the press of France was clamoring to give Ludendorff, the most prominent exponent of the hated Prussian militarism, carte blanche to strangle the new freedom in Russia "which menaced a system of social injustice by which all the bourgeoisies live."

Without transition, the imperialist war turned into a war of the imperialisms against the peoples. With the approval of the Allied high command a German army was rushed to the aid of the White Guards of Finland and helped to exterminate the forty thousand Socialists of Helsingfors. Rumanian boyars, who had run like hares when Mackensen entered Transylvania, were encouraged by Franchet d'Esperey, who commanded the Salonika front, to seize the choicest Magyar estates after the Hungarian army had demobilized as a token of good faith. That was their recompense, not for winning victories, but for trampling working-class leaders to death in the streets of Budapest. Had not Woodrow Wilson vetoed the idea, the offer of the German high command to suspend operations in all theaters of war, and jointly march on Moscow to wipe out the Bolshevik regime, would have been accepted. . . .

But now the German bourgeoisie began sending up alarm signals. Clemenceau knew his history. He remembered that in 1871, before peace was concluded between France and Germany, Bismarck had loaned Adolphe Thiers the necessary cannon to extinguish the Commune of Paris. In December, 1918, the "Tiger of France" returned the compliment by stipulating that 50,000 German machine guns were to be excepted from destruction to enable Ebert and Noske to shoot down the Spartacists in Berlin and the soviets in Bavaria. The German bourgeoisie was permitted to organize a civic guard of 400,000 men, the so-called *Reichswehr* (of which the world was to hear more), because England insisted that total disarmament would deliver the Reich up to Socialism.

Europe's bourgeoisies consented to every complicity in order to maintain the established social order. The essential fact of the history of 1919 which does not figure in official chronicles, consists in the singlemindedness of the ruling classes of every country to arrest the march of humanity towards Socialism. . . .

REFERENCES

[1] Paul Allard, *Comptes-rendus sténographiques des séances secrètes de la Chambre des députés*, 1917-1918.

[2] The Crown Prince states in his memoirs that a French aviator dropped a bomb in the neighborhood of German headquarters just once. "After retaliation we were never bothered again," he adds.

[3] The massacre of these Imperial Russian troops is mentioned by Winston Churchill in his history of the World War.

[4] *Enquete sur la situation de la métallurgie*: official government publication, substantiated in *Neueste Nachrichten* of Leipzig, Oct. 10, 1917.

[5] André Ribard, *La France, histoire d'un peuple*, Editions Internationales, Paris, 1938, p. 335.

[6] Jean Galtier-Boissière et René Lefebvre, *Crapouillot, numero spécial*, article "*Les Marchands de canons contre la nation*," Paris, 1933, pp. 40-46.

[7] Pierre Bruneau, *Le Role du haut commandement au point de vue economique de 1914 à 1921*, Paris, 1921, p. 55 *et seq.*; also report by M. Laurent Eynac in the Chamber of Deputies, *Journal officiel*, Feb. 14, 1921.

[8] Admiral Consett, *Les Triomphes des forces économiques*, Paris, 1927 p. 126.

World War II

THE PEARL HARBOR PUZZLE*

"You would do America a favor if you would shoot yourself," wrote a former Missouri circuit judge, "as you are certainly of no use to yourself nor the American people."

That is just one example of the many hostile, bitter, and paranoid letters sent to Rear Adm. Husband E. Kimmel after he was relieved of his command of the U.S. Pacific Fleet 10 days after the attack on Pearl Harbor. Some less emotional critics in Congress called for Kimmel's court martial, and a board of inquiry (the Roberts Commission) accused him of "dereliction of duty."

Despite eight separate investigations into the Pearl Harbor puzzle many

*Editorial, *The Arizona Republic*, May 20, 1968.

of the pieces are missing and may never be known. Others are the subject of great controversy.

But what now seems clear, from the vantage point of more than 26 years, is that Admiral Kimmel had been made a scapegoat by the Roosevelt administration, exactly as he contended all these years.

What we know about the Pearl Harbor affair is that the U.S. had broken the secret Japanese code and therefore had every reason to expect an attack on a U.S. installation. We also know that this military intelligence was withheld from Kimmel . . . the official explanation being that it was withheld for fear of alerting the Japanese that their code had been broken.

In any event, there was no "dereliction of duty," as the Roberts Commission charged.

But the overriding question is whether or not the information was withheld, as several major historians have contended (among them, the esteemed Charles Beard), in order to launch America's wartime involvement against Japan amid nationwide outrage over the "sneak attack" that knocked out 18 ships and killed 3,435 Americans.

This question probably can never be answered satisfactorily. Nevertheless, those who support this proposition point to the following entry in Secretary of War Henry L. Stimson's diary, dated Nov. 25, 1941: "The question was how we should maneuver them (Japan) into the position of firing the first shot without allowing too much danger to ourselves."

And they point to FDR's extra-legal measures, in both the Atlantic and Pacific, that nudged America toward war even while Roosevelt was pledging peace and declaring that our boys would never fight on foreign soil.

For the rest of his life, Husband Kimmel proclaimed his innocence, insisting that he was victimized by an administration which was bent on involving the U.S. in a war with Japan. "My principal occupation—what's kept me alive—is to expose the entire Pearl Harbor affair," he said in 1966.

Early last week, at age 86, Admiral Kimmel died. He did not receive in his lifetime the official vindication to which he felt he was entitled. But, in the relative calm of the post-war period, he did serve to remind the American nation that—whatever the ultimate facts about Pearl Harbor—the administration that moved rapidly to make a human sacrifice of him was anything but candid with the American people as the nation headed for a showdown with Japan.

THE HIROSHIMA BOMB*

Only those at some distance from the explosion could clearly distinguish

*Adapted from Robert Jay Lifton, *Death in Life*: Survivors of Hiroshima (New York: Random House, Inc., 1967), pp. 19–30.

the sequence of the great flash of light accompanied by the lacerating heat of the fireball, then the sound and force of the blast, and finally the impressive multicolored cloud rising high above the city. This awesome spectacle was not without beauty—as recorded by the same history professor, who witnessed it from a suburb five thousand meters (a little more than three miles) away:

> A blinding . . . flash cut sharply across the sky. . . . I threw myself onto the ground . . . in a reflex movement. At the same moment as the flash, the skin over my body felt a burning heat. . . . [Then there was] a blank in time . . . dead silence . . . probably a few seconds . . . and then a . . . huge "boom" . . . like the rumbling of distant thunder. At the same time a violent rush of air pressed down my entire body. . . . Again there were some moments of blankness . . . then a complicated series of shattering noises. . . . I raised my head, facing the center of Hiroshima to the west. . . . [There I saw] an enormous mass of clouds . . . [which] spread and climbed rapidly . . . into the sky. Then its summit broke open and hung over horizontally. It took on the shape of . . . a monstrous mushroom with the lower part as its stem—it would be more accurate to call it the tail of a tornado. Beneath it more and more boiling clouds erupted and unfolded sideways. . . . The shape . . . the color . . . the light . . . were continuously shifting and changing. . . .

Even at that distance, he and others experienced what is called the "illusion of centrality," as is succinctly suggested by a later poem originally written in the classical tanka style:

> Thinking a bomb must have fallen close to me, I looked up, but it was a pillar of fire five kilometers ahead.

This illusion, usually attributed to the sudden loss of a sense of invulnerability, is actually an early perception of death encounter, a perception which the atomic bomb engendered at enormous distances.

The bomb was completely on target and exploded, with a force equivalent to twenty thousand tons of TNT, eighteen hundred feet in the air near the center of a flat city built mainly of wood. It created an area of total destruction (including residential, commercial, industrial, and military structures) extending three thousand meters (about two miles) in all directions; and destroyed sixty thousand of ninety thousand buildings within five thousand meters (over three miles), an area roughly encompassing the city limits. Flash burns from the heat generated by the release of an enormous amount of radiant energy occurred at distances of more than four thousand meters (two and a half miles), depending upon the type and amount of clothing worn and the shielding afforded by immediate surroundings. Injuries from the blast, and from splintered glass and falling debris, occurred throughout the city and beyond.

The number of deaths, immediately and over a period of time, will probably never be fully known. Variously estimated from 63,000 to 240,000 or more, the official figure is usually given as 78,000, but the city of Hiroshima estimates 200,000—the total encompassing between 25 and 50 percent of the city's then daytime population (also a disputed figure, varying from 227,000 to over 400,000). The enormous disparity is related to the extreme confusion which then existed, to differing methods of calculation, and to underlying emotional influences, quite apart from mathematical considerations, which have at times affected the estimators. An accurate estimate may never be possible, but what can be said is that *all of Hiroshima immediately became involved in the atomic disaster.*

Two thousand meters (1.2 miles) is generally considered to be a crucial radius for susceptibility to radiation effects, and for high mortality in general—from blast, heat, or radiation—though many were killed outside of this radius. Within it, at points close to the hypocenter, heat was so extreme that metal and stone melted, and human beings were literally incinerated. The area was enveloped by fires fanned by a violent "fire-wind"; these broke out almost immediately within a radius of more than three thousand meters (up to two miles). The inundation with death of the area closest to the hypocenter was such that if a man survived within a thousand meters (.6 miles) and was out of doors (that is, without benefit of shielding from heat or radiation), more than nine tenths of the people around him were fatalities; if he was unshielded at two thousand meters, more than eight of ten people around him were killed. Mortality indoors was lower, but even then to have a 50-percent chance of escaping both death or injury, one had to be about twenty-two hundred meters (1.3 miles) from the hypocenter.

Those closest to the hypocenter could usually recall a sudden flash, an intense sensation of heat, being knocked down or thrown some distance, and finding themselves pinned under debris or simply awakening from an indeterminate period of unconsciousness. *The most striking psychological feature of this immediate experience was the sense of a sudden and absolute shift from normal existence to an overwhelming encounter with death.* This is described by a shopkeeper's assistant, who was thirteen years old at the time of the bomb and fourteen hundred meters from the hypocenter:

> I was a little ill ... so I stayed at home that day. . . . There had been an air-raid warning and then an all-clear. I felt relieved and lay down on the bed with my younger brother. . . . Then it happened. It came

very suddenly. ... It felt something like an electric short—a bluish sparkling light. ... There was a noise, and I felt great heat—even inside of the house. When I came to, I was underneath the destroyed house. .... I didn't know anything about the atomic bomb so I thought that some bomb had fallen directly upon me. ... And then when I felt that our house had been directly hit, I became furious. ... There were roof tiles and walls—everything black—entirely covering me. So I screamed for help. ... And from all around I heard moans and screaming, and then I felt a kind of danger to myself. ... I thought that I too was going to die in that way. I felt this way at that moment because I was absolutely unable to do anything at all by my own power. ... I didn't know where I was or what I was under. ... I couldn't hear voices of my family. I didn't know how I could be rescued. I felt I was going to suffocate and then die, without knowing exactly what had happened to me. This was the kind of expectation I had. ...

. . . .

A Protestant minister, himself uninjured, but responding to the evidence of mutilation and destruction he saw everywhere around him during extensive wanderings throughout the city, experienced his end-of-the-world imagery in an apocalyptic Christian idiom:

> The feeling I had was that everyone was dead. The whole city was destroyed. ... I thought all of my family must be dead—it doesn't matter if I die. ... I thought this was the end of Hiroshima—of Japan—of humankind. ... This was God's judgment on man. ...

And a woman writer, Yōko Ōta:

> I just could not understand why our surroundings have changed so greatly in one instant. ... I thought it might have been something which had nothing to do with the war, the collapse of the earth which it was said would take place at the end of the world, and which I had read about as a child. ...

This sense of world-collapse could also be expressed symbolically, as in the immediate thought of a devoutly religious domestic worker: "There is no God, no Buddha."

For many, immersion in death was epitomized by olfactory imagery—by memories of "the constant smell of dead bodies," and the lasting nature of those memories: "I can feel the smell of those dead bodies in my nostrils even now." The survivor originally experienced this "smell of death" not only from corpses around him but from the general odor of mass open cremations soon carried out by authorities (both for the prevention of disease and in accordance with Japanese custom); however derived, it became psychologically interwoven with the entire atomic bomb experience.

These cremations could even give rise to a certain amount of "atomic bomb gallows humor," as in the case of a professional cremator who, despite severe burns, managed to make his way back to his home (adjoining the crematorium), and said he then felt relieved because "I thought I would die soon, and it would be convenient to have the crematorium so close by."

Beyond death imagery per se, there was a widespread sense that life and death were out of phase with one another, no longer properly distinguishable—which lent an aura of weirdness and unreality to the entire city. This aura was often conveyed by those who had been on the outskirts of the city and entered it after the explosion, as was true of an electrician, then in his mid-forties, working at a railroad junction five thousand meters from the hypocenter.

> I was setting up a pole ... near a switch in the railroad tracks. ...
> There was a flash ... a kind of flash I had never seen before, which I
> can't describe. ... My face felt hot and I put my hands over my eyes
> and rushed under a locomotive that was nearby. I crawled in between
> the wheels, and then there was an enormous boom and the loco-
> motive shook. I was frightened, so I crawled out. ... I couldn't tell
> what happened. ... For about five minutes I saw nobody, and then I
> saw someone coming out from an air-raid shelter who told me that
> the youngest one of our workers had been injured by falling piles ...
> so I put the injured man on the back of my bicycle and tried to take
> him to the dispensary. Then I saw that almost all of the people in
> that area were crowded into the dispensary, and since there was also
> a hospital nearby, I went there. But that too was already full. ... So
> the only thing to do was go into [the center of] Hiroshima. But I
> couldn't move my bicycle because of all the people coming out from
> Hiroshima and blocking the way. ... I saw that they were all naked
> and I wondered what was the matter with them. ... When we spoke
> to people they said that they had been hit by something they didn't
> understand. ... We were desperately looking for a doctor or a
> hospital but we couldn't seem to have any success. ... We walked
> toward Hiroshima, still carrying our tools. ... Then in Hiroshima
> there was no place either—it had become an empty field—so I carried
> him to a place near our company office where injured people were
> lying inside, asking for water. But there was no water and there was
> no way to help them and I didn't know what kind of treatment I
> should give to this man or to the others. I had to let them die right
> before my eyes. ... By then we were cut off from escape, because
> the fire was beginning to spread out and we couldn't move—we were

together with the dead people in the building—only we were not really inside of the building because the building itself had been destroyed, so that we were really outdoors, and we spent the night there. . . .

This rote and essentially ineffectual behavior was characteristic of many during the first few hours in those situations where any attempt at all could be made to maintain a group cooperative effort. People were generally more effective in helping members of their immediate families or in saving themselves. This same electrician, an unusually conscientious man, kept at his post at the railroad over a period of several weeks, leaving only for brief periods to take care of his family. Again his description of the scene of death and near-death takes on a dreamlike quality:

> There were dead bodies everywhere. . . . There was practically no room for me to put my feet on the floor. . . . At that time I couldn't figure out the reason why all these people were suffering, or what illness it was that had struck them down. . . . I was the only person taking care of the place as all the rest of the people had gone. . . . Other people came in looking for food or to use the toilet. . . . There was no one to sell tickets in the station, nothing . . . and since trains weren't running, I didn't have much work to do. . . . There was no light at all, and we were just like sleepwalkers. . . .

Part of this aura was the "deathly silence" consistently reported by survivors. Rather than wild panic, most described a ghastly stillness and a sense (whether or not literally true) of slow-motion: low moans from those incapacitated, the rest fleeing from the destruction, but usually not rapidly, toward the rivers, toward where they thought their family members might be, or toward where they hoped to find authorities or medical personnel, or simply toward accumulations of other people, in many cases merely moving along with a gathering human mass and with no clear destination. Some jumped into the rivers to escape heat and fire, others were pushed into the water by the pressure of crowds at the river banks; a considerable number drowned. Many seemed to be attracted to the disaster center, overcoming numerous obstacles—such as spreading fire and, later on, guards posted at various points to prevent any influx of people—and made their way through the debris, often losing sight of their ostensible rescue missions in their aimless wandering.

As Dr. Hachiya described the scene in his classic, *Hiroshima Diary*:

> Those who were able walked silently toward the suburbs in the distant hills, their spirits broken, their initiative gone. When asked whence they had come, they pointed to the city and said, "That

way": and when asked where they were going, pointed away from the city and said, "This way." They were so broken and confused that they moved and behaved like automatons.

Their reactions had astonished outsiders who reported with amazement the spectacle of long files of people holding stolidly to a narrow, rough path when close by was a smooth, easy road going in the same direction. The outsiders could not grasp the fact that they were witnessing the exodus of a people who walked in the realm of dreams.

One of these "automatons" walking in the "realm of dreams," a watch repairman, at the time of the bomb in his twenties and three thousand meters from the hypocenter, describes his own mindless merging with a group of victims:

> All the people were going in that direction and so I suppose I was taken into this movement and went with them. ... I couldn't make any clear decision in a specific way ... so I followed the other people. ... I lost myself and was carried away. ...

The phrase he and others used, *muga-muchū*, literally "without self, without a center," suggests an obliteration of the boundaries of self. The physical state of many greatly contributed to this obliteration: complete or near-nakedness (partly because of clothes blown off by the blast and partly through being caught in an early-morning state of undress), various injuries and forms of bleeding, faces disfigured and bloated from burns, arms held awkwardly away from the body to prevent friction with other burned areas. Fellow survivors characterized such people (and by implication, themselves) as being "like so many beggars," or "like so many red *Jizo* standing on the sides of the road," implying that their identity as living human beings had been virtually destroyed.

Indeed, a few *hibakusha* described being rendered literally unrecognizable: one girl of thirteen, whose face was so disfigured by burns that when she returned home, her parents did not know who she was—until she began to cry; and another, one year older, was not only similarly disfigured but also unable, probably on a psychological basis, to see or speak:

> My mother and I were taken to [a nearby] island. ... I couldn't see and couldn't say anything—that is what I heard later. ... My eyes were not injured. I think I closed my eyes when the bomb fell. My face was so distorted and changed that people couldn't tell who I was. After a while I could call others' names but they couldn't recognize me. ... We were considered the very worst kind of patients. ... Of the thirty-five people put on this island, only two survived.

Dr. Hachiya also noted the "uncanny stillness" permeating the hospital where he was, for a time, both director and patient:

> An old woman lay near me with an expression of suffering on her face; but she made no sound. Indeed one thing was common to everyone I saw—complete silence. . . . Miss Kado [a nurse] set about examining my wounds without speaking a word. No one spoke. . . . Why was everyone so quiet? . . . It was as though I walked through a gloomy, silent motion picture. . . .

Yōko Ōta referred to this silence right after her description of the "end of the world," and more explicitly equated it with a general aura of death:

> It was quiet around us . . . in fact there was a fearful silence which made one feel that all people and all trees and vegetation were dead. . . .

And a grocer, himself severely burned, conveyed in his description this profound sense of *death in life*, of ultimate death-life disruption:

> The appearance of people was . . . well, they all had skin blackened by burns. . . . They had no hair because their hair was burned, and at a glance you couldn't tell whether you were looking at them from in front or in back. . . . They held their arms bent [forward] like this [he proceeded to demonstrate their position] . . . and their skin—not only on their hands, but on their faces and bodies too—hung down. . . . If there had been only one or two such people . . . perhaps I would not have had such a strong impression. But wherever I walked I met these people. . . . Many of them died along the road—I can still picture them in my mind—like walking ghosts. . . . They didn't look like people of this world. . . . They had a special way of walking—very slowly. . . . I myself was one of them.

The other-worldly grotesqueness of the scene, the image of neither-dead-nor-alive human figures with whom the survivor closely identifies himself, is typical. One man put the feeling more directly: "I was not really alive."

Related to the sense of death in life was a total disruption of individual and social order—of rules governing what is expected of one and whom one can depend on. Thus, the severely burned thirteen-year-old girl mentioned before (later to become a hospital worker) was assigned with her classmates to do "voluntary labor" on the fire lanes sixteen hundred meters from the hypocenter, and was as much disturbed by the sudden breakdown of teachers' standards of responsibility for their pupils as she was by her own injuries:

> I felt my body to be so hot that I thought I would jump into the
> river. ... I couldn't tell what was going on, but everything seemed
> strange. ... The teacher from another class, a man whose shirt was
> burning, jumped in. And when I was about to jump, our own class
> teacher came down and she suddenly jumped into the river. ... The
> river was filled with people and I could not swim very well, so I was
> afraid of jumping. ... At that time we felt quite lost. ... Since we
> had always looked up to our teachers, we wanted to ask them for
> help. But the teachers themselves had been wounded and were
> suffering the same pain we were.

Such disruption reaches deeply into psychic experience, and can produce
strange and desperate behavior—as it did in a young noncommissioned
officer stationed in the center of Hiroshima, but on leave in the suburbs
ten thousand meters away when the bomb fell:

> We were under military order to return to our unit immediately in
> case of any attack or emergency, so I returned almost without
> thinking. ... At first I couldn't get through ... so in the evening I
> started out again. This time I didn't try to help anyone but just
> walked through them. I was worried about the Army camp because
> according to what ... people told me, it had simply gone up in
> flames and disappeared. I was also a bit ashamed of having taken
> such a long time to return. But when I finally got back to the camp,
> just about everyone was dead—so there was no one to scold me. ...
> The first thing I did to give water to three people lying on the
> ground who were badly hurt—but a high-ranking officer came and
> told me not to give water to wounded people if they were suffering
> from burns. ... Next thing I did was to look for the ashes of the
> military code book—since we had a military order to look for this
> book even if it were burned, as it was a secret code which had to be
> protected. Finally I located the ashes of the book, and wrapped them
> in a *furoshiki* and carried this around with me. I wanted to take it to
> military headquarters as soon as possible, but when I finally did take
> it there the next morning, the officer scolded me for doing such a
> stupid thing. ... I was fresh from the Military Academy and my head
> was full of such regulations. ...

He stuck to military regulations so inappropriately, not only because he
was "fresh from the Military Academy" and unusually conscientious (even
compulsive), but also because he was inwardly not yet able to accept the
full dimensions of what had taken place and was behaving *as if* a familiar
form of order still existed.

Rather than total disorder, the decimation of the city created an
atmosphere so permeated by bizarre evidence of death as to make whatever
life remained seem unrelated to a "natural order" and more part of a

"supernatural" or "unnatural" one. These impressions emerged in frequently expressed imagery of a Buddhist hell, here described by a young sociologist exposed at twenty-five hundred meters:

> Everything I saw made a deep impression—a park nearby covered with dead bodies waiting to be cremated . . . very badly injured people evacuated in my direction. . . . The most impressive thing I saw was some girls, very young girls, not only with their clothes torn off but with their skin peeled off as well. . . . My immediate thought was that this was like the hell I had always read about. . . . I had never seen anything which resembled it before, but I thought that should there be a hell, this was it—the Buddhist hell, where we were taught that people who could not attain salvation always went. . . . And I imagined that all of these people I was seeing were in the hell I had read about.

Most "unnatural" of all was the sudden nonexistence of the city itself—as described by the history professor:

> I climbed Hijiyama Hill and looked down. I saw that Hiroshima had disappeared. . . . I was shocked by the sight. . . . What I felt then and still feel now I just can't explain with words. Of course I saw many dreadful scenes after that—but that experience, looking down and finding nothing left of Hiroshima—was so shocking that I simply can't express what I felt. I could see Koi [a suburb at the opposite end of the city] and a few buildings standing. . . . But Hiroshima didn't exist—that was mainly what I saw—Hiroshima just didn't exist.

And two days after the bomb Dr. Hachiya groped unsuccessfully for language which could comprehend the unnatural order he observed:

> For the first time, I could understand what my friends had meant when they said Hiroshima was destroyed. . . . For acres and acres the city was like a desert except for scattered piles of brick and roof tile. I had to revise my meaning of the word destruction or choose some other word to describe what I saw. Devastation may be a better word, but really, I know of no word or words to describe the view from my twisted iron bed in the fire-gutted ward of the Communications Hospital.

. . . .

"I WAS HORRIFIED"*

Reactions by students in a central Missouri high school after viewing the film "Hiroshima and Nagasaki: 1945":

Sane World, July 1970, p. 3.

There is nothing to say. Only horror—and the real horror is of those who could see and not believe that it is an evil thing. War is no longer an excuse for weapons such as these. If nothing is done there will be only one end—and no one to make a film like this.

It feels too much to feel. It is not so much death as the way of dying—instant, unprepared without reason—or slow and painfully maiming—against with no explanation why.

* * *

I was horrified. I hadn't before realized the terror and the destruction involved. I had heard about the bombings of Hiroshima, but I had never read or seen a movie about it. It was horribly gory—on many parts I had to close my eyes. Although I could hardly watch it I think it is good to at least hear—because it really makes you think about and evaluate this act by the United States. I was astounded at the reaction of the people themselves—they were so "quiet"! I cannot imagine the force which the bomb had—it is beyond my power of comprehension—the immense amount contained. I do know that I would not want another bomb of this type to be dropped on anybody for any reason.

* * *

God, how could we do this to them? I feel like crying or something but it won't do any good. What is the human race? How, how could we do this to those innocent people. Forgive me for saying this but Goddam war, any war! I feel that so strongly, I can taste it, I am sick, sick to death.

Why can't there be peace? There never has been any, and I get the scared, terrified feeling that there never will be any, either. I hurt, very deeply inside.

The word "peace" keeps running through my mind.

* * *

What can you say about such a film? Does anybody really think any form of government is worth all that destruction and all those human lives? It makes me sick to my stomach to think that I'm an American and we dropped that bomb. To see human life literally molded by fire and to think we did that, it makes me wonder if we are really human or are we animals fighting for ourselves with no respect for anyone else.

This also scares me because I think Viet Nam may eventually turn out that way.

My reaction to this film can only be described by the way my stomach felt afterwards. One cannot realize how alarming and depressing such an episode in history can be. Man is a savage and not fit for this world or any other world to destroy human life with such instantaneous cruelty. After this film I felt great apprehension and distrust towards the world and its leaders. This world will surely destroy itself in the near future. I cannot help feeling pessimistic when I know there are bombs and missiles planted near my home.

* * *

I am utterly sick. I'm frightened. It was so horribly realistic. My God, I just can't quite grasp the fact that my country has done that to humanity. We were the war criminals. We killed, slaughtered at an instant 200,000 men, women and children. Did we know what we were doing? My God, we couldn't have. Or else this country better be obliterated for the world's sake and for humanity's sake. This country makes me sick.

* * *

I have tremendously mixed up feelings about this film—all I keep saying over and over again is "why?" What is so horrible about communism that we go to the point of this horror (for lack of a better word)? It would be so easy to hate what ever country did it—except that we did it—and many, many people admire Truman for doing this—and many advocate the same for Vietnam. I'm sitting here fighting back tears—it was truly horrible—yet I'm very glad I saw the movie—as I missed *War Game*—because before I had always heard well, we dropped the bomb. It was probably horrible, but, by God! We stopped those Japs from killing our fathers and brothers. WHY CAN'T PEOPLE ACCEPT THAT FACT THAT WE'RE ALL BROTHERS?? WHY?? I also realize that because the United States did this I feel twice as emotional—which means that I don't practice what I preach. I seem to have this mental block that keeps saying "no, we didn't do it. . . . We're great," but that's something you have to face, I guess—it's like finding out your mom was about 11 when you were born and that she was a real slut or something. I'm really so numb right now that I'm rattling so I'll stop.

* * *

The silence . . . people blankly looking at their charred bodies flexing blackened fingers slowly, painfully, gloves of silk coming off to the touch, melted eyes, water and soup and mercurochrome painted on every wound, yet doing no good.

What about the mental burns?

Those were whole human beings ... and we won their surrender that way ... my God, what have we done?—What are we doing now?

Does life all boil down to a race to kill everyone and everything faster, more effectively? What really matters? What can one do? "Inevitability?"

The Cold War

THE COLD WAR MANIA *

Nobody knows whether the Cold War could have been prevented had Roosevelt lived. But Roosevelt was barely in his grave when the collaboration with the Soviet Union that he fostered was formally abandoned. Even a man like Henry L. Stimson did not at first credit the idea that the Russians might have reason to react negatively to our secret development, unilateral possession, and first use of the atomic bomb, though Stimson was one high official who showed some concern about our early Cold War policies. Henry Wallace was another, but Wallace's opposition was often more naive than reasoned.

Ignoring our own (and Churchill's) agreements with the Russians about Eastern Europe, which did not work out the way we expected, we interpreted Soviet actions there as a prelude to further expansion. Then came all the controversy about the "betrayal" at Yalta. According to that myth, we had "given" Eastern Europe to the Russians, who then "destroyed" democracy there. But one cannot give what one does not have to give, and it was easy to forget that at the time of the Yalta conference our forces had not yet crossed the Rhine whereas the Red Army had overrun Eastern Europe and was already at the gates of Berlin. Nor can one destroy what does not exist. Eastern Europe was in chaos after the war and, except for Czechoslovakia, the Eastern European countries, which before the war had suffered under fascist and pro-Nazi governments, had no experience with, nor the fundaments necessary for, Western-style democracy.

*Adapted from Fred Warner Neal, "Government by Myth," *The Center Magazine* 2(November 1969):2–7.

One thing led to another in the Cold War. The Berlin blockade was seen as "a Russian march to the English Channel." It was treated as though we bore no responsibility for the reparations and the currency disputes that led up to it. Again, when the Czechoslovak Communists took over the government of their country, the West assumed—with no factual basis—that here was evidence of Soviet military aggressiveness. The West ignored the fact that the Czech Communists had a freely elected plurality and that there were no Soviet troops in Czechoslovakia and had been none since 1946. Every secretary of State since 1948 . . . has cited the 1948 Communist *coup d'état* in Czechoslovakia as conclusive proof of Moscow's military aggressiveness.

Communist activity everywhere was seen as "Soviet aggression." The United States' containment policy was officially launched as the Truman Doctrine after the British told Washington they were not strong enough to organize the kind of government (monarchy) they wanted in Greece. The American reply was to send troops to save the Greek throne from "Soviet aggression" in the name of democracy. To this day, the Greek revolutionaries' defeat is cited to document the success of American policy in containing Russia. The fact was that from the beginning, far from conniving with the Greek Communists, Stalin, for his own purposes, actually opposed their revolutionary effort. He forbade his satrapies to aid them, and this before any hint of American intervention. In accordance with Lenin's doctrine that a revolution should not be attempted when the "objective conditions" for its success are not present, Stalin concluded—perhaps wrongly—that such conditions did not exist even in the uncertainties of postwar Greece.

Stalin was, in fact, a major antirevolutionary force. He discouraged Tito from trying to set up a communist regime in Yugoslavia. He discouraged Mao from trying to start a revolution in China. He even discouraged Togliatti from trying to win the Italian election of 1948. And it was his expulsion of Tito from the Cominform (which is what actually happened, rather than Tito's "escaping" from Soviet clutches) that shut off Yugoslav aid to the Greek Communists. That aid had been sent against Stalin's wishes. Stopping it was a major, if not *the* major, factor in the failure of the revolution in Greece. Stalin's policy was antirevolutionary, defensive, isolationist, inward-looking. It was also, of course, intransigent and often uncoöperative.

It is true that many of these facts, later easily documented, were not always readily apparent in the immediate postwar years. But neither were there any real facts to bolster the assumption of a vast Soviet military threat.

Looking back, it is not easy to explain the American fear of the

Russians, a fear that swiftly became an article of faith. It is no wonder that Stalin was defensive. The Soviet Union came out of the war with its heartland devastated, its manpower decimated, its agricultural and industrial potential drastically reduced, its air force virtually limited to fighter planes, its navy non-existent, and with no atomic bomb. By contrast, the United States in 1945 was stronger than ever. Its industrial-military potential had grown. Its air force controlled the skies, its navy controlled the seas. The United States had military bases around the world. The United States was sole possessor of the atom bomb.

There is also the myth that the Russians did not demobilize. In fact they demobilized extensively. Of course, the Russian army after the war, as before the war, was considerably larger than our own.

Today some of our young scholars doubt that Americans were really afraid of the Russians and question the sincerity of United States leaders of that time. They are wrong—the American fear of the Soviet Union was real enough. It can perhaps be better explained by a psychiatrist than a political scientist, but it did exist at the highest levels of American government. Young historians underestimate the extent to which statesmen can be irrational. . . .

The myth of the danger of Soviet military aggression became official dogma. When the Korean war broke out, almost no one doubted that it presaged Russian aggression in Europe. When the communists took over China, Dean Rusk described the action as "Russian colonialism."

Since we were so certain of the Soviet's aggressive intentions, diplomacy atrophied. American foreign policy became military policy, not as a result of some plot by the generals but because that was the way civilians thought. Almost unnoticed, the danger of "Soviet aggression" became the danger of "communist aggression," and then finally the threat of "internal aggression." The result was a "preventive intervention" syndrome, which led ultimately to Vietnam. The National Security Council's infamous "NSC-68" of 1950 outlined the need for American global intervention to counter Soviet global intervention (and revolutions generally). NSC-68 did not actually propose sending American troops to Vietnam, but its premises justified doing so.

As this unfolded, the liberal intellectuals were explaining to the American people how serious it was and advising them how to cope with it. Fears that our increasing militarization might threaten liberal humane values at home and abroad were turned aside with the assertion that we had to oppose Soviet communism in order to defend these values. It was explained over and over again that the United States had a responsibility to protect freedom and was required to do whatever was necessary to fulfill it. Increasingly, new social-science types specializing in Soviet and national-security studies—and well indoctrinated in the basic assumptions of anticommunism—streamed into the State Department, the Pentagon, the C.I.A., and into private institutions like the Rand Corporation and Hudson Institute, until, with the advent of the Kennedy Administration, they entered the White House itself.

In many ways, the Kennedy Administration was the high-water mark of these modern liberal intellectuals in power. Their main concern was how to cope with the Soviet threat more "effectively" than the Republicans—witness, for example, their early talk about a non-existent missile gap. Eisenhower had promised more effective anticommunism at any cost. In the eyes of the intellectuals around Kennedy, it was necessary to be tougher if we wanted to survive. McGeorge Bundy presided over this White House power elite, while Walt Rostow was left to draw up the plans for counter-insurgency.

Counselled by these Cold War intellectuals, President Kennedy began his foreign policy as a prisoner of Cold War myths. He had hardly taken office before he warned Americans that we might have to go to war over Laos. The Berlin crisis, coming soon afterward, was more serious but equally phony. The Administration, from Kennedy on down, repeated over and over again that the Russians threatened to drive us out of Berlin, which was simply not true. At no time was consideration given to Khrushchev's suggestion for a new legal arrangement for Berlin with the continued presence of American troops. As a result, our German policy, which on the eve of the U-2 affair had shown signs of flexibility under Eisenhower, never recovered.

Kennedy, however, was surely the most intelligent of the postwar Presidents. He was the only one who began to question the assumptions about Soviet military aggression. The Cuban missile was the only dangerous challenge to basic American interest he faced. Resolving it apparently gave Kennedy time to think; he then went further than any other leading American had done to ask for a reconsideration of our basic assumptions about the U.S.S.R. I don't know who killed John Kennedy, or why, and I am inclined to doubt the conspiracy theory, but whoever was responsible for his death surely saved the foreign-policy apparatus from the most serious threat it has ever had. Whether Kennedy would have gone on to apply common-sense restraint to Rostow's counter-insurgency plans, one cannot say. The original counter-insurgency concept of giving aid and know-how to established and democratic governments beset by revolutionaries could, under certain conditions, be a useful adjunct to foreign policy. Under Johnson, of course, counter-insurgency became a nightmare. It was applied to governments that were neither established nor democratic, and in the case of the Dominican Republic and Vietnam, it led to full-scale military intervention.

Some liberal intellectuals still oppose our policies not because they are wrong and based on fundamental misconceptions, but because they do not work. The activist college students who made a crusade out of Eugene McCarthy's Presidential campaign constituted the most meaningful opposition to our foreign-policy assumptions. They failed . . .

Sometimes we seem to be changing devils, redirecting our paranoia. . . . In the meantime, the danger of thermonuclear war is not less but greater. If the ABM/MIRV schemes are put into operation, for example, it may well be that even the theoretical possibility of controlling nuclear weapons will vanish. And one must remember that the assumed Soviet danger is still cited to justify this latest proposal. The testimony of Pentagon leaders before Congress daily outdoes itself to emphasize the threat. Senator Henry Jackson summed up the underlying rationale in a *Reader's Digest* article entitled "Russia Has *Not* Changed Her Ways." It seems clear that until the central myth is attacked, in depth, there is reason to doubt the possibility of new foreign-policy directions.

. . . .

THE HAWKS VERSUS THE DOVES*

The Dove idly swirled his sherry and stared out the restaurant window at the busy streets of the capital below.

"I know, I know," he said, irritably brushing his longish, greying hair behind his ear with the palm of his hand. "But how can we be sure this anti-ballistic missile system of ours would work?"

"Frankly, we can't," admitted the Hawk, a square-jawed general, his broad chest covered with battle ribbons. "But they can't be sure either. And hopefully, that may be enough to deter them from launching a first strike against us."

"Oh, come now," said the Dove. "I can't believe all this talk that they're developing a first-strike capability. Surely, they're as afraid of a nuclear war as we are."

"Their people, maybe. But do you really trust their leaders? We've seen them march into one country after another to prop up their puppet regimes. Never forget that they've vowed to destroy us."

The Dove looked uneasy. "But they'd never risk a nuclear war," he said. "What makes you think they're planning to strike first?"

The Hawk leaned forward in his chair. "They've openly admitted that they're targeting their missiles, not on our cities, but on our missile installations."

*Arthur Hoppe, *The Scottsdale Daily Progress*, June 17, 1969.

The Dove relaxed and smiled. "Well, I'd certainly rather they blew up our missiles than our cities."

"Not if you think it through," said the Hawk grimly. "If they were really concerned with our striking first, why target on our missile installations? If we fired first, our silos would be empty. The only conceivable reason is that they are planning on wiping out our missiles in a surprise attack. They could then destroy our defenseless cities at will."

The Dove frowned. "But surely . . ."

"Another thing," said the Hawk. "They admit they're constantly improving the accuracy of their missiles. They claim they can now hit within 400 yards of their target. There's no point in such accuracy if you're aiming at a city. It would only be valuable in a first strike against our missile installations."

"I can't believe . . ."

"They admit they already have enough land and undersea-based missiles to inflict unacceptable damage on us in a second strike. And yet they are constantly building more. Why? They seek our total annihilation."

"You make them sound like madmen."

"They may well be. Why else would they be developing diseases for which there's no cure and nerve gases for which there's no defense? Why else would they be working on multiple warheads to treble the existing nuclear terror?"

"Perhaps, in the upcoming disarmament talks . . ."

"You know they're stalling about opening disarmament negotiations. They've as much as admitted it. Why? I tell you, we've no choice but to step up our missile building program. We must maintain nuclear parity no matter what the cost, or face extinction."

The Dove sighed. "It will mean curtailing our domestic programs in order to maintain a balance of terror," he said. "But I suppose you are right. You can count on my support."

He stared moodily out the window for a moment at a Russian family happily crossing Red Square.

"Tell me this, General Zhukov," he said, shaking his head. "Why can't these American madmen be more like us?"

The Vietnam War

The next six selections deal with the Vietnam war. Although massive American involvement is now a thing of the past, there are many things about the war that have an enduring meaning. This is true even when what is said relates to the time-bound conflict itself. The first two pieces were written toward the end of the war (December 1972), but they are permeated with a timelessness that is thought-provoking; they originally appeared as part of a Saturday Review *symposium titled "The Consequences of the War."*

AN EROSION OF MUTUAL TRUST *

In 1972 there are not many Europeans left who still care to remember that ten, even seven, years ago they supported America's war effort in Vietnam. It is not the fashion nowadays to remember. But there was undeniably a great deal of support, and I was one of the supporters. Late in 1965 I published an article on Lyndon Johnson's intervention in Indochina, embarrassingly entitled "The Necessary War." The argument was deceptively simple: successful aggression begets more aggression, so no aggressor must go unchecked. In the Forties and Fifties the containment of Russian Communism in Europe had been the main task. In the Sixties and Seventies priority would have to be accorded to containing Chinese Communism in Asia. If the Americans did not stand up for Saigon, they could not very well be expected to stand up for Berlin.

All this was conventional wisdom at the time. Like a lot of conventional wisdom, it turned out to be quite wrong—for the simple reason that it rested on a number of fallacious assumptions. *Fallacy number one* relates to the nature of the conflict. Vietnam was not a war instigated from outside, fanned by Moscow or Peking; it was not the beginning of a major Chinese thrust southward by armed revolution. It was originally a civil war fostered by a regime in Hanoi that happened to be both nationalist and Communist and could, by dint of the latter, count on a minimum of aid from Russia and China.

Fallacy number two derives from this. It seemed logical to transfer the imperative of containment from the Old World to Southeast Asia. But Indochina was not Western Europe. American efforts alone never had a chance of succeeding in fortifying and holding the line—basically because there was no commensurate effort on the part of the Vietnamese. It was a hopeless task to promote democratic reform while prosecuting a war and

Adapted from Theo Sommer, "An Erosion of Mutual Trust," Saturday Review 55(December 1972):37–38.

even more hopeless to promote the retarded process of Vietnamese nation building by waging an all-out military campaign.

Fallacy number three has to do with the strategic philosophy underlying the U.S. operation. Escalation was wrong for two reasons. First, piecemeal deployment of American troops never offered any prospect for decisive success on the battlefield because every increment of U.S. war-fighting capability could be countered by an increase in the enemy's fighting strength. Second, as George Ball wisely observed early on, once the United States had actively committed itself to direct conflict with Hanoi, it could not be certain of controlling the scope and extent of escalation. By the same token, the brazen idea that a country such as Vietnam could be reduced from the air was all wrong from the very outset. Anyone who had experienced aerial bombardment during the Second World War or had read the U.S. bombing surveys on Germany and Japan knew that it was not only vile but bound to be ineffective, even counterproductive.

Fallacy number four is intimately connected with number three. Long before Lyndon Johnson ordered the suspension of air attacks against North Vietnam, it was glaringly apparent that the instruments of war were no longer proportionate to the aims of war. Anyone who ever visited Vietnam—as I did twice during the Sixties—must have wondered whether laying the country waste in a process of step-by-step vandalization could ever add up to peace, or even pacification. The war, the longer it ran on, blighted all the honorable motives that had ever been adduced or produced in its justification.

The Vietnamese gamble was a moral one so long as a successful outcome appeared to be a reasonable likelihood. It became immoral, a kind of reckless shooting craps with destiny, when nagging doubts first hardened into the certainty that in the end there could be only different degrees of failure and no such thing as success in any meaningful sense of the term.

I did not see all this back in 1965; but I did in 1968. By then it was clear that America had climbed on a tiger's back and that dismounting would prove to be a highly painful exercise. The curious thing is that the Vietnam War had outlived itself long before its formal conclusion became visible. The Cold War backdrop of confrontation, against which Dean Rusk had originally projected the conflict, suddenly dissolved when Richard Nixon ushered in his era of negotiations with Moscow and Peking. What earlier had looked like an entr'acte of global contention abruptly shrank into regional insignificance—another Biafra rather than a second Korea. Anyone killed in action between Cape Camau and Vinh Linh after Henry Kissinger's first trip to Peking died for better terms of surrender, not for victory.

Where has the war led the world? Astonishingly enough, the community of nations finds itself in pretty much the same spot it was in before the conflict started. There is a kind of competitive détente among all the principal actors on the world stage, with some limping behind, others nosily and noisily pushing forward.

The Vietnam War has prevented nothing, but it did delay some major international developments by seven or eight years—especially the formation of the new triangular (or perhaps, if one includes Japan and Western Europe, pentagonal) pattern of present-day world politics. It coincided in France with the heyday of Gaullist obstruction to the speedy integration of Europe and in Russia with the obsessive fear of ideological subversion that in 1968 led to military intervention in Czechoslovakia. In fact, the war may have contributed to some of these phenomena. At any rate, it compounded all of them.

But the world community suffered another loss, and this is perhaps the most momentous outcome of the Vietnam War: America has become unsure of her own purpose. Thus her allies have become doubtful of America's dedication to what used to be known as the "common cause." There is no denying the fact that the same allies who were originally impressed by America's steadfast commitment to Vietnam soon started losing confidence in America's judgment. And the result was an erosion of mutual trust within the Atlantic Alliance. . . .

EACH DAY IS A SEPARATE ORDEAL*

"The people of Vietnam do not like the past," a Chinese scholar wrote centuries ago. These words were written for me in Vietnamese by a fifty-eight-year-old schoolteacher in Cantho. So lightly did he press on his pencil that I cannot now see the tiny accents over the words: *viet nhon bat hieu co.* It was his way of reminding me of how the Vietnamese have loathed and fought foreign domination—one thousand years of Chinese rule, nearly a century under the French, and a decade of American "assistance and advice," as he put it. The Vietnamese appreciate irony. It is these last years that have sickened the schoolteacher and made him a man of great sadness. He did not speak his mind to the boys in his mathematics class because Vietnamese men go to jail for such opinions.

In Cambridge, where I have been living since my return from Vietnam in June, I read the morning newspapers and remember that classroom and

*Adapted from Gloria Emerson, "Each Day is a Separate Ordeal," *Saturday Review* 55(December 1972):52–55.

wonder how many of those students were drafted and died at Quangtri or Dongha, on Route 1 or on Route 13, in Binhduong or at Cuchi. The teacher feared for them during the long hours he taught them geometry, as he had feared for ten classes before them.

"It is not the past that haunts me now. It is the future that makes me tremble," he said. We spoke in French.

In the graveyard called South Vietnam, where officially the population is said to be seventeen million but is surely much less by now, you do not ask a Vietnamese about the future. They do not need to go into an even deeper darkness.

The future is not next year for them but tonight at five o'clock when there is enough rice to eat—or not nearly enough. It is tomorrow at 6 a.m. Nothing is taken for granted. Each day is a separate ordeal. Oddly enough, it is not the faces of refugees that I remember but that of a tiny, smiling cook who worked for some Americans in Saigon. One night she suddenly burst into tears after telling me how the price of tinned milk and rice had once more risen.

"We will all die," she said. I think she meant that the Vietnamese would die from worry and exhaustion, from scrambling and scrounging and waiting for the next blow.

Hell for the Vietnamese is not in the North, as many Americans might think, where U.S. bombings and battle deaths and the ghosts of missing men would have made a weaker nation—one less persuaded of its worth and its purpose—hemorrhage to death. They are better off there than in the South. Ellen Hammer, in her classic *Struggle for Indochina, 1940-1955*, writes: "No Vietnamese can forget that Ho Chi Minh was the first Vietnamese leader to declare the independence of Vietnam. He declared an independent state in September 1945 and a free state in March 1946. When Ho Chi Minh went to war, he seemed to be the heir to the nationalist tradition of his people."

In the North they have Ho. They had him when he lived, and they have him after his death. Almost nothing will convince them that this war is not a moral crusade, and that can only strengthen them. Long years of bombing by the richest and most powerful nation in the world has shown them that their survival is a triumphant victory. Man has won over the machine. This is their banner.

The Vietnamese hell is in the South. And there it cannot be described by statistics that overwhelm and numb the mind—400,000 Vietnamese civilians killed and 900,000 wounded between 1965 and 1972, as many as eight million villagers uprooted from their homes. South Vietnam, for me, is not a nation but a territory in which huge numbers of displaced persons live, persons who have been abused and betrayed by their government, its officials, and its allies. To survive in the chaos and rot of South Vietnam, one must not be too poor or too honest; a man must cheat. It is a country not only of the poor but of the bewildered and frightened, who see clearly that there is no one to restore order to their lives and no one to counsel and defend them. In the cities—the swollen, sickly places where refugees have bad dreams—you can see most clearly what has broken down. A man can only hope to get by if he pays and collects small bribes. *Tien ca phe,* or "coffee money," the Saigonese call it.

Often the most desperate war widows or parents of the dead or wounded must be able to pay coffee money or else risk long delays before receiving legitimate benefits. Just to receive an application form at the Ministry of War Veterans building in Saigon to file for a pension meant, when I was last in Vietnam, giving the clerk 200 piasters—and the price has surely gone up.

"We are very miserable," Mrs. Nguyen Thi Quang, a twenty-six-year-old widow who has five children, said to me last year.

There must be Americans as miserable as Mrs. Quang was, but I have not met them. Her husband, a government soldier, was killed on February 14, 1970, in a thirty-minute fire fight in the Mekong Delta. She came to Saigon with her five children to fill out the papers for her pension, hoping this would speed things up. When I saw her, she had more than sixty required documents in a big, red folder. One corner of it had been bitten off by a rat. It worried Mrs. Quang very much that, if the papers became soiled, they would be invalid. She paid her coffee money and received a lump sum of 60,000 piasters, which was then worth about $500.

"For days I wept because of the complications," she said. "On the day when I received the money it seemed no tears were left inside me." In addition to the lump sum, she received a war widow's pension of $41, which, owing to inflation, then had the purchasing power of $12 a month—in one of the most expensive cities in the world.

We American reporters in Vietnam knew how expensive the city was, but, of course, with our American-scaled salaries and expense accounts, prices did not terrify us. I remember when I discovered, to my horror, that a young Vietnamese named Truong Hong Bac, who did laundry, was often eating the bread and a leftover fried egg on my plate after breakfast so he could save the equivalent of 27 cents a day, which is what he would ordinarily have had to spend for his own breakfast. Bac was ashamed of this. He told me that because of rising prices he thought he soon would not be able to eat even one good meal a day.

Nowhere in the South did life proceed decently, with any degree of dignity. It is true that for centuries the average Vietnamese has never been a position to control his own environment and that he has traditionally been reluctant to act on his own initiative. Over the centuries he has been taught to accept authority at every stage of his existence, starting with his father. But this comforting framework has collapsed in the South, leaving nothing but greedy men victimizing the most frail.

....

The disorder and unease of South Vietnamese society have bred a selfishness that seems almost inhuman. I remember, with deep disgust, that in 1970 the survivors of the Mylai massacre had to sell the last of their possessions so they could pay the required bribes to the village office just to obtain the necessary papers for refugee resettlement benefits. They were not being compensated for the massacre, only for having been moved from their homes to another site. Indeed, the government of President Nguyen Van Thieu never acknowledged that there had been a massacre of Vietnamese civilians by American soldiers on March 16, 1968.

A sixty-year-old woman, too frightened to give me her name, said she had sold a pair of gold earrings given to her by her "mother's mother" to raise the 1,000 piasters needed for the bribe. She said this without self-pity but with a slight trace of contempt.

The village clerks of Sonmy (where the hamlet of Mylai was located) would have been astonished to have been punished for their merciless behavior. In their eyes they were doing it only to make sure their own families would not suffer. A man, after all, cannot live these days on the wages of a clerk. How often I heard this.

Before I left that cursed village in Quangngai Province, a forty-two-year-old man named Do Cam made a polite request. That was one of the few times when a Vietnamese spoke to me on behalf of others.

"I beg you to carry out your duties cleverly so that, when you leave, nobody in this hamlet will be in trouble with the government," Mr. Cam said. I promised.

The effects of the war have been so deep and so disruptive—I do not speak of bomb craters but of the Vietnamese view of themselves and of their world—that it is hard for me to imagine, even with peace, how a healing process could take place in my lifetime. A member of the Provisional Revolutionary Government's delegation to the Paris peace talks once told an American that the work of rehabilitating and restoring the South and its people would have to be the work of "many generations." The wreckage, seen and unseen, is very great.

It is not, perhaps, the bomb craters that have left the worse scars. A walk through the streets of Saigon can be more disturbing than flying over War Zone C, as the Americans used to call it, looking down at the earth. I am not an ecologist, but maybe it is possible that the good, rich earth of Cochin-China, as it was once called, will heal. I am not so sure the people can.

". . . WE COULD FINALLY EAT IN PEACE"*

They were the days that would culminate on March 16, that terrible March 16: My Lai massacre. Do you remember the testimony of the ones who took part in it? "Everyone who went into the village intended to kill. The order was to destroy My Lai to the last chicken, nothing must be left alive there. . . ." "We had collected men, women, children and babies in the middle of the village, like a little island. Lieutenant Calley came and said: 'You know what you've got to do, don't you?' Then he came back a little later and said: 'Why haven't you killed them yet?' I said I thought he wanted us to keep an eye on them, that's all. And he said: 'No, I want them dead.' And he began firing at them and told me to fire at them as well. So I loaded my M-16 with four clips which made sixty-eight shots altogether, and shot at the groups. I must have killed about ten or fifteen. . . ." "There was an old man in the shelter. He was shriveled up and very old. Sergeant Mitchell cried: 'Kill him.' And then someone killed him. . . ." "At the entrance to the village there was a pile of corpses. And there was a very small child wearing a short little shirt and nothing else. And this little kid came up to the corpses and picked up the hand of a dead woman—his mother, I guess. Then one of the GIs behind me knelt down in the firing position and got him with a single shot. . . ." "They were firing at everyone, at everything, without any reason—for instance, at the huts which were burning. White guys and black guys. But no one fired at the GIs, not a single civilian fired. We met no resistance, none at all. Besides, I didn't see one boy old enough to. . . ." "I couldn't believe my eyes. Two children were walking along the path; one must have been five and the other about four. A GI fired at the smaller one and then the bigger one threw himself on the body to protect it. The guy fired six shots at him. Calley's men did some strange things. They set fire to the huts and waited for the people to run outside so they could shoot them . . ." "When the whole thing was over Billy and I settled down to eat. But near us there was this band of wounded Vietnamese and some of them were still wiggling and moaning. Then Billy and I got up and finished them off. And we could finally eat in peace. . . ."

. . . .

*Adapted from Oriana Fallaci, *Nothing, and So Be It*: A Personal Search for Meaning in War. (Garden City, N.Y.: Doubleday & Co., Inc., 1972), pp. 188–189.

THE PASTOR'S PEN *

On the morning of June 9, 1942, ten truck loads of German Security Police under the command of Captain Max Rostock arrived at the tiny Czechoslovakian village of Lidice not far from Prague. The police surrounded the village and began, systematically, to kill every man and boy over 16 years of age (172 in all) in reprisal for the death, by bombing, of Reinhard Heydrich, chief of Security Police.

Seven women were taken to Prague where they were shot. All the rest of the women of Lidice, who numbered 195, were taken to the Ravensbrueck concentration camp, where seven were gassed, three "disappeared," and forty-two died of ill treatment. Four women of the village who were about to give birth were first taken to a maternity hospital in Prague where their newly born infants were murdered and they, themselves, then shipped to Ravensbrueck.

The children of Lidice were either sent to the concentration camp at Geisenau or, after suitable examination by Himmler's "racial experts" selected to be sent to Germany to be brought up as Germans under German names.

The Security Police burned down the village, dynamited the ruins and leveled it off. Lidice became a symbol of Nazi savagery of a sort which was manifested in even more terrible fashion in other European villages with names like Televaag (Norway) and Oradour-sur-Glace (France).

For the massacre of the people of Lidice Captain Rostock was hanged in Prague as a war criminal in 1951.

Early on the morning of March 16, 1968, American troops of Charley Company, First Platoon, under the command of Lt. William Calley, Jr., arrived by helicopter at the village of My Lai 4 in South Vietnam. In their sweep through the village the American troops shot and killed over 100 unarmed villagers, including old men, women and children. The village of My Lai was burned to the ground and ceased to exist.

Today, Lt. Calley stands convicted of the massacre at My Lai. Like Captain Max Rostock who commanded on the fateful June day at Lidice, Lt. Calley faces the prospect of, alone, bearing the guilt of these "war crimes."

But just as Captain Rostock's execution did not absolve the German nation and people of the guilt for Lidice—for that is where the guilt ultimately rested—so the execution of Lt. Calley will not absolve the

*Program note by Rev. Alfred M. Smith, Sunday bulletin, Scottsdale (Az.) United Methodist Church, April 6, 1971.

United States and its people of the guilt for My Lai which we must all ultimately bear.

The question which haunts me in the aftermath of the My Lai exposure is this: Does My Lai reveal that the Germans who perpetrated such acts of savagery in World War II, were, after all, just as good as we? Or, does My Lai reveal that we are, after all, just as bad as they?

Either way you phrase it, it is a frightening question.

BEYOND ATROCITY*

When asked to speak on recent occasions, I have announced my title as "On Living in Atrocity." To be sure, neither I nor anyone else lives there all or even most of the time. But at this moment, in early 1971, an American investigator of atrocity finds himself dealing with something that has become, for his countrymen in general, a terrible subterranean image that can be neither fully faced nor wished away. There is virtue in bringing that image to the surface.

In one sense, no matter what happens in the external world, personal atrocity, for everyone, begins at birth. It can also be said that some of us have a special nose for atrocity. Yet I can remember very well, during the early stirrings of the academic peace movement taking place around Harvard University during the mid- and late 1950s—about two hundred years ago, it now seems—how hard it was for us to *feel* what might happen at the other end of a nuclear weapon. Whatever one's nose for atrocities, there are difficulties surrounding the imaginative act of coming to grips with them.

After six months of living and working in Hiroshima, studying the human effects of the first atomic bomb, I found that these difficulties were partly overcome and partly exacerbated. On the one hand, I learned all too well to feel what happened at the other end of an atomic bomb. But on the other hand, I became impressed with the increasing gap we face between our technological capacity for perpetrating atrocities and our imaginative ability to confront their full actuality. Yet the attempt to narrow that gap can be enlightening, even liberating. For me, Hiroshima was a profoundly "radicalizing" experience—not in any strict ideological sense but in terms of fundamental issues of living and dying, of how one lives, of how one may die.

*Adapted from Robert Jay Lifton, "Beyond Atrocity," *Saturday Review* 54(March 27, 1971):23–25ff.

Whatever the contributing wartime pressures, Hiroshima looms as a paradigm of technological atrocity. Each of the major psychological themes discernible in Hiroshima survivors—death immersion, psychic numbing, residual guilt—has direct relationship to the atrocity's hideously cool and vast technological character. The specific technology of the bomb converted the brief moment of exposure into a lifelong encounter with death—through the sequence of the survivor's early immersion in massive and grotesque death and dying, his experiencing or witnessing bizarre and frequently fatal acute radiation effects during the following weeks and months, his knowledge of the increased incidence over the years of various forms (always fatal) of leukemia and cancer, and finally his acquisition of a death-tainted group identity, an "identity of the dead" or shared sense of feeling emotionally bound both to those killed by the bomb and to the continuing worldwide specter of nuclear genocide.

The experience of psychic numbing, or emotional desensitization—what some survivors called "paralysis of the mind"—was a necessary defense against feeling what they clearly knew to be happening. But when one looks further into the matter he discovers that those who made and planned the use of that first nuclear weapon—and those who today make its successors and plan their use—require their own form of psychic numbing. They too cannot afford to feel what they cognitively know would happen.

Victims and victimizers also shared a sense of guilt, expressed partly in a conspiracy of silence, a prolonged absence of any systematic attempt to learn about the combined physical and psychic assaults of the bomb on human beings. Survivors felt guilty about remaining alive while others died, and also experienced an amorphous sense of having been part of, having imbibed, the overall evil of the atrocity. The perpetrators of Hiroshima (and those in various ways associated with them)—American scientists, military and political leaders, and ordinary people—felt their own forms of guilt, though, ironically, in less tangible ways than the victims. Yet one cannot but wonder to what extent Hiroshima produced in Americans (and others) a guilt-associated sense that if we could do this we could do anything, and that anyone could do anything to us—in other words, an anticipatory sense of unlimited atrocity.

If these are lessons of Hiroshima, one has to learn them personally. My own immersion in massive death during investigations in that city, though much more privileged and infinitely less brutal, will nonetheless be as permanent as that of Hiroshima survivors themselves. As in their case, it has profoundly changed my relationship to my own death as well as to all collective forms of death that stalk us. I had a similarly personal lesson regarding psychic numbing. During my first few interviews in Hiroshima I felt overwhelmed by the grotesque horrors described to me, but within the short space of a week or so this feeling gave way to a much more comfortable sense of myself as a psychological investigator, still deeply troubled by what he heard but undeterred from his investigative commitment. This kind of partial, task-oriented numbing now strikes me as inevitable and, in this situation, useful—yet at the same time potentially malignant in its implications.

By "becoming" a Hiroshima survivor (as anyone who opens himself to the experience must), while at the same time remaining an American, I shared something of both victims' and victimizers' sense of guilt. This kind of guilt by identification has its pitfalls, but I believe it to be one of the few genuine psychological avenues to confrontation of atrocity. For these three psychological themes are hardly confined to Hiroshima: Death immersion, psychic numbing, and guilt are a psychic trinity found in all atrocity.

Hiroshima also taught me the value and appropriateness of what I would call the apocalyptic imagination. The term offends our notions of steadiness and balance. But the technological dimensions of contemporary atrocity seem to me to require that we attune our imaginations to processes that are apocalyptic in the full dictionary meaning of the word—processes that are "wildly unrestrained" and "ultimately decisive," that involve "forecasting or predicting the ultimate destiny of the world in the shape of future events" and "foreboding imminent disaster or final doom."

In the past this kind of imagination has been viewed as no more than the "world-ending" delusion of the psychotic patient. But for the people of Hiroshima the "end of the world"—or something very close to it—became part of the actuality of their experience. Thus one survivor recalled: "My body seemed all black; everything seemed dark, dark all over . . . then I thought, 'The world is ending.'" And another: "The feeling I had was that everyone was dead. . . . I thought this was the end of Hiroshima—of Japan—of humankind." Those witnessing Nazi mass murder—the greatest of all man's atrocities to date—called forth similar images, though they could usually perceive that the annihilating process was in some way selective (affecting mainly Jews or anti-Nazis or other specific groups). As Hiroshima took me to Auschwitz and Treblinka, however, I was struck mostly by the similarities and parallels in the overall psychology of atrocity.

Yet similar end-of-the-world impressions have been recorded in connection with "God-made" atrocities, as in the case of survivors' accounts of the plagues of the Middle Ages:

> How will posterity believe that there has been a time when without the lightings of heaven or the fires of earth, without wars or other

visible slaughter, not this or that part of the earth, but well-nigh the whole globe, has remained without inhabitants. ... We should think we were dreaming if we did not with our eyes, when we walk abroad, see the city in mourning with funerals, and returning to our home, find it empty, and thus know that what we lament is real.

The plagues were God-made not only in the sense of being a mysterious and deadly form of illness outside of man's initiation or control but also because they could be comprehended as part of a God-centered cosmology. To be sure, scenes like the above strained people's belief in an ordered universe and a just God, but their cosmology contained enough devils, enough flexibility, and enough depth of imprint to provide, if not a full "explanation" of holocaust, at least a continuing psychic framework within which to go on living. In contrast, Hiroshima and Auschwitz were carried out by men upon men, and at a time when old cosmologies had already lost much of their hold and could provide little explanatory power. Survivors were left with an overwhelming sense of dislocation and absurdity: Like the GI quoted earlier in relationship to Mylai, something for them was "missing"—namely, meaning, or a sense of reality. With Hiroshima and Auschwitz now part of man's historical experience, it is perilously naïve to insist that our imaginative relationship to world-destruction can remain unchanged—that we can continue to make a simple-minded distinction between psychotic proclivity for, and "normal" avoidance of, that image.

Yet, whatever the force of external events, there is a subjective, imaginative component to the perceived "end of the world." Hiroshima survivors had to call forth early inner images of separation and helplessness, of stasis and annihilation, images available from everyone's infancy and childhood, but with greater force to some than to others. There is, therefore, a danger, not just for Hiroshima survivors but for all of us, of being trapped in such images, bound by a psychic sense of doom to the point of being immobilized and totally unable or unwilling to participate in essential day-by-day struggles to counter atrocity and prevent the collective annihilation imagined.

Psychological wisdom, then, seems to lie in neither wallowing in, nor numbing ourselves to, our imaginings of apocalypse. A simple example of the constructive use of the apocalyptic imagination is recorded by Eugene Rabinowitch, from the beginning an articulate leader in scientists' anti-atomic bomb movements. Rabinowitch describes how, when walking down the streets of Chicago during the summer of 1945, he looked up at the city's great buildings and suddenly imagined a holocaust in which sky-scrapers crumbled. He then vowed to redouble his efforts to prevent that kind of event from happening by means of the scientists' petition he and others were drawing up to head off the dropping of an atomic bomb, without warning, on a populated area. The effort, of course, failed, but this kind of apocalyptic imagination—on the part of Rabinowitch, Leo Szilard, and Bertrand Russell, among others—has made it possible for at least a small minority of men and women to name and face the true conditions of our existence. (Bertrand Russell had earlier exhibited the dangers of the apocalyptic imagination when he advocated that we threaten to drop atomic bombs on Russia in order to compel it to agree to a system of international control of nuclear weapons.) For we live in the shadow of the ultimate atrocity, of the potentially terminal revolution—and if that term is itself a contradiction, the same contradiction is the central fact of our relationship to death and life.

We perpetrate and experience the American atrocity at Mylai in the context of these apocalyptic absurdities and dislocations. The GI's quoted description suggests not only that atrocity can be a dreamlike affair (in this sense, resembling the quoted passage about the plague) but that it is committed by men living outside of ordinary human connection, outside of both society and history. Mylai was acted out by men who had lost their bearings, men wandering about in both a military and psychic no man's land. The atrocity itself can be seen as a grotesquely paradoxical effort to put straight this crooked landscape, to find order and significance in disorder and absurdity. There is at the same time an impulse to carry existing absurdity and disorder to their logical extremes as if both to transcend and demonstrate that aberrant existential state.

Atrocities are committed by desperate men—in the case of Mylai, men victimized by the absolute contradictions of the war they were asked to fight, by the murderous illusions of their country's policy. Atrocity, then, is a perverse quest for meaning, the end result of a spurious sense of mission, the product of false witness.

To say that American military involvement in Vietnam is itself a crime is also to say that it is an atrocity-producing situation. Or to put the matter another way, Mylai illuminates, as nothing else has, the essential nature of America's war in Vietnam. The elements of this atrocity-producing situation include an advanced industrial nation engaged in a counter-insurgency action, in an underdeveloped area, against guerrillas who merge with the people—precisely the elements that Jean Paul Sartre has described as inevitably genocidal. In the starkness of its murders and the extreme dehumanization experienced by victimizers and imposed on victims, Mylai reveals to us how far America has gone along the path of deadly illusion.

PRISONERS OF PEACE *

This piece by Shana Alexander is startlingly up-to-date despite its publication two years before this book goes to press. Ms. Alexander answers the question "Who won the Vietnam war?" thus: "Nobody won because the war isn't over." That became all too clear when, early in 1975, the quarter century old Vietnam war heated up once again. ". . . the war that will not end" said a headline in the Boston Globe *(5 Jan 75).*

World War I had the Rainbow Division. World War II had Iwo Jima and the Bulge. Even Korea had the men of Changjin Reservoir. But until last week the longest and most dismal of all America's wars had victims, casualties and the faceless brutalities and braveries common to all wars, but no heroes at all. Well, we have them now.

One of Melvin Laird's last and finest acts as a Washington bureaucrat was to scrap a monstrous mouthful of Pentagonese—Operation Egress Recap—and retitle it Operation Homecoming. The new label for the prisoners' return gave one a faint foreshadowing that some measure of grace was also about to return to American life.

When the first batch of prisoners came bounding down the airplane steps, in so much better shape than anyone had been led to expect, joy was universal. Even press and politicians wept. . . .

Unlike American soldiers in war movies, these POWs did not ask: "Who won the World Series?" Instead they asked: "Who won the war?"

Of all the high-flown phrases cranked out about Operation Homecoming, none was sadder and more revealing than the military's carefully prepared reply: "South Vietnam didn't lose, and North Vietnam didn't win."

This is the language of Alice in Wonderland, the logic of Kafka and the voice of "1984." I think these first-returned men deserved a straight answer, not another riddle.

Surely what they really wanted to know when they asked who won was "Did *we* win or lose?" Why else save to win had they been there so long, and given so much? It is also doubtful that men whose professional duty had been to drop bombs from airplanes cared much whether northern peasants had beat southern peasants, or vice versa.

Nothing more cruelly exposes the hollowness of America's own position in the war than this tragic question and answer. For if nobody lost and nobody won, which is what this official reply says, then the war becomes officially meaningless. More than 46,000 Americans died for a circular

*Shana Alexander, "Prisoners of Peace," *Newsweek* 81(5 Mar 73):32.

sequence of justifications. And Captain Heck, the bomber pilot who after flying 156 missions refused to fly the 157th, was right when he said: "I have come to the conclusion that no war is ever worth what it costs to win it."

Still another way to answer the question "Who won?" is to say, "Nobody won because the war isn't over." Since the "cease-fire" the level of combat has increased. No wonder, despite Homecoming's joys, that the old Egress Recap label continues to haunt the mind. The egress part is clear enough, but what does "recap" mean? Is it something like tire recapping? After hearing nearly identical statements of loyalty and patriotism from each man, one wondered if they had not been brainwashed more in twenty hours on the plane home than in all the years in camp; as if what had been recapped was the prisoners' heads. The POWs often seemed to be offering only name, rank and serial number to the American public.

Our joy in having the prisoners back goes beyond relief at their safety, and the surprise of their excellent physical and mental health. Part of what we feel comes from our admiration for their personal character. One of the many ironies of this meaningless, disastrous war—disastrous *because* meaningless—is that, having sat out the permissive '60s in the skies and jungles of Vietnam, these POWs now appear to us to embody precisely those moral qualities of honor, patriotism, discipline and purpose which many of us feel have largely disappeared from American life. The penultimate irony may be that no one suffers this disappearance more keenly than Mr. Nixon himself.

A nation cannot long sustain a war its own people don't believe in. The South Vietnamese themselves long ago re-established the truth of that old cliché. But Americans too have needed something to believe in, and many who found the Communist-containment line insufficient also reject the peace-with-honor gambit. Operation Homecoming has given those Americans something to pin their belief on.

As heroes of the Vietnamese war, these POWs are precious to us in a most special way. If it is not possible to hail them as conquering heroes, then we will hail them as survivors. For hail them we must, lest the entire episode in Indochina be seen as the national disgrace it is. The final irony may be that after eight cruel years as prisoners of war, they have now become hostages of propaganda, prisoners of peace with honor.

No War – No Peace

Our consideration of war as an instrument of national policy concludes with a series of pieces indicating what the military has in store for us now and in the future. We find that deterrence theory is bankrupt, that our much-praised renunciation of biological warfare is a myth, that MIRV is as likely to start war as to prevent it, and that the SALT "disarmament" talks were actually agreements for massive arms development. The one bright note that come to mind is the 1974 American role in the Mid-East. Surely no fair person decries Secretary of State Kissinger's peace-making efforts between the Israelis and the Arab states. But what about his 1975 New Year's threat that America will intervene militarily if high oil prices seriously threaten the living level of the industrialized West? And, given "the military mind," what does the future hold? Will a few survivors envy the dead? Or will a doomsday machine end the whole show? Those who conclude that doomsday-type atomic weapons are so destructive they will never be used would be wise to remember that not all observers are so rational. A hint of the mentality prevailing in some high circles was provided by the late southern senator who asserted, in reply to critics of a Pentagon request for tactical nuclear devices, "If we have to start all over again, I want Adam and Eve to be Americans, not Asians or Europeans."

WHAT IS SECURITY? *

Richard Barnet is a widely recognized authority on national security and arms control problems. A graduate of the Harvard law school, he helped establish the prestigious independent research and education center called The Institute for Policy Studies. He has served with the State Department and the U.S. Arms Control and Disarmament Agency.

Since 1946 the taxpayers have been asked to contribute more than one trillion dollars for national security. Each year the federal government spends more than 70 cents of every budget dollar on past, present, and future wars. The American people are devoting more resources to the war machine than is spent by all federal, state, and local governments on health and hospitals, education, old-age and retirement benefits, public assistance and relief, unemployment and social security, housing and community development, and the support of agriculture. Out of every tax dollar there is about 11 cents left to build American society.

Nations, like families, reveal themselves through budgets. No personal document tells more about a man's values or his hopes and fears than the family budget. Similarly, the way to size up a nation is to examine the

*Adapted from Richard J. Barnet, *The Economy of Death* (New York: Atheneum, 1969), 5–7, 29–33, 59, 73–74.

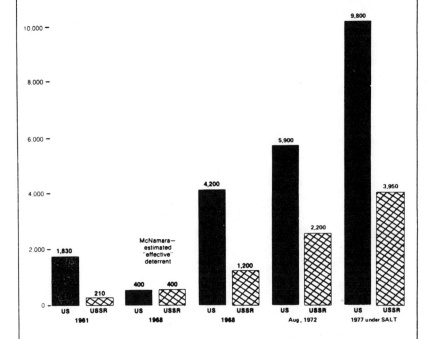

THE NUCLEAR ARMS RACE *

Number of Nuclear Warheads Deliverable by Intercontinental Ballistic Missiles (ICBM's), Submarine-Launched Ballistic Missiles (SLBM's) and Intercontinental Bombers

US 1961: 1,830 — USSR 1961: 210
US 1968: 400 (McNamara—estimated "effective" deterrent) — USSR 1968: 400
US 1968: 4,200 — USSR 1968: 1,200
US Aug, 1972: 5,900 — USSR Aug, 1972: 2,200
US 1977 under SALT: 9,800 — USSR 1977 under SALT: 3,950

Since World War II, the United States has spent $1.3 trillion on military programs. The Soviet Union has spent an estimated $1 trillion. A large part of these huge expenditures has been used to build nuclear weapons.

When both countries signed the SALT accords in 1972, they agreed to limit defensive missiles to very low levels and to stablize the number of offensive missiles for five years. However, SALT does not halt the nuclear arms race.

*Source: SANE WORLD (Society for a Sane Nuclear Policy).

national budget. But the real cost of America's search for security through armaments cannot be adequately measured in money. Ordinary mortals, even rich mortals and the Congressmen who vote the appropriations, cannot understand what a trillion dollars is. To comprehend the magnitude of our investment in killing power, we need to look at what we have sacrificed for it. The Economy of Life in America has been starved to feed the Economy of Death.

The result of this gigantic investment in security has been to make the American people among the most insecure on the planet. Perhaps the most important index of this fact is that Americans are more afraid to walk the streets of Washington than the streets of Saigon. These feelings are a direct reflection of an increasingly violent society. College presidents are beginning to administer their universities with the aid of armed helicopters. A carnival of anger has swept across the ghettos of every American metropolis; the fragile nature of our civilization is attested by the burned and looted stores of the inner city. Teachers, garbage men, and taxi drivers have taken turns in bringing America's largest city to standstill. The President of the United States no longer dares to travel among the people.

An incipient civil war has already begun. Young against old. Suburb against inner city. Black against white. According to the President's Violence Commission, an American is four times more likely to be a victim of violence than a West European. In his [first] inaugural address President Nixon alluded to the crisis of spirit in the United States and counseled people not to shout at one another. But good manners, important as it is to restore them, are no answer to the American crisis. As a college president recently observed on the day he resigned in the wake of a student rebellion, "A society that does not correct its own ills cannot expect peace."

The pattern is tragically familiar. The world historian Arnold Toynbee, who has traced the fate of the great empires of the past, finds that most have gone down to defeat not by invasion from without but because of social dissolution within. Mighty nations that do not respond to the needs of their own people have traditionally tried to solve problems and overcome frustrations through violence abroad and repression at home. In the process, they have hastened their own exit from center stage. The greatest security problems for a nation are the hostility and frustration of its own citizens. . . .

How does the arms race work?

The experience of the last twenty-five years makes clear that an attempt to stockpile nuclear hardware beyond what is conceivably needed to destroy the adversary's cities sets off a frantic escalation of the arms race on both sides.

Imagine the following conversation in the Kremlin. A Soviet general with a secret intelligence report on U.S. war plans gleaned from a careful reading of *The New York Times* demands an urgent audience with his

Chairman. He then informs him that the U.S. is proceeding to increase its
nuclear-missile stockpile from 4500 to 11,000 by building MIRV, the
hydra-headed missile that can hit several pre-selected targets at once, and at
the same time is also building ABM.

"Why are they doing a thing like that?" asks the Chairman.

"Don't have a clue," replies the general. "Or, rather, we've got too
many clues. The Americans give a new reason for building these forces
every time someone shoots down the old reasons."

"I don't like it. Do you think they are trying for a surprise attack?"

"They'd be crazy to try even with twenty thousand nuclear warheads.
They could never knock out all our retaliatory missiles. But maybe they
don't know that. They say they do, but you can't trust them. We must
assume that MIRV might destroy nearly all our present missile force. We'd
better err on the safe side and build both MIRV *and* ABM. Nothing less
will convince the Americans that getting into a nuclear war with us is
dangerous."

Meanwhile, back in the White House, Secretary Laird lays a sheaf of
top-secret photographs before President Nixon: "Looking over the development in the current deployment of the SS-9 [the late-model Soviet intercontinental missile] leads me to the conclusion that with their big warhead
and the testing that is going forward in the Soviet Union, this weapon can
only be aimed at destroying our retaliatory force."

"This looks like a security gap to me," says Nixon. "How many do they
have?"

"They'll have maybe five hundred by 1976. It looks like they're trying
for a first strike, and make no mistake about that. We need to increase our
yearly spending on nuclear forces by at least ten billion."

The only difference between the two conversations is that while the
Kremlin discussion is imagined, the White House discussion is reconstructed
from actual public statements. Because each side is uncertain about the
intentions of the other and the consequences of a "degraded deterrent" are
so disastrous, both overdesign and overbuild their forces. When one side
builds too much, the other assumes that it too must prepare for the worst.
When both sides arm themselves against their own strategists' most
pessimistic fantasies, the arms race spirals. Thus the attempt to gain
absolute safety in a nuclear war by building more weapons makes nuclear
war more likely. When both sides are in crash programs, there is a growing
risk that one or the other will panic and try a "pre-emptive attack,"
however irrational. One of the many specious arguments for building more
missiles and particularly the ABM is to protect against a small attack
launched by an "irrational man." It is hard to think of a more unstable
atmosphere for an unstable man than the continuing arms race.

MIRV is peculiarly dangerous because it increases uncertainty on both sides. Neither the Pentagon nor the Kremlin knows how many separate warheads are concealed in its adversary's missiles. Each plans for the worst and thus makes a reality of the other's nightmare. The losers are the American and Soviet peoples. Both are taxed in new and higher amounts to support a system in which the only sure result is that in the event of nuclear war more people will be killed. Since the actual number of warheads concealed in a missile nose-cone is unknown, the introduction of MIRV greatly complicates the problem of inspection and makes arms control almost impossible. As Clark Clifford put it in his final statement as Secretary of Defense:

> We stand on the eve of a new round in the armaments race with the Soviet Union, a race which will contribute nothing to the real security of either side while increasing substantially the already great defense burdens of both.

With this regrettable development noted, the Secretary went on to list his "strategic requirements." In addition to MIRV for the land-based Minuteman, the taxpayer needs Poseidon, which is a MIRVed version of Polaris, to shoot from submarines; SRAM (Short-Range Attack Missile) to launch from bombers to overcome Soviet air defense and to protect the bomber from any suggestion of obsolescence; SCAD (Subsonic Cruise Armed Decoy), another aspect of the bomber-rejuvenation program; ULMS, a new sea-based missile system for use when it is trade-in time for Poseidon; and the marvelously resilient advanced manned bomber, which appears to be impervious to rejection. This hardware list, which is being expanded by the Nixon Administration, costs about $10 billion a year, and within the next five years the annual cost is likely to be almost twice that amount. The total cost of these programs could come to more than $100 billion in all. That is a sizable invest.nent for something that "will contribute nothing to the real security" of the American people.

. . . .

The economy of Death defies logic. A piece of technology like the ABM is virtually discredited again and again by every former science adviser to the President, a number of Nobel Prize physicists, and several former high officials of the Defense Department itself. Yet the juggernaut moves on. If one rationale for building a new weapons system is exposed as nonsense, others spring up to take its place. The Secretary of State talks about détente and coexistence, and the Secretary of Defense demands the build-up of a first-strike force. The Pentagon demands billions to counter a nonexistent Chinese missile force while ghetto and campus rebellions, police riots, and political assassinations tear away at American society. Why?

The institutions which support the Economy of Death are impervious to ordinary logic or experience because they operate by their own inner logic. Each institutional component of the military-industrial complex has plausible reasons for continuing to exist and expand. Each promotes and protects its own interests and in so doing reinforces the interests of every other.

. . . .

The Armed Services have developed an elaborate packaging system to market their principal products to the public. Fear, of course, has been the biggest seller. It is packaged in a variety of ways. The National Security Seminar of the Industrial College of the Armed Forces, for example, has held 293 seminars in 161 cities, attended by more than 175,000 reserve officers and civilians. America "is faced by the greatest danger the world has ever known—the cancer of communism," Captain William A. Twitchell of the U.S. Navy told an understandably nervous audience at a typical National Security Seminar in Sioux Falls, South Dakota, in 1963. Colonel Charles Caple of the Air Force assured the people of Sioux Falls that any Soviet leader would have the same aim: "to destroy our way of life. We cannot coexist with these people." Representatives of industry, labor, business, education, religion, the professions, government, and civic and women's organizations are encouraged to attend as a patriotic duty.

There are 6140 public-relations men on the Pentagon payroll. The information branch of the Public Affairs office of the Department of Defense alone, with a budget of $1.6 million, employs more than 200 officers and civilians located in the Pentagon and in key cities around the country. The Office of Information for the Armed Forces has a $5.3 million budget which is used for a global radio network that reaches vast civilian as well as military audiences. The Armed Services Radio and Television Service operates 350 stations in 29 countries and 9 U.S. territories, spends $10 million a year and has 1700 employees. It is the largest broadcasting network in the world. Another agency for merchandising the Pentagon is the Armed Forces Motion Pictures, Publications and Press Service, which not only prints 8.5 million copies a year of some 70 military publications but also produces film clips and tapes for commercial TV and radio stations.

DETERRENCE THEORY*

The author of this consideration of "security through strength" has a Ph.D. in political science from Harvard University and is a former CIA official; his "An Open Letter to the Silent Majority" appears subsequently.

Nothing ought send a man with common sense up the wall like the claims of deterrence theorists and Pentagon enthusiasts that the Bomb is safe and will keep war from coming because men are dependably sensible and rational. Explicit in deterrence theory are the assumptions that human behavior and choices are calculable (". . . if we have this and they have that, and we do this and they do that, . . ."); that people and states calculate choice and behavior carefully and having done so are not substantially prone to error, neurosis, or irrational compulsion or impulse; or that the nuclear-bomb-missile deterrence system makes men more rational and sensible than they inherently are. Ask any taxi driver, advertising executive, nurse in an alcoholic or hard-drugs ward, riot squad leader, husband, wife, child, historian, political writer, psychologist, or psychiatrist!

From the beginnings of the age of democracy, since the French Revolution of 1789 when Napoleon dispelled the dreams of the Age of Reason, and the operations of capitalism shattered the free-market myths of Adam Smith, men have perceived that side by side with their reasonable natures nonrational powers and drives dwelt that are not easily tamed, nor easily prevented from exploding into soul- and society-shattering catastrophe. One must laugh, if weakly, at the proposition that humans are primarily rational; it's no less outrageous than the other obsessions with which we're concerned, and its hold on men lies in its staggeringly outrageous nature—the big lie—not in its logical merits.

The political theorists and jurists tell us that man without law and justice would be a wolf to man; that the fabric of statutory and common law constitutes a continuum in history that is a delicate social creation registering and organizing selected interactions among man's nature, drives, and aspirations; that the law's reason and the philosophy of democracy are rooted in both optimistic and pessimistic views of man; and that checks and balances and limited government are essential in democracies because of irrational drives for power.

Psychologists and psychiatrists have systematized observations of man's primal, wild streaks in treatises on crowd psychology, aggression,

*Adapted from Sidney J. Slomich, *The American Nightmare* (New York: The Macmillan Company, 1971), pp. 87–92.

nationalism and chauvinism, fascism's submissiveness, and regressive, primitive need in times of social and political insecurity to find identity and protection in submission to charismatic, domineering leaders, institutions or things—Hitler, Stalin, arms, missiles, technology. This side of man is no less real than the rational and purposeful represented by the concept of superego. Man is healthiest when expressing and realizing individual and biological drives within society, and primal, destructive impulses and drives emerge when man is separated or separates himself from social purpose. The concept of schizophrenia involves splitting from other men and plunging into artificial but comfortable tensions of fantasy worlds.

The so-called security of the nuclear-tipped missile defense system, based as it is on a view of man at variance with his true nature, is inaccurate, unrealistic and dangerous. Only the deluded can state or believe, in view of psychology's findings, that human nature is so rational and predictable that there is slight likelihood in the near future of either side's precipitating or blundering into a mass nuclear exchange, much less accidents or series of them claiming the lives of millions. What is required to maintain the missiles and to keep them from blowing up men is so inhuman that it's unrealistic to expect indefinite success.

Let us look at the lives men must lead to preserve, guard, and command these weapons. It strains belief that the Spanish, East Coast, and other Air Force accidents have not brought about catastrophe. The protection of anomic weapons makes healthy men anomic—tense, isolated, fearfully insecure, and the pressures keep building up and up and up. Penned in the ground with the missiles, with a few fellow men, always on the watch for breakdown in themselves and companions, always on the watch for the deadly blip or message that the Others are attacking, always worrying about confirming their reactions and those of others, always worrying about how they are doing. It's not, shall we say, fun. These men are always worrying about what it is they are doing, and they're aware, at least subconsciously, of screening from experiences differences between what they see in life and in the press and what they're told by their commanders. The world's burdens are literally upon them, but the world pays no attention, doesn't care; they're alone, preoccupied with possibilities of death. There is little relationship between what men do in the warning and command and control centers, the B-52s, below ground with the Minutemen, riding beneath the waves with Polarises, and the things they were taught at home and at school. Even Dick and Jane have nothing on it. It's no life for men and the possibility of catastrophic eruptions cannot be precluded.

How does one know whether and how long a man ought to remain in such circumstances? What's the breaking point? Have there been many close calls of which we don't know? How good is the psychological and psychiatric supervision? Is there any? How good is the screening of the FBI and the Office of Special Investigations (Air Force)? How good are the consulting psychologists and psychiatrists and how reliable? They are no less human than those they judge. Who screens the guardians checking out the psychological health of the guardians guarding the nuclear-tipped missiles aimed at the Russians and guarding us? According to the Associated Press in 1967, the Air Force had 26,500 officers and 85,000 enlisted men "in positions requiring human reliability clearance."[1] That's a lot of men to worry about, and they're far from all of them.

Communications within the nuclear deterrence system, among the missile commanders and their staffs and higher authority up to the White House is almost certainly excellent—as excellent as human engineering can make it. But how good are the communication systems with our adversaries? Or has all the talent, energy, and money gone to minimize communications contact in self-contained loops, so that we're crawling deeper into our own cocoon and they into theirs, huddling in the deadly technology of Final Solutions? The record does not reassure, and it may have been only accidental that the confrontations of October 1962 did not lead to nuclear holocausts.

As Mr. Sorensen[2] and Professor Schlesinger[3] so clearly and dramatically wrote in their accounts of the crisis, timing, decisions among alternative courses of action, and basic political-military strategy and approaches were severely affected by the nature of communications with the Soviets and even with the U.S. Embassy in Moscow. Propagation conditions affecting short-wave radio transmissions made instantaneous communication with the ambassador in Moscow impossible. With all the thousands of advisers, communications systems, memoranda, meetings, ulcers, worries, paper and all the rest of it was almost unilaterally resolved when President Kennedy chose to interpret an open to-whom-it-may-concern radio broadcast from Nikita Khrushchev as the half-capitulation the United States required as settlement. A less sensitive and less temperate leader could have interpreted Khrushchev's broadcast differently, and the crisis would have dragged on with unpleasant consequences—possibly air strikes and invasion of Cuba days later.

Only after this crisis did the United States and the Soviet Union set up a hot line to assure at least some direct communication in time of stress. A year or two later, however, it was put out of operation at least partially by adolescents in New York City, who cut it while prowling in the sewers.[4] There wasn't much of a back-up and a system of communications that could be put out of commission by two teenagers wasn't much of one. Subsequently in 1969 it was supplemented by direct teletype communications maintained by ITT World Communications on a twenty-four hour basis via submarine cables and land lines.[5] Still an accidental series of atomic explosions or simple forms of subversion might destroy them, while ionospheric propagation through short-wave remains slow and chancy.

In efforts to establish optimum command and control circuits and communications with forces in Vietnam, as well as with strategic nuclear and other forces, the Department of Defense through one of its sub-agencies—alone outnumbering the staff of the Arms Control and Disarmament Agency and probably the whole corps of foreign service officers—has spent hundreds of millions, including the purchase of satellites.

We have, then, anxious attention to retaliatory nuclear force communications requirements and reluctant, petty, almost random assurances regarding communications to prevent a universal holocaust. There are nuclear retaliatory "defense" satellites, but there is no nuclear standby peace satellite. Where would we be today without the ABC journalist John Scali who played such a crucial role in the life-and-death negotiations in October 1962, while multibillion dollar military and civilian communications megabureaucracies wallowed in impotence and were unable to help the President and his associates?

There were, then, in the hours of extremity only human answers and human relationships; common sense, judgment of the fitness of things and trust and belief in mutual desire to live. If and when the nuclear beasts are tamed and cast into the nether depths, as demons of fear and hate are cast back within the depths of our souls, it will be because we have established real social, political, cultural, economic, and other living links with our adversaries, in addition to expanded technical ones like special reserve conventional and satellite communications and many, many bilateral and multilateral peace-keeping links on earth. If it is done it will be because of change, because of rejecting the technological obsession.

But if we do not change, if we do not look for meaning to ideas and to politics instead of to things and possessions, if we persist in our blindness and particularism, if we do not again become alive to our traditions and better selves, we will burn our wives, our children, our friends, our societies, our great monuments to lost sanity, the fields and trees, the innocent animals, all to cinders. Foul death clouds will descend and float about the cinders of what was once a great, wide, beautiful, pulsating, life-intoxicated world.

REFERENCES

[1] "Pentagon Removes 10,000 Undesirables," *Los Angeles Herald-Examiner*, May 17, 1967.

² *Kennedy* (New York: Harper & Row, 1965), chap. xxiv and esp. p. 727.

³ *A Thousand Days* (Boston: Houghton Mifflin, 1965), chap. xxxi and esp. pp. 825–30.

⁴ "Hot Line Knocked Out by Seven Teen-agers," *Los Angeles Times*, May 17, 1965.

⁵ San Francisco *Chronicle*, March 17, 1969.

TEST-TUBE WARFARE, THE FAKE RENUNCIATION *

It will be three years in November since President Nixon officially renounced the use of biological weapons, directed the destruction of stockpiles, and ordered the discontinuance of further research into germ warfare. Yet, despite these Presidential directives, there has been an increase in Defense Department spending on research and development of chemical and biological weapons.

The Army is readying ranges for open-air testing of nerve gases—the same poisons that accidentally killed 6,400 sheep in Utah. The Defense Department remains amply endowed with government-owned facilities for chemical and biological warfare research. "In addition," says a study by James M. McCullough, Life Science Specialist at the Congressional Reference Service in the U.S. Library of Congress, "there have been university, private, and industrial laboratories working under Defense Department contracts on chemical and biological weapons." The study cites a governmental inventory of facilities that includes: the Edgewood (Maryland) Arsenal for "research and development on chemical agents and weapons and chemical warfare defense equipment and techniques"; the Chemical School at Fort McClellan, Arkansas, which conducts "some limited testing of agents"; the Rocky Mountain arsenal in Denver for the "production of chemical munition"; the Newport (Indiana) Chemical Plant "for the production of chemical agents"; the Dugway Proving Grounds in Utah for "field tests of chemical and biological agents"; the Naval Biological Laboratory in Oakland, California, for "biological warfare defense-related research"; the Air Force Proving Ground in Eglin, Florida, for "chemical and biological warfare research, development and test"; and the

*Adapted from Daniel S. Greenberg, "Test-Tube Warfare, the Fake Renunciation," *World* 1(15 Aug 72):26–28.

Naval Weapons Laboratory in Dahlgren, Virginia, for "chemical and biological warfare defense and safety research."

The quest for what is really happening in CBW must start with recognition of a fact that has been publicly stated but often overlooked in the euphoria produced by Mr. Nixon's assorted renunciations of CBW: The U.S. has not disavowed *chemical* warfare. It has disavowed only "first use" of it, which means that the Army—which is the principal custodian of CBW activities—is free to proceed with the development of gases and delivery systems. The U.S. acknowledges that it is doing this at budgetary levels little different from the spending that preceded Mr. Nixon's applause-winning announcements. Thus, if the publicly stated budgetary figures are to be believed, the total "chemical program" spending for research, development, test, and evaluation (RDT&E) is projected at $32.9-million for the current fiscal year; in 1970, the figure was $33.5-million.

Although some items within the total annual CBW budgets have decreased over the 1970–73 span, it is worth noting that the yearly RDT&E figure for "lethal chemicals" has risen from $4.3-million to $8-million, following sizable increases in previous years. In heavily censored testimony before the Senate Armed Services Committee last February, Lt. Gen. William C. Gribble, Jr., Army chief of research and development, made clear that the Army's interest in CBW is as strong as ever. "I think the scientists and the laboratory facilities that are engaged in this work are a national asset in terms of providing an emergency response should that ever be required," he said. "We must keep up with the state of the art...."

The same hearing brought out the fact that the Army plans to spend "a large part" of a $9.5-million budgetary item for improvements in the Dugway testing grounds. And recently, as part of the effort to promote public faith in the President's disavowals of CBW, Dugway was opened to newsmen for the first time in fifteen years. The most interesting product of the guided tour, however, was the commanding general's announcement that, as UPI reported it, "We are doing all we can short of atmospheric testing to find out what we need" concerning nerve gas.

. . . .

The Presidential ban on biological weapons was followed by the destruction of large stocks of a variety of grisly materials for producing disease in humans, livestock, and crops, all of which helped further the impression that the U.S. is getting out of the BW business. Actually, however, the Army retains authority for conducting "defensive" research; and while the President is being praised for ordering the old germ warfare labs converted to peaceful purposes, the Army has been shifting some of its staff operations to the Dugway Proving Grounds.

Budgetary figures, as well as gripes by laid-off workers at the old Fort Detrick laboratories, clearly indicate that the BW effort has been sharply scaled down. Nevertheless, within the category of "defensive" research, the spending plans are far from paltry. "Biological" research this year is projected at $4.2-million, compared with $7.7-million in 1970, while in the category of "defensive equipment" the current sum is $7.6-million. $7.6-million represents a drop of only $7-million over the four-year period.

The crucial question, of course, is whether the "defensive" role allows for experimentation on storage and delivery of biological organisms, as well as for the development of new biological agents. The Defense Department says that such work has been discontinued and that activities at Dugway are confined to "threat analysis"—the development of detection techniques, protective systems, and health countermeasures. The fact is, however, that the Army is the sole interpreter of the term "defensive," and its activities are conducted out of public scrutiny.

The Defense Department's own figures for procurement of chemical and biological systems, as distinct from the separate category of research, provide grounds for skepticism concerning the U.S. disavowal of these weapons. In 1970, the total for procurement was publicly stated to be $149.3-million, of which a substantial portion was for the purchase of herbicides for Vietnam. The exact figure for herbicides on an annual basis is obscured in the bookkeeping; but in response to an inquiry from Senator Gaylord Nelson (D-Wis.), the Air Force—which was responsible for buying the stuff and spraying it in Vietnam—reported overall expenditures of $134,049,005 for the purchase of the so-called Orange, White, and Blue herbicides.

. . . .

(Anyone who doubts the military capacity for blatant evasion of Presidential directives might refer to an official government history, *Science and the Air Force*, published in 1966. At one time, the book points out, the Bureau of the Budget decreed that the Air Force could no longer spend money on basic research. Research spending was continued nonetheless—by charging the costs off to development of a new bomber. "For all the Budget Bureau knew," the book gloats, "the $4.7-million it approved was for research connected with the development of this aircraft, clearly within the realm of applied research. But in reality, this money was handed over to OSR [Office of Scientific Research] to use, as originally planned, for basic research.")

. . . .

Negotiations for arms-control agreements with the Soviets have frequently foundered on the issue of inspection, with the U.S. insisting that its own inspectors, or perhaps an international group, have the right to conduct on-the-spot checks of compliance. Yet back home, the U.S. government seems unconcerned about verifying whether its army is in fact abiding by Presidential directives to engage only in "defensive" research. The Executive's disregard for Congress in military and foreign affairs has been so thoroughly demonstrated as to eliminate any realistic prospect for effective Congressional scrutiny. When Congress has questioned the military use of weather modification in Southeast Asia, for example, Defense's long-standing reply has been, in effect, that it is none of your business.

If there is ever an inspection agreement with the Soviets on CBW, it will have an ironic benefit: The American public will have reason to believe government accounts of what is going on in U.S. military laboratories.

THE MYTH OF MIRV*

... What is MIRV (Multiple Independently Targeted Re-entry Vehicle)? Why is the military so anxious to have it, and why have forty-two Senators sponsored a resolution urging the President to seek an agreement with the Russians to ban further tests?

Briefly, MIRV is a "missile bus" whose "passengers" are nuclear bombs. It enables a single booster to deliver as many as fourteen bombs, each one accurately aimed at a different target. The targets can be 50 or 100 miles apart, perhaps even more. Both we and the Russians have the know-how to produce MIRVs; none have been deployed yet, but testing is proceeding on both sides.

It is generally agreed that from a military viewpoint, MIRV is an effective weapon. Unlike ABM, which critics contend may not work and will not add to our defense, MIRV almost surely will work and potentially represents a tremendous increase in striking force. The opposition to MIRV is based on the conviction that it will lessen our security by severely escalating the arms race, and will increase the danger of nuclear war.

Much of the administration's case for ABM is based on the assumption that the Russians, by installing MIRVs in their big SS9 missiles, could threaten the reliability of our "nuclear umbrella" by the middle 1970s. The principal purpose of our own MIRVs, according to the Pentagon, would be to ensure our ability to penetrate any expanded Soviet ABM. The Defense

*Adapted from Leo Sartori, "The Myth of MIRV," *Saturday Review* 52(Aug. 30, 1969):10–15, 32.

Department plans to install MIRVs in about half our Minuteman ICBMs, and is refitting most of the Polaris submarine fleet with the new Poseidon missile, also to be equipped with MIRVs.

Critics point to the planned deployment of MIRV and ABM as a typical example of the futility of nuclear escalation—the dog chasing its own tail. We will install these weapons in response to the Russians' planned deployment, and they will install them in response to our own deployment. In the end both sides will be less secure, and the balance of terror will be more unstable than ever.

The best way to avoid this latest round of escalation is to agree with the Russians to stop testing MIRV. The opponents reason that neither side would stake its survival on an inadequately tested weapon. Therefore, if testing stops we can be confident there will be no deployment. But neither side would agree to a test ban if it felt the other side had already tested enough to go ahead with deployment. Since the United States is rapidly approaching this critical stage, a test ban must be agreed to quickly if it is to have any chance of success.

But even if we get an agreement not to test, how will we know the Russians aren't cheating? Fortunately, with spy satellites and other modern surveillance techniques, each side can detect with some confidence a test of a multiple warhead missile by the other. We have recently detected a Soviet test of this kind in the Pacific Ocean. On the other hand, a ban on deployment of MIRVs would be much more difficult to police. It is probably impossible to determine, without detailed on-site inspection, whether a missile in its silo contains one warhead or many. The issue of on-site inspection has been a major stumbling block in past negotiations. The Soviets have traditionally resisted it, and even we, who have always expressed our willingness to allow inspections, might well be reluctant to submit to the kind of search required to verify that MIRVs have not been installed. Yet, without adequate verification, a deployment ban would be meaningless. Thus, unless testing stops soon, the prospects for a MIRV agreement appear dim.

What are the military advantages of MIRV? Clearly, one gets more warheads with the same number of silos and boosters, but on the other hand the individual warheads must be smaller. In fact, the *combined* yield (megatonnage) of all the weapons in a "MIRVed" missile is less than the yield of the single weapon which the same missile could carry. The reason for the loss is the extra weight that must be carried in the form of heat shields and casings, as well as the more complicated guidance and propulsion systems required with MIRV.

The decreased yield is naturally a disadvantage: small weapons cause less destruction than large ones. But the reduction is not in direct proportion to the yield; the area of destruction of a one-megaton bomb, for example, is *more* than half as great as that of a two-megaton bomb.

Despite the reduction in total yield, the increased number of warheads makes MIRV attractive to the military. There are two main purposes for which MIRV would be useful, one essentially defensive and the other potentially aggressive. The first is in a retaliatory strike against an enemy's cities. Except against the very largest cities, many-megaton weapons are superfluous; much of their destruction would take place outside the city. And the crippling effect on a country of several small nuclear weapons landing on different cities is far greater than that of a single large bomb which completely devastates just one city. ("Small" here can still mean many times the size of the Hiroshima bomb.) MIRV therefore provides greater retaliatory strength with the same number of missiles.

If the opponent has an ABM defense, MIRV confronts the defense with a larger number of incoming objects; the chance that at least one of the warheads reaches its target is greatly increased. MIRV can therefore be regarded as a penetration aid. But for this purpose, independent targeting is unnecessary. The function of exhausting an ABM defense can be accomplished equally well by a less complex form of multiple-warhead missile called MRV (multiple re-entry vehicle). In MRV the individual warheads are not independently targeted, but are all fired at the same target in the manner of a shotgun blast. We now have MRVs in a number of Polaris submarines.

The second possible use of MIRV would be to attack the other side's missiles. For such a purpose, accuracy is all-important and yield is only a secondary consideration. A hardened ICBM silo can survive even a many-megaton burst a few miles away, whereas even a weapon of a few kilotons will destroy the silo if it lands close enough. Consequently, a MIRVed missile containing, say, five warheads can potentially destroy five of the opponent's ICBMs, whereas the same missile carrying a single large warhead can destroy, at most, one. By installing MIRVs, one side therefore greatly increases its capacity to strike at the other side's missiles, provided the accuracy is high enough. (A system without independent targeting is not suited to this purpose and is therefore considered less provocative.)

The first generation of MIRVs probably would not be accurate enough to permit one-on-one targeting; two and perhaps more warheads would have to be targeted on each enemy ICBM to assure its destruction. But once MIRVs are deployed, the door would be opened to further improvements that are already in the research and development stage. Such improvements could reduce targeting errors to unbelievably small distances, and could be installed with no noticeable change from the outside. The threat to opponents' missiles would then be very severe.

It is a paradoxical fact of life in today's nuclear age that weapons aimed at missiles are considered far more aggressive than weapons aimed at cities. The reason is simple: weapons aimed at cities are presumably intended for retaliation only; whereas those aimed at missiles can be used in a pre-emptive first strike. (They can also be used in what is called a "counter-force second strike." If an enemy launches a moderate attack, using only some of his missiles, one may choose to respond by attacking his remaining missiles, thus depriving him of the opportunity to launch a second round. Counterforce second strike is therefore a defensive strategy. Unfortunately, there is no way to convince the other side that one's missiles are intended only for counterforce second strike, and not for an aggressive first strike.) In a surprise attack, the all-important objective would be to destroy the opponent's missiles, thus denying him the ability to retaliate. If a country intended to launch such an attack, the installation of MIRVs would be an important step toward acquiring the capacity to do so. This is the most alarming feature of MIRV.

How does installing MIRVs differ from just increasing the number of one's ICBMs? As far as striking capability is concerned, the effect is pretty much the same. But there are at least two ways in which the destabilizing effect on the strategic balance is likely to be greater. First, neither side can ever be sure, once MIRV deployment has begun, how many weapons the enemy has; as a result, each is almost sure to overestimate the other's strength, and accordingly to overrespond. Thus the spiral of escalation and counter-escalation will expand at a faster rate. The feeling of relative security that comes from knowing the strength of one's opponent will be gone forever once the MIRV era begins.

The second feature peculiar to MIRV is that it enhances the premium on striking first in a crisis situation, making war more likely. The reasons for this will be described later.

In order to evaluate the arguments for and against MIRV, it is necessary to have in mind some picture of the present strategic balance—the strengths of the two superpowers in deliverable nuclear weapons. One statistic points up the enormity of the nuclear arsenals: *a single B-52 bomber carries more explosive power than has been used in all the wars of history.* And we have more than 600 B-52s, as well as about 1,000 land-based ICBMs, and more than 600 long-range missiles carried by Polaris submarines. All these missiles carry warheads in the megaton range (one megaton is the equivalent of one million tons of TNT, about fifty times the yield of the

Hiroshima bomb that killed 100,000 people.) Altogether, we have more than 4,500 deliverable nuclear weapons. It has been estimated that 400 one-megaton warheads could kill seventy million Russians and destroy about three-quarters of Soviet industry. (These figures refer to immediate destruction only, and do not include the widespread effects of fallout, contamination, epidemics, and so on, that surely would follow.)   The Soviet arsenal is also immense. Their ICBM force has expanded in recent years and now approximately equals ours in number. Although we are still considerably ahead in submarine missiles and nuclear bombers, as well as in total deliverable warheads, there is no doubt the Russians could devastate us if they tried.

In this situation, with each side having so much strength, numerical superiority means little. Each country insists that its strategic force is not an offensive weapon, but is intended only to "deter" the other side from attacking. At the moment, the ability of each power to retaliate after any attack is unquestioned; thus an uneasy stability rules. This state of mutual deterrence can be upset only if one side becomes capable of destroying so many of the opponent's weapons in a surprise attack that the opponent is unable to retaliate effectively. The ability to launch such an attack is known as first-strike capability.

It is not hard to imagine how desperate our situation would be if the Soviets ever obtained a first-strike capability. Even if they never actually launched a single missile, the mere threat of an attack would be sufficient to force important concessions throughout the world, perhaps even to make us surrender. The prospect that the United States might acquire a first-strike capability must appear equally ominous in the eyes of the Russians. Understandably, then, any move by one side that even vaguely threatens to lead to a first-strike capability is viewed with great apprehension by the other. The trouble is that each side sees its own arms expansions as purely defensive, while attributing aggressive intentions to similar actions by the opponent. . . .

. . . .

We are told that the Russians are developing MIRV in an attempt to obtain a first-strike capability, whereas our MIRVs are intended purely for retaliatory (defensive) purposes. No doubt a Soviet counterpart of Secretary Laird is pointing to the American MIRV development as an indication of our aggressive intentions, while proclaiming the defensive intent of the Soviet program. In the climate of mutual suspicion that has prevailed since the beginning of the cold war, this situation is hardly surprising. Each side attaches great significance to actions or utterances by the opponent that reinforce its fears. For example, a preoccupation with high missile accuracy must be particularly worrisome to the other side. A retaliatory strike against cities does not require extreme accuracy; the threat of a thermonuclear bomb exploding anywhere in New York City or Moscow provides an equally effective deterrent. But high accuracy is essential for an attack on missile silos. The Soviets must therefore have viewed with great alarm Secretary Laird's recent request for additional appropriations to accelerate work which will "improve significantly the accuracy of Poseidon guidance, thus enhancing its effectiveness against hard sites." Such a statement by a Soviet Politburo member would surely be cited by Mr. Laird as proof of the Russians' first-strike intentions.

If each country believed the other's proclamations of peaceful intent, the arms race would soon be over. This, unfortunately, is not a likely prospect. But irrespective of the motives on either side, it seems clear that we would feel more secure if the Soviets did not have MIRVs, and they would feel more secure if we didn't have them. It is equally clear that if one side proceeds with MIRV deployment, the other inevitably will also.

Therefore, an agreement that prevents the deployment of MIRV is in the best interest of both countries.

Critics of MIRV claim that it is more than just an escalation; that its deployment by both sides will actually make nuclear war more likely. The reasoning is as follows. Nuclear war can break out in a number of ways; a cold-blooded surprise attack by one side, during a period of calm, is not the only way or even the most likely one. A more plausible sequence of events begins with a crisis involving the major powers. The leaders of both countries are under great pressures. It has always been an axiom of military theory that the attacking side has an initial advantage. This is particularly true in a nuclear confrontation: Even though neither side has a first-strike capability, the country that strikes first would likely suffer fewer casualties and less destruction. The pressure to get in the first blow is reinforced by the fear that the opponents may be planning to do so. As the tension mounts, the leaders of one country may be persuaded by their military staff to strike first and accept, say, thirty or forty million casualties, rather than risk total annihilation if the other side should attack.

All this is true with or without MIRV; unless there is substantial disarmament we are sentenced to live indefinitely under such a threat. But if both sides have MIRVs the advantage to the attacker is materially increased; hence the chance that a crisis may end in disaster is also increased.

A simplified example explains why possession of MIRV by both sides increases the temptation to strike first. Suppose each side has exactly 1,000 land-based ICBMs (without MIRV). If side A wishes to attack, it may target one of its missiles on each of B's. Suppose the chance that a given missile destroys its target (called the "kill probability") is 75 percent; this allows for the possibility of misfire, targeting error, and so on. Even if A were to fire his entire force in a first strike, he could expect to knock out only 750 of B's missiles. The surviving 250 would be more than enough to enable B to retaliate. Thus, A is deterred. Obviously, so is B. This corresponds roughly to the present situation.

Next, suppose both sides have installed MIRVs in their arsenals with ten warheads per missile. Each side now has 10,000 warheads in the same 1,000 silos as before. Because the warheads are smaller each one is less likely to knock out a silo; the kill probability is reduced, say, to 50 percent. But A can target many warheads on each of B's silos. He can fire, say, 800 of his missiles, keeping 200 in reserve. The 800 missiles contain 8,000 warheads, so eight bombs can be aimed at each of B's 1,000 sites. Even though each weapon is only 50 percent effective, the chance that all eight will fail is extremely small, only about one in 250. According to the laws of averages, only four of B's missiles will survive, while A has 200 left. Evidently, B can obtain the same advantage by firing his missiles first.

The preceding analysis is admittedly oversimplified. It ignores submarines and bombers, which are important. It assumes that B does not fire his missiles on warning, which he could well do, and the kill probabilities used are higher than present-day accuracy makes possible. But such values are not out of the question for tomorrow, and the example illustrates an essential point: Because a single incoming missile is capable of destroying many MIRVed warheads in the ground, there is a great premium on getting missiles into the air first, when the other side is MIRVed. This is clearly a destabilizing factor in any crisis.

In this example, if B's 10,000 warheads were in individual silos, a far greater fraction would survive any attack that A could mount. Thus a good case can be made for the argument that if we were genuinely threatened by Russian MIRVs, deploying more Minutemen would be a much more logical response than putting in our own MIRVs.

As the example indicates, MIRV is a step toward a first-strike capability. In fact, in the hypothetical situation described, *both* sides have a first-strike capability *at the same time*. If combined with future breakthroughs in anti-submarine warfare and in air defense, MIRV could one day make that dread possibility a reality. One can imagine the pressures that then would arise in any crisis, with each side knowing that it had at least a good chance of getting away with a surprise attack, and that the opponents did also.

WILL THE SURVIVORS ENVY THE DEAD? *

Those who conclude that nuclear warfare is so horrible no nation will resort to it should read Herman Kahn's On Thermonuclear War *written as part of his work for the government-subsidized Rand Foundation. With total dispassion, Kahn analyzes the possibilities of nuclear conflict, viewing it as simply another problem waiting for solution. His discussion of radiation meters indicates his calm acceptance of "the unthinkable."*

... Probably the most important special equipment that would be needed—and the least improvisable—would be radiation meters of various kinds. These are not only useful during and immediately after the attack; they are necessary for many basic and important postwar activities. Meters could play an essential role in maintaining the morale and the risk-taking capacity of the cadres who would be exposed to radiation. It is easy to see why this is so.

The radiation from fallout has curious and frightening effects. Most people already know, or will know in a postattack world, that if you get a fatal dose of radiation the sequence of events is about like this: first you become nauseated, then sick; you seem to recover; then in two or three weeks you really get sick and die.

Now just imagine yourself in the postwar situation. Everybody will have been subjected to extremes of anxiety, unfamiliar environment, strange foods, minimum toilet facilities, inadequate shelters, and the like. Under these conditions some high percentage of the population is going to become nauseated, and nausea is very catching. If one man vomits, everybody vomits. It would not be surprising if almost everybody vomits. Almost everyone is likely to think he has received too much radiation. Morale may be so affected that many survivors may refuse to participate in constructive activities, but would content themselves with sitting down and waiting to die—some may even become violent and destructive.

However, the situation would be quite different if radiation meters were distributed. Assume now that a man gets sick from a cause other than radiation. Not believing this, his morale begins to drop. You look at his meter and say, "You have received only ten roentgens, why are you vomiting? Pull yourself together and get to work."

*Herman Kahn, *On Thermonuclear War*, 2nd ed. (Princeton, New Jersey: Princeton University Press, 1961), pp. 85-86.

DOOMSDAY MACHINES *

Here is another piece from Sidney Slomich, author of the foregoing item titled "Deterrence Theory." Here, Dr. Slomich describes what the likely results will be if present "defence" trends continue. He writes as if he is looking back just before the doomsday machines are exploded.

So is it in the wildly predatory international world of dawning 1980: machines of death, built and maintained in the psychosis that they will preserve men's life, dominate and possess men. Men labor in fragmentation to support the state, and the state labors to renovate and modify the deadly machines toward greater and greater levels of achievement. Just as dehumanized work in skyscraper cells, encapsulated modes of locomotion and pillbox houses of loneliness possess the "first-class" white citizens of suburbia, so do the nuclear bombs and missiles—promised never to be used—possess the spirit of the sovereign state of the United States of America and the atomized, isolated, frantically lonely, and psychologically technologized motes that constitute the supreme popular sovereign, once believed to be freedom's heirs and heralds by the world and themselves.

These men huddle in fear and wrap themselves in their rockets, for their doomsday weapons guarantee security and identity. The perfection of weapons comes before everything, while expressions of humanity and individualism come after everything. Human life is indescribably cramped, while weaponry is indescribably awesome. Capacities for destruction, if not for life, are magnificent. It's an awesomely powerful dybbuk, this technological obsession.

On the eve of 1980 weaponry far exceeds the dreams of its most ambitious proponents in the Pentagon, think tank, or patriotic profit-making industry of the 1970s.

The American Secretary of Defense, Robert Strange McNamara—who often spoke about restraint and the need for peace in human affairs, but who led the fight in Vietnam with enthusiasm until he learned it would not work, and who was the great architect, the Cardinal Richelieu of the nuclear age—shortly before leaving office and after several years of enthusiastically building them, eloquently spoke about the need to stop building nuclear missiles or ABMs. The Secretary, in a magistral address in San Francisco in September 1967, stated that the United States then possessed over two thousand strategic weapons: a thousand Minutemen in

*Adapted from Sidney J. Slomich, *The American Nightmare* (New York: The Macmillan Company, 1971), pp. 30-36.

their United States silos, six hundred B-52 bombers, hundreds of Polarises riding beneath the oceans (and more being built), and fighter bombers capable of delivering atomic bombs on target like milk to the back porch. Behind these delivery systems each with its own nuclear-tipped little present, tens of thousands of additional bombs lay stored for safekeeping, lest those rockets or planes be lost, mislaid, or not reach teeming destinations. Since an antiballistic missile system couldn't work well against adversaries with comparable killingly efficient missiles and rockets, all systems being subject to saturation, the Secretary, with regret, went along with the deployment of an ABM against only the Chinese who didn't have any or many missiles and who weren't good at it—yet.

Mr. McNamara's successors in the Pentagon believed in his logic and modes of thinking, if not his emotional reservations. They proceeded to develop ever better missiles and anti-missiles in the early and mid-seventies, and place them in the concreted ground, beneath the seas, and fly them around in aircraft, attended by hordes of jumpy, inert, bored, but certified clean-cut young men—guaranteed by FBI standards of what was right and healthy not to plunge into paroxysms leading to unauthorized button-pressing. The numbers of the missiles increased ten-fold. Bristling death-dealing submarined cocoons in the polluted oceans bore thousands more. Great, black pterodactyls, bat-winged bombers screaming sonic booms onto friendly and enemy towns alike bore still more thousands, while on the seabeds in concrete amid what remained of life were more.

They took lots of servicing in money and organization, for those in office accepted the need for continual improvement or upgrading, lest the Others make a Breakthrough. National allocations for defense quadrupled over those of 1971, rising to over $300 billion per year by 1978. A grimly intense security police, assisted by new corps of local patriotic-minded police, closely checked the backgrounds of certified button pressers. There had, after all, been a minor accident in the mid-seventies—though only six million died—when one certified, clean-cut, stable type, who was a missile guardian in Montana, after tuning in the latest Billy Graham Crusade affirming that the Second Coming was at hand and the world was ending, decided to give Christ a hand by shooting off two Minutemen IVs. That took out Kiev and almost ended it all before the President convinced the Soviet Premier that it was an accident and he really didn't mind losing Houston and Cape Kennedy too much. The FBI and its friends worried about the crazies—the ones who didn't like missiles—and their servants, and those who might do something irrational to upset the industrial, distributive, technological, and educational structure building, improving, maintaining and expanding those missiles.

The work of the FBI and police had, however, been considerably eased by the adoption of the Twenty-seventh Amendment, which established it a capital crime to criticize strategic missilery or agitate for arms control and disarmament.

Multimegaton missiles, multiply warheaded and independently targetable, rode in hundreds of orbits, and all the nuclear powers were represented. The Russians had "Arise Ye Prisoners of Starvation," in blinking red lights. Thanks to a cleverly phased orbit it was not visible in the U.S.S.R. The Chinese spelled out the title of their newest peace anthem: "The Yellow World Will Surge to Victory on Tides of Blood So Red." The Americans in red, white and blue lights spelled out the meaning of the First Amendment, a product considered suitable for export only.

Meanwhile, as sons and daughters rode the freeways in drug- and alcohol-induced fogs and as the missiles rode in orbit, huddled frozen in the ground, swayed in the dying seas, and sang jingles from space, United Nations delegates, able to face reality after ingesting Glibidex—the new tranquilizer with a brand-new and artificial molecular structure combining essences of alcohol, opium, LSD and methadone—spoke bravely of individualism, international order, necessities of doing something about the weapons, and the need for a new revolutionary consciousness to bring about institutional change. Outside hordes of individuals from the Associated International John Birch Societies, the American Fascist Legion, the Unified Youth Leagues to Propagate Anti-Semitism and affiliated enthusiasts pissed on the flower-beds, shook their fists toward the buildings, and screamed: "Communists, faggots, anarchists, killers, liberals, nigger-jews, atheists, lovers" and other imprecations.

As they screeched, the intelligence people were meeting in the well-appointed rooms of a grand hotel in Europe and exchanging information on internationalists, peaceniks, disarmament experts, militant blacks, theologians, liberals, humanists, historians, editors, poets, normally feminine women, crusaders against alcoholism and indiscriminate drug use, athletes, and other social or political undesirables.

Because of proliferating weapons and even larger numbers of warheads on all sides and the continuing nagging doubts regarding the efficacy or reliability of so-called defense systems, the United States in 1978 began work on a Doomsday Machine, which was announced on the eve of 1980 after two years of frantic development that had brought to the sometime smog-free plains of Pasadena four thousand of the best engineering, scientific, and instrumentation people in the country.

It was only a fancy old cobalt bomb, but what a bomb! The very best! A real Buick of a bomb! It was announced that the bomb was evidence of the country's desire for peace and that if anyone made an attack upon the United States it would go off, destroying the world with it.

The Soviets, having come to similar conclusions regarding deterrence strategy and the probable efficacy of their defense systems, developed their own cobalt Doomsday Machine and also placed at proper depths beneath the Atlantic and at proper distances from the shore a number of properly dirty bombs set to go off in the event of an attack on the U.S.S.R. Their explosions would so contaminate the atmosphere being borne around the world by prevailing westerly winds that they would destroy all life.

Since the main concern of the 275 million in the United States was security, as was also the case in the colleague nations of the Soviet Union, China, Cuba, and elsewhere, identity and value were oriented around the remarkable weapon systems demanding tight and completely managed reciprocating relationships among their parts, including the men within them. Since the humanities and traditional social sciences had nothing to do with engineering and designing and controlling weapons, and since they were properly suspect as providing sources of discontent, Locke, Socrates, Lincoln, Jefferson, Voltaire, and Shakespeare were duly taken from school and university curricula, their writing having been attacked as unscientific and mushy. In 1978 all were banned, along with the Sermon on the Mount. The Thirty-seventh Amendment, ratified by the fiftieth state on July 5, 1979, made it a capital crime to teach or advocate social science, save as a means to measure and devise techniques for socially acceptable control. A year earlier the Pentagon had established courses in Genetic Reconstitution and Social Rehabilitation at hundreds of flourishing R.O.T.C. campus departments. They were advanced pursuant to the principles established in the Thirty-second Amendment, which made it the inalienable right of all citizens to learn systems analysis and systems management.

Finis

Then came the Lord and His hosts and He looked down upon the earth.

"They befoul, they degrade the Men in them, the sparks of Me given freely," said the Lord. "They hear no reason and no love, and drive to evil. I weep for the young, and those still unborn, for their sires passed on to their children the sparks of Divine I have given, but they twist and refuse the future. I have done what I can. I must withdraw My Grace."

On earth a tube blew out in an orbiting five-megaton hydrogen bomb put up the week before by the Soviet Union. A short circuit and then a small explosion caused the craft to veer from orbit, reenter the atmosphere and sail toward Paris. A Soviet command and control crew, high on vodka and LSD, missed the periodic computer report and denied anything was wrong when Moscow began calling in alarm.

Moscow sent a hostile reply to Washington's inquiry. The White House ordered eighteen rockets shot toward Moscow and four toward Peking. What the Hell.

The American President must prove his manhood. Before the twenty-two American missiles hit their marks, there were four times that number from Cuba, China, and the Soviet Union flying toward the United States. But before they hit, the rest of the American arsenal went into the air, while IBM engineers warmed and congratulated themselves on good, real-time responses. Then the Doomsday Machines went off. The winds were favorable. In four days there were no more men, nor were there animals, and a foul death cloud radiated over what was once a pulsating, life-intoxicated world.

In memory of Moses, Socrates, Aeschylus, Christ, the visions of Prometheus, and Don Quixote and all the untold life-loving sons and daughters of Man, there was no one to turn the prayer wheel, take the Sacraments, meditate with the Oversoul, say the Kaddish.

Racism

In the preceding sub-part, war was described as the most spectacular example of power used arbitrarily. But there is another phenomenon that is more unequivocally arbitrary. It is *racism*, which may be defined as the belief that significant human abilities are basically racial in nature and that therefore some racial groups are inherently inferior. This belief is arbitrary—i.e., not in accordance with reason—because there is a mountain of data to prove that behavioral differences associated with race are in reality a matter of cultural variation and social structure. When reared similarly, the members of radically disparate racial groupings behave similarly in all socially important respects.

Despite the fact that professional behavioral scientists, with few notable exceptions, have long concluded that there is no important necessary relationship between race and behavior, racism continues to plague humankind. This observation is illustrated in heart-rending detail by the articles which follow. We take up first the treatment of Jews in the West. Anti-Semitism has, of course, long been a prominent feature of Christian culture, as suggested paradoxically in the January 1975 Vatican statement which, by offering guidelines for improving Roman Catholic-Jewish relations, inadvertently pointed to the enmity which has prevailed so often in the past. "Christian" anti-Semitism has usually taken the form of "gentlemen's agreements" that seem relatively harmless to those unaware of historical events. But experience suggests that:

> Anti-Semitism, however mild and gentlemanly, which fosters the dehumanization of Jewish-Gentile relationships, paves the way, in turn, for the active anti-Semite. All available evidence points to the fact that the Nazi anti-Semite had his way in Germany largely because of the prevalence of gentlemanly anti-Semitism.*

We therefore begin with two examples of "gentlemanly" anti-Semitism in America; following these pieces there are two examples of what happens when casual anti-Semitism gets out of hand, as it has so often in the past.

*E. Digby Baltzell, *The Protestant Establishment*: Aristocracy and Caste in America (New York: Random House, Inc., 1964), p. 325.

Anti-Semitism, Gentlemanly and Otherwise

THE POINT SYSTEM *

... Detroit's oldest and richest suburban area is the five-community section east of the city collectively called Grosse Pointe (pop. 50,000). Set back from the winding, tree-shaded streets are fine, solid colonial or brick mansions, occupied by some of Detroit's oldest (pre-automobile age) upper class, and by others who made the grade in business and professional life. Grosse Pointe is representative of dozens of wealthy residential areas in the U.S. where privacy, unhurried tranquility, and unsullied property values are respected. But last week, Grosse Pointe was in the throes of a rude, untranquil expose of its methods of maintaining tranquility.

The trouble burst with the public revelation, during a court squabble between one property owner and his neighbor, that the Grosse Pointe Property Owners Association (973 families) and local real estate brokers had set up a rigid system for screening families who want to buy or build homes in Grosse Pointe. Unlike similar communities, where neighborly solidarity is based on an unwritten gentleman's agreement, Grosse Point's screening system is based on a written questionnaire, filled out by a private investigator on behalf of Grosse Point's "owner vigilantes."

The three-page questionnaire, scaled on the basis of "points" (highest score: 100), grades would-be home owners on such qualities as descent, way of life (American?), occupation (Typical of his own race?), swarthiness (Very? Medium? Slightly? Not at all?), accent (Pronounced? Medium? Slight? None?), name (Typically American?), repute, education, dress (Neat or Slovenly? Conservative or Flashy?), status of occupation (sufficient eminence may offset poor grades in other respects). Religion is not scored, but weighted in the balance by a three-man Grosse Pointe screening committee. All prospects are handicapped on an ethnic and racial basis: Jews, for example, must score a minimum of 85 points, Italians 75, Greeks 65, Poles 55; Negroes and Orientals do not count.

. . . .

Time 75 (April 25, 1960):25.

THE CLUB AND THE CORPORATE ELITE *

... At noon every day in the week, the men at the top of the executive suites in the city of Pittsburgh gather for lunch in a great brownstone pile which has housed the Duquesne Club since 1889. As one old-timer at the club remarked: "The way to tell if a fellow's getting along in any Pittsburgh company is to see if he's yet a member of the Duquesne. As soon as his name goes up for membership, you know he ought to be watched. He's a comer."[1] According to Osborn Elliott, whose book *Men at the Top* is an excellent and intimate study of the mores of modern American business leadership, there are four prerequisites for membership in the Duquesne: "$1,000 initiation fee, $240 annual dues, at least nominal Christianity, and the blessing of your employer, preferably to the extent of his being willing to pay the bills."[2]

The Duquesne Club lies at the very core of the associational organization of leadership in Pittsburgh. In fact, it has been argued by the club's management in the federal courts that income from dues should not be taxable because it is a business organization. One club member of five years' standing, for instance, "has paid perhaps $30 worth of personal bills himself in that time, while his company has picked up tabs totaling about $6,000."[3] Not only do the large corporations usually support their executives in membership costs; they often have an important say as to whom the club accepts among their younger and rising executives. . . .

Membership in the Duquesne is not only a mark of a man's inclusion within the inner circle of top management. Within this inner circle of executive leadership—and reminiscent of one's days in the Navy during the war, where officers' bars from Norfolk to New Caledonia were differentiated by rank—"a man can be marked by name, rank, serial number (and salary), according to where he eats in the club." By and large, the lieutenants of industry are found lunching on the ground floor, while the higher brass are found upstairs. . . .

Here indeed is a distinctly American institution where close primary relationships are forged between top management men who have the power of decision over transcommunal corporate activities which affect the lives of men and women all over the world, from the Atlantic to the Pacific, from the Monongahela to the Amazon. It is, too, a kind of associational aristocracy-by-ballot which is ideally suited to a dynamic and democratic

*Adapted from E. Digby Baltzell, *The Protestant Establishment* Aristocracy and Caste in America (New York: Random House, Inc., 1964), pp. 362–365.

society's continual need to assimilate new men of talent and power into the top levels of established leadership.

But at the same time this aristocratic function fails, at clubs like the Duquesne, to reach out beyond the boundaries of nominal-Christian affiliations. In the long run, these caste boundaries will inevitably create embarrassing situations which will be downright dysfunctional to the organization and recruitment of leadership. Even today there is in Pittsburgh an executive at the very top level of leadership in one of the nation's major corporations who has never been taken into the Duquesne because of his Jewish origins (even though he has never been associated in any way with the city's Jewish community). But as this executive's high functional position would ordinarily demand Duquesne Club membership, other arrangements have had to be made. In other words, although it may seem absurd, he is *allowed* and *encouraged* to entertain important business associates in his company's private suite on the upper floor of the Duquesne. And he does this in spite of being barred from membership in the club! It may seem hard to believe that such a dehumanizing situation would be tolerated either by this talented executive of Jewish antecedents or by his gentile office colleagues who are also leaders at the Duquesne. But apparently the 1,700 resident and 850 nonresident members of the Duquesne would be contaminated if even one gentleman of Jewish origins were to be made a member of the club. . . .

REFERENCES

[1] Osborn Elliott, *Men at the Top*. New York: Harper & Brothers, 1959, p. 164.

[2] *Ibid.*

[3] *Ibid.*

SAMMY ROSENBAUM LIGHTS TWO CANDLES *

In his memoirs, Simon Wiesenthal describes how he tracked down Adolf Eichmann and other Nazis, and helped to gather evidence to convict them. One of his most touching stories was obtained from a Mrs. Rawicz, who came from the small town of Rabka in the Carpathian Mountains of Poland. The German occupation forces came to Rabka in 1939 and soon began to persecute the Jewish residents, including especially the Rosenbaum family whose father and head was a poor tailor.

*Adapted from Joseph Wechsberg, editor, *The Murderers Among Us*: The Simon Wiesenthal Memoirs (New York: McGraw-Hill Book Company, 1967), pp. 264-267.

... The family lived in two musty rooms and a tiny kitchen in an old, dark house. But they were happy, and very religious. Sammy learned to say his prayers. Every Friday night he would go with his father to the synagogue, after lighting the candles at home. Mother and Sammy's sister Paula, three years his senior, stayed at home and prepared dinner.

That sort of life became only a memory after the Germans occupied Poland. In 1940, the SS set up what it called a "police school" in former Polish Army barracks in the woods that surrounded Rabka. . . .

SS *Untersturmführer* Wilhelm Rosenbaum from Hamburg was made school commander. Rosenbaum was a true SS type: cynical, brutal, convinced of his mission. He would walk around town with a riding crop. "When we saw him in the street we got so frightened that we would hide in the nearest house entrance," the woman from Rabka remembered. Early in 1942, SS man Rosenbaum ordered all Jews in Rabka to appear at the local school to "register." The Jews knew what that meant. . . .

In the schoolroom in Rabka, SS *Führer* Rosenbaum looked through the list of names. "Suddenly he beat his riding crop hard on the table," the woman from Rabka told me. "Each of us winced as though we had been whipped. SS man Rosenbaum shouted: 'What's that? Rosenbaum? Jews! How dare these *verdammte Juden* have my good German name? Well, I'm going to take care of it!' " . . .

He threw the list back on the table and strode out. From that day on everybody in Rabka knew that the Rosenbaums would be killed; it was only a question of time. People in other places were known to have been arrested and executed because their name was Rosenburg, or because they were Jews and their first name happened to be Adolf or Hermann. . . .

It was a Friday morning in June 1942. The eyewitnesses, two of whom now live in Israel, cannot remember the exact date, but they know it was a Friday. One of the witnesses had been working in the house across from the playground behind the school. He saw what happened. Two SS men escorted "the Jew Rosenbaum," his wife, and their fifteen-year-old daughter Paula. Behind them came SS Führer Rosenbaum.

"The woman and the girl were marched around the corner of the schoolhouse and then I heard some shots," the witness has said under oath. "I saw how SS man Rosenbaum began to beat our Rosenbaum with his riding crop. He shouted: 'You dirty Jew, I'll teach you a lesson for having my German name!' Then the SS man took his revolver and shot Rosenbaum the tailor. He shot him twice or three times. I couldn't count the shots; I was too horrified."

Earlier, the SS men had come for the Rosenbaums in a small truck. Rosenbaum, his wife, and their daughter were around the table in the front room having breakfast. Sammy was already at a large stone quarry in nearby Zakryty, where he'd been sent as a forced laborer after his twelfth birthday. All Jewish men had to work, and Sammy was now classified as a man. But he was weak and undernourished and couldn't do much except sort out the stones and put the smaller ones on a truck.

The SS sent an unarmed Jewish policeman to the quarry for Sammy. They often sent Jewish policemen to arrest other Jews when they were too busy with their curriculum at the police school. The Jewish policeman later told the Jewish charwoman at the school exactly what had happened. He'd gone out to Zakryty in a small horsedrawn cart. . . .

Sammy looked up at the Jewish policeman. "Where are they?" he asked—"Father, Mother, and Paula. Where?"

The policeman just shook his head.

Sammy understood. "They're dead." His voice was low. "I've known for a long time that it was going to happen. Because our name is Rosenbaum."

The policeman swallowed, but Sammy didn't seem to notice.

"And now you've come for me." He spoke matter-of-factly. There was no emotion in his voice. He stepped up and sat down on the seat next to the Jewish policeman.

The policeman was unable to say a word. He had expected the boy to cry, perhaps to run away. All the while he was riding out to Zakryty the policeman has wondered how he could warn the boy, make him disappear in the woods, where the Polish underground might later help him. Now it was too late. The two SS guards were watching with guns in their hands.

The policeman told Sammy what had happened that morning. Sammy asked if they could stop for a moment at his house. When they got there, he stepped down and walked into the front room, leaving the door open. He looked over the table with the half-filled teacups left from breakfast. He looked at the clock. It was half past three. Father, Mother, and Paula were already buried, and no one had lit a candle for them. Slowly, methodically, Sammy cleaned off the table and put the candlesticks on it.

"I could see Sammy from the outside," the Jewish policeman later told Mrs. Rawicz. "He put on his skullcap, and started to light the candles. Two for his father, two for his mother, two for his sister. And he prayed. I saw his lips moving. He said *Kaddish* for them."

Kaddish is the prayer for the dead. Father Rosenbaum had always said *Kaddish* for his dead parents, and Sammy had learned the prayer from his father. Now he was the only man left in his family. He stood quietly, looking at the six candles. The Jewish policeman outside saw Sammy slowly shaking his head, as though he'd suddenly remembered something. Then Sammy placed two more candles on the table, took a match and lit them, and prayed.

"The boy knew that he was already dead," the policeman said later. "He lit the candles and said *Kaddish* for himself."

Then Sammy came out, leaving the door open, and quietly sat down on the cart next to the policeman, who was crying. The boy didn't cry. The policeman wiped away the tears with the back of his hand and pulled the reins. But the tears kept coming. The boy didn't say a word. Gently he touched the older man's arm, as if he wanted to comfort him—to forgive him for taking him away. Then they rode out to the clearing in the woods. SS *Führer* Rosenbaum and his "students" were waiting for the little boy. "About time!" said the SS man.

. . . .

SENTENCE: 20 MINUTES PER MURDER *

Sporadic violence such as that experienced by Sammy Rosenbaum and his family was soon supplanted by a systematic attempt by the German forces to exterminate all Jews. Death camps were established for this purpose. One of the most notorious of the camps was Treblinka, located in a Polish forest. In 1970, Treblinka's former commander, Franz-Paul Stangl, was convicted of being responsible for the death of the 400,000 victims who had been "processed" through the camp during the Stangl regime. Despite the enormity of his crime, Stangl could not be sentenced to more than 15 years because of an extradition agreement with Brazil where Stangle had been hiding; he was betrayed by his son-in-law for a $7000 reward. A sentence of fifteen years works out to penalty of approximately 20 minutes for each murder. Even more important is the symbolic significance of Treblinka and the other death camps. They illustrate one of the likely consequences for humanity when purely technical efficiency is the ruling guide for the appointees in a bureaucratic hierarchy.

. . . The savage efficiency of Treblinka, surpassed only by Auschwitz, brought death to well over 700,000 people who were gassed, shot, beaten and tortured to expiration by the SS and its Ukrainian guards. Yet the man responsible for developing Treblinka's murderous factory through the introduction of modern industrial techniques—the man who said he discouraged "pointless" sadism—has told the court: "You can ask me any questions you like. I have done nothing to anybody that was not my duty, and my conscience is clear."

Now 62, thin and alert, Stangl maintains the bearing of a small-town schoolmaster. Earlier in this lengthy trial he was shown a large plan of the camp; he did not hesitate for a moment to elaborate on his record, even to the most minute and grisly details. Indeed, the entire war-crimes case, the

*Adapted from Thomas Land, "20 Minutes Per Murder," *The New Leader* 53(Nov. 16, 1970):3-4.

biggest ever handled by German courts, has been marked by an odd detachment from the awful human consequences of Treblinka's efficiency. It sometimes seems that the trial is a study commission of disinterested scholars, conducted for the benefit of future historians, rather than a means of administering justice.

Counsel for the defense argued that the attentive little man in the dock had no alternative to processing people on the conveyor belt of death. When Stangl took over the camp, his lawyer said, "There were bodies lying about all over the place, no proper system of burial. . . ."

But by the time Stangl had established his new system, according to the testimony of a survivor, "it took no more than three quarters of an hour, by the clock, to put the victims through their last voyage, from the moment the doors of the cattle cars were unbolted to the moment the great trap doors of the gas chambers were opened to take out the bodies.

"Three quarters of an hour, door-to-door, compared to an hour and a quarter, sometimes even as much as two hours with the old system; it was a record."

The huge black-and-white plan of the camp came alive as witnesses took the stand to testify. Perhaps Stangl, too, was able to recall the friendly, green railway station where the tracks ended and the painted clock on the wall always showed three o'clock. As they were herded off the trains, many of the victims still believed they were on their way to colonizing the East.

Before the travel-worn families could catch their breath, men and women were separated and rushed through a series of check points. At one, you were told to hand over your coat, hat and suit in exchange for a string; at the next you were ordered to tie your shoes together with the string and hand them over; then your underwear was taken, your hair cut off, and your privates searched for money and jewels. Finally, whip-wielding guards would chase you—winded victims are killed quicker by gas—along a road, and in a state of helpless panic, into the gas chambers.

To make the extermination machine function, Stangl had to establish a large prisoner work force at the bottom of the camp's social triangle (the SS being on top and the Ukrainian guards in the middle) to handle the bodies and prepare the valuables, clothes and hair for transport to Germany. Here, at last, the industrialist of death failed. Degraded to the point where they had become mere useful slaves to the system, these living dead of Treblinka successfully mutinied against their well trained, armed and fed guards in August 1943. It was this revolt and the ensuing escapes that gave the trial its first-hand testimonies.

. . . .

Black Degradation in America

The American slave system, which began during the Colonial period and was ended 200 years later only as a war measure, has been described as the most degrading form of slavery ever known to humankind. The black Africans brought to America for sale into slavery were deliberately separated from accompanying family and tribal members; social isolates, it was concluded, would be less likely to be troublemakers. As slaves, the blacks were treated purely as property, even being defined as such in official documents and legislation. After emancipation during the war between the states, occupationally and educationally disadvantaged blacks—now Americans all, their African cultural heritage almost totally forgotten—were cast loose in a society whose ruling elements had a long tradition of using the weak so as to enlarge the advantages of the strong. The result was that black Americans, taken as a group, became a pariah group designated by a term, "nigger," which has come to symbolize anyone forced to live in a degraded manner. It is little wonder that the result has been a "black rage" that has at time erupted in riots, burnings, and demands for reparation. Evidence of these and related matters are demonstrated in the following selections. We begin with a few which give the historical background of black anger and despair.

SHE WEEPETH SORE IN THE NIGHT*

Solomon Northup was a free, black American living in New England in the 1840s when he was sent by his employer to complete a business transaction in Washington, D.C. While in the capitol city, Northup was abducted by slave traders and sold into bondage in the Deep South. After escaping twelve years later, Northup published an account of what had occurred. His Twelve Years A Slave *created a sensation, helping to generate the social conditions which led immediately to the Civil War. Among the stories told by Northup, the one about "Eliza" is particularly poignant. Eliza has been purchased by a new master; her daughter Emily is retained by "Freeman," who refuses to sell her to the mother's purchaser. Eliza previously lost her son Randall to another slave owner.*

. . . It would be a relief if I could consistently pass over in silence the scene that now ensued. It recalls memories more mournful and affecting

*Adapted from Solomon Northup, *Twelve Years A Slave*: Edited by Sue Eaken and Joseph Logsdon (Baton Rouge: Louisiana State University Press, 1968), pp. 57–60.

than any language can portray. I have seen mothers kissing for the last time the faces of their dead offspring; I have seen them looking down into the grave, as the earth fell with a dull sound upon their coffins, hiding them from their eyes forever; but never have I seen such an exhibition of intense, unmeasured, and unbounded grief as when Eliza was parted from her child. She broke from her place in the line of women, and rushing down where Emily was standing, caught her in her arms. The child, sensible of some impending danger, instinctively fastened her hands around her mother's neck and nestled her little head upon her bosom. Freeman sternly ordered her to be quiet, but she did not heed him. He caught her by the arm and pulled her rudely, but she only clung closer to the child. Then, with a volley of great oaths, he struck her such a heartless blow, that she staggered backward, and was like to fall. Oh! how piteously then did she beseech and beg and pray that they might not be separated. Why could they not be purchased together? Why not let her have one of her dear children? "Mercy, mercy, master!" she cried, falling on her knees. "Please, master, buy Emily. I can never work any if she is taken from me; I will die."

Freeman interfered again, but, disregarding him, she still plead most earnestly, telling how Randall had been taken from her—how she never would see him again, and now it was too bad—oh, God! it was too bad, too cruel, to take her away from Emily—her pride—her only darling, that could not live, it was so young, without its mother!

Finally, after much more supplication, the purchaser of Eliza stepped forward, evidently affected, and said to Freeman he would buy Emily, and asked him what her price was.

"What is her *price? Buy* her?" was the responsive interrogatory of Theophilus Freeman. And instantly answering his own inquiry, he added, "I won't sell her. She's not for sale."

The man remarked he was not in need of one so young—that it would be of no profit to him, but since the mother was so fond of her, rather than see them separated, he would pay a reasonable price. But to this humane proposal Freeman was entirely deaf. He would not sell her then on any account whatever. There were heaps and piles of money to be made of her, he said, when she was a few years older. There were men enough in New Orleans who would give five thousand dollars for such an extra, handsome, fancy piece as Emily would be, rather than not get her. . . .

When Eliza heard Freeman's determination not to part with Emily, she became absolutely frantic.

"I will *not* go without her. They shall *not* take her from me," she fairly shrieked, her shrieks commingling with the loud and angry voice of Freeman, commanding her to be silent.

Meantime Harry and myself had been to the yard and returned with our blankets, and were at the front door ready to leave. Our purchaser stood near us, gazing at Eliza with an expression indicative of regret at having bought her at the expense of so much sorrow. We waited some time, when, finally, Freeman, out of patience, tore Emily from her mother by main force, the two clinging to each other with all their might.

"Don't leave me, mama—don't leave me," screamed the child, as its mother was pushed harshly forward. "Don't leave me—come back, mama," she still cried, stretching forth her little arms imploringly. But she cried in vain. Out of the door and into the street we were quickly hurried. Still we could hear her calling to her mother, "Come back—don't leave me—come back, mama," until her infant voice grew faint and still more faint, and gradually died away, as distance intervened, and finally was wholly lost.

Eliza never after saw or heard of Emily or Randall. Day nor night, however, were they ever absent from her memory. In the cotton field, in the cabin, always and everywhere, she was talking of them—often *to* them, as if they were actually present. Only when absorbed in that illusion, or asleep, did she ever have a moment's comfort afterwards.

She was no common slave, as has been said. To a large share of natural intelligence which she possessed, was added a general knowledge and information on most subjects. She had enjoyed opportunities such as are afforded to very few of her oppressed class. She had been lifted up into the regions of a higher life. Freedom—freedom for herself and for her offspring, for many years had been her cloud by day, her pillar of fire by night. In her pilgrimage through the wilderness of bondage, with eyes fixed upon that hope-inspiring beacon, she had at length ascended to "the top of Pisgah," and beheld "the land of promise." In an unexpected moment she was utterly overwhelmed with disappointment and despair. The glorious vision of liberty faded from her sight as they led her away into captivity. Now "she weepeth sore in the night, and tears are on her cheeks: all her friends have dealt treacherously with her: they have become her enemies."

"A RED RECORD " *

Ida B. Wells-Barnett was a brave black American who traveled through the South during the post-reconstruction period to record the events that typified race relations of the day.

*Adapted from Ida B. Wells-Barnett, *On Lynchings*: Southern Horrors; A Red Record; Mob Rule in New Orleans (New York: Arno Press and *The New York Times*, 1969; reprint of three pamphlets published between 1892 and 1900), pp. 7-8, 28-29, 31-32.

The student of American sociology will find the year 1894 marked by a pronounced awakening of the public conscience to a system of anarchy and outlawry which had grown during a series of ten years to be so common, that scenes of unusual brutality failed to have any visible effect upon the humane sentiments of the people of our land.

Beginning with the emancipation of the Negro, the inevitable result of unbridled power exercised for two and a half centuries, by the white man over the Negro, began to show itself in acts of conscienceless outlawry. During the slave regime, the Southern white man owned the Negro body and soul. It was to his interest to dwarf the soul and preserve the body. Vested with unlimited power over his slave, to subject him to any and all kinds of physical punishment, the white man was still restrained from such punishment as tended to injure the slave by abating his physical powers and thereby reducing his financial worth. While slaves were scourged mercilessly, and in countless cases inhumanly treated in other respects, still the white owner rarely permitted his anger to go so far as to take a life, which would entail upon him a loss of several hundred dollars. The slave was rarely killed, he was too valuable; it was easier and quite as effective, for discipline or revenge, to sell him "Down South."

But Emancipation came and the vested interests of the white man in the Negro's body were lost. The white man had no right to scourge the emancipated Negro, still less has he a right to kill him. But the Southern white people had been educated so long in that school of practice, in which might makes right, that they disdained to draw strict lines of action in dealing with the Negro. In slave times the Negro was kept subservient and submissive by the frequency and severity of the scourging, but, with freedom, a new system of intimidation came into vogue; the Negro was not only whipped and scourged; he was killed.

Not all nor nearly all of the murders done by white men, during the past thirty years in the South, have come to light, but the statistics as gathered and preserved by white men, and which have not been questioned, show that during these years more than ten thousand Negroes have been killed in cold blood, without the formality of judicial trial and legal execution. And yet, as evidence of the absolute impunity with which the white man dares to kill a Negro, the same record shows that during all these years, and for all these murders only three white men have been tried, convicted, and executed. . . .

. . . .

Miss Wells-Barnett describes a black man who, after being accused of murdering a four-year-old white girl, is hunted down in another state and brought by train back to Paris, Texas:

... Arriving here at 12 o'clock the train was met by a surging mass of humanity 10,000 strong. The Negro was placed upon a carnival float in mockery of a king upon his throne, and, followed by an immense crowd, was escorted through the city so that all might see the most inhuman monster known in current history. The line of march was up Main street to the square, around the square down Clarksville street to Church street, thence to the open prairies about 300 yards from the Texas and Pacific depot. Here Smith was placed upon a scaffold, six feet square and ten feet high, securely bound, within the view of all beholders. Here the victim was tortured for fifty minutes by red-hot iron brands thrust against his quivering body. Commencing at the feet the brands were placed against him inch by inch until they were thrust against the face. Then, being apparently dead, kerosene was poured upon him, cottonseed hulls placed beneath him and set on fire. In less time than it takes to relate it, the tortured man was wafted beyond the grave to another fire, hotter and more terrible than the one just experienced. . . .

Words to describe the awful torture inflicted upon Smith cannot be found. The Negro, for a long time after starting on the journey to Paris, did not realize his plight. At last when he was told that he must die by slow torture he begged for protection. His agony was awful. He pleaded and writhed in bodily and mental pain. Scarcely had the train reached Paris than this torture commenced. His clothes were torn off piecemeal and scattered in the crowd, people catching the shreds and putting them away as mementos. The child's father, her brother, and two uncles then gathered about the Negro as he lay fastened to the torture platform and thrust hot irons into his quivering flesh. It was horrible—the man dying by slow torture in the midst of smoke from his own burning flesh. Every groan from the fiend, every contortion of his body was cheered by the thickly packed crowd of 10,000 persons. The mass of beings 600 yards in diameter, the scaffold being the center. After burning the feet and legs, the hot irons—plenty of fresh ones being at hand—were rolled up and down Smith's stomach, back, and arms. Then the eyes were burned out and irons were thrust down his throat.

The men of the Vance family having wreaked vengeance, the crowd piled all kinds of combustible stuff around the scaffold, poured oil on it and set it afire. The Negro rolled and tossed out of the mass, only to be pushed back by the people nearest him. He tossed out again, and was roped and pulled back. Hundreds of people turned away, but the vast crowd still looked calmly on. People were here from every part of this section. They came from Dallas, Fort Worth, Sherman, Denison, Bonham, Texarkana, Fort Smith, Ark., and a party of fifteen came from Hempstead county, Arkansas, where he was captured. Every train that came in was loaded to its utmost capacity, and there were demands at many points for special trains to bring the people here to see the unparalleled punishment for an unparalleled crime. When the news of the burning went over the country like wildfire, at every country town anvils boomed forth the announcement.

. . . .

Reverend King is quoted by a New York newspaper:

... "I followed the procession and wept aloud as I saw little children of my own race follow the unfortunate man and taunt him with jeers. Even at the stake, children of both sexes and colors gathered in groups, and when the father of the murdered child raised the hissing iron with which he was about to torture the helpless victim, the children became as frantic as the grown people and struggled forward to obtain places of advantage.

"It was terrible. One little tot scarcely older than little Myrtle Vance clapped her baby hands as her father held her on his shoulders above the heads of the people.

" 'For God's sake,' I shouted, 'send the children home.'

" 'No, no,' shouted a hundred maddened voices: 'let them learn a lesson.'

"I love children, but as I looked about the little faces distorted with passion and the bloodshot eyes of the cruel parents who held them high in their arms, I thanked God that I have none of my own.

"As the hot iron sank deep into poor Henry's flesh a hideous yell rent the air, and, with a sound as terrible as the cry of lost souls on judgment day, 20,000 maddened people took up the victim's cry of agony and a prolonged howl of maddened glee rent the air.

"No one was himself now. Every man, woman and child in that awful crowd was worked up to a greater frenzy than that which actuated Smith's horrible crime. The people were capable of any new atrocity now, and as Smith's yells became more and more frequent, it was difficult to hold the crowd back, so anxious were the savages to participate in the sickening tortures.

"For half an hour I tried to pray as the beads of agony rolled down my forehead and bathed my face.

"For an instant a hush spread over the people. I could stand no more, and with a superhuman effort dashed through the compact mass of humanity and stood at the foot of the burning scaffold.

" 'In the name of God,' I cried, 'I command you to cease this torture.'

"The heavy butt of a Winchester rifle descended on my head and I fell to the ground. Rough hands seized me and angry men bore me away, and I was thankful.

"At the outskirts of the crowd I was attacked again, and then several men, no doubt glad to get away from the fearful place, escorted me to my home, where I was allowed to take a small amount of clothing. A jeering crowd gathered without, and when I appeared at the door ready hands seized me and I was placed upon a rail, and, with curses and oaths, taken to the railway station and placed upon a train. As the train moved out some one thrust a roll of bills into my hand and said, 'God bless you, but it was no use.' "

When asked if he should ever return to Paris, Mr. King said: "I shall never go south again. The impressions of that awful day will stay with me forever."

. . . .

A DOUBLE BURNING*

Mr. White, the long-time executive secretary of the National Association for the Advancement of Colored People, describes one of the cases which finally aroused the conscience of the nation.

... The New York *Tribune* of February 8, 1904 tells of a double burning in Mississippi:

> Luther Holbert, a Doddsville Negro, and his wife were burned at the stake for the murder of James Eastland, a white planter, and John Carr, a Negro. The planter was killed in a quarrel. . . . Holbert and his wife left the plantation but were brought back and burned at the stake in the presence of a thousand people. Two innocent Negroes had been shot previous to this by a posse looking for Holbert. . . . There is nothing in the story to indicate that Holbert's wife had any part in the crime.

Benjamin Brawley, in *A Social History of the American Negro*, quotes the Vicksburg, Mississippi, *Evening Post*—which, obviously, can be relied upon not to add anything to the account of what actually happened—as to a new refinement introduced into the killing of Holbert and his wife—the use of corkscrews. This is the story:

*Adapted from Walter White, *Rope and Faggot* (New York: Arno Press and The New York Times; 1969 reprint of the 1929 Knopf original), pp. 35–36.

When the two Negroes were captured, they were tied to trees and while the funeral pyres were being prepared they were forced to suffer the most fiendish tortures. The blacks were forced to hold out their hands while one finger at a time was chopped off. The fingers were distributed as souvenirs. The ears of the murderers were cut off. Holbert was beaten severely, his skull was fractured, and one of his eyes, knocked out with a stick, hung by a shred from the socket ... The most excruciating form of punishment consisted in the use of a large corkscrew in the hands of some of the mob. This instrument was bored into the flesh of the man and woman, in the arms, legs and body, and then pulled out, the spirals tearing out big pieces of raw, quivering flesh every time it was withdrawn."

One may well imagine that death, even in the form of burning at the stake, must have been welcomed gladly by the man and woman as relief from such bestiality. This is what Mississippians did, not only to Holbert, who, at most, was guilty of killing his opponent in a quarrel, but to Mrs. Holbert, who was innocent of any connexion with the murder.

. . . .

Conditions were improved by the 1920s and 1930s, but they were far from perfect, as indicated in the following selections from the writings of Walter White and Anna Hedgeman. Mr. White was able to gather his information firsthand because he successfully passed as Caucasian. Mrs. Hedgeman, having been born and reared as a member of the sole (and middleclass) black family in a small Minnesota town, did not face truly rampant racism until she went to Mississippi to take her first teaching job.

ROPE AND FAGGOT*

Arkansas . . . Henry Lowry, a Negro of Nodena, had been held in virtual peonage for more than two years by a white landowner. When Lowry, on Christmas Day, 1920, demanded payment of wages due him, he was cursed and struck by the landlord and shot by the landlord's son. Lowry thereupon drew his own gun and killed the landlord and his daughter, who stood near him. Escaping to Texas, he was arrested. The Governor of Arkansas assured him protection from mob violence and a fair trial; so Lowry waived whatever rights he possessed involving interstate rendition. The two Arkansas officers sent to bring him back from Texas ignored the Governor's orders to take Lowry by the shortest route to Little Rock for safe keeping and took him by way of New Orleans and Mississippi. At Sardis, Missis-

*Adapted from White, *Rope and Faggot*, op. cit., pp. 23-25, 27-29.

sippi, a mob, waiting and obviously advised of the route, "overpowered" the officers. Lowry in their possession, word was sent to other members of the mob who were dining comfortably at the fashionable Peabody Hotel at Memphis. The newspapers were advised in time to issue early afternoon "extras" giving full details as to time, place, and other arrangements for the forthcoming lynching.

Ralph Roddy, a reporter for the Memphis *Press*, a daily newspaper, was sent to cover the event. His story, appearing in the *Press* of January 27, 1921, bore the head: "KILL NEGRO BY INCHES." Here is what Roddy saw and wrote:

> ... More than 500 persons stood by and looked on while the Negro was slowly burned to a crisp. A few women were scattered among the crowd of Arkansas planters, who directed the grewsome work of avenging the death of O. T. Craig and his daughter, Mrs. C. P. Williamson.
>
> Not once did the slayer beg for mercy despite the fact that he suffered one of the most horrible deaths imaginable. With the Negro chained to a log, members of the mob placed a small pile of leaves around his feet. Gasoline was then poured on the leaves, and the carrying out of the death sentence was under way.
>
> Inch by inch the Negro was fairly cooked to death. Every few minutes fresh leaves were tossed on the funeral pyre until the blaze had passed the Negro's waist. ... Even after the flesh had dropped away from his legs and the flames were leaping toward his face, Lowry retained consciousness. Not once did he whimper or beg for mercy. Once or twice he attempted to pick up the hot ashes in his hands and thrust them in his mouth in order to hasten death.
>
> Each time the ashes were kicked out of his reach by a member of the mob. ...
>
> As the flames were eating away his abdomen, a member of the mob stepped forward and saturated the body with gasoline. It was then only a few minutes until the Negro had been reduced to ashes. ...

William Pickens, in the *Nation* of March 23, 1921, told of one additional note of consideration shown Lowry by his murderers: "... the Negro said never a word except when the mob brought his wife and little daughter to see him burning." Despite the fact that the plans for the execution had been widely published hours before the actual burning, not only was no attempt made to prevent the lynching, but Sheriff Dwight H. Blackwood of Mississippi County, in which Nodena is located, was quoted by the *Press* to the effect that "Nearly every man, woman and child in our county wanted the Negro lynched. When public sentiment is that way, there isn't much chance left for the officers. ..."

Georgia. "Southern chivalry" draws no line of sex. An unscrupulous farmer in south Georgia refused to pay a Negro hand wages due him. A few days later the farmer was shot and killed. Not finding the Negro suspected of the murder, mobs began to kill every Negro who could even remotely be connected with the victim and the alleged slayer. One of these was a man named Hayes Turner, whose offense was that he knew the alleged slayer, a not altogether remarkable circumstance, since both men worked for the dead farmer. To Turner's wife, within one month of accouchement, was brought the news of her husband's death. She cried out in her sorrow, pouring maledictions upon the hands of those who had thrust widowhood upon her so abruptly and cruelly.

Word of her threat to swear out warrants for the arrest of her husband's murderers came to them. "We'll teach the damn' nigger wench some sense," was their answer, as they began to seek her. Fearful, her friends secreted the sorrowing woman on an obscure farm, miles away. Sunday morning, with a hot May sun beating down, they found her. Securely they bound her ankles together and, by them, hanged her to a tree. Gasoline and motor oil were thrown upon her dangling clothes; a match wrapped her in sudden flames. Mocking, ribald laughter from her tormentors answered the helpless woman's screams of pain and terror. "Mister, you ought to've heard the nigger wench howl!" a member of the mob boasted to me a few days later as we stood at the place of Mary Turner's death.

The clothes burned from her crisply toasted body, in which, unfortunately, life still lingered, a man stepped towards the woman and, with his knife, ripped open the abdomen in a crude Caesarean operation. Out tumbled the prematurely born child. Two feeble cries it gave—and received for answer the heel of a stalwart man, as life was ground out of the tiny form. Under the tree of death was scooped a shallow hole. The rope about Mary Turner's charred ankles was cut, and swiftly her body tumbled into its grave. Not without a sense of humour or of appropriateness was some member of the mob. An empty whisky-bottle, quart size, was given for headstone. Into its neck was stuck a half-smoked cigar—which had saved the delicate nostrils of one member of the mob from the stench of burning human flesh.

. . . .

MURDER IN BIRMINGHAM *

"The design, sequence, structure, drama and fulfillment of reconciliation

*Adapted from Anna Arnold Hedgeman, *The Trumpet Sounds*: A Memoir of Negro Leadership (New York: Holt, Rinehart and Winston, 1964), pp. 3–6.

[of the races], is focused upon the Crucifixion." These words were spoken by a white Episcopalian layman and attorney, to a startled audience of six hundred priests, ministers and rabbis at the Chicago Conference on Religion and Race in January 1963.

The impact of his words returned to me in full force as I stood months later in the Negro church in Birmingham, Alabama, where four little children had been murdered on the preceding Sunday at the Sunday school hour. Bits of glass peppered the floor amid scattered Sunday school books; Bible verses were still on the blackboards. One long side wall of the old church had caught the major force of a dynamite blast. A traditional stained glass portrayal of Jesus the Christ had once hung on the center wall. The dynamite had wrecked this portrait. His face was gone, His heart was ripped out, and His vital organs were torn from his body.

The broken symbol of Jesus brought back the ancient Biblical words, "And it was the third hour when they crucified Him . . . and when they had mocked Him they stripped Him of His purple cloak . . . and they crucified Him and divided His garments among them . . . and at the ninth hour Jesus cried with a loud voice, 'My God, my God, why hast Thou forsaken me?' "

The African slaves understood this Crucifixion story and expressed it in such songs as, "Were You There When They Crucified My Lord?" They understood His cruxifixion because they themselves were living it out as slaves in a strange land, stripped of their clothing, their dreams, their family and tribal relationships, their language, their direction of their own bodies and their opportunity for fulfillment.

It came to me clearly that crucifixion is the full meaning of the demonstrations which have rocked Montgomery, Little Rock, Jackson and Birmingham, and the rumbles one hears in Chicago, Detroit, New York and Los Angeles. It is also the meaning of the fear, dismay, questioning and often amazement with which whites are greeting the so-called Negro Rebellion.

Standing there by the broken figure of Christ, I realized that the continuing rebellion of the Negro presented an extraordinarily awesome challenge. Centuries ago, the Crucifixion had actually been an opportunity by which fearful, faithless, defiant, hopeful and trusting men found their way toward the Resurrection. Could these four crucified children and the broken figure of Jesus so reach into the souls of all of us that the potential of the Resurrection might again be comprehended in our living?

Part of the answer came as we walked through long lines of Alabama State Patrolmen, with guns trained not on the guilty white community but on the funeral procession and the three little white caskets (the fourth little girl had been buried the day before). As we entered the church to the strains of ancient Christian hymns, I could think only of Jesus' words, "My God, my God, why hast thou forsaken me?"

At the church door we were handed a small white black-bordered order of service. After the listing of the names of the three little girls who had been murdered on Sunday, September 15, 1963, we read the words, "Come unto me, all ye that labor and are heavy laden, and I will give you rest."

"Carol Denise McNair, 12, was born in Birmingham . . . was a member of the 16th Street Baptist Church where she attended Sunday School and sang in the Young People's Choir . . . She showed great leadership ability . . . loved children . . . and liked to read." The order of service goes on to say. "She was suddenly taken on High on Sunday, September 15, 1963 at 10:25 A.M. in the church which she attended amid the children whom she loved, as they was preparing to join in with other youths in singing songs of praise to the God she loved." And then there is a quotation, "There is no death, what seems to be, is mere transition to eternal life, with Christ."

Addie Mae Collins, 14, was also a member of the Youth Choir of the 16th Street Baptist Church and was in the intermediate department of the Sunday School. Beneath the story of her short life there was a poem which said, "Under each rank wrong, somewhere there lies the root of Right; that each sorrow has its purpose . . . But as sure as the sun brings the morning, Whatever is—is best."

The third little girl, Cynthia Dianne Wesley, 14, was described as the adopted daughter of Mr. and Mrs. Claude A. Wesley. The word "adopted" caught at my heart, for the story of the way in which Negroes have always helped children and relatives is one of the great untold "self-help" stories of America. Cynthia came from a family of eight children. She, too, was "a member of the intermediate class of the same Sunday School and was preparing to serve as a newly elected member of a Youth Usher Board . . . when she was summoned to peaceful rest." The poem which follows the story of her tiny life is called "Immortality" and has for its last two lines the words, "Mourn not, oh Grief, and Faith, lift up thine head; Lo, it is dawn with her. She is not dead."

The service was in the mood of grief and faith. I was glad that the opening scripture was read by a white minister, the Rev. Joseph Ellwanger, pastor of St. Paul Lutheran Church, for it meant that there was a courageous white minister in the community and that Negroes could still listen to a white minister.

Although there was comment on the brutality involved in all of the acts of violence—the 31 unsolved bombings in the state of Alabama, the tragic death of Medgar Evers in Mississippi, and the day-by-day brutalization of Negroes who are American citizens—there was no sense of defeat or despair. There was instead the acceptance of responsibility as children of God toward the witness which could bring the Resurrection.

As we came out of the church, some of us who did not go to the gravesite paused and looked again at the guns trained on the funeral procession. Many young people who had been standing outside the overflowing church for several hours began to sing softly "We Shall Overcome."...

. . . .

The next three selections are representative of the multitude describing various facets of white-black relationships during the turbulent 1960s. The outward manifestations of black rage are now different, but it would be folly to assume that the quietness of the 1970s suggests that black Americans have become apathetic. In reality, they have simply adopted different tactics to try to obtain what they have wanted all along—namely, the freedom to work toward creating a decent life-style, which is supposedly part of the birthright of every American.

NO HONOR IN A NATION COMPROMISED*

... I believe that Dr. Martin King, with his strength to love, with his courage to face any peril, with his capacity of being able to hate the evil deed without hating the evildoer, was a truly militant man.

Many of his critics would not have had the bravery which was a hallmark of his leadership.

Yes, Dr. King was a man of unusual heart.

And he needed heart.

How he must have needed heart as he saw faith in nonviolence dying.

How he must have needed heart when the power structure ignored his fervent pleas for motion and progress to prove to the restless masses that the nonviolent ethic could work.

How much heart he must have needed when the victories being won—if only temporary victories—were being won only because rioting and violence and looting had aroused the consciousness but not the conscience of America.

How he must have needed heart when intellectually bankrupt men tried to indict him as a Communist or a tool of the Communists.

*Adapted from testimony by the late Jackie Robinson at a Congressional hearing, 8 Apr 1968. Source: *Human Resources Development*, Part I (Washington: U.S. Government Printing Office, 1968), pp. 3-6.

You ask how group dynamics can be activated in the Negro community. Dr. King could have told you.

He tried to tell you so many times.

I mean no disrespect for my Nation's legislators, but I must say, in all candor, that the Congress of the United States is one of the important segments of the power structure which has failed the cause of justice.

Of course, I do not mean to indict all of the Representatives and Senators.

Some of the finest fighters for justice belong to the Congress.

But there are still enough Members in both Houses who have the combined strength to thwart the progress of equality and justice in America.

. . . .

What kind of positive group dynamics can you expect from youngsters on those street corners or even in the churches, schools, and homes when a bill to provide open housing for all is kicked around like an old ball, even though some of these homes would be havens for the disproportionate number of black troops offering their lives in Vietnam?

And when a Thurgood Marshall is nominated for the Supreme Court bench by the President, these youngsters see him humiliated, disrespected, and badgered with insulting questions by men unable professionally to sit on the same forum with him.

Those youngsters must say to themselves: "What chance have I, if this can happen to a giant with the talent of a Thurgood Marshall?"

That is why, today, you hear big business complaining that, despite their efforts to give jobs to minority group members, they are faced with only a tiny number of applicants.

Young black people just do not believe that it is "for real" when told that barriers once raised against them have been lowered.

. . . .

And I know that no matter how much fame or fortune a black man has in America, he really has not got it made, until the most humble black man and the most humble white man has it made.

So long as this is true, what kind of positive group dynamics can we anticipate from the ghetto.

We can expect dynamics; the dynamics of looting, the dynamics of rioting, the dynamics of escapism as expressed in resorting to narcotics, the dynamics of crime not only against whites, but against blacks as well.

And I warn you that although we must never knuckle under to anarchy —I warn you that getting tough with troops and with weapons is not the way.

I warn you that—out there in those streets—and this was true before Dr. King was assassinated and it will be true when this trouble dies down—out there in those streets are young, black kids, not propagandized by any group, not subsidized by any conspiracy, just black youngsters who aren't afraid to die.

I've had them tell me that they'd rather die in the streets of America than in Vietnam.

I've heard them say: "I am not afraid to die; I'm barely living now."

I've heard them declare that they are not willing to wait any longer for the hearts of men to change.

And while I deplore violence in any form, and while I do not endorse rioting and looting, I don't intend to bury my head in the sand about the pure, sheer sincerity of these black kids and their conviction that they are right in their cause.

I respect that sincerity—just as I respect those young, black athletes who say in one breath: "I would give my right arm to win an Olympic medal," but who say, on the other hand, that they can find no honor in competition so long as their Nation is willing to do business as usual with South Africa.

. . . .

VIETNAM #4*

a cat said
on the corner

the other day
dig man

how come so many
of us
niggers

are dying over there
in that white
man's war

they say more of us
are dying

*Attributed to Clarence Major; original source not known.

than them peckerwoods
& it just
            don't make sense
unless it's true
that the honkeys

are trying to kill us out
with the same stone

they killing them other cats
with

you know, he said
two birds with one stone

FIGHTING FOR PEACE*

Black Panther Party chief of staff David Hilliard speaks to a coalition peace rally in San Francisco and reveals how extreme the desperate can get.

There's too many American flags out here, and our Minister of Information, Eldridge Cleaver, says that the American flag and the American eagle are the true symbols of fascism. ALL POWER TO THE PEOPLE. Black power to Black people, Brown power to Brown people, Red power to Red people, and Yellow power to Ho Chi Minh, and Comrade Kim Il Sung, the courageous leader of the 40,000,000 Korean people.

The Black Panther Party takes the position that we want all Black men exempt from military service and that we believe that Black people should not be forced to fight in a military to defend a racist government that does not protect us. We will not fight and kill other people of color in the world, who like Black people are victims of US imperialism on an international level, and fascism domestically. So recognizing that, recognizing fascism, recognizing the occupation of all the pigs in the Black community, then it becomes evident that there's a war at home, there's a war of genocide being waged against Black people right here in America.

So then, we would like to ask the American people do they want peace in Vietnam. Well, do you? (audience) "Yes." Do you want peace in the Black communities? (audience) "Yes." Well you goddamned sure can't get

*Adapted from David Hilliard, "If You Want Peace, You've Got to Fight for It," *The Black Panther* (Nov. 22, 1969):2.

it with no guitars, you can't get it demonstrating. The only way that you're going to get peace in Vietnam is to withdraw the oppressive forces from the Black communities right here in Babylon. So that we have a suggestion for that, we have a proposal, we have a message for that. We have a petition that we're circulating on a national level to control the pigs in the Black community; and we know that those pigs are not going to move of their own volition. We know that those think that the Black Panther Party is just making up shit, that they're distorting history when we say that this country is fascist. But I think just a little reexamination of your history will show to you, the American people, that the history of this country promulgates and it sets a precedence for any fascism that has ever taken place on the stage of world history.

Adolph Hitler was a fascist. The man was an animal. The man was a monster. He was a jingoist, a war-mongerer. But Adolph Hitler did not create fascism. Adolph Hitler did not create the Black Legion. Black people were enslaved and killed in the millions before Hitler even came on the scene. The Red man was exterminated in this country, and Hitler don't take responsibility for that. So that this country has a blood stained history. This country is a country that was built on war, it was built on the ruins, it was built on the sweat and blood of its Black people. So that the history of the Black Panther Party, the ideology of the Black Panther Party is nothing more than the historical experiences of Black people in this country translated by war of Marxism-Leninism. Because we recognize that Marxism-Leninism is not a philosophy for Russians, it is not a philosophy for Chinese, but it's a philosophy for any people that's moving against an oppressive power structure such as the capitalistic fascist system of the American society. And we have adopted that. And that we're putting it into practice because it has proven beyond a doubt that it's truly in the service of the proletariat.

. . . .

We say down with the American fascist society. Later for Richard Millhouse Nixon, the motherfucker. Later for all the pigs of the power structure. Later for all the people out here that don't want to hear me curse, because that's all that I know how to do. That's all that I'm going to do. I'm not going to ever stop cursing; not only are we going to curse, we're going to put into practice some of the shit that we talk about. Because Richard Nixon is an evil man. This is the motherfucker that unleashed the counter-insurgent teams upon the Black Panther Party. This is the man that's responsible for all the attacks on the Black Panther Party nationally. This is the man that sends his vicious murderous dogs out into the Black community and invade upon our Black Panther Party Breakfast

Program, destroy food that we have for hungry kids and expect us to accept shit like that idly. Fuck that motherfucking man. *We will kill Richard Nixon, we will kill any motherfucker that stands in the way of our freedom.* We ain't here for no goddamned peace, because we know that we can't have no peace because this country was built on war. And if you want peace you got to fight for it.

————————

With the next group of selections, we attend to the black-white situation in the 1970s. All of the pieces have current significance although some of them were written several years ago.

NATIVE RESERVES*

... What the rural South had begun, the urban North completed. The black diaspora began in the late nineteenth century, burgeoned in the twentieth, hit floodtide during two world wars. The Negro population, as late as 1940, was three-fourths Southern and mostly rural; today, nearly half the nation's 22 million blacks live in the North and two-thirds are clotted in and around the nation's cities. And they came to the cities a peasant class, with nothing more than the muscle of their backs and the impossible dreams in their heads.

The cities, of course, have cheated the black man's hopes. But myths die hard, and the myth that the urban North is the promised land is not dead yet. Whites commonly assume that the North's higher welfare rates are the central attraction—the sort of utterly logical and utterly narrow judgment that comes from reading bar graphs too literally. Anything looks better to Negroes who live in unpainted shacks papered over inside to keep the wind out, who sleep three, four or five to a pallet made of a fertilizer sack stuffed with raw cotton, who sustain themselves and their kids on a diet of grits and beans and rice. And many Negroes still imagine that the rainbow ends in Memphis or Chicago or Newark; it is not the welfare statistics who write home. "All the boys hear all this talk about Up North and they just take off," says 17-year-old Arthelia Hulett, a farm boy in Alabama's Lowndes County. "All the money is Up North. There just ain't no money here."

*Adapted from pp. 8–9 of "The Negro in America, What Must Be Done," *Newsweek* (Nov. 20, 1967): entire special issue.

The riots and the grievances they revealed may at last have fractured the myth: the flow of migrants into Watts has ebbed from 1,000 a month before the holocaust there to 400 a month since. Yet still the trek goes on. Until this autumn, Velma Hatcher, 19, had a $50-a-week job at a small raincoat factory in Selma—enough to live on and even to squeeze out the payments on a shiny new yellow Camaro. But the plant's mostly Negro work force, Velma among them, went on strike, and the company brought in non-union replacements. There was nothing else available in Selma; there was the car she wanted desperately to keep; there were the letters home from a cousin in Flint, Mich., about the easy, high-wage jobs in the auto industry. And so, one teary October morning, Velma packed up, soothed her mother ("Soon as I pay for my car I be back home") and pointed North. "Velma didn't want to go North," her mother says, "but she didn't have no choice. She's tried lots of places up there, but she ain't had no luck yet. She wish she were back here, I know."

The story is repeated countless times: the rainbow ends in a ghetto hopelessly mired in the culture of poverty and the pervasive climate of failure. Most high-wage jobs, where they are available to Negroes at all, are for people with high-school diplomas and marketable skills, not Southern farm hands or Northern dropouts. So demoralized are the ghetto schools that it scarcely matters whether a student quits (as perhaps half do) or sticks through till graduation; half the job applicants at a hiring center in Boston's Roxbury ghetto have at least some high-school education, but the average grade level is fourth grade. Most galling of all is the ghetto itself—a monochromatic preserve which, as the Negro psychologist Kenneth Clark notes, makes it brutally plain to the black man how little his society values him.

His housing is old, crumbling, rat-ridden, so desperately overcrowded that—at the density rate of parts of Harlem—the entire U.S. population could be squeezed into three of New York City's five boroughs. Garbage festers uncollected on the sidewalks; building codes go unenforced; the streets are not even paved in parts of Houston's black quarter. "The ghettos in America are like the native reserves in South Africa," says Ralph Bunche. "They symbolize the Negro as unacceptable, inferior and therefore kept apart."

They symbolize his powerlessness as well. Very nearly everything in the ghetto—its tenements, its stores, its politics, even its brothels and its numbers banks—are owned by whites downtown. Symbols of power become fiercely important: few whites understand the rut Negroes feel when, whatever the merits of the case, an Adam Powell is expelled from Congress or a Muhammad Ali is stripped of his heavyweight crown.

And casual slights become traumatic. Once, on a visit to Watts, Robert

F. Kennedy tried to strike up a talk with two baleful youths in Malcolm X sweatshirts. "They finally began to talk," Bobby recounts, "how they lived, why they hated white people. The garbage on the streets which was never picked up. One lived with his mother, he was 19, he decided to complain to the department of sanitation ... They said, 'How old are you?' When he told them 19, they said you have to be 21 to complain. He told me, 'You can draft me and send me to Vietnam but I can't complain here!' The hatred left his face and you could see the hurt—what we'd done to him."

And finally everything crumbles. A bottle of muscatel becomes an anesthetic, narcotics a refuge, casual sexuality and violence the twin proofs of manhood for Negroes who cannot furnish the customary evidence: the ability to provide for a wife and children. Families break up. Illegitimacy becomes a norm: half of Harlem's babies last year were born out of wedlock. Welfare dependency grows: six Negro children in ten subsist at least part of their lives on the dole. Failure becomes a self-fulfilling prophecy: men wander aimlessly from one dead-end, low-wage job to another, quitting on the flimsiest real or imagined provocation since they expect to be fired anyway. Crime proliferates, most of it directed at other Negroes. Arrest records are cheaply accumulated, dearly lived down. Police and Negroes look on one another with mutual paranoia: cops often see Negroes as innately amoral, and Negroes commonly view cops as head-knocking bullyboys.

In the end, says anthropologist Elliot Leibow in a brilliant study based on a year-long live-in on a Washington ghetto street corner, a man's wife and children can become a symbol of his own failure as a man—and the easy, transient camaraderie of the corner becomes an irresistible lure. At the moment he submits, says Liebow, "he comes into his full inheritance bequeathed him by his parents, teachers, employers and society at large. This is the step into failure from which few if any return, and it is at this point that the rest of society can wring its hands or rejoice in the certain knowledge that he has ended up precisely as they had predicted he would."

For the corner is only a way station on the journey to the end of the line. At 17, Gary Robinson and nineteen other boys from his Harlem block joined the Air Force, and he has tried to keep tabs on them ever since. One beat his child to death with a shoe and was executed. Others have died of narcotic poisoning, or gone to prison on charges ranging from mugging to murder, or simply vanished. Only five are still in society: two cops, a doorman, a hustler and Robinson himself. Today, a cool, trim and handsome young man of 32, Robinson is a poverty worker in Boston, trying to place the ghetto poor in jobs or job training. Sometimes his wards fail him; one of them, a man newly lined up for a hothouse job, shuffled across Robinson's path one morning, generously nursing a toothache with muscat wine and offering amiably, "Sure, I'll be workin' tomorrow ... A man's got a right to do a little hurtin', ain't he?" And Robinson does not get angry, because he looks at them and sees his own past: running with a teen gang at 12, puffing pot at 13, doing 28 days in The Tombs at 23 for possession of marijuana. His mother came to see him in jail and cried, and Robinson decided to go straight. And now he agrees: "A black man's got a right to hurt."

. . . .

BLACK AND WHITE RACISM*

... If we are going to *know* the truth which makes us free, we must *tell* the truth about racism. White folks are not the only racists in the country today. Black folks are racist also. And their racism is not only directed toward white folks, but also against other Negroes. I do a comedy routine about moving into a white neighborhood. The first day I receive some callers on my front porch. Not the white racists, but the colored delegation. Dr. Jones standing there with his lips tucked in. The delegation has come by to make sure I act right and don't embarrass them in this white neighborhood. Dr. Jones says, "You have to watch yourself out here and remember the white folks are watching us." And I say, "What are you doin', stealin' or something?"

Sophisticated Negroes are embarrassed by the actions of their poor black brother in the ghetto, but are not embarrassed by the actions of poor whites in their ghetto. That is racism. But it is not a Negroid characteristic. It is the normal result of living under a system of oppression. After a period of time, the oppressed man begins imitating the behavior of the oppressor. It was not uncommon in the concentration camps of World War II for the Jewish prisoners to imitate the Nazi soldiers when their backs were turned. Some of the Jewish prisoners would cut their clothes in the same way the German uniforms were fashioned. They would misuse fellow prisoners in the manner of their Nazi oppressors. Imitating the behavior of the oppressor is a way of escaping one's own oppression. Negroes who have made a few advances within the system of oppression are frequently prejudiced toward other Negroes whose behavior reminds them of the worst the oppressive system has to offer.

*Adapted from Dick Gregory, *The Shadow That Scares Me* (New York: Pocket Books, 1968), pp. 38-40, 141-142.

If I had to choose between losing my wife to a white man and losing her to a black man, I would choose the black man, because I would not want to face the embarrassment of my friends reminding me that a white man stole my wife. Yet I know I am making a racist choice. A simple illustration will show the extent to which unconscious racism victimizes every human being in this country. My secretary and I boarded a plane in Chicago on our way to Newark. The plane was crowded and there were no two seats together available. My secretary took one single seat and I took another. I happened to be sitting next to a white woman and we began talking about the social problems of America. I mentioned that I thought the number one problem in America was racism. She was visibly relieved to hear me say this and she said, "You are so right. You know, I wanted to get up and give the young lady who is with you my seat. But I was afraid you would think I didn't want to sit next to you."

Suppose two airplanes took off at the same time; one filled with white passengers and the other filled with black passengers. If you had to decide which plane would crash, what would your choice be? Most white folks will choose the all-black plane and most Negroes will choose the all-white plane. That is racism. . . .

If a man put a tight shoe on his foot, so that the shoe continually rubs against the foot, he will get a corn. If he wears the tight shoe long enough, the corn will turn into a callus. Man does not want to have a corn or a callus on his foot, but Nature says that nothing shall rub against her own. If a man still persists in wearing the tight shoe, the callus will swell, getting harder and tougher, and eventually the shoe will wear out. I have never seen the shoe which would be able to wear out one of Nature's feet.

America has put a tight shoe on the Negro and now he has a callus on his soul. The Negro wants and needs a new shoe. America owes him that, because she took the Negro barefoot from Africa and put the shoe on him that was manacled to the plow which planted her cotton and to the ties that built her railroads. The greatness of America was built on the back of the Negro whose shoes still do not fit well enough to enable him to walk like a man.

Suddenly America seems to be willing to give the Negro a new pair of shoes. But she has disregarded the callus on his soul. Suppose a man wears a size 8 shoe, but all of his life he has been pushed into a size 7½. It is not enough to say you are going to give this man a brand-new size 8 shoe. Rather, you have to give him a size 9 or 10 and work on his corns and bunions until he is ready once again to wear the size 8. The Negro in America needs more than a new shoe. He needs a special shoe and the care of a doctor. The Negro needs special treatment.

When America decided that she must solve the missile gap, she did not entrust the solution of the problem to Senators and Congressmen who had never had a course in nuclear physics. Rather America went all over the world and assembled the best minds money could buy. Only highly trained and specialized scientists could solve the missile gap. America laid the problem before these brilliant minds and said honestly: "This is the problem. We don't know how to solve it. The solution is up to you."

When the ghettto becomes a laboratory instead of a battleground, the social problem in America can be solved. America must listen honestly to the cries of the ghetto and apply the best available minds to the solution of the problem. Top sociologists, psychiatrists, and social scientists are needed rather than blue ribbon panels to investigate the cause of riots. Civil disorder is Nature's violent reaction to the tight shoe system of oppression in America. And until social pediatricians do the necessary footwork, civil disorder will continue.

. . . .

A TERRIBLE INDICTMENT*

Dr. Kenneth Clark, a psychologist and a black American, interviews essayist-novelist James Baldwin, also black; after covering other matters . . . .

CLARK: . . . Now I'd like to go back to the point that you made that the Harlem that you knew when you were growing up is not the Harlem now and see if we can relate this also to the school.
BALDWIN: Let's see. Let's see if we can. It was probably very important for me—I haven't thought of this for a long time—it was important at the point I was going to P.S. 24—the only Negro school principal as far as I know in the entire history of New York was the principal—a woman named Mrs. Ayer, and she liked me. And in a way I guess she proved to me that I didn't have to be entirely defined by my circumstances, because you know that every Negro child knows what his circumstances are though he can't articulate them, because he is born into a republic which assures him in as many ways as it knows how, and has got great force, that he has a certain place and he can never rise above it. And what has happened in Harlem since is that that generation has passed away.

*Adapted from Kenneth B. Clark, *The Negro Protest*: James Baldwin, Malcolm X, Martin Luther King talk with Kenneth B. Clark (Boston: Beacon Press, 1963), pp. 6–8.

CLARK: Mrs. Ayer was sort of a model in a sense.

BALDWIN: She was a proof. She was a living proof that I was not necessarily what the country said I was.

CLARK: Then it is significant, Jim, that we do not have a single Negro principal in the New York public school system today.

BALDWIN: And it is *not* because "there ain't nobody around who can do it," you know. One's involved in a very curious and a very serious battle concerning which I think the time has come to be as explicit as one can possibly be. The great victims in this country of an institution called segregation (it is not a southern custom but has been for a hundred years a national way of life) the great victims are white people, the white man's children. Lorraine Hansberry said this afternoon—we were talking about the problem of being a Negro male in this society—Lorraine said she wasn't too concerned really about Negro manhood since they had managed to endure and to even transcend some fantastic things, but she was very worried about a civilization which could produce these five policemen standing on the Negro woman's neck in Birmingham or wherever it was, and I am too. I'm terrified at the moral apathy, the death of the heart, which is happening in my country. These people have deluded themselves for so long that they really don't think I'm human. I base this on their conduct, not on what they say, and this means that they have become in themselves moral monsters. It's a terrible indictment. I mean every word I say.

. . . .

A GROWTH OF SOCIAL MEANNESS *

. . . Behind the mass of [1972] electoral sentiment there are, at one end, urgent problems and, at the other, a growth of what I'd call social callousness, perhaps social meanness. The urgent problems have to do with safety in the streets—any liberal or radical who by now denies the reality of this problem is simply deluding himself (or staying off the streets). McGovern never really responded to or seized upon this matter; his high moralistic stance seemed too distant for millions of whites who may not think of themselves as prejudiced but who nevertheless look over their shoulders when they notice a group of black youngsters behind them.

. . . And most troubling of all has been the almost complete evaporation of the widespread good feeling toward blacks that one could detect only a

*Adapted from Irving Howe, "Picking Up the Pieces," *Dissent* 20 (Winter 1973): 7-12.

decade ago; indeed, the replacement of this feeling by a mixture of fear and contempt, a tacit acceptance of some notion of innate inferiority that leads "them" to drugs, mugging, violence, family disintegration, etc.

This new attitude toward the blacks is a terrifying phenomenon, not least of all because it subsists on a vicious circle of hostility. The *New York Times*/Yankelovich poll, which proved to be quite accurate, asked people: "Do you feel that minority groups are receiving too much, too little, or just about the right amount of attention?" Answers to this question are more likely to yield authentic responses than answers to formal questions about civil rights. And the responses are illuminating. Even after four years of what black leaders have assailed as "benign neglect" of minority needs, four out of every ten voters answered, "too much attention." And of these, almost 80 percent said they would vote for Nixon. A third of the Democrats polled said they would defect to Nixon, and of this group over half said blacks have been getting "too much attention." Compared with recent elections, there were twice as many Democratic defectors as usual and the defectors are twice as likely to resent minority-group gains.

Race, it now seems, was the dirty little secret of the campaign—and those intellectuals who supported Nixon because, as they proclaimed, he had been "prudent" in his four years of office were right in a way that (one hopes) they did not quite grasp.

. . . .

A NEW TIME OF CRISIS*

Yesterday—May 17— was the 18th anniversary of the Supreme Court's decision in *Brown v. Board of Education*, in which the Court held that "in the field of public education the doctrine of 'separate but equal' has no place" and commanded an end to the segregation of children by race in public schools. Today—May 18—in a less noted landmark, the 76th birthday of the Supreme Court's decision in *Plessy v. Ferguson*, which propagated the doctrine of "separate but equal" in the first place. Despite its explicit rejection in *Brown*, the system of segregation authorized by *Plessy* has had remarkable staying power.

Most of the years since *Brown* have been a period of pain and sacrifice for black parents and children struggling to overcome the barriers of massive resistance, delay and evasion thrown up by state authorities. It is

*Adapted from William Taylor, "School Desegregation: a New Time of Crisis," *ADA World* (June 27, 1972):14-16.

only in the past few years that significant progress in integrating the schools has been made—though we are still far short of dismantling the dual school system, notwithstanding President Nixon's claim that the process has been "substantially completed."

Now we have entered a new time of crisis in school desegregation efforts, a crisis in the form of attempts to delay and ultimately severely restrict the use of busing as a means of accomplishing integration. The action that Congress takes on these proposals may well determine whether *Brown* is finally implemented or whether it is consigned to the graveyard of history while the racist doctrine of Plessy is resurrected to govern our lives for the foreseeable future.

This is not an overstatement. For, while it is asserted correctly that busing is only one instrument for accomplishing school integration, it is equally clear that in most areas of the nation the public schools will remain segregated for many years unless transportation continues to be available as a remedy. It is in the cities of the nation, particularly the large ones, that busing is an indispensable tool for integration because residential patterns are so highly segregated. Yet these are the same cities in which the bulk of the black population of the country now lives; (according to the 1970 census, 37 percent of all black citizens now reside in the 25 largest cities of the nation). Indeed, in many large cities, to make integration a meaningful possibility for any but a handful of students will require not simply the availability of busing, but application of the principles of metropolitan desegregation declared in the Richmond and Detroit cases.

Accordingly, when the . . . Administration seeks in H.R. 13916 to postpone the implementation of court orders requiring busing and in H.R. 13915 to ban permanently any increase in busing at the elementary school level, *it is quite simply and directly seeking to foreclose the possibility of an integrated education for the mass of black and white students.*

This ban would apply to the most modest of desegregation plans—those involving the *voluntary* transfer of students from schools in which they are a majority to those in which they are a minority, if additional transportation were required. It also would inhibit development of new facilities— education parks or magnet schools—designed both to foster integration and in other ways to improve the quality of education for all children, since these facilities also would require some degree of busing.

Since H.R. 13916 clearly would postpone vindication of constitutional rights for large numbers of children, it can pass constitutional muster—if at all—only upon the most compelling demonstration of an overriding governmental interest in delay. It is here that the performance of the Nixon Administration has been so shockingly cynical and inadequate.

In the first instance the President . . . claimed that "many lower court decisions have gone far beyond what . . . the Supreme Court has said is necessary." But the Administration . . . failed to cite any cases, and an examination of the decisions that have caused the greatest controversy does not provide support for its claim. To the contrary, the great bulk of recent decisions in both the North and South are fully consistent with the principles declared in *Brown* and elaborated upon in such cases as *Green v. New Kent County, Holmes v. Alexander,* and *Swann v. School Board of Charlotte-Mecklenburg.*

What has happened is that as segregation laws and policies have fallen, courts have been impelled to examine the actions of school authorities and other governmental officials to determine the contribution they have made to the continuation of segregation. The conclusions reached by federal courts have been remarkably consistent. They have found that in deciding where to locate new schools, where to place boundaries, what steps to take to relieve overcrowding, what kinds of transfer policies to adopt, school officials have frequently chosen a course of action which could not but produce racial separation in the schools.

Further, courts have found, on the basis of extensive evidence, that school authorities have based their attendance zones upon patterns of housing segregation that were fostered in large measure by government action. In Detroit and Pontiac as well as in Richmond, it was shown that black people do not live in central cities simply out of choice or only because they lack sufficient money to go elsewhere or even because of private practices of discrimination.

The proof of government's role goes back to the 1930s and 1940s when the Federal Housing Administration, helping to create new suburbs, told developers that you could not have a "stable" community or a good community unless it was racially and economically homogeneous. The federal government made it clear in official pronouncements that not only must neighborhoods be segregated but schools as well, and that restrictive covenants, zoning laws—and even busing—must be used if necessary to keep them that way. To the present day the same FHA-assisted housing remains substantially segregated and even new subsidized housing, authorized by the Housing and Urban Development Act of 1968, is being built and operated on a segregated basis.

What is the Administration's response to this detailed proof? In a brief filed in the Richmond case, more than three weeks after the President had pointed an accusing finger at the federal courts, the Department of Justice begins its argument with the incredible statement that "we have not had the opportunity to scrutinize the record."

If the Justice Department had taken the trouble to examine the record in Richmond or other cases, it would have discovered that what the courts are dealing with, North and South, is not racial separation that is accidental or fortuitous or adventitious. It is a government policy of *racial containment*, which locks black people into lives of hopelessness and despair. And what we are seeking is not "artificial racial balance." Rather it is a means for government to undo the damage it has done to little children and to give them at least a fighting chance to lead decent and rewarding lives.

If the Administration has been insensitive to the rights of black children and reckless in its characterization of court decisions, one might at least expect that it would be prepared to document its allegation that orders requiring busing have seriously disadvantaged large numbers of school children. After all, the proposed congressional finding in Section 2(a)(2) of H.R. 13916 that busing orders have caused "substantial hardship" and "have impinged on the educational process" lies at the heart of the moratorium legislation. If it is not substantiated, there can be no basis at all for postponing implementation of constitutional guarantees.

Yet, astonishingly, the Administration has not offered specific facts to document its claim of "substantial hardship." To the contrary, the record of these hearings is filled with evidence:

• That transporting children to school by bus is a prevalent and traditional practice throughout the nation.
• That very little of it is done for purposes of desegregation.
• That transportation costs are a relatively small part of education budgets.
• That only a minute portion of recent increases in transportation costs are attributable to desegregation.
• That busing is the safest means of conveying children to school.
• That the times and distances involved in desegregation orders are consonant with busing for other purposes.

A survey of busing in 14 districts, conducted by the Center for National Policy Review, showed that among these districts, six experienced no increase in the duration of average bus rides as a result of implementation of court ordered plans (Arlington, Jackson, Oxnard, Pontiac, San Francisco and Savannah). The greatest increase in time was from 20 to 45 minutes in Tampa. Three districts experienced an increase of between 10 and 20 minutes (Manhasset, Nashville and Norfolk).

In no district was the average ride longer than 45 minutes after the implementation of a desegregation plan. The median average ride before implementation was about 20 minutes. The median average ride after implementation was about 27 minutes.

Even in cases involving metropolitan relief, the logistics may be no more difficult than desegregation plans for a single district. Bradley v. School Board of Richmond, a case in which I am privileged to serve as co-counsel, is the one decision in which a plan has been worked out in detail. There, the court-approved plan would put the metropolitan area's 104,000 public school children into six subdistricts. The maximum length of time for any trip would be 45 minutes in five of the six subdistricts and one hour in the sixth. The latter is a rural area of Chesterfield County where long distance rides of an hour or more are already common. Very few children actually would travel the maximum time—times which are well within limits set by the Virginia State Department of Education 25 years ago. And the number of children to be transported would increase by no more than 10,000— from 68,000 to 78,000.

Nor is there any basis in the record for Congress to conclude that court orders requiring busing "have impinged on the educational process." Again, the evidence shows quite the contrary: that school desegregation has been of significant educational benefit to black and other minority children and that where (as in almost all integration plans) schools are composed primarily of children of advantaged backgrounds, the performance of advantaged students has not been impaired by the presence of students of disadvantaged backgrounds. As a matter of fact, HEW's own report on the "Effectiveness of Compensatory Education," issued April 20, makes substantially the same point. While putting the best face they can on the prospects that compensatory efforts can result in significant educational gains (against the largely discouraging experience with such efforts so far) the authors explicitly disavow the view that compensatory programs are an adequate substitute for integration. After reviewing the evidence that desegregation brings achievement gains, their repeated plea is that both remedies are needed. If a federal agency under such strong political pressures to make contrary findings reaches these conclusions, what is left of the Administration's case?

. . . .

The next two pieces illustrate the gross insensitivity of vast numbers of white Americans to the black situation. The first selection is penned by Hubert Locke, a Presbyterian minister, a black who was formerly a campus pastor at Wayne State University; he describes racism as a serious viral disease. The second piece is by another sensitive black American, Mr. Roger

Wilkins, who was Assistant Attorney General in the Johnson Administration and is now with the Ford Foundation.

A DEADLY VIRUS*

... The easiest to diagnose and the most common variety of the virus, the Horatio Alger strain has been developed from that common experience of most white Americans whose forebears came to these shores in generations past, plugged into the Protestant ethic (i.e., they worked hard, lived frugally, saved their money and prayed on Sunday) and, in one or two generations, became instant American success stories. This brand of racism is quickly identifiable by such sincere but self-righteous comments as, "My parents or my family worked hard to get where we are. No one gave anything to us. If these blacks want equality, why don't they work for it the same way we had to?"

It may be true that, with the exception of those aristocrats whose wealth, jobs, and family status are an accident of genes, most Americans have had to work hard for whatever they have. But no segment of the American populace has had to work at being equal ... except, of course, the nation's black people. Somehow in that peculiar mentality reserved for white America, it has been given to black Americans to "prove" themselves, to demonstrate in advance their worthiness of being treated like human beings. And this is made the more ironic by the fact that black Americans were the one segment of the nation who for two hundred years were systematically stripped of any vestige of humanness. They were sold like cattle, forbidden to learn to read and write, denied any semblance of family life, bred like mink when their diminishing numbers were needed to survive an expanding cotton economy, finally emancipated after their continued servitude had plunged the nation into war and there seemed, in Lincoln's words, no other way to "preserve the Union"—and then told, for the next one hundred years, to prove themselves equal.

If the unmitigated gall that characterizes this position is not apparent, then perhaps the practical realities will be, and while they are ancient history perhaps, for the record they bear repeating. Most white Americans worked their way to the top when there was still a vast supply of unskilled jobs available in this nation. The white workers, mainly immigrants, who

*Adapted from Hubert G. Locke, *The Care and Feeding of White Liberals*: The American Tragedy and the Liberal Dilemma (New York: Newman Press, 1970), pp. 28–30.

manned the mills and factories from the 1880s to the 1930s also produced the sons who went to college, entered the professions and helped to create the new technology which, among other things, made unskilled labor a useless commodity. Black workers did not get into business and industry in any significant numbers until after the Depression, just a generation before business and industry began to discover it could turn out its products more cheaply and efficiently (i.e., with less labor problems) by using machines instead of men. Therefore, in today's automated, technological society, telling an unskilled black worker with a 5th grade education to work his way to the top is about as crass as telling a kid in the Soap Box Derby that he has the privilege of competing in the Indianapolis 500.

An additional fact of life also often escapes the memories of the millions of America's mini-Horatio Algers. When the Irish in 19th-century Boston saw signs saying "No Irish need apply," they could go home and practice losing their brogue. Polish Americans could drop the "ski" from their names (and many did), Italians could learn to cook with less garlic, and Jewish Americans could manage to deftly conceal the Yiddish News behind the New York Times. But the possibility of black Americans concealing their blackness, except by generations of race-mixing, is the ultimate in impossibility. A few white visionaries have been brash enough to suggest such an option for resolving America's racial dilemma, but few black persons have ever taken the suggestion seriously, a fact for which most white people have been profoundly grateful.

. . . .

GENTLEMANLY WHITE RACISM*

... When it was all over, a number of men had tears in their eyes, even more had lifted hearts and spirits, but a few were so dispirited that they went upstairs to get drunk. We had just heard the President and Vice-President of the United States in a unique piano duet—and to many Gridiron veterans, it was a moving show-stopper. To a few others, it was a depressing display of gross insensitivity and both conscious and unconscious racism—further proof that they and their hopes for their country are becoming more and more isolated from those places where America's heart and power seem to be moving.

*Adapted from Roger Wilkins, Boston *Globe*, 2 Apr. 70.

The annual dinner of the Gridiron Club is the time when men can put on white ties and tails and forget the anxiety and loneliness that are central to the human condition and look at other men in white ties and tails and know that they have arrived or are still there.

The guests are generally grateful and gracious. But the event's importance is beyond the structures of graciousness because it shows the most powerful elements of the nation's daily press and all elements of the nation's government locked in a symbolic embrace. The rich and the powerful in jest tell many truths about themselves and about their country. I don't feel very gracious about what they told me.

Some weeks ago, to my surprise and delight, a friend—a sensitive man of honor—with a little half-apology about the required costume, invited me to attend the dinner.

The first impression was stunning: almost every passing face was a familiar one. Some had names that were household words. Some merely made up a montage of the familiar faces and bearings of our times. There were Richard Helms and Walter Mondale and Henry Kissinger and George McGovern and Joel Broyhill and Tom Wicker and William Westmoreland and John Mitchell and Tom Clark (ironically placed, by some pixie no doubt, next to each other on the dais) and Robert Finch and Ralph Nader, and of course, the President of the United States.

One thing quickly became clear about those faces. Apart from Walter Washington—who, I suppose, as Mayor had to be invited—mine was the only face in a crowd of some 500 that was not white. There were no Indians, there were no Asians, there were no Puerto Ricans, there were no Mexican-Americans. There were just the Mayor and me. Incredibly, I sensed that there were few in the room who thought that anything was missing.

There is something about an atmosphere like that that is hard to define, but excruciatingly easy for a black man to feel. It is the heavy, almost tangible, clearly visible, broad assumption that in places where it counts, America is a white country. I was an American citizen sitting in a banquet room in a hotel which I had visited many times. (My last occasion for a visit to that hotel was the farewell party for the white staff director and the black deputy staff director of the United States Commission on Civil Rights.) This night in that room, less than three miles from my home in the nation's capital, a sixty-percent black city, I felt out of place in America.

This is not to say that there were not kind men, good men, warm men in and around and about the party, nor is it to say that anyone was personally rude to me. There were some old friends and some new acquaintances whom I was genuinely glad to see. . . .

But it was not the people who so much shaped the evening. It was the humor amidst that pervasive whiteness about what was going on in the country these days that gave the evening its form and substance. There were many jokes about the "Southern strategy." White people have funny senses of humor. Some of them found something to laugh about in the Southern strategy. Black people don't think it's funny at all. That strategy hits men where they live—in their hopes for themselves and their dreams for their children. We find it sinister and frightening. And let it not be said that the Gridiron Club and its guests are not discriminating about their humor. There was a real sensitivity about the inappropriateness of poking fun that night at an ailing former President, but none about laughing about policies which crush the aspirations of millions of citizens of this nation. An instructive distinction, I thought.

There was a joke about the amendments to the Constitution (so what if we rescind the First Amendment, there'll still be twenty-five left), and about repression (you stop bugging me, I'll stop bugging you), and there were warm, almost admiring jokes about the lady who despises "liberal Communists" and thinks something like the Russian Revolution occurred in Washington on November 15th. There was applause—explosive and pro-longed—for Judges Clement Haynsworth and Julius Hoffman (the largest hands of the evening by my reckoning).

As I looked, listened, and saw the faces of those judges and of the generals and of the admirals and of the old members of the oligarchies of the House and Senate, I thought of the soft, almost beatific smile of Cesar Chavez, the serious troubled face of Vine Deloria, Jr., and the handsome, sensitive faces of Andy Young and Julian Bond of Georgia. All those men and more have fought with surely as much idealism as any general ever carried with him to Saigon, with as much courage as any senator ever took with him on a fact-finding trip to a Vietnam battlefield, or even as much hope, spirit, and belief in the American dream as any Peace Corps kid ever took to the Andes in Peru. But the men I have named fought for American freedom on American soil. And they were not there. But Julius Hoffman was.

As the jokes about the "Southern strategy" continued, I thought about the one-room segregated schoolhouse where I began my education in Kansas City. That was my neighborhood school. When they closed it, I was bused—without an apparent second thought—as a five-year-old kinder-gartener, across town to the black elementary school. It was called Crispus Attucks.

And I thought of the day I took my daughter when she was seven along the Freedom Trail in Boston, and of telling her about the black man named Crispus Attucks who was the first American to die in our revolu-tion. And I remember telling her that white America would try very hard in thousands of conscious and unconscious ways both to make her feel that her people had no part in building America's greatness and to make her feel inferior. And I remember the profoundly moving and grateful look in her eyes and the wordless hug she gave me when I told her, "Don't you believe them, because they are lies." And I felt white America in that room in the Statler-Hilton telling me all those things that night, and I told myself, "Don't you believe them, because they are lies."

And when it came to the end, the President and the Vice-President of the United States, in an act which they had consciously worked up, put on a Mister Bones routine about the Southern strategy with the biggest boffs coming as the Vice-President affected a deep Southern accent. And then they played their duets—the President playing his songs, the Vice-President playing "Dixie," the whole thing climaxed by "God Bless America" and "Auld Lang Syne." The crowd ate it up. They roared. As they roared I thought that after our black decade of imploring, suing, marching, lobbying, singing, rebelling, praying, and dying we had come to this: a Vice-Presidential Dixie with the President as his straight man. In the serious and frivolous places of power—at the end of that decade—America was still virtually lily white. And most of the people in that room were reveling in it. What, I wondered, would it take for them to understand that men also come in colors other than white? Seeing and feeling their blindness, I shuddered at the answers that came readily to mind.

. . . .

ON BEING BLACK IN WHITE AMERICA*

This brief piece was written by a Time *magazine bureau chief who had been a counselor for Walter Vendermeer before Walter, at age 12, died from an overdose of heroin. Let this one story stand for the many illustrating the totally destructive effect that white racism has on a multitude of black Americans. It is true that young Walter's difficulties were compounded by family and personality shortcomings, but who would be so foolhardy as to deny that these shortcomings too were largely the product of racism? Indeed, it seems realistic to express wonder that the black Americans who achieve a measure of happiness are as numerous as they are; it is near miraculous there are not countless Walters.*

*John Schoonbeck, "Why Did Walter Die?" *Time* 94 (Dec. 26, 1969): 12.

When Walt was five months old, his father was deported to Surinam for violating immigration laws. The child spent the rest of his short life looking for a father surrogate. His search was limited to the area around Harlem's West 116th Street, where—like many children who grow up there—he learned about hustling, dope and sex before he was ten. Often he subsisted on potato chips, baloney and sodas.

At the Floyd Patterson House, Walt was the youngest of ten children in my group, but by far the toughest and most severely disturbed. Nobody knew quite what to do for Walt. He needed enough to eat, clothes to wear, adults to model himself after, toys to play with, a place to live. He needed and asked for lots of love, support and dependability. He got none of these—and it enraged him. He had learned to suspect everyone, and if he thought he was being crossed or cheated, his anger was uncontrolled. At first, he would kick a door, his eyes lowered; then he would smash things and curse. Eventually he would work himself up to a fight. Once I tried to get him in a shower to cool him off; after half an hour he succeeded in putting me in the shower. We knew that his emotional problems were beyond our capacity to treat. In October 1968, Family Court ordered Walt remanded to the custody of his mother, Mrs. Lilly Price. Neither the boy nor his mother was present at the court hearing.

Walt was the fifth of ten children from his mother's several marriages. Only Walt and four others still lived with her, and she supported them on a $412 monthly welfare check. About two months ago, after the family was evicted from their apartment for not paying rent, they moved into a single dingy room in a friend's home. There was only one bed for all six of them.

"Walter hadn't been going to school," says his mother, "but he went out and sold papers or carried groceries. He didn't support us—he just bought the things he wanted, like a pair of socks."

Violence is a fact of life to the children of West 116th Street, but in the weeks just before his death, Walt had more than his share. Earlier this month, someone dropped a brick on his head, and the wound had to be stitched. A few days later he was hit by a car, suffering scratches and bruises. A week after that, he fell from a fire escape.

The coroner who examined Walt found scar tissue under the skin of the boy's arm, indicating that he had shot heroin before. There was no evidence of the needle tracks common to hard-core addicts. Still, Walter weighed only 80 lbs.; so a double injection of heroin—the suspected dosage—would have been enough to depress his breathing and kill him. Was he deliberately given too powerful a dose? Maybe he had threatened a pusher, many of whom are his own age. Or did he perhaps know exactly what he was doing?

One thing is certain—Walt had no trouble getting the stuff. Take a ride down 116th Street sometime; see the pushers openly peddling heroin to young blacks for $2 a bag. If you go on a mild gray day, you will see doped youngsters nodding listlessly in doorways. This was Walt's Main Street; it was all he ever knew.

When he was found on the bathroom floor of a neighborhood rooming house, he was wearing one of those Snoopy sweatshirts so popular with kids of his age. It bore the inscription: "I wish I could bite somebody . . . I need a release from my inner tensions!" It was not just heroin that killed Walter. Maybe, like many another child born black in the ghetto, he died of his whole life.

"The Only Good Indians I Ever Saw Were Dead"

Thus spake General Philip Sheridan during the latter part of the 19th century. But his sentiment was not unique. It rather accurately sums up the long-prevailing white American attitude toward the people whose natural resources were coveted. The resulting aggression by whites was such as to lead Adolf Hitler to declare that German treatment of Jews was no worse than what happened to American Indians at the hands of whites. Even if that were not true, it seems clear that the "pioneer spirit" so praised in movie legend was actually a rather consistent policy of genocide, thievery, and illegal military endeavors. Thus, when Kit Carson was sent to hunt and kill the Navajo in 1864, he also burned their hogans, killed their livestock, and finally cut down the peachtrees they had planted. The ultimate result of the various actions may be seen on a multitude of Indian reservations today where the residents attempt to live—if one can rightly call it that—without even the most basic of necessities and, what is perhaps more important, without hope. Harvard nutritionist Jean Mayer has commented that not one of the Southwestern reservations has ". . . that most necessary of human commodites—decent food." Consequently, Indians have an abnormally high rate of infectious diseases: 8 times the national average of infant deaths from gastroenteritis, 18 times more strep throat, 6 times as much mumps, and quite commonly tuberculosis (which has all but disappeared among white Americans). Other consequences of our long-standing

*Indian policies are described in the accompanying selections. The first piece
gives typical examples of the way that Indian lands have been taken from
them by stealth or force. The second selection, "The Sand Creek Massacre," is particularly sad because it describes a group of Cheyenne who,
totally trusting the American forces, were shot down as they huddled
beneath the stars and stripes they'd been told would protect them. The
final selection indicates that conditions today are still deplorable, to state
the case as lightly as one decently can.*

THE LAST OF INDIAN LAND *

... Between the years 1887 and 1966 the Indian land base has decreased
from 138 million acres to 55 million acres. Indian land remains the subject
of continual and unrelenting expropriation—most frequently in the name of
progress.

*Indian land is cheaper, easier and less dangerous, politically to take. So
it is taken.* Construction engineers, road builders and dam erectors have an
uncanny knack for discovering that the only feasible and economical way
to do what must be done will, unfortunately, necessitate taking the Indian's land. These principles always apply:

1) that private property interests must give way to larger considerations
of public policy and social needs, and

2) that such a yielding should be structured to minimize the harm to
private interests in general and to protect the interests of the majority.
"The Greater Good" always hobbles the Indian. When a choice must be
made as to whose private property will be taken for public purposes—an
Indian's land or a non-Indian's—the Indian is invariably the loser.

Such was the case with the Indians of Fort Berthold, North Dakota in
their fight to keep the United States Army Corps of Engineers from
flooding their land. The opening of Garrison Dam in the spring of 1953
was a final, bitter defeat over the Three Affiliated Tribes which for six
years fought its construction. The dam flooded one-fourth of their reservation, 154,000 acres.

Although wary when reclamation officials at the Interior Department
first told them what the Army had in mind, the Indians decided to settle

*Adapted from Edgar S. Cahn, editor: Jerry J. Berman, W. Dayton
Coles, Jr., Nancy Esposito, F. Browning Pipestem, Associate Editors, *Our
Brother's Keeper*, The Indian in White America (New York: New Com-
munity Press, Inc., 1969), pp. 69–72.

the problem reasonably and within the purview of the law. Experts in the Bureau of Reclamation had drawn up an alternative to Garrison Dam which achieved the same purposes, inundated less valuable land, was equally feasible, and which required no intrusion on Indian treaty rights. After a series of consultations, the Army and the Interior Department led the Indians to believe the alternative would be accepted. It wasn't.

In response the Indians scraped together money and hired their own experts to devise a third plan. The tribes even offered to donate the lands they would lose to this dam—saving the government time and money—but the BIA would not endorse the plan. The Bureau of Indian Affairs received orders from the Secretary of Interior to refrain from involving the Department in further controversies with the Corps. The Army refused to consider the Indian offer.

When it became apparent that the Indians would resist the dam-building, the Government promised to provide 150,000 substitute acres of land downstream—land of equal value. The Indians were unenthusiastic. Fort Berthold was their ancestral home; further, the site for Garrison Dam had been declared unsafe by a Corps of Engineers study. Once the Indian lands had been taken and the reservation flooded, the Government "forgot" its offer. The Indians were left with no substitute land whatsoever.

The Army flooded the tribes' most fertile bottom lands, which were the basis of the entire reservation's economy. Left untouched were the harsh upland plains, barren for lack of water and with temperatures that reach 40° below zero. Beyond this, the site for the dam and the reservoir was so chosen that the waters partitioned a unified, compact territory (inhabited by a relatively prosperous cattle-raising people) into five divided and unlinkable sectors.

As at many other reservations, land at Fort Berthold had, years before the Garrison Dam crisis, been divided and parceled out in fractions among the Indians, and some had been acquired by non-Indians. Although a survey showed that 80 percent of the Indians wished to remain on their reservation, the flooding forced many to move and the checkerboarding of the land severely limited the Indians' farming and cattle-raising. The Government promised a consolidation program, but never delivered.

So the Indians went to Washington seeking justice, with the BIA opting for a quick and minimal settlement. In the original negotiations, they were promised access to the Court of Claims should the ultimate award prove inadequate. After much negotiating, they received only $12,605,625, no mineral or other use rights were retained, and future access to the Court of Claims was denied. Five years after the Indians gave up the lands, a rich oil deposit was discovered. They received no royalties.

Relocation of the Indians was carried out by the Army without regard for community or family, in alphabetical order. Kinship groups and native villages were dispersed. An early promise that the construction of the dam would assure lower electricity rates was never fulfilled. Wells which the Army drilled for the Indians turned black and brackish; the water was unusable. Indians were forced to buy water at 25 cents a barrel and haul it for miles.

After relocation was complete, the Bureau of Indian Affairs decided unilaterally to donate sections of Indian lands to churches and private schools. Without appraisal, the Bureau announced it would pay the tribe only $2.50 per acre for the land it seized and gave away. In 1968, a federal court found that this action violated the Indians' rights under the first and fifth amendments of the Constitution.

Today, 16 years after the opening of Garrison Dam, Fort Berthold is still in emotional and economic shock. In an effort to reestablish the old communities, tribal members travel up to 120 miles each weekend to attend reservation pow-wows, where tents are clustered along the lines of the old settlements. Unemployment stands at 60 percent. As of 1968, welfare payments have jumped to $573,022. Prior to Garrison, however, welfare costs were never over $5,000 for any year. Life styles have been destroyed. An older member of the tribe lamented, "We seem to need to be told what to do, like children. We have been made dependent. As Bureau of Indian Affairs personnel change, we get changes in policies. . . . We sort of wait to see how the new policy will go and we go with it. A generation seems caught. The old way is gone, but there is no adequate employment for a new way."

What happened in North Dakota is not unique. The catalogue of instances in which Indian land has been taken for the public good extends to California, Arizona, Idaho, Montana, New York, South Dakota, Pennsylvania and elsewhere. Indian communities have been sacrificed to flood, irrigation and hydroelectric projects. . . .

. . . .

THE SAND CREEK MASSACRE*

. . . The Cheyennes who were camped on Sand Creek heard from the Arapahos that an unfriendly little red-eyed soldier chief had taken the

*Adapted from Dee Brown, *Bury My Heart at Wounded Knee*: An Indian History of the American West (New York: Bantam Books, 1970), pp. 83–89.

place of their friend Wynkoop. In the Deer Rutting Moon of mid-November, Black Kettle and a party of Cheyennes journeyed to the fort to see this new soldier chief. His eyes were indeed red (the result of scurvy), but he pretended to be friendly. Several officers who were present at the meeting between Black Kettle and Anthony testified afterward that Anthony assured the Cheyennes that if they returned to their camp at Sand Creek they would be under the protection of Fort Lyon. He also told them that their young men could go east toward the Smoky Hill to hunt buffalo until he secured permission from the Army to issue them winter rations.

Pleased with Anthony's remarks, Black Kettle said that he and the other Cheyenne leaders had been thinking of moving far south of the Arkansas so that they would feel safe from the soldiers, but that the words of Major Anthony made them feel safe at Sand Creek. They would stay there for the winter.

After the Cheyenne delegation departed, Anthony ordered Left Hand and Little Raven to disband the Arapaho camp near Fort Lyon. "Go and hunt buffalo to feed yourselves," he told them. Alarmed by Anthony's brusqueness, the Arapahos packed up and began moving away. When they were well out of view of the fort, the two bands of Arapahos separated. Left Hand went with his people to Sand Creek to join the Cheyennes. Little Raven led his band across the Arkansas River and headed south; he did not trust the Red-Eyed Soldier Chief.

Anthony now informed his superiors that "there is a band of Indians within forty miles of the post. ... I shall try to keep the Indians quiet until such time as I receive reinforcements."[1]

On November 26, when the post trader, Gray Blanket John Smith, requested permission to go out to Sand Creek to trade for hides, Major Anthony was unusually cooperative. He provided Smith with an Army ambulance to haul his goods, and also a driver, Private David Louderback of the Colorado Cavalry. If nothing else would lull the Indians into a sense of security and keep them camped where they were, the presence of a post trader and a peaceful representative of the Army should do so.

Twenty-four hours later the reinforcements which Anthony said he needed to attack the Indians were approaching Fort Lyon. They were six hundred men of Colonel Chivington's Colorado regiments, including most of the Third, which had been formed by Governor John Evans for the sole purpose of fighting Indians. When the vanguard reached the fort, they surrounded it and forbade anyone to leave under penalty of death. About the same time a detachment of twenty cavalrymen reached William Bent's ranch a few miles to the east, surrounded Bent's house, and forbade anyone to enter or leave. Bent's two half-breed sons, George and Charlie, and his half-breed son-in-law Edmond Guerrier were camped with the Cheyennes on Sand Creek.

When Chivington rode up to the officers' quarters at Fort Lyon, Major Anthony greeted him warmly. Chivington began talking of "collecting scalps" and "wading in gore." Anthony responded by saying that he had been "waiting for a good chance to pitch into them," and that every man at Fort Lyon was eager to join Chivington's expedition against the Indians.[2]

Not all of Anthony's officers, however, were eager or even willing to join Chivington's well-planned massacre. Captain Silas Soule, Lieutenant Joseph Cramer, and Lieutenant James Connor protested that an attack on Black Kettle's peaceful camp would violate the pledge of safety given the Indians by both Wynkoop and Anthony, "that it would be murder in every sense of the word," and any officer participating would dishonor the uniform of the Army.

Chivington became violently angry at them and brought his fist down close to Lieutenant Cramer's face. "Damn any man who sympathizes with Indians!" he cried. "I have come to kill Indians, and believe it is right and honorable to use any means under God's heaven to kill Indians."[3]

Soule, Cramer, and Connor had to join the expedition or face a court-martial, but they quietly resolved not to order their men to fire on the Indians except in self-defense.

At eight o'clock on the evening of November 28, Chivington's column, now consisting of more than seven hundred men by the addition of Anthony's troops, moved out in column of fours. Four twelve-pounder mountain howitzers accompanied the cavalry. Stars glittered in a clear sky; the night air carried a sharp bite of frost.

For a guide Chivington conscripted sixty-nine-year-old James Beckwourth, a mulatto who had lived with the Indians for half a century. Medicine Calf Beckwourth tried to beg off, but Chivington threatened to hang the old man if he refused to guide the soldiers to the Cheynne-Arapaho encampment.

As the column moved on, it became evident that Beckwourth's dimming eyes and rheumatic bones handicapped his usefulness as a guide. At a ranch house near Spring Bottom, Chivington stopped and ordered the rancher hauled out of his bed to take Beckwourth's place as guide. The rancher was Robert Bent, eldest son of William Bent; all three of Bent's half-Cheyenne sons would soon be together at Sand Creek.

The Cheyenne camp lay in a horseshoe bend of Sand Creek north of an almost dry stream bed. Black Kettle's tepee was near the center of the village, with White Antelope's and War Bonnet's people to the west. On the east side and slightly separated from the Cheyennes was Left Hand's

Arapaho camp. Altogether there were about six hundred Indians in the creek bend, two-thirds of them being women and children. Most of the warriors were several miles to the east hunting buffalo for the camp, as they had been told to do by Major Anthony.

So confident were the Indians of absolute safety, they kept no night watch except of the pony herd which was corralled below the creek. The first warning they had of an attack was about sunrise—the drumming of hooves on the sand flats. "I was sleeping in a lodge," Edmond Guerrier said. "I heard, at first, some of the squaws outside say there were a lot of buffalo coming into camp; others said they were a lot of soldiers." Guerrier immediately went outside and started toward Gray Blanket Smith's tent.[4]

George Bent, who was sleeping in the same area, said that he was still in his blankets when he heard shouts and the noise of people running about the camp. "From down the creek a large body of troops was advancing at a rapid trot . . . more soldiers could be seen making for the Indian pony herds to the south of the camps; in the camps themselves all was confusion and noise—men, women, and children rushing out of the lodges partly dressed; women and children screaming at sight of the troops; men running back into the lodges for their arms. . . . I looked toward the chief's lodge and saw that Black Kettle had a large American flag tied to the end of a long lodgepole and was standing in front of his lodge, holding the pole, with the flag fluttering in the gray light of the winter dawn. I heard him call to the people not to be afraid, that the soldiers would not hurt them; then the troops opened fire from two sides of the camp."[5]

Meanwhile young Guerrier had joined Gray Blanket Smith and Private Louderback at the trader's tent. "Louderback proposed we should go out and meet the troops. We started. Before we got outside the edge of the tent I could see soldiers begin to dismount. I thought they were artillery-men and were about to shell the camp. I had hardly spoken when they began firing with their rifles and pistols. When I saw I could not get to them, I struck out; I left the soldier and Smith."

Louderback halted momentarily, but Smith kept moving ahead toward the cavalrymen. "Shoot the damned old son of a bitch!" a soldier shouted from the ranks. "He's no better than an Indian." At the first scattered shots, Smith and Louderback turned and ran for their tent. Smith's half-breed son, Jack, and Charlie Bent had already taken cover there.[6]

By this time hundreds of Cheyenne women and children were gathering around Black Kettle's flag. Up the dry creek bed, more were coming from White Antelope's camp. After all, had not Colonel Greenwood told Black Kettle that as long as the United States flag flew above him no soldier would fire upon him? White Antelope, an older man of seventy-five, unarmed, his dark face seamed from sun and weather, strode toward the soldiers. He was still confident that the soldiers would stop firing as soon as they saw the American flag and the white surrender flag which Black Kettle had now run up.

Medicine Calf Beckwourth, riding beside Colonel Chivington, saw White Antelope approaching. "He came running out to meet the command," Beckwourth later testified, "holding up his hands and saying 'Stop! stop!' he spoke it in as plain English as I can. He stopped and folded his arms until shot down."[7] Survivors among the Cheyennes said that White Antelope sang the death song before he died:

> Nothing lives long
> Only the earth and the mountains.

From the direction of the Arapaho camp, Left Hand and his people also tried to reach Black Kettle's flag. When Left Hand saw the troops, he stood with his arms folded, saying he would not fight the white men because they were his friends. He was shot down.

Robert Bent, who was riding unwillingly with Colonel Chivington, said that when they came in sight of the camp "I saw the American flag waving and heard Black Kettle tell the Indians to stand around the flag, and there they were huddled—men, women, and children. This was when we were within fifty yards of the Indians. I also saw a white flag raised. These flags were in so conspicuous a position that they must have been seen. When the troops fired, the Indians ran, some of the men into their lodges, probably to get their arms. ... I think there were six hundred Indians in all. I think there were thirty-five braves and some old men, about sixy in all ... the rest of the men were away from camp, hunting. ... After the firing the warriors put the squaws and children together, and surrounded them to protect them. I saw five squaws under a bank for shelter. When the troops came up to them they ran out and showed their persons to let the soldiers know they were squaws and begged for mercy, but the soldiers shot them all. I saw one squaw lying on the bank whose leg had been broken by a shell; a soldier came up to her with a drawn saber; she raised her arm to protect herself, when he struck, breaking her arm; she rolled over and raised her other arm, when he struck, breaking it, and then left her without killing her. There seemed to be indiscriminate slaughter of men, women, and children. There were some thirty or forty squaws collected in a hole for protection; they sent out a little girl about six years old with a white flag on a stick; she had not proceeded but a few steps when she was shot and killed. All the squaws in that hole were afterwards killed, and four or five bucks outside. The squaws offered no resistance. Every one I saw dead was scalped. I saw one squaw cut open with an unborn child, as I thought, lying by her side. Captain Soule afterwards told me that such was the fact. I saw the body of White Antelope with the privates cut off, and I heard a soldier say he was going to make a tobacco pouch out of them. I saw one squaw whose privates had been cut out. ... I saw a little girl about five years of age who had been hid in the sand; two soldiers discovered her, drew their pistols and shot her, and then pulled her out of the sand by the arm. I saw quite a number of infants in arms killed with their mothers."[8]

(In a public speech made in Denver not long before this massacre, Colonel Chivington advocated the killing and scalping of all Indians, even infants. "Nits make lice!" he declared.)

Robert Bent's description of the soldiers' atrocities was corroborated by Lieutenant James Connor: "In going over the battleground the next day I did not see a body of man, woman, or child but was scalped, and in many instances their bodies were mutilated in the most horrible manner—men, women, and children's privates cut out, &c; I heard one man say that he had cut out a woman's private parts and had them for exhibition on a stick; I heard another man say that he had cut the fingers off an Indian to get the rings on the hand; according to the best of my knowledge and belief these atrocities that were committed were with the knowledge of J. M. Chivington, and I do not know of his taking any measures to prevent them; I heard of one instance of a child a few months old being thrown in the feedbox of a wagon, and after being carried some distance left on the ground to perish; I also heard of numerous instances in which men had cut the private parts of females and stretched them over the saddle-bows and wore them over their hats while riding in the ranks."[9]

REFERENCES

1. U.S. Congress. 38th. 2nd session. Senate Report 142, p. 18.
2. U.S. Congress. 39th. 2nd session. Senate Executive Document 26, p. 25.
3. *Ibid.*, p. 47. U.S. Congress. 39th. 2nd session. Senate Report 156, pp. 53, 74.
4. *Ibid.*, p. 66.
5. George Bent to George E. Hyde, April 14, 1906 (Coe Collection, Yale University).
6. U.S. Congress. 39th. 2nd session. Senate Report 156, pp. 66, 73.
7. U.S. Congress. 39th. 2nd session. Senate Executive Document 26, p. 70.
8. U.S. Congress. 39th. 2nd session. Senate Report 156, pp. 73, 96.
9. *Ibid.*, p. 53; Berthrong, Donald J. *The Southern Cheyennes.* Norman, University of Oklahoma Press, 1963, p. 220.

PIECES OF A PUZZLE*

We began our investigations—not in Washington, and not by reading official reports—but by listening to Indians. On reservations, around ceremonial camp fires, in hogans or houses or huts, on the banks of the Columbia River, in upper state New York, Alaska, New Mexico, California, Oklahoma, the Dakotas, Nevada, the base of the Havasupai canyon—those are the places where we began to listen. The report reflects that perspective—the perspective of those voices we heard—of a composite picture pieced together by a core staff and dozens of researchers, who logged in tens of thousands of miles in the course of the past 10 months.

We do not begin reports with a recitation of isolated achievements—dollars spent, roads paved, sanitary facilities built. For those are dwarfed by an overriding reality that came through countless stories and was subsequently corroborated by extensive analysis of reports, statistics, and studies documenting the extent of poverty, injustice and deprivation.

The report begins where we began—with anecdotes seemingly unrelated, yet all part of a larger picture—with pieces of a puzzle.

On a Chippewa reservation in the Northwest, the children are busily writing a class composition. Their topic is on the blackboard: "Why we are all happy the Pilgrims landed."

At the Pine Ridge Reservation in South Dakota, the second largest in the nation, $8,040 a year is spent per family to help the Oglala Sioux Indians out of poverty. Yet, median income among these Indians is $1,910 per family. At last count there was nearly one bureaucrat for each and every family on the reservation. Over 60 percent of the reservation's work force is without steady employment.[1]

The chief of the Cherokee Indians is picked by the President of the United States—not by the Cherokees. He is W. W. Keeler. He is only fractionally Indian. He cannot even speak to his tribe in its native Cherokee language. But he is Chairman of the Board of Phillips Petroleum Company, an Oklahoma-based oil company that has acquired extensive mineral holdings from Indians in Oklahoma.

Major properties in Palm Springs, California, are owned by the Agua Caliente Indians. To protect these owners from their own improvidence, the Bureau of Indian Affairs permitted state officials to declare nearly

*Adapted from Edgar S. Cahn, editor; Jerry J. Berman, W. Dayton Coles, Jr., Nancy Esposito, F. Browning Pipestem, Associate Editors, *Our Brother's Keeper*, The Indian in White America (New York: New Community Press, Inc., 1969), pp. 1-4, 6-10.

two-thirds of them incompetent to manage their own affairs, and to provide guardians or trustees to act for them. It took nine years of complaints to move the BIA to investigate. In 1968 the Secretary of Interior revealed that trustees had been pocketing an average of one-third of the proceeds from the land. In some cases, trustees had been awarded fees as high as 340 percent of the total receipts.

Haskell Institute, an old Indian college, makes a heavy contribution to the economy of Lawrence, Kansas. At a local restaurant, however, an employee refused to serve the college students. Reminded of the 1964 Civil Rights Act, she responded, "We only have to serve niggers."[2]

Suicides among Indian teen-agers average three times the national rate: on some reservations the suicide rate reaches 10 times the national average. Senator Walter Mondale of Minnesota, describing a visit of Senator Robert F. Kennedy to the Fort Hall, Idaho, Reservation recalls: "We were told that suicides had occurred as early as 10 years of age." Two days after the Indian Education Subcommittee visit, a 16-year-old Indian boy with whom the late Senator Kennedy had chatted committed suicide. He took his life in the county jail, where he had been placed without a hearing and without his parents' knowledge, accused of drinking during school hours. He hanged himself from a pipe extending across the cell. Two other Indians from the same reservation had committed suicide in the same cell, using the same pipe, in the previous 11 months. One was a 17-year-old girl from the same school.

Welfare workers have forcibly removed Indian children from their mothers at Devil's Lake Reservation, North Dakota, placing them with white families. One observer said Indian children run and hide at the approach of unfamiliar cars, and Indian adults reportedly are afraid to speak out for fear they will lose their children. Families claim they have been removed from welfare rolls to force them to surrender their children for placement off the reservation.

In the State of Washington, Indians who once were prosperous now go hungry because the State will not allow them to fish. The State of Washington spends up to $2,000 per salmon to protect these fish for sportsmen and commercial fisheries, which catch over 90 percent of the salmon. But it refuses to permit the Indians, who catch less than 10 percent of the salmon, to continue to fish. The right to fish forever was promised to the Indians by the United States Government in exchange for taking away Indians' land.

An Indian child in the State of Washington objected to the American history text that called her ancestors "dirty savages." The girl was then summarily expelled from the public school there. The reason: the child was "uncontrollable." The mother was forced to send her daughter all the way to Oklahoma to the Bureau-run Fort Sill, Oklahoma, Boarding School. Hundreds of other "uncontrollable" and "problem children" are routinely shipped thousands of miles from home—some from Alaska to Oklahoma—to BIA boarding schools. They see their parents once a year, if that often.

. . . .

Indians in California are reluctant to take part in federal poverty programs for fear they later will be billed for the cost of the programs. Their fear is justified. Over the past two decades they have been repeatedly charged for federal expenditures in California relating to Indians during the 19th century. The charges are deducted from money owed to the Indians for land seized by the Government. In many instances, the goods provided to Indians were shoddy. In some cases they never were delivered. To this day, the California Indian Legal Services Program financed by the Office of Economic Opportunity has been unable to secure a guarantee from the Government that legal services which it provides to Indians will not be billed to them in the future.

The more the story varies, the more it remains the same—and slowly, a coherent picture emerges.

. . . .

As trustee, governor and benefactor of the Indian, the Bureau of Indian Affairs is a pervasive presence in the Indian world. The Indian's life can be measured in encounters with his Keepers as they make their appointed rounds. The BIA domain touches most states and covers more than 50 million acres which belong to the Indians. The BIA effectively governs the 400,000 Indians on the reservations, and heavily influences the lives of 200,000 living elsewhere. At the huge and fort-like Pine Ridge, South Dakota reservation, an observer likened the Bureau's presence to the British occupation of equatorial Africa.

. . . .

The Bureau, unique among federal agencies, is the federal, state and local government of the Indians, and supplants or dominates the private sector as well. It is realtor, banker, teacher, social worker; it runs the employment service, vocational and job training program, contract office, chamber of commerce, highway authority, housing agency, police department, conservation service, water works, power company, telephone company, planning office; it is land developer, patron of the arts, ambassador from and to the outside world, and also guardian, protector and spokes-man. Based in Washington, D.C.; the Bureau's 16,000 employees are lo-cated in outposts extending like tentacles westward from the Potomac.

The BIA Commissioner has his own "cabinet" in Washington—six depart-ments or branches, each with a staff: Community Services, Economic Development, Education, Administration, Engineering and Program Coordi-nation. This structure is duplicated on a regional level in Area Offices, headed by Area Directors. It is duplicated a third, and even a fourth, time at the reservation—or agency and sub-agency—level. Behind every official looking over every Indian's shoulder, there are several layers of officials looking over each others' shoulders.

. . . .

The BIA defines who is an Indian. It defines tribes, and can consolidate tribes at will. The Shoshone and Bannock peoples, for instance, have been forced to live together at Fort Hall Reservation, Iowa, and deal with the Bureau as one tribe. The Bureau decides how tribal membership is deter-mined and supervises admission to tribal rolls.

Nowhere is the BIA's authority better demonstrated than in its power over tribal and individual Indian trust property. The use of Indian land is controlled by the Bureau, as are sales, exchanges and other land transac-tions. The Bureau prescribes the number of cattle which may graze on a parcel of land. It approves leases, controls prices, terms and conditions. Often the leasing process is initiated not by the owner of the land, but by the person desiring to lease it. Leases have been approved without the owner's consent and *only* the Bureau—not the tribe or individual owner—is empowered to cancel a lease. Under certain circumstances the Bureau can sell timber on Indian land without the owners' consent, and get grant rights of way and permission to build roads, pipelines and even dams.[3]

Even the Indian's personal property is controlled by the Bureau. The Indian may be an adult—and perfectly sound in mind and body. But he still can be treated by the Bureau as legally incompetent to manage his own affairs.

Mere supposition by a Bureau official that an Indian might prove indiscreet in handling money, might be exploited, or might at some future point be unable to provide for himself—any of these is considered reason enough to relieve the Indian of control over his possessions. Once the Indian is deemed incompetent he cannot even draw money from his own bank account without obtaining approval from a BIA guardian. The deci-sion is virtually unchallengeable.

The Indian can, however, count on being treated as "competent" for at least one purpose—to sell his land. He may not be competent to lease it or to mortgage it, but if he needs money he will find the BIA most willing to help sell his land. When an Indian is hungry and desires welfare assistance, the Bureau may devise an acceptable pretext for authorizing the sale or may simply declare his land—land held in trust for him and his heirs forever—an "available asset" which he must utilize before qualifying for welfare. Once he has sold the land, the Bureau insists that the Indian spend the money from it before qualifying for welfare—but with restrictions. The money becomes subject to BIA control; it is doled out to the Indian at the welfare rate, which is usually below subsistence level.

In its own fashion, the Bureau looks after the education of its younger wards. The BIA operates boarding schools for some Indians, and contracts with local schools for the rest. But what lawyers call *in loco parentis*— "parents by proxy"—has disturbing implications when children are taken from their parents and transported as far as 6,000 miles from Alaska to Oklahoma boarding schools. The Bureau decides where Indian schools will be built and who will attend them. In the case of a Bureau school in Oregon, no Oregon Indian children or Indian children from the Northwest are permitted to attend. The Bureau can close a school and dispose of it without consent of the tribe it serves whenever it is judged that "the good of the service will be promoted thereby."[4]

Tribes must secure the consent of the Bureau to meet and discuss their constitutions. The Bureau decides whether a tribe's chosen form of government is acceptable, and nearly all tribal government decisions must be reviewed by BIA officials.

Even when exercised illegally, the total power of the Bureau is virtually unchallengable and unreviewable. Where the normal citizen has three avenues of redress—political, judicial, administrative—the Indian has none.

REFERENCES

1. Letter from Howard Kahn to Enos Poorbear, President, Oglala Sioux Tribal Council, May 16, 1968. Marshall Kaplan, Gans, and Kahn, "Description of Pine Ridge." *Oglala Sioux Model Reservation Program: The Development Potential of the Pine Ridge Indian Reservation.* p. 4, 1968.

2. "Haskell Students Face Discrimination," *The University Daily Kansan,* December 13, 1968.

3. *U.S.* v. *Creek Nation,* 295 U.S. 103, 110 (1935); 25 C.F.R. 151.1 *et seq.* (1968); 25 U.S.C. §§ 415, 415 (c) (1964); 25 C.F.R. §§ 131.5 (a); 25 C.F.R. § 131.2; 25 C.F.R. §§ 131.14; 25 C.F.R. §§ 141.7 (1968); 25 U.S.C. § 373 (1964).

4. 25 U.S.C. § 292 (1964).

Mexican-Americans

After black Americans, those of Mexican descent constitute the largest "racial" minority in the United States. The word "racial" is in quotation marks because there are important differences of opinion about whether or not people originating in Mexico can properly be referred to as a homogeneous racial grouping; many are purely Indian, but some are apparently Caucasian descendants of Spanish immigrants. It is, of course, the Mexican-Americans who are basically Indian who have had the status of a disadvantaged minority. Some of the relevant details are given in the two selections which follow.

SPANISH IS WRONG*

You know it almost from the beginning: speaking Spanish makes you different. Your mother, father, brothers, sisters, and friends all speak Spanish. But the bus driver, the teacher, the policeman, the store clerk, the man who comes to collect the rent—all the people who are doing important things—do not. Then the day comes when your teacher—who has taught you the importance of many things—tells you that speaking Spanish is wrong. You go home, kiss your mother, and say a few words to her in Spanish. You go to the window and look out and your mother asks you what's the matter?

Nada, mama, you answer, because you don't know what is wrong. . . .

Howard A. Glickstein, then Acting Staff Director of the Commission asked witness Edgar Lozano, a San Antonio high school student, whether he has ever been punished for speaking Spanish at school. Yes, in grammar, in junior high, and in senior high schools, he answers.

". . . they took a stick to me," says Edgar. "It really stayed in your mind. Some things, they don't go away as easy as others."

Edgar relates with some bitterness and anger the times he was beaten by teachers for speaking Spanish at school after "getting a lecture about, if you want to be American, you have got to speak English."

Glickstein tries to ask Edgar another question and the boy, this time more sad than angry, interrupts and says:

*Adapted from U.S. Commission on Civil Rights, *Stranger in One's Land* (Washington, D.C.: U.S. Government Printing Office, Clearinghouse Publication No. 19, May 1970), pp. 4 and 6.

"I mean, how would you like for somebody to come up to you and tell you what you speak is a dirty language? You know, what your mother speaks is a dirty language. You know, that is the only thing I ever heard at home.

"A teacher comes up to you and tells you, 'No, no. You know that is a filthy language, nothing but bad words and bad thoughts in that language.'

"I mean, they are telling you that your language is bad. ... Your mother and father speak a bad language, you speak a bad language. I mean you communicate with dirty words, and nasty ideas.

"... that really stuck to my mind."

Edgar, like many Mexican Americans before him, had been scarred with the insults of an Anglo world which rejects everything except carbon copies of what it has decreed to be "American." You start being different and you end up being labeled as un-American. An Anglo-oriented school in a Mexican American barrio can do things to the teachers, too. Bad communication can sorely twist the always sensitive relation between teacher and pupil.

Under questioning from David Rubin, the Commission's Acting General Counsel, W. Dain Higdon, principal of San Antonio's Hawthorne Junior High School, 65 percent Mexican American, asserted that he felt there was something in the background or characteristics of the Mexican Americans which inhibits high achievement.

Mexicans or Mexican Americans, Higdon told the Commission, have a "philosophical concept" in dealing with life which says *lo que dios quiera*, "what God wishes."

An Anglo, on the other hand, Higdon continued, says "in God we trust," not "this is how it shall be and you are limited."

"... you have unlimited horizons," Higdon explained to the Commission. "And whenever some situation befalls me [as as Anglo], I say it is my fault. Whenever some situation befalls a Mexican American, he may say it is his fault, but more generally and from a heritage standpoint he would be inclined to say, *lo que dios quiera*."

Rubin: Would it be fair to say that you feel there are genetic factors involved which account for the differences in achievements, that mixture of genes causes differences in people?

Higdon: Well, when you were in my office, I made that statement to you and I will stick by it. ...

The Mexican American child learns early that he is different. Then he learns that speaking Spanish prevents his becoming a good American. It's at this time, perhaps, when he most needs sensitive guidance. Yet, how do some teachers see the role of their profession?

Rubin: Did you state in an interview with me and with another staff

member that the obligations of the teacher were first to complete paper-
work and secondly to maintain discipline?

Higdon: Yes, sir, I did.

Rubin: And thirdly, to teach?

Higdon: Yes, sir.

. . . .

BROWN POWER*

There is an invisible nation hidden in our midst. The nearly 10 million
Mexican-Americans in the United States constitute the country's second
largest racial minority—a silent minority until very recently.

But they are rapidly becoming politically organized, and it seems quite
possible that in the next few years, at least in the Western United States,
they will match and surpass black people in militancy and political
strength.

Of late, Chicanos (as they call themselves) have begun to be "visible" all
over the Southwest. For example:

—Cesar Chavez and his pacifist United Farmworkers union, on strike
against large, corporately owned farms, have elevated to an international
scale their boycott of table grapes.

—Thousands of Chicano high school and college students all over the
Southwest have formed militant organizations, protested school conditions
and participated in walkouts. Denver's Rudolfo "Corky" Gonzalez, the
nation's most popular Chicano leader in the eyes of young militants, has
called for a nationwide school walkout next Sept. 16.

—Reies Lopez Tijerina, controversial founder of the Alianza Federal
(alliance of Free City States), made national headlines in 1967 when his
followers used gunfire to press their claim to territory of Tierra Amarilla in
Northern New Mexico.

—There have sprung up militant organizations of *barrio* (any area where
poor Spanish-speaking people live) youth, such as the California Brown
Berets who are modeled after the Black Panthers.

The movement invites comparison with the black power movement. The
results are startling:

Chicanos are the largest minority in the Southwest, from Colorado to

*Adapted from Kathy Mulherin, "Chicanos Turn to Brown Power: 'Five
Years behind the blacks, but we'll catch up very fast," *National Catholic
Reporter* 5(June 4, 1969):1, 5.

Mexico, from California to Texas. In California alone the three million Chicanos outnumber blacks two to one.

And their condition is worse. In Los Angeles, for example, their average annual income is $1,380, lower than the $1,437 for blacks. Only the American Indian has a lower income than the Chicano. And the Chicano receives only an average of eight years of schooling, compared with 10 years for blacks and 12 for whites.

The experience of the black power movement has not been lost on the Chicano. Said one professor: "We are about five years behind the blacks, but we will catch up very fast."

So far, a striking feature of the brown power movement is the absence of the many internal splits that plague the black and white radicals. Deep and common cultural roots seem to make the Chicano movement healthier, more flexible and more naturally communal than other radical groups.

As one Chicano told me: "We have always had our own community, so we have never suffered the feelings of *isolation* the black man feels."

The need for roots forces the black radical to expend much emotional energy over the question of how to treat his African culture which the white slaveowner tore away from him. But the Chicano feels psychologically unwounded because he has stubbornly kept his roots intact.

In the past few weeks, I have traveled several thousand miles around the Southwest, interviewing leaders such as Corky Gonzales and Reies Tijerina, young students and barrio militants, and poor farmers. I discovered a vigorous, complex people whose physical features, life styles and politics reflect the *mestizaje*—the mixture—which produced them: Spanish, Indian, and North American. Luis Valdez, founder of the United Farm Workers' *Teatro Campensino* (Rural Theater), has written:

La Raza, the race, is the Mexican people. Sentimental and cynical, fierce and docile, faithful and treacherous, individualistic and herd-following, in love with life and obsessed with death, the personality of the *raza* encompasses all the complexity of our history. The conquest of Mexico was no conquest at all. It shattered our ancient Indian universe, but more of it was left above ground than beans and tortillas. Below the foundations of our Spanish culture, we still sense the ruins of an entirely different civilization. ... A Mexican's first loyalty—when one of us is threatened by strangers from the outside—is to that *raza*."

But all this is only the soil of political organization. It was Cesar Chavez who, in recent times, first began to cultivate that soil when he organized the Delano farm workers not simply as victimized workers, but specifically as Mexicans. His campaign succeeded far better than previous efforts, and it helped to unleash a wave of energy which is creating the Chicano movement.

Frequently compared to Mahatma Gandhi for his gentle long-suffering (he has been afflicted with severe illnesses since his long fast last year, a fast he undertook to mobilize and unify support for his union), and passionate dedication to his people and the principles of nonviolence, this quiet, sad-eyed man has become in the last four years, an inspiration for thousands of Chicanos all over the West.

They were moved not only by Cesar's example but by the symbolic genius of his organization which spoke to their Mexican roots. Luis Valdez writes of the grape pickers' dramatic march from Delano to Sacramento in the spring of 1967:

"The pilgrimage to Sacramento was no mere publicity trick. The *raza* has a tradition of migrations, starting from the legend of the founding of Mexico. Nezahualcoyotl, a great Indian leader, advised his primitive Chichimecas, forerunners of the Aztecs, to begin a march to the south. In that march, he prophesied. ... they would begin to build a great nation. The nation was Aztec Mexico. ... Mexican grape pickers did not march 300 miles to Sacramento, carrying the standard of the *Virgen de Guadalupe*, merely to dramatize economic grievances. ... The Virgin of Guadalupe was the first hint to farmworkers that the pilgrimage implied social revolution. During the Mexican revolution, the peasant armies of Zapata carried her standard. ... Beautifully dark and Indian of feature, she was the New World version of the Mother of Christ. ... The people's response was immediate and reverent. They joined the march by the thousands."

The UFW produced the first newspaper of the movement, *El Malcriado*, and the first theater: today, there are 17 such newspapers, a Chicano Press association and at least six theater groups modeled after the *Teatro Campesino*.

If Chavez and the UFW provided the initial thrust for the movement, its current style and direction are better represented by Denver's Crusade for Justice and its director, Corky Gonzalez. It is, so far, the movement's most important organization, and Corky is easily the Chicano's most influential national leader.

Gonzalez, small, dark and trim, with curly black hair, a thick mustache and serious black eyes, was one of the nation's top 10 featherweight boxers from 1947 to 1955. Today, 40 years old, the father of eight children and given to wearing black T-shirts and black pants, he still exhibits the fighter's qualities of highly concentrated discipline and passion.

Such qualities come in handy in a city like Denver. Predictably, the city center is filling up with blacks and Chicanos who together will account for 20 percent of the area's population by 1970.

Here, as elsewhere, Chicanos are the least educated and the poorest—the city's over-all unemployment rate is 3 percent but for Chicanos it is 10 percent. A few more facts: 55 percent of Chicano homes in the *barrios* have six or more children; 50 percent of the Chicano population is under 19 years of age; 75 percent of the inmates in Denver prisons are Chicanos.

Driving into Denver from the airport, one passes successively through clearly divided residential areas—white suburbs, black middle-class, poor black, and finally, Chicano *barrios*.

There are many long, low, red brick apartment buildings, each with thin scruffy children playing on narrow strips of grass bordering the sidewalks. There are also many seedy brick and wooden houses with porches supported in weary dignity by dingy gray columns reminiscent of an earlier time, and a more genteel era.

Even with this background of poverty, neither Corky nor his followers in his organization, the Crusade for Justice, began as militants.

For years they tried to work within the Democratic party in Denver; Corky was a ward captain, he ran for mayor, the crusade once took over the Democratic party county and state conventions, and at one point, Corky was even a War on Poverty director.

Now he says: "We gave up on that political scene—the party system is a two-headed monster that eats at the same trough. The Chicano has to drop out of 'their' politics and create his own. . . . (This is) a controlled society in which the *gringo* (Anglo) makes all the major decisions. . . . As a result, my people have been politically destroyed and economically exploited."

His experience makes him wary of government programs—"there are always strings attached"—and he points with pride to the fact that the crusade's 26-room headquarters, a great musty box of a former Baptist church, was acquired nine months ago and is slowly being paid for without any grants from public or private agencies.

"Some of our people work for government agencies," says Emilio Dominguez, second in command in the crusade, "and we like to use them if we can." Dominguez, a middle-aged man with long hair and a beard who is by turns serene and irascible, chuckled wickedly as he told how his wife had insisted on conducting a federally supported summer project from crusade offices, "so we got all our phone bills paid that way!"

The crusade headquarters is a comfortably shabby labyrinth of classrooms, auditoriums, offices, recreation rooms and a curio shop. A newspaper, *El Gallo* is put out; there are classes in Mexican and Indian culture and history, in poetry, dancing, drama, Karate, judo and boxing. Crusade officers meet in one room, teen-agers sit around laughing and joking in another, and in the kitchen, someone is cooking up a batch of tortillas for a hungry visitor or for a poor family unfortunate enough to arrive in town on a weekend when the welfare office is closed.

Crusaders try to inform their people of their welfare rights, help them with grievances against school and city officials, find jobs for *barrio* youths. One gentle and sorrowful man, D. C. de Herrera, investigates police brutality cases.

The crusade has its playful moments too. This year's Mother's Day celebration was a vivid illustration of the warmth and affection between Chicanos of all ages and political attitudes.

The day began with a mass offered by Father Craig Hart (called Padre Corazon) on the stage of the auditorium. Music was provided by a good-natured, hardy band called *Los Vigilantes*, composed of a father and his four children, who were 5 to 15 years of age.

Father Hart asked everyone to gather around the altar and matter-of-factly encouraged participation. The people responded eagerly—the mass was in English, punctuated by simple Mexican religious folk songs. The mood was relaxed and informal as young people spoke about their mothers and their intentions. At communion, Father Hart greeted each person by name as he distributed consecrated portions of a corn tortilla.

After mass, I talked with Father Hart; he is a handsome and disarming young man with calm brown eyes and an easy grin. Earnestly, he talked about his own definition of religion. "It's the people's attempt to *hear* life ... that means the world is religious, because the world is becoming—freeing itself. These people here are religious all the way, but not in the official sense. They go to mass for important reasons—when somebody's baptized, married or buried."

When I asked whether the crusade received support from the church in the area, he frowned and shook his head. "And last week, when I was arrested (for sitting in at the State Legislature with fourteen others to protest that body's indifference to Chicano problems), the bishop said I was acting as an individual! Toleration isn't enough! The bishops have to speak out!"

Downstairs in a basement recreation room decorated with mural paintings of Aztec Indians, there was a noisy and cheerful party going on. Corky made a little speech in which he described his speaking tour of California campuses and he gently admonished: "Some of our old people say (about the youth), 'they're not doing it like we want to do it' but the young people are ahead of it—they're gonna lead it. . . . We have to catch up with the youngsters . . ."

Japanese-Americans

The most massive single act of American government lawlessness oc-curred early in 1942 when approximately 110,000 Americans of Japanese descent, most of them native-born citizens, were forcibly removed from their homes on the west coast and interned in concentration camps (which the government referred to as "relocation centers"). The root cause of this incredible violation of the Constitution was the anti-Oriental racism that had gripped American westerners for several generations. Even those we now think of as "liberals"—men such as Earl Warren and Senator Henry Jackson—agreed that the Japanese-Americans must be moved. And not just moved—pushed out precipitously before they could possibly settle their affairs or make decent arrangements to see that their hard-earned property would be cared for in their absence.

BIGOTRY UNLIMITED*

We begin with several brief items that suggest the racial climate of opinion prevailing during the early '40s:

"I'm for catching every Japanese in America, Alaska, and Hawaii now and putting them in concentration camps. . . . Damn them! Let's get rid of them now!—Congressman John Rankin,

Congressional Record, 19 Feb. 42.

LOS ANGELES, Dec. 6 [1943] (U.P.)
—By a 14 to 1 ratio, Southern Californians in a poll conducted by the Los Angeles Times, today favored deportation of all Japanese from the United States and a ban upon further Nipponese immigration.

"It takes 8 tons of freight to kill 1 Jap"

Southern Pacific R.R. billboard, 1943

"I am proud that I am an American citizen of Japanese ancestry, for my very background makes me appreciate more fully the wonderful advantages

*These and similar items appear in Maisie and Richard Conrat, *Executive Order 9066: The Internment of 110,000 Japanese Americans* (Los Angeles: California Historical Society, 1972).

of this Nation. I believe in her institutions, ideals and traditions. . . . I trust in her future. . . . She has permitted me to build a home, to earn a livelihood, to worship, think, speak and act as I please—as a free man equal to every other man.

Creed of the Japanese-American
Citizens League, 1940.

"A JAP'S A JAP"—GEN. DEWITT*

This selection begins with some of the testimony offered by General DeWitt, commanding officer of the Western Defense Command, at a Congressional hearing held in California during the spring of 1942:

. . . The general said he "didn't care what they did with the Japanese as long as they don't send them back here. . . . It makes no difference whether the Jap is a citizen or not. He's still a Jap and can't change."[1] "A Jap's a Jap. There is no way to determine their loyalty. . . . This coast is too vulnerable. No Jap should come back to this coast except on a permit from my office."[2]

Representative Anderson later inserted a longer portion of DeWitt's testimony into the Congressional Record. The general told the subcommittee:

> I haven't any problems except one—that is the development of a false sentiment on the part of certain individuals and some organizations to get the Japanese back on the west coast. I don't want any of them here. They are a dangerous element. There is no way to determine their loyalty. The west coast contains too many vital installations essential to the defense of the country to allow any Japanese on this coast. There is a feeling developing, I think, in certain sections of the country that the Japanese should be allowed to return. I am opposing it with every proper means at my disposal. We can handle individuals if there aren't too many. No Japanese can come back now for any purpose except by permit from my headquarters. There are a number of Japanese in the area who are in hospitals, too sick to be moved, or in mental institutions, but very few. We let them come in in an emergency to visit the sick and those in mental institutions. We also let them come to relocation centers. The great difficulty is that if you let an individual Japanese in for any reason at all, you establish a precedent and the whole question begins to develop and ramify so you can't stop it.[3]

*Adapted from Audrie Girdner and Anne Loftis, *The Great Betrayal*: The Evacuation of the Japanese-Americans During World War II (New York: The Macmillan Co., 1969), pp. 277–278, 303, 327–328, 378–380, 480–482.

In mid-April, aside from hospitalized patients, and a few wives of Caucasians, only eight Nisei were allowed in an official capacity in the Western Defense Command. Seven were translators for the Federal Communications Commission, and one was an interpreter for the Immigration Department. All of them were required to wear identification at all times. Yet DeWitt felt it was necessary to investigate the past activities of the Japanese already evacuated from the West Coast. In the summer of 1942, a research division with a staff of over fifty people had been organized to study the group. Working with old vernacular newspapers, ship manifests, records of Japanese organizations and banks, the researchers, who were still at work when the war ended, recorded some 500,000 separate items of information on the dossiers of 115,000 persons.[4] There is no record of the use to which this great mass of material was put.

General DeWitt's testimony on April 13 did not go unnoticed. Representative Henry M. Jackson of Washington quoted his racial indictment with approval in Congress two days later. The editorial writer on the camp newspaper at Amache decided DeWitt was trying to justify the mistake he had made in evacuating the Japanese. "Pity him and don't waste your anger," he wrote.[5] On April 15, the Washington *Post* published an editorial entitled, "A Jap's a Jap," which gave the opinion that "The General should be told that American democracy and the Constitution of the United States are too vital to be ignored and flouted by any military zealot. The panic of Pearl Harbor is now past. There has been ample time for the investigation of these people and the determination of their loyalty to this country on an individual basis. Whatever excuse there once was for evacuating and holding them indiscriminately no longer exists."

This was the opinion of the War Department. Colonel Scobey wrote a letter to the San Diego County Supervisors, in which he said, "The War Department feels that the retention of 100,000 people in relocation centers at the expense of the government in time of war is not only unjust to those who can establish their loyalty, but it is an unnecessary expense. . . . To condemn the Japanese in this country as a whole for the actions of the Japanese militarists does not seem to be just or appropriate."[6]

On April 19, less than a week after his statement before the House Naval Affairs Subcommittee, General DeWitt was forced to reverse his previous stand by issuing a proclamation allowing Nisei servicemen on furlough to enter the Western Defense Command. Cries of alarm greeted this proclamation, and the general's about-face was noted and commented upon. "What an utterly incomprehensible and contradictory policy for the War Department to adopt," Representative Jack Z. Anderson told the Congress on May 5. "Mr. Speaker, I am of the opinion that General DeWitt did not issue that proclamation of his own free will." At the April 13 hearing, a witness had asked, "What is the idea of putting the Japanese in the United States Army at all? Is that a matter of military policy? Did the War Department decide that? Not some civilian agency agitation?"

General DeWitt had answered, "I don't know anything about that. I have had nothing whatever to do with it. Manzanar and Tule Lake are kept under my observation as they are in the prohibited area. Recruiting parties were sent in by the War Department to obtain volunteers, and I do not want to be understood as in any way criticizing that action. At one time we had a great many Japanese in military units on the west coast. They were all, at my request, transferred out by the War Department to other organizations."[7]

. . . .

Girdner and Loftis mention some of the typical scenes in the "reloca-tion" centers:

. . . A young doctor in the service visited his family in camp. "I'll never forget the winter that he came," says his sister. "He had to accompany one of his patients back to the coast, and he brought his little boy, and he stopped off to see us in the camp. It was rather ironic. He was a Captain in his dress uniform. Here he was, serving his country, and we were inside. He didn't say anything. He was a quiet one, very much like my father. I guess he thought it was ridiculous. That's what we all thought."

Yori Wada wrote about trying to find his family at Jerome:

Arriving about midnight I sloshed around in the rain and red mud among black tar-papered barracks searching for 22-11-D. Half an hour later I found it. My knock, a light turned on, my sister's face in the half-opened doorway, and I was home.
Tadaima kaeri mashita (I have just come home) has been my customary greeting whenever I came home from Cal. Now it came unconsciously from my lips.
Oh, kaite kitake (oh, so you've come home) was Mother's greeting as she got up from the Army cot. It struck me suddenly and without warning that she had aged, aged ten years in two. Her face was covered with countless wrinkles, her former jet-black hair was streaked with gray, those deep brown eyes were tired, her body thinner. Oh, Mother, I wish I could have spared you this. Surely Americans couldn't approve of this. But Mother smiled at me and I answered.[8]

. . . .

Here, Girdner and Loftis mention Gordon Hirabayashi who has since become a well-known sociologist; his son also took the conscientious objector stance during the Vietnam war:

... A few Nisei were conscientious objectors who refused to serve because of general convictions against war, among them, Gordon Hirabayashi, who figured on the curfew case before the Supreme Court. He had served nine months in a county jail in the state of Washington followed by three months in a federal penitentiary for violation of the curfew and evacuation orders. On his release he worked for the American Friends Service Committee both in Spokane and in the relocation centers under the direction of Floyd Schmoe, former professor of forestry at the University of Washington. Hirabayashi married Schmoe's daughter in July, 1944, and in September was in court again for refusing to fill out the special selective service questionnaire for persons of Japanese ancestry and for subsequently failing to report for his preinduction physical examination. As a Quaker, he refused service on religious grounds, but he also objected to the questionnaire as discriminatory. It was, he believed, "an outright violation of both the Christian and American principles of justice and democracy."[9] Since he refused alternative service in a make-work camp, entering a plea of *nolo contendere*, he was sentenced to an additional twelve-month term in prison as a conscientious objector. . . .

. . . .

Here we see some of the complications of the California political scene:

... A number of California politicians became distraught over General DeWitt's edict of April, 1943, which allowed Nisei soldiers on furlough to go into the area of the Western Defense Command. But despite a few unpleasant headlines, such as the San Francisco *Examiner*'s welcome, "SOLDIERS OF NIP ANCESTRY ALLOWED TO ROAM ON COAST,"[10] most Nisei soldiers, though sometimes anticipating reaction, attracted little notice except when seen by old friends in their home towns. Masao Kanemoto (now Judge Wayne Kanemoto) who had volunteered for the 442nd Regimental Combat Team, returned to visit exactly a year to the day after he had been evacuated. He was walking down the street in a uniform that did not fit very well, when he saw a Navy officer and saluted. It turned out to be an old school acquaintance, a football player who had gone to San Jose High School at the same time he had. The Navy man stopped and said, "Why you're Mas Kanemoto, aren't you?" They talked a while, and then the Navy officer remarked that he had heard all the people of Japanese descent and their families had been evacuated from their homes. "How are they treating you?" he wanted to know. Kanemoto, impressed by his concern, told him their treatment was satisfactory, that the government had restricted their freedom, but their treatment in camp was all right. The next morning, Kanemoto read in the paper that his friend had just returned from Guadalcanal and had almost lost his life in a dangerous patrol. Seeing Japanese transports coming, he had to give warning. The planes came after him, and he escaped only by skimming over the water. He was awarded the Navy Cross for gallantry. Kanemoto, thought, reading this in the paper, "If anyone had wanted to be prejudiced against the Japanese, I guess he had reason to be. But he was the one who came forward to talk to me. So I felt very good about that, and have never forgotten it." Kanemoto himself was on his way to India where he served in the China—Burma—India theater as an interpreter.

In August, 1944, Stanford University approved the hiring of fourteen Japanese language instructors who were to come from Manzanar. At the time the Army had decided to draft Nisei out of camp after the initial success of the volunteer divisions, Dillon Myer was in Pasadena where he met with a small group to discuss a number of matters relating to relocation. Herbert V. Nicholson, the Quaker minister and member of the Friends of the American Way, told him he felt it was absolutely wrong to draft men from concentration camps. The moment they started the draft, he said, they should open the camps and tell the internees they could leave and go back to the Pacific Coast if they wished. Myer agreed, but pointed out that one branch of the government could not tell another what to do. Nicholson asked who could then, and Myer said, "You," suggesting he go to the War Department to talk with John J. McCloy. Not long after, Nicholson was on his way to Washington, stopping at various relocation camps as well as Camp Shelby where Nisei soldiers of the 442nd—often called McCloy's "baby"—were in training.

During a forty-five minute interview with McCloy and two Army officials, the Assistant Secretary of War thanked Nicholson for his suggestions, but said that he received a constant stream of letters urging him to keep the Japanese off the West Coast. These letters were mostly mimeographed sheets with signatures, evidently distributed by organizations, but they had to be counted. McCloy pointed to two baskets, one for letters favoring rescission, which was empty, and one for letters against, which was full. According to Nicholson, McCloy then said, "If you'll fill this basket on my desk with letters from people on the West Coast urging the return of the Japanese, we'll do something about it."

Nicholson at once telegraphed the Friends of the American Way, and letters and telegrams began pouring in from Pasadena. Then he went to Philadelphia, asking the Friends' Service Committee to start letters, and to New York, contacting the Federal Council of Churches. On his way home he contacted Japanese in eastern cities and relocation camps and suggested they urge Caucasian friends to do the same thing. Letters which Issei could send to their friends were mimeographed. By July thousands of letters reached McCloy's office, and he wrote saying Pasadena had sent more letters than any other community. Would they sponsor a Nisei girl student from one of the camps?

Representatives of their group sounded out Pasadena Junior College, asking them how they felt. Polls of the student body, the faculty, and the school board showed that over 90 percent favored the proposal.

Hugh Anderson, an officer in Friends of the American Way, requested of General Bonesteel, head of the Western Defense Command, that a Nisei college girl, a bright and attractive nineteen-year-old named Esther Takei, be sent from the Amache center. He had already conferred with the girl's parents in the camp. Ten days after the request was made, the young woman, who made the trip alone by train, was in the Pasadena home of Mr. and Mrs. Anderson.

She arrived on September 12, 1944, prepared to enter Pasadena Junior College. Despite her warm reception in most quarters and her subsequent popularity with the faculty and student body, a storm of protest broke out in the community and for five weeks it was not known what the outcome would be.

A parade of cars kept going by the Anderson house. Letters and phone calls made life tense for the family, but for every hostile message there were some of encouragement. Still, the pressure from the "domestic patriots" made it necessary for Anderson to remove Miss Takei and his wife and four children from the house.

Actually, California law was very specific on the right of all citizens to attend public schools, as was pointed out repeatedly by John W. Harbeson, principal of the junior college. But little support came from the Pasadena Board of Education, the ministerial leadership, or the Chamber of Commerce.

. . . .

Girdner and Loftis conclude with a consideration of the wider political meaning of the Japanese-American "relocation":

... When Roosevelt, in a broad interpretation of his powers as wartime Commander-in-Chief, signed over the rights of the West Coast Japanese to the control of the military, the action, approved by Congress and the Supreme Court, gave national and official sanction to policies pursued over the years by West Coast anti-Orientals. One of the effects of the government's intervention was to lift the mask of patriotism from the faces of the agitators, who then argued more openly on the grounds of self-interest. "A full assertion of the ordinary rights of citizenship would have shamed and weakened the lynch spirit," Eugene Rostow wrote in 1945, assessing the role of the judiciary.[11]

At the time of the Supreme Court consideration of the evacuation, Justice Murphy in his *Korematsu* dissent called the majority decision "a legalization of racism." Korematsu's attorney argued, "If of *white pedigree* these [citizenship] rights are considered to be indestructible, if of *yellow*, destructible. ... There is no higher title in America than that of 'citizen.' "[12] But to admit that race prejudice was a factor would seriously weaken the validity of the military judgment that the majority upheld; therefore it was discounted as the Court ruled on grounds of military necessity alone.

A 1942 legal opinion foreshadowed the Supreme Court argument which justified precautionary arrest: "Perhaps ninety-nine peaceful Japanese plus an unascertainable one who would signal to a submarine would add up to a sufficient reason to evacuate the whole."[13] Three years later Eugene Rostow indicted the Supreme Court's endorsement of this doctrine. "The exclusion program was undertaken," he wrote, "not because the Japanese were too numerous to be examined individually, but because they were a small enough group to be punished by confinement. ... The idea of punishment only for individual behavior is basic to all systems of civilized law. A great principle was never lost so casually."[14]

"In wartime judges wear epaulets under their robes," the attorney, Wayne Collins, has commented. Traditionally, the Court gives the military a free hand in time of war and restores the balance in favor of civilian rights in peacetime. After the subjugation of the South in 1866 a strongly Union Supreme Court issued a classic ruling in *Ex Parte Milligan*, a *habeas corpus* case involving a conspirator working for the South in Kansas. The ruling contradicted a wartime verdict approving a military trial for a group who conspired to assassinate Lincoln. In *Ex Parte Milligan* the Court decreed:

> .... The right of trial by jury is preserved to everyone accused of crime who is not attached to the Army, or Navy, or Militia in actual service.
> Martial law cannot arise from a threatened invasion. The necessity must be actual and present, the invasion real, such as effectually closes the courts and deposes the civil administration.
> .... Martial rule can never exist where the courts are open, and in the proper and unobstructed exercise of their jurisdiction. It is also confined to the locality of actual war. ....[15]

In by-passing the implications of the *Milligan* ruling in the evacuation cases, the Court gave sanction to the idea of limited, undeclared martial law in three respects: extension in time of controls after the military crisis of Pearl Harbor was past; extension in space of controls covering a good-sized portion of the western United States; and in effect, by denial of various civil guarantees in areas where civil government was still in operation in most ways for most people.

Less than a year after V-J Day, however, the Supreme Court handed down a decision in *Duncan vs. Kahanamoku*, which modified the judgment in *Korematsu* and the other Japanese evacuation cases—that the military holds precedence over the rights of individuals in wartime—and restored the principle of *Ex Parte Milligan*. The Court decreed that while martial law could operate in a crisis such as Pearl Harbor when civilians could be tried by military tribunals, after the turbulence was over, the governor in conjunction with the military did not have the authority to keep up such controls "for days, months or years," closing all the courts.[16]

The implications for *Korematsu* were not mentioned, although some commentators feel that if *Korematsu* had been heard at this time, in 1946, rather than in 1944, the outcome would have been different. Justice Frank Murphy, concurring with the majority opinion written by Justice Black in *Duncan* came close to naming the evacuation question explicitly when he described the racial bias involved in *Duncan*: although one-third of the population in Hawaii was of Japanese ancestry, members of the group were not considered fit for jury service in the lower courts. He stated further, "Abhorrence of military rule is ingrained in our form of government. ... This supremacy of the civil over the military is one of our great heritages. It has made possible the attainment of a high degree of liberty regulated by law rather than by caprice. ... From time immemorial despots have used real or imagined threats to the public welfare as an excuse for needlessly abrogating human rights. That excuse is no less unworthy of our traditions when used in this day of atomic warfare or at a future time when some other type of warfare may be devised."[17]

Perhaps only a few students of the law such as Rostow saw *Duncan vs. Kuhanamoku* as a significant modification of the principles enunciated in the evacuation cases. But Justice Robert Jackson, who had dissented in *Korematsu*, wrote shortly before his death in 1954: "I think the Court can never quite escape consciousness of its own infirmities, a psychology which may explain its apparent yielding to expediency, especially during wartime,"[18] and Justice William O. Douglas, who concurred with the majority, later altered his judgment, writing, "The power in time of war to take those extreme measures was sustained in decisions of questionable authority."[19]

It has been said that any denial of the rights of a single group cheapens citizenship for all. Edward Ennis, formerly with the Justice Department, called the evacuation "one of the most spectacular breakdowns ... of government responsibility in our history."[20] The destructive effect of the episode has been mitigated due to a favorable combination of international and domestic circumstances as well as to the actions of the persevering and the indomitable spirit of the Issei and Nisei. The apologies have been made, the reparations attempted, the claims settled, and the citizenship of the renunciants restored, but the evacuation cannot be relegated to a dusty corner of history. As a departure from American principles that was endorsed by the highest tribunal of the land, it will stand as an aberration and a warning.

. . . .

REFERENCES

1. Fresno *Bee*, April 14, 1943.
2. San Francisco *Chronicle*, April 14, 1943.
3. *Congressional Record*, Vol. 89, Part 3, 78th Congress, 1st Session, p. 4006, quoted by Rep. Jack Z. Anderson on May 5, 1943.
4. Jacobus tenBroek, Edward N. Barnhart, and Floyd W. Matson, *Prejudice, War, and the Constitution*, University of California Press, Berkeley and Los Angeles, 1958, pp. 159-160.
5. *Congressional Record*, Appendix, Vol. 89, Part 10. 78th Congress, 1st Session, p. A2810.
6. Galen Fisher, "A Balance Sheet on Japanese Evacuation," *The Christian Century*, August 18, 25, September 1, 8, 1943.
7. *Congressional Record*, Vol. 89, Part 3, 78th Congress, 1st Session, p. 4006.
8. Yori Wada, "Beyond the Horizon," *California Monthly*, December, 1943.
9. Palo Alto *Times*, July 1, 1944.
10. San Francisco *Examiner*, May 28, 1943.
11. Eugene V. Rostow, "The Japanese-American Cases—A Disaster," *Yale Law Journal*, Vol. 54, June, 1945.
12. Brief for Appellant, *Fred Toyosaburo Korematsu vs. United States of America*, United States Ninth Circuit Court of Appeals, December 9, 1942, pp. 92-94.
13. Charles Fairman, "The Law of Martial Rule and the National Emergency," *Harvard Law Review*, June, 1942.
14. Rostow, *loc. cit.*
15. *Ex Parte Milligan*, December, 1866, U.S. Supreme Court Reports, Vol. 18, Lawyers' Edition, p. 281.

16. Justice Hugo Black, majority opinion, *Duncan* vs. *Kahanamoku*, Supreme Court Reporter, Vol. 66, West Publishing Co., St. Paul, Minnesota, 1947, p. 611.
17. Justice Frank Murphy, concurring opinion, *Duncan* vs. *Kahanamoku*, *ibid.*, pp. 616-19.
18. Robert H. Jackson, *The Supreme Court in the American System of Government*, Harvard University Press, Cambridge, Massachusetts, 1955, p. 25.
19. William O. Douglas, *An Anatomy of Liberty*, Trident Press, Pocket Books, Inc., New York, 1964, pp. 32-33.
20. Hearings Before Subcommittee No. 5 of the Committee of the Judiciary, House of Representatives, 83rd Congress, 2nd Session on HR 7435, p. 35.

And now the nation, through its elected representatives, demonstrates how deeply it regrets having so mistreated a large block of American citizens several decades ago:

AP Dispatch, Aug. 5, 1972:

WASHINGTON—Japanese-Americans asked Congress yesterday to remove a legal lock which is keeping up to 2,000 of them from recovering family savings deposited before World War II in a Japanese bank's U.S. branches.

Confiscated assets of the Yokohama Specie Bank, about $4.5 million, remain in Justice Department hands, yet Japanese-Americans "with legitimate claims . . . are barred from recovering their hard-earned savings," Rep. Spark M. Matsunaga, D-Hawaii, told the House commerce and finance subcommittee. . . . Masaoka urged swift congressional action because prospective beneficiaries who were interned during World War II are currently an average of about 80 years old.

AP, Aug. 8, 1972:

. . . .

The Justice Department endorsed the bill on condition that it be revised to give the attorney general final power to decide the validity of claims, instead of involving a federal court. The subcommittee agreed to this revision. The money would be returned without interest.

The Stigmatized - - Society's Scapegoats

Traditionally, a *stigma* was regarded as a loathsome physical condition that burdened some unfortunates—a missing nose, for example. But, as Erving Goffman has illustrated so cogently, there are also purely social sigmata—i.e., cultural definitions asserting that whole categories of people are shameful or rightfully censured even though they may be innocent victims of historical or current events. They are thus treated arbitrarily since their disadvantaged social state has no reasonable relationship to their behavior.

One of the most important social functions of the stigmatized is to act as society's scapegoats. The scapegoat of ancient legend was an animal driven into the wilderness symbolically bearing away the sins of the community. Today, a scapegoat is a person or group that is regarded as blameworthy and thus *properly* caused to suffer; such suffering is functionally useful to those inflicting it since they are graphically reminded of their relative purity and righteousness.

When people engage in scapegoating, it is obvious that they cause a problem for many of the innocent. More important, however, is the fact that scapegoating is in effect a pseudo answer to a problem situation. Such answers permit problem-generating conditions to continue unchallenged while at the same time giving people the illusion that they are doing something constructive. Thus, the unreasonableness of scapegoating compounds a variety of problems and tends to block meaningful reform.

Facets of these themes are illustrated by the following selections which describe a variety of the kinds of people who are stigmatized in modern society: those who deviate from sex norms in one way or another, the mentally retarded, women, drug users, war resisters, the aged, etc. Certain types of non-exploitive sexual deviants and drug addicts are particularly obvious illustrations of the concept "crimes without victims." Such "crimes" as homosexuality and addiction, where freely consenting adults alone are involved, are crimes purely by legislative definition since there are no "victims" in the usual sense. Perhaps even more important, when drugs are illegal an addict is motivated to see that friends and relatives become addicted so he will be better able to "push" and thus support his own addiction. This incentive does not exist in England where drug addiction

Old and Alone

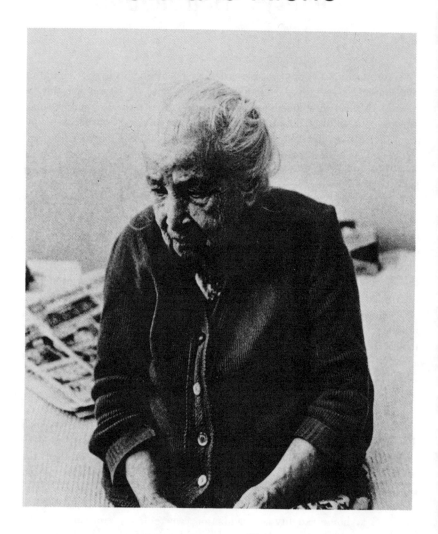

per se is not a crime; why should an addict pay the inflated prices of a black market when he can get his supplies with a medical prescription? And, it should be noted, England has fewer than 2000 heroin addicts. This surprises the innocent who have concluded that drugs are so attractive people will use them proportionate to their ease of access. Not so (generally speaking), since most people are aware that an addict's life, even that of a legal addict, typically becomes unrelieved degradation.

THE MODEL PSYCHIATRIC SCAPEGOAT—THE HOMOSEXUAL*

. . . was there ever any domination which did not appear natural to those who possessed it?

—John Stuart Mill[1]

The concept of mental illness is analogous to that of witchcraft. In the fifteenth century, men believed that some persons were witches, and that some acts were due to witchcraft. In the twentieth century, men believe that some people are insane, and that some acts are due to mental illness. Nearly a decade ago, I tried to show that the concept of mental illness has the same logical and empirical status as the concept of witchcraft; in short, that witchcraft and mental illness are imprecise and all-encompassing concepts, freely adaptable to whatever uses the priest or physician (or lay "diagnostician") wishes to put them.[2] Now I propose to show that the concept of mental illness serves the same social function in the modern world as did the concept of witchcraft in the late Middle Ages; in short, that the belief in mental illness and the social actions to which it leads have the same moral implications and political consequences as had the belief in witchcraft and the social actions to which it led.

As a prime case in point, Szasz discusses the homosexual:

. . . .

Our secular society dreads homosexuality in the same way and with the same intensity as the theological societies of our ancestors dreaded heresy.

*Adapted from Thomas S. Szasz, *The Manufacture of Madness*: A Comparative Study of the Inquisition and the Mental Health Movement (New York: Harper and Row, 1970), pp. xix, 242-249, 256-259, and references.

The quality and the extent of this aversion is revealed by the fact that homosexuality is considered both a crime *and* a disease.[3]

. . . .

The laws of our states prohibit homosexual behavior in much the same way as the laws of fifteenth-century Spain prohibited the practice of the Jewish religion. The results are also analogous. In Spain, the number of persons who admitted to being Jewish decreased precipitously, but vast numbers of individuals, called "Judaizers," practiced their forbidden religion in secret. Similarly, while there are few self-confessed homosexuals in our society, many persons practice their prohibited sexual activities in secret. . . .

. . . .

As the man with Jewish religion was considered not fully human, because he was not Christian—so the homosexual is considered not fully human because he is not heterosexual. In both cases, the individual is denied recognition as a human being in his authentic identity and selfhood —and for the same reasons: each undermines the beliefs and values of the dominant group. The Jew, by virtue of his Jewishness, refuses to authenticate Jesus as the Son of God, and the Roman Catholic Church as the unquestionable representative of God on Earth. The male homosexual, by virtue of his homosexuality, refuses to authenticate woman as the desirable sex object, and the heterosexual as the unquestionable embodiment of sexual normality. This is why the homosexual is not recognized as having the same rights as the heterosexual—just as the Jew was not recognized as a fully human being in many Christian societies, and as the mentally ill are not so recognized in contemporary American society. This injustice is slowly being recognized, as evidenced by a demonstration of the Student Homophile League "to protest the fact that the rights of the Declaration of Independence have yet to be granted to American citizens who are homosexuals."[4]

The homosexual seeking to emigrate to this country finds that he is unwelcome. I shall examine a 1967 decision of the U.S. Supreme Court on the deportability of an alien solely on the basis of homosexuality for the evidence it provides for my thesis that homosexuality is a kind of secular (sexual) heresy.

The case is that of Clive Michael Boutilier, a Canadian national, who was ordered deported by the Immigration and Naturalization Service.[5] The order for deportation having been sustained in the lower courts, Boutilier appealed to the Supreme Court. In a six-to-three decision, the Court upheld the order.

Boutilier was first admitted to the United States on June 22, 1955, at the age of twenty-one. His mother, stepfather, and three of his brothers and sisters live in the United States. "In 1963 he applied for citizenship and submitted to the Naturalization Examiner an affidavit in which he admitted that he was arrested in New York in October, 1959, on a charge of sodomy, which was later reduced to simple assault and thereafter dismissed on default of the complainant."[6]

Thus far, then, Boutilier had not been identified as a homosexual, in accordance with due process of law. However, he was foolish enough—at least from the point of view of gaining permanent admission to this country—to admit that he was a homosexual. "In 1964, petitioner, at the request of the Government, submitted another affidavit which revealed the full history [sic] of his sexual deviate behavior."[7] In this affidavit, Boutilier admitted that his first homosexual experience occurred when he was fourteen years old, and that between the ages of sixteen and twenty-one he "had homosexual relations on an average of three or four times a year." Boutilier also stated that "prior to his entry he had engaged in heterosexual relations on three or four occasions."

Evidently, this was an insufficient frequency of heterosexual activity to satisfy the U.S. Government. Accordingly, in 1964 the Government submitted an affidavit "to the Public Health Service for its opinion as to whether petitioner was excludable for any reason at the time of his entry."[8] The statutory reason for this request was paragraph 212 (a) (4) of the Immigration and Nationality Act of 1952 (66 Stat. 182, 8 U.S.C., paragraph 1182 [a] [4]), which specifies that "Aliens afflicted with psychopathic personality, epilepsy, or a mental defect . . . shall be excludable from admission into the United States." The question put before the Public Health Service was whether homosexuality constitutes "psychopathic personality."

The Public Health Service, after subjecting Boutilier to examination by its physicians, issued a certificate "stating that in the opinion of the subscribing physicians petitioner 'was afflicted with a class A condition, namely, psychopathic personality, sexual deviate,' at the time of his admission."[9] Upholding this judgment of the physicians and of the lower courts, the Supreme Court observed that "The legislative history of the Act indicates beyond a shadow of a doubt that the Congress intended the phrase 'psychopathic personality' to include homosexuals such as petitioner."[10] Since "The Government clearly established that petitioner was a homosexual at entry,"[11] ruled the majority of the Justices, his exclusion comports with the requirements of law and must be upheld.

. . . .

The fact that Boutilier's identification as a homosexual required the expert assistance of physicians merits special comment. Does the physician, in such a situation, have a moral duty to inform the subject of the nature and purpose of the examination and of the physician's obligations to his employer? In Western socieites, the physician occupies an important position of trust. Unlike the policeman, the tax examiner, or the district attorney, the doctor is looked upon as the ally of the sick individual—not the agent of the powerful state.[12]

It follows, then, that whenever the physician represents an interest other than that of the person whom he examines, the subject will be misled unless his tacit assumptions about the situation are corrected. In other words, the physicians who examined Boutilier for the Government had a choice of whether or not to tell him that: (1) they were agents of the Government, charged with ferreting out whether Boutilier was a homosexual; (2) if Boutilier was one, they would so inform their employer; (3) if they reported that Boutilier was a homosexual, he would be barred from entering the United States; and (4) if, in view of these circumstances, Boutilier wished not to incriminate himself, he could do so. Of course, I do not know whether the physicians in question did or did not give Boutilier any of these options. If they did not, they deceived their "patient."

Aside from the immorality of this kind of "medical" procedure, it is important to note that Boutilier's examination by Public Health Service physicians and their report were but gestures in a pseudoscientific ritual.[13] First, the examination could have had no rationally valid aim: Boutilier already admitted that he was a homosexual; how, then, could his "medical examination" reveal anything else? Second, the report only authenticated, with an official, medical signature, what the Court had already known: homosexuality had been *defined* as "sexual deviation" and "psychopathic personality" by the appropriate agencies of the U.S. Government; how, then, could the "medical examiners" report anything else?

Nevertheless, it may be argued that, like typhoid fever, homosexuality is a medical diagnosis, and that the physician's moral responsibility for the use to which this diagnosis is put is the same as that of any other citizen. I cannot agree with this view. It is the physician, not the ordinary citizen, who makes the diagnosis; hence, his responsibility for its use, like the policeman's for the use of his gun, is infinitely greater than that of a bystander.

The argument that homosexuality is a medical diagnosis is faulty on another ground as well. The physicians who examined Boutilier were not called upon to render a diagnosis, but to identify a person as deportable. This is not just my personal opinion; it is the view of the Justices who wrote the majority opinion for the Court. Arguing in opposition to those who would claim that psychopathic personality is too vague a term, the Court held that: "It may be, as some claim, that 'psychopathic personality' is a medically ambiguous term, including several separate and distinct afflictions. ... But the test here is what Congress intended, not what differing psychiatrists may think. *It was not laying down a clinical test, but an exclusionary standard* which it declared to be inclusive of those having homosexual and perverted characteristics."[14] (Italics added.)

The physicians who examined Boutilier and reported their findings to the Government were thus not expected to diagnose their subject but to decide whether he fitted into "an exclusionary standard" set by Congress. Is this a morally legitimate activity for physicians? If, as it appears, they merely rubber-stamp a decision made by nonmedical personnel, what is their real function? The answer to this question throws further light on the degraded status of the homosexual in American law.

. . . .

The history of the Inquisition and of systematic anti-Semitism leaves no doubt that society's official scapegoats are persecuted not because they have committed prohibited acts, or even because they might commit such acts, but because they are considered "enemies within." To destroy such internal enemies is a patriotic duty and a morally meritorious act just as it is to resist and destroy external enemies. It is therefore worse than futile—senseless or even aggravating—to try to prove the moral worth or social usefulness of particular persons, once it is established that they are members of a class of officially designated scapegoats. Heinrich Heine and Albert Einstein did not enhance the position of the Jews in Nazi Germany; if anything, they aggravated it. Persecutors sometimes deal mercifully with an erring and guilt-ridden victim who abases himself before his oppressors; what they cannot forgive is a blameless and virtuous victim, whose very innocence is an intolerable offense to his tormentors and who must, therefore, be destroyed without mercy. In short, men either obey the Rule of Law, or they do not. If they do not, the victim is punished not because of what he did, but because of who he is. Our mental health practices represent a massive re-embracing of this collectivistic and sadistic principle of social control.

This decision of the Supreme Court is significant, not only for the way it symbolically enshrines the homosexual as society's scapegoat, but also for the kind of "scientific" support it relies on for doing so. Many eminent authorities have expressed themselves on the subject of homosexuality; yet out of this spectrum of available opinion, the Court has selected the judgments of the medical and psychiatric employees of the U.S. Government, itself a party to the action before the Justices. If a case before the Court involved freedom of religion or the press, the Court might well have looked to authorities of all kinds, both living and dead, American and foreign. We can only speculate about why it has not done so in this case. Perhaps it was afraid of what it might find: in particular, that it might be unable to conceal, behind a rhetoric of psychiatric diagnosis, that it is not being called upon to evaluate a man medically but to dehumanize him legally.

Had the Court looked for its information on homosexuality to Lindner, instead of to the U.S. Public Health Service, it would have discovered that in our society "... nonconformity and mental disease have become synonymous. ... Hence, the rebellious, the Protestant—in short, the nonconformist—is considered sick and subject to all the arts science can muster or fashion to cure him of his 'sickness.' ... Declaring the homosexual mentally ill, therefore, brings him within the compass of this regressive view and the range of all the 'therapies' devised to insure his conformity. It may masquerade as a boon to the invert and a humanitarian modification of historic prejudice and hate; it is, in fact, but another way to obtain the conformance—this time in the area of sex behavior—our dangerously petrifying institutions demand."[15]

Or, had the Court looked to Sartre, it would have found that "Human relations are possible between homosexuals just as between a man and a woman. Homosexuals can love, give, elevate others and elevate themselves. It's surely better to get into bed with a boy friend than to go traveling in Nazi Germany when France has been defeated and strangled."[16]

But views such as Lindner's or Sartre's would not have supported the decision of the majority of the court in its concept of the homosexual as a socially dangerous psychopath, nor that of the minority in its concept of the homosexual as a sick man afflicted with a dreaded disease.

The Supreme Court decision in the Boutilier case illustrates Sartre's view that "The homosexual must remain an object, a flower, an insect, an inhabitant of ancient Sodom or the planet Uranus, an automaton that hops about in the limelight, anything you like except my fellow man, except my image, except myself. For a choice must be made: if every man is all of man, this black sheep must be only a pebble or must be *me*."[17] It is nothing less than obscene to talk about the homosexual as a sick person whom we are trying to help so long as, by treating him as a defective thing, we demonstrate through our actions that what we want him to be is a useful, rather than annoying, *object for us*; and that what we will not tolerate is his wanting to be an authentic *person for himself*.

The history of the statute under which Boutilier was deported provides further support for the view that the homosexual is a scapegoat. From the dissenting opinion we learn that "The provision for exclusion of persons afflicted with psychological [sic] personality replaced the section of the 1917 Act, 39 Stat. 875, providing for the exclusion of 'persons of constitutional psychopathic inferiority.' "[18] The purpose of that clause was to keep out "persons who have medical traits which would harm the people of the United States if those traits were added to those in this country who unfortunately are so afflicted."[19] This claim, that our legislators and judges discriminate against homosexuals in the belief that they are applying the findings of a modern and liberal psychiatric science to the making of policy for the national welfare, makes this an even more monstrous blunder.

I may, however, be using the word "blunder" falsely here. There is reason to believe that both those who draw up this kind of legislation, and those who enforce it, know full well what they are doing. When the immigration law under which Boutilier was excluded from the United States was being considered in Congress, in response to "the House's request for its opinion on the new provisions, the Public Health Service noted that: 'The conditions classified within the group of psychopathic personalities are, *in effect, disorders of the personality.* . . . individuals with such a disorder may manifest a disturbance of intrinsic personality trends, or are persons *ill primarily in terms of society and the prevailing culture.*' "[20] (Italics added.).

All this, I submit, is an open admission that social nonconformity is considered an illness; that physicians in the employ of the U.S. Government are empowered to diagnose such illness; that the Congress may then impose specific penalties on persons suffering from such illness; and that the Supreme Court will legitimize the constitutionality of such discriminatory legislation, singling out for repression individuals "afflicted" or incriminated with a specific disease. In short, this is a kind of medical witch-hunting, doctors persecuting "patients" for their alleged or real medical heresies. Thus has the physician replaced the priest, and the patient the witch, in the drama of society's perpetual struggle to destroy precisely those human characteristics that, by differentiating men from their fellows, identify persons as individuals rather than as members of the herd.

REFERENCES

1. John Stuart Mill, *The Subjection of Women*, p. 229.
2. Thomas S. Szasz, *The Myth of Mental Illness.*
3. See Thomas S. Szasz, Legal and Moral Aspects of Homosexuality, in Judd Marmor (Ed.) *Sexual Inversion*, pp. 124-139.
4. Stephanie Harrington, Homosexual sortie: An anonymous crusade, *Village Voice*, May 25, 1967. p. 10.

5. *Boutilier* v. *Immigration and Naturalization Service*, 387 U.S. 118, 1967.
6. Ibid., p. 19.
7. Ibid.
8. Ibid., p. 120.
9. Ibid.
10. Ibid.
11. Ibid., p. 122.
12. See Thomas S. Szasz, *Psychiatric Justice*, especially pp. 56–82 and 264–272.
13. See this chapter, p. 246, and Chapter 14, especially pp. 266–268.
14. *Boutilier* v. *Immigration and Naturalization Service*, p. 124.
15. Robert Lindner, *Must You Conform?*, p. 65.
16. Jean-Paul Sartre, *Saint Genet: Actor and Martyr*, p. 225.
17. Sartre, p. 587.
18. *Boutilier* v. *Immigration and Naturalization Service*, p. 133.
19. Ibid.
20. Ibid., pp. 134–135.

". . . IT ISN'T WHAT IT SEEMS"*

. . . To find oneself regarded as a mental retardate is to be burdened by a shattering stigma. Indeed, for the former patient, to be labeled as a mental retardate is the ultimate horror. They reject it with all their will. Their own words best indicate how the stigma weighs upon them.

> (A woman) When I got out of that place it was horrible. I knew everybody was looking at me and thinking that it was true what they thought I was. I couldn't stand for people to think that about me. That's a terrible thing for people to think. Nobody could stand to have people thinking about them like that. That's why I started to take dope (heroin). I used to cry all the time because of what people were thinking about me, so my friend gave me this dope and said it would make me feel better. It did, too. I didn't worry about nothing while I was on. But that's the reason I started taking it—nobody could stand what those people were thinking.

*Adapted from Robert B. Edgerton, *The Cloak of Competence*, Stigma in the Lives of the Mentally Retarded (Berkeley and Los Angeles: University of California Press, 1967), pp. 205–6, 209, 218–219.

(A man) When I was in the colony I was always worried. I'll admit it. You know, I was worried did they really think I was like them others. The ones that couldn't do nothing or learn nothing. I used to think that I'd rather be dead than be like them. I found out OK that nobody thought I was really like them others. I wasn't no mental problem or nothing like them others. If I was like them others, God, I would have really killed myself. Anything's better than that. Having no mind and not being able to think or understand nothing. God, that's really the worst thing.

(A man) I don't believe that anyone from the hospital has it easy outside. There's problems from being in that place. I mean with people you meet. They take me as if I'm not a smart person. That's what makes me so provoked. And I mean they act like I don't understand things, which I do understand things. That's a terrible thing; I'd never do that to anybody. I don't know why I have to suffer like this. Sometimes I'd rather be dead than have people act like I'm not a smart person.

(A woman) I don't even want to think about that colony. Some of the people there were so odd, I don't know why. And I used to wonder, God, if I stay here any longer I'm gonna turn out the same way. That used to scare me. When the doctor sent me here I guess he thought I was mentally unbalanced, but in my part I don't think I was. Afterward I seen that I don't think I was. And that's what bothers me. Why does everything happen to me? Why did I have to go to that place? Sometimes I go to the father, but all he does is tell me to pray. The worst thing is always trying to hide it from everybody. I just don't want nobody to know I was in that mental State hospital. I'm ashamed of it. Maybe it wasn't my fault for being there but I'm ashamed that I was ever there. I pray all right. I pray that nobody will ever find out about me.

. . . .

It should also be pointed out that it is misleading to attempt to bring the lives of these retarded persons into the perspective of "social deviance." These former patients are not social deviants who have rejected the normative expectations of the "outside," normal world. They espouse no counter-morality. Quite the contrary, their every effort is directed toward effecting a legitimate entry into the "outside" world. To do so they will lie and cheat, but they practice their deceptions in order to claim a place in the "normal" world, not to deviate from it. Their behavior, in fact, represents the very antithesis of social deviance.

. . . .

In the efforts of ... former patients ... to evade the stigma that they feel and fear, we see an eloquent testament to man's determination to maintain his self-esteem in the face of overwhelming cultural rejection and deprecation. If we accept the unanimous findings of the behavioral and psychological sciences concerning the fundamental importance of self-esteem for any human being, then we can understand the dilemma in which these former patients find themselves, and we can appreciate their achievement in finding what is for them a cloak of competence.

The most fitting epilogue for this discussion is found in the plaintive yet defiant words of one of these retarded persons: *"I've got a tendency of an ailment but it isn't what it seems."*

DID YOU EVER HEAR THE ONE ABOUT THE FARMER'S DAUGHTER?*

This is a portion of one of Studs Terkel's justly-famed interviews. The interviewee is a thirty-year old, single woman whose official work title is "script supervisor/producer." She works at a large advertising agency and has won several awards and widespread recognition for her expertise and thoroughness. The particular importance of this interview is that it shows so clearly that even women who have reached the top in their profession must still often engage in demeaning maneuvers if they hope to avoid some of the uglier consequences of male chauvinism.

. . . A face-man is a person who looks good, speaks well, and presents the work. I look well, I speak well, and I'm pleasant to have around after the business is over with—if they acknowledge me in business. We go to the lounge and have drinks. I can drink with the men but remain a lady. (Laughs.)

That's sort of my tacit business responsibility, although this has never been said to me directly. I know this is why I travel alone for the company a great deal. They don't anticipate any problems with my behavior. I equate it with being the good nigger.

On first meeting, I'm frequently taken for the secretary, you know, traveling with the boss. I'm here to keep somebody happy. Then I'm introduced as the writer. One said to me after the meeting was over and the drinking had started, "When I first saw you, I figured you were a—you know. I never knew you were the person *writing* this all the time."

*Adapted from Studs Terkel, *Working*: People Talk About What They Do All Day and How They Feel About What They Do (New York: Pantheon Books, A Division of Random House, 1974): 67–72.

(Laughs.) Is it a married woman working for extra money? Is it a lesbian? Is it some higher-up's mistress?

I'm probably one of the ten highest paid people in the agency. It would cause tremendous hard feelings if, say, I work with a man who's paid less. If a remark is made at a bar—"You make so much money, you could buy and sell me"—I toss it off, right? He's trying to find out. He can't equate me as a rival. They wonder where to put me, they wonder what my salary is.

Buy and sell me—yeah, there are a lot of phrases that show the reversal of roles. What comes to mind is swearing at a meeting. New clients are often very uptight. They feel they can't make any innuendoes that might be suggestive. They don't know how to treat me. They don't know whether to acknowledge me as a woman or as another neuter person who's doing a job for them.

The first time, they don't look at me. At the first three meetings of this one client, if I would ask a direction question, they would answer and look at my boss or another man in the room. Even around the conference table. I don't attempt to be—the glasses, the bun, and totally asexual. That isn't the way I am. It's obvious that I'm a woman and enjoy being a woman. I'm not overly provocative either. It's the thin, good nigger line that I have to toe.

I've developed a sixth sense about this. If a client will say, "Are you married?" I will often say yes, because that's the easiest way to deal with him if he needs that category for me. If it's more acceptable to him to have a young, attractive married woman in a business position comparable to his, terrific. It doesn't bother me. It makes me safer. He'll never be challenged. He can say, "She'd be sensational. I'd love to get her. I could show her what a real man is, but she's married." It's a way out for him.

Or there's the mistress thing: well, she's sleeping with the boss. That's acceptable to them. Or she's a frustrated, compulsive castrator. That's a category. Or lesbian. If I had short hair, wore suits, and talked in a gruff voice, that would be more acceptable than I am. It's when I transcend their labels, they don't quite know what to do. If someone wants a quick label and says, "I'll bet you're a big women's libber, aren't you?" I say, "Yeah, yeah." They have to place me.

I travel a lot. That's what gets very funny. We had a meeting in Montreal. It was one of those bride's magazines, honeymoon-type resorts, with heart-shaped beds and the heated pool. I was there for three days with nine men. All day long we were enclosed in this conference room. The agency account man went with me. I was to talk about the new products, using slides and movies. There were about sixty men in the conference room. I had to leave in such a hurry, I still had my gaucho pants and boots on.

The presentation went on for an hour and a half. There was tittering and giggling for about forty minutes. Then you'd hear the shift in the audience. They got interested in what I was saying. Afterwards they had lunch sent up. Some of them never did talk to me. Others were interested in my life. They would say things like, "Have you read *The Sensuous Woman?*" (Laughs.) They didn't really want to know. If they were even more obvious, they probably would have said, "Say, did you hear the one about the farmer's daughter?" I'd have replied, "Of course, I'm one myself."

The night before, there was a rehearsal. Afterwards the account man suggested we go back to the hotel, have a nightcap, and get to bed early. It was a 9:00 A.M. meeting. We were sitting at the bar and he said, "Of course, you'll be staying in my room." I said, "What? I have a room." He said, "I just assumed. You're here and I'm here and we're both grown up." I said, "You assumed? You never even asked me whether I wanted to." My feelings obviously meant nothing to him. Apparently it was what you *did* if you're out of town and the woman is anything but a harelip and you're ready to go. His assumption was incredible.

We used to joke about him in the office. We'd call him Mr. Straight, because he was Mr. Straight. Very short hair, never grew sideburns, never wore wide ties, never, never, swore, never would pick up an innuendo, super-super-conservative. No one would know, you see?

Mr. Straight is a man who'd never invite me to have a drink after work. He would never invite me to lunch alone. Would never, never make an overture to me. It was simply the fact that we were out of town and who would know? That poor son of a bitch had no notion what he was doing to my ego. I didn't want to destroy his. We had to work together the next day and continue to work together.

The excuse I gave is one I use many times. "Once when I was much younger and innocent, I slept with an account man. The guy turned out to be a bastard. I got a big reputation and he made my life miserable because he had a loose mouth. And even though you're a terrifically nice guy and I'd like to sleep with you, I feel I can't. It's my policy. I'm older and wiser now. I don't do it. You have to understand that." It worked. I could never say to him. "You don't even understand how you insulted me."

It's the always-having-to-please conditioning. I don't want to make any enemies. Only of late, because I'm getting more secure and I'm valued by the agency, am I able to get mad at men and say, "Fuck off!" But still I have to keep egos unruffled, smooth things over ... I still work with him and he never mentioned it again.

He'll occasionally touch my arm or catch my eye: We're really sympatico, aren't we baby? There may be twelve men and me sitting at a meeting and they can't call on one of the girls or the receptionist, he'd say, "Let's have some coffee, Barbara. Make mine black." I'm the waitress. I go do it because it's easier than to protest. If he'd known my salary is more than his I doubt that he'd have acted that way in Denver—or here.

Part of the resentment toward me and my salary is that I don't have a mortgage on a home in the Valley and three kids who have to go to private schools and a wife who spends at Saks, and you never know when you're going to lose your job in this business. Say, we're having a convivial drink among peers and we start grousing. I'm not allowed to grouse with the best of them. They say, "Oh, you? What do you need money for? You're a single woman. You've got the world by the balls." I hear that all the time.

If I'm being paid a lot of attention to, say by someone to whom I'm attracted, and we've done a job and we're in New York together for a week's stretch, we're in the same hotel, suppose I want to sleep with him? Why not? Here's my great double standard. You never hear it said about a man in my capacity—"He sleeps around." It would only be to his glory. It's expected, if he's there with a model, starlet, or secretary. In my case, I constantly worry about that. If I want to, I must be very careful. That's what I'm railing against.

This last shoot, it was an exasperating shot. It took hours. We were there all day. It was exhausting, frustrating. Between takes, the camera man, a darling man, would come back to where I was standing and put his arms around me. I didn't think anything of it. We're hardly fucking on the set. It was his way of relaxing. I heard a comment later that night from the director: "You ought to watch your behavior on the set with the camera man." I said, *"Me* watch it? Fuck that! Let *him* watch it." He was hired by me. I could fire him if I didn't like him. Why *me*, you see? *I* have to watch.

Clients. I get calls in my hotel room: "I want to discuss something about production today that didn't go right." I know what that means. I try to fend it off. I'm on this tightrope. I don't want to get into a drunken scene ever with a client and to literally shove him away. That's not going to do me any good. The only smart thing I can do is avoid that sort of scene. The way I avoid it is by suggesting an early morning breakfast meeting. I always have to make excuses: "I drank too much and my stomach is really upset, so I couldn't do it right now. We'll do it in the morning." Sometimes I'd like to say, "Fuck off, I know what you want."

"I've had a secretary for the last three years. I hesitate to use her ... I won't ask her to do typing. It's hard for me to use her as I was used. She's

bright and could be much more than a secretary. So I give her research
assignments, things to look up, which might be fun for her. Rather than
just say, 'Here, type this.'

"I'm an interesting figure to her. She says, 'When I think of Women's
Lib I don't think of Germaine Greer or Kate Millett, I think of you.' She
sees my life as a lot more glamorous than it really is. She admires the
externals. She admires the apartment, the traveling. We shot two commer-
cials just recently, one in Mexico, one in Nassau. Then I was in New York
to edit them. That's three weeks. She takes care of all my travel details.
She knows the company gave me an advance of well over a thousand
dollars. I'm put up in fine hotels, travel first class. I can spend ninety
dollars at a dinner for two or three. I suppose it is something—little
Barbara from a Kansas farm, and Christ! look where I am. But I don't
think of it, which is a funny thing."

It used to be the token black at a big agency was very safe because he
always had to be there. Now I'm definitely the token woman. In the
current economic climate, I'm one of the few writers at my salary level
getting job offers. Unemployment is high right now among people who do
what I do. Yet I get calls: "Will you come and write on feminine hygiene
products?" Another, involving a food account: "We need you, we'll pay
you thirty grand and a contract. Be the answer for Such-an-such Foods."
I'm ideal because I'm young enough to have four or five solid years of
experience behind me. I know how to handle myself or I wouldn't be
where I am.

I'm very secure right now. But when someone says to me, "You don't
have to worry," he's wrong. In a profession where I absolutely cannot age,
I cannot be doing this at thirty-eight. For the next years, until I get too
old, my future's secure in a very insecure business. It's like a race horse or
a show horse. Although I'm holding the job on talent and responsibility, I
got here partly because I'm attractive and it's a big kick for a client to
know that for three days in Montreal there's going to be this young
brunette, who's very good, mind you. I don't know how they talk about
me, but I'd guess: "She's very good, but to look at her you'd never know
it. She's a knockout."

I have a fear of hanging on past my usefulness. I've seen desperate
women out of jobs, who come around with their samples, which is the way
all of us get jobs. A lot of women have been cut. Women who had soft
jobs in an agency for years and are making maybe fifteen thousand. In the
current slump, this person is cut and some bright young kid from a college,
who'll work for seven grand a year, comes in and works late every night.

Talk about gaps. In a room with a twenty-two-year-old, there are areas in which I'm altogether lost. But not being a status-quo-type person, I've always thought ahead enough to keep pace with what's new. I certainly don't feel my usefulness as a writer is coming to an end. I'm talking strictly in terms of physical aging. (Laughs.) It's such a young business, not just the consumer part. It's young in terms of appearances. The client expects agency people, especially on the creative end, to dress a certain way, to be very fashionable. I haven't seen many women in any executive capacity age gracefully. . . .

POSTSCRIPT: *Shortly afterward she was battling an ulcer.*

HAIRY LEGS*

Some women in San Francisco helped a sister recently, and dealt with a problem that we all share.

On Nov. 5, Mary Alice Carlson, a student at San Francisco State, was called to go to work at Aquatic Specialties, 24th and Vicente, as a saleswoman. She had applied for the job along with several other women a week previously. One of the owners, * * * * * hired her, telling her to begin work two days later. The job consisted of cleaning dead fish from the tanks, learning the names of different species, and waiting on customers.

She came to work at 2:00 p.m. About five-thirty, * * * asked her to come into the back room for a talk. She did. He told her that he didn't think she was going to "work out here," and, in fact, that she was fired. She asked him why.

At first he refused an explanation, but she demanded that he give her some reason, so finally he told her it was because of her "grooming." What, she asked, was wrong with her grooming? (Mary Alice was wearing a clean, simple, straight dress, flat shoes. She was neat and clean.)

* * * told her, "You don't shave your legs."

Mary Alice was stunned. She asked if she was incompetent on the job. She couldn't believe that she was actually being fired because she didn't shave her legs. However, it was true.

She asked how it was that he had hired her (as he claimed at the time) over 16 other applicants when, after all, he had interviewed her and

*Adapted from Sheilah Drummond, "Hairy Legs Freak Fishy Liberal," *Berkeley Tribe* (date unknown).

apparently had not been offended at that time by her unshaven legs. He said he had not noticed this at the time or he wouldn't have hired her.

* * * said that he felt rather badly about the whole thing and so he would be willing to pay Mary Alice for a whole day instead of just three hours. Mary Alice delined the payoff and left for home, feeling a sense of unreality about the whole thing, as if she'd somehow gotten mixed up in someone else's scene.

. . . .

DRUGS—A COMMENTARY ON SOCIETY*

Let's play guess-the-drug.

1) What widely used substance answers this description: "Its mechanism of action on the brain and other body organs is unknown; it accounts for thousands of deaths and illnesses each year, and it produces not only chromosomal breakage, but actual birth defects in lower animals"?

2) Which drug "strongly stimulates the central nervous system with excessive doses producing tremors, convulsions, and vomiting"?

3) What might you take to get "increased alertness and mental activity and a greater capacity for muscular work . . . a very potent mood-elevator or euphoriant and perhaps the strongest antifatigue agent"?

Now the answers. How many said LSD for No. 1? Well, you're wrong. Heroin? Wrong again. It's aspirin. But don't worry, birth defects have been observed only in *lower* animals.

No. 2 sounds rather gruesome, doesn't it? It's nicotine.

No. 3 seems to be potentially valuable for combating fatigue and depression. But somehow American doctors haven't gotten around to prescribing cocaine. They probably will, though. It's not that they have anything in principle against dispensing addictive drugs.

What I have just done is to describe selectively the properties of certain drugs (the full descriptions are in Joel Fort's *The Pleasure Seekers*) in such a way as to manipulate your response to them. Two broadly accepted and totally legitimate drugs were presented as fiendishly dangerous, while a discredited and illegal substance sounded medically viable.

We are very easy to manipulate, we magazine scanners, TV gazers, billboard blinkers, Bargainhunters Unanimous, and Hypochondriacs Unlimited of America. For example, much of the prevailing mythology

*Adapted from Linda Hess's review of Joel Fort, *The Pleasure Seekers*, The Drug Crisis, Youth and Society (Indianapolis: Bobbs-Merrill, 1970), in *Saturday Review* 53(14 Mar 70):34–35.

about marijuana in this country, and even internationally, was perpetrated by one man, Harry Anslinger, who headed the Federal Bureau of Narcotics for about thirty years and still represents the U.S. in the United Nations Commission on Narcotic Drugs. Anslinger worked up a kind of frothing evangelical crusade against the devil-weed, complete with hair-raising hand-bills associating marijuana with every kind of crime, violence, personal and physical degradation.

But unlike most stump-thumping preachers, Anslinger pulled the strings that governed a growing federal agency, large amounts of public money, and the votes of many legislators eager to believe that something they could package, label, and outlaw was responsible for the disintegration of morality and the rebellion of youth in America. They would have done better to look into each other's eyes. The slogan "Marijuana is more dangerous than the hydrogen bomb" has effectively alarmed Congressmen even though, as Dr. Fort remarks, "they have never been particularly concerned about the hydrogen bomb itself."

I am tempted to dwell on the marijuana issue because it is so current, because every day so many lives and dollars are being wasted, because of present laws and official attitudes, against which evidence has mounted so overwhelmingly. But that would be unfair to Joel Fort's book, which goes far beyond polemics on any particular issue. Fort surveys the whole range of Mind-Altering Drugs ("MADs") to reveal how deeply our culture is committed to chemical cure-alls, stopgaps, and escapes, how confused and hypocritical are our attitudes toward drugs, and how relentlessly the real crises in our country keep building while we dope ourselves up on myths and socially approved concoctions.

The MADs Fort talks about are alcohol, opium, caffeine, amphetamines, LSD-type drugs, sedatives, and tranquilizers. He describes the extent of use, forms of abuse, legal controls, chemical composition, and action in the body (so far as this is understood) for each of these categories.

The facts and figures he gives on alcohol are, well staggering:

> Pouring down American throats yearly are roughly 650 million gal-lons of distilled spirits, 100 million barrels . . . of beer, 200 million gallons of wine, 100 million gallons of moonshine . . . and vast amounts of legal homemade wine and beer.
>
> At least six million of our citizens are alcoholics or . . . chronic excessive users. . . . One-third to one-half of all arrests by police in America are for chronic drunkenness . . . Cirrhosis is the sixth leading cause of death in this country . . . as many as 20 per cent of the inmates of state mental hospitals are there because of chronic psycho-sis due to alcoholic brain damage, an *irreversible* condition. . . .

> Between 50 per cent and 70 per cent of the . . . deaths and . . . injuries each year from automobile accidents involve or are caused by alcohol.

And so on. How can the same legislators and judges who ignore the monstrous abuses of booze dare to imprison people for distributing or possessing marijuana, which is not physically addictive, not dangerous to body organs, not even fattening? In the familiar steppingstone theory of addiction narcotics police try to link pot to heroin. Why don't they ever point out that nearly all heroin addicts "used as their first potent mind-altering drugs alcohol and nicotine, both of them *illegally* in their early teens"?

Eldridge Cleaver hits it in *Soul on Ice*, talking about his first imprisonment, at eighteen, for possession: "I had got caught with a bag full of love—I was in love with the weed and I did not for one minute think that anything was wrong with getting high. I . . . was convinced . . . that marijuana was superior to lush—yet the rulers of the land all seemed to be lushes."

Fort points out the barbarousness of making criminals of drug users, a practice which he equates with "burning witches at the stake or putting mentally ill in dungeons." He urges that all drug use be handled as a sociological and public health matter, and predicts that within a decade his view will be the consensus.

. . . .

As I write this, I am at once angered and saddened by a recent newspaper article. It is about what the author calls Diane Linkletter's "LSD-induced suicide." Not even *allegedly* LSD-induced. The story naively exposes the blindness, fear and guilt that cause people to point desperately accusing fingers at a drug, when the real villain is much deeper and closer.

Diane's parents seem to have known nothing about their daughter. At eighteen she eloped to Mexico; they had no idea of what had happened till she came back wanting an annulment. As for her drug usage, frequent depressions and suicidal thoughts, "they never dreamed what had been going on."

The writer of the article joins the parents in blaming LSD for the tragedy. In perfectly straight tones he tells us, "Diane's family background was exemplary. She was . . . raised in an atmosphere of money, social position, togetherness and a good home life where excessive partying and drinking had no place. They were religious and church-going."

Money, social position, and church. And a set of exemplary, or shall we say typical, parents who never dreamed what was going on with their daughter.

Switch back to Joel Fort. "Youthful drug use ... is a barometer and a commentary on the society, reflecting the failure of the family, the schools, and the 'leaders' ... Our youth are herded, processed, harassed, coerced, infantilized, rejected, drafted, criminalized, and otherwise prevented from self-realization ... Drugs are ideal [smoke screens]. ... The more they are talked about and used to monopolize public attention, the less the candidate or office holder needs to talk about the real criminal, social, and health problems of the society."

CAPTAIN HOWARD LEVY*

The army tries and convicts Captain Howard Levy, M.D., for refusing, on humanitarian grounds, to train Green Beret marines for duty in Vietnam:

... At precisely 0900 hours, on a bright Wednesday (the Army called it 10 May 67), in T-9536, a small frame building painted military yellow propped atop one of Fort Jackson's slight knolls, the United States Army took Dr. Howard Levy to task for being a flower child.

The court-martial began on the anniversary of the birth of the Confederacy and ground on through Armed Forces week. With the sounds of bayonet and combat courses—new "pacification teams" readying themselves for Vietnam—drifting into the crowded 82-seat courtroom, Levy's defense rested its case on Memorial Day. On 3 June 67, Dr. Levy was sentenced to three years at hard labor.

The Army hauled down from Washington its top law officer, Colonel Earl V. Brown, who ran the trial from a little raised box overlooking the court's maroon carpet which didn't go at all well with the building's eleemosynary green interior walls. Brown, a likable enough man in a distant-uncle sort of way, slurred "Parties-ready-to-proceed?" like a drill sergeant's order, a phrase he has probably mouthed more times than he would care to remember in his 17 years as an Army lawyer.

"The government is ready, sir." It was Captain Richard Shusterman, the Army's prosecutor. Shusterman and his assistant, Captain Blair Shick, wore

*Adapted from Don Duncan, with J. A. C. Dunn, "Notes Toward a Definition of the Uniform Code of Military Justice, as Particularly Applied to the Person of Captain Howard Levy," *Ramparts* 6(July 67):48–56.

identical summer gabardine uniforms, neatly pressed. Their eyeglasses both had gray plastic government-issue frames. Both men are 28, both Philadelphia lawyers who actually come from Philadelphia.

Hedge-hog mounts of books and paper crowded the two tables occupied by Levy's defense. Even though everyone knew Levy would be found guilty, he had two Army defense lawyers and two civilian lawyers. The Army defended him because that is part of the procedure of military justice, even though the accused should be found guilty. Captain Charles Sanders, a young, shiny-toothed Southerner, headed Levy's Army defense corps, assisted by Captain Walter Jones, a tall, silent young man with black-rimmed spectacles who seemed to do little during the trial but run Levy's tape recorder and occasionally paw through a huge brown suitcase crammed with defense documents.

Charles Morgan Jr., the American Civil Liberties Union southern regional director from Atlanta, headed Levy's civilian defense, which took as its prime goal getting enough material on the record for appeal to a civilian court. A fat man with a pink, morning-scrubbed look on his face, Morgan by midday was beginning to show broad patches of sweat forming under the arms of his olive drab suit. Captain Levy sat next to Morgan, looking as uncomfortable in uniform as a man can look, and next to him was his other lawyer, Laughlin McDonald, who, it turned out during the course of evening sessions after the trial, is an accomplished folksinger.

In a Camelot gesture, Colonel Brown pressed a button which sounded a buzzer in a back room. Everyone in the building rose, as if at a Catholic mass, and waited for the court-martial board—ten field grade officers whom the New York Times' Homer Bigart branded "ten Toby Mugs"—to enter through a heavy maroon curtain, hung ceremoniously with a tieback, simulating a stage.

The court filed in, slowly . . . .

In the front row of spectator seats behind Howard Levy were his parents, Seymour and Sadie—small, middle-aged, unobtrusive, friendly and worried. Mrs. Levy has large, desolate green eyes, a low, confidential note in her voice, and a voracious appetite for crossword puzzles. Mr. Levy was suntanned, with a thin, sandy little moustache and a large lump on his left forehead, the result of having once been hit by a baseball bat, which gave his face an off-balance look. His voice is deep and hoarse; he used words like "animus," "obdurate" and "adduce," and invited you to call him Sy. He and his wife lavish affection on anybody they like, but for some reason the gods have not smiled much on the Levys lately: they had an automobile accident the first day of their son's trial, and $439 worth of damage was done to their car (they were driving out to Fort Jackson from downtown Columbia, and Seymour Levy missed a stop sign because he was looking for direction signs). Their New York apartment was burgled shortly after they arrived in Columbia, and Mrs. Levy explained several times that she had specifically asked "that newspaper" not to publish their address for just that reason. "Well, into every life a little rain must fall," Seymour Levy said. For his sake you wish them a little sunshine. They are gentle people.

As the chrome handcuff snapped around the physician's wrist, a wail went up from spectators in the courtroom. Unable to direct the hands of the healer for its own ends, the military had shackled them.

That histrionic scene was the finale in the theatrical court-martial, but it wasn't the way the Army had meant to stage it. Colonel Brown, who had tried to make the Army out as the paragon of reason during the trial, looked duly amazed as a burly lieutenant colonel crashed through the swinging gate of the spectator's section seconds after the verdict had been announced and grabbed the doctor by the arm. Lt. Colonel Chester Davis, the hospital administrator, and a former patient of Dr. Levy's, his pink face turned deep red, the paunch over his belt buckle quivering, said that the doctor was under arrest. Levy looked distastefully at Davis's hand. "You don't have to hold my arm," he said.

"Where are you taking him?" Morgan demanded. Davis didn't answer; he was trembling. "May he be accompanied by counsel?" His voice choked, Davis said, "He will not be accompanied by counsel." "May he be accompanied by military counsel, then?" Davis said no, then reached for the handcuffs. Captain Shusterman, the prosecutor, blinked. "Sir, that's not necessary," protested Captain Sanders, Levy's military attorney. "But he's a doctor!" shouted a spectator in the courtroom, and Davis rushed the manacled Levy out the door and into a waiting military police car.

At that moment, the code of Uniform Military Justice showed its true colors. All the easy dignity and military propriety with which Brown and Shusterman had tried to imbue the court-martial's proceedings were shattered. The arbitrary manacling of Dr. Levy was an act of raw power, showing the hard layer of what seemed to be pure hatred for the troublesome doctor beneath the Army's hitherto gentlemanly facade.

It is ironic, reflecting on this scene, that Howard Levy was the one convicted of conduct unbecoming an officer and a gentleman.

. . . .

Note: In 1973, a Federal Appeals Court, on grounds of unconstitutional vagueness, dismissed all but one charge against Dr. Levy—the one: disobeying a direct order. However, in June 1974, the U.S. Supreme Court upheld all aspects of the sentence imposed upon the doctor.

OLD AGE IN PRESENT-DAY SOCIETY*

The characteristic mark of the adult's attitude towards the old is its duplicity. Up to a certain point the adult bows to the official ethic of respect for the aged that has, as we have seen, asserted itself during the recent centuries. But it is in the adult's interest to treat the aged man as an inferior being and to convince him of his decline. He does his best to make his father aware of his deficiencies and blunders so that the old man will hand over the running of his affairs, give up advising him and submit to a passive role. Although the pressure of public opinion forces the son to help his old parents, he means to rule them as he sees fit; and so the more he considers them incapable of managing for themselves the fewer scruples he will feel.

It is an underhand, sly manner that the adult tyrannizes over the dependent old man. He dares not give him orders openly, for he has no right to his obedience: avoiding a frontal attack, he manipulates him. Naturally, he always says he is acting in the old man's own interest. The whole family abets him. The old man's resistance is worn down; he is overwhelmed with paralysing attentions; they treat him with ironic kindness, talking in childishly simple terms and even exchanging knowing winks over his head; they let slip wounding observations. If persuasion and artifice fail to make him yield, they do not hesitate to use lies or a bold, decisive stroke. For example, they will induce him to go to a rest-home, 'just to try it', and then abandon him there. The wife and the boy who are dependent on the adult can defend themselves better than the old man: the wife renders service—bed-service and the housework—and the boy will grow into a man capable of calling the adult to account; the old man will do nothing but travel downwards to decrepitude and death. He is a mere object, useless and in the way: all they want is to be able to treat him as a negligible quantity.

The interests at stake in this struggle are not solely of a practical nature: they also have a moral aspect—there is a desire that the aged should conform to the image that society has formed of them. They are required to dress themselves in a certain way and to respect outward appearances. More than in any other, it is in the sexual aspect of life that this repression makes itself felt. When the old Prince Sokolski thinks of marrying again in *The Adolescent* his family mounts guard over him; they do so out of interested motives but also because they are utterly shocked by the idea. They threaten to put him into a madhouse; in the end they keep him shut

*Adapted from Simone de Beauvoir, *The Coming of Age*. Translated by Patrick O'Brian (New York: G. P. Putnam's Sons, 1972), pp. 218–220.

up at home: he dies of it. I have known similar tragedies in middle-class families of this century.

Daughters often feel resentment with regard to their mothers, and their attitude is much the same as that of sons to their father. The least ambivalent affection is that of a daughter for her father and of a son for his mother. They are capable of great self-sacrifice for a beloved parent who has grown old. But if they are married, the influence of the spouse often limits their generosity.

Where there is no personal connexion, adults feel a contempt not unmixed with disgust for the aged: throughout the centuries, as we have seen, comic authors have exploited this feeling. Since the younger man looks upon the ancient as a caricature of himself, he makes fun of him, so as to break the connecting bonds by means of laughter. Sadism sometimes comes into this mockery. I was taken aback in New York, when I went to the well-known show in the Bowery, where horrible old women in their eighties sing and dance, lifting up their skirts. The audience roared with laughter: what exactly was the meaning of all this mirth?

Nowadays the adults take quite another kind of interest in the aged: they have become objects of exploitation. In the United States more than anywhere else, but also in France, there are greatly increasing numbers of nursing-homes, rest-homes, residences, villages and even towns where elderly people who have the means are made to pay as much as possible for an often inadequate comfort and care.

In extreme cases the old lose whatever they do: they are the victims of the contradictions inherent in their status. In the death-camps they were the first to be chosen for slaughter; seeing that they had no power to work they were given no chance of any kind. . . .

OUT TO PASTURE*

MACARTHUR PARK—The lunch hour is over, and this patch of green near downtown Los Angeles is quiet now. The young girls have eaten their sack lunches and are back taking dictation and selling hosiery. The young men are back on the job, too. As the afternoon stretches toward evening, the park is peopled mostly by those no longer working, no longer young.

The elderly come slowly, and usually alone, from the cheap hotels and

*Adapted from Barbara Isenberg, "To Be Old and Poor is to be Alone, Afraid, Ill-Fed and Unknown," *The Wall Street Journal* 87(15 Nov 72): 1 and 16.

rooming houses nearby, passing the pawnshops, eateries and movie houses on their way into the park. Here they sit on splintered green benches, rarely talking to each other, rarely turning away from the main path where each hopes something interesting might happen.

It seldom does.

"Why am I here?" says Joe, a 72-year-old retired house painter. "I am here because I have no place else to go." Shielding his face from the sun with a trembling hand, he surveys the silent people on the benches around him. "We are old now," he says, "and we've been put out to pasture with no hope and not even enough hay." There is no bitterness in his voice. That is just the way it goes, he seems to say.

. . . .

Joe, who makes do on $176 a month from Social Security, is a member of one of the nation's most distressed minorities—the more than 20 million Americans who are over 65. It is a minority that expands daily by 1,000. The problems facing these legions grow apace with their numbers.

Not the least of these is a pervading feeling of uselessness, of being shelved and ignored by a society enamored of youth. The retirement dinner is not just a mark of appreciation, a farewell gesture by co-workers; it can also be a consignment to oblivion—and, frequently, to poverty.

Fully half the elderly have incomes averaging less than $75 a week. Many live on far less. A study by New York City's Office for the Aging found that in 1968 one-third of the households in the city headed by people 65 and over subsisted on less than $2,000 a year. Social Security is clearly the only income for millions of the aged, and even recent boosts in benefits will not alleviate grinding poverty. Twenty percent of very little is—very little.

Some of the elderly poor lived decently while they were working, but were booted into mandatory retirement without adequate reserves. Now, they watch anxiously as inflation and rising taxation eat away at small fixed incomes. Others, who always had to struggle, have to struggle even harder. They are caught "between depleting resources and increasing lifetimes," says Jack Ossofsky, executive director of the National Council on Aging in Washington. "The poor never saved for rainy days because it rained every day of their lives. Now, with just Social Security, they have to repeat month by month the miracle of Chanukah, when one day's oil lasted eight days."

So, like Joe the retired painter, the aged poor drift to the inner cities, to neighborhoods like the ones surrounding MacArthur Park. They come by necessity, not by choice; only in neighborhoods like these can they find low rents and easily available shopping and services, important to people for whom even a few blocks may be too far to walk and for whom 25 cents for the bus is an expenditure to be carefully weighed.

So, in neighborhoods that the younger and more affluent have deserted, the elderly poor quickly fill the old hotels and rooming houses, competing with drunks and drug addicts for space, yielding the parks and the streets after dark because they are afraid. Like Sylvia, a 66-year-old widow who lives in terror of what darkness might bring. She does not, ever, go out at night. Alone in her room, suffering from acute depression, she surveys a future that she sees as hopeless.

There are many Sylvias, many parks, in the big cities. The MacArthur Park area isn't the worst of them. It was one of the city's more fashionable residential districts before World War II, and it still lacks most of the grime and squalor of deteriorating inner-city neighborhoods elsewhere. And the 32-acre park itself remains a sunny, palm-studded place, pleasing to the eye.

But the neighborhood has run downhill. According to 1970 census data, it now is a warren of cheap apartments, most of them one or two-room units that rent for $45 to $100 a month; the median rent is $79, 20% lower than the city-wide median. The number of units that lack plumbing in the rooms is four times the city-wide average. And, according to the Los Angeles Police Department, the MacArthur Park area has one of the highest crime rates in this city.

The shabby apartments are packed with the poor elderly—the average age in one census tract near the park is 64—and most of them live alone, as do five million of the total U.S. population over 65. Coupled with their sense of uselessness, their solitude breeds despair. Some fight it. They haunt the U.S. and state courthouses for trials, picking up a legal education that astounds attorneys and become fans of particular judges and lawyers whose cases they never miss.

Many go to the park regularly; it is their outdoor living room, their only recreation. Still others fill the days with the organized activities of senior citizens groups, fighting loneliness at the ballroom of the Elks Club with foxtrots done to the ballads of long ago. And a few are lucky enough to get work. Says an old man clerking at one of the cheap hotels: "I know that if I couldn't do this, I'd go on the bottle. I'd be drinking all day to make the time go."

But when night comes, when the drunks and addicts and thieves have the park and there is no place to go and nothing to do, the loneliness takes over. "It's not too bad during the day," an oldster recently told psychiatric nurse Terese Gilbert here, "but when it gets dark . . . well, you could just jump out a window."

Many of the aged are gnawed by the fear not that they will die, but that they will die unnoticed by anyone. It is a fear well founded. "At least a third of the elderly we find in the central city have no friends or family who care about them," says Lois Hamer, director of the Program of Retired Citizens, a privately financed volunteer group that seeks to help the aged here. She tells of writing a letter to the son of a bedridden old woman, pleading with him to visit her. He replied bluntly that he simply wasn't interested.

So some of the elderly do pass through life without notice. Recently, Miss Hamer's volunteers found one woman seriously ill who had been in bed a full week. No one knew; no one cared. She was taken to a hospital. She was fortunate. Many die before the volunteers, or anyone else, find them.

Many of the elderly poor are so deeply withdrawn that they consciously avoid human contact, psychiatrists say. The oldsters sit side by side in the lobbies of the threadbare hotels watching TV, but they don't speak to each other. Or they spend almost every day looking out the windows of their rooms at a world they won't be part of again. In interviews with the elderly in one hotel near MacArthur Park, University of Southern California graduate student Victor Regnier found that some defined their "neighborhood" as the hotel itself—and a few evidently considered it limited by the four walls of their rooms.

To many, these rooms are the only security they have, so they cling to them beyond reason. At this moment a 93-year-old woman is slowly starving herself to death in an apartment near MacArthur Park; she is unable to get out to buy any food, and she refuses to accept any help from anyone.

Even this kind of "security" is marred by fear. Many of the elderly say they are afraid to ask landlords to fix broken plumbing, peeling wallpaper or other problems, lest the rent be raised. Even a $5 boost can send them out into the streets in a painful search for new quarters that are cheaper. The fear of fire is a major one; one old woman constantly seeks reassurance from her social worker, tells her again and again of a fire three years ago, worries constantly that she will be unable to get out this time because she is arthritic.

Many of the aged poor are depressed to the point of mental imbalance. The people who live near MacArthur Park all seem to have suffered sudden losses occurring over a relatively short time span: loss of a feeling of usefulness when they are retired or cannot work, loss of a wife or husband, loss of income, good health, status, friends. For many, it is more than they can take.

Like Tom, who is 67. He is poor, and he has no living relative now. Independent and in good health all his life, he now is troubled by both arthritis and failing vision; he is in mortal fear of blindness, and even more than that, of losing his independence because of it.

Tom goes to a mental health clinic. Most of the elderly with similar problems don't obtain the early help that would permit them to remain in society, psychiatrists say. Nationally, one of every four suicides and one in every four admissions to state mental hospitals are people over 65, says Dr. Robert N. Butler, a Washington psychiatrist who is an expert on the problems of the aged.

Nutrition is a staggering problem and contributes to the poor health of many of the elderly. It is a particular problem in the MacArthur Park area, where most of the food stores are small, higher-priced outlets rather than supermarkets. Some hotels serve decent meals at low prices, but most don't. Even hotplates can't be used in some of the older buildings because their wiring can't take the current load.

So, many of the elderly eat what they can get, or afford, not what is good for them. Miss Hamer of the Program of Retired Citizens gives a typical day's menu for too many of the elderly poor: for breakfast, a roll and coffee with all the milk and sugar that can be poured into it. For lunch, the same. For dinner, the same, with maybe a piece of pie.

Some live mainly on what they can buy from the vending machines in their hotel or apartment lobbies. Social workers and volunteers find others, often the frail who cannot make repeated trips out of their rooms, living almost entirely on bread and butter.

Others eat dog food. "They can get two meals out of a can," says Robert Frost, an official of the National League of Senior Citizens in Los Angeles. "Where else could they get so much protein for so little money?"

. . . .

WHAT BECAME OF THAT PENSION?*

I had always expected to live out my retirement years in Philadelphia. My wife and I still call it home. I held a highly responsible job there. As I looked forward to those years of doing volunteer work in the community, I felt reassured that the company I worked for had a pension plan that would provide us adequate means.

This pension plan, I have learned the hard way, was built on sand. I

*Adapted from Moriz Dreyfus, "Other Side of the Coin: What Became of That Pension?" *The Arizona Republic*, 24 Jan 72.

made every attempt to meet its terms of eligibility—even to moving away from Philadelphia—but it has left me pretty much out in the cold.

* * *

I had worked in Philadelphia for a garment concern. After 32 years I had risen through the ranks and to become vice president for sales. In 1960 my wife and I faced a cruel choice. That year the firm was gobbled up by a manufacturing company in Rochester, N.Y.

Those few employees who were not let go had to agree to move to Rochester or forfeit their pension benefits. Overcoming our reluctance to leave our home town, my wife and I made the difficult move to that cold, strange city in upstate New York. I was 59.

Once in Rochester, I made two bleak discoveries. My new employer's pension benefits would be only 50 percent of what the Philadelphia firm had assured us, and if my wife outlived me she would get nothing. Yet everything was not hopeless.

For one thing, the Rochester company would not force me to retire at the age of 65, as I would have in Philadelphia; for another, the company bought for me, as it did other executives, an $80,000 life insurance policy that would provide my wife a financial cushion if my death preceded hers.

* * *

Once again we were in for a surprise—and a bad one. In 1969 my life insurance coverage was arbitrarily reduced to $35,000.

Within a year that company, too, was bought out. Our new bosses announced that all employees over 65 must retire forthwith. That meant me, since by now I was 69. Sure, they gave me a retirement party; lots of presents—a color TV set, gold watch and the assurance of pension payments amounting to $314 a month.

One other little farewell present wasn't so good: my life insurance coverage, already reduced from $80,000 to $35,000, was slashed again—this time to $11,000.

One year later the cushion disappeared entirely. After this firm had, in turn, been sold to a Texas conglomerate, my life insurance policy was canceled outright. Further, my pension shrank from $314 a month to $169.

* * *

Nearly everyone who has seriously studied our pension system agrees that it needs overhauling. Ralph Nader has called it a "scandalous swindle." Subcommittees of both houses of Congress, after two years of hearings, have lambasted private pension plans. A majority of 40 million employes covered by such plans, according to one congressional report, will never collect one penny of retirement payments.

The explanation is that pension plans are totally unregulated—despite the fact that their assets, estimated at $150 billion, are about double the holdings of all of this country's mutual funds.

Rep. John H. Dent, D-Pa, chaired the subcommittee of the House Committee on Labor that investigated this "swindle." He made this analysis: "If you remain in good health, and if you stay with the same company until you are 65, and if the company is still in business and if your department has not been abolished, and if your job has not been made technologically obsolete, and if you have not been laid off for too long a time, and if there is sufficient money in the fund—you will get your pension."

His Senate counterpart, Harrison A. Williams Jr., D-N.J., labeled the pension system as we know it "a glorified filing system."

The Williams-Javits bill was introduced to provide regulatory supervision. It received wide backing in the Senate, but political infighting prevented its passage. . . .

. . . .

Note: Since the foregoing appeared, pension-protecting legislation has been adopted at the Federal level. The legislation is minimal and does nothing to alleviate the plight of the multitudes of people whose "pensions" turned out to be phantom.

Red Tape

A formal social organization in which the roles and statuses of participants are carefully specified is often termed a "bureaucracy." These organizations are typically governed by purely rational values—i.e., by a business-like attention to achieving given goals. But such achievement often leads to an impersonal application of rules that may be totally inappropriate in particular cases. Thus, "The Bureaucrat" has become the model of the unreasonable person, the individual who regards rules as sacred writ. The result, all too often, is that ordinary citizens who must deal with bureaucracies come away feeling they have been had. Is there any more frustrating experience than the glassy-eyed stare of the rigid bureaucratic personality who is afraid to deviate even slightly from "the rules"? But, as the accompanying articles suggest, the difficulty is not always attributable to individuals; it is sometimes simply a function of the impersonal bureaucratized process. In any case, the result is the same: the personal and social problems that arise as a consequence of the rigidity of bureaucracies and/or bureaucrats.

FAINTLY PERVERTED*

... Every time a group of oppressed people rises up and tries to change their situation, someone gets anxious. I am reminded of a project in which residents of an old people's home began to take an interest in the residents of a home for the mentally retarded located nearby. Great idea, for who is better qualified to spare a little patience and give a little love than a lonely old person? Everything went smoothly, just informal visits, quiet reading hours, old voices raised in barely remembered lullabies.

The tragedy was that it was too good to be left alone. Someone decided it had to be organized, formalized, structured, observed, and supervised by responsible authorities. Classes were instituted to teach the old people how to handle retarded children. Printed schedules for visits and what would take place on those visits began to appear. The showing of too much

*Adapted from Sharon R. Curtin, *Nobody Ever Died of Old Age* (Boston: Little, Brown and Co., 1972), pp. 212-214.

physical affection was discouraged, and it was implied that there was something faintly, well, you know, *perverted* about the whole enterprise.

I don't really know the end of the story; the woman who told me about it just said she soon lost interest. It was true, she told me, that she had a favorite among the children and spent most of her time with her. "But they made me feel guilty about loving that child, as if an old fool like me and a young fool like her couldn't have any need to love and be loved. They said we had to do things just so, and that took all the love out. . . . Maybe they were right. I couldn't be around to care for that child forever, but I didn't think it would actually harm her to have a little affection. They made me feel that I'd done something wrong."

Anyone with any experience with institutions could have told that old lady what she did wrong. She stepped outside of total dependence on the institution, and took the child with her. The integrity and power of the institution, as felt by its staff, was threatened. So the Kafkaesque "they" resumed control, and in the process, destroyed something quite beautiful. Even if the project, in some modified form, continues, the relationship between the old people and the retarded children will remain part of the total institution, less human, less spontaneous and less enjoyable. Instead of the old people doing something they want to do, and taking pride in that act, they will feel exploited, used as unpaid labor.

I wish that old people in that home had not let themselves be defeated; but I suspect they didn't know until too late that the battle was on. And if you think about what life in most of those institutions we have built for our aged is like, maybe they were beaten before they started. The old are supposed to be a burden, not a resource.

. . . .

DEAR COMPUTER *

A Consolidated Edison billing computer kept sending a woman customer notices that her gas and electricity would be cut off unless she paid $0.00. Despite protests to the utility that their figures showed she owed nothing, the notices continued. Finally, the woman, who asked not to be identified, wrote a check for $0.00. The computer has not replied, she said.

Los Angeles Times, Feb. 20, 1973.

WE CAN'T HELP HIM *

John Wilson of Washington, D.C. lived within a few blocks of embassies and grand houses. But his house was not grand: it consisted of a single room, ten by fifteen feet—home for John, his wife and five of his ten children (the other five had to be boarded with an aunt). The room cost him $65 a month.

John worked as a dishwasher in a downtown hotel—an occupation yet to be reached by the minimum wage law that has been on the United States statute books for twenty-five years. His work week: six days. Pay: $57.

Every Saturday he took home $53—and paid $15 of it to his landlord.

John had a wish. He wanted to get his ten children back under one roof. Not an unreasonable wish. At one point they had all been together, crammed into two rooms, with the side use of a kitchen and a bath (cost: $35 a week—$152 a month). But then the landlord counted the children—nine, then, and a tenth on the way—and had thrown him out.

His one hope lay in public housing. A poor man, he was told, could get a large enough apartment for $45 a month. He applied. For a long time, no answer. Then a form-letter reply:

> "We regret to inform you that, after careful examination of the facts presented in your application, we have found you to be ineligible for the following reasons ... (and in ink below) INSUFFICIENT FUNDS."

The judgment: John Wilson was too poor to pay $45 a month for a six-bedroom apartment. *The sentence:* John Wilson must continue paying $65 a month, half again as much, for a single room inadequate to house even half of his children.

But the story does not end there. When the situation was brought to light by the *Washington Post,* public housing officials said they had been misunderstood. John Wilson, they explained, wasn't exactly ineligible. It was just that there weren't any apartments for people with such low incomes. But they would put him on the waiting list. Along with 6,000 other families. There are only four vacancies a year in the six-bedroom category. There are a hundred and one applicants for six-bedroom apartments. Even with a top priority rating, officials said it would take John Wilson six years to get an apartment.

*Adapted from Phillip Stern and George de Vincent, *The Shame of a Nation* (New York: Ivan Obolensky, Inc., 1965), pp. 106 and 108.

THE RIGHT HAND KNOWETH NOT . . .*

In the last two years the Defense Department cranked out 12 films, all on the same subject: "How to brush your teeth!" Ten more films were produced from within the Pentagon in that period on another subject, venereal disease.

These, according to a highly critical report made public yesterday, are among many examples of how the federal government is spending millions and millions of dollars of the taxpayers' money each year for the production of films and other audio-visual material. The films and the equipment needed to produce them often are duplicated by other agencies, and the government itself does not seem to know just how much is being spent.

Even individual government agencies apparently do not know what is being produced or how much is being spent within their own department.

It all adds up to another example of massive—and expensive—government bureaucracy that no one seems able to control, to say nothing of coordinating.

. . . .

"WHO GIVES A DAMN?"**

The book from which this selection is taken is Mr. Hickel's view of why he was forced to resign as Secretary of Interior during the first Nixon administration. It is apparent that Hickel's keen interest in protecting the environment conflicted with corporate interests; the latter prevailed.

... The morning of May 1, 1969, was a spring morning at its best in Washington. The grass sparkled with dew and the world looked fresh and clean. As I walked out of the home I had recently bought in the Maryland suburb of Kenwood, I felt good. We had moved into the house less than a week earlier after living for nearly four months in an apartment at the Sheraton-Park Hotel, two floors below Vice President Spiro Agnew's apartment.

I stepped into my limousine and my driver, Hilton Coleman, began the thirty-minute run to Andrews Air Force Base, where I boarded an Air

*Adapted from *Washington Post* Service dispatch, Aug. 10, 1972.

**Adapted from Walter J. Hickel, *Who Owns America?* (Englewood Cliffs, N.J.: Prentice-Hall, Inc., 1971), pp. 203-204, 206-208.

Force jet. By 8:15 A.M. we were rolling down a runway headed west to the Pacific—bound on a special mission for the President.

I had received President Nixon's approval for a trip I considered of considerable importance to the nation: a 14,000-mile fact-finding mission to Micronesia, the Trust Territory of the Western Pacific, for which the Department of the Interior has administrative responsibility.

. . . .

Mine was the first trip to the Trust Territory taken by a Secretary of the Interior in seven years. As we visited some of the major islands—Saipan, Truk, Tinian—I was impressed by the cordial personal welcome extended to us by these warm and outgoing people. I was particularly taken by their beautiful and friendly children, and I loved every minute I spent with them. Harking back to my earlier experiences in Alaska, I tried, throughout my trip, to stress that Micronesians needed and deserved a much louder voice in their own affairs. And I exhorted them to "dream big dreams."

On Monday, May 5, I stood on the outdoor stage of a mission school and spoke to the people of Saipan who had gathered before me, plus thousands of others throughout the islands who were listening to the Micronesian Broadcasting System: "You will help develop the legislation which will end the trusteeship and build a lasting political partnership with us." I pledged immediate steps to improve the Micronesian judicial system, ease tariff barriers and travel restrictions, gear up for major educational and health programs and invite new investment capital to the islands: "For years you have had little voice in your government. This is wrong. Only when the people lead their government can that government be great and people prosper. And while that work goes forward, land will not be taken from Micronesians for any government purpose without full consultation with all parties involved and full and adequate compensation to land owners."

"Full compensation" was an extremely important point, one that would put me in conflict with some of the White House people later, especially Dr. Henry Kissinger, assistant to the President on national security affairs. But we left Saipan that night and headed for home with a feeling of pride and accomplishment. We had made *contact*. We had established rapport. The people of the Trust Territory and I understood each other. It was a human thing. I tried to symbolize this rapport by swearing in High Commissioner Ed Johnston in Saipan, the seat of the territorial government, rather than in Washington, D.C., 6,778 miles away, where the ceremony had always taken place before.

I believed then, and I believe now, that the people of the Trust Territory had the right to own and dispose of their own land with full agreement and compensation. If I now ask "Who Owns America?" then the Micronesians have every right to ask "Who Owns Micronesia?"

. . . .

In Micronesia, the overriding desire and need of the people is to own their own land. That is all they have. But Henry Kissinger argued that the United States had to have the right of eminent domain—the right to condemn what Micronesian land we wished; to build what bases and other facilities we wished, with little regard for the moral (if not legal) rights of the people who inhabited this land.

We had this argument out at a meeting that took place in Secretary of State William Rogers's office. Along with Rogers, Kissinger and myself, Harrison Loesch and Mitch Melich were there. I might have gone along with almost anything less than the argument for eminent domain—such as negotiated purchase or lease of land. We had established military bases in Turkey and Spain without right of eminent domain. What right did we have to invoke eminent domain on the Micronesians? They had little enough land for their own needs, and their very livelihood depended on that land and the surrounding ocean. They wanted to work with us. They told me in Saipan that all they wanted was a voice in our decisions.

But Kissinger's answer in Rogers's office was: "There are only 90,000 people out there. Who gives a damn?"

. . . .

PART 2

Inequitable Distribution

It will be recalled that the second major aspect of injustice, as the term is being used here, is inequitable distribution of the means to well-being. This does not imply that in the just society all participants are precisely equal in their access to such ingredients of well-being as monetary income and health care. To achieve such absolute equality would require totalitarian control over conception and over birth-to-death educational experiences so that all would develop strictly equal abilities. Controls of this type would destroy liberty *which is another prime element of justice. Hence, the most that the just society can do is to insure that a) all societal members have a* fair *access to the means to well-being and a* realistic possibility of *using the means, and b) no individuals or sub-groups have the opportunity to accumulate private property in amounts sufficient to give them unwarranted power over others. That our society denies these essentials of justice to large segments of the population is amply and sadly demonstrated by the following readings which are categorized in terms of four headings: The Faces of Poverty, The Rich Get Richer, Health Alone is Victory, and The Environmental Crisis.*

189

The Faces of Poverty

Here we begin a series of pieces depicting the multi-faceted nature of poverty. In the first selection, Lutheran pastor Arthur Simon—whose book has provided an apt title for present purposes—attacks common myths about the poor: that their apathy is just a cover for laziness, that they "have it made," that they could clean up if they really wanted to, and so on. Following this relatively abstract article, there are a number telling how the poor cope—or fail to cope—with their actual living situations. Since so many American poor are black, we begin with reports about them by attorney Peter Schuck and psychiatrist Robert Coles; and journalist Dale Wright tells about East-coast migrant workers who are largely black. But many white Americans—not to speak at the moment of Indians or Mexican-Americans—are also poverty stricken, as illustrated in the pieces by reporter Ben Bagdikian and (once again) Pastor Simon. Finally, Sylvia Porter writes about the vicious credit traps lying in wait for those least able to defend themselves.

It should be noted that all of the conditions mentioned in the various selections included here have been made almost indescribably worse by inflation. Already at rock bottom, the poor have no way to make reasonable adjustments when inflation tightens the screw. Thus, as indicated to the Senate Select Committee on Nutrition and Human Needs, in June 1974, when one poor man was asked what he felt would be at least a minimum improvement in his situation, he said he would like not to have to eat any more dog food.

MYTHS ABOUT THE POOR*

... The myths and stereotypes people employ indicate that the poor have never been so misunderstood. That should not surprise us. For one thing, they have become a minority group for the first time in our history, and we misunderstand minorities. In addition, we no longer live next door to the poor, but in our own class ghettos, and separation breeds suspicion.

*Adapted from Arthur R. Simon, *Faces of Poverty* (St. Louis: Concordia Publishing House, 1966), pp. 65-68.

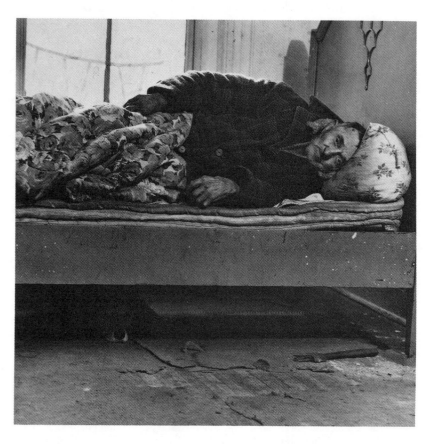

Can we afford to explore
the heavens when there's still
a hell on earth?

Above all, we are impressed with the increasing wealth of our nation, a wealth in which most have shared, and we are therefore prone to assume that anyone who really wants to can shake off the restrictions of poverty. Failure to do so, we instinctively believe, is a mark of moral weakness.

This misunderstanding helps to make poverty a dead end for people because it prevents us from facing the problem honestly and working for solutions. Below are some standard expressions of this misunderstanding.

1. *The poor are lazy. Let them make it the hard way like I did.* This stance assumes two things. It assumes that "I have made it the hard way." When this assumption is analyzed, it almost always turns out to be erroneous or highly exaggerated. We are too ready to give ourselves the credit when circumstances and opportunities may have been stacked in our favor. For example, how can we equate the chances of a white baby with the chances of a Negro baby? The evidence does not permit it.

It also asserts that those who don't "make it" are lazy. But what is the evidence? During World War II unemployment became virtually nonexistent because jobs were available. During most of our history there has been a shortage of labor in the country. When labor is in demand, few are idle. The lesson of life is that personal achievement is impossible apart from opportunity. Destroy or curtail opportunity, and you reduce achievement.

2. *Why don't they go out and get jobs?* There are not enough jobs to go around. Most unemployed people do hunt for jobs, but the hunting is often for nonexistent positions, and one cannot be expected to play this game indefinitely. If you think otherwise, try it for a few years. Many jobs, because they pay little or are seasonal do not furnish a living wage. Naturally the unskilled, the ill-educated, the aging, and dark-skinned minorities suffer the most from this.

3. *People on relief have it too good.* Let no one kid you. People on relief live far below the margin of poverty, and they can't afford any extras—as a look at an itemized list of necessities for welfare recipients demonstrates. This is living pared down to the bone. However, you cannot blame a family on welfare for wanting to watch television, even if they pay for it in food and clothes, because it may offer them their one escape from an otherwise dismal existence. To such a family a TV set is far less expendable than for most of us who have a wide range of choices in recreation and entertainment. If occasionally a person on welfare spends money foolishly—on liquor or perhaps expensive flowers—it reflects a wish to escape one's fate or an agonizing desire to participate in a bit of America's abundance, even though it means more suffering in the end.

4. *Why don't they move out of the slums?* Where can they go? And how would they find work there? And how could they live until they do? The trend in jobs is to the city, so people must move to centers of

employment. And when one is poor, he lives where the rent is cheap. For millions of Americans it means there is no alternative to the slums.

5. *Why don't they at least clean up?* To many, uncleanliness is the final insult. "Cleanliness is next to godliness," they say (though the truly godly have never been so preoccupied with cleanliness). But on the Lower East Side cleanliness is next to impossible; at least there are formidable obstacles. Being crowded together in small living units with virtually no closet space is one. Waging war with soot is another. Inadequate service from the city sanitation department, population density, and emotional torment are others. However, the idea that poor people are dirty is a stereotype that does disservice to the majority of them, who do rather well against impressive odds.

What strikes one about the myths that lie behind such questions is not only that they block understanding but that they reflect a fierce self-righteousness. The moral superiority they assume and the ease with which they presume to expose the faults of the poor raise the question whether those who make such judgments know the meaning of grace.

At the same time it is often overlooked that the poor have strengths and virtues. The poor are not impressed with formalities or with the kind of sophistication that tends to obscure rather than reveal persons. They are less apt to be prisoners of pride, more apt to be open about themselves, about life and its problems. They are better braced for disappointment, more humble in failure. Death is no stranger to them, and the poor are often much closer to it, more honest about it than others. They are in touch with the smell of the street, the violence and passions of men, the sufferings of their neighbors. As a result they are often more able than others to sort out and pay attention to actions that really matter and less apt to get hung up on things for appearance's sake.

Furthermore, a poor man who is dirty and lazy is a sick man, and we ought to have a double sense of responsibility: not to feed his sickness by isolating him and putting him on the dole but to help him get well. Especially we ought to take steps to see that the children of such a man are not locked into the same pattern of hopelessness.

A basic blunder in trying to understand the poor is the failure to take into account the raw material out of which they must shape their lives. An aspiring junior executive in his corporation was fired, but for months, while he was unemployed, he got dressed and left the house in the morning as he always did so that he would not have to tell his teen-age children he was unemployed. If humiliation and guilt can do that to a professionally trained man, imagine what it means to a man to face his family month after month, perhaps year after year, with no job and no likelihood of a job or able to look forward at best to the most minimal support for his family. Think of the burden of the man who knows he is probably trapped for good in the slums and will never be able to lift his family out of poverty; who realizes that the very situation he is in is likely to predestine his children to the same.

In this situation a whole pathology of poverty develops which is sicker than anything like it a generation ago. The sense of failure and uselessness it produces may have a whole host of repercussions. It may drive a man to seek an escape in alcohol or to abandon his family. His children are more apt to grow up disturbed, restless, and unable to get along in school. They are more likely to be disillusioned about the future—frustrated when they see the growth of the nation but realize that they are not being equipped to have a productive share in it. They may turn to drink, dope, sex, crime, or any combination of these. A girl may crave affection and want desperately to escape prisonlike conditions—and become the victim of the very thing that perpetuates her imprisonment. She has a lover and gives birth to children, in or out of wedlock, and soon finds herself saddled with incredible responsibilities for which she is not prepared. She becomes old and worn out before her time. It is easy to stand morally aloof and criticize her deficiencies; but where do we get the idea that those of us who are prone to criticize, given the same circumstances, would not be just as apt to get caught in the same web?

We can ignore these agonizing truths rather than acknowledge our responsibility for them, but then we should know we are throwing our weight on the side of making poverty a dead end for people.

. . . .

TIED TO THE SUGAR LANDS*

. . . In the weeks before Christmas, at the height of the "grinding," or harvest, season, the sugar fields hum with activity. The 5,000 cane workers, as well as unemployed workers from nearby towns lured by the seventy-hour work weeks, bend to the feverish rhythm of the harvest—cut the cane with a harvester, load the cane with a loader, pick up the "scrap" cane by hand, haul the cane with a tractor, hoist the cane with a derrick, drive the cane to the raw sugar mill. And always the insistent refrain—get the cane to the mill before the first frost sours and ruins it.

By mid-January, the cane fields are desolate again. The cane workers

*Adapted from Peter Schuck, "Tied to the Sugar Lands," *Saturday Review* 55(6 May 72):36–42.

stand inside their shacks, gazing out at the interminable rain that trans-
forms the gummy, alluvial earth into an unapproachable swamp of cane
stubble. There is no work on such days, and such days are common well
into the spring. The cane worker knows that he will be fortunate to get in
twenty hours of work a week in January and February, aerating the soil
and shoveling earth away from the drains in the field. He knows, too, that
he will be idle much of the time until September, just before the grinding
season begins once again. But he also knows that there is nowhere else for
him to go.

Rooted in the rich delta soil, the cane worker is immobilized by a
deprivation extreme even for the rural South. He is a skilled operator of
sophisticated machinery; yet on the average he earns only $2,635 a year to
sustain a family of six. This is $1,900 less than the poverty level for a farm
family and almost $1,000 less than the average for farm-worker families,
widely recognized as the most deprived remnant of the nation's poor.

Federal assistance programs do not mitigate the cane worker's distress,
for in the sugar belt, the federal pipeline runs less to the workers than to
the large growers. South Coast Corporation and Southdown Lands, Inc., are
the two largest sugar growers in Louisiana. Subsidiaries of giant absentee
conglomerates (Jim Walter Corporation of Tampa, Florida, and Southdown,
Inc., of Houston, Texas), the two received $297,981 and $186,213 respec-
tively in direct federal subsidies for the 1969 crop year, but federal
assistance is far less generous to their plantation workers.

A 1970 survey showed that 79 percent received *no* federal assistance whatsoever. Despite the cataloguing of a morass of misery—inadequate diet,
overcrowded housing, and grossly deficient medical care—the cane families,
as working people, are not eligible for welfare. By early 1972 most parishes
had accepted food stamp programs, but these programs are often administered with a niggardliness and hostility that virtually negates their impact.
With only three aides to administer 1,300 cases, the program's director in
Lafourche Parish expresses dismay at newly liberalized regulations. "They
just rammed these down our throats," he says, flourishing his program
manual. "These people will just have to wait six weeks until we can take
their applications. Then we have to check them out. We've got files on
these families two inches thick. We know exactly what they're doing."
Emergency cases? "A second priority. First, we weed out the cheaters.
Second, we do emergencies. Then, new cases. Those are our orders from
Baton Rouge, approved by the USDA."

The sugar growers and the USDA (United States Department of Agriculture) are the two forces that determine the cane worker's fate. His ties
to the grower are rooted in utter economic necessity. His ties to the federal
agency are rooted in nearly four decades of law. The Sugar Act made him

a ward of the department in the early 1930s; his exclusion from the Wagner Act, with its provisions protecting union organizing, has perpetuated that dependency. [Ed. note: The 1974 Congress did not renew the Sugar Act.]

The result is a diffuse triangular relationship in which the growers and the department each deem the other responsible for the worker's welfare. But in the end, no one—least of all the cane worker—is, in fact, responsible.

In the cane lands the question of race is inescapable, for the 5,000 cane workers and their 25,000 dependents are nearly all black and Baptist. Living in plantation housing, often buying in plantation stores, the sugar worker, descended from generations of sugar workers, still speaks of himself in the language of bondage—he is "tied" to the plantation. He is the "slave" of the grower; he is "not free to go."

The growers, white and Catholic, dominate the politics of the parishes as they have for generations. Their mode of conduct is *noblesse oblige*. Murphy Foster, son of a governor and U.S. senator and one of Louisiana's most prominent growers, leans back in his chair in a dimly lit office festooned with hundreds of *Playboy* nudes sent to him over the years. "Niggers are the happiest creatures on God's green earth," he says. "I've worked with these people for thirty years, and if they have a problem, they know to come to me."

At the New Orleans offices of the American Sugar Cane League, the national association of growers, vice president Gilbert Durbin talks of growers' concern for worker welfare. Most growers, he stresses, supply their field workers with "free" housing on the plantations, housing that, he estimates, is worth $50 to $70 a month. They often let workers who are disabled or too old to work in the fields simply go on living there. Though Durbin insists housing conditions are good, the 1970 survey showed that in plantation housing three-quarters of the houses had no toilets and were rat-infested; half had leaking roofs and not even cold running water. "I've seen that housing," said a Terrebonne Parish telephone worker. "No one would live there who had any choice in the matter."

On the South Coast plantation in St. Mary Parish, even a cursory view of the housing provides a profoundly shocking confirmation of the telephone worker's words. Though Durbin insists that some new housing is being built, extensive decrepitude is the norm. Some shacks are said to date back to slavery times. At night the glow of bare light bulbs shows through gaps in the cabin walls. Rats, revealed by car headlights, scurry across front yards. Ancient roofs and floors sag and tremble to the touch. One Southdown worker smiles when asked about his home. "My father is seventy-nine and has lived here all his life. He says it was here long before he was born. The roof leaks no matter how much I patch it. We need an overcoat in the kitchen and a board under the refrigerator to keep it from falling through the rotting floor. If my little girl runs through the living room, the whole thing shakes. What's wrong with it? Hell, nothing's right with it." Does Southdown make needed repairs? "Well, the overseer says the house isn't worth repairing. We can't demand repairs since we don't pay rent."

Whatever its quality, the growers do not provide the housing simply out of good will. Until 1955 the Sugar Act *required* them to supply it to their field workers, so the housing is already there. "Free" housing, some growers concede, is simply a substitute for wages that would otherwise have to take the form of cash.

Free housing and a seasonal job tie the sugar worker to the plantation. In addition, many workers are deeply, perhaps irreversibly, in debt to their growers. ... The web of debt is impenetrable, for it is woven from life's necessities. Typically, a worker's medical care is billed directly to the plantation and deducted from his paycheck. Many growers charge for utilities in the "free" housing. Workers often buy food on credit at stores located on the plantations. Once "company stores" run by the growers, the stores are now frequently leased to outsiders—a dubious improvement from the workers' point of view. The company store charged exorbitant prices, but extended interest-free credit. The leased stores have lower prices but crippling rates of interest. The wife of a field worker on Sterling Sugar Company's St. Mary Parish plantation buys food at the leased store: "If I buy five dollars' worth of groceries there, six dollars is deducted from my husband's pay. Everybody automatically pays an extra twenty percent."

Many field hands receive nothing on payday but a pay slip showing that their net indebtedness has increased over the pay period. Others consistently receive $20 per month in cash regardless of their total earnings. The rest is taken out to amortize a debt that may or may not have gone up over the pay period. Over and over the outsider hears the sugar workers' refrain: "I never see cash."

During the rainy season, some growers seek outside work for their field hands. But according to Stanley Beverly, an OEO-funded job specialist in St. Mary Parish, only two other industries of any consequence exist in the area—oil and gas, and carbon black. Both hire few blacks, have little turnover, and, until recently, insisted on high school diplomas. For the black cane workers, with an average of two years schooling (28 percent have no schooling at all), these jobs are agonizingly beyond reach. Industrialized and job-rich Morgan City is nearby, but workers are attracted there from sixty miles up the bayou, giving employers their pick of laborers from six or seven parishes.

Blacks from the sugar plantations do not fare well in this competition. Often outside employers will not hire them until they have housing off the plantation; yet, without an outside job, the workers cannot move off the plantation. Job-seeking itself can be costly. Recently a plantation worker in St. Mary Parish took the required physical examination for a job in town. When he returned to his home on the plantation, the owner, apparently informed by the examining physician, evicted him for disloyalty.

Under the circumstances, it is not difficult to understand why only 10 percent of the cane workers do get outside jobs during the long rainy season, or why overt expressions of discontent are muffled. But the paralysis and the placidity are deceptive. Job-developer Beverly thumbs through the thick tile of applications for outside jobs on his desk. "If they could get a job off the plantation, they would leave in a second," he says. "I don't know of one who would stay."

Officially, the growers' position is that sugarcane workers enjoy perfectly adequate working and living conditions. The responsibility for any deficiencies, they insist, lies squarely with the U.S. Department of Agriculture. Even Bishop Maurice Schexnayder, the seventy-six-year-old Catholic prelate with ecclesiastical jurisdiction over the area, shares his view. Nudging his crimson skullcap farther back on his head, he says, "There is no suffering among sugarcane workers. Under the Sugar Act, the Department of Agriculture sees to that."

This theme—that USDA is the ultimate guarantor of the workers' welfare—is a familiar one in the sugar belt and has a firm basis in law and politics. Since 1934 the Louisiana cane industry has flourished under the protective wing of the Sugar Act. The act establishes an unusual and elaborate regulatory mechanism, one that the industry gratefully accepted from the Roosevelt administration following near disastrous bouts with crop diseases and foreign competition in the late 1920s and a critical weakening of sugar markets in the early Thirties. It requires USDA to restrict the quantities of raw sugar marketed annually in the United States, reserving a specific quota for each domestic producer as well as import quotas for designated foreign nations. The import quotas keep the domestic sugar price at a "premium" of about three cents a pound above the world price. That premium was worth almost $400-million to growers in 1971. In addition, the act provides for annual subsidies to growers to limit their production. Those payments totaled $93-million in fiscal 1970. Together, these two subsidies to the sugar growers total about $500-million annually.

But the generous Sugar Act exacts a *quid pro quo*. In return for these massive subsidies ("You people never seem to understand that these are *not* subsidies," fumes grower Murphy Foster only moments after denouncing the food stamp program. "They are benefit payments"), the act requires that the growers fulfill certain minimal conditions. The most critical of these conditions for sugar workers is that growers must pay "fair and reasonable" wage rates. As President Roosevelt put it when he sent the bill to Congress, if the sugar industry is to receive the benefits of a quota system, then "it ought to be a good employer."

To ensure fair wages, the act requires that USDA itself annually determine the wage rates of sugar workers. Thus, every July the department holds public hearings on wage rates in the Lousiana sugarcane area. Every year representatives of the American Sugar Cane League testify to rising costs, shrinking profit margins, and gloomy industry prospects, none of which are publicly supported with hard data, and all of which preclude a wage increase. Every year Dr. Joe R. Campbell of Louisiana State University appears at the request of the league to present statistics on yields, costs, returns, prices, etc., for sugarcane farming, statistics that omit, however, such key data as the salaries owners pay themselves and the rising values of their cane land. Every year one or two witnesses testify on behalf of the cane workers, describing the impoverished circumstances in which they work and live. And every year, just before the harvest in October, the department issues its wage determination granting a token increase.

This year's wage determination indicates in whose interests USDA issues its rulings. Growers, for the first time in memory, recommended a wage increase; USDA awarded an increase *smaller than the growers recommended.* Then the department made the increase effective only *after* the harvesting season was over, thereby nullifying its effect during the months when the field hands perform the great bulk of their year's work. ... The peculiar circumstances of this wage determination aside, sugar workers wonder how USDA can reconcile its statutory mandate to set for workers a "fair and reasonable" wage with a worker's actual annual income of $2,635—*cum* hovel. Is the USDA fearful that higher wages would accelerate technological unemployment of workers? That seems doubtful, since even growers concede that mechanization of harvesting operations has gone about as far as it can go, and according to the Sugar Cane League, the mechanization of planting operations is still in the experimental stage. Would higher wages drive sugar growers out of business? There is no evidence for this. Caneland values continue to climb, reflecting the growing profitability of sugar allotments attached to the land. World demand for sugar normally increases about 3 percent a year. This year it increased about 4 percent, pushing the price of sugar futures to their highest point in nine years. In early January the domestic raw sugar price reached 9.1 cents per pound, the highest monthly average since 1964.

In the end, politics is a more likely explanation than economics for USDA's policy. The Sugar Act notwithstanding, USDA simply does not regard farm workers as part of its constituency. By habit, tradition, and inclination, the department has learned to take the bureaucratic path of least resistance, a path that leads to those politically vocal growers with large-scale operations. The Sugar Act, with its highly unusual mandate to protect the powerless, simply bends before the political momentum.

. . . .

Crawford Percle has run the neat white office of the Agricultural Stabilization and Conservation Service (ASCS) in Napoleonville, Assumption Parish, for about twenty-five years. As head of the USDA outpost charged with implementing the Sugar Act regulations, Percle occupies a key position in local affairs. His gaze shifts from the Nixon poster on the wall to his visitor, who has just asked to see the farm-worker complaint file. "I don't think I've *ever* received a farm-worker complaint in this parish," he replies. No, he concedes, he has never informed workers about their right to submit grievances. (The nature of the USDA-mandated grievance procedures leads one to wonder what difference it would make. Under these procedures a farm worker who believes that he has not been paid in accordance with Sugar Act requirements may file a complaint in the ASCS parish office. The parish committee—which by law includes *only* growers— "shall arrange for such investigation as it deems necessary" and make a recommendation. Appeal from this recommendation lies with the ASCS state committee—likewise limited by law to growers and by tradition to the larger growers. If the farm-worker is tenacious enough to appeal a second time, his complaint may finally reach a nongrower, a deputy administrator of ASCS in Washington.)

No notice of new wage rates made effective several weeks earlier is posted in the office. Do the workers know about it? "I mailed information on the new rates to the growers. They'll tell the workers, I guess." . . . . The grower, the sugar worker, and USDA—these disparate forces constitute the three polar points in the constellation of local sugarcane politics. It is a closed and stable structure—one that has proved profitable, durable, and remarkably resistant to change. "It's been going on for one hundred and fifty years," says one resident of Franklin. "Only today it's legal."

If the past is any guide to the future, the cane workers will escape this system, not by changing it, but by leaving it for New Orleans, Chicago, or New York. But this is possible only for the young. For the many thousands left behind, hope for a better life in the fields will depend wholly on outside intervention.

COLA AND NOTHING ELSE*

[Author Coles introduces his subject:] *There is in my experience no better*

---

*Adapted from Robert Coles, *Still Hungry in America* (New York: World Publishing Co., 1969), pp. 42–47, 85–86, 88, 98.

way to comprehend the way millions of poor Americans live than to get them talking about water and cola. Their most devastating problems come to light as they talk, problems that have to do with poor sanitation, disease, hunger, and perhaps most awful of all, the twin sense of loneliness and lowliness. Here, from my tapes, speak white men and black men, white mothers and black mothers. Americans all, they share a common fate:

Yes, a Coke costs. But everything costs and even if you don't have money, you have to pay. You get the money somehow, or mostly you just do work for somebody, and he pays for your Cokes and your flour, if you know what I mean. Me, I work in the house, and the boss man, he don't give me much money, but he helps us out, yes he does, with the food. He tells the grocer to give us some things, and he does, and he don't never bill us, no sir.

* * *

Around here, you have to be careful. You go get water, and it turns out contaminated. That's right. I tell my wife to give the kids water after she's boiled it, and in between to use a Coke or like that. A lot more people would be dead if we had to depend on river and spring water. The coal, the acid from strip-mining, it's getting into all our water.

* * *

Yes, the nurse told me that milk is best, way better than Coca-Cola. I said if she thought so, maybe she could come around here with a gallon or two, every day, and then I'd use it for sure. She said we should be smart, and sacrifice, and buy milk when we can, with the money we spend on Cokes. Then what do we do in between, I asked her. What do we do while we're saving up money to buy milk—tell our kids to be patient, and wait until we've got something for them to drink, maybe in another few days? Maybe those coal companies could give each one of us a gallon of milk every week; they'd still be making a fortune on what they take out of this here land. Even if I had the money to get a cow, and get milk from her, I couldn't let her around here to graze. She'd get poisoned by what they've done to our land; it's covered with slime, with the landslides those machines have caused. I hope the people who use our coal know that we don't get a cent out of it and can't afford milk, no, and our county, it's being torn into bits by what they do.

* * *

No, I don't think the Cokes hurt them. I think they feel better with a Coke. They have the bottle to hold, and it keeps them out of mischief, and they're glad to have something of their own. I'll tell you. My little boy, he got himself attached to an orange-pop bottle. It was the first time he ever had orange-pop—no, he's never had orange juice—and he liked it so much that he kept asking me for more, more, more. I said there wasn't any more, not for now. Well, you know, he wasn't really asking, I mean speaking. He was too young. He just grabbed and grabbed, and I thought, oh my, he really does like the orange flavor, and we'll have to try to get some more. My sister is up in Chicago, you know. And she works in a factory there, and she eats real oranges, and she says she can keep a bowl of fruit around, and why don't I come up there. But she wrote it was bitter cold there, and besides she don't be with her kids at all; it's my aunt who's there and takes care of them, so she can work, and they lives all in that two rooms they've got, and nowhere for the kids to go, or anywhere else. So it's bad all over, that's what I believe. The man at the store said that sure you might get better food up there, but with the sun and all down here, you don't need so much. No, I don't believe he was fooling me. He seemed to mean it; though I admit I wondered myself how the kids could get by on the sun and as much food as *he'd* let me have from his store. So, thank God for the commodities the government gives us.

. . . .

[The author continues:]
Almost every child we saw was in a state of negative nitrogen balance; that is, a marked inadequacy of diet has led the body to consume its own protein tissue. What we saw clinically—the result of this condition of chronic hunger and malnutrition—was as follows: wasting of muscles; enlarged hearts; edematous legs and in some cases the presence of abdominal edema (so-called swollen or bloated belly); spontaneous bleeding of the mouth or nose or evidence of internal hemorrhage; osteoporosis—a weakening of bone structure—and, as a consequence, fractures unrelated to injury or accident; and again and again, fatigue, exhaustion, weakness.

These children would need blood transfusions before any corrective surgery could be done—and we found in child after child (and in adults, too) the need for surgery: hernias; poorly healed fractures; rheumatic and congenital heart disease with attendant murmurs, difficult breathing, and chest pain; evidence of gastrointestinal bleeding or partial obstruction; severe, suppurating ear infections; congenital or developmental eye disease in bad need of correction.

The teeth of practically every child we saw—and of their parents, too—were in awful repair—eaten up by cavities and often poorly developed. Their gums showed how severely anemic these children are; and the gums were also infected and foul-smelling.

Many of these children (and again their parents) were suffering from degenerative joint diseases. Injuries had not been treated when they occurred. Bleeding had taken place, with subsequent infections. Now, at seven or eight, a child's knee joint or elbow joints might show the "range of action" that one finds in a man of seventy who suffers from crippling arthritis.

In child after child we tested for peripheral neuritis—and found it, secondary to untreated injuries, infections, and food deficiencies. These children could not feel normally—feel pressure or heat or cold or applied pain the way the normal person does. What they do feel is the sensory pain that goes with disease; pricking, burning, flashes of sharp pain, or a "deep pain" as one child put it.

The children were plagued with cold and fevers—in Mississippi, in late May—and with sore throats. They had enlarged glands throughout the body, secondary to the *several* infections they *chronically* suffer. Some of them showed jaundice in their eyes, which meant that liver damage was likely, or that hemolysis secondary to bacterial invasion had occurred.

What particularly saddened and appalled us were the developmental anomalies and diseases that we know once were easily correctable, but now are hopelessly consolidated. Bones, eyes, vital organs that should long ago have been evaluated and treated are now all beyond medical assistance, even if it were suddenly—*incredibly* is the word the people themselves *feel* rather than use—available. In some cases we saw children clearly stunted, smaller than their age would indicate, drowsy and irritable.

In sum, children living under unsanitary conditions without proper food, and with a limited intake of improper food, without access to doctors or dentists, under crowded conditions in flimsy shacks pay the price in a plethora of symptoms, diseases, aches, and pain. No wonder that in Mississippi (whose Negros comprise 42 percent of the state's population) the infant mortality rate among Negroes is over twice that of whites; and while the white infant mortality rate is dropping, the rate for Negroes is rising.

Perhaps more valuable and instructive were the comments of five Mississippi doctors who were asked by the state's governor, Paul B. Johnson, to visit the same counties we visited—"in response to certain charges of starvation and conspiracy in the state of Mississippi." Many people in the state, not only doctors and politicians, felt that once again "outsiders" had come upon the Delta and the South to tranish and malign its "traditions," to single out unfairly this area, that region—when all over the country certain people have trouble finding work, a decent place to live, and even enough food to appease their hunger, their children's hunger. Let our own doctors go see what really exists, Mississippi's governor said—and by prompting such a step he provided the kind of leadership the nation certainly craves and doesn't always find. Here are some observations from the medical report submitted to Governor Johnson, and then to the United States Senate:

The situations encountered were indeed primitive. In one locality eight families were found to share one faucet and one privy. The mother of one of these families stated that she obtained surplus commodity food and that her welfare check was seventy-one dollars per month. She said she had been unable to get work for some time. Her monthly rent is fifteen dollars. She has no children in either of the Head Start programs, but her house does have electricity and a new refrigerator. Sanitation in the area was not acceptable by modern standards. Six of her eight children were seen. Several of them had infected lesions and all appeared to have some degree of anemia, but none was on the verge of starvation.

At one house visited, there was one outdoor privy serving "nine or ten families." Not far away was a single water faucet which constituted the only water supply for the same people. Garbage and refuse were strewn about the premises and the smell of human excrement was unmistakable. . . .

Hospital facilities for indigent patients are virtually nonexistent. . . .

[One boy commented to Coles:]

Things as they are around here—well, they're not too good. That's what my momma says to me. They're not too good. She says someday they might get better. She says they would, they'd get better if we went up there to Chicago. She and my daddy, all the time they say no, it's bad there too, or yes, we're going tomorrow, or maybe next week. Then something comes up, and we never seem to leave; we never get there, to Chicago; or anywhere that I can see; just here; and once a month into the town, to get food for to eat for the month; and to church, we go every Sunday there;

and that's all. Or, I forgot school. Some days I'll go, and some days not. The teachers want you all dressed up, and they tell me it's not only that I haven't got the right clothes, it's that I have this bad thing on my head—it's a rash, and it may be something catching, she says, "For all I know it may be catching," that's what she said, yes sir. So if it gets better for a while—yes sir, it does—I'll try me the school. I'll wear my brother's shoes. They're mine, too; but he says they're his because he's the older one. And I'll go. Once I was there all week.

HARVESTING DESPAIR*

... The migrant farm workers I knew best harvest the fields in the Atlantic Coast states. They are for the most part native-born Negroes from the Deep South—Florida, Georgia, Alabama, the Carolinas, and some from Mississippi and Texas. But I also traveled and worked with off-shore Puerto Ricans, West Indians, Mexicans, Bahamians, and a scattering of Anglo-American whites. They begin their seasonal journeys in late January or early February with south Florida citrus crops, then move from field to field, through tomatoes and potatoes in Florida; corn, snap beans, and cucumbers in the Carolinas; berries and fruits in Virginia and Maryland; then perhaps vegetable crops again in Delaware, New Jersey, and New York. Many follow the crops into northern New England and Canada, where, in late November and early December, they help bring in another potato harvest.

When the last of these crops have been harvested, it is back again to the Deep South where the cycle starts over again. All of these workers, no matter what their origin, no matter what the color of their skin, have one thing in common: they are a miserable, forgotten lot. Few really care about them; most would prefer to ignore them.

Once the crops are in and packaged in baskets, or bound up in bags, or bottled and canned at the processors', there is no further need for the hand harvester and the women and children he brought along with him on the bus or truck or broken-down automobile that labored up the road. He is unwanted in the farm community which purchased his labor so cheaply; he is a misfit, often a burden on the urban center nearby. He is inarticulate, the possessor of few skills, disorganized, rootless; and because of his migrancy and the accident of his birth as a Negro, a Puerto Rican, a Mexican or West Indian, he is a minority within a minority....

*Adapted from Dale Wright, *They Harvest Despair*: The Migrant Farm *Worker* (Boston: Beacon Press, 1965), Preface, 8-13, 49, 52-53, 99-101.

Red was a seasonal farm worker. I had met him just after dawn that morning at the head of a long row of tomatoes in a field just outside Homestead, Florida—a busy, Dade County back-country village some thirty-five miles southwest of Miami. From Homestead and the surrounding villages and vegetable fields which line both sides of the country roads come the dining-room-table supplies for—well, everywhere.

I had arrived there in mid-April about the time the last wave of the early spring migrant tide was ebbing northward, "up the road, on the season." And I moved along with the migrant farm-labor army of stoop workers as they grubbed and lifted and sweated from the rich earth a large portion of the nation's—indeed, of the world's—harvest.

I got to know the tall, angular man with the big hands as well as one man can hope to know another in a few brief hot spring days. The story of his life, and that of his wife and small children, was one of misery and squalor; of hunger and hardship; of disinterest and despair; of days and weeks of hard labor under a punishing sun, for shamefully low wages. Indeed, the tragic chronicle of Red's forty-odd years of occupying so transiently each tiny successive fragment of somebody else's land, where he stood, or labored, or rested through all the dreary days of his life, appalled me, and I had thought myself rather well insulated against shock.

There were times in my all-too-short association with this particular harvester when I was aware of my intrusion into his life; my intimate, sometimes impertinent questions, were invasions of that privacy which ought to be sanctified, inviolate for every human being, not the least of all for Red. He had benefited so little from life; there was no reason to think, to dream, that his share of its rewards would ever be greater. Yet, there was within me the omnipresent urge—call it a mission if you like—to search out a particular kind of truth; a purpose which transcended the irreverence of trying to pry into another man's soul.

. . . .

I visited with him and his woman and their brood of five barefoot, half-naked little children in the tin-and-tarpaper shanty that somebody else owned near Goulds, another Florida back-country farm village along the highway up the road on the way to Miami. And I found this migrant farm family carbon-copied with unhappy frequency many times over during the spring and summer and early fall of a long, close, painstaking look at the itinerant harvester along the Atlantic Seaboard. What I found in thousands of miles of travel, in many weeks of living and working and sleeping and, not infrequently, suffering with the gatherers of crops made me angry and sick. Just minutes away from the glittering, good-timing wealth of Miami

Beach—and, later, just commuter-train distance away from the neon-lit vulgarity of Manhattan's Times Square—I saw the horrifying ugliness of poverty amid plenty. I saw Red and folks like him cheated out of their paltry wages for labor honestly done. I saw men and women and children crudely exploited by growers whose fields they harvested, and by migrant labor-crew leaders who brought them into those fields. I found that slavery had not been abolished. One hundred years after Abraham Lincoln had proclaimed emancipation in one of the great documents of our time there had not been deliverance. The American Promise remained woefully unfulfilled.

I rebelled at what I saw and experienced in the fields and farm-labor camps along the East Coast. I was shaken and grieved that the misery of marginal existence continued unrelieved in my lifetime. I was convinced that neither the declaration of War on Poverty—nor all of the other undeclared skirmishes—were likely to emancipate the itinerant gatherers of crops.

Red was one of the foot soldiers in that vast army, yet he was alone. The tall fellow's grave quietude suggested that he was a thoughtful man. He was at the same time a contradiction, displaying a recognizable intelligence, an inherent incisiveness in the face of almost total illiteracy.

"I don't remember," he said, "jus' how far I got in school. It weren't far, though—maybe a couple of grades or so, up in the Carolinas." He paused in mid-row, straddling the plants, hooked his thumbs in his waistband and pondered a moment. Then he observed: "Mus' be a whole lot of people in this country doin' the same kind of work as me. They ain't got no trade or nothin' an' so they got to do what they can. They can't be lawyers or preachers. They can't get out of the fields and into school to learn. So they jus' picks and totes and labors like this, till the bossman tells them to stop."

He unhooked his thumbs from his belt, and waved his hand over the field as he continued, "Maybe if I'd got a chance to stay in that school up in the Carolinas longer, I could have been the bossman of this here field. Then it would be me to tell folks when to start and when to stop and pay them off at the end of the day."

He kicked at an overripe tomato with his army-surplus-store shoes and squinted into the slanting rays of the sun. His spectacles slid down his nose and the rows and the people and the trees in the distance faded out of focus.

"Them children of mine . . . ," he said, pressing the glasses into place again with his forefinger, ". . . look like they got to come into these fields soon as they able, same as I did. Don't look much like they'll get any schoolin' no place. Sure like to see one of them boys be a preacher an' take the Word of the Lord aroun' to folks need religion. Needs a sight more of it myself. Ain't had time enough to stop long enough to git to the Good Book an' learn how to straighten myself out. Ain't no tellin'; one of them chil'ren maybe got enough sense to be a schoolteacher or somethin'. One of my kinfolk's a teacher in Georgia. That woman's got learnin'. She puts on a clean dress everyday and don' have no part of this pickin' an' liftin' on the road, on the season. That's the way to git by. Seems like my woman's all the time pregnant—or gittin' over it."

Twin girls had died early in infancy. They were buried, Red recollected, out back of a labor-camp shanty somewhere up the road—in one of the Carolinas. It was a source of the deepest regret to him that the course of his travels had not taken him back to the Carolina bean patches and the shanty where the babies had taken ill and died—of malnutrition and the lack of proper medical attention. Red lamented, "They passed away in the night from c'nsumption, long before they was old enough to know what it was all about. One went on Sunday, when we wasn't workin' in the fields; the other one died the next Wednesday—just like that. They was cryin' and squawlin' for their mother's breast one minute; then the next minute they was gone."

The lighting of a cigarette from a wrinkled, sweat-sodden packet did not interrupt Red's rare, fleeting moment of soul-baring. He continued: "The undertaker and the doctor said they got it from me. I been had it a long time. Ain' got no money for medicine or hospitals. Got all them chil'ren wants to eat. The old woman, she's porely, too, so I keeps on pickin' 'matoes—or whatever other kind of work they is to be done. Maybe this time, when the season is down, I'll git to a clinic someplace . . . maybe git me some pills. That's what I needs . . . some of them little pills and a bottle of cough syrup. That ought to stop this coughin' an' this pain in my chest. Sometimes I feels awful bad from the pain. Can't git my breath . . ."

He drew deeply from the cigarette, inhaled, coughed up a ragged cloud. "I hurts somethin' fierce here inside," he said. He crossed his arms tightly over the lower part of his chest. The misery that lived inside the tall man was painfully inscribed on his face. "Sometimes I hurts so bad," he said, "I can't hardly work in the fields. But there's them kids, an' my woman, Emily, she can't do nothin' to help. They all got to eat. Who's goin' to feed them . . . ?"

Thoughts of his family were more overpowering than the aches in his chest. "Emily's a good one," he said. "Works when she can. But she can't do much. Got too much misery in her joints. Can't tote a basket when she gits it filled up to the top. They tells me it's arthritis. Comes from sleepin' in a cold shanty one winter up in Virginia. Got stuck there after Christmas one year when she was havin' one of them kids."

There was George, he added, who was seven; and Marie, who was just four. They had developed coughs like his own ". . . back there two, three months ago, when it was cold at night in that shack in Goulds, an' there wasn't nothin' around to make no heat."

He wiped a bare forearm across his mouth and shrugged. "Maybe we'll all git to a clinic someplace and see 'bout some of them little pills. That ought to do it, them little pills.

". . . or maybe not."

Those were some of the grim facts of one migrant farm family's life: of the seven in the Alonzo Fisher family, four—Red himself, his wife, and two of the children—needed immediate, intensive medical care, considerably more than just little white pills from an outpatient clinic. Chances that they would get attention were, indeed, slim. The odds pointed, in fact, to quite the opposite: that Red's condition and that of his wife and children would deteriorate rapidly; that the other three still-unafflicted children might contract the rumbling cough that started down in his guts and came up in mucus flecked with blood.

. . . .

Here is another migrant family who, needing work, traveled with great difficulty to a place where they'd been told "They're hiring." They weren't.—Ed.

Robert Andrew Robinson unburdened himself of his family's belongings—the bedspread bundle of dirty laundry and the cardboard beer carton—and dumped them into a pile before one of the shanties. He led his wife, Mattie, the sleeping Adolphus in her arms, to a seat on the steps. Virginia Lee tagged along, carrying her rubber doll in one hand and clutching her tattered picture book in the other.

The sun angled obliquely over a corner of the camp clearing. The irrigation pump engine chugged with a mechanical, sometimes irregular tempo, spouting water through a large pipe to foam into a ditch on the way to the corn and tomato plants.

Robert leaned one shoulder against the wall of the cabin, thrust both hands into his pockets and eyed his family.

"Mattie," he said, "the bossman told us there ain't nothin' ready to pick here for a while. There ain't no food here neither, an' no stove to cook it on if we had some. Look like we got here too soon." He kicked a miniature furrow in the soft dirt, "We got to get somethin' to eat . . . an' quick!"

Mattie looked first at her husband, then at the baby. "That sure is the truth," she said. "He'll be mighty mean if I have no milk for him."

. . . .

There was no food about the place. The cabins were in no way ready for occupancy. Except for the irrigation pump, there was no water supply; nor were there toilets or other sanitary facilities. The last inhabitants of the camp had left the place in disarray, with miscellaneous debris and litter scattered around the shanties.

Robert dug a two-pound Maxwell House Coffee can ("It's good to the last drop!") out of a mountain of equipment in the rear of one of the crew leader's trucks. He scooped a shallow hole in the dirt with a broken-handled hoe he found under one of the shanties. With brush and leaves and bits of paper, he built a fire in the hole, then placed four discarded vegetable tins at each corner. Over them he laid a rectangular sheet of metal roofing which he had found somewhere in the clearing.

Robert went about his task purposefully, methodically, as though he had a plan. Mattie watched as though she had seen it all done before. I watched with quiet amazement.

Despite all of his shortcomings, Robert was a resourceful man and that quality reinforced my own regard for him.

Dry wood and brush soon blazed under the sheet-metal roofing and Robert walked down the dirt road leaving the fire in his makeshift open-air stove to grow hotter. A few moments later he returned with two cabbages which he had torn from their roots in a nearby field.

He filled the coffee-can cookpot with water from the irrigation pump, then with his pocketknife, cut one of the cabbages into bite-size pieces and dumped them into the can. He placed it carefully on the stove and squatted beside it to wait.

After a time the hot water softened the unsalted cabbage and it was ready, as ready as it ever would be—the first meal for the Robinson family since they'd departed Homestead many hours—and more than three hundred miles—earlier.

Robert lifted the infant from his mother's arms to give her the first turn at the cookpot. With the pocketknife he had handed her she speared a few chunks of cabbage and put them into her mouth. She rolled them around for a moment, then began chewing slowly, reluctantly, hesitantly. At last she gave the pocketknife back to her husband.

Mattie Robinson had been weary when she climbed into Rudy Thompson's crew bus in Homestead, but now I saw a human being completely consumed by discouragement. She brushed her knotted, early-gray hair back with her hands as she fought with all the courage she could muster to hold back the tears. She locked her fingers tightly behind her back and looked away from her husband.

She pondered her plight: a long trip to nowhere, to poverty and hunger amid plenty. It was the way it had been before; it was the way it was now; it was the way it would be tomorrow.

This was the way of a migrant farm family.

At last the woman wept silently. Great tears welled up in her eyes, rolled heavily down both dark cheeks, and collected in pools in the wrinkles at the sides of her mouth. When the baby began to cry, she bent to take him from his father, and the tears fell onto the hot sheet-metal cookstove he had built.

Mattie didn't notice where her tears fell; she didn't hear them sizzle and dance and sputter away. She still wept silently, and a shudder began at the top of her head and fell like a dark shroud down over the length of her tired, sagging body.

Robert was unaware of his wife's fleeting confrontation with despair. He had been busy spearing pieces of boiled cabbage with his right hand while holding his son in his left arm.

. . . .

And still another family—Just to the left of the entrance way leading to the camp was the community water pump. It served all of the fifty to sixty tenants who lived there. The pump was mounted on a concrete slab and before it produced more than a trickle of water it had to be hand-cranked vigorously for three or four minutes. Then the water came in a gush and splashed over a pail provided to catch the drippings, and into pools around the slab.

A little farther along the wide roadway, to the right, was a long one-story building; it, too, was covered with simulated red-brick shingles. It was the only multiple dwelling in the camp. There were three adjoining apartments under the same roof, each with its own entrance.

A screen door, fallen away from one of the entrances, leaned against the front of the house. Three brick chimneys, one for a cookstove in each unit, rose skyward from the top of the building. Smoke from wood stoves—in midsummer—vanished into the breeze from two of the chimneys.

Mrs. Isabelle Johnson, the mother of three, occupied the two-room unit in the center of the long building.

She shooed the flies away from an infant asleep in a cot and declared, "That child ain't got a chance. His daddy and me want to give him the best, but we can't do no better than this."

Mrs. Johnson had been a tenant at the camp for three years. She had moved there with her husband on her first visit to central New Jersey on the season.

"Well, it was like this," she explained. "My husband got laid off from his job at that sawmill near Essex, Virginia. There was this busload of people going through, so we got on. We heard all the talk about a lot of work in the fields in New Jersey at good wages. We didn't have nothing to lose, so we got on and came here.

"The first year wasn't so bad," the young mother related, "And we moved into this place kind of temporary. Me and my husband both worked in the tomato fields. Then when potatoes were ready, we picked up behind the digging machine. We even bought a secondhand car and George drove it back and forth to the different jobs he found. But I started having babies one right after the other and now we can't get out of this place. Can't find no landlords that take farm people with children, so we got to stay here."

Mrs. Johnson and her husband, George, paid $15 weekly rent for the two rooms they lived in. There was no bath, no indoor plumbing, and no sanitary facilities—only the community outhouse to the rear, which they shared with the rest of the tenants. The only time they knew that a landlord existed was when he sent a rent collector around on Saturday morning. The owner rarely appeared. The couple wanted desperately to return to Virginia with their children, where they would be with the rest of their families and friends, but because of the weekly rent, expenses for food and medicine and other necessities, they were unable to save enough for the trip.

"We're stranded here in this awful place," Mrs. Johnson lamented, "and there just ain't a thing we can do."

. . . .

BIG-CITY HILLBILLIES*

"You mean you want to take a look at a hillbilly!"

Homer Burleigh, thirty-three, from Anniston, Alabama, hefty, freckle-faced and sandy-haired, dressed in T-shirt, dark slacks, loafers and for the moment immobile with resentment, blocked the doorway to his flat. Like 20,000 other Southern whites living in the two and one-half square miles

*Adapted from Ben H. Bagdikian, *In the Midst of Plenty*, The Poor *in America* (Boston: Beacon Press, 1964), pp. 29–30, 36–40.

of Chicago's Uptown, he had his pride, his problems, and an innate suspicion of the Eastern city slicker.

Homer Burleigh finds it hard to stay angry for long and he led the way inside. Four of his five children, ages two, three, five, and seven (a ten-year-old boy was still in school), ran about in bare feet, dressed only in underpants. Mrs. Burleigh, a wan, hard, very pregnant woman, also was barefooted. The five-year-old boy chanted to the visitor, "You got on a necktie. You got on a necktie."

He walked into a small kitchen, sat down, rubbed a large hand over his face and sighed. He was in trouble and he knew it and he was, after the first resentment, anxious to talk about it. His trouble was not just the meagerness whose clues lay about: the drab four rooms, a living room with two pieces of furniture—television set and, opposite, old sofa; two bedrooms with four beds for seven people; the "extra room," a horrid chamber painted throughout—ceiling, walls, closet, doors—in a mottled grey and black; and a back room with a good kitchen table and four chairs, refrigerator, and kitchenette. Homer Burleigh was penniless, about to be evicted, maybe even jailed. Much of this was his own fault, the panicked response to crises. But basically he was living through the recurring ritual of the poor in which they are reminded that theirs are fragile, leaky vessels in the sea of life, barely able to keep afloat with the best of luck and in danger of sinking with the slightest storm. Homer Burleigh made mistakes when the margin of safety with which he had to live permitted no mistakes whatever.

On one side there was the Burleigh family, which had not done so badly. A complete country boy who hadn't finished the fourth grade had gone to the city and from nothing made himself a skilled industrial worker with respectable wages. On the other side was the turbulent social sea from which they tried constantly to escape—the Uptown world of Chicago, reminder of the probability of poverty. This was the urban world of the Southern white and the refugee from Appalachia.

. . . .

Neither one of them can remember just when or how the change occurred but sometime between that first week seven years before and the day Homer sat at the kitchen table and told about it, their lives took a downturn. For one thing, they had four children, which with Millicent's son, made a household of seven. Expenses began to climb, in lurches with each child. They needed a bigger apartment than the neat three-room flat they had the first year and this meant more furniture. As their needs went up for more bedrooms, they were pushed into a category of apartment that is in short supply, which meant that they began drifting downward in quality of neighborhood and of building. Medical bills, which they never had considered a normal running expense, somehow became a constant drain, at first just for the deliveries and then for baby illnesses.

There was no single period when these problems emerged into their consciousness. But it bore down on them in the late 1950s when business took a turn for the worse. Homer felt it in the machine shop where he worked.

The men were cut back on hours a week, Homer being among the first to suffer because it was a relatively small shop with men of more seniority in it. When he was cut back to three days a week he couldn't pay for his rent and food and everlasting car payments.

So despite the urging of his boss to stay on a little longer until business improved, Homer struck out for another job that would pay a full week's work. He found one at once. Again he did well because he is a hard worker and an engaging fellow with initiative and a certain brassy friendliness. But when the new shop cut down on the workweek, Homer was among the first to feel the reduction because he was the most recently hired. He left for another shop to get a full week's work. In each place his lack of seniority made him the first hit by reduced time. A home economist could have told Homer that he simply didn't earn enough money to support a family of seven properly and an ingenious one might even have drawn a curve to show precisely when the Burleigh fertility outran the Burleigh income. All Homer knew was that no matter what he did, he didn't have enough money. Yet he was trying as hard as ever.

He was working in a machine shop making $85 a week, when the sores began. These were strange running sores, first under his arm and then in his groin. Even before this he knew he was facing a financial crisis of some sort. His take-home pay was about $300 a month. Rent took $110 of this. The car, by now a 1954 Pontiac, took $60 a month. This left $130 for everything else, which for a family of seven is not enough for the most economical complete diet. Yet he also had to extract from this amount clothes, gasoline and oil, medical care.

He shifted to a plastic molding plant where, for a time, the take-home pay was higher, but it, too, sagged down to about $300 a month. He began falling behind on his car payments. Then he claims he lost his car-payment booklet with his receipts, showing he had paid $400 of the total of $1200, and when the finance company resissued a new book it showed him owing the full $1200. The finance company threatened to attach his pay. His sores gave him more and more trouble and got infected from the dust in the plastic factory. A doctor told him he'd have to stop that kind of work. At this point he committed folly. He applied for a new Social Security number under which to get his pay, thus, he thought, escaping the clutches of the finance company. He says the finance company then seized the car on the street but told Homer he still owed them $1200.

It is difficult to be sure what did happen. Homer is a hard worker but he is not a creature of cold rationality. He is not too hard on himself in the car episode and he may have been all wrong. But car dealers and finance companies have perpetrated documented frauds on the innocent immigrants and on some not so innocent. Welfare workers, for example, confirmed the case of a Mexican-American from Texas who bought a six-year-old car that had a true value of about $400. The dealer charged him $800 for it, plus a flat $240 carrying charge, plus ordinary finance company interest on the whole amount, including the carrying charge and $120 insurance that they took out for him. He had made four monthly payments of $75 each and had paid $200 for a set of four new tires when he had an accident, rolled over, and ruined another car. He was in the hospital when he learned that the finance company had claimed the wreck, declared it a total loss (although the new tires presumably were usable), and threatened court action to recover all the money the man allegedly owed. At the same time lawyers for the man whose car the Mexican-American had ruined, brought suit because the $120 for insurance was for collision only, not for liability. The finance company protected their interest in the car but not the owner's.

Homer Burleigh, car gone, job almost gone, finally turned to welfare, for the first time after seven years in the city. The welfare worker told him it would be two weeks before the payments would start, so Homer worked out the two weeks. His welfare came to $261 a month and this would not pay the rent and food for them all, so from time to time toward the end of the month, Millicent would go to a nearby Presbyterian Church for free food.

The wheels of bureaucracy turned. Six months after the welfare payments started Homer was notified that he would lose his payments and would be charged with fraud. He thought they had caught up with his new Social Security number. But they had not. He was charged with having received unreported pay while getting welfare. He had. It was the pay for the last two weeks of work, after he had applied for aid to dependent children but before the payments began. The day he talked at the kitchen table, the last of the final welfare payment had been spent and in four days he was to be evicted from his flat for non-payment of rent.

"If the arm continues this way, and if they don't give me assistance, I'm going to have to put the kids in a home." His eyes filled. "These kids are young. They don't know all these problems. But that older boy, he's pretty bright. You can't keep things from him forever. Anyway, we haven't been able to pay the rent and Monday is the end. When they move us onto the sidewalk, the kids will know, all right."

And so the lines of failure seemed to converge for Homer Burleigh: a motherless home full of contention, almost no formal education, an impoverished landscape to grow in with no hope for a young man, a pattern of wandering to where there was money without making a permanent commitment, a drifting of life without heed for the consequences of more children. But he was not an evil man, nor a lazy one. His was simply the fragile vessel of endemic poverty, never strong enough to withstand a prolonged storm. And his children seemed doomed to go forth in a similarly brittle craft.

. . . .

STRANGERS AND PILGRIMS*

When Carl Miller and Eileen Nelson exchanged marriage vows in a Methodist parsonage on Independence Day 1945, they made a covenant with poverty.

Carl, 37, was working as a maintenance man in a war plant near Flushing in New York City. Eileen, 30, worked in a factory that turned out bullets. Together they brought home $130 a week, a good income even during the war. Like typical newlyweds, they were optimistic about the future and thought that their marital union gave evidence of fine and prosperous years ahead.

Neither of them knew that never again would they come within striking distance of their wartime wages. Neither realized that in a short time they would be standing on the sidelines as the prosperity of the postwar world passed them by. They could not guess that they would become an unwilling part of the massive, impersonal problem of poverty in America.

. . . .

The question that insists on intruding is "Why?" Why were the Millers swallowed up by poverty? Why were they unable to claim a decent share in the expanding wealth of the richest nation on earth? The usual answers testify falsely and bewitch us with a sense of moral aloofness that evades the real problem of poverty in America today. Contrary to widely accepted

*Adapted from Arthur R. Simon, *Faces of Poverty* (St. Louis: Concordia Publishing House, 1966), pp. 3, 6-16, 21.

myths about poor people the Millers were not shiftless, dishonest, or immoral. They did not even carry the stigma of color. They had no desire to freeload on the public. They wanted to work. Yet they were drawn into poverty much like a drowning man is drawn into the vortex of a whirlpool.

. . . .

"Carl and I met in the Greyhound bus terminal lunch counter in Flushing, next to my father's real estate office. He was always nice to me, never fresh. I never had to be afraid. He was kindly and I could tell he really cared. We both had suffered, and we understood each other."

In August 1945, a month after the Millers were married, Japan surrendered, and wartime contracts were canceled. Both Millers found themselves out of work.

Mr. Miller got employment as a dishwasher and pot-cleaner in Flushing at $36 a week—quite a letdown. During the next half year he had two other dishwashing and mopping jobs. He would quit and try to find better employment, but without success, until he was down to working in a spaghetti plant for $20 a week.

During these months living accommodations were a problem. The Millers began their married life in an attic. Then they were able to secure two furnished rooms for $21 a week, but the expense made it unbearable—especially when Mr. Miller was earning $20 a week in the spaghetti plant.

"We saw an ad in a newspaper about the Sanford Towers. It was a big apartment house on Union Street. Carl worked there as a porter and fireman for about seven months. We got two rooms and a bath in the basement, plus $50 every two weeks. I was carrying Eric and going around in men's trousers helping Carl. The people in the house were friendly to us and gave us some food and baby clothes. We liked it there, but the superintendent began pestering me, so we decided to move," Mrs. Miller said.

The Millers found themselves caught in a web of circumstances they could not understand or control. They wanted desperately to improve themselves, but after the war it was not easy for a man with a glass eye and no skills. They felt rootless and frustrated and sometimes thought that any change would be a chance to get ahead.

After a couple of unsatisfactory dishwashing jobs, Mr. Miller got a job at a restaurant as a busboy and dishwasher at $30 a week, working nights. The job lasted a year. "I was laid off because all the employees had to take a physical exam, and I had varicose veins. They didn't bother me then though."

The Millers were able to manage on $30 a week, although they were paying $15 a week rent. "We lived on 'Bum's Hill.' That was my name for it, " she said. "We called it 'Bum's Hill' because it had nothing but that kind of people—the worst women and the worst men. We couldn't wait to get out." But Mrs. Miller had only two months to go with Eric, so they waited.

Eric was born in Aunt Esther's house in Queens Village July 7, 1946. The plan was to have the baby at Aunt Esther's home with a doctor in attendance. Eric arrived before the doctor did.

"The doctor just checked me and gave me some sleeping pills, but I threw them away. When Carl came there was still the afterbirth, and he cleaned it all up. It didn't faze him a bit. I always felt better when he was near.

"We moved from 'Bum's Hill' and for the next six months lived in the cellar of my father's real estate office. Dad had put some old furniture there after my mother's death, and so we fixed up the cellar to live in. There were no windows, but the rooms were big," Mrs. Miller recalls.

"Finally we got a place on Union Street, three rooms in an old building. The rent was $40 a month. We lived there 4½ years."

Shortly after they moved to Union Street, Mr. Miller was able to find better employment. He secured work at a restaurant on Manhattan's west side as a dishwasher and cleanup man for $45 a week. Situated above it was a machine shop.

"After two months I got a job in the machine shop for $55 a week sweeping floors and running envelopes through a machine. I had that job for nearly five years. Then I had to leave," Mr. Miller says. "They wanted me to stay. I was worried about getting another job, so I stayed as long as I could; but my veins were popping out, and my legs swelled up so bad I had to quit."

About two years before Mr. Miller quit his job at the machine shop the Millers moved from their home in Flushing to the west side of Manhattan. In doing so they were opting for an oppressive, nomadic style of life that would saddle them with incredible difficulties. They had no way of knowing this, however. They moved for several reasons. First of all, word got around that the buildings in their area were going to be torn down because they were dilapidated, and the Millers had no reason to expect that the new buildings would be erected for their income level. A more pressing reason, however, was the same thing that draws most people into the heart of the city—work. They wanted to get closer to Carl's machine shop. "The job wore me out, and the long trip home standing on a crowded train didn't do me any good. I hoped that by moving close to the machine shop I could keep on working there." That hope turned out to be short-lived. This was in 1951, and Eric was five years old.

The Millers left their apartment with whatever possessions they could carry, took the subway to Manhattan, and got a newspaper to see what was advertised. They went to a hotel on West 49th Street and saw a room for $23 a week. The room looked so bad that they walked out. The Millers didn't know what to do next, so they asked a taxicab driver. He took them to a place on 8th Avenue and 47th. They were there about four months.

Mr. Miller tells it this way: "The manager was nice. He would give us the shirt off his back. But he had a bum crowd. Transient men and women. Not Bowery bums, but people who didn't live like we do. We had one room and a bath for $21 a week, but it was a terrible room, and we had to eat out."

The hotel "office" is above a corner bar. The stairs are squeaky, the halls are unbelievably narrow. The wood and furnishings seem to exude 19th-century air. The rooms are tiny, and toilet facilities shared. There are dozens of small, cheap hotels like this west of Times Square in the vicinity of the machine shop where Carl worked, and the Millers were due to get acquainted with many of them in short order.

For the next five months they tried a succession of such hotels, but always with the same frustration. "We wanted to settle down and live like ordinary folks, but to get an apartment you need to pay a month's rent and a month's security. We never had enough money for that, and we didn't want to beg from anybody. We wanted to make it on our own. We had a little pride," Mr. Miller said.

The Marie Antoinette on West 63d Street became an oasis for a year. There they had two furnished rooms and a bath for $25 a week—nearly half of Carl's salary. The contrast between this and the places they had been staying made them happy. "There were wonderful people there. It was one of the nicest hotels in New York. Carl was working, and I could keep my head up," Mrs. Miller recalls. They were stalling off the inevitable, however. Mr. Miller's feet and legs got so bad he had to quit his job at the machine shop. Since he was unemployed, there was no way for them to pay the rent, and the hotel manager advised them to go on welfare. That was in 1953.

"We would have none of it," she insisted. "Instead, we found a hotel on Ninth Avenue near Times Square that offered a room for $14 a week. Carl was getting an unemployment check of $45 a week. It was a wretched place."

In the meantime Mr. Miller got in touch with Jimmy Phillips, a man for whom he had worked as a watchman four years before his marriage. Phillips was then supervisor of a large warehouse building on 43d Street between 11th and 12th Avenues. He knew and respected Carl and got him started on a 2-days-a-week job, and gradually over a period of four months worked it up to a regular 5-days-a-week job. In the meantime the Millers made it by squeezing pennies and eating their main meal each day at a Salvation Army center. The meals cost 20 cents apiece. Even so, once they were so broke that they left the hotel and slept for a few nights on some potato sacks in the loft of the building where Carl worked. Phillips gave the Millers some money for food over the weekend until their check came.

"We had a roof over our heads, we had a bite to eat, and somebody cared," said Mrs. Miller, laughing. " 'Well, we're all together,' Carl would say. He always felt that way. As long as we were together that was the most important thing. So I didn't mind sleeping on burlap bags or eating hamburgers. But I couldn't do it with any other kind of man."

Before long Mr. Miller was working a 7-day week for Phillips and making $87 take-home pay. He was a watchman, but did odd jobs as well. With this income they were able to break the cycle of cheap hotels and get a furnished apartment on West 45th Street in Hildona Court, where they lived for four years. Two rooms and a bath cost them $28 a week. Why didn't they try to get a normal, unfurnished apartment? "We should have, but we just couldn't save money," Mrs. Miller explained. "It would mean going back to the cheap hotels for a while, and I was very nervous. I just couldn't take it anymore. I always had to worry about the people in those hotels, and sometimes tell somebody off. I had to have a Bible in one hand and a boxing glove on the other." Emotionally weary, the Millers found temporary refuge from the world in their new quarters.

On July 18, 1957, about three years after the Millers came to Hildona Court, Susan was born at the Polyclinic Hospital. To finance the new arrival, the Millers took out a $300 loan from a finance company at an inflated rate of interest.

Eric was eight years old when the Millers moved into Hildona Court. Since they were moving around so much, or expecting to move, Eric's mother taught him to read a little and to count, but he had never gone to school. In the lobby of the hotel they met Mrs. Price, a retired school-teacher who was disabled. She asked if she could teach Eric privately, so for more than three years he had a private tutor in Mrs. Price. Eric liked her and ran errands for her in exchange. Even after she was bedridden she continued to teach Eric.

In 1959 the Millers received another jolt. United Parcel purchased the property of the block between 11th and 12th Avenues where Carl worked. Less than two years after Susan was born, wreckers came and demolished the buildings and, along with the buildings, Carl's job.

"Jimmy Phillips wanted to help us," said Mr. Miller, "so he talked to the foreman of Associated Wreckers and told them not to hire a watchman because I was a good one. For 10 weeks, while the wreckers were working,

I stayed on at the same pay. When the building was level, I talked to the foreman about getting a job, but there were no openings. I tried over and over to get a job as a watchman, but nobody would hire me."

Mrs. Price wanted them to contact Mrs. Miller's brother, who was managing a nursing home in Florida. She refused, so Mrs. Price phoned him on her own. "Are you going to send money?" she asked. He sent them $20 with a letter in which he wrote, "God helps those who help themselves." Mrs. Miller said she wasn't angry but felt sorry that her own brother didn't understand. "Sometimes you can't help yourself," she wrote him. She felt lost.

— Mrs. Price sent Mr. Miller to "Big Joe," the announcer on "The Happiness Exchange" radio program. "He helped lots of people," said Carl. "We used to listen to his program. People whose homes were burned out or who were in accidents would be on the program, and people would send in money. But he told me our case wasn't bad enough for his program, and he told us to go on welfare." Mrs. Price had been suggesting welfare too, but the Millers had resisted it until now. Welfare stamps you as a failure, and people think you are lazy. But now they had no choice, so the Millers became a welfare case.

"When Carl lost his job he got $45 a week unemployment, so we had already moved into a small hotel again," said Mrs. Miller. "Then a welfare investigator found a place for us in the West Village [lower Manhattan], an apartment facing the waterfront. It was three small rooms on the fourth floor of an old tenement. The rent was $90 a month. From the window you could see the cars going by on the West Side Highway. Welfare helped us out with an $80 check for furniture, but we had to wait for the check. We slept three nights on the floor." Susan was now about 2 and Eric 12.

It was a much better home than the cheap hotels they had been living in. It was also a sign of defeat, a sign that society would help them exist but would not permit them the self-respect of working.

"We moved into the West Village in December of 1960, just a few weeks before Christmas. We were waiting for the next unemployment check, but it didn't come. We began to panic. We went around the corner to Benny's grocery store and explained. He let us take $40 worth of groceries on credit. It was like an old home town in the country there. Benny was good to us. But no check came the next week either, or the next. Marie, the woman behind the counter in Benny's, took up a collection of $17 to help us. Then the police came with a Christmas tree and toys for the children. Some ladies from a church gave us things. It was three weeks before the checks came, all three at once! Nobody knew what we went through." That was two days before Christmas.

Eric began public school when the Millers moved to the West Village.

"It was a bad school, a lot of gangs," Eric explained. "A lot of kids went into the '600 schools' [for problem children] from there. Sometimes the kids would hit the teachers. The teachers had no control. The kids were like a pack of animals. They would throw things at the teachers." Eric remembers that this was especially true in a shop class with one teacher they disliked. "They threw boards and tools at him. They broke vises and windows and pulled down his bulletin boards. They ransacked his closet and sometimes tried to punch him one. He had some court cases going, he told me. He said he had it easier when he taught in Harlem. The school had lots of Negroes and Puerto Ricans, but the white kids were just as bad. Most teachers had better control than he did. Maybe they were afraid and tried not to show it. He was afraid."

Eric didn't like the school, but he did all right in his studies. He learned the hard way that New York City, like other cities, offers the worst schools to the poor.

In September of 1961 the Millers decided to get off welfare. They still had three months to go on unemployment checks, plus $175 returned to them from income tax payments. They hoped that this sum, plus unemployment checks, would give them enough time for Carl to get a job. So they told the investigator, and they were dropped immediately.

It was a mistake. "We knew we couldn't pay $90 a month rent," Mrs. Miller explained, "so we found a place closer by on Bleecker Street, two tiny rooms and a bath for $32 a month. With the $175 we were able, for the first time, to lay out two months' rent.

"It was six flights up. It was the worst building we ever lived in. The day we moved in Eric fell through a broken fire escape to the fifth floor fire escape, and we had to take him to the hospital. There were beatniks and women next door, dope parties, and bums sleeping on the roof. The stairs and the hallways were crumbling, the plaster was falling down.

"By Christmas we were down almost to nothing again, and Carl couldn't find a job. The man who ran a delicatessen across the street gave us some food. The police helped us out too. So did some people from Our Lady of Peace. All along we met people who cared. God cared for us, and He used people to do it. Sometimes we were frightened, but somebody always came along and helped.

"When we were down to nothing we had to go back to welfare. At welfare they told us we should have come sooner, but I can't keep something in my bag and go to welfare."

While the Millers were on welfare, Mr. Miller would report for job openings to the welfare rehabilitation center on the Lower East Side, a short distance across town on lower Manhattan. "Sometimes they called me in every week or every other week, sometimes every day. They'd send me out to apply for jobs all over the city. Sometimes the places would make me take exams. Sometimes I just filled out application forms when I applied. Usually they sent me out for jobs I just couldn't handle. It was crazy. Others would be there to apply for the same job, and the younger men always got 'em."

This proved to be a discouraging ordeal for Mr. Miller. His vision and his varicose veins were against him. So were his age, his lack of education, and his work record. By this time he knew very well that few employers considered him employable, and each trip was a humiliating reminder of that fact. Mr. Miller had often been job hunting on his own, but with constant rejection, and it was also an expensive undertaking because of the travel fare and meals involved.

. . . .

It was while the Millers were on 13th Street that I met them. They lived there for a year and a half. Like most old tenements, it left a lot to be desired. The building was not well kept. It had strong odors and was noisy. "The children on the street broke open mailboxes. Strangers came into the building all the time. Maybe they were peddling dope," Mrs. Miller suggested. "There were a lot of fires in the building, and that scared us. The lady who lived below us with her children sometimes fought with the men who came to see her, and we didn't want to have any of it. Then, when Eric was bitten by termites from the closet and had to go to Bellevue for treatment, we decided we had enough. So for weeks we went up and down the streets looking for a better place. We found a 3-room apartment on 10th Street. Since the rent there was cheaper, welfare was happy to let us move."

Here the Millers have lived since September 1963—on a $100.60 check twice a month, paying $62.00 a month for rent.

That leaves them $138 a month for food and other expenses. Although welfare may give an emergency allotment for clothing or furniture, the Miller's regular checks still amount only to $1.16 a day per person for ordinary living expenses—which is less than most of us spend for food alone.

Since going on welfare early in 1962, Mr. Miller has had two part-time jobs. For six months he worked at the Men's Shelter on East Third Street. The Men's Shelter is a city-owned building near the Bowery which feeds 2,000 to 2,500 derelicts every day, and until recently housed 580 of them each night. It isn't a pretty place. Mr. Miller waited on these pitiable men from behind the counter. "I gave them coffee and soup and sandwiches. I worked five days a week from 1 to 5 p.m. and earned $1.45 a day. They let me keep it and didn't take it off the welfare check. It wasn't much, but it helped. I liked the work. Then a rash broke out on my face and neck, and I was let go. They told me I could have the job back when my face cleared. After a few months, when my face cleared, I went back, but they told me the job had been taken by someone else. I tried three times to get the job back." It still upsets Mr. Miller.

He also worked for one day a week for about half a year in a garment factory, sweeping floors and cleaning toilets. Most of the workers there were women, and they made ladies' and children's pajamas. "It was filthy work. They didn't have the proper equipment, and I had to pick up dirt from the ladies' rooms by hand. I made $9.72 a week, and welfare let me keep it. Then I got those terrible skin sores around my lips. They began to swell, and I was ashamed to let anybody see me. I think I picked up the skin infection at work."

Even part-time work can make a big difference for a family on welfare. It can give a man a sense of being useful.

Ever since Mr. Miller was 14 and had his left eye removed, he wore a glass eye. Although a glass eye doesn't help anyone's vision, it does wonders for one's appearance and morale. Glass eyes are also easy to break when you take them out to wash them. While the Millers were at Bleecker Street, Mr. Miller broke his glass eye. "I contacted our welfare investigator about it, but while I was waiting I got an infection in my eye. I had to go to the Polyclinic Hospital to have a little surgery done, and have it cleaned and drained. My eye socket took about three weeks to heal, and I had to go to the hospital several times a week for treatment. Then the hospital gave me a slip for welfare for a new eye. They told me to get the slip to welfare right away and get the glass eye as fast as possible, because the eye socket was starting to shrink and close up. I sent the slip to them, but didn't hear anything. I started to worry and called them up. They told me I would have to have a special form. I went to the hospital, but there they told me their slip was okay. About a month went by, and by this time the hole had partially closed, and all I could be fitted for was a 'baby eye.'" The eye is, in fact, so small it can hardly be seen. His left eye is sunken, almost completely shut, and constantly drains pus.

This problem is further complicated by the fact that Mr. Miller's vision is failing in his right eye. He has to use a magnifying glass to read. He was fitted with glasses once by welfare, but the frames were purple and looked like ladies' glasses. The time and the red tape involved in getting glasses from welfare is also discouraging. ("What you have to go through to get a pair of glasses!") Besides, Mr. Miller doesn't think the glasses helped him much, so he settles for a magnifying glass.

. . . .

Although he doesn't mention it often—he is the "silent sufferer," as Eric describes him—not being able to work is demoralizing for Mr. Miller and for the family. "I've worked since I was 14," he says. "I wasn't lazy. I got a lot of satisfaction out of my work. It kept my mind occupied and I was able to take care of my family. I always wanted to work. There are so many that want to work and can't get work. There are a lot of people in the same situation, and they can't get work either. I still want to work."

Wanting to work is not enough, however. More than we may care to admit, ours is a society in which the fit survive, and our notion of fitness is often irrational and morally deficient. In many respects the Millers measured up. They were white, and both came from middle-class families. They grew up in a world which expected them to make their way, and they were determined to do just that. But life became something like a whirlpool for them. Poor health and lack of skills sucked them to the bottom. And now the specter of second-generation poverty haunts the Miller children, who are prepared by hurt to face society's increasingly stringent demands.

Even today, though he is 57 years old, unskilled and handicapped, there are socially useful jobs Mr. Miller could do to make himself and his family feel worthwhile, but we do not have the imagination to let him be useful. Instead we label him "unemployable." We pay him to be useless and heap upon his family an indignity which few of us would be able to bear.

In doing so we invest in human misery.

CREDIT TRAPS FOR THE POOR AND INNOCENT*

An Atlanta slum resident borrowed $1,152.72 from a small finance company a while ago and signed a note for $1,632, including interest to be repaid over two years. During this period the finance company persuaded him to accept several additional small cash advances, bringing his total debt to $1,805.85.

But after he had paid off $1,405, he discovered his outstanding balance was $2,040. It was costing him $3,445 to borrow $1,805.85! What happened?

What happened was that this slum resident was a victim of "flipping"—a vicious but entirely legal credit trap commonly found in U.S. ghettos today.

"Flipping" means refinancing a small loan to raise a small amount of extra cash and, in the process, incurring steep finance fees which are repeatedly applied to the full original amount of the loan.

*Adapted from Sylvia Porter, syndicated columnist, Feb. 17, 1971.

A far less costly alternative would be a new loan for the amount of extra cash needed—but the uneducated slum dweller does not know this. Nor does he know how to read the fine print on a complicated installment sales contract. Nor can he even understand the bold-type statement of interest charges required under the Truth in Lending Law.

For you, a middle-income borrower, getting a loan is a simple process of going to a nearby bank and signing a note pledging to repay under specified terms. If you're late on a payment, you generally have a grace period of 10 days or so, and even if you go beyond this period you usually pay no more than a minor penalty.

For the ghetto resident, though, borrowing may be a nightmarish never-never land of thug collection tactics, intolerable harassment, the constant threat of losing his possessions—and job. And despite all the sermonizing by the well-to-do, often a $5 or $10 loan is a matter of life or death.

As consumer credit has soared to $126 billion a year, so have credit traps reached unprecedented dimensions.

Among the strictly illegal practices which plague the ghetto dweller even at this time of supposedly stiff regulations are: being induced to sign blank installment credit contracts; not being told the full purchase price or interest costs by the salesman; not being given a copy of his sales or installment loan contract.

In addition, many slum dwellers can't find ANY legitimate source for a small loan and are at the mercy of loan sharks who will charge rates ranging from 1,000 percent a year—UP. Many have no idea of how to get a lawyer to defend them in court and are terrified of lawyers in general. Many are simply resigned to the inclination of the courts to dispose of their legal problems as quickly as possible and without regard to real justice.

Credit today is seldom extended in the ghetto on an individual's ability to handle it wisely and to repay it on time and seldom at interest rates you and I would consider even remotely within the range of reasonableness. In contrast, the unscrupulous ghetto lender knows every possible angle of self-protection under today's laws and he certainly has no scruples about deception and brutality.

. . . .

The Rich Get Richer

Inequities in the distribution of the means to well-being are compounded by a well-known phenomenon that can be termed "The Law of the Two Leasts": Financial benefits accrue to those needing them least; debts pile up among those least able to pay. The working details of this "law" are illustrated by the accompanying articles. Erwin Knoll shows that Federal subsidies provide multi-billion dollar benefits for the wealthy and only a pittance for the far more numerous poor. A specific example is given in the brief excerpt titled "Tax-Deductible Lunch." The result is that despite assertions to the contrary, there are some signs of declining real income equality among Americans, as suggested by the quotation from Thurow and Lucas and the adaptation from Gabriel Kolko's book, *Wealth and Power in America*. Kolko's observations are followed by a series of items taken from the daily and weekly press; the title for them, "Shafting Mr. Poor and Mr. Average," obviates need for further explanatory comment here. Finally, perhaps by way of pouring salt in a wound, there is a description of the way that the Social Security system, which was set up to aid the helpless, has evolved so that it has become a burden to the youthful poor and a boon to the elderly rich.

IT'S ONLY MONEY*

... How sweet it is. The Sugar Act of 1948, designed "to protect the welfare of the U.S. sugar industry," provides for direct cash payments from the U.S. Treasury to producers of sugar beet and sugar cane in the continental United States, Hawaii, and Puerto Rico. The cost to the taxpayers in fiscal 1971: $83.6 million.

Flying High. Under the Federal Aviation Act of 1958, "to promote the development of air transportation to the extent and quality required for the commerce of the United States, the Postal Service, and the national defense," the Government reimburses air carriers for any losses they may incur. Last year, reimbursements totaled $57.2 million.

*By Erwin Knoll, "It's Only Money," *The Progressive* 36(Mar 72): 23-26.

Sail on and on. The Merchant Marine Act of 1936, "to promote the development and maintenance of the U.S. Merchant Marine," authorizes cash subsidies to U.S. shipping companies whose vessels are used in foreign trade. In fiscal 1971, the payments came to $223.8 million.

These three items—three relatively minor items—are from an incredible compendium of public subsidies for private interests prepared by the staff of the Joint Economic Committee. The 222-page study, *The Economics of Federal Subsidy Programs,* available for $1 from the U.S. Government Printing Office, Washington, D.C. 20402, is recommended reading for Americans who will soon be bending over their income tax returns. It helps explain where much of the money goes.

At least $63 billion was spent on subsidies in fiscal 1970, according to the Committee staff's admittedly "crude" and "conservative" calculations, which did not include such benefits as welfare and aid to the blind, or such free services as medical care for merchant seamen. Still, $63 billion was almost a third of the money spent by the Federal Government that year—$308 for every man, woman, and child in the United States, $1200 for every family.

"This mammoth subsidy system represents a mindless means of spending taxpayers' money," says Democratic Senator William Proxmire of Wisconsin, the chairman of the Joint Economic Committee. "There is virtually no analysis of economic benefits and little analysis of the cost of these programs. Neither Congress nor the Executive Branch determines if alternate programs can do a better job. There is no effort to see if the market place would be a more efficient way to achieve the goals. There is no evidence collected to analyze each subsidy program in relation to the costs and benefits of other pressing needs.

"In fact, there is not even the most elementary examination of whether these subsidy programs actually achieve the goals they were designed to achieve. The Government spends less time and attention in determining the cost and priorities of most Government subsidy programs than the average housewife spends in determining the priorities of her weekly household spending."

Subsidies are a mystery—"hidden from public scrutiny," as the staff of the JEC observed. The term subsidy itself is shunned like the plague by the drafters of special-interest legislation, and appears nowhere in the massive Budget of the Government of the United States. Despite its huge cost and formidable impact on the American economy, the subsidy system has been virtually ignored by economists; the JEC report is the first book-length study to appear in English. Even defining "subsidy" is a problem; after wrestling with the subject, the JEC staff came up with this "simple" definition: "A subsidy is any one-way governmentally controlled income transfer to private sector decision-making units that is designed to encourage or discourage particular private market behavior." The complicated definition runs to a page and a half.

That definition encompasses the sugar, shipping, and airline subsidies previously cited, and scores more like them. It includes payments to dairymen and beekeepers whose products are damaged by pesticides (about $5.5 million this year), as well as favorable tax treatment for individual capital gains (at least $7 billion). It covers special housing for disabled veterans and special depreciation allowances for major corporations. It embraces the "cost deficiency" in the second class mail rates paid by newspapers and magazines, which the Postal Service estimated at $136 million in fiscal 1970.

"It cannot be too strongly emphasized," the JEC staff noted, "that the label 'subsidy' does not make a Government program automatically good or bad. If the public supports the objective of the subsidy—such as increased housing assistance—and the subsidy achieves that objective efficiently and equitably, it is a good subsidy. If it does not meet those tests, it is a bad subsidy. Only informed public debate and analysis can determine if a subsidy is good or bad." But to put it mildly, as the JEC study did, "there appears to be a bias in the system toward producer rather than consumer subsidies."

Four major forms of subsidy were identified:

• Cash subsidies—direct payments from the Treasury—amounting to $10 billion to $13 billion a year and designed to enhance the profits (or diminish the losses) of certain industries, to discourage the production of certain farm crops, to build fish ponds and irrigation systems, to send students to college, and to achieve many other purposes, some of which are not even spelled out in the legislative history of the authorizing statutes.

• Tax subsidies, diminishing Federal revenues by at least $38 billion a year in order to aid businesses, investors, homeowners, credit unions, banks, and life insurance companies.

• Credit subsidies, costing $4 billion to $5 billion a year and providing low-interest loans for housing, education, farming, hospital construction, rural electrification, and purchase of U.S. military hardware.

• Benefit-in-kind subsidies, worth about $10 billion annually, which provide goods and services including mail delivery, food, public housing, airports, public lands, industrial machinery, trees, and other items.

Some of the specific subsidies identified in the study prompted questions and comments from Proxmire:

¶ Agriculture, $5 billion. "Do these subsidies benefit the average farmer or the corporate giants?"

¶ Medical care, $9 billion. "How can we be providing subsidies this large and still have so much dissatisfaction with medical care?"

¶ Manpower programs, $2.5 billion. "How much of the benefits are just windfalls to business firms?"

¶ International trade, $1 billion. "Where is the proof that any of these subsidies increase exports?"

¶ Housing, $3 billion. "What share of these benefits go to the poor?"

¶ Natural resources, $3 billion. "It is not at all clear that the subsidies in this area have improved the environment."

¶ Transportation, $1 billion. "One is struck by the large amounts of aid given air and water transportation and, in contrast, the small amounts given to urban mass transit."

¶ Commerce and economic development, $20 billion. "The lion's share of this consists of tax subsidies to business, many of which are quite questionable."

The $63 billion in subsidies identified by the JEC staff are "just the top of the iceberg," said Senator Fred R. Harris, Democrat of Oklahoma, who testified during three days of subsidy hearings conducted by Proxmire in January. Two Brookings Institution economists, Joseph A. Pechman and Benjamin A. Okner, told the Committee that tax loopholes and "erosions" in the individual income tax alone account for $77 billion in lost revenues. They estimated that income taxes could be slashed by forty-three percent across the board "if all the eroding features of the tax law were eliminated."

Author Philip M. Stern, whose book on tax loopholes, *The Great Treasury Raid*, was a best seller in 1964, called the Internal Revenue Code "the largest of all welfare bills"—particularly for the rich. Working from the Pechman-Okner data, he calculated that each of the nation's wealthiest families—those with income of more than $1 million a year—has its taxes reduced by $14,000 a week as a result of deductions and preferences written into the tax law. The saving for the nation's poorest families—those earning less than $3,000 a year—is thirty cents a week.

Families with incomes of more than $100,000 a year—about three-tenths of one percent of the U.S. population—receive "tax welfare benefits" of more than $11 billion annually, Stern noted—about four times the Government's annual expenditure for food stamps to feed the poor, and about 1,000 times the Federal outlay for health programs serving migrant farm workers. The total "tax welfare benefits" for families earning less than $10,000—almost forty-six percent of the population—amount to less than $8 billion.

"It would be unthinkable," Stern testified, "for Congress to even consider a proposal to vote welfare grants of $14,000 a week for the wealthiest versus thirty cents a week for the nation's poorest families. Yet Congress has done indirectly—in the tax laws—what it would never dream of doing directly."

Why does Congress do it? An answer was provided to the Committee in dramatic testimony by Senator Harris, who dropped his Presidential candidacy last year because of a lack of campaign funds. The subsidy system, he suggested, is inextricably intertwined with the financing of politics, and it is sustained equally by Republicans and Democrats, conservatives and liberals.

Liberals who do not depend on large campaign contributions from the oil industry find it "not too difficult . . . to talk about doing something about the oil depletion allowance," Harris noted. "But liberals do get a lot of money from Wall Street. So it was no surprise that Joseph Duffey, former president of the Americans for Democratic Action who ran for U.S. Senator from Connecticut in 1968, chilled some of his best contributors to the point of zipping tight their pocketbooks when he included reform of the capital gains tax in his list of tax reforms needed."

In his own short-lived Presidential campaign, Harris revealed, a principal backer "became increasingly alienated by my talk about decentralizing the shared monopolies which dominate thirty-five percent of American industry and which artificially set prices far above competitive market levels, perhaps as much as twenty percent." The supporter wanted Harris to stick to such "safe" subjects as drug addiction and the Vietnam war.

"The political phenomenon I am describing," Harris said, "explains why our Government is approaching such paralysis. For now it is very difficult to get American politicians, including many who are quite liberal, to advocate more than just *tinkering* with fundamental wrongs or simply *adding* a little more to existing New Deal-type programs. If one group is gaining unfair advantage, the reaction of most legislators is not to end that injustice but to seek similar advantages for their constituents. We see this everywhere. If the trucking industry gets a subsidy from the highway trust fund, Congress's answer is not to end that subsidy but to grant comparable subsidies to other modes of transportation. If the oil industry gets a depletion allowance, the response is not to end that abuse but to pass the abuse on to other extractive industries. And so on. The whole process snowballs until we end up with $63 billion plus in subsidy programs and with a Government that begins to stagger and fall from its own weight."

"How is it that the average citizen puts up with such an unfair system?" Proxmire asked, but the answer was evident in the Committee's staff study and hearings. The average citizen has no idea of what is going on. He staggers under his tax burden, grumbling about pathetically small "giveaways" to the poor and totally unaware of the generous giveaways to the rich.

"All subsidies should be openly disclosed and evaluated for the American public," Proxmire says, and his Committee is pondering several plans for an annual review of the subsidy system. Some three dozen more detailed studies of specific subsidies have been commissioned, and additional hearings are to be held this spring. All this may help spread the word, but the process will not be easy. The JEC's staff study and the January hearings received scant attention in the mass media, and Proxmire complained that at one point in the hearings, three of the four correspondents at the television table seemed to be fast asleep.

A dull and tedious business, subsidies. After all, it's only money. Easy come, easy go.

TAX-DEDUCTIBLE LUNCH*

... The worker's paycheck power has shrunk regularly since 1954. The erosion of purchasing power becomes almost a fixed part of the American scene, so the average worker who established his standard of living when he was single or was first married finds now that he can maintain it only by having saved when he was younger, which he probably didn't do; or by moonlighting on a second part-time job; or by having his wife work, in spite of the obstacles to doing so; or by continued pressure for even larger wage increases.

The tax-reform measure of 1969 did nothing to correct the unequal tax treatment of work-connected expenses of wage earners compared to the favored treatment given high-salaried white-collar company executives. For example, a worker cannot claim a deduction for driving a car to and from work, even when no public transportation is available to him. The company executive, however, may have the free use of a company limousine and chauffeur without having to pay any taxes for these services. The wages the worker spends for his lunch to fuel up for the afternoon are fully taxable. On the other hand, the executive can take a friend to lunch in an expensive restaurant, deduct this expense, and pay no taxes on it, by merely showing that it is a business-related luncheon. Even the wear and tear on shoes and clothing the worker incurs while at work is not tax deductible.

*Adapted from Michael M. Schneider, "Middle America: Study in Frustration," *The Center Magazine* 3(November–December 1970):2–9.

There is no provision for tax relief as family education costs rise, either in terms of the average three hundred dollars a year it costs to send a child to school or the larger cost of sending a child to college. In some states income is redistributed from lower-income to higher-income groups to subsidize education for the children of the latter group. . . .

. . . .

DECLINING EQUALITY?*

Conservative observers have hailed the rising incomes of American workers as evidence that "free enterprise works." The system, it is claimed in addition, leads to ever greater equality, as is evidenced in the decline of incomes received by the rich relative to those received by the poor; for example, in the 22 years from 1947 to 1969, the average income of the most affluent 20 percent of American families fell from 8.6 to 7.3 times that of the least affluent 20 percent of families. In commenting on these figures, Thurow and Lucas observe:

Relative incomes are only one measure of dispersion, however. Constant and even falling relative differences are compatible with increasing absolute differences in a world with rising incomes. In 1947 the average income of the richest 20 percent of all families was $10,565 higher than that of the poorest 20 percent of all families; in 1969 it was $19,071 higher (in 1969 dollars). The real gap between the poorest and richest 5 percent of all families rose from $17,057 to $27,605 (in 1969 dollars) despite the sharply declining difference in relative incomes.

INCOME INEQUALITY**

It is difficult to know what to conclude about trends in relative income for various groups of Americans. Various studies make such sharply diver-

*Lester C. Thurow and Robert E. B. Lucas, *The American Distribution of Income*: A Structural Problem; A Study Prepared for the Use of the Joint Economic Committee, Congress of the United States (Washington: U.S. Government Printing Office, 1972), p. 7.

**Adapted from Gabriel Kolko, *Wealth and Power in America*: An Analysis of Social Class and Income Distribution (New York: Praeger Publishers, 1962), pp. 127-129.

*gent claims that one often has no alternative to depending on his own
ideological predilections. Kolko's ideology, as illustrated below, tells him
there is great and pervasive inequality in American life. In any case, "Mr.
Average" gets "royally shafted," as suggested in the potpourri that follows
the Kolko observations.*

Insofar as economic power in the United States derives from savings and
income, it is dominated by a small class, comprising not more than
one-tenth of the population, whose interests and style of life mark them
off from the rest of American society. And within this class, a very small
elite controls the corporate structure, the major sector of our economy,
and through it makes basic price and investment decisions that directly
affect the entire nation.

"The historic ethos of American life" may be "its bourgeois hungers, its
classlessness, the spirit of equality," as Louis Hartz suggests in *The Liberal
Tradition in America* (1955), but these are surely not the dominant
realities in its social and economic structure.[1] American society is based on
a class structure, and it pervades most of the crucial facets of life.

More than any other factor, the American class structure is determined
by the great inequality in the distribution of income, an inequality that has
not lessened although the economy's unemployment total has dropped
from 12 million to a much smaller but still substantial figure. A sharp
inequality of income has remained despite a generation of encroachments
by law, wars, and crises at home and abroad. If the form this inequality
takes has been modified by expense accounts, undistributed profits, undeclared income, and similar complex measures, the nature of the phenomenon has not been altered.

The economically determined class lines in American society have been
reinforced by the failure of the lowest-paid groups (largely blue-collar
workers) to increase their relative income share since 1939—contrary to the
common academic notion that they have. Their occasional ascents to a
higher-income bracket usually result from the entry of wife or child into
the labor market. And, perhaps most significant of all, the movement of
the children of blue-collar workers into white-collar occupations is not
necessarily a step upward, since white-collar workers are losing ground in
their income standing.

Inequality of income is reflected in inequality of consumption, an
inequality so great that contemporary social theories on the "democratiza-
tion" or "massification" of symbols of economic status hold little relevance
to the America of this decade. On the one hand, nearly one-half of the
population is financially able to meet only its immediate physical needs,
and the larger part of this group, nearly one-third of the nation, are in

want of even basic necessities. On the other hand, a small section of the population, at most the top tenth, lives in the prosperous and frequently sumptuous manner that most social commentators ascribe to the large majority of Americans. And within this small section, there exists an economic elite variously described as the "sports-car," "country-club," or "Ivy League" set, depending on its particular tastes. Here are found the major owners of stock and the corporate managers, sharing the same social life and the same set of values.

Sharp inequalities in consumption are the pervasive fact of the American class structure. Privacy and comfort in housing are privileges of the well-to-do, and an increasing number of $250,000-and-up homes are being built throughout the United States—at a time when the few old mansions of the Astors and Morgans are being sold, purportedly because of loss of wealth, but actually because of changes in taste. The type of car one drives is a fairly accurate index of social class; the expensive sports car is purchased when an ordinary car will no longer impart sufficient prestige. Steaks are standard fare in the upper-income ranks; hamburger—which now accounts for one-quarter of beef consumption as opposed to one-tenth before World War II—is the staple of the luckier among the lower-income groups. Life is longer for the wealthy, whose money spares them from some diseases and in general gives them superior medical care. Last of all, higher education at the best institutions perpetuates the advantages of wealth in succeeding generations, while among the poor, vast reservoirs of talent and creativity go unexploited. . . .

REFERENCE

1. Louis Hartz, *The Liberal Tradition in America* (New York: Harcourt, Brace & Company, 1955), p. 206.

SHAFTING MR. POOR AND MR. AVERAGE

The daily and weekly press regularly carry items indicating the variety of ways that "Mr. Poor" and "Mr. Average" get shafted, to use the phrase adopted by the late Stewart Alsop. The following brief pieces are representative of their type. The message clearly conveyed by them is that our "progressive" income tax system is in truth regressive. But the shafting of Mr. Poor and Mr. Average does not stop with taxes, as you will see.

MR. AVERAGE GETS IT

Stewart Alsop, *Newsweek*
77(April 19, 1971):132

... Mr. Average is ... at least vaguely ... aware that a lot of very rich people pay no income tax at all—301 with incomes over $200,000 a year, at last count—and that many more pay less proportionately than he does. And he is vaguely aware that the government is making a lot of the rich richer—on defense contracts (on which, according to a recent government report, profits often top 50 percent) and on federally subsidized housing, shipping, farming and so on.

....

The way the economic pie is sliced is what politics is mostly all about. This country badly needs a radical left that will stop nattering about how wonderful the Berrigan brothers are, and loudly demand, instead, that the system stop shafting poor Mr. Average ..., otherwise, Mr. Average will sooner or later move angrily toward the radical right.

LET THEM EAT HEAT

Environmentalist Professor Barry
Commoner, *New York Times* Service,
Oct. 7, 1971.

... all the power that goes into New York heats it, including the power for the air-conditioners which cool buildings but heat streets. "The result is an image of people who can't afford air-conditioners living in the heat of those who can."

LOOPHOLES FOR THE RICH

AP dispatch,
Jan. 3, 1972.

Despite congressional efforts to close tax loopholes, 112 Americans with incomes above $200,000 paid no federal income taxes in 1970, Rep. Henry S. Reuss, D-Wis., said yesterday.

Reuss, long an advocate of tax reform, said three of the nontaxpayers reported 1970 incomes of more than $1 million.

He did not identify any of the free riders in his statement, which he said was based on preliminary information supplied at his request by the Treasury Department.

"The Tax Reform Act of 1969 was supposed to end this grand-scale tax avoidance, but it is obvious now that it hasn't done so," said Reuss.

However, in 1969, the last year before the reform act took effect, 300 persons with incomes in excess of $200,000—52 of whom made more than $1 million—paid no taxes.

Reuss estimated that between $20 billion and $30 billion in additional revenue could be raised each year if the tax laws required everyone to pay his fair share of taxes.

Reuss and Rep. James Corman, D-Calif., are cosponsoring a tax reform bill that would raise about $19 billion by plugging loopholes, he said, and about $10 million more could be brought in by repealing new tax benefits for businessmen enacted this year and taxing the income of foreign subsidiaries of U.S. firms on a current basis.

The chief provision in the 1969 act that was supposed to end tax avoidance by the rich was a requirement for a minimum tax. Reuss, calling the minimum tax "a love tap," said it hasn't done the job.

"What we ought to do is simply close the loopholes that oilmen, wealthy executives, real estate speculators and those with great inherited wealth use to escape taxes," he said. "We need tax reform, Phase II."

NEW TAX BREAK FOR UPPER INCOMES

Sylvia Porter, syndicated
columnist, April 30, 1970

To hundreds of thousands of you in the upper-income brackets of business and the professions, the single most important reform in the 1969 Tax Reform law isn't a reform at all. Instead, it's an utterly new, tremendous tax break which at the start of the reform drive wasn't even dreamed of.

Specifically, it's a new tax rate ceiling of 60 percent on the income you earn in 1971 and an even lower tax rate ceiling of 50 percent on the income you earn beginning in 1972 and continuing thereafter.

In short, starting only 19 months from now, your earned income can't be taxed at rates higher than 50 percent. (At the same time, your other taxable income will still be taxable at regular rates up to the 70 percent maximum.)

Meanwhile, the maximum tax on your long-term capital gains up to $50,000 a year (unreduced by the deductible half) will remain at 25 percent, but the rate on the amount over $50,000 will rise so that beginning in 1972 the effective maximum on your long-term capital gains above $50,000 will go up to 35 percent.

Once the top rate for earned income is cut from the regular 70 percent to 50 percent, a top-bracket individual will get a $200 tax saving for every $1,000 of additional earned income taxed at 50 rather than 70 percent—and the drastic reshuffling in rate relationships well may lead to drastic rejuggling of tax strategies.

LOOPHOLES AGAIN

UPI dispatch,
March 27, 1972

Rep. Henry S. Reuss, D-Wis., said yesterday that 18,646 Americans used special loopholes to pay an average of less than 7 percent tax on at least $100,000 each in 1970 income.

Reuss, a member of the House Banking and Currency Committee and the Joint Economic Committee, said the 18,646 persons did not include the 394 Americans with 1970 incomes of over $100,000 who paid no federal tax at all.

Reuss said in a statement that he based this conclusion on an analysis of data from the Treasury on operation of the so-called "minimum tax" provision of the 1969 Tax Reform Act. The provision was intended to insure that all persons with very high incomes paid at least some federal income tax.

"This is just one more illustration of the gross inequity of our federal tax system," Reuss said. "Here we have thousands of wealthy Americans piling up $100,000 a year and more from capital gains, oil depletion allowances, stock options, real estate tax shelters, and other tax loopholes, and paying a tax on it of less than 7 percent—the same percentage paid by a wage-earner making $6,500 a year!'"

He said that by "the most conservative assumption possible," the wealthy Americans taking advantage of "loophole" income paid an average tax of 6.76 percent. But he said it was more reasonable to assume that the incomes averaged over $150,000 each, which would mean an average tax percentage of under 4 percent.

"As it stands now," he said, "the minimum tax administers just a small 'love tap' to wealthy tax avoiders. They can continue to use tax loopholes if they will just pay a small admission fee for the privilege."

. . . .

POOR PAY TAXES AT 50% RATE

UPI dispatch,
March 19, 1971

The biggest tax bite is felt by the poorest families in America, those with incomes of less than $2,000, who pay 50 percent of their earnings in taxes, Census Bureau figures showed yesterday.

Herman P. Miller, chief of the population division who made the disclosure in a New York speech, put the blame on regressive state and local sales and property taxes that, unlike income taxes, are not scaled according to ability to pay.

Thus, families forced to spend most of their meager earnings on basic necessities pay the highest percentage of earnings, 27.2 percent, in state and local taxes, Miller said.

By comparison, he said, the rate steadily declines as income rises, where families earning $50,000 or more a year, and presumably saving or investing a share of their income, pay only 6.7 percent in state and local taxes. . . .

Miller, who delivered a paper at a symposium on "The Affluent Consumer" sponsored by the National Industrial Conference Board in New York, defined income for all brackets as earnings only, and excluded government "transfer" payments to individuals in welfare and Social Security payments.

If such transfer payments are included for the under-$2,000 families, they would double income on the average, and lower to 25 percent the portion of their income paid out in taxes.

The tax bite for families more comfortable financially is not much greater. Families in the $4,000-to $6,000-a-year category have tax payments totaling 26 percent of income, including transfer payments. It is 30 percent for those with incomes from $15,000 to $25,000 a year.

Using Miller's definition of income as earnings only, the average tax bite is: $2,000-$4,000, 34.6 percent; $4,000-$6,000, 31 percent; $6,000-$8,000, 30.1 percent; $8,000-$10,000; 29.2 percent; $10,000-$15,000, 29.8 percent; $15,000-25,000, 30 percent, and $25,000-$50,000, 32.8 percent.

LICENSED TO NOT PAY

Santa Barbara Community
Union, Jan. 28, 1972

In California—the lowest paid County employees and the poorest people on welfare have to pay motor vehicle taxes if they want to drive to work—but NOT the billion dollar Bank of America or the giant General

Motors Acceptance Corp! (General Motors just happens to be the world's RICHEST corporation, and Bank of America is the world's BIGGEST privately owned bank.) Even churches and other non-profit organizations have to pay, but the money-rich banks are EXEMPT, under State law. Thus GMAC, which qualifies as a 'Bank' for some odd reason, pays not a PENNY in license fees for its large fleet of motor vehicles. These vehicles are given so-called 'public' service plates—based on some legal loophole 'buried in antiquity,' to quote a DMV official. . . .

THE POOR PAY MORE AND RECEIVE LESS*

In this brief excerpt from a longer piece by Connecticut Senator Abraham Ribicoff, the specific percentages and dollar figures have changed since the Senator wrote. The situation is even worse now and will apparently deteriorate further before significant changes occur. In the interim, the poor suffer grievously while the rich can use their full Social Security income to gild the lily of their investment dividends.

. . . Social Security taxes are regressive, forcing low-paid workers to surrender a much higher percentage of their income than highly paid employees. The injustice arises because everyone covered by Social Security is taxed 5.2 percent of his first $9,000 of earnings, but not taxed at all for any earnings in excess of that figure.

This formula is fine for Harry Smith, who makes $40,000 a year. His Social Security contribution comes to $468, or 1 percent of his total income. But for Joe Taylor, who makes only $9,000, and also pays $468, this is 5.2 percent of his salary—a rate five times greater than that paid by Harry Smith. There is no justification for this difference. Social Security should be reformed so that everyone pays a more reasonable share of their income and receives more adequate benefits.

Another inequity in the Social Security system is the limitation imposed on income received by Social Security pensioners. Many elderly persons are eager to work and help support themselves. But the government discourages work by penalizing them for every dollar earned above $1,680 a year.

Consider a widow receiving Social Security benefits. She receives $150 a month from the program. Then she takes a job that pays her $3,600 a year. For every two dollars she earns over $1,680 and up to $2,880, she

*Adapted from Abraham Ribicoff, "The Alienation of the American Worker," *Saturday Review* 55(22 Apr 72):29–33.

must forfeit one dollar in Social Security benefits. Above $2,880 she loses benefits on a dollar-for-dollar basis. This limitation applies until the age of seventy-two, when she will be allowed to earn any amount without losing Social Security benefits.

The effect of this earning limitation penalizes the working class. While our working widow is losing benefits for every dollar earned, our friend Smith is allowed, on retirement, to receive all of his income from investments, stocks, bonds, copyrights, patents, rentals, dividends, and pensions without losing a penny of Social Security benefits even if his outside income is $100,000. Two million elderly workers, meanwhile, are losing some or all of their Social Security benefits, for which they paid a higher percentage of their salaries. This is wrong and must be changed if Social Security is to be a program that meets the needs of the lower middle class. Proposals are now pending before Congress to raise the income ceiling, but this is only a start in the right direction. . . .

Health Alone is Victory

Among the basics of well-being, good health is probably the most all-encompassing, as suggested by Sir Walter Scott's observation, "Ill health ... is defeat. ... Health alone is victory." With good health, almost anything can be handled. But the contrary is also sadly true—without good health, ordinary tasks become difficult at best; and difficult ones become impossible. The affluent few no doubt understand this, but it can be fully appreciated only by those in straightened circumstances. As Abraham Ribicoff indicates in the first adaptation which follows, only about five million Americans can "afford" to be ill—that is, can afford decent health care. Few of such Americans can comprehend what it must be like to live as does the person described by Robert Coles in the second adaptation—a mother who is never sure she can find a hospital to take her in when her children are about to be born; a mother who is too poor to find help when her baby is desperately ill. It is stories and experiences of this type that lead to angry outbursts such as those penned by Abbie Hoffman and John Wilkinson. Famed anthropologist Margaret Mead is also angry, but expresses herself with restraint in speaking to a Congressional committee. Dr. Mead's testimony is followed by several selections describing the political irresponsibility and corporate greed that contribute to poor, and sometimes literally death-dealing, health conditions among Americans. These conditions frequently affect all, even the wealthy.

HEALTH CARE AND THE AMERICAN WORKER*

... For about five million affluent Americans, major sickness or injury may be an inconvenience or personal tragedy—but not a cause of bankruptcy. These people don't sweat out questions such as, Should we pay the rent this month or the hospital? The grocer or the doctor? Is a sick child something we can afford this winter or next? They don't think about collection agencies, hospital attorneys, and bankruptcy courts. They spend little time worrying about whether they will lose their health insurance if they are laid off during a rough economic period.

*Adapted from Abraham Ribicoff, "The Alienation of the American Worker," *Saturday Review* 55(April 22, 1972):29-33.

For more than 200 million Americans, however, these matters are a constant, gnawing worry. The symbol of medicine is no longer the Red Cross or the physician's insignia, but the dollar sign. Between 1960 and 1970 hospital costs almost tripled and doctors' fees nearly doubled. The average day in the hospital that cost $32.23 in 1960 cost $79.83 in 1970. The complete physical that cost $57 as recently as 1968 cost $100 in 1970.

If developments in health insurance had kept pace with the increases in cost, that would have relieved the problem significantly. But health insurance programs did not keep pace. In the face of rising costs, twenty-four million Americans still have no hospital insurance at all. That is one in every seven persons under the age of sixty-five. One in five Americans—or thirty-five million people—are without surgical insurance. . . .

AND THEN SHE WENT*

. . . The time I worry is later, because it's a question of whether we can get into a hospital or not. Some don't try. They've been turned away, or they believe they will. But I've gone down there, and I tell them I live in the country, and please can't my child just be born there in the hospital, and I'll go home the same day, or the next, if that's what they want. And twice they've been good to me and let me stay, and the other times I've had to go. It's up to the nurse; she runs the place. She has that doctor in her pocket. If she's in a good humor, she'll let you see him, and if not, well she tells you that hospitals take money to run, and why don't we quit begging. Now if you're real sick, I think maybe they're supposed to take you, and to deliver you also—they're supposed to.

But as I say, they either do or they don't, and you never know when you're walking up the stairs if you'll be walking back down again in five minutes, bleeding or not. One time I fainted and my husband, he had to drag me out, and he said the nurse, she told him I was faking, putting on some kind of act to scare her, and it wouldn't work. "You niggers sure must think we're dumb, falling for that. Go faint someplace else." That's what I heard later that she said. But there are good people, too—you know. Once my husband took me all the way to Birmingham, and they were real nice there. They told me I'd been a bad girl, and I hadn't taken care of myself much at all. They told me I had swollen ankles, and why did I put

*Adapted from Robert Coles, *Still Hungry in America* (New York: World Publishing Co., 1969), pp. 15-19, 27-28.

all that salt on my food, and did I know it was hurting me, and my baby, too. They told me I wasn't eating right. They could tell even before they took their tests, and didn't I know that I was going to have a baby, and he needed to eat, and even if I didn't care much about myself, I should think of him. Lord, they scolded me; but let me tell you, they were real good to me. They started in, and they took the blood, and had me give them some of my water to test, and they measured my blood pressure and listened to me all over. They said my heart was making funny noises, bad ones, but thank God the baby, he sounded all right in there, because they listened to him, too. And they sent me right on upstairs. They didn't ask me a single question, I mean whether I had a dollar to my name. They said I was sick, and I should get better, and that was all they cared about. And it was near time for me to deliver, so they did everything. I mean they got rid of the water and I lost weight. They said if I didn't we'd both die, the baby and me, especially the baby, so I was lucky to come there. I near died, eating their food, I'll admit. We're just not used to having a lot of it, but with no salt. It tasted funny, and a lot of the stuff—well, I'd just never seen it before—them pieces of meat with hardly no fat and milk all the time and they'd give you puddings and things like that, to build up your bones or something, they said.

They say Birmingham is a mean town, a real mean town. That's what I used to hear as a girl; but I tell everyone it's not so. I mean, it doesn't have to be. At least it wasn't for me, that one time. Of course the next time we came there, with my girl Rachel in me, they were just like around here. The man at the desk—he wasn't no doctor or anything, I could tell—he told me to turn myself around and go right back where I came from. Then I tried to explain to him what was the case, and that I had a record there, but he didn't want to listen. He told me that I'd better watch my step. And he said they didn't have room for any more people on the "nigger ward," and if I got in last time, well I was lucky. My husband was getting ready to say something else when the man reached for the phone— and well, we both didn't say a word more. We turned about real fast and walked out. All the way home I thought they might be following us, and we wouldn't hear the end of it; but they never did, and we were happy you know, after all that, to have Mrs. Thomas come along and deliver me, like before. I tried to stop with the salt, like I remembered I should and maybe that helped, because Rachel was born a real good child, yelling and screeching she did. But then she died, a few months later. Yes sir, she did.

. . . .

As a clinical investigator . . . I have to conclude rather stiffly that we'll

never know exactly what caused Rachel's death—what "took" Rachel.
Eventually I did persuade Rachel's mother to describe the death. . . :

She was doing fine, real fine. I thought she was going to be fine, too. I did. There wasn't a thing wrong with her, and suddenly she was in real trouble, bad trouble, yes sir, she was. She started coughing, like her throat was hurting, and I thought she must be catching a cold or something. I thought I'd better go get her some water, but it wasn't easy, because there were the other kids, and it's far away to go. So I sent my husband when he came home, and I tried to hold her, and I sang and sang, and it helped. But she got real hot, and she was sleepy all right, but I knew it wasn't good, no sir. I'd rather hear her cry, that's what I kept saying. My boy, he know it too. He said, "Ma, she's real quiet, isn't she?" Then I started praying, and I thought maybe it'll go the way it came, real fast, and by morning there won't be anything but Rachel feeling a little tired, that's all. We got the water to her, and I tried to get her to take something, a little cereal, like she was doing all along. I didn't have any more milk—maybe that's how it started. And I had a can of tomato juice, that we had in case of real trouble, and I opened it and tried to get it down her. But she'd throw it all back at me, and I gave up, to tell the truth. I figured it was best to let her rest, and then she could fight back with all the strength she had, and as I said, maybe by the morning she'd be the winner, and then I could go get a bottle of milk from my boss man and we could really care for her real good, until she'd be back to her self again. But it got worse I guess, and by morning she was so bad there was nothing she'd take, and hot all over, she was hot all over. And then she went, all of a sudden. There was no more breathing, and it must have been around noon by the light. . . .

THE DOCTOR REVOLT*

I've always had this thing about Doctors and Hospitals. My father was a distributor of physician and hospital supplies. I grew up with doctors and doctor talk all around me. In a previous life, I worked for two years in a mental hospital as a psychologist and later in yet another life as a drug detailman calling on physicians. I had gotten to know doctors pretty well and my impression was, with very few exceptions, that they were a

*Adapted from Abbie Hoffman, "The Doctor Revolt," *Win* (Feb. 15, 1969): 7–9.

dedicated, well-meaning group of rotten, conceited, dumb, racist, bastards. Their politics is on a level, say, to that of the British Admiralty in the late nineteenth century.

Moreover, the hospital structure which plays such a key role in the training and subsequent life of a physician encourages archaic medical thinking in spite of all its new found gadgets. The Board of Trustees of any hospital in America would make the Board of Trustees of Columbia look downright revolutionary, and the Hospital Board runs its institution with a tight fist. Suspension from a hospital staff means black balling from an entire region and possibly from the whole country. The black-balled physician is still free, of course, to practice medicine, but without a hospital staff position, his ability to gain intensive care treatment for his patients is severely curtailed. The stakes for rebellion are high. In addition, the material incentives for a physician who keeps his nose clean are so high that very few, very few indeed, step out of line. There is another factor which tends to make them reactionary and that is their training. Usually medical schools draw on students who have majored in one of the sciences; when they get them, a period of intensive study, internship, and residence follows that might last ten years. This might be followed by another two years in the Army for males. And so by the time the typical physician is ready to go into practice, he is about thirty-five years old. During all those years, he has been exposed to little outside the field of medicine. His training, including undergraduate school has cost in the neighborhood of $30,000. It is no wonder then that the temptation to hang up a shingle and begin charging patients twenty-five to fifty dollars for an appointment that might last ten minutes and a thousand or two for an operation that might take an hour or less, is extremely high. Physicians 35–40 are hungry after years of financial deprivation. Older physicians are surrounded by a team of consultants, accountants, business secretaries, collection bureaus, and medical journls that function solely to advise the doctor on the modern operating techniques concerning a patient's wallet. Hypochondriasis, that eternal money-maker, still forms the backbone of many a physician's practice.

I write all this lying in a hospital bed during my third week of hepatitis. When the disease first hit me, I went to see Dr. Irving Oyle. Dr. Oyle is a rarity in the world of medicine. He is totally dedicated to curing patients and doesn't give a shit about money. A few years ago he was running a successful practice out on Long Island with all the right kind of patients. Somehow it wasn't giving him the kind of gratification he wanted so he closed up shop and headed for the ghetto in New York's Lower East Side. As for practicing medicine, the Lower East Side must seem more like the wild west. Firmly entrenched in a storefront that one could easily mistake as one of the Motherfucker dens, Dr. Oyle carries on a lone struggle to bring medical care to an area that could use 50-100 Dr. Oyles.

From the time he ordered me into the hospital to the time we finally located a bed took six days. He told me of a fellow doctor who had a heart attack patient who waited three days before space could be found in a hospital.

Finally another doctor friend of mine located a bed in Albert Einstein Hospital in the Bronx, and I was bundled up at 1:00 a.m. and sped to the hospital. The doctor feared that if I waited until morning the space might be gone.

Let's turn now to the finances. Because sympathetic doctors who know me pulled certain strings, I am going to escape this mess financially clean. Otherwise this treatment would cost somewhere in the neighborhood of $2,500 and this is without an operation or any medication. There is a kid down the hall with an unusual blood ailment that has hospitalized him for two months. When he is through, his cost, which his parents must pay, will run in the neighborhood of $15,000.

A month ago, I had a rasping cough and went to the clinic at St. Vincents Hospital. It was eleven dollars to see a physician, and an hour and a half wait. He prescribed an X-ray appointment that, because of a crowded schedule, was three weeks from that date. When I showed up, the hospital demanded sixteen dollars for the X-ray, and again cash in advance (I also found out it would be another eleven dollars when I came back to get the physician's report on the X-ray results). I stormed out after a big shouting match and never had the X-rays taken. For a simple cough, treatment was to be at least $38, not counting another $5 for medication prescribed and probably another $5 more the second time I saw the physician. So there it is, $50 for a cough, about $2500 for hepatitis, $1,000-$10,000 for an operation, and, well, it's a good thing they don't charge those poor bastards for heart transplants. Couple this with the astronomically high cost of medicine in this country and, you can see that when the doctor looks up from his desk and tells you hospitalization is required, going home and shooting yourself might, in the long run, prove less painful. That is, of course, if you haven't read *The High Cost of Dying.*

The strange part about this mess is that if you are really poor you are not too bad off. That is if you live in New York or one of a dozen or so other states that have a welfare program that entitles you to full medical treatment. These states also have a Medicaid program that provides relatively complete care if you are under 21 or over 65 years of age and make less than $2300 per year. Then there is the federal Medicare program for persons over 65. These programs do require applying with complicated forms and delays that can take up to six months. Still, public hospitals are fantastically understaffed and overcrowded. In addition, few hospitals make attempts to reach out into the community and the poor are reluctant to go to a hospital which is excessively authoritarian, paternalistic, and white.

Then there are the various health insurance plans which range in cost from $200–$400 per year and again have restrictions as to the limit in terms of type and length of care, but will cover most conditions.

Without any of these three deals going for you, and unless you have millions or your brother is a doctor, you have a hell of a problem if you get seriously ill. . . .

MEDICINE MEN *

Is Medicine more than a tribal dance? Do doctors really *do* anything, except for a few selected radical surgeries and some pediatric medicine? Do they really have any success in lengthening the span of life? René Dubos, for one, denies both, or that there's any point to this whole shamanistic display at all. Life expectancy in Europe (and the total population), for example, began to expand markedly before very few of the "modern" advances in medicine had been made. Stopping throwing garbage in the street probably did more good than all the medical men in the world. My own impression is that all this "medicated survival" probably only adds about two weeks to the general life expectancy of the population. You may have a dramatic success in the case of a few persons, but you might kill twenty thousand others with your operation. A recent report said that ten thousand people died last year from completely unnecessary operations. I'm certain that figure is grossly underestimated. These things ought to be looked into. I have a strong feeling that most people ought to have imitated the Christian Scientists, who, by and large, stay away from doctors. Christian Scientists no longer refuse to have a child with an imminently rupturing appendix operated on. But they do retain a great aversion to the medical profession and the number of times they go to a physician is quite small. And yet they have one of the highest life expectancies in the United States. Of course one could say they comprise a self-selecting group; but then what you're saying is that they are healed on grounds other than medicine. What do you select? Instead of selecting doctors you select something else. They pay no attention to medical

*Adapted from John Wilkinson, "This Whole Medical Matter," *Center Report* 5(April 1972):24–25.

chauvinism, and live longer. You can select economic grounds, and it's true that rich people do live longer; but in this case not because they're rich and have other advantages. What are those other advantages? Specify them and you may find why they live longer. But the reason they do, whether it does them credit or not, is not medical. While I'm being outrageous, let me suggest that physicians have always killed more people than they have cured. George Washington and John Keats didn't survive blood-letting. They ought to have had transfusions—and think of all the cases of cancer that are probably just beginning to appear from the routine use of X-rays for two generations.

A medical man recently told me half jocularly, "I don't have my patients in Hospital X." And I asked him what *do* you do with them? He said he puts them in Hospital Y. Then I asked him what was the benefit of that. He said, "Because people die in Hospital Y from what we diagnose and not some other disease. In Hospital X they die of what was never diagnosed." And then seriously he said to me, "I don't know if we should put people in hospitals at all, they could so easily get a murderous case of infectious hepatitis or of staphylococcus; those infections have grown so virulent that on balance, except in the extremest case, where somebody is going to die anyhow, they should stay away from those slaughterhouses."

. . . .

THE REDISCOVERY OF HUNGER IN AMERICA*

We need to face the simple facts: The American people are less well nourished, as a whole, than they were 10 years ago.—Dr. Margaret Mead, December 19, 1968.

With this statement, Dr. Margaret Mead opened the investigation of the Select Committee on Nutrition and Human Needs into the problems of hunger and malnutrition in the United States. Dr. Mead told of a comprehensive wartime nutrition program. By the end of World War II, she said,

Nutrition had become a word that nobody dared to be against— like motherhood. We had set up entirely new patterns of eating in many parts of the country where we had had the most deficient

*Adapted from Select Committee on Human Needs, U.S. Senate, The Food Gap: poverty and malnutrition in the United States. Washington: U.S. Government Printing Office.

diets. We had wiped out the major deficiency diseases * * * and in the face of the affluence of the early 1950s, by 1960 it was possible to say that the major nutritional disease in the United States was overnutrition.

We wiped out those diseases through effective cooperation among Government, private industry, the news media, and voluntary agencies. But our increased affluence made us careless. It produced massive nutritional complacency. Today middle-class America has forgotten about proper nutrition, while poor America simply cannot afford it.

Explaining this massive effort to end malnutrition followed by years of nearly total inattention to the problem, Dr. Mead said:

> What we do in the United States is first to say that we face a terrible crisis. Then we roll up our sleeves and we do something about it and we can do something about it very well and very fast. The worse it seems, the better we do something about it. We then say we have done a wonderful job and relax and go somewhere else. * * * This is what we did with nutrition.

In 1964, we declared, "unconditional war on poverty in America" and launched a campaign to educate, train, employ, house, clothe, provide legal services, a headstart, health care and family planning for 39 million poor Americans. But we left out of this battle plan what may have been its most important single campaign—the elimination of hunger and malnutrition. We failed to realize that adequate nutrition is an absolute prerequisite to normal human development. We did not suspect what now seems obvious: that hungry children cannot learn and that hungry adults cannot work. We did not then understand what Dr. Charles Lowe, chairman of the Committee on Nutrition of the American Academy of Pediatrics, was to tell us in February 1969:

> It is not poverty per se which must be [our] concern, but rather, the fact that poverty carries with it a variety of social and economic disabilities. We have a sequence of aberrations, each of which feeds upon the others. This morbid chain must be broken * * * the readily accessible link is also the most critical. Were we to insure that infants, children, and pregnant mothers of this country receive adequate nutrition, we could interrupt the cycle and remodel the future. Infant mortality and prematurity rates would decrease. With this there would come to our children improved growth and development, certainly of body and probably of intellect. Educational accomplishment and achievement would improve and, with this, economic status would rise.

We did not realize that vitamin deficiency and other diseases attributable to malnutrition were still prevalent among America's poor.

While we may argue over the extent to which ending hunger will help eliminate poverty, we can be sure that so long as we fail to do battle against hunger in America, we will never win a war against poverty.

. . . .

Conclusions of the Select Committee. The testimony the select committee has received, the field interviews its members and staff have conducted and studies undertaken by the staff and by consultants for the committee lead to these major findings and conclusions.

1. Medical Evidence of Malnutrition. Clinically validated malnutrition exists in serious proportions in the United States and is a particularly acute problem among infants, preschool, and schoolchildren from low-income families.

2. Effect on Child Development. Coupled with other social and economic factors, hunger and malnutrition as found in this country can and does have a direct and major adverse affect on the normal physical and mental development of young children. The clear evidence that malnutrition is a major and perhaps the primary factor in retarded intellectual development of poor children is in itself enough to make action imperative and to require that immediate measures be taken to assure that every pregnant woman, every infant, every preschoolchild, and every schoolchild who risks suffering from hunger and malnutrition receives an adequate, nutritious diet.

3. Economic and Social Consequences. The human costs to our society of failing to meet the hunger problem—the emotional and psychological effects of hunger on families that cannot meet their food needs—are incalculable. The economic benefits which would result from the elimination of malnutrition among our poverty population, however, can be estimated in terms of higher educational achievement, increased work productivity and declining incidence of disease, infection, and death. The elimination of poverty-related hunger and malnutrition would, according to a recent Bureau of the Budget estimate, result in a three-fold return on our taxpayers' investment.

4. Malnutrition and Disease. Malnutrition is both a major cause and a common result of ill-health. Prolonged malnutrition lowers human resist-

ance to disease and subjects its victims to more frequent and more serious illness. Similarly, the chronically ill person is more likely to suffer from malnutrition. This is true both because prolonged illness may reduce a person's desire or ability to properly nourish himself and because certain afflictions, such as parasitic infections, may rob their victims of the nutritional value of whatever food they do obtain. Because of this two-way correlation between malnutrition and disease, there exists a parallel correlation between poor health care and poor nutritional status. Poverty level families are thus trapped in a vicious cycle. Since they are poor they are likely to be malnourished and therefore are likely to require more medical care than normal. Yet, also because they are poor, they are unlikely to be able to obtain adequate health care, and therefore become even more vulnerable to malnutrition. Given the circular nature of this problem, it is critically important that improved medical treatment and sanitation facilities be provided simultaneously as nutrition is improved. Failure to improve the delivery of health services to the poor, to produce the medical personnel qualified to deal with nutrition related diseases, and to focus the attention of our health clinics on the malnutrition-disease relationship, greatly reduces the effectiveness of present efforts to provide every American with a fully nutritious diet.

5. Nutrition Practices. Despite sharply rising incomes over the past decade, malnutrition has increased among Americans at all income levels. Knowledge of proper nutritional practices and the lack of information of what constitutes good nutrition has declined over the past 10 years. If malnutrition is to be eliminated, particularly among the poor, rising incomes and expanded food assistance programs must be coupled with increased awareness of the basics of proper nutrition.

6. The National Nutrition Survey. The national nutrition survey of the incidence and location of hunger and malnutrition in the United States should be expanded and completed. It should not be ended after completion of the present 10-State survey. The survey should provide as quickly as possible, though sampling techniques, a report on the nutritional status of the entire American population. It should also focus particularly upon the nutritional problems of 38 million poor and near poor Americans; special surveys should be conducted to establish the extent and severity of malnutrition among particular population groups; and the nutritional results of federal food assistance and health programs should be monitored and evaluated. The survey should become a permanent, continuing tool and its results should be periodically reported to the Congress and the American people.

7. Poverty-Related Hunger. Millions of American poor and near poor risk suffering the effects of serious hunger and malnutrition for one overriding, major reason: lack of enough personal and family cash income to purchase the food necessary to provide themselves an adequate diet.

8. The Failure of Family Food Assistance. In relation to the dimensions of the problem, the impact of the two major Federal food assistance programs, the food stamp and commodity distribution programs, has been minimal. They have neither served a significant proportion of those in need of assistance, nor been administered to provide sufficient food or food stamps to enable the few who do participate to provide themselves and their families with an adequate diet. They have been neither funded nor administered to alleviate the problem of poverty-related hunger. . . .

'DEFECTIVE' PRODUCTS CHARGED TO NINE FIRMS*

WASHINGTON—Nine companies accused of posing potential "serious health problems" by selling defective foods, drugs and other products were named yesterday by Rep. Les Aspin, D-Wis.

One of the firms, Mrs. Smith's Pie Co., refused to give the Food and Drug Administration (FDA) access to records needed to determine if some coconut cream pies were contaminated by bacteria that can cause illness and even death, the General Accounting Office (GAO) charged in a report Sept. 14.

The charge was denied by a spokesman for the firm, which had $76 million in sales in all 50 states last year.

"We have never refused FDA access to anything we have, whether in the form of records, products or raw materials," Carl G. Denton, vice president for production, said from company headquarters in Pottstown, Pa.

The firm of Parke-Davis, the report claimed, delayed for 11 days a recall of "super-potent" digitalis, a prescription heart stimulant, thus contributing to the FDA's inability to recover 84,000 pills, or 42 percent of those distributed.

Parke-Davis, a Detroit-based subsidiary of Warner-Lambert Pharmaceutical Co., had no immediate comment.

The GAO based its report on a review of 91 FDA seizures of adulterated, misbranded or illegally marketed products. Sixty-nine percent of the merchandise deemed defective was removed from the market, the congres-

The Washington Post Service, Oct. 4, 1972.

sional watchdog agency concluded; the remaining 31 percent apparently was sold.

The GAO—citing problems created for the FDA by a lack of authority necessary to get access to many records, to detain suspect shipments from interstate shipment and to force recalls of defective products—said that a total of 3,300 firms refused to cooperate with more than 10,000 requests made by FDA inspectors in the period mid-1968 through mid-1971. In four out of five cases, companies denied access to records, the report said.

The GAO, as is customary, illustrated the problems with anonymous examples. Rep. Aspin then asked the agency and the FDA to name the nine firms involved; the FDA did so.

In a statement yesterday, Aspin accused the companies of having "consciously sabotaged FDA efforts to remove contaminated foods and drugs from the shelves."

In the Mrs. Smith case, the GAO charged, the bakery relied on a supplier some of whose eggs were found to contain salmonella bacteria. In addition to acting against the supplier, the FDA sought bakery records supposed to show the results of testing for salmonella in pies that already had been distributed, the GAO said.

Charging that the bakery refused to let the FDA see the records, the GAO said the inspectors consequently were unable to find out if the pies contained salmonella, if Mrs. Smith's own procedures for testing for the bacteria were adequate, and even if tests had been performed.

In the Parke-Davis case, the GAO said, the firm would not accept the FDA's test findings that digitalis pills were "super-potent," but insisted on making an analysis of its own. The resulting 14 week delay made the ultimate recall "less effective," the agency said.

The GAO also charged that:

—Guerra Nut Shelling Co., Hollister, Calif., refused to provide the FDA with shipping data on walnuts contaminated with fecal bacteria.

—Nationwide Chemical Co., Concord, Calif., refused to supply shipping records on an inadequately labeled drain opener which, according to consumer complaints to the FDA, had caused skin burns and, in one case, serious facial scars.

—American Hospital Supply Co.'s Harleco Division, Philadelphia, refused to supply data on about 20 chemicals used for medical diagnoses that it was recalling.

—Cedar Lake Foods, Cedar Lake, Mich., sold 30 of 51 100-pound bags of flour that the FDA had requested it to hold for completion of a seizure action after finding the flour "contaminated with filth."

—Laser, Inc., Crown Point, Ind., sold 3,960 ineffective thyroid capsules that the FDA did not have authority to detain after the agency initiated a seizure action which took 30 days to complete.

—Modern Macaroni Co., Honolulu, processed noodles in an "insect and rodent infested plant"; the FDA tried to seize 5,436 packages, but the firm sold all but 684 in the 33 days it took for a seizure action to be completed.

—Stayner Corp., Berkeley, Calif., produced an unidentified prescription drug that failed federal standards for dissolution—"a moderate-to-serious health hazard." The firm waited 55 days before initiating a recall the FDA requested, allowing an estimated 75,000 tablets to reach the public.

HIDDEN INGREDIENTS *

Federal regulation of meat and poultry is heavily biased toward the principle that what the consumer cannot see cannot hurt him. The plant inspector is primarily concerned with bruises, tumors, fecal contamination, enlarged livers, stray feathers—defects which he can see, touch, or smell. But of far greater potential danger to the consumer's health are the hidden contaminants: bacteria like salmonella and residues from the use of pesticides, nitrites, hormones, antibiotics, and other chemicals used in food production and processing.

Here the inspection failures are more often errors of omission than commission. Monitoring meat for chemical residues has traditionally been limited to spot checks for a few compounds, often with analytical equipment either too insensitive or too time-consuming to catch contaminated meat before it reaches the consumer. There is no regular monitoring of salmonella or other microbiological contaminants in meat and poultry plants in the United States. Yet at least thirty diseases, including brucellosis, hepatitis, trichinosis, and salmonellosis, are transmissible to man through meat, milk, poultry, eggs, and other foods of animal origin.

Changes in the technology of food processing have increased the risk of microbiological poisoning, as more fully processed foods are offered to the consumer and as the time span between processing and consumption continues to increase. The increased density of animal populations for both feeding and processing and the contamination of their environment have also increased the hazards. In the absence of microbial standards, strict

*Adapted from Harrison Wellford, *Sowing the Wind*, A Report from Ralph Nader's Center for Study of Responsive Law on Food Safety and the Chemical Harvest (New York: Grossman Publishers, Inc., 1972), pp. 125–128.

adherence to the sanitation rules set out in the USDA *Inspectors Handbook* reduces the spread of bacteria within the processing plant. But as we have seen, the inspectors who apply these rules on the production lines are sometimes not backed up in USDA when the plant managers complain, and even if they do gèt cooperation from USDA and the processor, the speed with which they must work weakens this front line of consumer defense.

The hazards from chemical contaminants are both more serious and less easily controlled. With the possible exception of a few stores specializing in organically grown beef, it is virtually impossible to buy meat which is not contaminated to some degree with synthetic chemical residues. Between 80 and 90 percent of all beef and poultry produced in this country is grown on a diet of antibiotics and other drugs from birth to slaughter. Three-fourths of all cattle in the United States are fed stilbestrol and other growth-stimulating hormones. Pesticides enter the human food chain when meat animals eat contaminated feed and water or are directly sprayed to control parasites and insects.

Both the FDA and the USDA keep watch on the levels of chemical in food but the technology of residue monitoring, as well as budget allocations for this task, is inadequate. For example, there are several highly poisonous chemicals which may be present in meat at levels too small to be discovered by present screening devices but too large to be safely consumed. Carcinogenic compounds, such as stilbestrol and nitrosamines, and the tetra-dioxin contaminant of the herbicide 2,4,5-T, a potent agent of birth defects in test animals, are three chemicals in this category.

The threat of chemical residues from pesticides, antibiotics, and hormones in meat and poultry is another side effect of the rapid application of chemical technology to agriculture. As with the use of pesticides on crops, the short-term effects on yields of hormones and antibiotics which increase the body weight of the animal are sometimes allowed to outweigh potential long-term hazards at the human end of the food chain.

The use of antibiotics and hormones has helped cause basic changes in cattle and poultry feeding practices. The practice of cramming immense populations of livestock into small areas is closely tied to the use of antibiotics in feed. Cattle are now confined by the thousands in feedlots where they must stand shank to shank in a mire of manure. Tens of thousands of chickens are raised under one roof in cages in which three or four birds are stuffed together in a 12″ by 18″ space. Veterinarians find that the incidence of respiratory diseases and other illnesses increases when animals are raised under such stressful conditions. Crowding also creates conditions favorable to the rapid spread of disease. While this feeding system may increase the efficiency of production to some extent, the farmer has to contend with increased fears of disease and epidemics in his animals. He therefore feeds them a substantial diet of antibiotics, tranquilizers, and other prophylactic drugs to suppress disease and relieve stress.

Corporate agriculture fears that its huge investments in feedlots and broiler houses would be threatened if discovery of unanticipated hazards to human health forced drastic restriction of the use of antibiotics and synthetic hormones. Their anxiety leads to tremendous pressures on the federal regulators and scientists who must evaluate the safety of agricultural chemicals. These pressures are doubly effective because the agencies which make the decision, FDA's Bureau of Veterinary Medicine and USDA's Consumer and Marketing Service, both have promoted the chemicalization of meat production. Questions about safety usually originate outside these agencies in the National Cancer Institute and other health agencies which have no direct voice in the decisions. For this reason, questions of safety in the use of animal drugs cannot be left to the experts in the federal agencies and laboratories on the assumption that objective science will prevail. The search for dangerous chemicals in meat leads into political thickets as dense as any in the Federal Trade Commission or the Interstate Commerce Commission.

Politics, for example, influence the question of which chemical residues are to be looked for in meat. Dr. James Stewart, until recently chief of chemical residue sampling at USDA, concedes this is often a political question. Money is given to the Agricultural Research Service in a lump sum and allocated according to whatever residue has caused the biggest stir in the media. When hormone pellets in chickens produced a scare in 1956–1957, the number of animals checked for stilbestrol and other growth-stimulating chemicals greatly increased. In the mid-sixties, the possibility that drug-resistant bacteria might result from the use of antibiotics in feed caused alarms, and sampling for antibiotic residues became the vogue. In 1970, since the mercury scare, USDA has initiated sampling for heavy metal residues, but planned to reduce monitoring of antibiotics and hormones, until dissuaded by public and Congressional criticism.*

In the past, the consumer has relied on scientists to provide answers to the question: what level of chemical residue in the food supply, when weighed against the economic benefit of its use, is an acceptable risk? But "acceptable risk" is ultimately a political judgment. Evaluation of balance of risks and benefits should be based on as complete and pertinent scientific data as possible, but decisions about how much risk the public is

---

*Dr. Stewart, an authority on pesticides and other residues in meat, resisted a planned cutback on monitoring for antibiotics and hormones. He apparently won the battle but lost the war. In the recent reorganization by new inspection chief Kenneth McEnroe, he was denied a planned promotion and assigned a new job with less responsibility.

willing to accept—e.g., weighing a potential cancer hazard against an increase in the price of beef—must be made by society and its political
leaders. The chemical industry and the producers and processors of meat
know this and direct their paid advocates in the trade associations accordingly.

THE HIGH-FILTH DIET, COMPLIMENTS

OF FDA*

Insects and rodents have befouled man's food for untold centuries, but
only in the last year have they done so with the publicly announced
official sanction of a Federal agency. That agency, ironically, is the U.S.
Food and Drug Administration, which is responsible for keeping impure
foods out of interstate commerce and out of the country.

Last March, after much prodding from consumers and Federal legislators
alike, who thought the public had a right to know just what amounts of
filth the FDA tolerates in food for human consumption, the FDA revealed
the figures for the first time. The menu all these years, the public learned,
included a stomach-churning assortment of insect parts and larvae, fish
cysts, mold, rot, rodent hair and excrement.

Until the public announcement last March, the FDA's filth tolerances
were a matter of unofficial policy within the FDA. In some cases, some
manufacturers knew what the FDA's unofficial tolerances were. In other
cases, they didn't. But the public didn't know at all. With the announcement in March, the unofficial policy took on the force of official sanction.
The public learned that the FDA, for example, allows approximately one
rodent pellet per pint of wheat, 10 drosophila or other fly eggs per
8½-ounce can of fruit juice. Peanut butter is acceptable up to a limit of 50
insect fragments or two rodent hairs per 3½ ounces. FDA's list of permissible levels of filth ranged from soup (the contaminants allowed in some
ingredients) to nuts (how rancid and moldy they can be). Those levels, the
FDA asserted, represent "natural or unavoidable defects . . . that present no
health hazard."

Reaction to the FDA's disclosure was swift and vocal, in Congress as
well as in supermarkets. "Maybe the FDA will tolerate these filth levels,"
remarked one legislator, "but I doubt that the American consumer will or
should."

Nevertheless, almost all of the FDA's filth tolerances today remain the

Consumer Reports 38(March, 1973): 152-154.

same as those announced a year ago. In CU's judgment, they are no more justified now than they were then. After a thorough review of those tolerances with experts on extraneous matter in foods, we find that the FDA's standards are grossly out of line with current food processing capabilities. Our investigation reveals that such levels of filth are far from "unavoidable"—and that some of them present a possible hazard to heatlh.

In certain foods, some defects are not preventable. A microscopic scale insect that grows on peppercorns is such an example. It is natural, in the sense that it is agricultural in origin and develops with the crop. It's unavoidable because current technology cannot effectively remove it from pepper before grinding. We are faced with two alternatives: either tolerate it or do without ground black pepper.

Many types of contamination, however, are quite avoidable. High levels of filth often result from using infested raw materials. Rat excreta or roach fragments in food are signs of improper storage or manufacturing practices. Yet, the FDA would have us believe that many such instances of contamination are acceptable—an "irreducible minimum after all precautions humanly possible have been taken," according to the agency. Ample evidence clearly contradicts that notion.

Peanut butter, that frequent staple of the school lunchbox, is a glaring example. When CU last tested peanut butter (CONSUMER REPORTS, May 1972), we found that 86 percent of our samples contained *neither* insect fragments nor rodent hairs. In peanut butter such defects are caused by preventable infestations—which most of the manufacturers of our samples *did* prevent. Yet, as mentioned earlier, the FDA still allows up to 50 insect fragments or two rodent hairs in 3½ ounces of peanut butter. It should be noted, moreover, that rodent hairs do not necessarily originate from shedding. Rats and mice lick themselves, so their feces frequently contain hairs. Finding short hair fragments in a finely ground product like peanut butter indicates that they probably entered in fecal pellets. How the FDA can classify such filth as "natural or unavoidable" remains a mystery to CU.

The gross level of rodent excrement permitted in wheat is similarly appalling. FDA's present tolerance of up to one pellet per pint does not even reflect average conditions found more than two decades ago, and conditions have improved since then. In a survey conducted in 1950-51, the FDA and Department of Agriculture found that 77 percent of wheat sampled contained no rodent pellets. Less than 10 percent of the samples contained one pellet or more per pint.

Rodent pellets get into wheat largely because of unprotected storage conditions, and such contamination represents a lack of infestation control. Since the survey was conducted, the trend in grain storage has been toward tighter structures: so there's no valid reason why the FDA should accept gross levels of filth in wheat. CU's food consultants confirm that reputable flour millers reject wheat that is as dirty as the FDA tolerance allows. But that does not guarantee that *all* producers will observe such self-imposed restrictions.

A comparable situation exists with corn meal. *Food Purity Perspectives*, a publication specializing in food sanitation science, notes that the FDA's current defect level for corn meal "is a closet skeleton handed down from 1940." At that time, corn meal was made from produce stored over long periods in corn cribs unprotected from rats and mice. Such storage conditions are comparatively rare now, but the FDA filth standards that were adopted to correct the situation that existed in 1940 have weathered the generation gap.

Currently, the FDA considers corn meal adulterated if 20 percent of the samples contain over five rodent pellet fragments per 50 grams (1¾ ounces) *and* if an additional 20 percent of the samples contain more than two such pellets or rodent hairs. In contrast, the degerminated corn meal industry accepts *no* pellet fragments in the product and also rejects it if an additional test shows more than one rodent hair. The industry also rejects corn meal with more than 20 insect fragments per 50 grams. The FDA, however, tolerates five times that much—100 insect fragments per 50 grams. Apparently, that is considered "natural or unavoidable" by the FDA.

Similarly unrealistic are the FDA's tolerances for chocolate products, which are allowed to contain up to 150 insect fragments per eight-ounce sample. Chocolate suppliers can provide a reasonably clean product to candy bar manufacturers, and they do so when their customers require it. Insect fragment counts in such instances will range from three to 10 (or even zero to 10) per eight-ounce sample. When customers don't insist on such tolerances, however, fragment counts often jump to a 30-to-80 level.

Although candy bars are usually clean, some manufacturers take more care than others. The FDA could raise the general level of care taken by adopting and enforcing a more realistic tolerance level, thereby protecting both the public and reputable manufacturers. But the agency still embraces its 150-fragment tolerance as an "irreducible minimum."

Up to now, many food processors have followed more exacting purity standards than those of the FDA. But official endorsement of unnecessarily high, out-of-date tolerances—and there are many on the FDA's list—is an open invitation to manufacturers to relax current standards. Meanwhile, those who were *not* observing such standards before will have less incentive to do so in the future. Some processors, in addition, might be tempted to mix relatively clean batches of food with contaminated ones to get the latter under the FDA's liberal filth limits. While such mixing is illegal, it's extremely difficult to police. By setting such high tolerances for filth, the FDA is, in effect, encouraging adulteration of foods rather than assuring their purity.

In defense of its position, the FDA points out that enforcement of maximum limits on filth is not the only weapon in its food policing arsenal. It leans heavily on manufacturing plant inspections to insure that food is being processed under sanitary conditions. Even if a product meets FDA purity standards, says the agency, its manufacture under insanitary conditions (unclean enough to contaminate the product or endanger health) renders it adulterated—and subject to seizure. Repeated infractions, if serious enough, may result in prosecutions or injunctions against the manufacturer.

In theory, a vigorous inspection program might well offset weaknesses in other policing methods. But how good are the FDA's inspection efforts? Unfortunately, an evaluation of those efforts conducted by the government's General Accounting Office (GAO) last year leads CU to only one conclusion: *deplorable.*

To judge the effectiveness of FDA's inspection program, GAO auditors accompanied FDA personnel to food plants in 21 states. Of 97 plants selected at random, only 30 met FDA standards of sanitary practice. Twenty-three plants were judged to have serious insanitary conditions, including rodent-infested raw materials, live insects on in-process raw materials and numerous live roaches and flies in manufacturing and storage areas. Twenty-eight were judged to have minor insanitary conditions, considered not sufficient to contaminate the product or endanger human health. The other 16 fell somewhere in between serious and minor.

According to the GAO report, the FDA sharply curtailed its inspection coverage after 1968 so that resources could be shifted to concerns the FDA considered more critical, such as botulism and drug hazards. As a result, in fiscal 1972 the agency had only 210 inspectors to police more than 60,000 food establishments.

In fiscal 1972, the FDA's understaffed force was able to inspect no more than 7500 of those 60,000 food establishments. At that rate, the agency admits, it could inspect each establishment an average of *only once every seven years.* Significantly, by the time of the GAO survey, the FDA's inventory of food establishments had become so outdated that 22 percent of the plants proposed for inspection in the survey had already gone out of business.

Congress has now hiked FDA's food policing budget, and the number of plant inspectors is being increased to approximately 500 in fiscal 1973. Despite that welcome addition, however, the FDA will be able to inspect each food establishment, on average, only once every three to four years.

In view of that inspection gap, unrealistic filth tolerances can only compound the difficulty of assuring food purity. And an increase in adulteration may pose more than an aesthetic problem. The FDA currently states that the filth it tolerates in food presents no hazard to health. That contention is no less than astounding when one examines what the FDA has previously said about the subject.

Few treatises on food hygiene so clearly and meticulously explain the necessity of preventing contamination as the FDA's "General Principles of Food Sanitation." In its 1968 edition, the FDA reiterated its warnings against filth:

"The defilement of foods by rodents and flies, notorious carriers of disease bacteria, introduces a real health hazard," notes the FDA. A form of liver disease, for example, is caused by an organism that inhabits the kidneys of rodents. It may spread to man, the FDA explains, through food or water fouled with rat urine. The Salmonella bacterium responsible for mouse typhoid also causes food poisoning among humans. "Infected mice may easily contaminate food products to which they have access," warns the FDA.

"Insects," the agency continues, "inject micro-organisms with their saliva; they deposit their contaminated excrement on foods; their bodies may carry untold numbers of organisms of disease or food spoilage."

In sharp contrast to its current disclaimer about filth hazards, the FDA in 1968 was emphatic about such danger. "Often the line of demarcation between a harmful and a filthy food is exceedingly narrow. Many sources of filth in food products are potential sources of disease organisms," the FDA explained. "Flies and roaches may harbor pathogenic bacteria and transmit infections to foods. Rodents, flies, and other insects closely associated with filth and insanitary conditions are capable of mechanically transferring pathogenic and spoilage organisms from such filth directly to food products."

If the FDA has evidence that the rodent and vermin population has been laundered since 1968, CU would be eager to share that data. Meanwhile, we can only regard the agency's current attitude as contradictory and grossly irresponsible. It is true, of course, that disease organisms are often washed out or destroyed during processing and cooking operations. But rodents and vermin don't always obligingly deposit their filth *before* the final cooking stage. Infestation can occur, for example, during the cooling period before food is sealed or packaged. And numerous processed foods, such as bakery items, spices, candy, and jams, are not recooked at home.

Some disease organisms, moreover, can survive the heat of cooking. The *C. perfringens* bacterium, for example, one of the most common causes of food poisoning, sometimes produces spores that may resist ordinary cooking temperatures. And heat-resistant strains of the organism are frequently found in rodent feces.

Of itself, a rodent hair or roach fragment or fly leg hardly constitutes an imminent threat to health. But when found in food, it is evidence of possible contamination by disease organisms. Such filth should not be casually dismissed, as the FDA evidently has decided to do.

The agency's liberal tolerances on mold in some instances may also introduce a possible hazard. Most shelled nuts, for example, are acceptable under FDA standards if no more than 5 percent show mold. But certain molds that grow on peanuts, pistachios and other nuts before processing can produce aflatoxin, a substance that has caused liver cancer in animals. There is also speculation that aflatoxin and other mold toxins may be associated with liver cancer in humans, although direct proof is lacking.

According to CU's food consultants, manufacturers normally reject moldy nuts before processing, and the FDA requires that products contaminated with aflatoxin (over 20 parts per billon) be destroyed. Nevertheless, there is no guarantee that sampling procedures to detect aflatoxin will catch every instance of contamination. Accordingly, until more is known about the potential effect of such toxins, CU believes that more restrictive tolerances on mold in foods would help to reduce public exposure to possible danger.

In short, CU views the FDA's current filth tolerances as an invitation to food adulteration and a possible hazard to health. We urge that they be revised as soon as possible to realistic levels, and that the public be given access to the pertinent data on which any new tolerances are to be based.

The Environmental Crisis

In the preceding sub-part, good health was described as the most all-encompassing basic condition needed for well-being. Some would dispute that claim, asserting that environmental factors are more fundamental. We need not take sides in this argument. It suffices to note that good health and environment are indissolubly related; we cannot be healthy in an unhealthy environment, and we cannot work to improve the environment if our health is sufficiently undermined by deteriorated surroundings.

That the environment is deteriorating is beyond argument. Indeed, as the following selections and much-noted energy and mineral shortage indicate, we are at an environmental crisis point. This point is made in Professor Mark Reader's "Life in Death," which serves as our introduction. His summary and predictive observations are illustrated by selections grouped into four sets: 1) A Potpourri of Death, 2) Heat Pollution and Nuclear Energy, 3) Assault on the Ocean, and 4) Looking Backward and Forward.

LIFE IN DEATH *

... As I see it, the parameters of our present-day circumstances are fixed by six irreducible facts and their consequences:

Firstly, human and most other life on this storied, marbled planet is about to come to an end. Both the pleadings of our scientists and the grievings of our senses tell us this. If we are not the last generation of living people on this earth, then we are giving birth to the one that is. An unusual situation exists, therefore: simultaneously, we are becoming conscious of the fact that we are witnessing the earth's first remembered survival crisis and that we, ourselves, are awaiting extinction. And, as we shall see, the implications of this awareness, upon both our perceptions and our behavior, are likely to be momentous.

Secondly, not everyone agrees that our situation is critical. Some reject our assessment because they romanticize history and human nature; some, because they cannot be sure about the magnitude of our difficulties and

*Adapted from Mark Reader, "Life in Death: On Surmounting the Environmental Crisis," unpublished paper, Fall 1972.

over-estimate our abilities to manage them; some, because they are caught in a web of parochial thinking and selfish interests; and some, because they have chosen to live inauthentic lives, the consequence of denying their own mortality and that of others. These doubts and denials complicate the terribly difficult task of survival, as they persuade many that their circumstance is not unique and, therefore, that they need not take extra-ordinary counter-measures to combat it.

Thirdly, it seems likely that we shall suffer an irreversible disaster within the foreseeable, rather than the remote, future. (A disaster becomes irreversible if it destroys a vital life-support system and all life dependent upon it for its existence.) *Thus, if we wish to prolong life beyond the present moment the decision-making, or lead-time in which to do it is short.* Gone are the days of childhood, when we were shocked to learn that life on this planet would end on some distant day when the sun exploded or the earth turned cold. As adults, we have become somewhat hardened to the prospect that life might cease momentarily.

Fourthly, the crunch of time and the magnitude of our problems dictates that we act before all of the "facts" are in and without the assurance that our actions will sustain us. We cannot wait for disaster to strike and take remedial action afterwards. Once a vital life-support system is knocked out, no one will be left to repair it. Once a species is lost, we cannot recover it. Thus, if we really wish to live beyond the present, we shall have to take risks in our daily lives, institute ways of skirting disaster, experiment with a host of survival plans, and get used to acting on the basis of imperfect information.

Fifthly, we have only limited human, natural and technological resources to commit to the struggle for existence. Scarcity—of skills and of viable options—still rules the human community. *This de facto power shortage implies that we must gear our collective decisions and actions to maximize life's chances and, simultaneously, free as many people as possible to engage in our mutual struggle for existence.* In the contemporary world, order and liberty cannot be separated. We cannot survive in a condition of slavery, nor one of license. If we are to have a future, we must be able to rely upon the thoughtful creativity of each other.

Sixthly, survival depends upon our ability to fashion a concrete survival scenario and get majorities of people of different social, political, economic, psychological and cultural backgrounds to accept it quickly. To accomplish this twin task, we must generate intelligent and effective political action. And this, in turn, means that we shall have to re-order priorities on both a national and global scale immediately. . . .

In many respects, therefore, our situation is Hobbesian: when faced with premature death, what must reasonable people do if they decide to survive? Or, to put the matter in more contemporary terms, how must the species act so that we might get past what Isaac Asimov calls a "Seldon crisis," a time in Galactic history when the universe's only promising life form is confronted with real and imminent destruction?

I intend to answer these questions as I explore the implications of each of these six theses further.

Many of you, I suspect, are skeptical about the extremity and bleakness of my *Weltanschauung.* For reasons that I shall try to make evident in a moment, you deny that life on earth is about to end for most, if not all, species—including our own. Yet to me, of all of my claims, this one is the least disputable. To me, evidence of an impending, irreversible disaster comes pouring in almost faster than any of us can assimilate it. We are in a state of shock. Death awareness has come upon us too suddenly. It is everywhere apparent and everywhere denied: in each off-shore oil spill and industrial "accident"; in the autopsies being performed on the world's waterways and sea life; in every smog alert that drives people off our streets; with each new species added to our expanding lists of endangered or extinct wildlife; in the sharp rise of electrical power failures; in the presence among us of shriveled plants and trees; in the herbicide, insecticide and mine-made poisonings of the land; in the unending flow of poured concrete that is covering up what was yesterday's choice farm and woodlands—and, throughout all of this, in the flood of apologies and excuses that act to justify a continuance of these death yielding activities as necessary for living.

How can anyone who has thrust his senses into our deteriorating environment deny our rush toward disaster? Yet people do. And I suppose there are reasons.

Most people deny death instinctively. For instance, there are many who see nothing new in our surroundings. They inform us that humankind has met and conquered death before and that it will do so again, as an unlearned reflex. They advise us not to worry. The struggle against death began with the origin of the species, they say, and has been fought and won by each generation since. Our present circumstances are no greater and no worse than those our ancestors overcame thousands of times. And anyhow, even if we do not survive this latest crisis, we shall be replaced in the life processes by a species better equipped to live than we.

I think this judgment is mistaken on every count. In the first place, while people have surmounted survival crises in the past, the whole of human, and most other, species have never been exposed to total and complete extinction at a single time. Individual peoples, tribes, plants, and animals, yes; but never, as far as I know, has the whole of biological life come under assault. The life-system itself, and not just a part of it, is now in jeopardy. Moreover, should some life survive a man-made catastrophe there is no assurance that it will be any "better" than our own. We are not, for the moment, permitted to make this kind of qualitative judgment. . . . More importantly, however, . . . is the central meaning of our own daily life experiences as each morning we breathe air that is dirtier than the day before and each night we watch a telecast about the mercury or lead found in the fish we eat. And this, too, I assume, is the meaning behind those reports (uttered so casually as to become all the more frightening) by astronaut Wally Shirra, telling of noticing the visible disclouring of our oceans during a 5-6 year period as viewed from space, or of undersea explorer Jacques Cousteau's remark that on a sunlit day underwater divers can see a thin film of oil riding on almost every sea, and of adventurer Thor Heyerdahl, aboard Ra II, sighting the garbage which now floats hundreds of miles into the mid-Atlantic.

Reluctantly, we must conclude that the whole—and not just some isolated and tangential part of life—is being threatened with destruction.

Secondly, this rather romantic and sanguine view about humankind conquering death previously, assumes that people carry about their persons a survival mechanism that triggers automatically in the presence of death. It assumes that people inevitably perceive threats to their personal existences. This is just not true as the history of our species, especially as it has been played out in this century, attests. When confronted with death many people will (a) acquiesce to it needlessly, passively and quiescently—as evidenced by their repeated failure to build for themselves very much more than a mining town existence and mentality since the advent of the industrial revolution (the willingness of millions of people to accept as necessary Los Angeles smog provides the latest such example), or (b) deny that they are the intended victim of disaster even when the signs are incontestable, as it was for the inmates of the concentration camps.

Thirdly, this argument assumes that humankind has always had at its disposal the tools necessary to overcome disaster. The latest version of this fantasy takes the form of asserting that we can do whatever we wish, given our technological advances. What is rapidly becoming evident about our technology, however, is that it—as much as anything else—is at the root of our survival problem and that, additionally, we have not yet produced sufficient people and/or other tools to manage it creatively. Thus, on the negative side, it has been our technology which has made possible the world's overpopulation and pollution problems; it has been our technology which has been responsible for the rising social and environmental costs of production; and it has been our technology which has been responsible for our inability to quite keep pace with the problems it creates.

As importantly, however, what many people fail to understand is that the tools they invent and the uses to which these tools are put depend upon human choice and decisions made within a sympathetic cultural environment. Thus, it is not our tools that have saved us in the past, but a culture which encourages people to invent and use them. History is dotted with peoples, like our own native American Indian populations, that have been decimated because their cultures did not permit the development of the technology they needed to survive. We are in similar straits today, heirs to a cultural life which is not sufficiently free, especially in the political realm, to guarantee the production and use of the innovative behaviors, skills and tools necessary for survival.

Thus, I think we can dispose of the objection of those who believe that people have always confronted and overcome death before and shall do so again. . . .

Nevertheless, while conceding that our situation is new, there are others who do not agree that it is as novel as I have proposed. Having lived with the spectre of universal catastrophe since the development of thermo-nuclear and bio-chemical weaponry, they view environmental catastrophes as no different from other ruinous possibilities that 20th century man has fashioned for himself.

Unfortunately, I cannot agree. And for two related reasons. Even as we built our thermonuclear and bio-chemical stockpiles during these last 25 years, very few of us expected that *in the ordinary course of events* we would unleash them and extinguish life thereby. Everyone knew that disaster could, and might still, overtake us but only if some person or nation had a thermonuclear "accident" or made a miscalculation about someone else's intentions, or if madness suddenly overcame those in political power. None of us expected that the outcome of normal living would culminate in universal, pre-mature and complete annihilation. None of us expected to be consumed in thermonuclear fires or felled by a mysterious nerve gas if only we minded our own business and got our neighbor to do the same. Our daily life styles reflected the fact that we bet against this contingency. The only reason that many people tended their own gardens for as long as they did was in the expectation that if they brought uncertainty into the world, their leaders would not be able to cope with it and would finger the bomb in panic. But now, virtually every informed judgment tells us that we shall destroy ourselves by conducting business-as-usual, by leading undisturbed and quiet lives, by not "rocking the boat."

Moreover, if you think about it, most people have never been com-pletely sold on the idea that a third world war would be the last one; that, automatically, it would compromise one of the earth's vital life support systems. We have thought this to be possible, but not inevitable. This, I suggest, is precisely why political and military leaders in all nations have couched their language in estimating the aftermath of a thermonuclear exchange and made game-plans for many such exchanges. They have tended to believe that although life for survivors of such a war might not be worth living, not all life would disappear. Few really have acted as if they thought that there would be no survivors, no life of any kind. And even those who did, who really believed that we had the capacity to kill off all living things, have bet that that *total* capacity would never be used. Thus, in considering the consequences of thermonuclear and/or bio-chemical exchanges, they have thought of total destruction as a possibility only, dependent upon our ability to unleash sufficient quantities of our destructive arsenals. They still do. They still fuss about first and second thermonuclear strikes.

But the environmental crisis is different. From an environmental point of view, it is clear that we shall inevitably destroy one of the basic building blocks that make and sustain life—like oxygen-producing plankton—simply by continuing the living processes that we have already set loose in the world. For environmentalists, then, extermination of all life becomes a calculable probability, no longer contingent upon accident but upon the life process itself.

But I detect growing impatience from others. I have overestimated the dangers, you say. While our pollution and population problems are serious, they are not as fatal as I suppose them to be. My arguments are designed to alarm and frighten, rather than to soothe and calm. I am acting like a latter-day millenarian, the most recent in a wearisome line of prophets of doom.

This may be the case, and I freely admit it. It may be true indeed that I and others have miscalculated the seriousness of our circumstances. And yet certain events in our shared lives support our estimation and not yours. Specifically, there is some reason for thinking that we are killing life and using up this planet at an accelerating rather than a constant rate. As far as I know, we have no reliable measures of this rate of acceleration, but it is likely to be sharp, given the mushrooming world population, rising standard of living for many, increased consumption necessary to sustain all, and earth destroying wars. Within this setting, ecological accidents and liabilities—*and not just our consciousness of them*—are likely to be increasing absolutely. It seems reasonable, therefore, to anticipate more and more Santa Barbara type oil leaks, more collisions of tankers in the English Channel and high seas, more Gulf of Mexico oil fires, and more massive industrial accidents in the immediate future.

My other reply to critics of this kind might be more telling, although less evidential, however. It is a modification of Pascal's wager. If we environmentalists are correct in our diagnosis about the extent and immediacy of our survival crisis, then by becoming alarmed about it we might be able to buy the time needed to prevent an irreversible disaster; if we are wrong, and no such disaster is in the offing, then we lose nothing by acting to prevent it. In fact, by acting as if an irreversible disaster was about to hit us, we are likely to improve both our environment and the quality of our daily lives in it. But if you are wrong, then our decision to act cautiously and deliberately (which is the implicit consequence of your general attidue) without haste and in good time, will simply hasten the advent of that disaster which we all wish to prevent. In other words, it is better to be slightly alarmist than slightly dead.

And this, I suppose, leads me to address those who take me as the fool. I shall begin by admitting that prophets of doom have appeared in each age of human history and that there have been entire epochs when people believed that the world was at an end—and that as far as we know they were all wrong. If all of them were wrong, therefore, what makes me think I am right?

If we examine the projections of these millenarians, however, we can flatly say that they were mistaken because they never took into account the only sort of evidence that matters in a projection of this sort: live, empirical, measurable evidence which transcends narrow and limited situations. They were without science. We can look back on these people as being parochial, projecting onto a global stage those circumstances and experiences that were uniquely theirs. But the same is not true of us today. If, for a moment, we use our imaginations to project ourselves into a distant and remote place, the facts of our present-day situation will not, and do not, change. From any angle, they show us that life on earth is perishing, that the planet is being plundered and polluted. This whole earth perspective—that most remarkable and unexpected gift from our space program—shows us that this once beautiful blue planet is being made lifeless by some of those who now inhabit it.

As I indicated earlier, however, I am sure there are others who, up to this point, have looked upon this whole discussion as a "cop out," as an apology for continuing the world's injustices. In it, they find all sorts of hidden and concealed motives. They detect a desire to thrust aside the unresolved problems of war, proverty, inequality and fear; or the subtle attempt to prop up a dying economic system that has been so ruinous to the human spirit and which is now faced with bankruptcy and internal decay; or, more primitively, that I am a nationalist, intent upon bolstering the wealth, power and prestige of my country at the expense of theirs.

Although I can assure these people of the sincerity of my motives, I cannot expect them to believe me. The only way to answer their suspicions, therefore, is to tell them that they are beside the point, and for two reasons. In the first place, it seems to me that not to live is infinitely worse than to live in the most miserable of circumstances and that, therefore, the first condition of attaining the good life, is life itself. But there is enough testimony against me on this point, so that I shall not press the case here. Instead, I shall argue that the only way that any of us are ever going to attain freedom and social justice for all is by attacking the survival crisis head-on. It is the interest of aching peoples everywhere—and that includes most of us—to unite with environmentalists. As we tap the secrets of survival we may also find ways of opening up the reservoirs of social justice. For the moment, however, I shall not try to argue the matter, although I believe it to be true. . . .

Lastly, I must answer those who, having confronted death—having seen that we are killing ourselves and all other living things with a constant and relentless passion, who really know that each of us is dead and that our children shall not live out their maturities—have decided, nevertheless, either to turn their faces to the wall in hopeless despair or to squeeze from life all they can in the little time remaining to them, even if it means foreshortening the life of someone else, including their own children. Theirs is an argument that I fear most, for theirs is an argument from action.

I do not know exactly how to reach these people other than to remind the hopeless that their despair guarantees that they, and I, will die more quickly than need be (their paralysis makes for a self-fulfilling prophecy), and to suggest to the exploiters that they are rapidly creating counterforces that are making their lives less secure, less profitable, less free and less enduring than they had imagined.

So much for criticism; I hope I have been fair with it and, in the process, have exposed many of the illusions under which we operate currently.

In summary, it is clear to me that all of the existing evidence, both scientific and sensory, tells us that our situation is new, perilous and immediate—and, ironically, that it has fallen upon us, a ragged assortment of beleaguered and bewildered people to do what the saints and heroes out of our historical past wanted to do and thought they were doing. We must save the world. While our ancestors accepted their calling with rejoicing (and might do so only because existence itself was never in doubt), we have been summoned to perform miracles out of reluctance, defeat and uncertainty. Without dramatizing our situation unduly, I think it is now evident that the fate of life in the known universe now depends upon the ability of ordinary people to perform extraordinary and heroic acts. The burden of survival has been passed to the common man and he (and we) are not likely to assume it unless we understand the nature and implications of this, our collective encounter with death.

A Potpourri of Death

Here are seven articles illustrating the great variety of ways that we are endangered by assaults on the environment. In the first two selections, the side effects of pesticides and chemical fertilizers are discussed. These first pieces are followed by one concerned with air pollution and one indicating that humans themselves, because of their sheer numbers, are the prime causative factor in environmental degradation. Finally, there are three selections describing the short-sighted exploitive practices which turn forests into deserts and destroy aspects of nature which can never be replaced.

OF CATS AND RATS, ROACHES AND SUCH*

. . . DDT is one of the most potent man-made bombs ever to explode in the insect world.

It has saved hundreds of thousands of human lives by wiping out the mosquitoes that transmit malaria. It has saved millions of dollars worth of man's crops from being consumed by armies of insects.

But now DDT is coming under government ban, and it underscores the fact that modern man's technology is often a two-edged sword. It can do as much or more harm than good.

Look, for example, to Borneo where the World Health Organization once used DDT to kill off malaria-carrying mosquitoes.

It killed the mosquitoes, but it didn't kill roaches, which accumulated DDT in their bodies. Long-tailed lizards, called geckoes, that roam the walls and floors of tropical houses, ate the roaches, as usual.

But the DDT from the roaches hit the nervous system of the lizards. They slowed down, became less agile. So cats caught them easily and ate them.

The cats died from the DDT in the lizards.

Rats started moving in from the Borneo forests, carrying the threat of an epidemic of plague.

*Adapted from Alton Blakeslee, "Of Cats and Rats, Roaches and Such," AP Science dispatch, 13 Nov 69.

So cats were flown out and parachuted into the villages to catch or drive away the rats. They did.

But then the roofs of houses started caving in. The lizards, you see, had also been eating caterpillars that made their meals from the roof thatching.

This story is told by Dr. LaMont C. Cole of Cornell University, an ecologist, a specialist studying nature's balance of living things and systems.

DDT is but one example of a technological blessing with a price tag that often is unknown or unpredictable at the outset.

CORPORATE FARMS:

THE GRASS ISN'T ALWAYS GREENER*

"These fish are living bombs. Anything that comes along and eats them is just doomed."

This dire warning by Dr. Denzel B. Ferguson about DDT-laden fish in the Mississippi River is only one small example of the effect American agribusiness is now having on this country's environment. The chairman of Mississippi State University's Department of Zoology estimates that mosquito-fish, slightly larger than minnows, today are carrying loads of agricultural poisons up to 120 times as large as once would have killed them.

Since World War II, southern plantations and farms have been growing larger and larger and relying more and more on machines and chemicals for mass production; hence larger pesticide runoffs. In their desire for bigness and what they term "efficiency," these corporate farmers are rapidly changing the entire structure of rural life in the south.

But this area of the country is not alone, for throughout the rural areas of all America, agribusiness and its political and academic allies are radically changing the landscape.

Over 2,000 farms and some 300 small businesses are closing down each week as more than 800,000 people each year migrate from the country into our already overcrowded urban centers. As this change takes place not only is the social structure being altered but there are clear signs that the environment is also being seriously endangered in a number of ways by the corporate invasion of agriculture.

It is estimated, for example, that agriculture today accounts for over 15 percent of all U.S. water pollution. These increased pesticide residues that

*Adapted from A. V. Krebs, "Corporate Farms: The Grass Isn't Always Greener," *Environmental Action* 4(24 June 72):3-6.

are poisoning our streams, rivers, lakes and oceans are also threatening the health of the men, women and children who still live and work in these fields, robbing them each day of a little more of their physical vitality.

Although the food from these fields is checked closely for pesticide residues by the Food and Drug Administration in an effort to protect the consumer, this does not mean that the consumer can be completely sure that there are not harmful substances in the food he eats. For in agribusiness's desire to mass produce and register impressive sales figures and profit margins, some foods are becoming questionable as to their quality and the possible health hazards they pose for human beings.

Ethylene gas, for example, used to speed up the growth of produce (green figs being brought to full size and ripeness in seven days, 58 days sooner than naturally ripened figs), has been shown, when used on tomatoes, to provide lower quality with less vitamin A and C and inferior taste, color and firmness. There is also strong evidence that diethylstilbestrol (DES), which is a growth hormone fed to cattle to make them grow faster, causes cancer in man.

And, as a recent report by the Agribusiness Accountability Project's Task Force on the Land Grant College Complex pointed out, researchers and agricultural scientists from the nation's 69 land grant colleges and universities are even today hard at work in their largely tax-supported laboratories developing new additives and methods, like ethylene gas and DES, for America's large food corporations and major chemical manufacturers.

Meanwhile, down on the farm, less and less care is being given to the land, as huge, impersonal conglomerates plunder blocks of acreage, sapping the soil's wealth and dumping their wastes into the rivers and lakes of the country.

. . . .

The very soil itself is also being damaged in many cases by agribusiness's fascination with heavy vehicles and mechanized harvesting equipment. Soil scientist Dr. William R. Gill explains: "As farm machines become more and more powerful and grow bigger and bigger, they increasingly compact the earth with their weight. This may even be offsetting the very aim of tilling—loosening the soil to promote plant growth.

Corporations, in efforts to irrigate their large tracts of land cheaply, are creating ecological problems relative to water supplies. In California, for example, the state and federal governments through a multi-billion dollar tax-supported water project want to divert to a peripheral canal 80 to 90 percent of the water which normally flows through the Sacramento-San Joaquin Delta into San Francisco Bay. This scheme would deliver irrigation water to the 600,000-acre Westlands Water District in the already agriculturally rich San Joaquin Valley.

Recipients of this federally subsidized water (at a cost of about $1000 an acre) are the Southern Pacific Co., Standard Oil Company of California, J. G. Boswell Co. (which has earned over $16 million alone in federal crop subsidies since 1966 for not growing cotton) and other large—and in most cases absentee—landlords. The water from the peripheral canal would also be used in ample supply to develop the desert regions of Southern California so that land salesmen can create new residential areas.

Meanwhile, the loss of water in the delta is potentially dangerous to the ecology of the entire San Francisco Bay Area. It is argued by defenders of the water plan that the water can be replaced by rivers in Northern California. That in turn, however, will necessitate a whole new series of dams and expensive water systems in what is now largely a wilderness area. But agribusiness is in large measure *the* economic determinator in California, as it is becoming throughout rural America, and it is unlikely this water project can now be stopped.

. . . .

DEATH BY BERYLLIUM*

This is one man's story, but it is also the story of scores of laborers in the beryllium industry and of millions of men and women in other industries who daily endure America's most polluted environment: the blue-collar workplace.

Robert C. Ferdinand is 43. He has lived among the gray ruins of these strip-mined hills all his life.

From 1957 to 1968 he worked at what is now known as the Kawecki Berylco Industries beryllium plant here. He has not worked a day since.

It is fair to say that KBI used Ferdinand's skills as a maintenance mechanic to increase its profits, and in return it gave him a modest wage and a death sentence.

Pale, hazel-eyed, still stocky, Ferdinand cannot even do the dishes without sitting down to rest. He barely can climb a flight of stairs. He cannot roughhouse with his five kids. Gripped by pain in every part of his body, he sits home with his wife Kathleen and waits for

*From Stewart Udall and Jeff Stansbury, "Beryllium Disease is Death Sentence for Factory Workers," *The Arizona Republic*, 21 Mar 71.

word from his lawyer that KBI—a firm which earned $4.4 million profit in 1969—finally has agreed to pay him $60 a week for total, job-induced disability.

Ferdinand has chronic systemic beryllium disease.

When the local chamber of commerce lured the beryllium industry to Hazleton in 1957, it made much of the fact that the new plant was the cleanest, safest in the world. But it was not nearly safe enough.

"That plant was a rat hole and still is," says Ferdinand. "The maintenance mechanics got the worst of it. We cleaned beryllium off the machines with sulfuric acid—what a combination that was.

"After two or three months on the job, I started to cough a lot. The cough got worse when I went into the areas where we crushed beryl ore, mixed beryllium fluoride with magnesium and soaked beryllium beads in nitric acid. You could see the orange fumes moving through the plant into the air outside.

"The company never let us know the results of its air-monitoring tests. After a bad leak or spill, they'd tell us to go back into the area before any new tests were run. When we complained, the safety director got angry and told us to wear our safety glasses, respirators and hard hats. But we could still taste the beryllium.

"In the early 1960s I got sick a lot, all rundown and coughing. One day the company doctor, Edward Henson, called me in to say that my lung X-rays two years before had shown white spots. He said it was probably bronchitis and had cleared up. But my health kept going downhill. Lots of other guys at the plant had the same symptoms.

"On April 2, 1968, we were pumping sulfuric acid into a measuring tank and it overflowed into a pitful of beryllium scraps and other chemicals. The reaction set off clouds of smoke, and I couldn't get out of there for three minutes. I coughed and threw up a lot. Oh, I was sick. On April 19 I had to quit work. Today I can't do anything. I'm like a dead dog."

Last year Ferdinand lost 40 pounds. A biopsy found a very high level of beryllium in his lungs—139 milligrams of metal per gram of lung tissue. Despite these facts, the company refuses to send Ferdinand any compensation checks—and the family is living on a monthly Social Security payment of $379.

Defending its policy, KBI argues that Ferdinand is only partially disabled from berylliosis, and, besides, there is no proof that he even has the disease.

"The presence of beryllium in the lungs has no diagnostic significance," says Dr. Henson, "and the quantity has no relevancy to the seriousness of the disease, if disease is present."

Sworn to the Hippocratic oath, Henson also is fond of pointing out that much of the beryllium people are exposed to comes from the soil and the burning of fossil fuels.

Ferdinand's own doctor, Herman H. Feissner Jr., stoutly defends the sick man's right to receive compensation.

"He's totally disabled from the beryllium he was exposed to at the plant," Feissner says. "Every symptom, every bit of work history shows this, but the company won't admit it because it doesn't want people to know about conditions inside the plant. It has sent Bob Ferdinand to clinic after clinic trying to prove I'm wrong. It has hired the best attorneys it can find to see that he doesn't get a cent."

And so Ferdinand's story is an indictment of many forces in our society:

—The medical profession, which learned about berylliosis in the 1930s but has done little to protect workers from the disease.

—The legal profession, far more beholden to companies like KBI than to workers like Ferdinand who can produce only a rare contingency fee. Ferdinand's present lawyer has yet to interview Dr. Feissner, whose medical evidence is embarrassing to the company.

—State compensation laws, which impose a crushing burden of proof on disabled workers. Ferdinand should not have to spend years trying to prove beyond a shred of doubt that he has berylliosis; the company should be forced to prove, if it can, that he does not have the disease.

—Environmentalists, who have yet to understand that the blue-collar workplace is our most tragic environment and blue-collar workers the most natural potential allies of the environmental movement.

—Industries, that still treat their workers as environmental guinea pigs. Recently, KBI has fought every move by the enlightened Oil, Chemical and Atomic Workers International Union to give beryllium workers control of their plant environment.

The company suggests that beryllium disease is a matter of individual sensitivity. Is it not more a matter of corporate insensitivity and fear?

These larger issues pale when you talk with Ferdinand and his wife, who has grown tragically wise in her three-year fight with lawyers, doctors and the KBI.

"They're desperately trying to find someone who'll say I don't have berylliosis," Ferdinand says, "but I feel it in my bones. My whole body aches, especially at night. I dread the evening."

And Kathleen: "I'm afraid to ask the doctor why Bob has all this pain. I don't want to know. All I care is that I have Bob now and I don't want to lose him."

THE HUMAN RACE HAS, MAYBE,

THIRTY-FIVE YEARS LEFT*

. . . .

In a year of poor harvest, the weight of the burthensome multitudes lies heavy upon the shoulders of the affluent. My grandfather had a book that his father gave him, presented upon his reaching young manhood; and whether it was given with a kind word or a black look, I can't say, but the title was *Where to Emigrate and Why*. My grandfather headed West—this at a time when emigration remained plausible for young men found to be surplus upon the home ground.

Today the crowd is global. There is no place to go. There has never been such a crowd, and in no time at all now, it's going to be twice as big. . . . Perhaps the mildest we can hope for is the suggestion of a prominent anthropologist that birth-control agents be applied liberally to the public water supply.

The case is this: Fifteen thousand years ago the earth probably held fewer people than New York City does today. The population doubled slowly at that time—say every forty thousand years. Today there are more than three billion people in the world and the rate of increase is almost a thousand times greater. Doubling occurs in less than forty years.

On a graph the human population line now rises almost vertically, which will not continue—there must be leveling off or decline. Leveling seems rational. Decline can be a landslide, as the history of the Irish and the lemming imply. . . .

In the United States a huge majority sees population as infinitely less threatening than crime and communism. Population crisis in America tends to become a cliché—a joke in the newspapers about standing room only in the year 2600. After which the matter may be dismissed—possibly it's something the Chinese are up to.

The City of the Future. . . . In Calcutta six hundred thousand people sleep, eat, live in the streets. . . . The American visitor sees these thousands lying upon the ground "like little bundles of rags"; sees "women huddling over little piles of manure; patting it into cakes for fuel, children competing with dogs for refuse"—and reacts with shock and revulsion. . . .

*Adapted from David Lyle, "The Human Race Has, Maybe, Thirty-Five Years Left." *Esquire* 68(Sep 67):116–118, 176, 179–180, 182–183.

Calcutta stands for three worldwide forces—burgeoning population; food shortage; a torrent of migration to the cities.

Today there are about five hundred million people in India. In thirty years or so there may well be one billion. Most Indians live in rural villages—but the villages are overflowing. The surrounding lands no longer produce enough food. The excess population drifts into the big coastal cities where there is hope of food; Calcutta has become an immense breadline where the starving from the countryside gather to feed on grain from American ships.

The vision of six hundred thousand people lying in the streets at night—a prostrate breadline waiting for Midwestern grain—must be burned into the mind if the fate of the third world (and of the United States) is to assume reality. Because as the population rises, the supply of grain is running out. This is true not only for India but for two-thirds of the human population. All over the third world the City of the Future is a place where the rural poor gather to await the grain handout from abroad, while it lasts.

From Calcutta, draw the implications for the third (so-called "under-developed") world—briefly, as follows:

• The 1960 population of the developed world was about 900,000,000; that of the third world ran over 2,000,000,000.

• The agricultural land resources of the two parts of the world are approximately equal.

• By the year 2000 the developed world must feed 1,300,000,000 on its half of the world's croplands. The third world will have to feed about 5,000,000,000 people on its half.

• The industrial states have moved on to high-yield agriculture, getting maximum production from the land. The third world must make the same transition—but there very well may not be time to make it before mass famine sets in.

The bind is this: There is a desperate need to cut population growth and to raise food production within the next three decades. The most urgent period will be the ten or fifteen years immediately ahead. All right, then, say the hopeful—birth control; but Cora Du Bois, an anthropologist with much experience in India, reports that ". . . any effective reduction of population growth among heavily breeding rural populations is not foreseeable in less than possibly fifty years. I believe this is a question on which it is wise to have no illusions."

Nor is the prospect for rapid increase in food supply much brighter. On the contrary, according to Lester R. Brown, an economist with the U.S. Department of Agriculture: "The food problem emerging in the less-developed regions may be one of the most nearly insoluble problems facing man over the next few decades."

There are, nevertheless, a few optimists. Some talk of farming the sea, eating plankton; but this will not help anyone soon. Anyway, says William Vogt, who is experienced, "Few of the people who advocate this, I am sure, have tasted plankton. . . ."

. . . .

Perhaps the most disturbing thing about the present world-population situation is the almost uniformly pessimistic outlook of so many very capable people who have examined the matter closely. Lloyd V. Berkner, a leading American scientist, remarked that in the third world, "We are probably already beyond the point at which a sensible solution is possible." Eugene R. Black, when he was president of the World Bank, said, "We are coming to a situation in which the optimist will be the man who thinks that present living standards can be maintained."

Dr. B. R. Sen, Director-General of the United Nations Food and Agriculture Organization, has said, "The next thirty-five years . . . will be a most critical period in man's history. Either we take the fullest measures to raise productivity and to stabilize population growth, or we will face disaster of an unprecedented magnitude. We must be warned . . . of unlimited disaster." . . .

The third world, then, is in acute danger of entering into a descending spiral where each successive failure reinforces the last in a descent toward chaos. The process may have begun. There is a tendency in the U.S. to believe it will be possible to isolate ourselves from this, retreat into the land of affluence. For a while perhaps.

Consider this: As of 1954 the United States was using about fifty percent of the raw material resources consumed in the world each year. The rate of consumption has been rising and by 1980 the U.S. could be consuming more than eighty-three percent of the total.

Today the U.S. is a net importer of goods. Its reliance on foreign trade grows each year. The third world, in the meantime, sees industrialization as the road to salvation; its demand for raw material can be expected to accelerate. Today we can soothe the hungry by offering a certain amount of food and aid. Tomorrow we will be competing for raw material and there will be no spare food to offer.

The prospect is not bright. As Professor Harold A. Thomas, Jr. of Harvard's Center for Population Studies put it, ". . . unless we engage ourselves today in problems of development of the poor nations, the conditions under which we live during the next two generations may not be attractive. The fuel required to sustain our mammoth technological apparatus may constitute a gross drain on the resources of the earth. Other societies cannot be expected to regard this favorably. A vista of an enclave of privilege in an isolated West is not pleasant to contemplate. Wise and human political institutions do not thrive in beleaguered citadels."

. . . .

BUCHAREST–1974*

... On August 19, 1974, the first World Population Conference convened in Bucharest, Romania, with more than 135 nations in attendance. The conference mission was of the utmost priority: to exchange diverse viewpoints on population policies and to reach common understanding regarding population growth levels. The thrust of the Plan of Action adopted during the 12-day gathering, though less than earth *shattering*, inculcated some hope of earth *saving*. A look at what transpired at the Population Conference, particularly the political points and the socioeconomic disparities between the developing nations of the world, reveals not only the major population issues confronting global society today, but also the key conflicts which must be resolved by the international community if we are entitled to expect a tomorrow.

That the United Nations General Assembly designated 1974 as International Population Year was in itself an action to be lauded. Admittedly, resolutions do not have the binding force of international law; nevertheless, the decision to meet in Bucharest demonstrated some feeling of consensus among nations: that population on a worldwide basis had reached a staggering figure. It took from the beginning of man until about 1830–10,000 years—for the world's population to reach one billion; the next century added the second billion; only 30 more years, to 1960, were needed to add the third; and the fourth billion will arrive by 1975. More alarming than this, experts have predicted that the global population will reach an overwhelming 7-1/2 billion by the year 2000—just a quarter century away.

Most industrialized nations view this prediction with shock and dismay, while the majority of developing nations perceive additional population growth as a boon to their economic development.

*Adapted from Nancy D. Joyner, "Bucharest–1974," *AAUW Journal* 68 (Nov 74):9-11.

The question to be resolved at the Population Conference was a crucial reconciliation of the two opposing views. Only a blind optimist could have failed to predict the inevitable reservations some nations have to an unequivocal declaration of a global program to control the world's population. What did emerge, however, was a curious blending of socio-economic objectives as primary goals, with population limitation—the presumed purpose of the gathering—taking a back seat in the diplomatic bargaining.

Perhaps more than anything else, the Conference made nations more aware of what the issues really are. The main goal of the industrial nations, to encourage governments to set up family planning programs by 1985, in hopes of reducing average family size, was thwarted by an "impromptu" alliance including the Communist countries, Latin American nations (where Roman Catholicism is the predominant religious faith), the Vatican, and some African and Arab nations. . . .

This "coalition" constituted a clear majority in opposition to a concerted international governmental push for scientific birth control dissemination and usage; they contended that socio-economic betterment, not population growth limitation, is the foremost world need today. In some instances, the desire to reduce population growth was viewed as a sinister plot to suppress progress within the developing nations. After all, some of these nations argued, industrialized nations achieved their unprecedented growth and prominence in the world community through population expansion. To limit the developing nations before they reach a "saturation" point in numbers of people is to sap their mainstay for achieving industrial "greatness." Despite the obvious fallacy of these arguments (the People's Republic of China sponsors an active government program for birth limitation, the success of which can be directly linked to economic and social progress), these nations made their feelings known in the outcome of the Conference's covenant: family planning was de-emphasized and socio-economic betterment was emphasized as much as possible.

International failure to place "population" at the heart of the planetary crisis struck deep into the concerns of women's rights advocates. Betty Friedan accused the developing nations of "forming an alliance to create a double standard and deny women their basic rights." Although not taking the "hard line" feminist approach of Ms. Friedan, Helvi Sipila of Finland, the first woman assistant secretary-general of the United Nations, commented that countries limiting family planning information and supplies "are infringing on the exercise of basic human rights." Yet the concerns of women were not entirely overlooked by the Conference, because a key point of the Plan of Action focused on the recognition of the right of women to be involved in economic development and to participate equally in all spheres of life. The linkage of women's equality and lower fertility rates was recognized; in doing so, the international community made it clear that socio-economic betterment entails not only industrial progress, improvement of educational, medical and housing facilities, but advancement in the status of women as well.

Caspar Weinberger, Secretary of HEW, remarked: "The fact that a population conference of 135 nations and many population and food experts has been held at all has been a great accomplishment." Admittedly, the airing of political and ideological views on the population issue was necessary and important, but the true test of the Conference rests with the peoples of the world. The Conference reaffirmed the basic human right of couples to decide freely the number and spacing of their children. Under the Plan of Action, governments need only see that birth control information and means are made available to their people, but governments are not committed to encourage birth control usage nor to suggest optimum family size. Although the majority of governments represented continue to view their national priorities as socio-economic progress first, population limitation second, they may soon find, as other nations can attest, that their people have a different ordering of priorities. As "Spaceship Earth" seems smaller, as food scarcities increase, as droughts and famines continue, as pollution levels and environmental problems rise, the need to improve life for the living may be the strongest personal incentive to smaller, happier and healthier families.

FROM FOREST TO DUMP*

Once, the Ocala National Forest was a wilderness Eden of pine trees that had stood tall when the nation was born, of hickory, sweetgum, magnolia and orchids, of giant live oaks with outstretched arms decked in Spanish moss.

It was here, amid fantastic beauty, that Marjorie Kinnan Rawlings found inspiration for "The Yearling," the Pulitzer Prize-winning story of a boy and his pet fawn. The South's largest deer herd roamed the forest. Bears fished in teeming waters. Wild turkeys galore roosted in the trees.

On misty mornings, the graceful white-tailed deer gathered to drink from the banks of pure, spring-fed streams that sparkled like diamonds and, as the evening shadows crawled through shaded glens, mirrored the red fire of the setting sun.

*Adapted from Ben Funk, "Ocala Forest, Once Inspiring, Is a Dump," AP dispatch, 2 Aug 72.

But that was before, by U.S. government policy, lumber and pulpwood interests, land developers, U.S. Navy bombers and wildlife poachers began a systematic exploitation. . . .

It was before the timber industry was allowed to "clearcut" thousands of acres of trees at a time, gashing great, ugly scars across the face of the tortured wilderness.

It was before developers began subdividing 65,000 privately owned acres inside the forest boundary, including almost all desirable waterfront on the largest of its 20,000 acres of lakes and ponds.

It was before the Navy staked out a 6,200-acre range for practice bombing and strafing that shattered the forest stillness, started fires raging through valuable hardwood timber, throwing wildlife into panic.

Today, except for a few spots—some maintained in virgin loveliness by conservationist owners—the Ocala is more of a huge, shoddy, trash-strewn land development than a true wilderness. Everywhere, signs proclaim that "the Heart of the Ocala" is for sale.

And now, says Lyman Rogers, president of the Coalition to Protect the Ocala Forest, the oil industry wants to blanket it with oil rigs and petrochemical complexes.

Rogers formed the coalition following his own discovery last year that the U.S. Bureau of Land Management had quietly leased 95 percent of the Ocala's 430,000 acres for oil drilling. Before the action became known, the Amoco Production Co. had staked out a site for its first well and was ready to put a bit in the ground.

The BLM also had leased out Florida's two other national forests, the Osceola and the Apalachicola, to the petroleum industry, but Rogers's group decided to make its stand at the Ocala, hoping for a historic decision that could help decide whether other beleaguered U.S. forests are to survive.

"The Ocala has undergone more stress than any other forest in America," said Rogers. "If we put on a fight to the finish now, there is something of value to save. The Forest Service has developed a 10-year plan to improve the Ocala, but the exploiters and the land developers are moving much faster than that.

"The oil companies would have us believe that the need to drill on public lands comes from a great oil shortage. Actually, they want to drill there because it's cheap. It costs a lot less to deal with the BLM than with hundreds of individual landowners."

. . . .

When Rogers broke the news of the oil leases, which he had accidentally obtained in a conversation with a well driller, Florida U.S. Forest supervisor Robert Entzminger defended the Ocala against oil industry encroachment. Shortly afterward, Entzminger was transferred to Utah.

In the public outcry that followed, Interior Secretary Rogers Morton ordered a one-year moratorium on oil drilling in the Ocala pending environmental impact statements and a public hearing, which had been required all along under the Environmental Policy Act. . . .

Frank Finison, who was transferred from Louisiana to take over Entzminger's post, quickly read the mood of Florida. In public meetings throughout the state, he sought citizen guidance in managing the forest for better use by people seeking escape in the wilderness from the congestion and pollution of the cities. Out of these sessions came a 10-year plan attacking all the old evils. "The big job," said Finison, "lies ahead."

The problems are overwhelming. One is to curb the appetite of the lumber and pulp industries, which have been given a tree-chopping free rein for decades. The success of a U.S. forest has always been gauged on its revenue from timber sales.

. . . .

Denuded slashes more than a mile long are shockingly visible from the highways. The Forest Service argues that new growth in the clearcut areas provide good browsing for deer. But with speeding traffic in clear view on the roads, the animals are afraid to leave the shelter of the woods to get to it.

Under the new Ocala plan, Finison said, cuttings will be allowed on no more than 80 to 100 acres and they must fit into the topography and terrain, with no openings onto the road.

Whether these restrictions will prevail against the timber lobby is open to question, however. In Washington, a proposed presidential order which would have banned clearcutting in public areas of scenic beauty was cancelled last January after meetings of administration officials and timber industry executives.

Demanding an investigation, Sen. Fred R. Harris, D-Okla., said, "We ought to know more about this seemingly incestuous relationship between the timber lobby and the government."

'THESE MURDERED OLD MOUNTAINS'*

The mining process where land is stripped away to reveal the minerals below has violently defaced the hillsides of Kentucky and other eastern states. Now, the same process is threatening the Dakotas and Montana, but

*Adapted from David Nevin, " 'These Murdered Old Mountains,' " *Life* 64(12 Jan 68):54–55, 66–67.

powerful mining interests have so far blocked meaningful control legislation. In his description of the results of strip mining in Kentucky, David Nevin implies what is likely to happen—indeed, has already begun to happen—in the plains states.

The sun was bright and warm the day the bulldozers came around the hill and ruined Cecil Combs. It was a simple matter and entirely legal. The men on the bulldozers were miners and they held title to the coal that lies in thick, rich seams with edges cropping out on the sides of the mountains. Combs could hear the coughing of the machines in the quiet mountain air long before they rounded the ridge that soars to the sky above his farm. To reach their coal, the miners shredded the rock with explosives and ripped the soil with the bulldozer blades and poured it all down on the croplands below. They destroyed the land, perhaps for a century to come, and in the process they destroyed Cecil Combs as well.

All that Combs had ever owned was his 30-acre farm on the steep slopes above Pigeon Roost Creek, which empties into Troublesome Creek in the Cumberland Mountains of eastern Kentucky. This is a strange and beautiful country with its tight folds of mountains curled one within the other like a maze, each separated by a deep hollow in which the people cluster in tight and isolated communities of hillside farms. They orient not to roads but to the noisy little streams in the bottom of each hollow that babble away the violent rainfall. Once, the water in these creeks was clear and game fish flashed in the sun and deer paused to drink. But that was long ago. The good times are gone now and the land is ravished.

The disaster visited upon it and upon Cecil Combs is called strip mining. Coal seams range throughout these mountains. Decades ago, when mining was entirely a matter of men going underground and digging, the owners of the property sold—often for as little as 50¢ an acre—the right to mine whatever minerals it might contain, which meant coal. Now the time has come to take the coal, but in this day of new earth-moving machines that range from powerful bulldozers in the mountains to gigantic shovels in flatter country, it is much less expensive to take it from the top.

This sort of operation is not limited to the Kentucky mountains or even to coal. Surface mining for coal and other minerals goes on at an accelerating pace. An estimated 3.2 million acres have already been disturbed, an area as large as the state of Connecticut.

. . . .

The violence done to Cecil Combs's 30 acres is repeated a thousandfold and more across the mountains of Kentucky. From the air you can see the timbered ridges, stretching for miles into the bluing haze with the yellow wounds of the miners' cuts clearly marked in their sides. The cuts follow the coal seam, rounding ridge after ridge. Sometimes they encircle a mountain, leaving a lonely island of trees on top, and sometimes, in a sort of cosmic contempt, the miners simply whack off the entire mountain top and leave it a mesa.

Rock containing sulphur often is exposed and it oxidizes. Rain water washes it into a mild solution of sulphuric acid that collects in reddish pools. It seeps into the water table and ruins wells. It runs down into the streams. The fish die and the grass along the banks surrenders and the trees that shade the stream fail to leaf the following spring.

The spoil bank leaks yellow silt into the streams. Gradually it covers their stony bottoms and the creeks begin to fill. Then they cannot contain the runoff of the heavy rainfall and they send floods of acid water over the fertile bottomlands and coat them with the sterile silt. In many places today, only cattails and other marsh plants prosper on what was the best garden land.

These conditions are fast becoming endemic to the Cumberland Mountains, and wherever the land is damaged, the society is damaged.

. . . .

The only workable answer so far is reclamation enforced by law, its cost simply part of the cost of mining the coal. In European strip mining, on land already at a premium, the dirt is set aside, the coal lifted and everything replaced in order, the rock and subsoil below, the top soil back on top. It is compacted, leveled, limed to counteract acidity, fertilized and planted. This really restores land but, at least from a strict economic point of view, such a program isn't feasible in the U.S.: it costs more per acre than the average per-acre price of land.

. . . .

To reassure myself that I had not misjudged the excesses and the damage of mountain strip mining, the last place I visited before leaving Kentucky was Pearl Grigsby's farm on Lotts Creek near Hazard. I found Grigsby on the rude road that miners had made through his hollow—against his wishes—for easy access to the notch they had cut above. . . .

I went onto the notch itself and stood over the slide that poured down on much of Grigsby's hollow. The ground was wet and I could hear water trickling. Now and then a miniature slide broke free of the mass with a wet thwacking sound, tumbled a few feet and stopped. It was yellow and orange and blue with clay. Sandstone boulders and torn timber poked out of it. On impulse I started down. It was steep and wet and slippery. My boots sank to the ankles—in places I went in to the knees—in viscous, shifting, gooey mud. I went down and down, around the boulders, under the broken trees, slipping, sliding, falling—and toward the bottom, planted knee-deep in mud, I turned to look at the mass now towering above me, wet and glistening in the failing light, and it was as threatening as the high wave of a following sea in that moment before it comes down on you.

That slide will not stop, law or no law. And all at once, I remembered an old mountain lawyer who, smiling cynically, used to drawl, "Mountain strip mining laws are kind of like letting a fellow go ahead and commit rape—provided he signs a bond guaranteeing to restore the victim to her original condition. It just can't be done."

HOW THEY KILLED THE BUFFALO*

Two of the most startling examples of human greed and shortsightedness occurred during the last half of the 19th century. It was then that Americans by the thousands engaged in a mass, wanton slaughter of the bison and the passenger pigeon. In the case of both species, the clear signs that extinction was nigh were noted but ignored by almost all observers. The immediate result was the near disappearance of the bison and the total extinction of the pigeon; the long-term consequence was a permanent, deleterious alteration of the natural environment. The sad description of what happened on the buffalo hunts was penned by Wayne Gard when he was an editorial writer for the Dallas Morning News.

Stories of the vast size of the buffalo herds that once roamed the Great Plains of the West sound like the imaginings of a Paul Bunyan. They would hardly be credited today except that they were attested by many reliable travelers and by early settlers.

. . . .

Many of those who saw the enormous buffalo herds in the West and assumed that they always would be there lived to see the plains cleared of them. Except for a remnant in the north, the whole slaughter was completed in little more than a decade. The near extermination of the buffalo came because his hide was worth a dollar or so to hardy hunters willing to take chances on being scalped by Indians.

For as long as they could remember, the Indians had been hunting buffaloes. The tribes living on the Great Plains were especially dependent on them for their meat, for robes for winter warmth, and for hides used in making tepees. When the early Spanish explorers first saw the buffaloes on the plains, they called them Indian cattle. . . .

*Adapted from Wayne Gard, "How They Killed the Buffalo," *American Heritage* (Aug 56):292–297.

Some of the early travelers in the West hunted buffaloes for sport as well as for meat. One such was Washington Irving, who, with several companions, went on a buffalo hunt in the Indian Territory in October, 1832. Irving, after several misses, downed an enormous bull with his pistol. He took the tongue on his saddle and carried it back to camp.

A number of European visitors traveled to the West to try their marksmanship on the shaggies. Among them was Sir William Drummond Stewart, who came from Scotland in 1843 to shoot buffaloes. In the Platte Valley he and his party found all they could want—a herd estimated at a million head. On some days when they finished shooting the prairie was strewn for miles with dead animals.

. . . .

The start of the great buffalo hunt is linked with the name of J. Wright Mooar, who became the mightiest of the hide men. Mooar, of Scotch ancestry, was born in Vermont in 1851. He traveled west in 1869 and, after working as a horsecar conductor in Chicago and as a carpenter at Rochelle, Illinois, went on to Hays, Kansas, in the fall of 1870. There he chopped cordwood for a government contractor on Walnut Creek, thirty miles south of the fort.

As this was buffalo country, Mooar soon joined in the more lucrative occupation of hunting. With five associates he equipped a small outfit, with two horse teams and one ox team. At that time the market for hides was limited largely to their use in making lap robes. Mooar and his fellow killed for meat. Mooar shipped the hind quarters to Quincy, Illinois, and to Kansas City, leaving the rest of each carcass, including the hide, to rot on the prairie.

In the winter of 1871-72, Mooar learned from another hunter, Charlie Rath, that the Leavenworth firm of W. C. Lobenstein had an order for 500 buffalo hides. A firm in England wanted them for experimental use in making leather. After Mooar had provided a quota of this order, he had 57 hides left. He shipped the surplus hides to his brother, John Wesley Mooar, who was a clerk in a jewelry store in New York, asking him to see if he could interest tanners in them.

The tanners were so interested that Wright Mooar soon had orders for all the hides he could deliver, and his New York brother went to Kansas to handle the business end of the enterprise. As more tanners discovered that buffalo hides made leather good for many uses, the demand became so great that a whole army of hunters surged into the buffalo ranges.

With Dodge City as the principal outfitting and shipping point, most of the hunters worked in small groups, going out with wagons for hauling back the hides. They used heavy rifles, some of them Sharps made especially for killing buffaloes. In some cases, two hunters worked together, sharing both the shooting and the skinning. In a bigger outfit, two or three expert marksmen might hire a larger number of less skilled men for the more menial work of skinning and drying.

The buffaloes, although suspicious of strange smells, had poor eyesight and were less alert than most game animals. If the hunter approached against the wind, usually he could come close to the herd without being noticed. Often he could kill many of the animals before the others sought safety in flight. Some hunters fired from the saddle, but more preferred to work afoot and thus have steadier aim and take more hides with less ammunition. The hunter tried to shoot the buffalo just behind the shoulder blade and to penetrate the heart. A wounded bull could be dangerous, but usually the rifleman could dodge long enough to place the mortal shot.

One of the Kansas hunters, who hired fifteen skinners, claimed to have killed 1,500 buffaloes in a week, 250 of them in a single day. Billy Tilghman took 3,300 hides in one season. With a long-range Sharps rifle, even an ordinary marksman could average fifty hides a day. At one place on the prairie a surveying party found 6,500 carcasses from which the hides had been stripped. The untouched meat had been left to rot or to be devoured by wolves. A Santa Fe railway conductor, J. H. Helton, said he could have walked for a hundred miles along the right of way without stepping off the carcasses. So great was the slaughter that in 1872 and 1873 the railroads hauled 1,250,000 hides out of Kansas and nearby territory.

This hide hunting, plus the killing of an estimated 350,000 head by Indians in that period, thinned the Kansas herds enough to make further shooting less profitable there. In search of new herds, J. Wright Mooar and John Webb saddled their horses and took a trip through the Texas Panhandle. For five days they rode through a sea of grazing buffaloes.

Their report excited the other hunters, but there was some hesitation because the Medicine Lodge treaties of 1867—by implication and interpretation—had reserved for the Indians all hunting grounds south of the Arkansas River. However, Texas, which owned the land now in question, had not been a party to the treaty. Mooar asked advice from the Third Infantry commander at Fort Dodge, Richard Irving Dodge.

"Boys," replied the officer, "If I were hunting buffalo I would go where the buffalo are."

That was enough for the hunters. Willing to risk the danger of Indian scalpers, they quickly formed parties and set out to the south. They were followed in the spring of 1874 by dealers in hunting supplies and hides. . . .

In the winter of 1876-77 an estimated 1,500 hunters were shooting buffaloes on the Texas plains, and by early spring Fort Griffin had about four acres filled with piles of hides waiting for the wagon trains to haul them to Fort Worth. In the latter town, one morning in May, 1877, a reporter noted a caravan of ten wagons coming in. "In front were eleven yoke of oxen driven by one man and dragging after them four large wagons, heavily laden. Two other teams, with seven yoke each, drawing three wagons, followed. There probably were 2,500 to 3,000 hides in the train."

In the same spring another Fort Worth observer was impressed with one lot of 60,000 hides piled high on a platform near the Texas and Pacific Railroad. During the season, Fort Griffin sent in about 200,000 hides, which brought the hunters about a dollar each. But the peak of the slaughter had passed, and the end was in sight. The hunters had broken up the great southern herd, leaving only scattered remnants.

In the winter of 1877-78 the skinners took more than 100,000 hides in Texas. This virtually wiped out the southern herd. The only noteworthy commercial hunting left was that in the northern plains in the early 1880s. Like many of his fellows, J. Wright Mooar put away his buffalo guns and turned to cattle ranching in Texas. His careful aim had downed 20,000 of the shaggies in eight years.

The widespread and wasteful slaughter had aroused shocked opposition, especially in the East. Several western states passed laws to curb the killing, but these measures came too late and were not strictly enforced. Realists in the West knew that the buffaloes would have to go before the hostile Indians of the Great Plains could be subdued and the ranges opened for cattle ranching.

Representative James A. Garfield expressed this view in 1874 when, in a debate in Congress, he reported that the secretary of the interior would rejoice, as far as the Indian question was concerned, when the last buffalo was killed. Early in the following year General Phil Sheridan put it even more clearly when he addressed a joint session of the Texas legislature, which was considering a bill to protect the buffaloes.

The hunters, said the General, ". . . will do more in the next year, to settle the vexed Indian question than the entire regular army has done in the last thirty years. They are destroying the Indians' commissary. . . . Send them powder and lead . . . let them kill, skin and sell until the buffaloes are exterminated. Then your prairies can be covered with speckled cattle and the festive cowboy, who follows the hunter as a second forerunner of an advanced civilization."

When the hunters had completed their slaughter, only the white bones remained strewn over the plains. Many a pioneer farmer and ranchman eked out his meager income in a drought year by gathering these bones and hauling them in his wagon to the nearest railroad town, where they were shipped off to be made into carbon or fertilizer.

In isolated valleys enough buffaloes were left to let the breed survive and to supply circuses and zoos and those ranchmen who liked to keep a few for sentimental reasons. . . . Yet the vast herds have vanished; they roam only in song and story and in the minds of a few old men with long memories.

Heat Pollution and Nuclear Energy

The next three articles discuss some of the problems associated with two of the alleged "solutions" to increased demands on energy sources. Observing the pollution caused by internal combustion engines, many have suggested that we make greater use of "clean" electricity, especially for propelling automobiles in crowded urban areas. However, production of electricity also causes pollution, particularly in the form of heat. Therefore, from a world standpoint there is little pollution gain in using electricity for energy since such use simply transfers the source of pollution from the locale of use to the locale of production. Those who see nuclear fission as a relatively cheap and non-polluting source of energy are also in for disappointment. As indicated in two of the accompanying selections, fission-based nuclear power apparently causes more problems than it solves. Even so, some observers are willing to take the risk—Dr. Hans Bethe, famed Cornell University physicist, declared on 14 Dec 74 (New York Times) that the energy crisis is so severe "We urgently need a non-fossil source of power. The only such source which is available and which has been developed for use is nuclear power from fission."

THE HEAT BARRIER *

Thermal pollution, as the term is applied most often today, refers to waste heat from the generation of electrical power. The adverse consequences of ejecting such heat into rivers, bays, and estuaries is indeed a matter for serious concern, but it is only one aspect of a more fundamental problem. Specifically, *all* human activities—from metabolism to driving (and stop-

*Adapted from Paul R. Ehrlich and John P. Holdren, "The Heat Barrier," *Saturday Review* 54(3 Apr 71):61.

ping) an automobile—result in the dissipation of energy as heat. In the case of a power plant, the heat delivered to the environment ultimately includes not just the waste heat at the site but all the useful output as well: The electricity itself is dissipated as heat in wires, filaments, the bearings in electric motors, and so forth. That all the energy we use—electrical and otherwise—is eventually degraded to heat is a consequence of the second law of thermodynamics. No technological gimmickery or scientific breakthrough can be expected to remove this constraint. Thus the thermal load imposed upon the surroundings where energy is consumed can be moderated only by manipulating the number of consumers or the per capita consumption of energy. The thermal loads where electricity is generated and where it is transmitted, on the other hand, can be tricity is generated and where it is transmitted, on the other hand, can be reduced by devising more efficient power plants and transmission systems. . . .

The consequences of man's introduction of heat into his environment can usefully be classified as local, regional, and global. On the local level, the principal effects are the disruption of aquatic ecosystems by the heated effluent from power-plant condensers, and climatic effects ranging from ground fogs (associated with evaporative cooling towers at power plants) to the urban "heat-island" phenomenon. The effects associated with power plants have been well publicized, and we will not pursue them here. On the other hand, the heat that man dissipates in his cities is neither as widely appreciated as a problem nor as well understood scientifically in its effects. . . .

We know that our cities are, on the average, somewhat warmer, rainier, and foggier than their rural surroundings. We also know that the rate of energy dissipation by man in the Los Angeles Basin, for example, is equal to nearly 6 percent of the solar energy absorbed over the same area. This is undoubtedly a significant perturbation. However, it is difficult to sort its consequences from other man-induced effects that accompany it, including the city's surface structure and heat-transfer properties and the usual haze of pollutants.

The most serious reason for concern over our apparent capacity to alter urban climates today is the warning it provides of intervention on a larger scale in coming decades. The possibility that man will become a climatic force to be reckoned with over large areas (coastlines, river basins, megalopolises) cannot be dismissed lightly. According to one recent estimate, the Boston-Washington megalopolis in the year 2000 will contain fifty-six million people on 11,500 square miles. Their dissipation of heat will be equal to 50 percent of the solar energy incident on that surface area in the winter, and 15 percent of the corresponding figure in summer. Nor can it be safely assumed that serious effects will not occur even before man's energy contribution reaches so large a fraction of the sun's over appreciable areas. Those who make that assumption—and many technologists have done so—overlook the fact that regional climates are often the result of numerous powerful forces operating in a rather finely tuned balance. In other words, the climate we perceive often represents a small difference between large numbers. Thus the important determinants of regional climate include the variation of solar heating with latitude and the winds and ocean currents driven by these differences, the variation in the heat balance on land and adjacent bodies of water, the role of river systems, lakes, bays, and oceans as thermal buffers, and so forth. Man will be an important force on these sorts of scales well before his energy dissipation is comparable to the total solar impact.

Our knowledge of the detailed operation of the meteorological system is as yet inadequate to predict the exact consequences of such human impact, but the onset of instabilities seems a distinct possibility: Local perturbations of sufficient size could trigger disproportionate fluctuations or semi-permanent changes on a continental or perhaps even hemispheric scale. It should be noted that the first casualty of sudden climatic change of any sort is likely to be agricultural productivity.

On a global scale, many other environmental problems loom larger than thermal pollution for the decades immediately ahead. Last summer's MIT-sponsored Study of Critical Environmental Problems identified some of the most serious ones: climatic effects of increasing loads of carbon dioxide and dust in the atmosphere, the accumulation of persistent pesticides and toxic heavy metals in terrestrial and oceanic food webs, and the rising input of oil to the oceans. Nevertheless, it is to be emphasized that large-scale thermal pollution is in principle (and in the long term) less tractable than any of these. For even if we should be clever enough and lucky enough to ameliorate or evade every other threat accompanying continued population growth and increasing consumption, the laws of thermodynamics would finally force a halt.

If the present global rate of increase in energy consumption—approximately 5 percent per annum—should persist for another century and a half, man's dissipation then would be equal to 10 percent of the solar energy absorbed over the entire surface of the globe, or one-third of the solar energy absorbed over land. Simple calculations suggest a corresponding mean global temperature increase of about 13 degrees Fahrenheit. Not all climatological authorities agree that thermal input can be translated into temperature change with any such degree of precision. However, all accept the inevitability of climatological and ecological disruption by the growing thermal burden.

MORATORIUM POLITICS: FINDING THE CRITICAL MASS*

In order to terminate a scandal like the premature licensing of nuclear power plants, it is necessary to be realistic.

Never before has a serious effort been made to halt a $40-billion industry dead in its tracks. Winning a moratorium on the deployment of nuclear power plants will require one of the largest citizen efforts of all time. It will require active pressure on Congress and on utility directors by about a million Americans who are enraged by the threat of nuclear electricity to our health, genetic integrity, and our national security—a million citizens who are willing to work against any candidate or utility director who fails to support a moratorium.

In order to exert pressure, the national constituency for a nuclear power moratorium must first do two things. It must identify the individuals who already support a moratorium, because nothing is so easily dismissed as a group which can't prove for whom it speaks. Second, the moratorium movement must enlarge its constituency, fast, while the country is still getting only a few percent of its energy from nuclear power.

Who is likely to join the moratorium movement? I think the potential allies would include religious leaders, health people, environmentalists, business and civic groups, farmers, veterans' groups, peace and disarmament people and civil liberties people. Let's consider them more closely.

Religious leaders. The nuclear power issue is essentially a moral issue, not a technical one. Radioactive nuclear pollutants which escape into the environment can kill and maim living creatures for centuries after we have enjoyed our electricity. One of the well-known effects of exposure to extra radioactivity is extra genetic injury. As John Francis of the Scottish Council of Churches has said: "The *minimum* morality of man is to leave the gene-pool of humanity intact."

Nuclear power plants today are creating long-lived radioactive poisons which will have to be kept out of the environment for 100,000 years. Unless stopped, the plants in the U.S. alone will have produced enough radioactive garbage and plutonium in the next thirty years to kill or maim almost every living thing on Earth. Will our generation make the future of life subordinate to the future of the nuclear power industry? Shall we make the future of life depend on success or failure in containing the radioactive by-products of nuclear electricity? In effect, the nuclear power

*Senator Mike Gravel, "Moratorium Politics: Finding the Critical Mass," *Environmental Action* 4(9 Dec 72):9-13.

industry has started to use the entire planet as a laboratory for its radioactive containment experiment, and us as its involuntary guinea pigs.

Objection to this experiment does not require technical expertise; it requires common observation of human fallibility, and an ability to distinguish hetween gambles which are proper and gambles which are immoral. Leading nuclear experts like Dr. Alvin Weinberg, director of Oak Ridge Nuclear Laboratory, Dr. Albert Crewe, former director of Argonne Nuclear Laboratory, and Dr. Hannes Alfven, 1970 Nobel Laureate in physics at University of California at San Diego, acknowledge that unsuspected or uncorrected deficiencies in nuclear power technology could create "catastrophe for the human race," "serious danger for the entire population of the world, " or "a total poisoning of the planet." Obviously, nuclear electricity is one of the most profound moral issues of our time.

Health people. I feel that natural-food people and other private citizens who cherish good health have been the most courageous activists in this issue so far.

I do not mean the official "guardians of public health" in the government, the National Academy of Sciences, or the National Council on Radiation Protection. They set the presently permissible dose of nuclear radiation in 1957 at a level which they estimated at that time might well cause a five to 10 percent increase in cancer and a quarter of a million "defective babies." Such consequences were apparently acceptable to them. Even today, they continue to support that dose-level, or they keep their objections wrapped safely in silence.

Chronic exposure of our population to the legally permissible dose of radiation could easily reverse all advances in public health during the last 25 years. In tacit acknowledgement of this outrage, the nuclear power people have started promising never to give us more than one percent of the permissible dose.

The whole trouble is that they are making promises which may be impossible to keep.

The 150 nuclear plants already planned or operating will produce more long-lived radioactivity in this country every year than about 130,000 Hiroshima bombs. Ask any nuclear enthusiast *what* gives him such confidence that imperfect human beings will manage to keep 99.99 percent of that radioactivity under perfect and perpetual control, and then evaluate the vacant answers carefully.

In its February, 1972 editorial, the American Journal of Public Health warned its readers that there needs to be "an increasing awareness of the consequences, actual or potential, that mistakes (in nuclear technology) may entail for present or future generations."

The probability that nuclear electricity will create irreversible nuclear pollution is beginning to trouble many experts in the biological sciences, but if such experts are too timid to rock the nuclear boat, their intellectual "awareness" will be utterly irrelevant.

Environmentalists. Many environmentalists have been fooled into thinking nuclear power is "clean," when in fact, it is the dirtiest technology conceived so far by man. Nuclear energy is "clean" only the way coal is "clean." They are *both* clean, provided you keep their deadly pollutants out of the environment.

Unfortunately, though nuclear pollutants are far more toxic than those from fossil-fuels, we do not have the foggiest notion how to cope with them. The Europeans continue to dump some radioactive waste in the ocean; we pump, dribble, and bury some of ours in the ground, release some to the air, and put the rest in tanks.

Failure of the cooling system for a single storage tank of liquid waste at the nuclear fuel-reprocessing plant in South Carolina, for instance, could require the evacuation of Washington, D.C., most of Maryland, most of Delaware, a good part of Virginia, West Virginia, and North Carolina. Few environmentalists yet know these things.

Environmentalists are concerned about the strip-mining of coal, but many do not seem to understand that open-pit mining for nuclear fuel is common. As the AEC awkwardly put it, "This operation requires the stripping off of all the often enormous rock quantities overlying the deposit."

The residues left from uranium mining and milling contain radium, with a radioactive half-life of 1600 years. Already there are 90 million tons of radioactive uranium "tailings," mostly from our weapons program, eroding into our Western river-systems. This unsolved problem will grow immense, and immensely alarming to environmentalists, if we go ahead with nuclear electricity.

Business and civic groups. These groups generally favor anything which is good for the economy. Since nuclear electricity poses an unprecedented threat to the economy, they are potential moratorium-supporters.

When those in business understand that a single nuclear accident can do twice the property damage of Hurricane Agnes, totally ruin the economy of a huge region of this country, and lead to an *un*planned nuclear shut-down from coast to coast, they may consider an immediate moratorium the *only* responsible position.

They may become the most ardent moratorium-supporters of all when they realize that most of their property insurance policies specifically exclude damage from nuclear power plants. Furthermore, the Price-Anderson Act (Section 170 of the Atomic Energy Act) sets the limit for a utility's public liability at $560 million per nuclear accident, with the taxpayers (including the victims) paying about 80 percent and the utility, 20 percent. Any damage over $560 million is simply not covered, although damage could exceed $7 billion per accident according to the AEC. And that figure could be an underestimate because power plants today are at least five times larger than the plant considered in the AEC damage estimate. Chambers of Commerce may start fighting nuclear power harder than anyone when they learn how Price-Anderson protection for the nuclear industry is leaving every other industry unprotected.

"But we need the power" is a refrain which will fade out as more people come to know that there are several safe and insurable ways to get "the power"; gasified coal, direct and indirect solar energy (including the wind), and geothermal heat could easily supply all of this country's energy demand (electrical and non-electrical) without the operation of a single nuclear power plant, ever. Incidentally, I predict that the alternatives to nuclear electricity will reach "commercial readiness" with breath-taking speed as soon as a nuclear moratorium seems certain.

Farmers. The country's farmers all stand to lose a great deal from nuclear electricity. The AEC's own "Brookhaven Report" estimates that one major nuclear accident (or act of sabotage) could radioactively contaminate 150,000 square miles of agricultural land, which is the equivalent of a square with one side reaching from Chicago to Cincinnati, or from New York City to Richmond, Va.

It is worth noting that the Bethlehem Steel Corporation intervened in January, 1972 against a nuclear power plant proposed near its billion-dollar steel complex east of Gary, Indiana.

Veterans' groups. Veterans' groups, like the American Legion, do not yet realize that nuclear power plants, each loaded with as much radio-activity as several hundred Hiroshima-bombs, can make this country indefensible. Nuclear power plants are vulnerable to conventional warheads from airplanes and submarines, not to mention sabotage and blackmail by terrorists.*

Peace and disarmament people. The AEC is officially concerned about a "black market" in nuclear fuel, especially plutonium, which is more valu-

---

*On November 15, after this article was written, hijackers who had seized a Southern Airways jet threatened to send the aircraft crashing into the Oak Ridge nuclear power plant in Tennessee. The plant was evacuated and though the threat was not carried out, it was obvious that the authorities had no way of dealing with the situation.

able than heroin or gold, and which makes excellent atom-bombs. The theft of plutonium could put private atom-bombs into the possession of terrorists, maniacs, gangsters, or foreign agents.

This probability is taken very seriously indeed by high government officials, who issue reports and regulations, but admit having no sure solution. The nuclear industry has already experienced trouble accounting for all the plutonium it handles; a loss-rate of one to two percent per year has been common.

It takes only 20 pounds of plutonium, or less, to make an atom-bomb. If we go ahead with nuclear electricity, we will have an inventory of about two million pounds of plutonium in this country by the year 2000.

By 1980, fifty countries will have enough plutonium from nuclear power plants and research reactors to make several thousand atom-bombs. Just a one-percent diversion of this plutonium per year into atom-bombs would make a farce out of the Nuclear Non-Proliferation Treaty.

Civil liberties people. In a nuclear economy, efforts to prevent diversion of plutonium may fail, no matter how greatly security measures are extended. When and if enough plutonium gets diverted for someone actually to make threats against this country with private atom-bombs, the emergency could easily provoke a nationwide panic and a martial-law situation lasting indefinitely. The possibility that nuclear electricity may end up wiping out our traditional American freedoms and civil liberties is a matter which deserves a great deal of consideration.

Most people who are unfamiliar with the unsolved problems of nuclear electricity react at first by saying, "If it is as bad as you say it is, the government would not permit it." Decent people tend to be complacent and to assume that the government is looking out for the people's best interests. I draw their attention to a 1971 booklet by the American Medical Association (AMA), which states that environmentally induced diseases are costing Americans about $38 billion a year; "an even greater price," the AMA points out, "is paid in human suffering and lives."

In allowing literally murderous levels of chemical pollution to develop in this country, the government clearly failed to look after the best interests of its citizens. In order to prevent *nuclear* pollution, citizens had better look out for themselves.

THE NUCLEAR SWORD OF DAMOCLES *

A short while ago another nuclear accident occurred. An underground

*Adapted from Lenore Marshall, "The Nuclear Sword of Damocles," *The Living Wilderness* 35(Spring 1971):17–19.

weapons test, supposedly self-contained, produced a radioactive cloud that traveled at least 450 miles, with fallout at its site that affected hundreds of people who had to be evacuated and decontaminated, and for whom ultimate damage cannot yet be ascertained.

During the years since Hiroshima—the short years previous to this newest atomic accident (which was the 17th underground test that has leaked, according to Atomic Energy Commission announcements)—we have recognized to our sorrow and terror that our entire planet has joined the wilderness in its struggle for survival; not only the wilderness but the whole world is in peril. Nothing, no matter how remote, is immune. Great tracts of fertile land, plant life and animal life in forests, plains, oceans, rivers, and lakes, have been joined by human life in the danger of extinction. The greatest threat to the continuance of animal, vegetable, and human existence comes from the nuclear sword of Damocles that hangs over our heads.

By great good luck, despite the minor accidents, there has not yet been a massive release. However, since sources of nuclear contamination are proliferating, the chances of a major disaster are also increasing; such a disaster could devastate a number of states and cause thousands more cases of cancer and genetic defects and deaths. There is a fundamental difference between radioactive pollutants and other pollutants such as DDT, NTA, oil, and automobile exhaust. All the latter are stable compounds, and there are possibilities of eliminating them or of rendering them harmless. But radioactive atoms are deranged atoms whose high-energy emissions from the nucleus cannot be stopped or, presto, made innocent by a lawsuit or a wave of a wand; they taper off at their own rate—240,000 years for radioactive plutonium 239, which happens to be a basic element in both the military and peaceful application of nuclear energy.

Cockroaches are said to withstand the effects of radiation quite nicely. Other animals, wild or otherwise, fare worse.

Since there is no way to turn off radioactivity, nuclear pollution is in a class by itself. Therefore, to whatever extent is possible, we must prevent any more of it from occurring.

We are already bearing the legacy of some earlier activities—radium from uranium mine wastes eroding into the Colorado and into other rivers, plutonium 238 in the atmosphere from a misfired navigational satellite (1964), and fallout from the atmospheric nuclear bomb tests. They are all, of course, still with us. For instance some of the radioactive cesium 137 will still be around 300 years from now and radioactive carbon 14 another 57,000 years. The strontium 90 fallout created by atmospheric tests was enough to work its way into the bones of almost every child tested for it in the Northern Hemisphere, according to Anthony Smith (*The Body*).

Since all radiation exposure is assumed to be harmful, whether it comes from bombs, medical X-rays, nuclear power plants, rocks, or the stars, what counts is the amount we accumulate and which we can still limit. The only hopeful thing to be said about this peril is that it is still possible to control it, keeping doses of radiation to safer permissible levels.

The biggest radioactive burial ground in the world lies in Nevada only 75 miles from Las Vegas, and consists of 250 square miles of contaminated desert surface pocketed with deadly plutonium 239. Under the surface, as well, lie hundreds of pools of radioactivity; some radioactive tritium is contained in the waters beneath the surface. This no-man's-land is mentioned in a paragraph within a report of the Atomic Energy Commission to the President's Council on Environmental Quality. If an earthquake or some other disaster, man-made or natural, were to strike this land, there is no knowing how vast would be the damage.

This is only one of many instances of pollutant destruction related to A.E.C. blasts and experiments. There is no way of estimating how much radioactivity is being released to the environment from all sources; however, what is known is that the amount of radioactivity and the damage from it are adding up. Since 1957 the A.E.C. to date has conducted over 200 tests in Nevada, plus two in Mississippi and two in Alaska. During 1970, through October 14, the United States detonated 23 underground bombs, the Russians six. An estimated 33 percent of the underground explosions vent some radioactivity into the air and, probably, gases seep to the surface eventually from all of them. Regarding Alaska, an A.E.C. contractor has calculated that the MILROW test in October 1969 could start discharging radioactive hydrogen into the ocean in six years and continue discharging for the subsequent 66 years. In 1966 ecologist G. G. Polykarpov warned that the oceans already have all the radioactivity that they can tolerate and that fish embryos show damage. Nonetheless new underground tests, the largest we have ever held, are being planned for Alaska, and in an active earthquake zone.

From sources other than nuclear bomb tests the danger and the damage proliferate. There are about 20 experimental nuclear power plants in operation in the United States now; the A.E.C. expects to license 450 to 650 more in the next 30 years. Each plant accumulates in one year as much long-lived radioactivity as in several hundred Hiroshima bombs. Construction and active preparations are presently occurring in 28 states and in Puerto Rico. Peaceful "Plowshare" underground bomb tests, proposed by the hundreds, would create contaminated gas, oil, and possibly copper for nationwide distribution. Pilot projects have been blasted in Arizona and Colorado; Wyoming is probably next. Nine "Plowshare" excavation bomb experiments for building canals and harbors have produced contaminants; a recent one produced radioactive air as far from the Nevada test site as Boise, Idaho. Thus the "peaceful atom," a kindly-sounding benefactor, may require a bit more assessment.

Radioactive material is being more and more widely used in industry, raising problems of disposal. In Florida, the country's first commercial nuclear sewage disposal plant is using radioactive cobalt. Storage of radioactive wastes is a mammoth problem. Altogether, there are over 100 million gallons of high-level radioactive waste stored in tanks in South Carolina, Idaho, Washington, and New York states. Storage tanks tend to disintegrate under the intense radioactive bombardment and heat; so far, 60,000 gallons have leaked from such tanks into the ground. The A.E.C. is working on techniques for solidifying the waste, but the process is so expensive that the A.E.C. hopes to dump millions of gallons of *un*solidified waste into underground excavations along the Savannah River. At the A.E.C.'s Hanford installation, there are open "dribble trenches" for so-called "low level" wastes. In March 1970, ducks drinking from these trenches were found to be so radioactive that eating them would give a person five times the annual "permissible" dose of radiation. And oysters at the mouth of the Columbia River are reconcentrating radioactive zinc released far upstream at Hanford. In New Mexico, radioactive waste is pumped into deep wells, stored, and allowed to seep into desert soil. Monitoring has sometimes been casual. At one commercial plant in West Valley, New York, after official denials of hazard, a group of citizens found radioactive levels in a creek to be 30,000 to 100,000 times higher than levels permitted by the A.E.C. During a test of the nuclear space rockets in Nevada in 1965, levels of air contamination on U.S. highway 95 between Reno and Las Vegas rose temporarily to 200,000 times their normal level.

When plutonium 239 falls on the test site in Nevada, the land is fenced off and posted. The problem is how to confine that plutonium to that fenced-off place, against wind and oxidation, for the next 240,000 years— when it will no longer be able to hurt us. Near Denver, Colorado, local scientists have proven that significant amounts of plutonium have escaped from the Rocky Flats plant where warheads are manufactured. After denying the possibility, the A.E.C. has confirmed the findings.

A recent medical report in the *Journal of the American Medical Association* states that among the young people of Rongelap Atoll in the Pacific who were accidentally exposed to fallout during the 1954 tests, the majority have developed thyroid abnormalities, many of them malignant.

Today's environmental crisis proves that much modern technology now actually functions to the detriment of society. It has become disoriented from society. Science and scientists are not omniscient; in fact many scientists are attached to special interests in government and industry. As Doctors John W. Gofman and Arthur R. Tamplin say of science and technology: "They offer credibility to the proposed ABM system and thereby offer thinkability to a nuclear war; they create the illusion that if we really get into trouble with our environment, science and technology will be able to rescue us; and they divert the scientific manpower away from more meaningful programs.". . .

Assault on the Ocean

These selections describe various conditions and practices which, if not altered substantially, will literally "kill" the world's oceans. The factual nature of the accounts give substance to the "fictional" pieces which conclude our consideration of environmental conditions.

OCEAN DESTRUCTION *

Underwater explorer Jacques Cousteau warned yesterday that the world is facing the destruction of its oceans. He estimated 30 to 50 percent of sea and plant life already have been damaged in the last 20 years.

"This is a frightening figure," Cousteau told the first session of the International Conference of Ocean Pollution, called by the Senate Commerce Committee.

Cousteau said his estimates were drawn from his personal experience of exploring the seas throughout the world.

He said that although people talk in terms of air, water and land pollution, "there is only one pollution."

"Everything (is) in the oceans," he said, noting that although water covers a large surface of the world water reserves are "really very small."

Government environmental agencies estimate that 48 million tons of pollutants were dumped in the seas in one year—1968—and the figure probably is larger now. Cousteau specifically named the waters of the Strait of Gibraltar as a dying area and predicted that "in a very few years, there will be nothing alive there."

Washington Star Service, Oct. 19, 1971.

He blamed some of man's other activities such as over-fishing and the digging up of plant life, for the deterioration of the oceans.

He said he believed people would be willing to spend $50 billion to $60 billion a year to curb pollution, because it is necessary for the survival of man.

"We know the cycle of life is intrinsically tied up with the cycle of water, so anything done against water is a crime against life."

The French explorer offered hope, if nations were prepared to act soon to restore the seas.

"Each time man has protected a species, the comeback has been successful," Cousteau said. "Nature is ready to respond," he said. "There is hope . . . if it is not too late."

CRISIS AT SEA:

THE THREAT OF NO MORE FISH*

The world is on its way to running out of fish. The endless riches of the sea that were supposed to mean salvation for the world's multiplying population turn out to be far from endless. They are being plundered by over-fishing so great that some stocks may be on an irreversible voyage to extinction.

For most of the earth's history, fish have had more than an even break. They could shelter in places fishermen could not go, or evade crude tackle with relative ease. But in the past two decades such automated marvels of electronic fish catchery as the American tuna seiner *Captain Vincent Gann* have radically altered the balance. Adopted by small nations as well as large, the new technology has led in the space of 20 years to a worldwide doubling of the quantity of fish caught. Today the haddock is gone from Georges Bank off the coast of New England and the yellowfin flounder from Alaskan waters, just as the herring was hunted out of the Baltic.

There is no good reason for any fish to become extinct. Actually, the world could safely catch twice as many fish as it does now, provided some simple rules of conservation were followed. But seaboard nations, including the U.S., are so tangled in tradition, in 18th-century concepts of "freedom of the seas" and in three-mile territorial limits that they have not been able to agree on sensible laws of fishery. . . .

*Adapted from Robert Brigham, "Crisis at Sea: The Threat of No More Fish," *Life* (Dec. 3, 1971):60–68.

The U.S. may lead in tuna fishing for the moment, but in most other kinds of fishing we rank as an underdeveloped country. Behemoths like the *Boevaya Slava*, a 575-foot Soviet factory ship, have outclassed our efforts and have brought the Russians within striking distance of the Japanese as the world's leading food-fishing nation. Fitted with all the processing and freezing equipment of a big onshore plant, the great ship is like a moving island, going wherever she is needed, taking in fish from her fleet of two dozen smaller catcher boats. . . .

. . . The fertile Georges Bank extends in sandy shallows 160 miles out from Cape Cod. A generation ago, New England fishermen were taking thousands of tons of haddock and cod and flounder from Georges every year, and hardly denting the supply. Ten years ago the Russians appeared, then the Poles, the Germans (East and West), the Spaniards and even the Bulgarians. At times their fleets totaled more than 500 vessels, many of these the new factory ships able to freeze everything they caught and to stay at sea for months.

. . . .

In the U.S., the immediate damage has been to people: to the men of Gloucester and New Bedford and other East Coast ports where the unemployment rates are among the highest in the country, to the veteran fishermen who no longer can expect their sons to follow in a tradition as old as the country, to owners who see their means of livelihood rotting away uselessly beside a wharf.

The long-term loss has been to the fishing grounds. Some biologists estimate that if all fishing stopped tomorrow, the haddock would never return to Georges Bank in the numbers that existed there just ten years ago. Like huge mechanical combines harvesting a field of wheat, the foreign vessels have raked over the grounds until they are now little more than a wasteland. One Canadian study defined the problem: "What is everybody's property is nobody's responsibility."

By 1970, when it was perfectly apparent they had wiped out nearly every living thing on the North Atlantic banks, the fishing nations involved got together and agreed on a quota system. It was no more than an admission of damage already done and is not likely to reverse the process of destruction. The foreign fleets came to the North Atlantic after they had cleaned out the Baltic and the North Sea. When they clean out the banks near our shores they will go elsewhere.

American fishermen have been powerless to halt the rape of their own fishing grounds, partly because the U.S., as a maritime power, has insisted on the three-mile territorial limit as a guarantee of free passage through all the world's oceans and straits. On this point we have the unfamiliar but wholehearted support of the Russians. Our dogged insistence on narrow limits is a major cause of the uncontrolled slaughter of fish. But this doesn't have to be the case.

... We could lead a return to sanity by sponsoring three measures ...:

■ Dual seaward limits for all coastal states: 12 miles as the limit of sovereignty, with an additional fishery conservation zone extending out to the point where the continental shelf slopes off into the ocean depths. Most fish live on the shelf, not in the depths. By placing responsibility for the world's fish stock in the hands of the nations bordering the seas, the world would take a practical step toward preservation and regulation. A coastal state should not be able to restrict all fishing to its own boats. But it should be able, through licensing, to limit the total catch to a sustainable yield.

■ International limits on the different species of tuna that would cut off the fishing worldwide when a set quota is reached. Tuna range through all the world's oceans, and tight conservation measures in one area mean nothing if it's open season at the fishes' next port of call.

■ Agreement that river-spawning fish such as salmon should never be caught on the high seas but only at the mouths of the rivers in which they are born and where they return to spawn and die. If salmon are netted during the oceanic part of their life cycle, it may well mean that when the time comes for them to return to their native rivers, none are left to strike up certain streams, while other rivers are glutted. Two improbable villains in the present situation are Denmark in the Atlantic and South Korea in the Pacific. Neither nation has a salmon river of its own and both insist on the right to catch salmon on the high seas. If their attitude wins out in the name of "freedom of the seas," the salmon may go the way of the whale.

There is no reason why laws cannot be written that would acknowledge the basic right of free passage and still allow for the conservation of the world's fisheries. In fact, unless such laws are written, we will be preserving only the right of passage over a dead sea.

THE DEATH THROES OF ESCAMBIA BAY *

Almost every day, fish churn the coffee-brown waters of Escambia Bay in violent death struggles. Then they pop to the surface, bellies up, fins rotted away, eyes falling out, blood oozing through skins.

*Adapted from "Escambia Bay, in Its Dying Agony, is a Victim of Pollution," AP dispatch, Dec. 2, 1971.

Sometimes they blanket the surface for miles, like driven snow. The stench is sickening.

Escambia Bay, in its dying agony, is a victim of pollution. Its suffering is shared by everyone around its shores.

This summer, massive fish and oyster kills have brought final destruction of a once bountiful seafood industry. Visitors who have been coming back year after year for the water sports read of the kills and cancel reservations.

Real estate values are falling. Homes on the bay, once in great demand, are going up for sale, but prospects sniff the wind and there are few takers.

"Without the water, this town is nothing," says an angry Lt. Buster Zangas of the Florida Marine Patrol. "And the water has been taken away.

"The bay has gone to hell. No sensible person would argue that fact. Day after day, the whole bay floats with dead fish. I've seen the bottom blanketed with dead fish like fluorescent paint. There can't be anything left.

"Every time there is a kill, the pollution boys say they are investigating to see what killed them. They know damn well what it is—and they know the answer. Plug those damn pipes."

The pipes to which Zangas refers are the outfalls of the Monsanto Chemical Co., manufacturer of nylon yarn; American Cyanamid Co., producer of acrylic fibers; Escambia Chemical Co., which turns out plastics and chemicals, and the Gulf Power Co.

These industries, a federal-state pollution task force, reported, are responsible for pollution that has strangled the bay. They were given until Jan. 1, 1973, to stop harmful discharges or shut down.

But the bay didn't have that much time.

"For all practical purposes, Escambia Bay is dead," says Harmon Shields, director of marine resources for the Florida Department of Natural Resources. "To bring it back is to do away with pollution."

Monsanto, Escambia and American Cyanamid discharge waste water containing nitrogen, phosphorus and potassium into the waters.

The chemicals overenrich the waters, causing explosive algae blooms. Oxygen is depleted in the process, toxic conditions develop and death runs through the entire chain of marine life.

Gulf Power, the task force said, adds thermal pollution by discharging hot water into the Escambia River and the bay.

Last Sept. 5, Escambia dumped 29,500 pounds of nitrogen into the bay, 10 times its normal daily discharge. Several massive fish kills followed. On Sept. 8, oyster fishermen preparing for an expected million-dollar harvest found the oysters all dead.

At a hastily called state hearing, Escambia admitted the discharge but refused to accept responsibility for the kills.

Chairman David Levin of the Florida Air and Water Pollution Control Board told the company's officials he was convinced that the dump contributed to the wipeout of the oyster beds.

But Levin said he didn't think Escambia could be punished because, "I don't think the evidence presented here would stand up in court."

At another hearing two weeks earlier, Shields had reported that his agency had no power to enforce pollution laws except in oil spills.

Pensacola courted industry after World War II, trading the water for payrolls. The giant Monsanto plant led the way to the bayside in 1951, lured by the water transportation facilities, a seemingly unlimited supply of good processing water, the climate and water sports which made it easy to get workmen. The Escambia plant went up in 1955, American Cyanamid in 1958.

For years, Escambia Bay took everything thrown into it—industrial wastes, untreated municipal sewage, fertilizer and pesticide runoffs from farms—and still it thrived.

In 1967 the kills began. A year later, Joe Quick, a state marine pathologist, found fish bleeding from open ulcers, with fins and tails eaten up.

"Compounds in the water were causing them to lose the slime which covers them and functions as an outer layer of skin," Quick said. "The loss produced red sores and left them open to attacks by bacteria and parasites."

This summer, marine losses were fantastic. Nineteen times, fish died by the millions. Dozens of smaller kills occurred. How many died this year?

"How can you estimate that when you see the entire surface of the bay covered with dead fish?" Zangas asked. "You could say 50 to 75 million. That wouldn't be accurate, but it wouldn't be too high, either.

"Private fishermen used to complain because the commercial boats were taking their fish. Hell, they could drag that bottom for a thousand years and not do the damage these industries have done.

"A man who went out there today and tried to fish for a living would starve to death."

Joe Blanchard, fisheries biologist for the Florida Game and Fresh Water Fish Commission, says that "all of a sudden in the past three years, this thing has become a monster."

All the companies report they are spending large sums in seeking ways to reduce pollution and contend that federal pollution officials are trying to drive them out of business. They say they are making progress in pollution abatement efforts.

But, at a recent state hearing, technical manager John Cramer said Escambia "does not know how to get a further reduction of nitrogen deposits."

And all the people can see is the dying fish and the dirty waters.

. . . .

Looking Backward and Forward

We conclude this depressing consideration of the environmental crisis with three accounts, the first factual and the last two nominally fictional. It would be pleasant to note that conditions and trends such as those described in the preceding selections have inspired government officials, industry tycoons, and citizens in general to engage in significant reform efforts. Unfortunately, the very opposite must be reported. As indicated in James Bishop's article, pollution "pays," hence polluters typically expend their energy on seeing how they can evade pollution regulations. That they are often criminally and self-defeatingly short-sighted seems almost too obvious to need mention. And, as shown in the second article by sociologist Amitai Etzioni, even the pressing energy crisis which became evident to all during 1974 has not prompted Americans to take a critically needed long view.

Although the last two selections are supposedly fictional, they are probably fairly accurate predictions of what lies ahead. Indeed, many of the conditions Stanford University Biologist Paul Ehrlich, author of "Eco-Catastrophe!," thought would not prevail until the mid- and late-seventies were appallingly evident before 1975: the red tides coming north from the Gulf states, the 1972 sharp decline in the Peruvian anchoveta beds, the Iceland fishing crisis and the tuna catches ruined by unacceptable DDT levels, the all but extinct great whales, the shellfish breeding grounds ruined by oil spills, etc. These and similar events and conditions are ominous signs that the doomsday contemplated by Ehrlich has an even greater chance of occurring—though the timing may vary to a degree—than he once thought.

DO LITTLE IF ANYTHING*

Pollution makes strange bedfellows—especially when the polluter is a heavy taxpayer.

*Adapted from James Bishop Jr., "The Polluter's Wedge: Give Out Jobs, Pay Taxes . . . and Don't Forget to Lobby," *Newsweek* Feature Service, 9 Feb 71.

In community after community the natural outrage of the householder at the pollution of the air he breathes and the water he uses is markedly allayed when the offending company has made itself a necessary—or at least a highly convenient—part of the financial status quo.

One big Midwestern steel plant is a case in point. The plant is the town's largest single employer, taxpayer and polluter.

Last year, the plant threatened to close down if it was required to meet stringent new local air pollution standards. Buying new equipment for the 55-year-old open-hearth mill, the company said, would be like buying a new engine for a rusty old car.

Though conservationists and local authorities called the threat a bluff, the chamber of commerce fretted that the economic consequences of the plant-closing would be worse than the fallout from the mill's stacks. And the local newspaper asked editorially: "What good is clean air and water, if no one has a buck to buy himself some bread?"

The 8,000 citizens of North Tarrytown, N.Y., were even more unhappy when civil charges were brought against the General Motors plant there for polluting the Hudson River. Though on a given day local residents can predict the color of the cars coming off the assembly lines by the color of the nearby river waters, they are also mindful of an interesting fact: GM pays half the local taxes.

Rayonaire Corp., a textile plant on Georgia's Altahama River, has been supporting the town of Jessup for years and polluting the river with its dyes at the same time. Now, threatened with closure by the state attorney general, the company is cleaning up—but not very well, according to Rock Howard, head of Georgia's Water Quality Control Board.

"They've cut corners, used their own engineers, instead of getting in people who really know what they're doing," Howard grumbles. But he is inhibited by the plant's many friends in Jessup.

"The local management is still playing the old game, wining and dining the citizenry and making themselves important to the town. It's a little town. A lot of people need work. The plant advertises in the local newspaper. . ."

Corporation executives, of course, did not become corporation executives as a reward for stupidity. Even as they come out publicly for an end to pollution, many are privately directing their lobbyists in Washington to weaken environmental controls and laws.

They are also maneuvering their own people—and occasionally themselves—into high positions on some of the public bodies which are supposed to call the polluters to account. Indeed, a majority of state pollution boards are heavily weighted with representatives of polluters, not only business but agriculture and local government.

Last year, for example, President Nixon set up the National Industrial Pollution Control Council in the Commerce Department. And one corporate bigwig on the council was with a company that, at the time of his appointment, had not complied with a 1966 state order to stop polluting municipal sewers with sulfurous wastes. . . .

ON INCREMENTING A HURRICANE*

Scientific studies of national decision-making have shown that democracies tend to abhor comprehensive planning and major shifts in strategy, preferring instead to "increment" or muddle through, making adjustments through a series of small steps aimed at moving away from a mess rather than at moving toward clearly stated, positive goals. Thus, a study of our country's federal budget shows that the allotment for most federal agencies will usually be within 10 percent of last year's—come hell or high water. National priorities may change, new crises may be identified; but as a rule agencies entrusted with new missions will grow only slowly, while the custodians of obsolescent missions and downgraded priorities are likely to continue to draw "their" billions.

It has been argued that it is the genius of democratic policy-making that it takes into account the large variety of needs and interests represented in the populace, and does not lend itself to a sudden shift to one side to the neglect of others. Thus, it is "undemocratic" to suggest cutting the NASA budget by a factor of 4 while quadrupling that of the Office of Energy. This would be "unfair" and unsettling to the industries that grew up around the space effort and to the congressional districts in which they are located. Gradual transitions, which do occur, allow for less painful adjustments. Finally, master plans often do not work anyhow, the future is too complex to be anticipated and molded, today's grand designs are tomorrow's discarded charts. Muddling through, the incrementalists conclude, is not just a fact of life, but the best way to live.

While much of what the incrementalists say is valid, there are moments when muddling through just will not do to get a country out of a serious predicament. France discovered this when it was invaded in 1939. The United States realized it had to double the defense budget, within *one* year, in terms of percentage of the gross national product, at the onset of the Korean War.

The energy crisis has so far elicited chiefly rather modest attempts at muddling. A year after the crisis broke we still have no national policy, let

*Amitai Etzioni, "On Incrementing a Hurricane," *Science* 186 (29 Nov 74):783.

alone a program commensurate with the problem. The ideas being kicked around, which are a long way from attaining even the status of policies, are quite incremental in nature.

Project Independence, aimed at making us self-reliant in 20 years, is little more than a slogan. Major decisions about the sources of energy to focus on, how to develop them, even whether independence is worth the gigantic costs it would exact, have in effect not been made. Most importantly, the American people have not yet been prepared for the fact that whichever way we turn—toward consuming a good deal less energy or paying *much* more for its development—the American way of life will have to be *significantly* adjusted over the next decade. Estimates of how much Project Independence will cost run to $700 billion.

While incrementing might well be the genius of democracy under most circumstances, to try to muddle through a hurricane is folly. The nation must be told that this crisis is not temporary and that it will require a not trivial reduction in the American standard of living, albeit not a radical one. It will require more master planning and national coordination than we tend to welcome in peacetime. It will require more leadership and less incrementation.

THE ASSAULT ON THE FUTURE *

... At Baker's Beach near San Francisco Bay, among purplish-green cypress, swirling winds, barrelling mist, and gentle sun, children, men, and women played and swam not long ago. Then into the Bay from the new towns south, east, and north came streams of oil and urine and plastic and acid and shit and paper and garbage. Like New York City's refuse, it was thought to be collected safely miles off shore, but the ocean rolls it right back through the Golden Gate, with an abandoned car here and there as cherry on the sundae. Monterey to the south, like San Francisco, a gold and pearled city on the hills, waits for the typhoid. Booming and beautiful green surf and spray hold hepatitis, and if you clamber among streams, rocks, cypress, and mist and sun at San Francisco's Land's End, hold your nose; for San Francisco's shit flowing past affluent Seacliff and Marina stinks no less than Harlem's or Calcutta's.

Who is working to keep the Bay and the oceans off New York and the shallows of the Gulf of Mexico from wholly becoming masses of slimy open sewage fronting cities where the poor live amid shipping slips and industries, while atop the towers and above the fumes visitors from subur-

*Adapted from Sidney J. Slomich, *The American Nightmare* (New York: The Macmillan Company, 1971), pp. 27–30.

bia eat, drink, and dance? And what is happening out in the oceans, in the deep below the coat of lead covering them and Antarctica's ice, which even the penguin's shuffle can't avoid? Heyerdahl has told us industry's plastic bottles and petroleum globs are all over the ocean, hundreds of leagues from land.

Rich man, poor man, silent majority man, who preserves and who resists preserving for sons and daughters the right to walk along the shore of the sea? Who will stop the dead march of fences and sugar-cube cell houses thrown along beach and hill and cliff and blocking off the wind's and water's wildness? Will Carolina's Cape Fear soon be Development Country, like the tracts marching up and down the Pacific Coast? Will our children even lose a place to put their footsteps when the need to leave the paths industry and society have machined? For relief of the spirit, for the breath of the wild, will they have recourse only to wildly careening rides in four-wheeled juggernauts over black-fumed covered freeways—a wild ride that makes them forget breathing?

Rich man, poor man, silent majority man, picture sons and daughters careening along the freeways on New Year's Eve as 1980 nears.

Like information bits on computer tapes, cars run up and down, back and forth along concrete strips through the fogs and dirt clouds outside, while drug- and alcohol-induced miasmas blow through their minds. It's too hard to find a place to walk, to play, to commune with the wild, to love, to talk, and to live as humans in a community with others; so in rage and frustration they careen in encapsulated private worlds amid illusions of floating and annihilating time and space, lest love—the life force within them with no place to go—blows out, tearing soul and body.

Suburbia—box after box, yard after yard after yard surrounded by fences and other boxes and yards—oozes by the freeway's frenzy and over ground that was once green to the gates of the city's towers.

Tract housing, cells of loneliness, isolate men—boxing them away from what remains of open space and sky and from the yellows, blacks and browns, while they communicate by moving among each other on computer-tapelike freeways in automobiles—the time's ultimate capsule of loneliness.

The cities are ghettos, although here and there are heavily guarded isles of affluence. Ethnic groups are separated from each other, isolated quantities in engineered social systems, like prison cell blocks or factory work gangs. Almost all who sleep in San Francisco, Boston, New York, Houston, and Cincinnati, are blacks, Mexican-Americans and Orientals, though a few poor and old diffident people huddle near the hills or shores where the dying brown surf still pounds.

The powerful heads of the managerial, financial, military and tourist processing classes, live in affluent isles properly imperial in their psychologies. Their protection is not withdrawn at night, but in the other sections police retreat to fortified station houses as darkness comes, so that wild adolescent males—powerless, with no cars for drugged release on the freeways and who are denied outlet and opportunity—can vent violence on brother and sister in modes not threatening society's and industry's stability. In the morning police, with ambulance and paddy wagon, cautiously move in to protect hordes of clerks, professional bureaucrats, and bureaucratized professionals barrelling in from suburbia to work in their daytime cells. At night they barrel back to suburbia's tracts in their loneliness capsules, leaving the streets of the city—once a community—to the street gangs, derelicts, beaten animals, and well-guarded tourists patronizing plush, artful, multiracial, and poly-sexual brothels managed by some of the city's finest systems engineers (municipal cultural affairs departments).

So it is the future that is assaulted by and fully structured in the present's terms: technologized, machined existence in suburbia; bureaucratized and exploited cities; human passions expressed in socially accepted violence in the cities and involuted, suicidal violence on the freeways; and society's groups separated from each other—lest they interact and, knowing humanity, achieve equality and love.

Having been fragmented by work and patterns of living, and having come to love their fear, men refuse to affirm that they have their lives and humanity in common: they refuse to interact, to build communities. Like ants in their hills, cogs in machines, information bits on computer tape, they hide from each other. Possessed by demons, dybbuks, by their own involuted and perverted creativity, they have decided they ought to like being possessed by possessions: houses in which they cannot truly live, automobiles which run them, and jobs fragmenting personality and individuality.

ECO-CATASTROPHE!*

The end of the ocean came late in the summer of 1979, and it came even more rapidly than the biologists had expected. There had been signs for more than a decade, commencing with the discovery in 1968 that DDT slows down photosynthesis in marine plant life. It was announced in a short paper in the technical journal, *Science*, but to ecologists it smacked of doomsday. They knew that all life in the sea depends on photosynthesis, the chemical process by which green plants bind the sun's energy and make it available to living things. And they knew that DDT and similar chlori-

*Adapted from Paul Ehrlich, "Eco-Catastrophe!" *Ramparts* (September 1969:24–28).

nated hydrocarbons had polluted the entire surface of the earth, including the sea.

But that was only the first of many signs. There had been the final gasp of the whaling industry in 1973, and the end of the Peruvian anchovy fishery in 1975. Indeed, a score of other fisheries had disappeared quietly from over-exploitation and various eco-catastrophes by 1977. The term "eco-catastrophe" was coined by a California ecologist in 1969 to describe the most spectacular of man's attacks on the systems which sustain his life. He drew his inspiration from the Santa Barbara offshore oil disaster of that year, and from the news which spread among naturalists that virtually all of the Golden State's seashore bird life was doomed because of chlorinated hydrocarbon interference with its reproduction. Eco-catastrophes in the sea became increasingly common in the early 1970s. Mysterious "blooms" of previously rare microorganisms began to appear in offshore waters. Red tides—killer outbreaks of a minute single-celled plant—returned to the Florida Gulf coast and were sometimes accompanied by tides of other exotic hues.

It was clear by 1975 that the entire ecology of the ocean was changing. A few types of phytoplankton were becoming resistant to chlorinated hydrocarbons and were gaining the upper hand. Changes in the phyto-plankton community led inevitably to changes in the community of zoo-plankton, the tiny animals which eat the phytoplankton. These changes were passed on up the chains of life in the ocean to the herring, plaice, cod and tuna. As the diversity of life in the ocean diminished, its stability also decreased.

Other changes had taken place by 1975. Most ocean fishes that returned to fresh water to breed, like the salmon, had become extinct, their breeding streams so dammed up and polluted that their powerful homing instinct only resulted in suicide. Many fishes and shellfishes that bred in restricted areas along the coasts followed them as onshore pollution esca-lated.

By 1977 the annual yield of fish from the sea was down to 30 million metric tons, less than one-half the per capita catch of a decade earlier. This helped malnutrition to escalate sharply in a world where an estimated 50 million people per year were already dying of starvation. The United Nations attempted to get all chlorinated hydrocarbon insecticides banned on a worldwide basis, but the move was defeated by the United States. This opposition was generated primarily by the American petrochemical industry, operating hand in glove with its subsidiary, the United States Department of Agriculture. Together they persuaded the government to oppose the U.N. move—which was not difficult since most Americans believed that Russia and China were more in need of fish products than was the United States. The United Nations also attempted to get fishing nations to adopt strict and enforced catch limits to preserve dwindling stocks. This move was blocked by Russia, who, with the most modern electronic equipment, was in the best position to glean what was left in the sea. It was, curiously, on the very day in 1977 when the Soviet Union announced its refusal that another ominous article appeared in Science. It announced that incident solar radiation had been so reduced by worldwide air pollution that serious effects on the world's vegetation could be expected.

Apparently it was a combination of ecosystem destabilization, sunlight reduction, and a rapid escalation in chlorinated hydrocarbon pollution from massive Thanodrin applications which triggered the ultimate catastrophe. Seventeen huge Soviet-financed Thanodrin plants were operating in underdeveloped countries by 1978. They had been part of a massive Russian "aid offensive" designed to fill the gap caused by the collapse of America's ballyhooed "Green Revolution."

It became apparent in the early '70s that the "Green Revolution" was more talk than substance. Distribution of high yield "miracle" grain seeds had caused temporary local spurts in agricultural production. Simultaneously, excellent weather had produced record harvests. The combination permitted bureaucrats, especially in the United States Department of Agriculture and the Agency for International Development (AID), to reverse their previous pessimism and indulge in an outburst of optimistic propaganda about staving off famine. They raved about the approaching transformation of agriculture in the underdeveloped countries (UDCs). The reason for the propaganda reversal was never made clear. Most historians agree that a combination of utter ignorance of ecology, a desire to justify past errors, and pressure from agro-industry (which was eager to sell pesticides, fertilizers, and farm machinery to the UDCs and agencies helping the UDCs) was behind the campaign. Whatever the motivation, the results were clear. Many concerned people, lacking the expertise to see through the Green Revolution drivel, relaxed. The population-food crisis was "solved."

But reality was not long in showing itself. Local famine persisted in northern India even after good weather brought an end to the ghastly Bihar famine of the mid-'60s. East Pakistan was next, followed by a resurgence of general famine in northern India. Other foci of famine rapidly developed in Indonesia, the Philippines, Malawi, the Congo, Egypt, Colombia, Ecuador, Honduras, the Dominican Republic, and Mexico.

Everywhere hard realities destroyed the illusion of the Green Revolution. Yields dropped as the progressive farmers who had first accepted the new seeds found that their higher yields brought lower prices—effective demand (hunger plus cash) was not sufficient in poor countries to keep prices up. Less progressive farmers, observing this, refused to make the extra effort required to cultivate the "miracle" grains. Transport systems proved inadequate to bring the necessary fertilizer to the fields where the new and extremely fertilizer-sensitive grains were being grown. The same systems were also inadequate to move produce to markets. Fertilizer plants were not built fast enough, and most of the underdeveloped countries could not scrape together funds to purchase supplies, even on concessional terms. Finally, the inevitable happened, and pests began to reduce yields in even the most carefully cultivated fields. Among the first were the famous "miracle rats" which invaded Philippine "miracle rice" fields early in 1969. They were quickly followed by many insects and viruses, thriving on the relatively pest-susceptible new grains, encouraged by the vast and dense plantings, and rapidly acquiring resistance to the chemicals used against them. As chaos spread until even the most obtuse agriculturists and economists realized that the Green Revolution had turned brown, the Russians stepped in.

In retrospect it seems incredible that the Russians, with the American mistakes known to them, could launch an even more incompetent program of aid to the underdeveloped world. Indeed, in the early 1970s there were cynics in the United States who claimed that outdoing the stupidity of American foreign aid would be physically impossible. Those critics were, however, obviously unaware that the Russians had been busily destroying their own environment for many years. The virtual disappearance of sturgeon from Russian rivers caused a great shortage of caviar by 1970. A standard joke among Russian scientists at that time was that they had created an artificial caviar which was indistinguishable from the real thing— except by taste. At any rate the Soviet Union, observing with interest the progressive deterioration of relations between the UDCs and the United States, came up with a solution. It had recently developed what it claimed was the ideal insecticide, a highly lethal chlorinated hydrocarbon complexed with a special agent for penetrating the external skeletal armor of insects. Announcing that the new pesticide, called Thanodrin, would truly produce a Green Revolution, the Soviets entered into negotiations with various UDCs for the construction of massive Thanodrin factories. The USSR would bear all the costs; all it wanted in return were certain trade and military concessions.

It is interesting now, with the perspective of years, to examine in some detail the reasons why the UDCs welcomed the Thanodrin plan with such open arms. Government officials in these countries ignored the protests of their own scientists that Thanodrin would not solve the problems which plagued them. The governments now knew that the basic cause of their problems was overpopulation, and that these problems had been exacer-

bated by the dullness, daydreaming, and cupidity endemic to all governments. They knew that only population control and limited development
aimed primarily at agriculture could have spared them the horrors they
now faced. They knew it, but they were not about to admit it. How much
easier it was simply to accuse the Americans of failing to give them proper
aid; how much simpler to accept the Russian panacea.

And then there was the general worsening of relations between the
United States and the UDCs. Many things had contributed to this. The
situation in America in the first half of the 1970s deserves our close
scrutiny. Being more dependent on imports for raw materials than the
Soviet Union, the United States had, in the early 1970s, adopted more and
more heavy-handed policies in order to insure continuing supplies. Military
adventures in Asia and Latin America had further lessened the international
credibility of the United States as a great defender of freedom—an image
which had begun to deteriorate rapidly during the pointless and fruitless
Viet-Nam conflict. At home, acceptance of the carefully manufactured
image lessened dramatically, as even the more romantic and chauvinistic
citizens began to understand the role of the military and the industrial
system in what John Kenneth Galbraith had aptly named "The New
Industrial State."

At home in the USA . . . the habitability of the cities diminished, as nothing
substantial was done to ameliorate either racial inequities or urban blight.
Welfare rolls grew as automation and general technological progress forced
more and more people into the category of "unemployable." Simultaneously a taxpayers' revolt occurred. Although there was not enough money
to build the schools, roads, water systems, sewage systems, jails, hospitals,
urban transit lines, and all the other amenities needed to support a
burgeoning population, Americans refused to tax themselves more heavily.
Starting in Youngstown, Ohio in 1969 and followed closely by Richmond,
California, community after community was forced to close its schools or
curtail educational operations for lack of funds. Water supplies, already
marginal in quality and quantity in many places by 1970, deteriorated
quickly. Water rationing occurred in 1723 municipalities in the summer of
1974, and hepatitis and epidemic dysentery rates climbed about 500
percent between 1970-1974.

Air pollution continued to be the most obvious manifestation of environmental deterioration. It was, by 1972, quite literally in the eyes of all
Americans. . . . The public had been partially prepared for the worst by the
publicity given to the U.N. pollution conference held in 1972. Deaths in
the late '60s caused by smog were well known to scientists, but the public
had ignored them because they mostly involved the early demise of the old

and sick rather than people dropping dead on the freeways. But suddenly our citizens were faced with nearly 200,000 corpses and massive documentation that they could be the next to die from respiratory disease. They were not ready for that scale of disaster. After all, the U.N. conference had not predicted that accumulated air pollution would make the planet uninhabitable until almost 1990. The population was terrorized as TV screens became filled with scenes of horror from the disaster areas. Especially vivid was NBC's coverage of hundreds of unattended people choking out their lives outside of New York's hospitals. Terms like nitrogen oxide, acute bronchitis and cardiac arrest began to have real meaning for most Americans.

The ultimate horror was the announcement that chlorinated hydrocarbons were now a major constituent of air pollution in all American cities. Autopsies of smog disaster victims revealed an average chlorinated hydrocarbon load in fatty tissue equivalent to 26 parts per million of DDT. . . . The Department of Health, Education and Welfare announced studies which showed, unequivocally that increasing death rates from hypertension, cirrhosis of the liver, liver cancer and a series of other diseases had resulted from the chlorinated hydrocarbon load. They estimated that Americans born since 1946 (when DDT usage began) now had a life expectancy of only 49 years, and predicted that if current patterns continued, this expectancy would reach 42 years by 1980, when it might level out. Plunging insurance stocks triggered a stock market panic. The president of Velsicol, Inc., a major pesticide producer, went on television to "publicly eat a teaspoonful of DDT" (it was really powdered milk) and announce that HEW had been infiltrated by Communists. Other giants of the petrochemical industry, attempting to dispute the indisputable evidence, launched a massive pressure campaign on Congress to force HEW to "get out of agriculture's business." They were aided by the agro-chemical journals, which had decades of experience in misleading the public about the benefits and dangers of pesticides. But by now the public realized that it had been duped. The Nobel Prize for medicine and physiology was given to Drs. J. L. Radomski and W. B. Deichmann, who in the late 1960s had pioneered in the documentation of the long-term lethal effects of chlorinated hydrocarbons. A Presidential Commission with unimpeachable credentials directly accused the agro-chemical complex of "condemning many millions of Americans to an early death." The year 1973 was the year in which Americans finally came to understand the direct threat to their existence posed by environmental deterioration.

And 1973 was also the year in which most people finally comprehended the indirect threat. Even the president of Union Oil Company and several other industrialists publicly stated their concern over the reduction of bird populations which had resulted from pollution by DDT and other chlori-nated hydrocarbons. Insect populations boomed because they were resistant to most pesticides and had been freed, by the incompetent use of those pesticides, from most of their natural enemies. Rodents swarmed over crops, multiplying rapidly in the absence of predatory birds. ... Man's air-polluting activities had by then caused gross changes in climatic pat-terns. The news, of course, played hell with commodity and stock markets. Food prices skyrocketed, as savings were poured into hoarded canned goods. Official assurances that food supplies would remain ample fell on deaf ears, and even the government showed signs of nervousness when California migrant field workers went out on strike again in protest against the continued use of pesticides by growers. The strike burgeoned into farm burning and riots. The workers, calling themselves "The Walking Dead," demanded immediate compensation for their shortened lives, and crash research programs to attempt to lengthen them.

It was in the same speech in which [the president at the time] ... after much delay, finally declared a national emergency and called out the National Guard to harvest California's crops, that the first mention of population control was made. [He] ... pointed out the United States would no longer be able to offer any food aid to other nations and was likely to suffer food shortages herself. He suggested that, in view of the manifest failure of the Green Revolution, the only hope of the UDCs lay in population control. His statement, you will recall, created an uproar in the underdeveloped countries. Newspaper editorials accused the United States of wishing to prevent small countries from becoming large nations and thus threatening American hegemony. Politicians asserted that ... [the presi-dent] was a "creature of the giant drug combine" that wished to shove its pills down every woman's throat.

Among Americans, religious opposition to population control was very slight. Industry in general also backed the idea. ...

Suddenly the United States discovered that it had a national consensus: population control was the only possible salvation of the underdeveloped world. But that same consensus led to heated debate. How could the UDCs be persuaded to limit their populations, and should not the United States lead the way by limiting its own? ...

Those who opposed population controls for the U.S. were equally vociferous. The military-industrial complex, with its all-too-human mixture of ignorance and avarice, still saw strength and prosperity in numbers. Baby food magnates, already worried by the growing nitrate pollution of their products, saw their market disappearing. Steel manufacturers saw a decrease in aggregate demand and slippage for that holy of holies, the Gross National Product. And military men saw, in the growing population-food-environment crisis, a serious threat to their carefully nurtured Cold War. In the end, of course, economic arguments held sway, and the "inalienable right of every American couple to determine the size of its family," a freedom invented for the occasion in the early '70s, was not compromised.

The population control bill, which was passed by Congress . . . [in the mid-'70's], was quite a document, nevertheless. On the domestic front, it authorized an increase from 100 to 150 million dollars in funds for "family planning" activities. This was made possible by a general feeling in the country that the growing army on welfare needed family planning. But the gist of the bill was a series of measures designed to impress the need for population control on the UDCs. All American aid to countries with overpopulation problems was required by law to consist in part of population control assistance. In order to receive any assistance each nation was required not only to accept the population control aid, but also to match it according to a complex formula. "Overpopulation" itself was defined by a formula based on U.N. statistics, and the UDCs were required not only to accept aid, but also to show progress in reducing birth rates. Every five years the status of the aid program for each nation was to be re-evaluated.

The reaction to the announcement of this program dwarfed the response to . . . [the president's] speech. A coalition of UDCs attempted to get the U.N. General Assembly to condemn the United States as a "genetic aggressor." Most damaging of all to the American cause was the famous "25 Indians and a dog" speech by Mr. Shankarnarayan, Indian Ambassador to the U.N. Shankarnarayan pointed out that for several decades the United States, with less than six percent of the people of the world had consumed roughly 50 percent of the raw materials used every year. He described vividly America's contribution to worldwide environmental deterioration, and he scathingly denounced the miserly record of United States foreign aid as "unworthy of a fourth-rate power, let alone the most powerful nation on earth."

It was the climax of his speech, however, which most historians claim once and for all destroyed the image of the United States. Shankarnarayan informed the assembly that the average American family dog was fed more animal protein per week than the average Indian got in a month. "How do you justify taking fish from protein-starved Peruvians and feeding them to your animals?" he asked. "I contend," he concluded, "that the birth of an American baby is a greater disaster for the world than that of 25 Indian babies." When the applause had died away, Mr. Sorensen, the American representative, made a speech which said essentially that "other countries look after their own self-interest, too." When the vote came, the United States was condemned.

This condemnation set the tone of U.S.-UDC relations at the time the

Russian Thanodrin proposal was made. The proposal seemed to offer the masses in the UDCs an opportunity to save themselves and humiliate the United States at the same time; and in human affairs, as we all know, biological realities could never interfere with such an opportunity. The scientists were silenced, the politicians said yes, the Thanodrin plants were built, and the results were what any beginning ecology student could have predicted. At first Thanodrin seemed to offer excellent control of many pests. True, there was a rash of human fatalities from improper use of the lethal chemical, but, as Russian technical advisors were prone to note, these were more than compensated for by increased yields. Thanodrin use skyrocketed throughout the underdeveloped world. The Mikoyan design group developed a dependable, cheap agricultural aircraft which the Soviets donated to the effort in large numbers. MIG sprayers became even more common in UDCs than MIG interceptors.

Then the troubles began. Insect strains with cuticles resistant to Thanodrin penetration began to appear. And as streams, rivers, fish culture ponds and onshore waters became rich in Thanodrin, more fisheries began to disappear. Bird populations were decimated. The sequence of events was standard for broadcast use of a synthetic pesticide: great success at first, followed by removal of natural enemies and development of resistance by the pest. Populations of crop-eating insects in areas treated with Thanodrin made steady comebacks and soon became more abundant than ever. Yields plunged, while farmers in their desperation increased the Thanodrin dose and shortened the time between treatments. Death from Thanodrin poisoning became common. The first violent incident occurred in the Canete Valley of Peru, where farmers had suffered a similar chlorinated hydrocarbon disaster in the mid-'50s. A Russian advisor serving as an agricultural pilot was assaulted and killed by a mob of enraged farmers in January, 1978. Trouble spread rapidly during 1978, especially after the word got out that two years earlier Russia herself had banned the use of Thanodrin at home because of its serious effects on ecological systems. Suddenly Russia, and not the United States, was the *bete noir* in the UDCs. "Thanodrin parties" became epidemic, with farmers, in their ignorance, dumping carloads of Thanodrin concentrate into the sea. Russian advisors fled, and four of the Thanodrin plants were leveled to the ground. Destruction of the plants in Rio and Calcutta led to hundreds of thousands of gallons of Thanodrin concentrate being dumped directly into the sea.

Mr. Shankarnarayan again rose to address the U.N., but this time it was Mr. Potemkin, representative of the Soviet Union, who was on the hot seat. Mr. Potemkin heard his nation described as the greatest mass killer of all time as Shankarnarayan predicted at least 30 million deaths from crop failures due to overdependence on Thanodrin. Russia was accused of "chemical aggression," and the General Assembly, after a weak reply by Potemkin, passed a vote of censure.

It was in January, 1979, that huge blooms of a previously unknown variety of diatom were reported off the coast of Peru. The blooms were accompanied by a massive die-off of sea life and of the pathetic remainder of the birds which had once feasted on the anchovies of the area. Almost immediately another huge bloom was reported in the Indian ocean, centering around the Seychelles, and then a third in the South Atlantic off the African coast. Both of these were accompanied by spectacular die-offs of marine animals. Even more ominous were growing reports of fish and bird kills at oceanic points where there were no spectacular blooms. Biologists were soon able to explain the phenomena: the diatom had evolved an enzyme which broke down Thanodrin; that enzyme also produced a breakdown product which interfered with the transmission of nerve impulses, and was therefore lethal to animals. Unfortunately, the biologists could suggest no way of repressing the poisonous diatom bloom in time. By September, 1979, all important animal life in the sea was extinct. Large areas of coastline had to be evacuated, as windrows of dead fish created a monumental stench.

But stench was the least of man's problems. Japan and China were faced with almost instant starvation from a total loss of the seafood on which they were so dependent. Both blamed Russia for their situation and demanded immediate mass shipments of food. Russia had none to send. On October 13, Chinese armies attacked Russia on a broad front. . . .

A pretty grim scenario. Unfortunately, we're a long way into it already. Everything mentioned as happening before 1970 has actually occurred; much of the rest is based on projections of trends already appearing. Evidence that pesticides have long-term lethal effects on human beings has started to accumulate. . . . Simultaneously the petrochemical industry continues its unconscionable poison-peddling. For instance, Shell Chemical has been carrying on a high-pressure campaign to sell the insecticide Azodrin to farmers as a killer of cotton pests. They continue their program even though they know that Azodrin is not only ineffective, but often *increases* the pest density. They've covered themselves nicely in an advertisement which states, "Even if an overpowering migration [sic] develops, the flexibility of Azodrin lets you regain control fast. Just increase the dosage according to label recommendations." It's a great game—get people to apply the poison and kill the natural enemies of the pests. Then blame the increased pests on "migration" and sell even more pesticide!

Right now fisheries are being wiped out by over-exploitation, made easy by modern electronic equipment. The companies producing the equipment know this. They even boast in advertising that only their equipment will keep fishermen in business until the final kill. Profits must obviously be maximized in the short run. Indeed, Western society is in the process of completing the rape and murder of the planet for economic gain. And, sadly, most of the rest of the world is eager for the opportunity to emulate our behavior. But the underdeveloped peoples will be denied that opportunity—the days of plunder are drawing inexorably to a close.

Most of the people who are going to die in the greatest cataclysm in the history of man have already been born. More than three and a half billion people already populate our moribund globe, and about half of them are hungry. Some 10 to 20 million will starve to death *this year*. In spite of this, the population of the earth . . . [grows by 70 million and up each year.] For mankind has artificially lowered the death rate of the human population, while in general birth rates have remained high. With the input side of the population system in high gear and the output side slowed down, our fragile planet has filled with people at an incredible rate. It took several million years for the population to reach a total of two billion people in 1930, while a *second two billion will have been added by 1975!* By that time some experts feel that food shortages will have escalated the present level of world hunger and starvation into famines of unbelievable proportions. Other experts, more optimistic, think the ultimate food-population collision will not occur until the decade of the 1980s. Of course more massive famine may be avoided if other events cause a prior rise in the human death rate.

Both worldwide plague and thermonuclear war are made more probable as population growth continues. These, along with famine, make up the trio of potential "death rate solutions" to the population problem—solutions in which the birth rate-death rate imbalance is redressed by a rise in the death rate rather than by a lowering of the birth rate. Make no mistake about it, *the imbalance will be redressed*. The shape of the population growth curve is one familiar to the biologist. It is the outbreak part of an outbreak-crash sequence. A population grows rapidly in the presence of abundant resources, finally runs out of food or some other necessity, and crashes to a low level or extinction. Man is not only running out of food, he is also destroying the life support systems of the Spaceship Earth. The situation was recently summarized very succinctly: "It is the top of the ninth inning. Man, always a threat at the plate, has been hitting Nature hard. It is important to remember, however, that NATURE BATS LAST."

PART 3

Defective Correctives

The third major element of injustice, as noted in the introduction to
this volume, may be summed up as "inadequate methods of rectifying
wrong." The society which has a multitude of problems is not necessarily
in serious difficulty if it also has effective methods of righting the existing
wrongs. But the society without such methods is doubly damned, plagued
as it is by its troubles and by inept attempts to surmount the troubles.
That this double damnation applies to our society is made painfully evident
by the following selections which are divided into seven categories: Is
Education the Answer?, Is the "System" the Answer?, Is Law and Order
the Answer?, Is "Free Enterprise" the Answer?, Is "Withdrawal" the
Answer?, Is Welfare the Answer?, and, is Revolution the Answer?

Is Education the Answer?

As indicated in the first of the following articles, Americans have a long-term illusion which takes the form "Education Cures All." This would be a fairly benign notion except that it leads to two difficulties: 1) constant disappointment, and 2) failure to change the system which is the root cause of problems (as well as of given forms of education). Actually, mass education has never successfully addressed itself to fundamental problems while still retaining the support of the power elite that typically controls state and local boards of education. Such boards insist that education concentrate on "essentials," which is a euphemism for "indoctrinate the young in the established norms." At the college level, on the other hand, there is some attempt on the part of a few liberal educators to lead students toward a critical analysis of their society; but this often results in internecine battles over academic freedom, "subversive" ideas, abrogated tenure rights, and the like. When seen in toto, thus, education as it actually exists in the United States today can in no sense be regarded as a realistic panacea for social problems.

INEQUALITY AND THE SCHOOLS*

This article is based on the findings reported in a controversial book by Christopher Jencks and his associates at Harvard University. They conclude that first-rate education given to poor people will not, as has been hoped by many significantly reduce economic inequality. The research underlying this conclusion is flawed, but the present article has the virtue of calling attention to the fallacy of believing that if schools alone are changed, then somehow society can be fundamentally altered.

Americans have a recurrent fantasy that schools can solve their problems. Thus it was perhaps inevitable that, after we rediscovered

*Adapted from Mary Jo Bane and Christopher Jencks, "The Schools and Equal Opportunity," *Saturday Review of Education* 55(Sept. 16, 1972): 37–42.

Robots

poverty and inequality in the early 1960s, we turned to the schools for solutions. Yet the schools did not provide solutions, the high hopes of the early-and-middle 1960s faded, and the war on poverty ended in ignominious surrender to the *status quo*. In part, of course, this was because the war in Southeast Asia turned out to be incompatible with the war on poverty. In part, however, it was because we all had rather muddleheaded ideas about the various causes and cures of poverty and inequality.

Today there are signs that some people are beginning to look for new solutions to these perennial problems. There is a vast amount of sociological and economic data that can, we think, help in this effort, both by explaining the failures of the 1960s and by suggesting more realistic alternatives. For the past four years we have been working with this data. Our research has led us to three general conclusions.

First, poverty is a condition of relative rather than absolute deprivation. People feel poor and are poor if they have a lot less money than their neighbors. This is true regardless of their absolute income. It follows that we cannot eliminate poverty unless we prevent people from falling too far below the national average. The problem is economic inequality rather than low incomes.

Second, the reforms of the 1960s were misdirected because they focused only on equalizing opportunity to "succeed" (or "fail") rather than on reducing the economic and social distance between those who succeeded and those who failed. The evidence we have reviewed suggests that equalizing opportunity will not do very much to equalize results, and hence that it will not do much to reduce poverty.

Third, even if we are interested solely in equalizing opportunities for economic success, making schools more equal will not help very much. Differences between schools have very little effect on what happens to students after they graduate.

The main policy implication of these findings is that although school reform is important for improving the lives of children, schools cannot contribute significantly to adult equality. If we want economic equality in our society, we will have to get it by changing our economic institutions, not by changing the schools. . . .

These findings imply that school reform is never likely to have any significant effect on the degree of inequality among adults. This suggests that the prevalent "factory" model, in which schools are seen as places that "produce" alumni, probably ought to be abandoned. It is true that schools have "inputs" and "outputs," and that one of their nominal purposes is to take human "raw material" (*i.e.*, children) and convert it into something more "useful" (*i.e..* employable adults). Our research suggests, however, that the character of a school's output depends largely on a single input, the characteristics of the entering children. Everything else—the school budget, its policies, the characteristics of the teachers—is either secondary or completely irrelevant, at least so long as the range of variation among schools is as narrow as it seems to be in America.

These findings have convinced us that the long-term effects of schooling are relatively uniform. The day-to-day internal life of the schools, in contrast, is highly variable. It follows that *the primary basis for evaluating a school should be whether the students and teachers find it a satisfying place to be.* This does not mean we think schools should be like mediocre summer camps, in which children are kept out of trouble but not taught anything. We doubt that a school can be enjoyable for either adults or children unless the children keep learning new things. We value ideas and the life of the mind, and we think that a school that does not value these things is a poor place for children. But a school that values ideas because they enrich the lives of children is quite different from a school that values high reading scores because reading scores are important for adult success.

Our concern with making schools satisfying places for teachers and children has led us to a concern for diversity and choice. People have widely different notions of what a "satisfying" place is, and we believe they ought to be able to put these values into practice. As we have noted, our research suggests that none of the programs or structural arrangements in common use today has consistently different long-term effects from any other. Since the character of a child's schooling has few long-term effects, and since these effects are quite unpredictable, society has little reason to constrain the choices available to parents and children. If a "good school" is one the students and staff find satisfying, no one school will be best for everyone. Since there is no evidence that professional educators know appreciably more than parents about what is good for children, it seems reasonable to let parents decide what kind of education their children should have while they are young and to let the children decide as they get older.

Short-term considerations also seem decisive in determining whether to spend more money on schooling or to spend it on busing children to schools outside their neighborhoods. If extra resources make school life pleasanter and more interesting, they are worthwhile. But we should not try to justify school expenditures on the grounds that they boost adult earnings. Likewise, busing ought to be justified in political and moral terms rather than in terms of presumed long-term effects on the children who are bused. If we want an integrated society, we ought to have integrated schools, which make people feel they have a stake in the well-being of other races. If we want a society in which people are free to segregate themselves, then we should apply that principle to our schools. There is, however, no compelling reason to treat schools differently from other social arrangements, including neighborhoods. Personally, we believe in both open housing and open schools. If parents or students want to take buses to schools in other neighborhoods, school boards ought to provide the buses, expand the relevant schools, and ensure that the students are welcome in the schools they want to attend. This is the least we can do to offset the effects of residential segregation. But we do not believe that forced busing can be justified on the grounds of its long-term benefits for students.

This leads to our last conclusion about educational reform. Reformers are always getting trapped into claiming too much for what they propose. They may want a particular reform—like open classrooms, or desegregation, or vouchers—because they think these reforms will make schools more satisfying places to work. Yet they feel obliged to claim that these reforms will also reduce the number of nonreaders, increase racial understanding, or stengthen family life. A wise reformer ought to be more modest, claiming only that a particular reform will not harm adult society and that it will make life pleasanter for parents, teachers, and students in the short run.

This plea for modesty in school reform will, we fear, fall on deaf ears. Ivan Illich is right in seeing schools as secular churches, through which we seek to improve not ourselves but our descendants. That this process should be disagreeable seems inevitable; one cannot abolish original sin through self-indulgence. That it should be immodest seems equally inevitable; a religion that promises anything less than salvation wins few converts. In school, as in church, we present the world as we wish it were. We try to inspire children with the ideals we ourselves have failed to live up to. We assume, for example, that we cannot make adults live in desegregated neighborhoods, so we devise schemes for bussing children from one neighborhood to another in order to desegregate the schools. We all prefer conducting our moral experiments on other people. Nonetheless, so long as we confine our experiments to children, we will not have much effect on adult life. . . .

WHAT AMERICA REALLY IS*

It is Wellesley, Massachusetts, but it could be any one of the small towns and cities in which . . . students and adults have found themselves in

*Adapted from Marc Libarle and Tom Seligson, editors, *The High School Revolutionaries* (New York: Random House, Inc., a Scanlan's Book, 1970), pp. xi–xiii, 68–72.

violent opposition to each others' beliefs, styles, and values, and minor incidents have exploded into vicious confrontations.

The famous "Wellesley Incident" begins innocuously enough in Wellesley High School with a special program in the gym devoted to the problems of racism and poverty in America. It ends several days later with students in faded blue jeans and worn sweaters, and adults in neat shirts and pressed jackets, climbing on the auditorium chairs, yelling and screaming at each other, waving their arms and calling for each others' defeat. Outside it is a cool spring night, but inside there is tension, anger, and fear. One boy is arrested and countless numbers of students, numb and bewildered by this spectacle of chaos and reprisal, are radicalized.

For three periods on the morning it began, students and teachers in the gymnasium saw documentary films and heard poetry by Langston Hughes. They listened to young men from the Boston ghettoes talk about slums and prejudice. Then, as they sat in hushed silence in chairs on the basketball court, they watched the Boston Theater Company perform a part of LeRoi Jones' play, *The Slave.*

Significantly, the school program on poverty and racism was punctuated with the anger of an author who used words like "shit" and "fuck" to communicate his opposition to a system and a society that has kept the black man oppressed.

The students were fascinated by the play, but—in an indication of what was to follow—teachers suddenly left the room or started to correct their tests and papers.

Later the word circulated ominously in Wellesley that the play was "revolting," and about a week later over thirteen hundred people showed up at the regular School Committee meeting to denounce the students for selecting such entertainment.

"Filthy," "vulgar," the adults yelled across the crowded auditorium toward the lonely moderator trying to ascertain whether school funds had been improperly used. Speakers went to the platform, the pros and cons of the play were hurled about the room like lethal darts. Members of the John Birch Society, Veterans of Foreign Wars, and the American Legion contributed staunchly and loudly to the program; finally the editor of the school paper mounted the stage.

"I think one of the things that is affecting you the most," said this A-student and star athlete, "is the word 'fuck.' " He quoted a line from the play ending in "fuck you" and the audience was stunned.

"Well, the first time I heard the word 'fuck'," he went on, "was when I was five years old and that was right here in Wellesley. In fact, I know some people in Wellesley who cannot say a sentence without using the word 'fuck.' "

"Get him out," cried a man in the audience. "Arrest him," yelled others. "Stop him!" "What right does he have?" The adults stood up, climbed on the chairs, and cried, "Arrest him."

A uniformed policeman, summoned by the audience, jumped up on the stage, grabbed the boy, and arrested him. The vice principal started to scream at the high school students standing in the front of the auditorium. "We're trying to build a good school and you're wrecking it," he cried as the policeman went off stage with the young editor. "You're the ones who're wrecking it," he repeated.

"This whole wall of angry shouting people rose up around us," said one white student later, recalling the angry scene. "It was really terrifying, and for the first time we began to realize what we were up against in our fight for freedom. Up until then we had confronted only one man, the principal or the vice principal, but here were hundreds of people screaming and yelling."

"Here was America right before our eyes," he went on, echoing the words of countless hundreds of high school radicals, forced into their radicalism by similar discoveries and observations. "This is what America really is."

This next except from Libarle and Seligson is by Paul Gayten, a seventeen-year-old student, black, who was attending East High Schol in Denver, Colorado; Mr. Gayten titles his piece "Keep on Pushing."

... I'm eighteen years old, and I come from a family of fourteen. My parents are living together in Springfield, Illinois, but I live by myself out here. It's easier on them if I live on my own, and any money that I make I send back to them. My father is a construction man. He builds homes and things like that.

In East High School there are about 200 black students out of 500. There are about three blacks out of over a hundred teachers. I wasn't happy at the school. In fact, I wouldn't say that anybody is happy at the school. You go there and try to learn, but it's hard for the black students to learn. Most of the teachers don't want to learn you. They learn white people more things than they do black. If you're black, I guess it's concluded that you stay back. And the teachers don't help you to pass. A lot of the teachers are racists as East High School. You go to class. If you come in late, you have to go down to the office and maybe get suspended. And if you get two suspension from there, you get kicked out of school for the week, until your parents can come in. And after your parents come in, the same thing next week. That's what happened to me. They kicked me out because I was late trying to get something from another teacher.

Well, see—you go to this class. If you have been out suspended or sick and you want to find out what you missed, you ask the teacher. Some teachers tell you to wait after class and get this information. After they kick you out of school they don't want to tell you what you missed. But it's different if there's a white kid who comes up and says that he was out of school sick, maybe like I was—sick for a long time. This white boy might say he was sick too, but really he just went around and didn't go to school. And he goes up there and asks the teacher, "Could you tell me what my back homework is, my makeup homework?"

She stops right in the middle of class and says, "Well, you do page 24, 25, and 26, and that's all."

I would go up there and ask her, "Could you help me with this 'cause I've been sick and out of school?"

Then she'll say, "Well, you wait after class and I'll give it to you."

You wait after class and probably the teacher has gone already. You wait. She says she has to run down to the office or something like that, and soon she's gone and you be late for the other class and you don't have a pass or nothing. And then you tell the next teacher that you were trying to get this stuff from Miss ———— and that she said wait after class, and she says, "O.K. Paul. Why don't you go on down to the office anyway to see about getting an excuse."

They know it's hard for me to get an excuse. My uncle say that's why they send me there in the first place. I go down there and talk with Mr. C————, the assistant principal. And he say, "Paul, this ain't the first time you been down to the office."

And I say, "I know this."

And he say, "You're going to have to be suspended from school."

I say, "For what?"

And he say, "For coming to class late."

I say, "I told you the reason I come to class late."

And he say, "You still getting suspended."

I finally say, "O.K., I don't give a damn, I'm going." You know how they make me mad. I studied hard, but it seemed they were all out to get me.

They send me on home, and I tell my uncle about it. And my uncle say, "Paul, you're just going to have to go ahead and live with it because you can't help it. That's how the teachers are there." So he gets me back in school. And then for about a week, everything going smoothly a little bit. But before I know it, again they are going to kick me out of school.

You see, my aunt was sick in the hospital, so I called long distance to tell my parents about it. I got out of my class; this nice black teacher let me out of my class with an excuse. But Mr. C———— came up to me and said, "Why aren't you in class?"

I said, "I got an excuse to be out of class 'cause my aunt is sick."

And he said, "You shouldn't be taking up school time. You don't belong here."

"Well." I said, "I'm going to talk to my mother. I don't care what you say, because my aunt is sick and I got to talk to her."

So he said, "Well, I got some paper for you, so when you get off the phone, you just come to the office and get ready to go on home."

I got fed up again. I say, "O.K., I don't care."

The assistant principal got my uncle believing that I'm just messing around in school. My uncle gets mad. "Well, Paul, you know you're getting in trouble like this."

So I say, "I'm calling my mother because your wife is sick and you're getting mad at me about it." I went and asked my teacher to tell Mr. C———— that he gave me an excuse to be out of class. So the teacher goes and says that Paul was excused from class.

The assistant principal say, "Well he was out in the hall messing around outside and out front. I'm kicking him out for that." So the teacher now gets mad. This is a black teacher, and he gets mad.

He say, "We gonna see something about this."

The assistant principal say, "Well, you're a teacher. Why don't you agree on what we're doing?"

And the teacher said, "That ain't fair, because black students should have the same rights as white students do. They're allowed out in the halls with passes."

The assistant principal then said, "Well, we're still kicking him out anyway. We don't care what you say. We're paying you, and you do what we want you to do or get out." This is one of the ways they make it rough on the black kids.

Blacks also get punished worse than the whites. I remember when I got in a fight with this white kid. The kid knocked into me in the hall, so I said something like, "Hey watch it, cowboy!" He had his hair and stuff like a cowboy. The cat got mad and tried to jump me and everything. We fought, and after I done whopped the cat and everything, they wanted to kick me out. And this white kid got to go to class.

"You go on to class: we'll do with him. We're gonna make sure we get this straight." They took me to the office and let him go on to class. They didn't even bring him to the office. In the office they're asking me, "Paul, why do you do this and everything?"

I say, "You know, he bumps into me, and then wants to get mad because I call him a name. And it wasn't like the kind of names I'm always called."

They say, "Well you're getting kicked out of school."

I say, "What are you going to do with him?"

They say, "We'll take care of him."

Before I know it, some brothers came to me and said, "Paul, he's still in school."

I was kicked out for a whole week. And then when I came back, I can't make up no homework, 'cause they don't let you. When you go to a teacher and tell her you're behind because you were suspended, they say, "Well, that's your tough luck. You should do things right. If you don't get it, if you don't know how to get ahead in school, you might as well not learn anyway." Some teachers tell you what the homework is. Maybe one or two, if they're black teachers. Black teachers try to help you out whenever you want. But a white teacher says, "That's your tough luck." It's almost like saying, "Why don't you go on somewhere. Go in a corner and hide somewhere cause you ain't getting nothing from me. If you fail, that's too bad."

BUSING IN BOSTON*

If the foregoing excerpts from The High School Revolutionaries *seem exaggerated, consider what has been happening in the Boston school desegregation fight, as suggested by the following two items taken from a Boston newspaper. The first describes a scene in Judge W. Arthur Garrity's courtroom when John Leubsdorf, counsel for the pro-busing forces, examines a witness, Mrs. Elma Carter, a black American and a biology teacher at South Boston High:*

> Mrs. Carter: "On December 6 . . . it was known that there was going to be a white assembly . . . . The assembly ended at the end of the third period . . . . At that time, they marched through the school . . . . At the landing of the second level, black students were held back. White students were allowed to pass . . . . They were chanting . . . ."
>
> Leubsdorf: "What were they chanting?"
>
> Mrs. Carter: "Niggers eat shit . . . . Twice I have used the Audio-Visual room for safety . . . . [That Friday] as I

*Adapted by T. F. Hoult from material appearing in *The Boston Phoenix*, 24 Dec 74.

proceeded down the corridor, I heard, 'Niggers go home, niggers go home.' Then it changed to 'Niggers eat shit.' When I got to the hallway, there was no one—no policeman, no aide. I proceeded to the Audio-Visual room, knowing I could find safety. They were going faster than me . . . . I went to the Audio-Visual room and pulled the projector . . . in front of me. The students saw me and started yelling 'nigger' and 'black bitch.' A white male teacher came to my assistance . . . ."

Mrs. Carter's testimony obviously shocks Garrity as much as the rest of the spectators. The order he issues at the end of the day specifically bans racial epithets in the schools. Although Garrity hates to issue orders when moral suasion might suffice, his order grants most of Leubsdorf's requests but leaves control of the schools and police with the local authorities—for the time being, at least.

Busing opponents are led by John Kerrigan who heads the committee controlling the schools of Boston. At an anti-busing rally:

John Kerrigan wanders around in a black windbreaker with the words "Boston School Committee Chairman" emblazoned on the chest, and "Bigga" inscribed on the arm. "Bigga," he explains, is an old Army nickname, given by his barrack-mates, who were awed by the size of his sexual organs. Or so he says.

After being found guilty of contempt, Kerrigan leaves Judge Garrity's Court:

When John Kerrigan reaches the now-empty corridor, he is once more full of swagger, brimming with more adolescent *macho* than he has displayed in weeks. He offers one reporter an enema . . . . Within earshot of a black television correspondent, he bellows, "Did you see [him]? He's a great proof of evolution. I bet he loves bananas." An elevator arrives to take him downstairs, manned by two policemen. On the first floor, he is disgorged into a mob of his most vehement, vocal supporters, the remnants of the crowd evicted from the 12th floor when the hearing started.

RULE FROM THE TOP*

I have just taken part in a dismaying meeting with a group of "West" Union High School System administrators ("West" being a pseudonym for the name of a large western city which, in terms of the apparent representativeness of its power structure and educational arrangements, could be almost any big city in the land). The only bright note is the hope that if the implications of the meeting become known to others, perhaps steps can be taken to alleviate similiar conditions elsewhere.

The meeting was concerned with civil liberties—a "long-hair" case—and, throughout the discussion, the administrators appeared to lack even the foggiest notion of the meaning of civil liberties in a democratic society. Two of them went so far as to laugh when the totalitarianism of their system was mentioned.

After the meeting, I attended a party which included a number of friends who are high-school teachers. Noticing my down-in-the-dumps attitude, they pressed for details. After I told the story, one particularly fine math teacher consoled me with the disquieting observation, "Don't worry—only the worst ones become administrators." This was a gross generalization, of course—and it wasn't even directed specifically at West—but it met no opposition from those at the party. The other teachers chimed in to agree that in their opinion it is quite reasonable to hypothesize that only the most authoritarian teachers are picked to be administrators. A few conspicuous exceptions were noted, but the teachers were unaminous in asserting that high-school and grade-school administrators, especially the former, are almost always selected from the ranks of those who believe that social control properly proceeds from "the top down," that the prime role of schools is to cultivate conformity, and that classroom decorum is more important than creativity. It was pointed out that athletic coaches, in particular, manifest the "proper" characteristics. Coaches generally have an unusually narrow educational experience that involves precious little concern with abstractions such as democracy and civil rights; they are trained to issue commands and to expect unquestioning obedience such as one would find in a traditional Prussian guard; and they frequently have a physique that intimidates the weak—all of which perhaps helps to account for the otherwise inexplicable fact that they are so often appointed to administrative positions.

And then I recalled what happened at a school-board meeting I attended in a nearby suburb just a few months before. Representatives of the

*Adapted from Thomas Ford Hoult, "Don't Worry, Only the Worst Become Administrators," *Changing Education* 4(Spring 1969):23–26.

American Federation of Teachers local were there to ask, as they had asked countless times before, that the school-board members sit down with the union members—as equals—and come to some mutually agreeable conclusions. But the board remained adamant; the board president proclaimed that the board alone would make all decisions on salaries and working conditions. He then announced a substantial improvement in the salary schedule and appeared surprised when the union spokesmen denounced the new schedule as symptomatic of an outworn system involving rule-form-the-top.

But not all the teachers representatives were opposed to the traditional control system. The president of the local education association rose to thank the board for its "magnanimous" action and went on to say something like; "And when we are speaking of salary increases, let's not forget our wonderful administrators—they deserve more than anyone!" While the superintendent flushed, and members of the audience squirmed and hung their heads as if in shame, one person announced: "That's the most blatant bit of bootlicking I've ever observed." But—and this was the most disconcerting point of all—the union representatives then flatly predicted that the bootlicker would undoubtedly be made a school principal. "He would have all the qualifications the board wants," one teacher said. "He'd have a craven attitude toward those who have authority over him, and a callous disregard for his fellow workers. He'd be a natural for 'lower' administration."

. . . .

But now I see that, so far as high-school systems are concerned, the union members were probably correct. The bootlicker type *does* seem to be a natural for administration in all too many secondary schools—or, at least this appears to be the case from the standpoint of those favoring a truly democratic society. Of course, If your fundamental value is authoritarianism, then you will see nothing wrong with making principals out of those who manifest licked-dog behavior when in the presence of their so-called betters; not will you see anything amiss in the responses of the West Union administrators in our meeting about long hair.

The meeting was called at the request of Stephen Ray (as I shall call him), executive secretary of the state branch of the American Civil Liberties Union. Ray had received an appeal from a high-school lad who needed just one credit to graduate but who was not permitted to register in the summer session on the grounds that his hair was "too long" and, according to interpretations based on the established dress code, long hair is a disturbing influence in the classroom. On the grounds of principle, the boy refused to have his hair cut; in effect, he asserted that the right to life in a democratic society includes the right to be free of interference with purely private behavior which cannot be shown to injure others. The boy asked the help of one teacher, who then volunteered to solve the immediate problem by having the boy assist her so he could receive his needed credit without having to appear in class. When he was still not allowed to register, the boy followed the established appeal procedure. Merely having an appeal route would appear to safeguard individual rights—but the West procedure is so long and complicated that, like many such arrangements, it too often makes a mockery of rights. The process involves so many steps, appointments, interviews, etc., that it tends to make a moot case out of any given situation; it is such as to discourage all but the rare few who have mature convictions, dogged determination, and limitless time and energy.

Despite the complications and the pressure of time, our long-haired youngster was persistent enough to "exhaust administrative remedies" so far as they were available, given the limited period permitted for "late registration." After being denied redress at every level, the boy asked the ACLU to help him, and the meeting was arranged. Ray then asked me—as an ACLU board member—to join him, along with another university professor, two cooperating lawyers, and a university student. The school-system representatives included the assistant superintendent, the director of administrative services, the principal of one high school and the associate principal of another, and an athletic coach (!) newly appointed as social studies coordinator. We—the ACLU group—were not told that our Friday meeting was being held the day *after* the last day when the boy would be permitted to register in any case, hence we did not know that in more senses than one we were gathered to talk into the wind.

The meeting opened with distribution of copies of the school-board's policy on student behavior and dress and with the related dress codes prevailing in the various high schools. All the codes called for boys to have "neat and *conservative*" haircuts. Such codes and haircuts are needed, said the administrators, because people who *dress* poorly *act* accordingly, and the educational process is impeded.

When asked for some reasonable evidence—evidence beyond guesswork and gossip and "my experience"—that education is hampered when people dress their bodies and hair as they please, we were given nothing but hostile stares along with firm statements that we didn't know whereof we spoke. We were asked if we favored abolishing *all* rules and we responded, "No—when there is clear empirical evidence that a regulation really makes a substantial contribution to the proper functioning of the school, then it is sensible. All other regulations—especially those established by administrative fiat—should be abandoned as inappropriate in a democratic society."

But—said one of the administrators—with such a minimum of rules, what would you do about the pupil whose dress violated a legal statute? We answered, "Let those who violate the law suffer the penalties of law, with apprehension and punishment being administered by the police and the courts; where schools assume the role of the police and of judges, they run the risk of making it appear that teachers and stick-wielders are synonymous."

My university colleague pointed out that college administrators also used to assume that student dress must be regulated. Now, however, dress codes have been abandoned, or are ignored, in all but the most backward Podunk Normal schools. And still there are no university riots centering around miniskirts and boys with long hair. Even at Berkeley and Columbia, relatively few students appear in public without being clothed, cut, and combed in accordance with prevailing middle-class standards. Those who violate the standards constitute a small—and often scorned—minority.

"But, have you ever taught in high school?" we were asked, and the implication was that, if we knew conditions "from the inside," we, too, would favor the existing rules. Not so, we rejoined—and we did not depend upon testimony from the one among us who *had* taught in high school. The proper answer to the "Vas you der, Charlie?" tactic is an old one: You do not have to eat a rotten egg to know something significant about its condition. One does not have to have syphilis to know that is something to be avoided. One need not have been a resident of Germany to justify denouncing Hitler. And, similarly, it is possible to make cogent criticisms of school systems without being personally involved in them.

At one point in the meeting, I expressed concern about the "tone" of the various dress and behavior codes. Where, I asked, is there any acknowledgement of the importance of dissent? We're not here to encourage dissent, said an administrator, adding something to this effect: "If we let students express dissent, we'd lose our jobs tomorrow." The assistant superintendent interjected his resentment about the opinions expressed by the long-haired boy—the boy said he likes to challenge his teachers. "And what is wrong with that?" we asked. Teachers can't teach if they have to respond to challenges, said the assistant superintendent.

At another point, when we had, so to speak, driven the administrators into a logical corner from which there was no reasonable escape, the assistant superintendent trotted out the last refuge of the defenseless bureaucrat—namely: "Our job is to carry out the policies of the board; we cannot be held accountable for what the board decides." We said, "Your responsibility, then, is to educate the board; perhaps the board members are not aware of current trends and needs." The administrators' answer boiled down to: "Our job is to *obey* the board, not educate it." (Shades of Nuremberg!)

Toward the end of what was all too clearly a useless get-together, I spoke of my deep concern with the implications of the meeting. "It seems to me," I said, "you men have no meaningful knowledge of the fact that this country was founded on dissent and challenge and difference, and that in social systems where dissent is forbidden or discouraged, those in control stand in constant danger of making frightful errors." I said it was apparent the West Union High School System was run in terms of totalitarian principles that would be appropriate in some societies but not in ours. In response to this charge, the principal grinned, almost as if he were thinking, "tough beans." "Your grin suggests," said one of my colleagues, "you don't think it matters that your system manifests many of the features one would expect in a prison." The grin faded and was replaced by the more usual hostile glare.

"I didn't realize our high schools were so totalitarian." the assistant superintendent observed in a very sarcastic tone of voice. "Are we unique in being totalitarian?" No, said one of the ACLU representatives— totalitarianism is rampant in the high schools of America and it is high time for a change at that level just as there was a previous change at the college level.

The chances of lessening the totalitarianism commonly found in high-school administration are hampered by the twin fears which appear to possess so many high-school administrators. One of the fears centers on the notion that if an administrator admits a particular rule is not justified, he may lose all control. The West administrators patently know that a boy's long hair, in and of itself, causes nothing significant; but they seem to view the hair rule as a symbol of the dominance they feel they can and should exercise. A related fear is the idea that anarchy will prevail if minutiae of behavior are not closely regulated—a fear which is based on the mistaken belief that human behavior is basically a function of technical law rather than of underlying cultural norms. It is important to note that for neither of these fears is there a scintilla of respectable empirical evidence.

But our group of administrators clearly felt that, since their minds were made up, it only confused the issue to speak of evidence. With every point we tried to make, we were rewarded with the glassy look of total resentment. Fundamental civil liberties, such as due process, free speech and free assembly, are inappropriate for students, the administrators implied. We got the impression that students should obey, not question; they should conform, not dissent; they should learn to manifest "conservatism!" With such attitudes apparently prevailing among those controlling the school system, it seemed appropriate for me not to resist the parting observation, as we left the meeting room, that the techniques being used in the West Union High School System are such as to maximize the chances that graduates will be the kind of meek conformists who provide the foundations needed for a dictatorship.

It is particularly disquieting that the administrator group apparently did not resent our charges about authoritarian procedures. They seemed mainly concerned that no one should interfere with their sacred rules! . . .

DON'T ASK QUESTIONS*

John Holt is one of the most prominent educators to call for a "deschooled" society—i.e., one in which there are no schools at which attendance is compulsory. The deschooled society does not mean one that has no schools per se. Mr. Holt and his confreres assert that what must be discarded is forced attendance, regardless of interest, in a standard curriculum. Such "education" often does more harm than good. Instead of the prison-like settings we designate as "public schools," deschooled advocates would offer tax-supported learning centers where interested citizens of all ages could go for help in solving problems, including reading difficulties.

Almost every child, on the first day he sets foot in a school building, is smarter, more curious, less afraid of what he doesn't know, better at finding and figuring things out, more confident, resourceful, persistent and independent than he will ever be again in his schooling—or, unless he is very unusual and very lucky, for the rest of his life. Already, by paying close attention to and interacting with the world and people around him, and without any school-type formal instruction, he has done a task far more difficult, complicated and abstract than anything he will be asked to do in school, or than any of his teachers has done for years. He has solved the mystery of language. He has discovered it—babies don't even know that language exists—and he has found out how it works and learned to use it. He had done it by exploring, by experimenting, by developing his own model of the grammar of language, by trying it out and seeing whether it works, by gradually changing it and refining it until it does work. And while he has been doing this, he has been learning other things as well, including many of the "concepts" that the schools think only they can teach him, and many that are more complicated than the ones they do try to teach him.

In he comes, this curious, patient, determined, energetic, skillful learner. We sit him down at a desk, and what do we teach him? Many things. First,

*Adapted from John Holt, "School is Bad for Children," *The Saturday Evening Post* [no vol. number] (Feb. 8, 1969):12, 14–15.

that learning is separate from living. "You come to school to learn," we tell him, as if the child hadn't been learning before, as if living were out there and learning were in here, and there were no connection between the two. Secondly, that he cannot be trusted to learn and is no good at it. Everything we teach about reading, a task far simpler than many that the child has already mastered, says to him. "If we don't make you read, you won't, and if you don't do it exactly the way we tell you, you can't." In short, he comes to feel that learning is a passive process, something that someone else does *to* you, instead of something you do for yourself.

In a great many other ways he learns that he is worthless, untrustworthy, fit only to take other people's orders, a blank sheet for other people to write on. Oh, we make a lot of nice noises in school about respect for the child and individual differences, and the like. But our acts, as opposed to our talk, say to the child, "Your experience, your concerns, your curiosities, your needs, what you know, what you want, what you wonder about, what you hope for, what you fear, what you like and dislike, what you are good at or not so good at—all this is of not the slightest importance, it counts for nothing. What counts here, and the only thing that counts, is what we know, what we think is important, what we want you to do, think and be." The child soon learns not to ask questions—the teacher isn't there to satisfy his curiosity. Having learned to hide his curiosity, he later learns to be ashamed of it. Given no chance to find out who he is—and to develop that person, whoever it is—he soon comes to accept the adults' evaluation of him.

He learns many other things. He learns that to be wrong, uncertain, confused, is a crime. Right Answers are what the school wants, and he learns countless strategies for prying these answers out of the teacher, for conning her into thinking he knows what he doesn't know. He learns to dodge, bluff, fake, cheat. He learns to be lazy. Before he came to school, he would work for hours on end, on his own, with no thought of reward, at the business of making sense of the world and gaining competence in it. In school he learns, like every buck private, how to goldbrick, how not too work when the sergeant isn't looking, how to know when he is looking, how to make him think you are working even when he is looking. He learns that in real life you don't do anything unless you are bribed, bullied or conned into doing it, that nothing is worth doing for its own sake, or that if it is, you can't do it in school. He learns to be bored, to work with a small part of his mind, to escape from the reality around him into daydreams and fantasies—but not like the fantasies of his preschool years, in which he played a very active part.

The child comes to school curious about other people, particularly other children, and the school teaches him to be indifferent. The most interesting thing in the classroom—often the only interesting thing in it—is the other children. But he has to act as if these other children, all about him, only a few feet away, are not really there. He cannot interact with them, talk with them, smile at them. In many schools he can't talk to other children in the halls between classes; in more than a few, and some of these in stylish suburbs, he can't even talk to them at lunch. Splendid training for a world in which, when you're not studying the other person to figure out how to do him in, you pay no attention to him.

In fact, he learns how to live without paying attention to anything going on around him. You might say that school is a long lesson in how to turn yourself off, which may be one reason why so many young people, seeking the awareness of the world and responsiveness to it they had when they were little, think they can only find it in drugs. Aside from being boring, the school is almost always ugly, cold, inhuman—even the most stylish, glass-windowed, $20-a-square-foot schools.

And so, in this dull and ugly place, where nobody ever says anything very truthful, where everybody is playing a kind of role, as in a charade, where the teachers are no more free to respond honestly to the students than the students are free to respond to the teachers or each other, where the air practically vibrates with suspicion and anxiety, the child learns to live in a daze, saving his energies for those small parts of his life that are too trivial for the adults to bother with, and thus remain his. It is a rare child who can come through his schooling with much left of his curiosity, his independence or his sense of his own dignity, competence and worth. . . .

THE COMING AMERICAN REVOLUTION*

The author of this piece was a tenured professor of philosophy at Arizona State University until he was fired in 1971 by the state Board of Regents. The Regents claimed Starsky was discharged because he illegally dismissed a class, but everyone knew that what really motivated the regents was Starsky's vigorous advocacy of revolutionary socialism. Early in 1973, a federal court judge ruled that the regents' action, in comparison with Starsky's ideas, was far more dangerous for the country and Starsky must be rehired; the regents have appealed the order.

. . . The technological level of present capitalist society created certain problems which have dramatically changed the functions of many of our old institutions. Universities have always been responsible for transmitting

*Adapted from Morris J. Starsky, "Campus Struggles and the Coming American Revolution," paper presented to the Southwestern Socialist Conference, Los Angeles, California, Nov. 28, 1969; mimeographed.

the ideas, values and culture of a ruling class to its next generation. If you are going to inherit an economic system you have to have a proper knowledge of it and an outlook appropriate to it. You have to know how to deal with the problems of that social system since you will be making all the important decisions in it.

It is not only the sons and daughters of the ruling class that are being trained in the large state universities and colleges around the country today. Most of the students in these institutions are from the working class. They are learning the skills and techniques required for operating the computerized means of production characteristic of advanced capitalist society. It is a sophisticated economy and it needs sophisticated workers. Incidentally, this is a contradiction of captialism that needs to be explored. The sophisticated worker of modern capitalism is not going to be easy to trick or fool with capitalist propoganda. The new technology and the new jobs require a new education. For example, they require a "new math." When the battle over new math was raging in Arizona, the conservatives called it a Communist plot designed to break down the family. Obviously, neither daddy nor mommy could handle the new math because their training was for an earlier period in the capitalist economic system. Jobs didn't require a knowledge of technical subjects based on the new math. Now there are many such jobs and the ruling class is adjusting its educational system accordingly. Thus, the university is playing a role analogous to the role played by the high school in an earlier period. It has become a factory whose raw material is an unskilled or semi-skilled high school graduate with a low exploitation rate and whose finished product is technically trained or trainable with a high exploitation rate. The product isn't going to inherit the system so he doesn't need to know very much about himself, his role and the world at large. All he needs to know is the ideological justifications for the system which he is going to serve and the proper motivations for his role in that system. After all, you can't expect capitalists to create a working class that is educated enough to challenge the right of the capitalists and their political stooges to run the country.

Advanced monopoly capitalism has not only created new job requirements, it has rendered large groups of people economically superfluous. Among these groups are young people. Thus, universities have become not only training and indoctrination centers, but also detention centers or holding pens for those whose skin color or income emancipates them from menial work. The technical training doesn't take four years; it doesn't even take four semesters. The "get a degree" ideology and the corresponding discrimination against those without degrees reveal the essential role of present universities. Young people are being kept in these institutions, isolated from society and in a subordinate status, because there simply are no jobs for them. At a time when young people are physically adults and emotionally ready for adult status, they are not only unemployed but unemployable by design.

Training and detention are two functions of the modern university. The third is research. The large corporations and the various agencies of government spend more money for research than for practically anything else. Thus, establishing a large state university is a way of distributing the cost of research and development through the capitalist class as a whole and a large section of the working class. That's what they mean when they say that education is an investment. Incidentally, this is why small businesses, mining and agriculture resist large univeristy budgets. They didn't when the bulk of the money went for research from which they could profit.

Universities, however, are not merely social overhead for the ruling class. They are state-capitalist enterprises. Universities are giant corporations and their incentive is profit from counter-insurgency, real estate, military hardware development and investments. The educational needs of the students and the community, which ought to be the primary concern of the university, is not a concern at all. How can it be? Capitalists and capitalist managers run the university. They establish schools of business administration, but no schools of union administration. They own large amounts of stock in corporations and control the university's investments as well. A recent study conducted by the Temporary N. Y. State Commission to Study Campus Unrest concludes that "... administrators seem to have forgotten that the purpose of the university is to provide knowledge. They prefer instead to emphasize the growth and management of the institution—without reference to students" (AP,11/27/69).

The university does the training, detaining and research for the corporations and the military. The products of the research are sometimes turned over to the capitalists outright. On other occasions joint business ventures are created to profit from the research. This usually includes privileged members of the faculty who then serve on committees to find ways of solving the problem of student unrest (see Ridgeway, *The Closed Corporation*). The products of the training are recruited either into the capitalists's profit machine or into his death machine. It is really the same machine. . . .

Those blacks, chicanos and Indians fortunate enough to pass the racist admission requirements of most universities find themselves in the most shocking situation of institutionalized racism and male chauvinism that anyone can imagine. American education is not only capitalist indoctrination, it is white-european-male-capitalist indoctrination.

It is important here that we distinguish between an *objectively* racist policy and a *consciously* racist policy. If you do not allow black people or brown people to attend your university, then you are following a consciously racist policy. On the other hand, if you have admission standards set by the needs of your economic system, and it just so happens that black and brown people do not meet these standards, then your policy is objectively racist and so is your economic system. The administrators of most large universities are not following a consciously racist policy. The faculty isn't either. Yet, both are following objectively racist policies; the latter in what they teach and how they teach it, the former in their refusal to use the resources and facilities of the university to aid in the liberation of oppressed national minorities. They refuse because the oppression of national minorities is built right into the system they serve, just as the oppression of millions of people around the world is built right into the system.

What all of this shows is that the problems of education underlying the campus struggles against the war machine, racism and meaningless education cannot be solved within capitalist society because the solution requires a revolutionary reorganization of educational structure and content which cannot be accomplished without ending the hegemony of the capitalist ruling class. . . .

What is at issue in the campus struggles is the question of what reason is and what reason demands of those who want to be reasonable. For revolutionaries, the reasonable, objective and neutral character of American universities is irrational, ideological and partisan. It is that kind of reason which hides behind the rhetoric of objective, value-free scholarship while it lives off millions of dollars from defense grants to find better ways to control, coerce and destroy people all over the world and even here at home. Liberal objectivity must be seen for what it is: a conceptual framework which constitutes and organizes facts in such a way that the only truths are ruling class truths and the only values are ruling class values. Neutrality too must be seen for what it is: assent.

The political content of our demands is not neutrality but commitment of the resources of the university to the liberation of mankind from oppression. Universities cannot be neutral because they are economically controlled institutions with limited resources. Decisions must be made about who is to be hired, what research is to be done and the like. These are political decisions. Now they are being made by men who serve the capitalist class and the capitalist state. . . .

DEGREES ARE NOT ALL*

Perhaps we should rethink an idea that is fast becoming an undisputed premise of American life: that a college degree is a necessary (and perhaps

*Adapted from Blanche D. Blank, "Degrees: Who Needs Them?" *AAUP Bulletin* 58(September 1972):261–266.

even a sufficient) precondition for success. I do not wish to quarrel with the assumptions made about the benefits of orthodox education; I want only to expose its false god: the four-year, convertible, all-purpose, degree-bearing college, aimed at the so-called "college age" population and by now almost universally accepted as *the* stepping-stone to "meaningful" and "better" jobs. Adding two degrees to the American Dream of two houses, two cars, and two children will not improve the quality of that dream nor the quality of those degrees. A recent television documentary called "And What If the Dream Came True?" was a poignant reminder that the American college is apparently not up to meeting the fundamental problems of our lives. This thoughtful reportage of the lifestyle and reflections of a typically wealthy suburbanite family, in which both parents were the products of our best higher education, seemed to reveal the possibility that college—American style—is, if anything, more likely to mold one to fit the technological culture (the presumptive villain of the piece) than to release one to cope with it in fulfilling and meaningful ways. College for this family (although college was hardly its major theme) was quite patently a one-stop affair on the road to a series of job and housing moves, none of which produced for the protagonists a sense of well-being or satisfaction. Yet this is reputedly an accurate report of what life is like for the American successes. And while it is becoming fashinable to rail at the hardware materialism that is rampant in the Dream, it has not yet become chic to call into question the software, by which I mean the degrees.

Yet if we continue to deify college degrees, to assume that we can produce better men for better living through collegry, then we will (unwittingly, to be sure) alienate many youths, destroy many universities, denigrate many socially useful types of work, and reverse our commitment to establishing a more egalitarian society.

More specifically, what is wrong with the current college-work cycle are the following anomalies: We are "selling" college to the youth group of America as a take-off pad for the material good life for which we are already infamous in that population circle. College is literally advertised and packaged as a means for getting more money through "better" jobs at the same moment that Harvard graduates are taking jobs as taxi-drivers. This is a seriously irresponsible promotion in many ways. It is a perversion of the true spirit of a university, a perversion of humane social ethic, and, at bottom, a patent fraud. To take the last point first, the economy is simply not geared to guaranteeing these presumptive "better" jobs; the colleges are not geared to training for such jobs; and the ethical propriety of the entire enterprise is very questionable. The current emphasis on college degrees is also subtly but irrevocably denigrating the actual and potential fulfilments inherent across a broad spectrum of work. In other words, we are by definition (rather than by analysis) establishing two kinds of work: work which is labeled "better" by having a degree requirement tagged to it; and all other nondegree work which, through this logic, becomes automatically "low level" or "dead-end."

This process is also destroying our universities, since we are encouraging (indeed, almost compelling) them to cater to this lock-step economic survival march. In so doing, the "practical curriculum" must become paramount, the students must become prisoners, and the colleges must become servants of big business and big government. Under these conditions the university can no longer be an independent source of scientific and philosophic truth-seeking and moral criticism. It is losing the essential environment which made possible its greatest social contributions. Ironically enough, moreover, we are in all this creating an elite that may be more rigid and anti-egalitarian than even the traditional castes of birth and wealth. . . .

The need for this rethinking . . . may be best illustrated by a case study.

Joe V. is a typical liberal arts graduate who took his college years "straight." That is, he "grooved" on philosophic questions, was fired by imaginative art and literature, and majored in political science. He was employed by a large New York City bank, where because he was a "college man" he was given the opportunity to enter the "assistant manager training program." This was a two-year stint in which the trainees were rotated among different bank departments to gain technical know-how and experience. The trainees were also given classroom instruction, including some sessions on "how to write a business letter." The program was virtually restricted to college graduates. At the end of the line, those successful in the enterprise could look forward to an assistant bank manager position in which the largest single activity is giving simple advice to bank customers and in which there is a modest amount of employee supervision. Joe searched for some congruence between the training program and the later job, on the one hand, and his college-whetted appetites and skills on the other. He found none. Indeed, the skills for the actual job had to be learned essentially on the job; and the skills engendered by college were not only irrelevant, but actually dysfunctional. That is, the research-seminar, paper-writing, analytic lifestyle of college had actually unsuited Joe for the lifestyle of an assistant bank manager. It seemed probable that it had even unsuited him for the lifestyle of a full-fledged bank manager.

In most instances necessity would have forced Joe to stay on with the bank. Had this happened, neither the bank nor Joe would have been as fulfilled as might be hoped. In giving Joe preference for the training program the bank had bypassed a few enthusiastic aspirants already dedicated to a banking career and daily demonstrating their devotion and competence in closely related jobs. In questioning his superiors about the entire enterprise, Joe could only conclude that the "top brass" had some very diffuse and not too well-researched or even well-thought-out conceptions about college men. The executives admitted that college itself did not insure the motivation nor the verbal or social skills they might need. They were not even convinced that simple English accompanied the degree-bearers. That was why they had letter-writing courses. Nor were they clear about the skills that were actually most desirable for their increasingly diverse branches. Yet they clung (blindly, it seems) to the college prerequisite.

This strange symbiotic cycle has been with us for a long time. It may have received its greatest impetus during the depression when business enterprises used the criterion of college degrees as a cheap and convenient way to cut down the long lines that surrounded every employment office. No matter what the job, college men got first preference. Selling ribbons at Macy's, pushing papers in the civil service—it was all the same. Indeed, it was at this time that the New York City civil service, for example, became the homeland for a very large number of overqualified college graduates who later rose to managerial posts but who remained forever embittered by the lack of symmetry between what they saw as their skills, training, and (most clearly) their ambitions and the rather meanly paid and unheralded jobs they held. A typical civil servant's sole hold on status was often the difficult exam system that he alone could master. There is, of course, a natural tendency to recruit in one's own self-image; but in the civil service, recruiting for college types became in some places, a surrogate for other status rewards.

What is more remarkable about this history is that the public at large should have so quiescently accepted this litmus test. Why a college degree should grant someone automatic first-call on a full dinner-pail in times of economic distress remains a mystery to me, particulary as it is no secret that college has always been (and even now remains) the particular preserve of the relatively well-to-do. Even in the event that college might become the preserve of the intellectual in lieu of the comfortable, I will still fail to see the moral imperative that to the gifted belongs all privileges. But despite the ethical implications, connections between degrees and "better" jobs continue to be forged and exploited by both sides of what is essentially a parasitic relationship.

During the sixties, and continuing unabated to this day, the mass media have done a "hard sell" by announcing that degree-holders earn an "extra $100,000" during their working lives. I doubt that this is an accurate reflection of the power of degrees as such. The statistic probably does reflect such "intervening variables" as the fact that all but 7 percent of our college graduates (speaking nationally) come from middle to upperclass homes. In other words, people whose fathers own businesses, whose uncles are in the professions, whose incomes permit them a leisurely period for job-hunting and so forth—these people can indeed rely on getting "better" jobs.

The college degrees may well be irrelevant. Yet "truth in advertising" does not restrain the outpouring of institutional service ads that appear as subway placards and radio spot announcements. Degree-granting institutions, moreover, run their own ads touting their programs under banners like "Get Ahead," and their hallways are festooned with similar come-ons.

It is easy to understand why business allows the colleges to act as recruiting, screening, and training agencies for them. Insofar as it works, it saves business money and time. They have virtually nothing to lose. Moreover, big business and big government are in a short-sighted way aided by the "class" society that the college prerequisite system helps to perpetuate. That is, the degree system helps to cement a stable and visible divide between a type of *arbeiter* class and an *angestellter* class. Such a divide reinforces the managerial need for a legitimized hierarchy. It reduces costly coerciveness, simplifies union negotiations, and in many other ways preserves for Caesar that which is Caesar's.

Why colleges allow themselves to act as servicing agents for business or other enterprises may not be as apparent. The first thing, however, to be clear about is that colleges are increasingly becoming conventional bureaucracies. It is inevitable, therefore, that they should respond to the first and unchallenged law of bureaucracy: Expand! Behind almost every new college program is the imperative of growth. The more, therefore, that colleges can persuade outside institutions to restrict employment in favor of their clientele, the stronger is the college's hold and attraction. . . .

SCHOOLS AND THE MELTING POT*

It is fashionable these days to point to the decline of the public school, as if there were a time in some golden past when the schools really served all of the people all of the time. Legend tells of the Little Red Schoolhouse that made equal opportunity available to children of every economic and social class, and, a little later in the nation's history, functioned as the primary instrument of the melting pot that offered poor immigrant children access to the fullness of American life. Today the schools are

*Adapted from Colin Greer, "Public Schools: The Myth of the Melting Pot," *Saturday Review* 52(Nov. 15, 1969):84–86, 102.

criticized for their failure to provide equality of opportunity to poor black children. The charge is true, but it is by no means the whole truth, nor is it new. The public schools have always failed the lower classes—both white and black. Current educational problems stem not from the fact that the schools have changed, but from the fact that they continue to do precisely the job they have always done.

What we are witnessing, in our current panic over urban education, is no more than an escalation of the criticisms made by school reformers since the turn of the century. The many innovations introduced over the past fifty years have made it easier for school systems to handle the huge numbers of students brought into the schools by compulsory attendance legislation and a job market requiring increasingly sophisticated talents, but they have not changed the basic function of the schools as the primary selector of the winners and losers in society.

The very fact that we can look with pride at more and more students going on to secondary and higher education reveals a system that with increasing efficiency benefits some and denies others in the bosom of its material prosperity. Public schooling cannot be understood, nor the current problems manifest in it, apart from a consideration of the predominant influence of social and economic class. For at least the last eighty years, socio-economic class, as signified by employment rates and levels, has determined scholastic achievement, as measured by dropout and failure rates.

From 1890, at least, the schools failed to perform according to their own as well as the popular definition of their role. In virtually every study undertaken since that of Chicago schools made in 1898, more children have failed in school than have succeeded, both in absolute and in relative numbers. The educators who collaborated on the Chicago study found an exceedingly high incidence of poor school performance. They were quick to look to foreign birth as an explanation, but immigrants spawned Americans and still, with each passing decade, no more than 60 percent of Chicago's public school pupils were recorded at "normal age" (grade level); the rest were either "overage" (one or two years behind), or "retarded" (three to five years behind). In Boston, Chicago, Detroit, Philadelphia, Pittsburgh, New York, and Minneapolis, failure rates were so high that in no one of these systems did the so-called normal group exceed 60 percent, while in several instances it fell even lower—to 49 percent in Pittsburgh, and to 35 percent in Minneapolis.

The truth is that the mobility of white lower classes was never as rapid nor as sure as it has become traditional to think. The 1920 census, for example, showed that even the favored English and Welsh migrants found half their number tied to the terrifying vulerability of unskilled labor occupations.

Americans of English stock (dominating national language, customs, and institutions) had 40 percent of their number working in coals mines and cotton factories.

And what of the school in all this? Clearly, according to the same body of data, a close relationship obtained between various group designations (native-born with and without foreign parents, and foreign-born), which revealed that levels of school retention in any given group coincided with that group's adult employment rate. Dropout rates for all groups, including the Negro, were in direct proportion to rates of adult unemployment. Further, the high degree of school achievement among Jews, which has confirmed our expectation of public schools, did not mean success for all Jews. Otherwise, why the remedial classes and dropout panic in several of the schools on New York's Lower East Side with as much as 99 percent "Hebrew" registration? Where the family was poor enough to take in boarders to cover rental costs, and desperate enough to join the city's welfare roles, then delinquency, prostitution, and child-labor were as much the burden of Jewish families, for whom such characteristics were real if not typical.

With rising industrial unemployment and an expanded technological economy, the school-leaving age increased so that the problem of caring for all grades of ability on the elementary school level escalated to the high school level. Vocational instruction programs were an inevitable corollary to the academic program and quickly became a symbol of the schools' stratification role. Today, the junior college serves as the junior high school had served earlier, operating to a large extent as an extension of secondary education, with back-seat status justified by the democratic rationale of monumental numbers to be catered to.

The pattern of school failure has been perennially uniform, but concern for it was by no means as great as the concern on the part of educators to get more pupils into school. In 1917, and again in 1925, federal compulsory education legislation put added strength behind various state actions to this effect. Compulsory school-leaving age moved from twelve to fourteen and then to sixteen, but always with the proviso that the two years at the top were dispensable for those who either achieved a minimal grade proficiency determined by the classroom teacher or, more importantly, could prove that they had a job to go to.

In 1919 Chicago gave 10,000 such work permits, in 1930 only 987. Between 1924 and 1930 the allocation of work permits in a number of cities was reduced by more than two-thirds. The school had not suddenly become essential to mobility, but a shrinking unskilled job market required fewer men less early, and so the schools were expected to fill the gap.

The assumption that extended schooling promotes greater academic achievement or social mobility is, however, entirely fallacious. School performance seems consistently dependent upon the socio-economic position of the pupil's family. For example, of high school graduates who rank in the top fifth in ability among their classmates, those whose parents are in the top socio-economic status quartile are five times more likely to enter graduate or professional schools than those of comparable ability whose parents fall in the bottom quartile. Similarly, while American males born after 1900 spend more years in school than their nineteenth-century predecessors, federal and other estimates indicate no concomitant redistribution of economic and social rewards.

Commitment to more and more schooling, beginning at kindergarten now (although only one in four of the eligible could go as yet) and continuing as long as possible, did nothing to modify the record of poor school performance. Compulsory attendance at higher levels only pushed failure rates into the upper grades throughout the 1920s and 1930s in such cities as Chicago, Boston, New York, Philadelphia, Detroit, and Washington, D.C.

Chicago noted a 65 percent increase among the "underprivileged" between 1924 and 1931. Elementary school backwardness stood at 61.4 percent, but 41 percent of all those entering ninth grade were seriously behind, too; in tenth grade the figure was 32 percent. Apart from such factors as pupil "feeble-mindedness" as an explanation, there were school difficulties to blame, too. Overcrowding in Detroit, where 13,000 were in half-day sessions and 60 percent in school were "inadequately housed" in 1925; in Philadelphia, Cleveland, and New York the same overcrowding, unsanitary conditions, and serious financial problems prevailed.

On a scale of nine semesters, Philadelphia high schools lost 65 percent of incoming students at the end of the first semester, lost another 32 percent at the end of the fourth and were down to 19 percent of the total in the final semester. In one instance, of a 339-pupil sample established for survey purposes, only ninety-one survived two years. Federal data on schools published in 1937 showed clearly the nationwide "cumulative elimination of pupils in school." While 1,750,000 American youngsters entered grade nine, 86.7 percent were still in school one year later; by grade eleven, only 72 percent were left, and finally 56 percent were graduated. Separate data for New York City showed just over 40 percent of ninth-grade classes graduating. In the late 1940s, George Strayer recorded the same old story in Washington, D.C., New York City, and Boston. Fifty percent of Boston's ninth graders failed to graduate; in New York the figure was up to more than 55 percent. In James Coleman's assessment of *Equal Educational Opportunity* in the nation (1966), in the Havighurst study in Chicago (1964), and in the Passow report in Washington, D.C. (1967), the narrative remains staggeringly unchanged.

The Negro, the individual farthest down, has epitomized the inexorable relationship of success and failure, inside and outside the school. The link between permanent unemployment or chronic underemployment and educational failure is black now, but blacks have inherited a whirlwind no less familiar to them than to lower-class whites. Employment conditions were most severe when it came to the Negro, and school failure rates were at once more glaring and more poignant. But, in effect, the public schools served Negro children as they served the vast majority of others: in Chicago, Philadelphia, Detroit, and New York, that has been the problem since 1890.

But if white lower classes have been vulnerable to the economic market place, the Negro, who worked sporadically and as a reserve force, was constantly a victim. If school success or failure had little meaning in the economic market place for whites, it bore no relevance whatever for blacks. As a result, Negro school failure was quickly isolated as a separate problem early in the twentieth century. When, in the 1940s, Negroes finally entered the lower levels of industrial employment from which they had been excluded, those levels had already become a shrinking sector of the economy, and the massive numbers of school dropouts had no place to go. And so it remained appropriate—even inevitable—to consider Negro school performance as a separate question. But the truth is that academic effort has never been relevant to the place of the poor in society. . . .

If the assumptions on which public education was founded have gone unexamined, the problem is now compounded by rising aspirations. We could afford failure in the schools as long as the economy had room for unskilled workers and as long as the lower classes accepted without protest what appeared to be their inevitable place. Now, however, there are practically no jobs left for the unskilled, and even if there were, the black lower class no longer is willing to accept only that kind of opportunity—not in a society in which real wealth is increasing so fast.

What this means, in effect, is that in a variety of different ways we have increased our demands on the schools. Thirty years ago the purpose of public education was culturally defined as little more than baby-sitting for all the children. Now, neither corporations, government, suburban parents, nor the black community are willing to accept the school as a mere custodian. Its purpose has been redefined by society: Not only must it serve all children, but it must graduate them all with salable skills.

We criticize the schools and look for change in the present distribution of costs and benefits; we are aware that other social institutions educate, and we have been aware for a long time of the selective nature of public education, but we nevertheless accept the notion that public schools are an assumed asset in the regeneration of society. We have adopted a history based on men and events chosen from the history of democratic ideas in education, while we ignore other men, whom we have labeled anti-intellectual. David Crockett and Horace Greeley, for example, leveled scornful tirades against the creation of elite institutions that served an emerging meritocracy. The land and money, they said, might instead have contributed to a real experiment in universal public education, to make public education truly public in its services, not merely in its uses. Schools have been public only in the sense that what happens in them is typical of what happens outside.

Having assumed the salutary past of the school, we have engaged in discussion and debate over the present efficacy of schools with no question but that schools must be; they are generic to the American landscape. These assumptions preclude debate and scholarly inquiry as to why we maintain schools and what we can reasonably expect of them. Until we can question the validity of these assumptions, we cannot begin to achieve the social restoration of which we speak so eloquently, but for which there is little precedent. We can only continue to generate rationalizations across a vareity of disciplines for a national commitment to an ideology that claims simply, but erroneously, that the public schools have always done what they are now expected to do. The truth is they never have.

Is the "System" the Answer?

No matter what is proposed as possible solutions to social problems, timid and tradition-oriented people caution, "You should stay within the system." That is, reformers should use nothing but generally accepted techniques for bringing about change. This might be good advice if it had any practical meaning. But if the system has generated a problem, or if the system itself is the basic problem, then "staying within the system" will avail almost nothing. The term "staying in the system" usually means don't make waves; don't cause a fuss; try *nothing* for the first time; change nothing significant; preserve the existing distribution of power and privilege. Of course, sometimes change is proposed by those in power. But when it is, the change is usually in a reactionary direction; as indicated in the selection by Hubert Locke, America's "silent majority" calls for a return to the 19th century when white dominance was almost unquestioned. The other selections give further dimensions of what "staying in the system" really means.

WHITE LIBERALS AS CONSERVATIVES*

A friend of mine recently remarked—and I believe quite correctly—that the tragedy of the white liberal in our time stems from the fact that he is really a conservative! He is a conservative because he clings to an idealized vision of American society, because he more than anyone else recites the national rhetoric about constitutional guarantees and liberty and justice for all, because he stubbornly refuses to acknowledge that most Americans— Mr. Nixon's "silent majority" if you will—have already made up their minds that these very principles are what's basically wrong with the nation. It's the silent majority that wants to change the Constitution and insists that the problem in America is too much freedom (i.e., permissiveness), especially where blacks and the young are concerned. Constitutional guarantees, so argues the silent majority, have gotten us nothing except the

*Adapted from Hubert G. Locke, *The Care and Feeding of White Liberals*: The American Tragedy and the Liberal Dilemma (New York: Newman Press, 1970), pp. 71-72.

protection of the criminal at the expense of the majority of "decent, law-abiding citizens!" And freedom in this nation, the argument continues, has produced an increasing crop of young, bearded, unbathed dope addicts, inflated welfare rolls, and growing lists of draft dodgers. The silent majority therefore wants change—it pushes for progress into a future which will be safe and secure because it is firmly entrenched in white hands—while the liberal finds himself in the awkward position of longing for the good old days (whenever that was) when people supposedly believed in the Declaration of Independence, the Constitution, and the Bill of Rights. It is the liberal, ironically, who wishes to conserve the past, and the silent majority (who have been traditionally accused of being the conservatives) who seek to press forward into a grand and glorious (i.e., white-dominated) future.

A LOT OF NONSENSE*

Cultural change, one is told, is supposed to come about through our democratic political system. If you have a good idea or if you want to make a change, you are supposed either to offer yourself as a political candidate or support a candidate who shares your idea. . . .

That is a lot of nonsense.

What happens in an election is no mystery. We have two political parties differentiated not by principle but by their constituencies. Both parties claim to be for progress, continuity, stability, economy, fairness. Both have particular constituencies, but both move toward the middle to absorb the undecided and independent voters. They do that so effectively that when the campaign comes down to the wire it is hard to distinguish between them. In 1960, John F. Kennedy ended his campaign sounding like a hard-line anticommunist cold warrior, and Richard M. Nixon ended his soundling like a civil-libertarian. In 1968, both Nixon and Hubert Humphrey supported "peace with honor" and "law and order with justice" because that is where the consensus was to be found at the time.

In short, our elections turn out to be competitions for marginal performing advantage within a consensus already established by the time the voters go to the polls.

A national delusion is that somehow it is the elections which generate that consensus. They don't. A good example of that is the Vietnam war issue. That war has fed upon our elections. Without elections we would not have had as long and flourishing a war as we have had. Every time an

*Adapted from Garry Wills, "Working Within the System Won't Change Anything," *The Center Magazine* 5(July/Aug 1972):34–37.

election approaches, those in power do not want to grate against all the patriotic instincts which say America cannot and should not lose a war. The more delicate that issue becomes and the more people's sensibilities might be inflamed, the more the candidates mute their voices, dissemble, and speak ambiguously. So, for years the Vietnam war was pushed into the background at election time. It happened again in the off-year elections. . . .

Insofar as changes occur, they occur between elections, not during elections. Again, take the Vietnam war and the change in public attitude toward the war. At first, only a few people opposed America's involvement. There were the teach-ins and the speeches. Then came books, marches, and advertisements. Then the moratoria. Finally the mass demonstrations. By this time a lot of people were taking a very hard, principled stand against the war—the kind of stand that doesn't get votes—and they kept hammering away at it. Eventually the people made it safe for the politicians to oppose the war, cautiously of course. But it was a long time from the first teach-in to the time when Bobby Kennedy was saying we should have a pause in the bombings.

None of the major changes in our society took place because of elections. Take the Volstead Act—both its passage and its repeal—take women's suffrage, or the coming of the New Deal. Nobody "voted in" the New Deal. Fiscally, Roosevelt's 1932 platform was conservative. He accused Herbert Hoover of spending too much.

Changes occur when a lot of people take stands on issues and when politicians then find they can introduce some of them into legislative action. Then the politicians get a retrospective vote of approval (as Roosevelt did in 1936) or disapproval (as Johnson did in 1968).

As part of our social mythology as to how changes take place, we say that if the system isn't working very well, we should get people to trust the system by making it more trustworthy, having fairer debates, getting more people to vote, having a more enlightened electorate. All these things may be good in themselves but they have nothing to do with change. The fact is that our electoral system is a vast, inertial, conservative force that provides order and stability, the recognizable and the familiar, at a time when putatively the system may be weakest—that is, when there may be a change in the government.

I suppose the best thing about our national electoral campaigns is that they do provide a sense of national identity; they tend to enlist national loyalty. But, of course, our electoral process also modulates differences to the point where in order to rise very high the candidates shed principles and provocative points of view.

It is rather encouraging, then, when we look for the forces of change, to find that people who start out as "freaks" generate change—Martin Luther

King starting the bus boycotts, the teachers and students who began the first antiwar teach-ins on Vietnam, the first woman suffragettes. Right now, changes are taking place because of the women's liberation movement. And changes are taking place on such matters as abortion and marijuana and amnesty. The way to change things, even to change the government, is to work outside the government.

NEEDED: A CAPTAIN OF THE SHIP*

In this early 1975 view from abroad, Englishman Simon Winchester looks back and compares the effects of two traumatic events: the November 1963 assassination of President John Kennedy and the August 1974 forced resignation of President Richard Nixon.

Not since 1963 has an American year come to be dominated by a single, tragic event. What happened in Dallas on that November afternoon came as the most terrible of bombshells: what happened in Washington on that sticky August morning was expected, prayed for, inevitable—a consummation, indeed, devoutly to be wished. The November horror brought to an end an era of American self-confidence and hope, and snuffed out a national spark; the August horror of this year, regrettably, did very little at all.

It neither cleansed nor improved not stirred nor, in truth, very much altered this country—this country that is at once dangerous and delightful, complacent and cathartic, emetic and energetic, hopeful and utterly hopeless. Richard Nixon's going was, in retrospect, little more than a televisual hiccup: had this society been a better one or one with a political system built more on honour than on power, Nixon would have gone with less spectacle long before. The suggestion that his summertime passage was an event that tested the system and found it to be working can be seen now, five months on, as being as unworthy a remark as it was untrue.

The former President, still lying pathetic and sickly in his tasteless hacienda, is unforgotten but not, in truth, unmissed. He was a frightful crook, of that there is now no doubt. He debased a worthy House, he invited paranoia into the Oval Office and let him sit on his desk, he took counsel with dishonesty and dinner with deceit. Every unspoiled inch of the taped petard that finally hoist the wretched man shows today his weakness and his indecision and his manipulative cunning.

The dates and times of all those conversations will, like the long lexicons of the affair—which will house words and phrases like enemies and

*Adapted from Simon Winchester, "Needed: A Captain of the Ship," *The Guardian*, 4 Jan 75.

twisting slowly slowly and deep six and down to the wire and fight like hell and I am not a crook and I know what I meant and my mother was a good woman to get out you son of a bitch—fade shortly into the oblivion they deserve. Perhaps, on second thought they may one day be regurgitated lovingly in some dreadful nostalgic nightmare by uncaring youths of a less innocent generation, but for now the words and the seamy characters and their childish, pathetic, half-cocked, crazed schemes for the aggrandisement either of themselves or of their cronies will be pushed into some dusty cave of breaking. Only the antihero of it all remains, dying very slowly, writing very fast, paying bigger bills than most Americans will ever see and living out the world's agony of shame and degradation.

And yet, when we see, and wince at, the alternative, are there not a few who miss him now? Washington is rarely a still city these days, but once in a while the breeze seems to stir with a faint rustle of "Will ye no come back again?" There is an unspoken feeling abroad that since the ideal—capability coupled with integrity—cannot now be realised in a nation that prefers to send its intellectual and moral dropouts to be its rulers, might it not be better, considering the crises of the times, to have a man at the helm who at least can do, can think, can act? That is one of the most awful legacies of 1974—the suspicion that Dick's final trick was to leave the ship uncaptained once he had walked the plank. There are a few now who would have him fished out of the shark-filled sea and lashed firmly to the tiller, watched constantly by the moralists of the era until the time comes, two summers hence, for America to choose again. And even then, recalling that America chose Richard Nixon and Wilbur Mills, there is no promise of necessary salvation in that course either.

. . . .

The motorcycle of state wobbles on still. The old driver who tried to dope the tank is gone, and a new one, unfamiliar to the machine, is on the seat. His left hand was firmly gripped on a Kissinger that a domestically troubled land seemed not to need any further, and his right was on a popular sentiment that, in the wake of that infamous and unpardonable pardon seemed to be turning to thin air. Mr. Ford was, at the close of the momentous year, being referred to alternately as a Boy Scout and a clown. Leadership and driving ability were wanted by everyone, and being offered by no-one—not even Nelson Rockefeller, who emerged somewhat tarnished from a set of confirmation hearings.

The nation was speeding fast to an unknown destination, the throttle open, the brakes worn, the steering uncertain, the road slick. The ditches yawning on every side, the driver, wearing a fez in place of a crash helmet, seemingly inept. The exhilaration was there, all right—the beauty of the flashing metal and the gleaming fire and the pulsating roar. But the prospects, with a nasty bend or two ahead, were not good. The women and the blacks and the practitioners of good who jumped into the sidecar in November once the ghoul was out of the way were still very much at year end in the sidecar. A driver was needed, and needed quick.

AN OPEN LETTER TO THE SILENT MAJORITY*

The author has a Ph.D. in political science from Harvard University and is a former CIA official.

Here is a story, my friends. One night a man dreamt that a monster was on his chest, choking him, trying to kill him. The man woke in terror and saw the monster above him. "What is going to happen to me." the man cried. "Don't ask me," replied the monster, "it's your dream."

Take your society, your law's integrity, and your country back from the experts. I have been an "expert" and I can tell you that experts gone wild—and they have—are like cancer. They know only one thing: more, more, more of the same. Nothing is more expert than cancer, nothing a better example of power without purpose. Cancer is ignorant, but, oh, it works, it grows.

I have been an expert, have lived among them in their anti-communities—could have rested among them. I hope I have left them well behind me. An expert sees his small piece of reality and little else. He confuses understanding with control and makes of the latter his single virtue. One of our leading social scientists has said that the chief accomplishment of this age is to have changed so many political problems into technical ones. We see in Vietnam, as at Auschwitz, the result of technical solutions to political problems.

I have been an expert. I hold a Bachelor's, Master's, and Ph.D. in Political Science from Harvard University, where I studied federal and municipal government in America, political philosophy, international law, Russian history, the Soviet economy, and international relations. I've done research for the Army on Czechoslovakia; I spent a number of years as an officer of the CIA; I worked on strategic problems, including Vietman, in Army think tanks—among them the Research Analysis Corporation; for

*Sidney J. Slomich, *The American Nightmare* (New York: The Macmillan Company, 1971), pp. 282–284.

similar private companies I've done research on communications satellites, on China, and on arms control; I've also done research on military assistance and foreign military training programs, the implications of which I tried to get the Department of Defense and Army to see even before the huge Vietnam intervention; I was senior scientist, then Director of the Arms Control and Disarmament Study Group at Cal Tech's Jet Propulsion, Laboratory, where I immersed myself in studies for NASA and ACDA on vital inspection and proliferation issues; I have studied and published on advanced technological applications to urban affairs; I have taught political theory and foreign policy at various California universities; I have studied educational policy and counseled foreign governments in urban affairs for the Stanford Research Institute; recently I have been serving as consultant on social goals, urban and suburban affairs, and the sources of aberrant social behavior, for a variety of private clients. For sixteen years I worked exclusively within the established foreign policy and governmental system, in public and private organizations, usually in circumstances involving heavy or nearly exclusive use of classified, secret materials. If my memoranda, studies, and reports, scattered all over Washington, were piled on each other they would probably constitute a small hill.

So I have been an expert, and I'm not bragging about it. I accepted the necessity of working within the system, believed that it was possible in that way both to affect the system itself constructively and to accomplish something. Only in the late sixties did I come to understand that government, business, and what is correctly called "the Establishment," were too inert, too committed to the shape of things as they have been to inaugurate human policies, that for change the people had to take government back to themselves. Only the people awakened and grasping power from these mindless megainstitutions, can effect change.

In 1964 I sat in disbelief in a Washington think tank, listening to a very well-financed Army proposal to develop a computerized electronic warning system to alert the Pentagon when a Latin American country was likely to go "Red," and—the system having been perfected on paper—to rent a whole Latin American country and army to test it out. This stupid and unbelievably naive project was the product of Ph.D.s, men who call themselves and are called scientists. When this project was discovered by Chileans who observed some strangely behaving researchers, it hit the press and was investigated by Congress. When, from the beginning, I criticized Project *Camelot*, I was asked, annoyedly, why I was always being so "negative." This is a particularly apt, yet typical, example of the allegedly scientific thinking that lies behind Vietnam and all the horrors it has brought to roost in this country and all over the world.

I could give many more examples, but I don't want to take up time with horror stories. Suffice it to say that over the last generation, especially the last fifteen years, the United States—at home and abroad—has been preoccupied not with human life and its purposes, but with ignorant power and control—that is to say with death—and has become, along with the Soviet Union, as a colleague in mindless adversity, the planet's greatest polluter, an agent of potentially total repression, and the greatest threat to continued human life the world has ever faced. I do not like to say these things, but one must speak plainly. There is a monster on our chest.

Is Law and Order the Answer?

It is commonly asserted that a multitude of social wrongs are best righted within a framework of "law and order." This would probably be true if legal processes were even roughly similar to the way they are pictured in idealistic accounts which speak of "equal treatment under the law," "rehabilitation," "civil rights and liberties," "legal justice," "police protection," and "orderly legal processes." But these are, at best, only sometime characteristics of law-and-order as it actually exists in the United States. As is indicated in painful detail by the accompanying articles, observations, and reports, American law-and-order very often boils down to what can be termed the two J's: *justice* for the strong and *jail* for the weak, with both J's being accomplished by police state tactics including illegal searches and detention, planted evidence, government secrecy and spies, and the use of agents provacateurs. Thus, except for the privileged few, law-and-order as presently administered—with some notable exceptions such as the Supreme Court's Miranda, Escobedo, and Gideon decisions—is quite obviously an inadequate means to rectify wrong.

It is also obvious that one of the most prominent characteristics of law-and-order is its arbitrariness. Therefore, the subject could just as easily have been considered in Part I of the present work. But an "arbitrary" decision was made to consider the subject in Part III so as to give special emphasis to the inadequacy of the claim that maintaining law and order is in itself somehow a fundamental answer to many social problems. This inadequacy, it is wise to keep in mind, is largely due to the arbitrariness and the illegal actions of many of the government officials who administer the law; perhaps the one word "Watergate" is sufficient to indicate that even some of those in the highest positions of trust, while crying loudly for the preservation of law-and-order, do not hesitate to undermine it if they judge that particular violations may be useful in helping to maintain their power. Such cynicism has led some observers to conclude that law-and-order has no significance other than as a cover for the greedy. But this is an erroneous conclusion. It is not the orderly processes of law that are enemies of justice; indeed, the very opposite is true. Life without order is brutish if not short. But legalities imposed from on high primarily to protect a disproprotionate distribution of privilege inevitably generate the problems associated with envy, deprivation, uncertainty, anger, and revenge.

Introduction

DEATH OF A CITIZEN*

Journalist Morgenstern's description of the death of one person symbolizes what law-and-order means for those who are weak, poor, and without special influence.

Until a few years ago this country's only government-subsidized art form was officialese, the art of saying almost nothing in almost impenetrable prose. Now a new, antithetical form of official art is emerging—the documentary report, more often than not written clearly and candidly by people who really want to be understood. It has come a long way since the pioneering work of the Warren commission, whose report suffered from great length and lack of a plot. Subsequent documents on such matters as urban riots, campus violence, racial polarization and pornography have given connoisseurs of the genre all they could ask for and more: wealth of incident, lucid narrative, solid structure, contemporary setting, calm commitment to truth. What's more, these reports meet the most rigorous criteria for pure art. They exist solely unto themselves, since nobody does anything about their conclusions.

One of the most recent documentaries is also the most esthetically advanced. It's called "A Report to the Mayor of New York on the Death of a Citizen, Julio Roldan," and it was written at the mayor's behest by William J. vanden Heuvel, chairman of the city's Board of Correction. Vanden Heuvel's narrative was put together from research done by eleven young attorneys, volunteer investigators looking for the truth about how Roldan, a 33-year-old Puerto Rican, died in the Tombs, Manhattan's House of Detention for Men. (Only New York is candid enough to call its detention house the Tombs, though similar tombs all over the country contain thousands of men and women being buried alive while they await trial.) Authorities at the Tombs, where Roldan was being held pending trial for attempted arson, insisted that he had committed suicide in his cell. The Young Lords, a militant Puerto Rican organization to which Roldan belonged, said he'd been murdered by guards. Clergymen of several denominations supported the Young Lords' demand for an investigation.

*Joseph Morgenstern, "Death of a Citizen," *Newsweek* 76(Dec. 7, 1970):14.

At the outset, then, this report on the death of a citizen promises to be a most popular work indeed, a mystery documentary. Mayor Lindsay wanted to know if it was murder or suicide, and so do we. If it was murder, then who was the killer and what was his motive? If it was suicide, what madness drove Roldan to do it. Who was Roldan, and what did he feel, say or do at the moment of his death? Even though the reading public has had its fill of prison stories lately, this one would seem to be a model of the old-fashioned tale told simply and dramatically through the experience of a single man.

In its early, seductive passages, the Roldan report seems to be doing just that. The salient facts of the dead man's life are sketched quickly. Born in Puerto Rico, 1936. Came to New York as a teenager. Attended a slum high school, dropped out. Served two years in the Army as a medical corpsman, honorably discharged in 1963. Roldan's service to the U.S. Army, the report says in its first hint of compassion, was "without blemish." After the Army Roldan lived with his brother, a Protestant minister in the Bronx. He studied for the clergy but soon dropped out again, fearing that religion was irrelevant to his people's problems. Poverty, injustice were radicalizing him. Months, years of shuttling between New York and Puerto Rico, living out of a knapsack at times, living for Puerto Rican independence. Arrested there in 1969 for flag-burning, fined $25. Joined the Young Lords in New York last summer at the age of 33, lived mostly at the group's mess hall, where he was chief cook. A prototypical political hero so far, though slightly old as Young Lords go.

Now the report reprints some of Roldan's poetry. "City of Strangers," in which he describes himself as "an earth rejected skum," and "Let's Get Together Because I Love You," in which he says "Together/We can save/ The World for our kids ..." Having established the hero's humanity so boldly, the report might next be expected to pattern itself on "Darkness at Noon" or maybe "The Prisoner of Chillon." But no, something subtle and strange happens to the narrative as Roldan and a buddy are picked up by three plain-clothes policemen in the entranceway of a Spanish Harlem apartment house. The classic hero gradually fades from view. The report turns from Roldan's unknowable interior life to the exterior life around him, to discernible facts, quotable statements, verifiable records. It's the technique of the new novel or the modern fact film. The report cannot reincarnate the hero, but it can and does provide an ordered account of the circumstances surrounding his death.

This objective technique has its frustrations and its rewards. We can't be sure if the arrest is a good one or a bum one, any more than we can be sure from the things we hear or read in the media if such groups as the Young Lords or the Panthers are good ones or bum ones. The police claim

Roldan and his friend were setting a fire, the defendants claim they were putting one out. We can't tell what Roldan feels like at his arraignment, but we learn from the record that he hasn't been allowed to make his own phone call, that he hasn't been allowed to discuss his case with his attorney before the arraignment. We don't know if Roldan is clinically sane when he yells to the judge that "there is no justice in this court," but we do know that the judge could not have sent him for psychiatric examination if he'd wanted to, since the city's facilities were filled up, and we also know that the conditions of Roldan's arraignment are objectively insane: a noisy, crowded courtroom, an attorney too rushed to make a routine argument for his client's release pending trial, an assistant district attorney handling 30 cases an hour and basing his bail request on unverified and incorrect police information, a judge so obviously overwhelmed by the case load that he devotes an average of 102 seconds to each defendant that day. When Roldan's attorneys asks for more time the judge replies: "I can't create the Utopia here."

Roldan's state of mind and body remain opaque, but it comes to light that he was given no medical examination at the Tombs because there weren't any facilities, that he was left alone in a cell despite increasing signs of desperation or derangement, and that a telegram of reassurance from the Young Lords was misrouted, presumably by innocent error, and never reached the presumedly innocent prisoner. We do not know what Roldan thought in his last moments of life in his cell in the Tombs, but we do know that the cell was Lower E-4, that a doctor pronounced the prisoner dead a few minutes past 8:30 a.m. on October 16, two mornings after Roldan had been arrested, that an autopsy surgeon gave a finding of undoubted suicide and that a pathologist retained by the Young Lords concurred "without reservation."

To that extent the report allows us some brief catharsis. It was suicide after all, technically speaking. Roldan was 63 inches tall, the bars of his cell ceiling were 66½ inches above the seat of his stool, and he swung by his belt in the space between. But catharsis is not the point, for this is not, it develops, a conventional mystery. We never learn from the report whether Roldan was innocent, guilty, sane, insane, nice or not nice. We can't even be sure in retrospect if he was a promising poet or a derivative one. What we do learn from the cool, persuasive text is that suicide can be induced by a judicial and detention system of sufficient inhumanity, that such a suicide is very little different from murder, that justice is not so much blind any more as stoned out of her head, and that we have in this country today immeasurably more order than law.

Black Americans and the Law

FIRST PRIZE*

As part of its 50th anniversary celebration in 1970, the American Civil Liberties Union conducted a writing contest for high school pupils who were asked to consider the subject, "The Bill of Rights: Is It for Real?" The first prize winner was Ms. Goldie Holt, Nashville, Tennessee. Her selection follows; although it does not deal directly with law and order, it nevertheless speaks eloquently about what "equal protection of the law" really means to many Americans.

Abraham Lincoln, after he freed us, didn't get to live long after it to see if he regret it or not. It kinds of tickles me to think that if that old mister just happen to raise up from his grave, he just might go and burn up that " 'mancipation Proclamation."

Shucks! I ain't the smartest in my school but I got awareness of whats going on!

When I looks around and sees some schools of the white and some of those of the blacks, why it just ain't right! But who's you going to tell it to? Some too proud to say that their school and theyselves been hyped. Some see the difference and either so scared you couldn't get them to say a word or they thinks on the facts a little too hard and just decides to quit. All the whil, that's just the way some whites wants them to do. All I can hear is, "We ain't zoning this, we ain't bussing that, and my children ain't going to be shipped to school like cargo."

Seems like to me that's just like saying, we gots to keep those people in they own territory, we ain't needing no racial harmony in this America, my children ain't going to school with no niggers. They've so far succeeded in keeping us in our own territory! And those whites unfortunate enough to live where we do ain't overlooked. (Seniors gets a choice, to which school to go to.) Ain't that nice to be so thankful of Who!

Take the school that I go to, All Creek Monsters and Mud Dabbers! We have some Purity there though, acting as instructors of education. Makes me think of those white men and women who done been to Africa as missionaries. To save lost black souls from theyselves.

*Goldie Holt, untitled, *Civil Liberties* (March 1971):3.

I remember once in class there was a girl named Barbara Blackmon. She had this speech to do and I never felt sorrier for a person before. She stood up there and sounded like a brand-new, freshly whitewashed Aunt Jemima telling Master's children they ought to praising him and licking his boots. After all he didn't have to even have to let us have a school!

"All this talk about integration," she says, "why there's much difference between black and white as night and day. God helps those that helps themselves. East is East and West is West and never the twain shall meet."

(Don't know where she got that.)

I never felt sorrier or sicker over a person before. She was too blind to see she was a Creek Monster too. And no 'mount of praise to the Man was making them love her any more.

Mud Dabber High School, I guess we were just a little too dark to mix with the Purity! We got to be some kind of monster! The People must be afraid we going to eat up they children. Or maybe they thinks we going to lead them astray. (I recalls a song we sung in Church, "Yield Not to Temptation.")

Once I lived in a neighborhood wheres the blacks lived on one block and whites on the next—this was integrated. The school I went to then was a Mr. Clean Jr. High School. They had themselves a Spaghetti supper to get money for the P.T.A. My mother had to work at night so I went alone. I gots myself a tray and went to a table I found in a corner. Next thing I knew was this girl who was in my math class comes over to me and ask me if she can sit down. I says yes. She sit down. We starts to talk then her mother comes and gets her real polite like. And while I was supposing to be not looking, I was. And I saw her being talked at and figured it was 'cause of me. I got up, took my tray to the window. I thought as I walked out they'd probably scald it for two hours. I just left that school and went to the Creek where us monsters and dabbers were supposed to be anyhow.

I'm the kind of person that has a love of nature. Since we ain't got much country around here I just hops on me a bus rides uptown and walks around up ther. The sights you see just to be looking and hearing! One minute you feel eyes just tearing you apart with hate then the next, some white man (whose face looked like two-hundred miles of bad luck) looking at you like you was grade double-A beef. Everytime, I just goes on 'bout my business and they don't even know hows they hurting me. Sometimes, I just walks around in a daze more or less like a zombie. And I don't know how to tell you about the pain I feel. There's all kinds of things going on in my mind—I'm lost.

Most time I just loose myself in the emptiness. My frigid heart leaps out for a piece of love. Suffer my soul so solidly so sadly—noone knows me from a tick or tack! And time has raped me of a soul.

There's a saying I been hearing all my life. It says you can't keep a good man down. I finds it ain't so! You can keep him down—way down. Normal is what normal be and they tells a black man he ain't normal. He can't be right cause he's too dark and black is evil. I guess it ain't nobody's fault, it's just the ways we been brought up. But seems like to me they should see that when they says you got the right to talk then shoots you down when you talks too loud, that when they says you got the right to assemble then calls the dogs, firehose, and troops on you, it ain't right! Things have come to that, though, and no one says they the blame! That Bill of Rights means something to me but that ain't no good. It got to mean something to everybody else.

I likes to read a lot, so I finds out more than everyday things. Who's that that said, a little learning's a dangerous thing? Some things I found out in those books though, kind of hard to tell from fact or lie. All these years I been wondering where the black man been while you all a fighting those wars, where's he been when all those inventions and patents been handed out. I found out that it was a black man that found out all that stuff about blood and plasma and then hisself died from too much loss of blood. I might been unaware of all this today if someone hadn't started shouting Black Power! That's when I started reading, trying to see through things 'stead of around them. Never even knew Cleopatria was from Africa and a black woman. I loves America too! But why shes been hiding myself from me? There's black blood well as white blood on this land and some of those European lands too! We have fought. We have died. And my Lord, how we have cried and hurt.

Good thing, I'm one of those people who thinks when they sees a cup half fulled its almost filled up instead of half gone or else I be saying—this country going to the waste, Communist infesting everything and body or why don't we just split this country in half—have the Mason-Dixon line down the middle! Colored on one side white on the other.

I realizes I'm just simple everyday people and what I says and thinks ain't no matter but I loves these states, that flag, and the people. Most of all, I loves that Paper that says: All men are created equal. I show enough be glad when everybody wakes up and starts to live with me!

EQUAL JUSTICE AS SHE REALLY IS*

Women who go around bombing buildings are held by the law to be a threat to the community. Jane Alpert, a white woman so charged, had her

*Source Unknown.

bail set at $20,000. Panther Joan Bird, a black woman charged with *conspiring* to bomb, had her bail set at $100,000. Miss Alpert's judge is Marvin E. Frankel; Miss Bird's is John N. Murtagh. Jane and Marvin and John and Joan.

TAKE IT TO COURT*

... critics ... say we should take our problem to court and fight the battle legally. I tried that and it didn't work. How can I get justice in a court where the judge is an elected official whose votes come out of an all-white neighborhood? When the judge knows he will have to have voter approval to get reelected, he cannot have an open and sympathetic ear for my problem.

And how can I get justice from a judge who honestly does not know that he is prejudiced? For example, many rich Negroes have gotten divorces in northern courts, but you have never read where a colored woman has gotten a large settlement from her rich colored husband. Yet the rich white man better not lose his wife or she gets all his money. So how is this judge going to give me justice when he can't even treat my woman right?

The courts and society have never treated my woman right. If my wife goes downtown and steals something, when she is caught she is called a hoodlum. If a white celebrity's wife gets caught stealing, she is a kleptomaniac. The black woman is listed with the crime rate and the white woman is placed on the sick list.

A white man and his wife can go to court and get a divorce. Say he is making fifty thousand dollars a year and they have three children. The court grants the wife custody of the children. If she marries another white man who is making fifty thousand dollars a year, do you think the father could go back to court and get custody of his children because his wife married again? Not a chance. But if I married her he could do just that. Such is the racism of the American court. I cannot take my problem there.

. . . .

Respect for law and order is a ... phrase which doesn't sound right to the man in the ghetto. Look through the United States Constitution and the Bible and you will find that neither document is concerned with law and order. They both talk about justice. Somehow these old knicker-

*Adapted from Dick Gregory, *The Shadow that Scares Me* (New York: Pocket Books, 1968), pp. 40–41, 69–70.

wearing cats who inked the Constitution knew that if you give a man 99.9 percent justice, he will give you law and order in return. But if you ask a man for law and order without placing him in a climate of justice, it is like asking him to breathe and placing him in a vacuum without any air, or telling him to bleed without giving him any blood.

Everything Nature demands of you, she gives you in advance. Then, if you violate her natural laws, you are in trouble. It is natural to expect men to live in peace and harmony within a climate of justice. Those who violate the law and order of an atmosphere of justice should be in trouble. But if this country is going to demand law and order before creating a climate of justice, it is going to have to hire one cop for every Negro in America and another cop for every white man. Such one-to-one policing sounds unnatural. But it is no more unnatural than demanding law and order while condoning the absence of justice.

America must learn that you can *postpone* justice, but you cannot *prevent* it. and the longer the postponement, the stiffer the penalty. For example, if I snatch your wallet tonight and get away, I am postponing justice. If I had been caught, I might have been sentenced to six months in jail. Since I got away, perhaps next week I will snatch your wallet again. If I get away, I am still postponing justice. Next year I may go for bigger stakes and in the process, shoot and kill you. This time I am caught and sentenced to the electric chair. I have gone from an earlier six months' maximum to the death penalty. The longer you postpone justice, the stiffer the penalty.

THE CIRCLES*

During the 1967 race riots in Detroit, city police cornered a small group of black men and white women in the Algiers Motel; the black men were abused, and three were killed and sexually mutilated by the police. Later, John Hersey interviewed the father of Aubrey Pollard, one of those who died in the incident; here is what the father said:

"I don't hate no policemans," Mr. Pollard said to me one day, speaking of the kind of justice black men and boys get in Detroit, "don't hate no judges, but if justice is going to be—when *I* do wrong, I gets fined, I suffer for it, and I don't expect any more. I could ask for leniency, but I really

*Adapted from John Hersey, *The Algiers Motel Incident* (New York: Alfred Knopf, 1968), p. 156.

don't expect it, because I'm poor. But as far as the Negro, he lives in the ghettos, he doesn't know anything else but the ghettos, his parents teach him that because he comes up that way from a little small fellow, to get what you can—grab, quick! The Negro is looked upon as a minority group. Anything that he does, everybody see it. If you think I'm lying, go down to court tomorrow. You'll see how many—now"—and he began to count white suburbs on his fingers—"out in Dearborn, they got their own court; Birmingham, they got their own court; Redford, they got their own court. Murder, regardless to *what* it is, unless there's a case where they bring it downtown, but they keeps it out. What does this do with the Negro? It puts him in a circle, puts him in one little circle. And everyone of them, he got to go down in front of Judge DeMascio, Judge Davenport, and the rest of them. It's a racket, that's all it is! It's the politicians. They work in a circle. You can see the money moving. You don't have to be blind unless you're stupid!"

BLACKS AND DISSENTERS*

This brief excerpt from a longer piece by Professor Skolnick suggests that there is often no clear line separating the two subjects, "blacks and the law" and "dissenters and the law." One of the reasons was stated by journalist Tom Wicker when he commented on "The Charlotte Three." This trio consists of three young and highly educated black American anti-poverty workers who were convicted of arson in North Carolina. The basis of the conviction was highly suspicious testimony by ex-convict police informers given special secret bonus payments by the prosecution. Wicker wrote: ". . . the case of the Charlotte Three has become something of a cause for those who know about it. They believe it to be one more of those vengeful miscarriages of justice by which comfortable society attempted to label urban unrest, racial disorders, campus disturbances and anti-war activity as the work of agitators and terrorists, rather than the result of economic and political injustices" (New York Times, 27 Dec 74).

. . . Revolutionary situations pose a terrible dilemma for the civil libertarian when he finds himself in sympathy with the motives of the revolutionaries, deplores violent means, and at the same time recognizes that an emphasis upon order may impede necessary and desirable social change. The dilemma is particularly agonizing when he finds himself increasingly unable to distinguish between contemporary morality and immorality.

*Adapted from Jerome H. Skolnick, "Black Separatism," *Chicago Today* 5(Summer 1968):16-21.

Which is preferable, the violent revolutionary act or the severe social sanctions that slowly, sometimes negligently, impinge upon masses of humans on the basis of racial or ethnic characteristics?

In this perspective, what should be the response to the black struggle? Principally, we must recognize that the needs and concerns of black people in our society are different from those of the comfortably situated white liberal. The black man living in the inner city is not so concerned with freedom of expression as an abstract ideal, nor in drawing fine distinctions between expression and action. He has real and immediate legal concerns that are not presently being satisfactorily attended to by institutions in the legal order. For example, after Dr. King's murder, disorders occurred in several cities, notably Chicago and Washington, D.C. Observers found serious deficiencies in the arrest and processing procedures. I myself saw bail proceedings in Chicago where the judge questioned the accused as to guilt or innocence before setting bail, and the Public Defender stood by and listened without objecting. (Under the circumstances, he may have had no other choice.) Even when arrestees could make bail, there was no one to collect it. In Washington, D.C., David Ginsburg reports that a study (by Ronald Goldfarb) found serious deficiencies in procedure: some prisoners were "lost" or unnecessarily detained for days; detention facilities were overcrowded; transportation was inadequate; and paper work was unbearably burdensome. Most significantly, curfew and arrest policies were ambiguous.

In the administration of criminal justice the poor man, black or white, is faced with a paucity of defense attorneys. A landmark Supreme Court decision like *Gideon*, requiring that every accused felon be accorded a defense attorney, is not as progressive a step as it initially appears. The function of the defense attorney in our adversary system is to provide, as stated by Dean Francis Allen, ". . . a constant, searching, and creative questioning of official decisions and assertions of authority at all stages of the process." In fact, however, we do not have an adversary system of criminal justice, but an overcrowded administrative system that depends upon the close-knit assistance of all functionaries, defense attorneys included. Our lower courts, especially, are a disgrace, with administrative concerns prevailing over concerns for justice.

In general, we do not have enough competition in the criminal law system, and we do not have enough competent lawyers. As a result, the right to counsel may not be, to the man faced with a criminal charge, what it appears.

The black man in the inner city is often faced with and by the example of police corruption in our urban centers. . . . Police corruption, precisely because of its wider ramifications, is a more politically sensitive issue than police brutality and police harassment. These latter problems are not limited to interactions with white policemen only. In fact, Negro policemen have been known to be even more brutal than white, and the black man has often even less of an opportunity sustaining a case of victimization against the Negro cop. Our inner-city black communities sometimes appear to be occupied countries, colonial outposts, with colonial police, black and white, living off graft, keeping an eye on the natives, and putting them in their place. . . .

Dissenters and the Law

SECOND PRIZE*

Here is the second prize winner in the ACLU contest described in connection with the above-quoted "First Prize."

A few weeks ago
I got a book
from the library
that told about
the Bill of Rights.

I read the section
about freedom of speech
while I was waiting
to see the principal
because I had distributed
an "underground newspaper."

I read the section
about freedom of the press
after I was threatened
with suspension from school
if I wrote another article
for the local newspaper
without the approval
of the administration.

I read the section
about cruel and unusual punishment

*Eric Crist, untitled, *Civil Liberties* (March 71):4.

the day I was kicked out of school
because of the length of my hair

As I read the section
about the right
to petition for redress of grievances,
the T.V. showed films
of cops using clubs
to break demonstrators' heads.

I started the section
about unreasonable search and seizure,
but after I had seen
a newspaper article
about a law authorizing
police to enter houses
in certain cases
without warning the occupants,
I decided I had read enough,
so I closed the book
and took it back
to the library,
where I put it
on a shelf marked:
                    FICTION

LAST SPEECH TO THE COURT*

*In 1921, Bartolomeo Vanzetti and Niccolo Sacco, two workingmen
immigrants from Italy, were tried and sentenced to death for a Boston-area
bankroll robbery-murder. Information developed later by such authorities
as Supreme Court Justice Felix Frankfurter strongly suggests that the two
men were convicted on the basis of faulty evidence. Although this became
known to the authorities in charge, the prejudice against Sacco and
Vanzetti—because of their socialist-anarchist political orientation—was so
virulent among the political elite that even world-wide protest demonstrations and a six-year appeal effort did not save the accused. They were sent
to the electric chair in 1927. Ever since, they have stood as an unforget-
table symbol of the helplessness of the weak dissenter in the face of
establishment-controlled legal processes. Vanzetti's last address to the*

*As printed in Walter Lowenfels, *The Writing on the Wall* (New York:
Doubleday and Co., 1969), pp. 138-139.

appeal court, when he knew that all was lost, has become one of the best-known statements by a political dissenter motivated primarily by the dream of making a more perfect society.

I have talk a great deal of myself but I even forgot to name Sacco. Sacco too is a worker from his boyhood, a skilled worker lover of work, with a good job and pay, a good and lovely wife, two beautiful children and a neat little home at the verge of a wood, near a brook. Sacco is a heart, a faith, a character, a man; a man lover of nature and of mankind. A man who gave all, who sacrifice all to the cause of Liberty and to his love for mankind; money, rest, mundane ambitions, his own wife, his children, himself and his own life. Sacco has never dreamt to steal, never to assassinate. He and I have never brought a morsel of bread to our mouths, from our child-hood to today—which has not been gained by the sweat of our brows. Never.

Oh, yes, I may be more witful, as some have put it, I am a better babbler than he is, but many, many times in hearing his heartful voice ringing a faith sublime, in considering his supreme sacrifice, remembering his heroism I felt small small at the presence of his greatness and found myself compelled to fight back from my throat to not weep before him—this man called thief and assassin and doomed. But Sacco's name will live in the hearts of the people and in their gratitude when Katzmann's and your bones will be dispersed by time, when your name, his name, your laws, institutions, and your false god are but a dim rememoring of a cursed past in which man was wolf to the man . . .

If it had not been for these thing, I might have live out my life talking at street corners to scorning men. I might have die, unmarked, unknown, a failure. Now we are not a failure. This is our career and our triumph. Never in our full life could we hope to do such work for tolerance, for joostice, for man's onderstanding of man as now we do by accident. Our words—our lives—our pains—nothing! The taking of our lives—lives of a good shoe-maker and a poor fish-peddler—all! The last moment belongs to us—that agony is our triumph.

THE DEFENSE OF THE CATONSVILLE NINE*

In March of 1968, Catholic priest Daniel Berrigan and eight other war protestors raided a draft board office in Catonsville, Maryland. They destroyed some of the files in an attempt to help impede the American war effort in Vietnam. The subsequent trial has been described by Father Daniel in a free verse form. In this excerpt from the description, Father

*Daniel Berrigan, *The Trial of the Catonsville Nine* (Boston: Beacon Press, 1970), pp. 81-95.

Daniel intersperses a quotation from an article written by a sociologist, C. Wright Mills.

DEFENSE

What was the impact of the act of your brother Philip Berrigan when he poured blood on draft files in Baltimore?

DANIEL BERRIGAN

I began to understand
one could not indefinitely obey the law
while social conditions deteriorated
structures of compassion breaking down
neighborhoods slowly rotting
the poor despairing   unrest
forever present in the land   especially among
the young people
who are our only hope   our only resource
My brother's action helped me realize
from the beginning   of our republic
good men had said no
acted outside the law
when conditions so demanded
And if a man did this
time might vindicate him   show his act to be lawful
a gift to society
a gift to history
and to the community
A few men
must have a long view
must leave history to itself
to interpret their lives   their repute
Someday
these defendants may be summoned
to the Rose Garden and decorated
but not today

DEFENSE

Could you state to the court what your intent was in burning the draft files?

DANIEL BERRIGAN

I did not want the children
or the grandchildren of the jury
or of the judge
to be burned with napalm

JUDGE

> You say your intention was to save these children, of
> the jury, of myself, when you burned the records?
> That is what I heard you say. I ask if you meant
> that.

DANIEL BERRIGAN

> I meant that
> of course I mean that
> or I would not say it
> The great sinfulness
> of modern war is
> that it renders concrete things abstract
> I do not want to talk
> about Americans in general

JUDGE

> You cannot think up arguments now that you would
> like to have had in your mind then.

DANIEL BERRIGAN

> My intention on that day
> was
> to save the innocent
> from death by fire
> I was trying to save the poor
> who are mainly charged with
> dying in this war
> I poured napalm
> on behalf of the prosecutor's
> and the jury's children
> It seems to me quite logical
> If my way of putting the facts
> is inadmissible
> then so be it
> But I was trying to be concrete
> about death   because death
> is a concrete fact
> as I have throughout my life
> tried to be concrete
> about the existence of God
> Who is not an abstraction
> but is someone before me
> for Whom I am responsible

DEFENSE

Was your action at Catonsville a way of carrying out
your religious beliefs?

DANIEL BERRIGAN

Of course it was
May I say
if my religious belief is not accepted
as a substantial part of my action
then the action is eviscerated
of all meaning   and I should be
committed for insanity

DEFENSE

How did your views on the Vietnam war take shape?

DANIEL BERRIGAN

My views on war and peace
arose in me slowly
as life itself
pushed hard and fast
I should like to speak of
5 or 6 stages   in my development
I was invited to South Africa
around Easter of 1964
There I had about two weeks
of intense exposure
to a segregationist police state
At one meeting in Durbin
I remember   the question being raised
What happens to our children
if things go so badly
that we have to go to jail?
I remember saying
I could not answer that question
not being a citizen of that country
but I could perhaps help
by reversing the question
What happens to us and our children
if we do *not* go to jail?
2   I visited eastern Europe twice
in 1964
meeting with Christians in Czechoslovakia   Hungary
                                                 Russia
This had bearing

on my development   I was coming to realize
what it might cost to be a Christian
what it might cost
even at home
if things were to change
in the direction I felt events were taking
even then
In the summer of 1965   I went to Prague
to attend the Christian Peace Conference
This was a kind of breakthrough
For the first time   a Catholic priest
sat in that vast assembly of Christians
from all over the world   from Marxist countries
from India   from Africa   from the east and west
talking about things
that diplomacy and power and the military
were not talking about
That is to say
How can we survive as human beings
in a world
more and more officially given over
to violence and death
I think the imperceptible movement
of my conscience
was pushed forward by that experience
3 I returned in the summer of 1964
and was assigned as editor and writer
at a magazine in New York
named *Jesuit Missions*
I was quite convinced
that the war in Vietnam
would inevitably worsen
I felt that a cloud
no larger than a man's hand
would shortly cover the sky
In the autumn of 1964
I began to say no to the war
knowing
if I delayed too long
I would never find the courage to say no
In that year
I underwent a kind of bootcamp

in the "new man"   becoming a peaceable man
in a time of great turmoil
New York was not an auspicious place
to be a peaceable Catholic priest
Cardinal Spellman was living
He had always supported American wars
He believed   I think this states his thought
that the highest expression   of Christian faith
was to bless our military
By his Christmas visits
to our foreign legions
he placed official approval
on our military adventuring
I had to say no to that too
I had to say no to the church

* * * *

Gentlemen:
Since we are among those pagans who take declarations seriously, we must
ask you as declared Christians, certain questions. . . .

Should you not stand up and denounce with all the righteousness and
pity and anger and charity and love and humility which your faith may place
at your command, the political and militarist assumptions now followed by
the leaders of the nations of Christendom?

Pagans are waiting for your answer. You claim to be Christians. What
does that mean as a public fact?

C. Wright Mills: A Pagan Sermon

* * * *

4   Finally
in the autumn of 1965
I was exiled from the United States
to Latin America
JUDGE
What do you mean, "exiled"?
DANIEL BERRIGAN
I was sent out   your honor
with no return ticket
As one of my friends expressed it

sending me to Latin America was a little like
tossing Br'er Rabbit into the briar patch
I visited ten countries in four and a half months
from Mexico to Southern Chile and then
up the western coasts
I discussed American involvement
in the political and social scene of those countries
I spent time with the students   the slum dwellers
with whatever government officials would talk
as well as with church leaders
In Mexico   a student said to me
We hate you North Americans   with all our hearts
but we know   that if you do not make it
we all come down   we are all doomed
I arrived in Rio in January of 1966
in the midst of devastating floods
In the space of a single night
the rains came down with torrential force
whole towns collapsed
people and shacks fell into a stew of death
I remember the next morning
slogging through the mud
in the company of a slumdweller
who was also a community organizer
He looked at me and said
My friend   millions for war in Vietnam
and this for us

JUDGE

What? Are you saying that the United States government
caused the flood?

DANIEL BERRIGAN

I think   the fact
was a bit more subtle than that
I think he was saying
the resources of America
which belong in justice
to the poor of the world
are squandered in war   and war preparation

DEFENSE

Now may I ask about your writings and publications?

PROSECUTION

What difference does it make how many books he has written?

DEFENSE
I show you the book *Night Flight to Hanoi*. Will you outline the circumstances out of which this book was written?
DANIEL BERRIGAN
5 The book marks
the next stage   of my development
In January of 1968   an invitation came
from the government of North Vietnam
Professor Howard Zinn and myself
were invited to Hanoi
to bring home   3 captive American airmen
For me to go to Hanoi
was a very serious decision
I believe   I have always believed
that the peace movement must not merely say no
to the war
It must also say
yes to life   yes to the possibility of a human future
We must go beyond frontiers
frontiers declared by our country or by the enemy
So I thought it would be important
to show Americans
that we were ready to risk our lives
to bring back American prisoners
because we did not believe
that in wartime
anyone should be in prison
or should suffer separation
from families
simply   we did not believe in war
And so we went

* * * *

What crime have I committed, I keep on asking?
The crime of being devoted to my people.

HO CHI MINH: PRISON DIARY

* * * *

In Hanoi I think we were the first Americans
to undergo

an American bombing attack
When the burned draft files
were brought into court yesterday
as evidence
I could not but recall
that I had seen in Hanoi
evidence of a very different nature
I saw   not boxes of burned papers
I saw parts of human bodies   preserved in alcohol
the bodies of children   the hearts and organs and limbs
of women

* * * *

EVIDENCE FOR THE PROSECUTION

The boxes of paper ash
The size of infant caskets
Were rolled in on a dolly,
Heaped there like cord wood
Or children after a usual
Air strike on Hanoi
I heard between heartbeats
of Jesus and his hangman
The children's mouth mewing
For the breasts of murdered women
The blackened hands beating
The box of death for breath.

DANIEL BERRIGAN

* * * *

teachers   workers   peasants   bombed
in fields and churches and schools and hospitals
I examined our "improved weaponry"
It was quite clear to me
during three years of air war
America had been experimenting
upon the bodies of the innocent
We had improved our weapons
on their flesh

JUDGE

> He did not see this first hand. He is telling of things
> he was told in Hanoi, about some things that were preserved
> in alcohol.

DANIEL BERRIGAN

> French   English   Swedish experts   doctors
> testified
> these were actually the bodies
> whose pictures
> accompanied the exhibits
> The evidence was unassailable
> The bombings
> were a massive crime against man
> The meaning of the air war in the North
> was the deliberate systematic destruction
> of a poor and developing people

JUDGE

> We are not trying the air war in North Vietnam.

DANIEL BERRIGAN

> I must protest the effort
> to discredit me on the stand
> I am speaking of what I saw
> There is a consistent effort
> to say that I did not see it

JUDGE

> The best evidence of what some "crime commission"
> found is not a summary that you give.

DANIEL BERRIGAN

> So be it
> In any case we brought the flyers home
> I think as a result of the trip to Hanoi
> I understood the limits
> of what I had done before
> and the next step that must come

* * * *

Calamity has tempered and hardened me and turned my mind to
steel.

HO CHI MINH: PRISON DIARY

* * * *

On my return to America
another event
helped me understand
the way I must go
It was the self-immolation
of a high school student
in Syracuse New York
in the spring of 1968
I had seen him once or twice
at the edge of a crowd
As I learned later
he had expressed a desire
to know me better
though this never happened
This boy had come to a point of despair
about the war   He had gone
into the Catholic cathedral
drenched himself with kerosene
and immolated himself in the street
He was still living a month later
I was able to gain access to him
I smelled the odor
of burning flesh
And I understood anew
what I had seen in North Vietnam
The boy was dying in torment
his body like a piece of meat
cast upon a grille
He died shortly thereafter
I felt that my senses
had been invaded in a new way
I had understood
the power of death in the modern world
I knew I must speak and act
against death
because this boy's death
was being multiplied
a thousandfold
in the Land of Burning Children
So I went to Catonsville
and burned some papers   because
the burning of children

is inhuman and unbearable
I went to Catonsville
because I had gone to Hanoi
because my brother was a man
and I must be a man
and because
I knew at length
I could not announce the gospel
from a pedestal
I must act as a Christian
sharing the risks and burdens and anguish
of those whose lives were placed
in the breach by us
I saw suddenly   and it struck with the force of lightning
that my position was false
I was threatened with verbalizing
my moral substance out of existence
I was placing upon young shoulders
a filthy burden   the original sin of war
I was asking them to enter a ceremony of death
Although I was too old
to carry a draft card   there were other ways
of getting in trouble with a state
that seemed determined upon multiplying the dead
totally intent upon a war
the meaning of which   no sane man could tell
So I went to Hanoi
and then to Catonsville
and that is why I am here

DEFENSE

Did you not write a meditation to accompany the statement
issued by the nine defendants at Catonsville?

DANIEL BERRIGAN

Yes sir

DEFENSE

Would you read the meditation?

DANIEL BERRIGAN

Certainly
"Some ten or twelve of us (the number is still uncertain)
will if all goes well (ill?) take our religious bodies
during this week

to a draft center in or near Baltimore
There we shall   of purpose and forethought
remove the 1-A files   sprinkle them in the public street
with home-made napalm   and set them afire
For which act we shall beyond doubt
be placed behind bars for some portion of our natural lives

in consequence of our inability
to live and die content in the plagued city
to say 'peace peace' when there is no peace
to keep the poor poor
the thirsty and hungry thirsty and hungry
Our apologies   good friends
for the fracture of good order   the burning of paper
instead of children   the angering of the orderlies
in the front parlor of the charnel house
We could not   so help us God   do otherwise
For we are sick at heart   our hearts
give us no rest for thinking of the Land of Burning Children
and for thinking of that other Child of whom
the poet Luke speaks   The infant was taken up
in the arms of an old man whose tongue
grew resonant and vatic at the touch of that beauty
And the old man spoke: this child is set
for the fall and rise of many in Israel
a sign that is spoken against
Small consolation   a child born to make trouble
and to die for it   the First Jew (not the last)
to be subject of a 'definitive solution'
And so we stretch out our hands
to our brothers throughout the world
We who are priests to our fellow priests
All of us who act against the law
turn to the poor of the world   to the Vietnamese
to the victims   to the soldiers who kill and die
for the wrong reasons for no reason at all
because they were so ordered by the authorities
of that public order which is in effect
a massive institutionalized disorder
We say: killing is disorder
life and gentleness and community and unselfishness
is the only order we recognize
For the sake of that order

we risk our liberty   our good name
The time is past when good men may be silent
when obedience
can segregate men from public risk
when the poor can die without defense
How many indeed must die
before our voices are heard
how many must be tortured dislocated
starved maddened?
How long must the world's resources
be raped in the service of legalized murder?
When at what point will you say no to this war?
We have chosen to say
with the gift of our liberty
if necessary our lives:
the violence stops here
the death stops here
the suppression of the truth stops here
this war stops here
Redeem the times!
The times are inexpressibly evil
Christians pay conscious   indeed religious tribute
to Caesar and Mars
by the approval of overkill tactics   by brinkmanship
by nuclear liturgies   by racism   by support of genocide
They embrace their society with all their heart
and abandon the cross
They pay lip service to Christ
and military service to the powers of death
And yet   and yet   the times are inexhaustibly good
solaced by the courage and hope of many
The truth rules   Christ is not forsaken
In a time of death some men
the resisters   those who work hardily for social change
those who preach and embrace the truth
such men overcome death
their lives are bathed in the light of the resurrection
the truth has set them free
In the jaws of death
they proclaim their love of the brethren
We think of such men
in the world   in our nation   in the churches

and the stone in our breast is dissolved
we take heart once more"
DEFENSE
Nothing further.

The Police and the Courts

"I WAS SO SQUARED . . ."*

A grisly crime, public outrage, pressured police. In Manhattan, the familiar pattern swirled about the twin murder of *Newsweek* Researcher Janice Wylie, 21, and Schoolteacher Emily Hoffert, 23. Yet last week the old pattern had a new result: a rare official admission of a near-miscarriage of justice.

The crime that frightened hundreds of New York career girls, not to mention their parents, occured on August 28, 1963, when Janice and Emily were slugged, bound and stabbed to death around noon in their East Side apartment. Detectives questioned 1,000 persons, all to no avail, until April 24, 1964. On that day, George Whitmore, 19, a myopic, pock-marked Negro drifter with an IQ of 60, walked up to a Brooklyn cop in an area where a nurse had barely managed to frighten off a rapist the night before. "What was all the shooting about last night?" asked Whitmore carelessly. For days afterward, he was answering, not asking questions.

Whitmore was hustled to the station house and grilled for 26 hours. Next day, the city's top police brass triumphantly displayed the youth before TV news cameras as the confessed perpetrator of three crimes—the attempted rape, the unsolved killing of a Brooklyn charwoman, and the Wylie-Hoffert murders. The nurse, police said, had identified Whitmore. As to the double murder, police said that Whitmore diagramed the career girls' apartment for them and was even carrying a snapshot of Janice Wylie that he had snatched from her dresser. To be sure, Whitmore recanted his detailed, 60-page confession when he was arraigned. But Chief of Detectives Lawrence McKearney was unworried. "We've got the right guy," he said. "No question about it."

Manhattan D.A. Frank Hogan's investigators were soon less sure. Before

*Adapted from *Time* 85(Feb. 5, 1965):60.

signing his confession, Whitmore claimed that he had plucked the snapshot from his father's junkyard in Wildwood, N.J., to "show my friends I've got a white girl." Last fall the D.A.'s men displayed the picture around Wildwood: it was easily recognized as that of a local girl named Arlene Franco, who had thrown it away. Keeping this development to themselves, Hogan's men also secretly discovered a witness who saw Whitmore in Wildwood, about 150 miles away from Manhattan, calmly sitting in a local restaurant on the day of the murder.

As for the confession, during psychiatric examinations at Bellevue Hospital, Whitmore painfully wrote that he had been "hit many times" by police interrogators. "Then I was so squared that I was shakeing all over. And before I knew it, I was saying yes. I was so squared if they would have told me my name was tom, dick or harry I would have said yes."

When a man is accused of several crimes committed in a short period, many lawyers feel that fair practice is to try him first on the most serious charge. With only the now-suspect confession to go on, the prosecutor took a different tack. In the murder trials, if Whitmore took the stand to repudiate his confession, prior convictions would be admissible evidence to impeach his testimony. By arrangement between the Brooklyn and Manhattan D.A.s, Whitmore was thus tried first in Brooklyn, where the nurse's identification would help nail him for attempted rape: the Brooklyn and Manhattan murder trials were scheduled to follow in ascending dramatic order.

After Whitmore was convicted on the rape charge last November, his mother fired his court-appointed lawyer; two other lawyers took the case for no fee. In turn, they persuaded veteran Criminal Lawyer Stanley Reiben to join them. Reiben and enterprising newsmen soon began poking hole after hole in the prosecution case. N.A.A.C.P. lawyers also joined Reiben in charging that the jurors in the first trial were influenced by Whitmore's race and the Wylie-Hoffert charges.

Last week the payoff came when police arrested a new suspect in the Wylie-Hoffert murders: Richard Robles, 22, an ex-convict and narcotics addict, whose habit is said to require "about five bags of heroin a day." (Daily cost: roughly $100 or more.) The evidence against Robles reportedly rests on the word of a friend-turned-informer, Nathan Delaney, 35, another addict with three criminal convictions.

Under New York law, Delaney is subject to a life sentence if convicted of a felony for the fourth time. Perhaps by no coincidence, Delaney began talking about Robles on being arrested for killing a drug pusher. He was soon cleared ("justifiable homicide"). According to some stories, Robles readily admitted during bull sessions at Delaney's flat that he had "iced" (killed) the Wylie and Hoffert girls while burglarizing their apartment. To nail Robles, the police got a court order allowing them to bug Delaney's flat and record Robles' conversations. Delaney also wore an underarm recording device for monitoring other chats with Robles. Whether or not it stands up in court against Robles, the Supreme Court has held such evidence to be admissible in state criminal trials.

Revealing Statement. On the arrest of Robles, D.A. Hogan finally issued a 1,400-word statement clearing Whitmore of the Wylie-Hoffert murders, though not of the Brooklyn murder, which is not in Hogan's jurisdiction. One of Hogan's assistants declared: "I am positive that the police prepared the confession for Whitmore just as his lawyers charged." And he added: "If this had not been a celebrated case, if this case hadn't got the tremendous publicity, if this was what we so-called professionals call a run-of-the-mill murder, Whitmore might well have been slipped into the electric chair and been killed for something he didn't do."

However honest, that was an oddly revealing statement, for according to the bar's canons of professional ethics, the great goal of prosecutors is always to seek justice rather than merely to compile convictions. . . .

SELECTIVE HARRASSMENT*

. . . consider an experiment conducted recently by a California State College professor. He selected 15 students with perfectly clean driving records, made them pledge to obey all traffic regulations, and turned them loose on the Los Angeles freeways in various types of vehicles having only one thing in common: a Black Panther sticker prominently displayed on the bumper. Within 17 days, every student had been stopped by the police—one black three times—for a total of 33 moving violations. The results were not surprising to anyone familiar with the realities perceived by many long-haired, hippie-garbed youths, for whom selective harassment by police is a constant condition of life in America. . . .

THE VIOLENT SOCIETY**

. . . many veteran policemen sincerely believe that what you need in our

*Adapted from a letter to the editor by Larry Darrel, *The New Leader* 54(Jan. 25, 1971):31.

**Adapted from Hallowell Bowser, "The Gentle Gendarmes," *Saturday Review* 53(March 28, 1970):22.

racially and ideologically tense society is a patrolman who commands respect with his nightstick and service revolver.

The police of other Western democracies, however, seem to get along fine using approaches that minimize violence. The standard explanation is that the people of these countries are racially and culturally homogeneous, hence quiescent and tractable. But until quite recent times, "racially homogeneous" Europe has had more than its share of bloody mob scenes, footpads and cut-purses, and sudden death in dark alleys. If things are better now, could this happy condition be in part a result, not the cause, of violence-minimizing police methods?

To visiting American hard-liners, there is something comic-opera about the European police scene, what with smiling policemen taking senior citizens on walking tours to point out pedestrian hazards; officers holding safety classes for bicyclists; and special forces men restraining overwrought demonstrators with smiling forbearance.

"Reading the Swedish press," Boston sociologist George Berkley has said, "An American is continually impressed by the way policemen handle unruly, violent, and frequently armed teen-agers [and cop-killers] without resorting to major force."

When European police do carry pistols, they use a modest 7.65 automatic that packs less wallop than the .32 handguns carried by New York City's policewomen. Most American policemen carry a formidable .38-caliber revolver, and many departments allow them to buy a Magnum—a handgun eminently suited (as one European police official has put it) to stopping an elephant. Other common U.S. police equipment includes the riot shotgun, Mace, and a sort of karate glove with lead weights built into it, "for instant defense."

These unnerving details are not spelled out here to make it look as if American policemen get their jollies from head-busting. On the contrary, the suspicion grows that deep-running flaws in our law-enforcement systems undercut the American policeman at every turn, inducing him to depend too heavily on violence as a deterrent, and depriving him of access to those public-rapport approaches that greatly ease the task of his European counterparts.

STREET JUSTICE IN ARIZONA*

This piece is preceded by an editor's note: "The writer giving this eyewitness acount is by no means a street freak. In fact, he has short hair

*Adapted from "Up Against That Wall, Punk, or I'll Cripple You," *New Times* 4(Tempe, Arizona), March 7, 1973.

and has lived in Tucson [Arizona] all his life, holding a respectable job and studying at the University. He must remain nameless because of his court case."

After all the cold, gray days, things were getting better and the promise of a warm evening with the woman I had met at the Shanty filled me with happiness. As we danced down the street laughter could be heard everywhere and life was good.

Our car was across the road and as we crossed over to it, a blue unmarked police car screamed to a halt. Four men in army fatigues leaped out and grabbing two longhairs, shouted, "Get your hands against the wall and freeze!"

The two guys just stood there, mouths open in surprise. "What did we . . .?"

"Get the hell up against that wall, punk, or I'll cripple you," howled a club-wielding trooper.

By this time a crowd was gathering and two more cop cars pulled up. The two freaks were handcuffed and thrown into a car and taken away.

"All right, clear the street. Everybody get out of here." The police were looking for blood.

I went to my friend Steve's car and waited for him. A cop beckoned to him to cross the street over to where he had his unmarked car parked. When Steve got there, the cop said, "Don't you know jaywalking is against the law? Give me some I.D. I'm going to give you a ticket. Wait here."

With that, he went into his car and began writing up a citation. I couldn't believe it and walked over to Steve saying, "It's a shame that some fucking idiot always overreacts and . . ."

The cop jumped out of his car, nearly dropping his notebook in excitement. Fire was in his eyes and he shouted at me wildly, "What did you say, buddy?"

"I wasn't talking to you, officer," I said.

"You got any I.D. wiseguy?"

"Sure," I said.

Whip it on me, baby," he said.

He retired to his car and soon erupted forth with a jaywalking ticket for Steve and a citation for loud and profane language and disorderly conduct for me.

I was astounded. As far as I knew, expressing an opinion to your friend (even if it contained a descriptive word) wasn't against the law. How could this be?

"Officer," I protested, "I don't understand what it is that I did. Will you please explain?"

"You said fuck you, buddy!" His eyes were wild and his excitement frightened me. I expected to get hit.

"I can't sign this thing when I don't even know what I did wrong . . ." Before I could finish the cop turned me around, pinned me up against the car with a club and handcuffed me viciously,. "You don't wanna sign it; then you're going to jail!"

I. was in a car being driven away from my friends before I even had a chance to explain.

. . . .

I was taken to a staging area behind a church where about a half-dozen marked cars and a paddy wagon were set up and people were being manhandled and photographed all around. The cops were laughing it up and having a grand old time. There were about five other longhaired males there who looked indignant and bewildered and it was obvious that no one knew what was happening. One cop seemed to have a conscience and looked very apologetic.

"You just happened to be in the wrong place at the wrong time," he told me. "Just flow with the program and you won't get hurt."

They stood us up against the paddy wagon and one by one we were photographed with a polaroid camera. "For our personal stash," one cop told me.

They replaced the steel handcuffs with a plastic tie that fell off after I was put into the paddy wagon because the cop who applied it didn't know how to do it right. When the paddy wagon was opened later for more prisoners, a cop saw my hands free.

"Get the hell out of there. You without the cuffs!" I stepped out of the van and the cop grabbed my coat and threw me on the ground.

"I'll make damn sure you don't slip out of this again, buster!" and with that he cinched the plastic down hard over the bones in my wrist while he knelt on the small of my back so I couldn't escape. The tie cut off the circulation to my hands. I was thrown back into the wagon, where I had to sit on my rapidly numbing hands for three hours while the purge of Fourth Avenue continued and the gestapo rounded up enough freaks to fill the van.

As I waited, unmarked cars came and went, depositing protesting, confused teenagers and freaks and then going for more. It was a nightmare of red flashing lights and wildmen in the disguise of policemen prowling the darkness.

One by one, the malicious jaywalkers, partygoers and innocent bystanders piled into the paddy wagon until it was full and we headed out to the Silverbell jail annex.

When we got there, the cop driving told us to walk quietly to the jail or we'd get shot. No questions asked, brother. . . .

Once inside the jail we were herded into a grey, clammy cell and, on into the night, were taken out one by one and booked. The jailers were looking harried.

"What the hell went on out there?" one asked me.

"You better be careful, fella, we're a hard core band of vicious criminal jaywalkers and you might get hurt," I said. The jailer looked at me with contempt and shoved me into a 40-by-12 foot cell with 80 other people who were already packed in Brisling Sardines. There was no room to lie down. The 16 bunks were long gone and all I could do was stand against the bars for the rest of the night and contemplate my fate. The stench of vomit and the three open and overflowing commodes made me feel sick.

The next morning about 6 a.m. we were herded into the dining room and fed a pigs breakfast of cornmeal mush, burnt sausage and watery coffee with no surgar served in a bowl. Retch.

After breakfast we went back to the cattlepen cell and waited. At 8:30 we boarded a bus with bars on the windows and trucked into town to be arraigned. . . .

The court room scene was a farce. Judge Mario Cota Robles handed out fines and two-day jail terms to those who plead guilty thinking that he would understand that they really hadn't done anything wrong. Cries of outrage and dismay came from those who were sentenced. The sad thing was that most of those who did plead guilty did so because they had no money for bond. If they had pleaded not guilty it could have meant a month or more in jail until trial on a charge for which the penalty was often only a day or two in jail and a small fine. Judge Cota Robles was obviously aware of this and wouldn't allow any questioning of his rulings. Most of the defendants were unaware of the laws they had broken and had no way of knowing how to plead. If they didn't say one way or the other the judge would throw them back into jail. This is justice?

When my turn came to plead I asked the judge to define the charges against me and to read the police report so I could find out what it was that I done wrong. He said he wouldn't and ordered me to plead one way or the other. I told him that he was making a mockery of the law and he said if I didn't plead right then he'd cite me for contempt. I said "Not Guilty" and asked him to appoint an attorney for me since I can't afford to hire one on my own. He denied my request saying that I probably wouldn't go to jail even though the penalty is up to two months in jail and a $300 fine.

I then asked if I could appeal his no lawyer ruling and he said, "You'll have to hire yourself an attorney to appeal my ruling that you can't be appointed a public defender." With a smile on his face the bail was set at $55.

After we were all arraigned and sent back to jail on the bus they started processing and fingerprinting. The law says that if you post bond you have to be let out right away. Well, my bond was posted at 10:30 in the morning right after court by Steve. At the jail they took the ones who had to stay in jail and processed them first and deliberately waited until last to take those of us who had been freed legally through bail or released after paying a fine. I paced the floors of that metal cage until nearly 3:30 that afternoon.

When I walked out of that jail at 3:30 I left something behind me that will never be replaced: my respect for the laws and police of this city. The so-called Establishment cries that its youth are disrespectful and have no regard for the law. All I can say is that the establishment is asking for trouble. There was no justice in that court. The rich go free and the young and poor suffer.

How am I to respect law that doesn't respect my basic rights as a human being? I have been manhandled, had to put up money I can't afford and face two months imprisonment for expressing an opinion to my friend. Wake up, America, Orwell's 1984 is not a cliché the left wing throws around to stir up trouble. It is up to you. What are we going to do to stop this terrible trend?

STREET JUSTICE IN NEW JERSEY*

The riot which occurred in 1967 in the black community of Newark, New Jersey, was described in the mass media as an uprising by "the people." The affair was, in truth, a "police riot," as described here by political activist Tom Hayden.

Clearly the evidence points to a military massacre and suppression in Newark rather than to a two-sided war. This was not only the conclusion of the Negroes in the ghetto but of private Newark lawyers, professors of constitutional law and representatives of the state American Civil Liberties Union. They have charged that the police were the instrument of a conspiracy "to engage in a pattern of systematic violence, terror, abuse, intimidation, and humiliation" to keep Negroes second-class citizens. The

*Adapted from Tom Hayden, *Rebellion in Newark* (New York: Random House, Inc., 1967), pp. 53, 58–60,

police, according to the lawyers' statement, "seized on the initial disorders as an opportunity and pretext to perpetrate the most horrendous and widespread killing, violence, torture, and intimidation, not in response to any crime or civilian disorder, but as a violent demonstration of the powerlessness of the plaintiffs and their class . . ."

Thus it seems to many that the military, especially the Newark police, not only triggered the riot by beating a cab-driver but then created a climate of opinion that supported the use of all necessary force to suppress the riot. The force used by police was not in response to snipers, looting, and burning, but in retaliation against the successful uprising of Wednesday and Thursday nights.

. . . .

In the aftermath of the riot it became clear that substantial citizens of Newark were aware of the magnitude of the police brutality issue. A Committee of Concern, including the Episcopal Bishop, the dean of Rutgers' Newark branch and the dean of Rutgers' Law School, the vice-presidents of the Prudential Insurance Company and of Newark's largest department store, declared that one of the major causes of the riot was the feeling among Negroes that the police are the "single continuously lawless element operating in the community." The solid citizens agreed that this Negro view had merit; indeed, they said "independent observers" agreed with it. Since their statement implied a prior awareness of the problem, the question could be asked why they had taken no action previously to solve the problem. If *Life* magazine could express worry that the Negro community did not turn in the snipers in its midst, would it not be proper to worry why the white community never turned in the violent element in its midst?

The riot made clear that if something is not done about the police immediately, the fears of white society will be transformed into reality: whites will be facing a black society that will not only harbor, but welcome and employ snipers. The troops did not instill fear so much as a fighting hatred in the community. Many people, of every age and background, cursed the soldiers. Women spit at armored cars. Five-year-old kids clenched bottles in their hands. If the troops made a violent move, the primitive missiles were loosed at them. People openly talked of the riot turning into a showdown and, while a great many were afraid, few were willing to be pushed around by the troops. All told there were more than 3000 people arrested, injured, or killed; thousands more witnessed these incidents. From this kind of violence, which touches people personally, springs a commitment to fight back. By the end of the weekend many people spoke of a willingness to die.

Jimmy Cannon was one such person. He was the uncle riding with ten-year-old Eddie Moss when the Guardsmen shot through the car and the young boy's head was ripped open. Jimmy put the car, blood, bulletholes and all, into a private garage as proof of what happened. Then he was beaten on the streetcorner by police who found him there. Jimmy learned how to fight during four years in the Marines. "I don't hold any grudges against you," he told a white person who interviewed him. "I'm just for rights, not for violence. This thing is wrong. I've faced a lot of things, but this is bad, and I just don't care anymore. I am to the point where I just don't care."

AGENT PROVOCATEUR FOR THE FBI*

The informer who collaborated with the Federal Bureau of Investigation in the raid on Camden draft board files said in an affidavit filed yesterday that the bureau had used him as a "provocateur."

The informer, Robert W. Hardy of Camden, N.J., said the raid last August 22 could not have occurred without his leadership.

His initial purpose in going to the FBI, he said, had been the opposite— "to stop the action."

He said the FBI, in constant touch with him for two months preceding the raid, told him to watch developments and paid for the gas, trucks, van, tools and groceries needed by those planning the project.

Hardy said the defendants lacked the know-how to carry out a raid on the draft files and seemed to have dropped the idea till he rekindled interest by instructing them, while working with the FBI, in how to detect and avoid burglar alarms, by providing ladders, tools and instruction on how to break into a fifth-floor window of the Camden post office building with the aid of tape and drills, by providing special bits for use on glass, by providing schematic drawings of the draft board office as well as the entire building, by renting vehicles and by outlining strategies.

The accused were arrested shortly after draft records were removed from the files. Some were arrested in the act of removing them. The defendants are free on bail on charges of conspiracy, breaking and entering, theft and destruction of government property and interfering with the Selective Service Act.

Hardy said he provided the affidavit after a meeting in Woodbury, N.J., with the Reverend Michael J. Doyle of Camden, a defendant who has been his parish priest, and David Kairys of Philadelphia, Father Doyle's lawyer.

*Adapted from *New York Times* Service dispatch, March 16, 1972.

The informer said he supplied the document "because it is important that the truth come out."

The informer said the FBI had assured him from the beginning that the arrests would be made before the raid actually took place, that his friends among the Camden 28 would be prosecuted for nothing more than conspiracy and that they would not go to jail.

FBI agents here told him the raid was allowed to proceed, he said in the affidavit, because "the higher-ups, someone at the little White House in California, they said, which I took to mean someone high in the FBI or Justice Department then in California, wanted it to actually happen."

Kairys siad that "this is not law enforcement, it is the FBI acting illegally as a political force."

"That the FBI was told to make it happen and then to sit and watch it happen indicates that the government was not interested in preserving those pieces of paper (draft records) but was trying to stop an antiwar movement," he said.

It is a case of manufacturing crimes to support repressive policies and the political futures of persons in power."

He said the "misuse" of informers was becoming a common FBI technique. He cited the role of Boyd Douglas, the FBI informer in the Berrigan case . . .

Kairys filed a motion this morning in federal district court in Camden, immediately across the Delaware River from Philadelphia, to dismiss the indictments against the Camden 28, attaching a copy of the Hardy affidavit. He charged entrapment in violation of the Constitution and federal law.

JUDGING THE JUDGES*

It is 11:43 a.m. on a Wednesday in late February. Spring is edging into Louisville, Ky., and on the street people have shed their coats and are nodding and smiling.

But in the courtoom of Circuit Judge R——— there are no smiles. A middle-aged barber, accused of wounding a man, is worried. His freedom and future are at stake.

On the witness stand his daughter, an attractive woman, tells the jury how the victim provoked the shooting by taunting her father and by getting youngsters to block the barbershop driveway with their bicycles to keep customers away.

*Adapted from Howard James, *Crisis in the Courts* (New York: David McKay Company, Inc., 1967), pp. 1-2.

As she testifies, an aging newsboy enters the courtroom and hawks papers.

With considerable rustling, Judge R_____ opens his newspaper to the comic page. After reading for several minutes he pulls the section out, folds it into a smaller square, and counts quietly to himself, apparently working the crossword puzzle.

The young woman seems nervous. She speaks rapidly.

Judge R_____ looks up from his paper and tells her to slow down. There is a note of irritation in his voice when, a few minutes later, he again orders her to speak more slowly, so the court stenographer can keep up.

The stenographer, who already has put down her pen and is checking her fingernails, says, "Oh, I gave up a long time ago."

When the defendant's daughter finishes, two other witnesses take the stand briefly. Judge R_____ denies the prosecution request to let a woman use the chalkboard to clarify her testimony.

At 12:38 p.m., the judge adjourns court for lunch until 2 p.m.

A visitor, after buying license plates in another office, has stopped by to watch. With adjournment he rises to leave before the jury has departed. Judge R_____ orders him stopped by a bailiff, brings him before the bench, and gives him a lecture on courtroom decorum.

What happened on this day in Louisville is unusual. But it is far from unique in the nation's state courts.

THE GILES-JOHNSON CASE*

It would be hard to find more devastating proof of the awful fallibility of the American judicial system than the seven-year saga of three young citizens of Maryland. An ugly little incident on a dark night in July, 1961, on a dubious lovers' lane in rural Montgomery County snatched two brothers, James and John Giles, and a friend, Joe Johnson, from anonymity and, in a malignant and terrible miscarriage of legal process, catapulted them all onto Death Row at the state penitentiary in Baltimore. They had been convicted of raping a teen-aged white girl and were condemned to die in the gas chamber. But their real crime against society—as this book will show—was to have been born black. That is another way of saying that the dominating white society of the United States of America in the last third of the twentieth century had, again, itself committed the unpardonable crime of racism.

*Adapted from Edward P. Morgan's introduction to Frances Strauss, *"Where Did the Justice Go?"*: The Story of the Giles-Johnson Case (Boston: Gambit Incorporated, 1970), pp. vii–xii.

But though man's continuing inhumanity to man makes a mockery of the term "civilization" in the context of human behavior, in this country and elsewhere, all is not quite lost. The doggedness of the individual human spirit is still a wondrous thing. Tyrants have never been able to extinguish it completely. Its vigor keeps an open society from becoming closed—though, paradoxically, even in modern America the ancient strangling prejudices of race coupled with the suffocating selfishness of our very affluence are putting the spirit of human freedom to the extreme test of endurance.

For the Giles brothers and Joe Johnson are alive and free today, not because of the majestic movement of justice through the courts, but because a stubborn handful of people, goaded by what Quakers call a conscience of concern, pursued injustice right up to the Supreme Court and down again. They won not by following the System but by bucking it at every turn—and nearly every turn was heartbreaking until the last. There was no national celebration of their victory. Indeed, ninety-nine percent or more of the American public undoubtedly are ignorant of the Giles-Johnson case to this day. But they should not be, if this republic is to be saved.

Before the last sentence is dismissed as the desperate hyperbole of an embittered do-gooder, let us ask ourselves, honestly, how much more evidence is it going to take to make us realize where we are headed? How many more Kerner Commission reports need to be published before we grasp the fact that we are fragmenting the country into separate, hostile groups forming Apartheid America? How many more life experiences of the Giles and the Johnsons of the land must be told before we concede that the noble motto, "Equal Justice Under Law," carved on the marble front of the Supereme Court building in Washington, is too often mocked in practice? As George Orwell would put it, some people are still more equal than others. We continue to operate on different standards of justice for the rich and the poor, for the Negro and the Caucasian.

Again and again this fact emerges in the record of the Giles-Johnson case. In October, 1963, at a hearing in the state capitol in Annapolis—which finally persuaded Maryland's governor at the time, J. Millard Tawes, to reduce the sentences of the three Negroes to life imprisonment—one of the defense attorneys, Robert Heeney, got to the sociological heart of the issue. "If I could change the color of the skin of one of these defendants," he said, "we would not be before you today."

To a supporting exhibit bearing the signatures of nearly 7,000 Maryland citizens and 1,500 more from the District of Columbia, there was an ironic footnote. This was in the form of a press clipping reporting the fact that on August 28, 1963—two years after the crime in Montgomery County and on the very day of the huge civil rights march on Washington—a young, white, gentleman tobacco farmer of southern Maryland named William Devereaux Zantzinger had been sentenced to six months in jail and fined $625 for manslaughter. In a drunken rage at a charity ball he had beaten a fifty-one-year-old Negro barmaid with a cane, causing her death.

The sexual element in racism seems to bring out the worst savagery of prejudice. Perhaps we have passed the time when a black man can be convicted of molesting a white woman by simply casting a glance in her direction. But when a Negro is suspected of the craven but titillating crime of rape, he is automatically presumed guilty unless and until he can prove his innocence. In the past this has been well-nigh impossible because the whole machinery of society was geared against the accused. And, as it was put by one of the dedicated attorneys who donated countless man hours to the defense without fee, Joe Forer, "Innocence is a relatively irrelevant factor of American Law."

And, in commenting on the turgid, tortured Supreme Court ruling which eventually, by the most circuitous and frustrating of routes, led to the freeing of the Giles boys and then Joe Johnson, Forer added: "The Court gets cases every day of terrible injustice which they don't attempt to review on the valid grounds that they can't correct all the injustices." But Forer tried to revive the spirits of the exhausted, puzzled, and forlorn defense committee by explaining that though they had neither won nor lost that round, "... I think that very inability of the Justices to decide this case indicates that the committee had made a dent on the public conscience. ... It [the case] was disturbing [to the Court] because it was an injustice the public had picked up."

The durability of this true, dispassionately told tale emerges, perhaps, no more from the nightmare of injustice it reveals than from its stirring chronicle of the quiet, patient courage the defense committee displayed through the years and years of dedication which finally made that "dent on the public conscience."

And to what palpable dangers this little band of citizens exposed themselves by the temerity of their challenge to the System! The consistency of the State's hostility to their efforts was appalling, but characteristic of an anachronistic Establishment on the defensive: trial court judges with minds wizened by the past repeatedly denying defense efforts to include the full story of that July night in the record. A state's attorney, either by laxity or design, but at any rate made secure in the arrogance of his attitude by prevailing standards of justice in Maryland, suppressing evidence as to the character of the teen-aged "victim." Obscene "nigger-lover" calls to committee members in the dead of night. Harassment of them, subtle or overt, by local police and attaches of the sheriff's office; Such as the not quite Gestapo-like arrest of Harold Knapp, a government scientist and one of the most indefatigable of the defense volunteers, on a warrant charging disturbances of the peace and sworn out by the girl's mother—but not acted upon until eight days after it had been issued and, by coincidence, at 10 p.m. after a day of court hearings which had driven Knapp to bed in a state of near exhaustion.

No wonder that the brother of Alice Alt, another volunteer, anxiously asked her at one point, "Need you get so involved?" But these volunteers simply could not stay uninvolved, even though they were confronted with such hopeless circumstances as the bewildered reluctance of the parents of the Giles brothers to do anything. They were of the generation that "kept their place" and locked their mouths shut, no matter how deeply the wrongs against them rankled. As Frances Strauss reports with pointed poignancy," . . . it never occurred to them that they had any personal rights."

Which bring to mind Edmund Burke's memorable observation that "for evil men to triumph it is necessary only for good men to do nothing." One is tempted to speculate that that piece of wisdom helped impel Winston Churchill to remind the British Parliament in the 1940's that democracy is the worst possible form of government—except all the others.

The lesson here is plain, yet one which it is not easy to forget, namely, that we cannot expect to enjoy the benefits of an open society without responding with the responsibility of personal participation.

Attorney Forer put it well in an extemporaneous résumé spoken to friends after their efforts had been finally crowned in quiet triumph with the full pardoning of the third defendant, Joe Johnson.

"I think that most of the people on the Giles-Johnson Defense Committee at the beginning," Forer said, "shared the kind of American view that our courts are infallible . . . somehow they think they can take some politician and put him on the bench and he'll get rid of all his prejudices, or turn into a genius, no matter how stupid he was before.

"Of course it's logical for people to feel that way; it makes them feel more comfortable to let the courts administer justice and handle life and death. . . . So it's easier to say 'Oh well, they'll settle it.' and that's one of the reasons why we don't have a better system for the administration of more justice."

. . . .

INDICTING THE GRAND JURY*

The grand jury sits in secret, a practice begun to protect the innocent. But the modern-dress version makes the secrecy strikingly reminiscent of

*Michael Tigar and Madeleine Levy, "An Eight-Point Indictment of the Grand Jury System," *Center Report* (December 1971):13-14.

the oath *ex officio* procedure which for a time threatened to still the first stirrings of the adversary system, the presumption of innocence and the right of public trial. The evils which were disowned in the creation of the right to a fair trial are, in fact, quite at home in the grand jury room: there is no right to notice of the scope and nature of the crimes being investigated; there is no confrontation of the witnesses who have led the trail of the investigation to the witnesses' doorstep and, collaterally, there is no possibility, much less no right, to cross-examine those witnesses. In essence there is trial in secret, and by inquiry.

There is the ordeal of examination without counsel, which even (Joseph McCarthy-type) Congressional committees never sought to impose. In the grand jury room, counsel is not permitted. True, the witness may ask the government lawyer to be excused and retire to the ante-room to consult counsel, but the atmosphere is heavily weighted in favor of the government. There is no judge or other supposedly impartial official present—only the grand jurors and government counsel.

There is trial by the ordeal of distance. A federal conspiracy prosecution may be brought in any judicial district in which the overt act in furtherance of the alleged conspiracy was committed. However, if the prosecutor's venue choice is too disadvantageous to the defense, the court can order a change of venue "for the convenience of parties and witnesses and in the interest of justice." There is no such corrective available for a venue choice in the site of a grand jury investigation. Thus, in certain cases, witnesses are required to bring their counsel with them and face their summary contempt hearings and jail terms at a great distance from home.

There are limitations on the right to bail and to appeal. A defendant charged with crime, even a serious offense, can usually—in the federal courts—secure prompt release on bail pending trial. A grand jury witness found summarily in contempt for refusal to answer can expect serious and often insurmountable difficulty in obtaining release pending appellate review. And the review available, under the 1970 crime bill, is truncated, providing in many cases no opportunity even to have the record of proceedings below transmitted to the appellate court.

The grand jury dispenses with the privilege against self-incrimination. By the consistent course of federal decision, a witness may decline to provide any information which may form a link in a chain of evidence incriminatory of him or her. When government casts wide its conspiracy net, and the inquisition begins into friendships and associations, almost any question is potentially productive of incriminatory testimony. To undermine the privilege against self-incrimination, the 1970 crime bill greatly expands the scope of the so-called "immunity" provision of the United States Code. Immunity laws have been recognized in American law since the late nineteenth century; in their "old form," they provide that a witness could be granted immunity from prosecution about all subjects of her or his testimony. Thus, even if the testimony were incriminatory, the witness could not be prosecuted and thus has, in theory, no need for a privilege against self-incrimination. Immunity may thus be used when A has information that will incriminate not only her or him, but also B whom the authorities really want to prosecute. The 1970 crime bill, however, provides not for complete immunity but for a partial, or "use" immunity. If A incriminates herself or himself, the government may not use the incriminatory testimony *itself* at a later trial of A, but there is no provision that having discovered the misdeed the government may not seek to prosecute it by gathering other evidence. This undermining of the privilege against self-incrimination has been held unconstitutional by the Court of Appeals for the Seventh Circuit and by United States District Judge Constance Baker Motley of New York.

Let us consider this problem in the broader context of a sixth objection: the grand jury inquisition destroys associational freedom by an assault upon political privacy. To begin, the grand jury's organ grinder, the government lawyer, has access to wire-tap and other electronic surveillance material which can be used as a basis for questioning and intimidating witnesses. The technology of privacy-invasion, and the public sense of its unbridled use, makes the grand jury on the loose doubly chilling. Another aspect of privacy-invasion arises from indiscriminate poking and prying into associational freedom. In an active political organization, meetings, friendships, discussions and interchange of ideas are the means by which business is done. Assume that one member is subpoenaed to testify. That member can invoke the privilege against self-incrimination as to his or her own activities, but not with respect to the activities, words or beliefs of others. To the real worry that in a student radical organization there is a paid FBI informer, is added the certainty that any member may, against his or her will, be made an informer in the secrecy of the grand jury room.

The grand jury is often convened to surveil a group or groups whom the Attorney General suspects, seeking some pretext for making a formal charge. Frequently, the indictments that do result are for offenses peripheral to the purported purpose of the grand jury, or are so ludicrously unsupported as to be *post hoc* apologies for having begun the investigation in the first place. The federal grand jury is more and more utilized to probe, expose and punish the exercise of political freedom by its immediate targets and chill dissent among all but the hardiest.

The federal grand jury has taken on a new dimension, uncontemplated by its creators and in defiance of its traditional role; it has become an evidence-gathering body once an indictment has been returned. Grand juries have continued in session long after voting indictments in an attempt to give government lawyers compulsory process for obtaining criminal discovery explicitly forbidden them by the Federal Rules of Criminal Procedure. Federal Rule 15 gives only defendants the right to take depositions to perpetuate testimony and Federal Rule 16(c) severely limits the right of government lawyers to discovery. The remainder of Federal Rule 16 limits the defendant's right to discovery. Thus, the use of the grand jury's power of subpoena is a clear evasion of the law.

OFFICER OF THE COURT*

Any lawyer today who considers himself an "officer of the court" when he's defending a political client is deluding himself. A court clerk has more rights as far as the judge is concerned than the lawyer in political trials. His role as an officer of the court means only that he is supposed to be an accessory in preserving the system as it exists today.

That system takes the political defendant out of his daily life and throws him into prison to await trial—makes him pay a penalty before he is ever tried or convicted.

Then he is railroaded into denying his innocence by our "compromise system of justice." Frequently a client says, "I am innocent." His attorney says:

"Let's be practical. I know the district attorney; he's not a bad guy. The judge and I used to play golf together. So I can make a deal for you. You can plead guilty to a lesser charge. Now, if you want to go ahead with a jury trial, it will take four or five days, and I'll have to charge you $500 a day."

This client makes $20 a day, and can't even afford to take those five days off work because he'll lose his job.

He pleads guilty to a crime when both he and his attorney know he is innocent. Is this justice?

This goes on every Monday morning in courts throughout the nation. We call it "expediting the calendar." When are we going to expedite the rights of human beings, which is the real job of officers of the court?

It literally takes a million dollar defense to get even a semblance of justice for a political client. This makes our legal system irrelevant for 60 million Americans. They cannot get justice in our courts.

The administration of justice is as far behind the times as is our economic system, which makes 40 to 50 million Americans live off charity

*Adapted from Charles R. Garry, "Who's An Officer of the Court?" *Trial* 7(Jan/Feb 1971):18–20.

or wait for war to come along to get employment. Our courts provide support for the economic system that creates a ghetto oppressed by our so-called vested interests. And this will go on until "power to the people" becomes a reality and there is democratic apportionment of wealth in this country.

Why do the courts support the present system? Who are the judges? Most are former district attorneys, insurance company or big business lawyers, political hacks. According to statistical studies, 10% of the bar controls 90% of the legal business, while the other 90% of the bar—the plaintiff's personal injury lawyers, the criminal defendants' lawyers, the probate lawyers and family lawyers—are fighting over less than 10% of the legal business. This 10% of the bar picks the judges and decides whether the rest should be disbarred.

In the case of federal judges, the situation is even worse, because they are picked for life. Some become drunkards, get senile, lose all concept of humanity. Some develop "federalitis"—you can't talk to them, you can't get rid of them.

Can we permit this archaic system to last? Sure, there are some good federal judges. But I am willing to sacrifice even the good ones to get a system under which bad judges can be challenged peremptorily because of prejudice.

If that happened once or twice, these judges would start becoming human beings and recognize lawyers as true officers of the court—not just errand boys in the courtroom.

Now the judge is an absolute monarch in his courtroom. There is really no way to get rid of him. Sure 28 United States Code §144 says you can refuse a federal judge, but it's almost impossible to do, because he passes on his own qualifications.

To compound the problem in federal court, the judge picks the jury. You can submit questions to the judge, but it's up to him.

In the Chicago 8 conspiracy trial, the defense submitted 160 questions. Judge Hoffman did not ask one. His idea of voir dire was: "Mr. Jones, can you be fair?" Is there anyone on the jury panel who cannot be fair?" Dead silence.

If Hitler were on that jury, he would have answered yes, he could be fair.

I have had federal judges take my voir dire questions and proceed to read them off, in one long paragraph, to the jury as a group. If no one raised a hand about it, that was that. But, if I were to ask a question like that of a witness, it would be objected to as a compound question.

The voir dire is very important. How else can a lawyer get a cross-section of the community? How else can he find out whether he can have some rapport with the jurors? Whether a prospective juror is biased against his client?

I used an extensive voir dire in the Huey Newton case. It is detailed in the book *Minimizing Racism in Jury Trials* (National Lawyers Guild, Box 673, Berkeley, Calif.).

Remember we live in a country where, according to the Kerner Commission Report, two-thirds of the people are either overtly or latently racist. This makes our legal system irrelevant for 60 million Americans. How can a black, brown, yellow, or red man get a fair trial?

Look at the Panther 21 in New York: The judge sets bail at $50,000 and $100,000. This is denial of bail. The defendants are in jail for months before trial. While in prison, they see white defendants charged with actually committing the overt acts they are charged with conspiring to commit, but never committed, and these white militants get $10,000 or $20,000 bail.

So, for 60 million Americans there is no justice. What can a lawyer expect to accomplish in such a situation? I don't think he can make the system work. It won't work until some basic changes are made in the society, and these changes won't be made through the courts.

The lawyer can only try to give temporary first aid, try to protect dissenting men and women, and in the process, try to expose the chicanery, the fraud, the sham, and the injustice that he encounters.

Lest I be accused of exaggerating, let me grant that the lawyer can make the system work when he is handling a common old fender-bending case or an ordinary rape or clean-cut murder case or even when he's representing the Maifia, who have a certain political power.

The judge who was a district attorney for 30 years will still treat him with respect. But just let him come into court with a political client, and the rules change. All he can hope to do is to convince one or two jurors that this defendant should not be railroaded into prison. The most he should expect is a "hung" jury.

Thus, the lawyer's role is to expose what's going on in the judicial system.

The lawyer must present his case with all the strength at his command. If there is disruption in the courtroom, it is the judge who is the cause of it, and the attorney must make him aware of it. I don't recall a single case, including the Chicago and New York cases, in which there was any interruption or disruption that was not brought on by the judge himself.

Judge Hoffman is a classic example. When the lawyers refused to be window dressing, he cited them for contempt. It is no answer to put a Kunstler in jail for representing clients who have come to the conclusion that America is failing in its responsibilities, that white militants must join their black, brown, red, and yellow brothers in fighting degradation.

As Huey Newton says, "You can put a revolutionary in jail, but you can't jail the revolution."

I know that some lawyers think what I've said is just propaganda. Brothers and sisters, if you think that, it's a lot later than you think. When black Americans have come to the point where they have no confidence in the white man's court, where the police come into the ghetto and brutalize them, where the judge railroads them to prison without a jury of their peers, then lawyers, as a primary part of the white establishment, must do something about it or they are failing in their own obligation to prevent oppression in the courtroom.

I sound very pessimistic, because when I look around at what's going on in our beloved America, I can see that lawyers have contributed to the chaos and oppression. We have become the spokesmen for the establishment, under the guise of "due process of law and democracy."

The only ray of light I see is the lawyers who are beginning to inquire. If we start inquiring and self-evaluating, we can begin to find an action-answer—not just rhetoric. Unless we change now, we are doomed.

I don't have the answers. Lawyers who take up this fight will find their own solutions as they become involved. Then, we will be able to stand up and say, "Yes, we are officers of the court."

ABRIDGEMENT OF THE CONSTITUTION*

... Democrats, goaded by the President and the attacks of the Vice President, proclaimed proudly that ... "every major anti-crime and anti-pornography proposal has been passed by the United States Senate." Among them:

The Organized Crime Control Act of 1970, which includes a provision permitting judges to impose thirty-year sentences on anyone convicted of a felony if the judge decides that the defendant is "a dangerous special offender"—meaning, in simple language, when the judge concludes that the person in question is a bad guy. The bill, moreover, abridges Constitutional safe-guards against self-incrimination and the use of illegally obtained evidence. In its analysis of the act, the Bar Association of the City of New York declared that the bill sweeps "far beyond the field of organized crime. ... The bill as presently drafted [and subsequently passed] frequently hits targets which were not intended and misses those which

*Adapted from Peter Schrag, "The Law-and-Order Issue," *Saturday Review* 53(Nov. 21, 1970):26, 86.

were. ... Even more disturbing is the impatience which [the bill] shows for constitutional safeguards."

The District of Columbia Omnibus Crime Bill, now signed into law, which gives police the authority to search premises with a warrant but without announcing their presence and demanding entry (the no-knock provision) and which many lawyers regard as a violation of Constitutional prohibitions against illegal search and seizure. The act also provides for preventive detention—the incarceration without bail of criminal suspects who appear, in the judgment of a magistrate, to be likely to commit further crimes if they were free. In effect, the act allows a judge to imprison a suspect before trial; although existing inequities of the money-bail system have resulted in the incarceration of thousands of legally innocent suspects, the D.C. act, rather than eliminating the injustices, institutionalizes them. The administration considers it a model for the nation.

Neither of these acts nor any others recently passed by Congress deal with the substantive inadequacies of earlier crime bills. ...

In all of their eagerness to improve "law enforcement," neither Congress nor the administration has ever shown serious interest in appropriating funds to reform prisons, which happen to be the most intensive breeding grounds of crime in America.

If the problem were limited to the danger of specific Congressional acts—dangers of omission and commission—it would be serious enough. But the climate produced by the rhetoric of the past year is likely to produce even more damaging effects. The cry for law and order has encouraged local prosecutors, police, and grand juries to crack down on dissenters, to intimidate unpopular figures, and to initiate criminal proceedings of dubious merit. Civil liberties organizations around the nation have noted sharp increases in the harassment of students, teachers, university administrators, writers, black people, and other minorities. Dissenters are finding it harder to get jobs or to keep them. Students—especially those with long hair—are searched at random by state police, and demonstrators are now being routinely photographed by police agents on the street.

The crime control acts passed by Congress, many of them initiated by individuals representing racial backlash, tend to hit poor people more severely than they do the affluent. It is the poor who cannot afford high-priced legal talent, cannot raise bail, and cannot defend themselves against the intricacies of the legal process; it is the poor who are more likely to be regarded as bad risks, as potential criminals, and as "dangerous special offenders." But it is also the poor—and the black—who are, and always have been, the special victims of local police raids, of unexplained shootings, and of violent acts inside or outside the station house. ...

PENTAGON PAPERS REVISITED*

*Although the "Pentagon Papers Trial" is now over and the defendants
exonerated, it would be unwise to forget it. By means of the trial, federal
government officials attempted to establish principles that are clearly
totalitarian: a provision for unlimited state secrets, legal punishment for
violation of executive orders, and charges of espionage without regard to
intent. These and other important aspects of the Papers affair were
succinctly described, toward the end of the trial, by John Kincaid who
participated in the defense effort.*

. . . The Founding Fathers regarded secrecy along with large standing
armies as serious threats to democracy. Secrecy, by its very nature, is
anti-democratic. It excludes people, including Congress, from decision-
making; curtails freedom of speech for government officials; insulates
government criminals from public justice; and places the public in the
position of having to make un- and ill-informed electoral decisions. Yet it
has been precisely in the name of national defense, of protecting Americans
from foreign tyranny, that the Executive Branch has constructed an iron
curtain of secrecy between itself and the people in order to conceal its own
international and domestic tyranny.

Last year Congressman William Moorhead noted that "there are 55,000
arms pumping up an down in government offices stamping 'confidential' on
stacks of government documents; more than 18,000 government employees
are wielding 'secret' stamps; and a censorship elite of nearly 3,000 bureaucrats have authority to stamp 'top secret' on public records." Rep. Ogden
Reid estimated that the Pentagon holds 18 piles of classified information as
high as the 555-foot Washington Monument.

William G. Florence, a retired Air Force officer with 43 years experience
as a Pentagon classification expert, has testified that at least 99.5% of these
documents do "not quality for classification and protection in the defense
interests of the nation." Yet the practice continues and, according to
Florence, "at least $50 million a year is still spent on storing, protecting
and inspecting unnecessarily classified defense information."

The mystique of state secrets has become so pervasive that even
Congress is spellbound. Not only is Congress often denied information even
upon request, but Congress has denied itself information. For example,
since 1949, none of the 200 bills introduced to make the CIA more
accountable to Congress has passed. In fact, only two even got out of
committee. When Senator Gravel released NSSM-1, "the Kissinger Papers,"

*Adapted from John Kincaid, "Do Not Probe Your Secret Govern-
ment," *Sane World* 11(December 1972):2.

to his colleagues, many accused him of breaking the law even though Congress has never passed a classification law.

Congress also practices its own form of secrecy. In 1971 the Senate Armed Services Committee held 79% of its meetings behind closed doors; the Agriculture Committee, 33%; the Foreign Relations Committee, 43%; and the House Appropriations Committee, 92%.

While the government is increasingly invading the privacy of foreign nations and American citizens, it is undertaking intensive in-house and judicial actions to secure its own secrets. Chief among these is the Pentagon Papers Trial. . . . The constitutional gravity of this case has been overlooked in the publicity surrounding its events and personalities.

The first charge is conspiracy to defraud the government by "defeating its lawful governmental function of controlling the dissemination of classified" information. Although "conspiracy to defraud" charges are common, this is the first case charging conspiracy to defraud the government of a function that is not clearly lawful. Criminal charges must be based on statute, but in this charge there is no statute. Congress has never given the President statutory authority to establish the classification system. The system was established by Executive Order for internal housekeeping purposes. People who compromise that system have previously been subject to administrative reprimand, not criminal prosecution.

In this case the government is claiming implied statutory authority based on the Freedom of Information Act, which contains an exemption clause regarding material "specifically required by Executive Order to be kept secret in the interest of the national defense or foreign policy." This novel interpretation of the Freedom of Information Acts lays the groundwork for an Executive decree system. If Ellsberg and Russo are convicted of breaking not a law but an Executive Order, then in seizing its full complement of "implied powers" the Justice Department will be able to prosecute others under this and other Executive Orders.

According to the 65-year history of U.S. espionage law, the disclosure of classified information is a crime *only* when that disclosure is made "with intent or reason to believe that the information to be obtained is to be used to the injury of the United States, or to the advantage of any foreign nation. . . ." Yet, in this case, for the first time, the government has cleverly excluded "intent."

The exclusion of "intent" means not only that Ellsberg and Russo will not be able to tell the jury why they xeroxed the Pentagon Papers (and thereby the moral and legal issues of the war). It also means that American citizens can now be charged with espionage for giving fellow American citizens information about "their" government. By excluding "intent" the government is placing the American people in the category of an alien power.

It should be noted that the copying and leaking of classified information are regular practices in Washington for which no one has ever been charged with "spying."

The theft charge is equally unprecedented. In the indictment the government charged Ellsberg with stealing the physical volumes and Russo with receiving this stolen property. But during the pre-trial period when it became indisputably clear that the government did not own the physical documents copied by Ellsberg and Russo, the government re-defined the indictment to charge them with stealing "the arrangement of the words on the pages and the ideas conveyed by that arrangement."

In a brief *amicus curiae* for ACLU, Melville Nimmer, the country's leading expert on copyright law, said that this is the first time in American history that the government has claimed a property interest in information. There is no precedent and no basis in law for the charge of stealing information from the government, and setting such a precedent now would overturn the rights of Americans as guaranteed by the Constitution.

TWO KINDS OF JUSTICE*

Three of the major defendants in the Watergate case—Herbert Kalmbach, Jeb Magruder, and John Dean—were released from prison after serving only a few months of their respective sentences. They and members of their families talked to newsmen:

Herbert Kalmbach, natty in a three-piece suit, told a news conference he had "renewed appreciation and confidence in the essential fairness of America's justice" and even hoped that his "actions have served to strengthen the pillars of justice."

Jeb Magruder was welcomed home with yellow ribbons round the old oak tree—actually a cherry—in his suburban yard. Neighbors gathered to greet him with a friendly banner.

Mrs. John Dean said it was a great way to start the new year and that her husband had been "sufficiently punished."

How easily is the world turned upside down! With an unexpected stroke of his pen, John Sirica—the old "hanging judge" himself, the scourge of Watergate—turned loose three of the major participants in the biggest political scandal in American history, one being seen by more and more people as having threatened the very foundations of democratic government.

*Tom Wicker, "American Justice," *The New York Times*, 10 Jan 75.

Mr. Kalmbach's response was worthy of a Kafka story. He got off with six months, mostly in quarters for Government witnesses, and as a result his confidence in the "fairness of American justice" is renewed. Some people spend more time than that in jail merely awaiting trial on minor larceny charges. Mr. Kalmbach, who sold an ambassadorship, fancies that his having pleaded guilty to a felony and a misdemeanor, as well as testifying against former colleagues, actually "strengthened the pillars of justice." But first, he and the Watergate gang came as close as anyone has to pulling down those pillars.

As for Mr. Magruder's neighbors, their generosity toward a good family and community man does them credit. Such generosity is virtually nonexistent, however, when the ordinary convict shuffles out of the prison gate in a state suit with a few grudging state dollars in his pocket and no job, little ability to get one, and no yellow ribbon around the stunted splinter that may pass for a tree in his ghetto neighborhood.

And if four months of minimum security confinement for John Dean is sufficient punishment for a man prosecutors say was the key man in the Watergate cover-up before he became the key man in the prosecution, what is it when a high school dropout gets fifteen years in New York for possessing more than an ounce of marijuana? What is it when black radicals like Jim Grant and T. J. Reddy get 25 and 20 years in North Carolina on arson charges by witnesses paid thousands of dollars by the Federal Government? What is it when Martin Sostre spends five of his seven years in four New York prisons in solitary confinement for refusing to knuckle under to prison rites like mail seizures and rectal searches?

It is being suggested, of course, that, as in the case of Richard Nixon, who goes free on $55,000 a year, the loss of high office and political power as well as public humiliation make up for soft prison terms (seven months for Mr. Magruder). Aside from the fact that anyone who goes to prison, whether for four months at Fort Holabird or ten years at San Quentin, suffers humiliation and the loss of his job and family associations, the outlook for clever, educated, well-groomed and facile men like these three is quite good in a celebrity-conscious and success-oriented society. Yesterday's scandal is tomorrow's lecture tour or best seller; old felonies can found new careers, as witness that busy entrepreneur, Spiro Agnew.

It is true enough that all these men ultimately helped the Government crack the Watergate case and convict the other culprits; but it also is true that they could have blown the whistle at any time but never did until faced with the necessity to save their skins as best they could.

In the cases of Mr. Dean and Mr. Kalmbach, bar associations could levy harsher penalties than the law has by barring them from legal practice. But to the millions of low-income, disadvantaged, unskilled and uneducated

Americans, so many of whom have good reason to view the law with fear and distrust, the whole episode is likely to be another demonstration that there is one kind of justice for them, and another for affluent, educated persons with good lawyers and "standing" in their communities.

The rest of us, without further recriminations against Mr. Dean, Mr. Magruder, or Mr. Kalmbach, might take time to ask ourselves what a crime really is. A street mugging is abhorrent, a break-in demands severe punishment; but are betrayals of public trust and subversion of the laws by officials sworn to uphold them really to be considered lesser crimes, on the practical scale of the penalties that result?

In Prison and Beyond

PRISONER #122054*

Photographer Danny Lyon spent 18 months in Texas prisons while photographing and talking to prisoners. Prisoner Billy McCune was most memorable.

Billy McCune was born in a shack across from Baylor University about forty years ago. His father was a World War I veteran, an epileptic who sold pencils and ice cream in front of the Waco County Court House. His mother was Luddie Kincaid. In his teens, Billy was adjudged to be feebleminded and sent to the Mexia State School for Feebleminded Children. After leaving the state school he entered the Navy and visited Sing Toa, China. Eventually Billy was discharged from the service for ineptitude.

In 1950, at the age of twenty-one, he returned to Fort Worth. Without work and without funds, he got a little money by breaking into parking meters. Then one night in a parking lot opposite the Liberty Theater in Fort Worth, Billy McCune raped a woman. It was the first and only serious crime of his life. The circumstances of his crime and the character of his victim were never completely clear. Billy stood trial for the crime of rape and, because of his outbursts during the proceedings, the young man was handcuffed and tried in chains. Billy was found guilty and sentenced to die in the electric chair.

The initial newspaper accounts of the crime described it as the brutal

*Adapted from Danny Lyon, *Conversations with the Dead*: Photographs of Prison Life With the Letters and Drawings of Billy McCune #122054 (New York: Holt, Rinehart and Winston, 1971), pp. 11-12, 196.

rape-beating of a Fort Worth housewife. Billy was placed in the county death house to await execution. One evening he cut off his penis to the root and, placing it in a cup, passed it between the bars to a guard. After being hospitalized, Billy was returned to the death house. Five times a date was set for his electrocution and five times the execution was postponed as a legal fight ensued to save Billy's life. Evidence was brought forward that seriously questioned the character of the victim and whether there had been any violence at the time of the crime. In the final appeal hearing before the judge, a relative of the victim questioned whether a rape had occurred at all. In 1952 his death sentence was commuted to life in prison.

Over eighteen years after those events took place I met Billy McCune in prison. The first seven years of his sentence he had spent in virtual solitary confinement, in the old segregation unit of the Walls. It was a maximum security unit within a maximum security unit designed for a few hundred of Texas' most dangerous convicts. When the unit was abolished he was transferred to the Treatment Center of the Wynne Farm, and that is where he is now.

In September 1970, at Rice University, Mr. Lyon's photographs and Mr. McCune's drawings were displayed; McCune wrote:

This is what I would say if I were allowed to be present on September 10, 1970. This pattern should cope with questions anyone might ask.

Dear and Respective Citizens of Texas. . . .

I have rotted away by physiological stress and strain by consumption. And I have learned through the reality of experience that the two little words with big meaning, 1. Pathos and 2. Ethos, mean. Surely if I ever come out of this grave I will do so a sadder and wiser aspect of the human organism, from the innerthoughts of reflections, which in the future tense shall be my retrospections.

Looking back at my ghost and phantoms of what I had lost and knowing in my heart I have nothing to show for it and when I think about my past, I am consoled by Winston Churchill's famous words, "I have nothing to offer but blood, toil and tears." So in my art and my expressions, my feelings of the type of life I have lived is all I have to offer to the art and literary world, how my eyes and ears react to stimulus from this point of intersection of so many quantitative variables. I now weigh about 130 pounds. Am sexually decapacitated. Have not a tooth in my mouth. Not too many strands of hair atop my noggin. I am growing old, tired (worn out) and sad mentally. I do not know how many days, weeks, months or years I have left of my inheritance from mother nature. I brain-wash myself and you people also that I have learned from the sad experiences of reality. So therefore, I say to you, *if it is now—after twenty years* within the hearts and minds of the authorities of this state to release the accused and convicted that it is my sincerest and profoundest hope and prayer to the unknown God to depart from the state and never return. I do *not* claim this present state as my native land, as my heritage and destiny. I feel no relation to it nor to any of its inhabitants. I have had many sad and unpleasant nightmares about dying here, bottled up in disection and being sent to Galveston. So you see, I pray to be freed under the inter-state parole system probably to New Mexico and should there be any question as to what I propose to do there in my new dimension, let me suggest it may be basic or essential to install me in a little part time job there with a humble shack to keep the grapes of wrath off my head.

So in conclusion, I, Billy G. McCune, behind the gray walls of Texas do now in advance, not knowing what will be your response on my effort (art composition) and the above without sophisticated technique in the prose of flattery, I am indeed impressed beyond description that people would lower their posterity by contributing this time and energy to a social misfit, a born loser and an outcast such as I, there be no retraction or happy reunion, and yet as one skeleton said to another in the catacombs of oblivion, I do not and am not presently in a condition to react to the art perspective. All I know is that all things work for the good for those with a grain of good. To you all these words: a time for crime, a time for punishment, torment and tears and pain. A time for work but not for play and at last the time to lie down in the dust and die, so good bye to one and all from B. G. M.   #122054

AMERICA'S HUMAN GARBAGE DUMPS*

Prison is the only garbage dump we have that is so repulsive we encircle it with barbed wire and a stone wall.

You get there in a closed van and the doors of the van don't open until the big iron gates have clanged shut behind you. You aren't released until a group of old men like no old men you ever knew decide you are something like a nice tractable person now. For years you don't touch the hand of a woman or child, wear clothing of your own choice, go somewhere on the spur of the moment; you don't eat what you feel like eating, talk to whomever you'd like to talk to, read a magazine you happen to see on the stand and find interesting. That is because there are no women and

*Bruce Jackson, "Beyond Attica," *Transaction* 9(Nov/Dec 1971):4, 6-7, 10.

children in prison (save those beyond the wire grills of visiting rooms), and all the clothing is the same in prison, and there are those walls and barbed wire and bars to keep you from going anywhere at all; it is because the only food you get is what the mess hall manages to set out that day or what you can hustle on the side; it is because conversations in prison are guarded or tight or secret and there are no telephones with which you may have casual chats with casual friends, and there are no magazine stands on which to find that potentially interesting magazine.

Prison is a place where all sorts of things are not there.

What is there hurts: sameness bars, guards on towers with guns, guards walking the halls with clubs who find you strange and alien and perhaps even hateful and evil because you've been adjudged a criminal by a group the law insists represents your peers. They look at you with fear or hate or contempt, perhaps only because you're a nigger or a spic or perhaps just because they don't know what is going on in your head, and that alone is frightening enough to make them hate you or fear you. And you them— hate and fear are always bilateral affairs. In addition to the guards are the people you must live with—other convicts: suspicious, mean, guarded and as frightened as you are perhaps, surely as mistrusting as you.

The days are short, the nights interminable. In most prisons in this country there is little for inmates to do, so men spend up to 18 hours of each day locked in small cells, waiting to be tired enough to sleep, waiting for sleep to descend long enough to break up the boring run of days in which almost nothing happens save an occasional letter from home, a fight to watch, an argument to have, a hustle to make.

What work there is in prison is usually demeaning and boring: inmates are paid humiliating wages (New York 30 cents a day, California up to a dollar for a few, Texas nothing at all) for tedious and often exhausting and usually uninstructive work (picking cotton, stamping out license plates on an ancient machine in extreme heat, pushing a mop, and—yes—even break- ing rocks).

A good inmate is one who makes no trouble for the institution. He may do whatever he wants—have homosexual affairs, run gambling concessions, deal dope, brutalize his fellows, peddle soft jobs—but so long as he is quiet about it and makes no trouble the administration cannot ignore, he will not be bothered by guards and he will be paroled out reasonably early in his sentence. A bad inmate is one who makes ripples, someone who complains about treatment or food or lack of educational opportunity or humiliation by guards; a very bad inmate is one who talks such things up among his fellows; an outrageously bad inmate is one who suggests to his fellows that they do not have to stand for such treatment, who tells them that the courts may have sentenced them to punishment by incarceration but that does not mean the prison authorities have any duty or right to punish them further. Such inmates do the maximum amount of time the law permits, for authorities—parole boards and such—feel they are not fit to be released in society for they have not learned how to "get along."

California for years has ridden along on the crest of a prison reputation that derived from some petty changes it made over 20 years ago. But California prisons are cesspools, where inmates with politically deviant ideas are locked away for years in euphemistically named "Adjustment Centers," prisons within prisons where men are locked in cells 23½ hours every day and given nothing to do, where guards and convicts engage in a spiraling game of mutual brutalization. There is no appeal from commitment to an Adjustment Center, there is no right to know why one was placed there or who one's accusers are, there is no chance to present evidence on one's own behalf. California has the indeterminate sentence—a pretty idea that says fit the punishment to the criminal and not the crime—that results in longer sentences than most other states, for the time in prison is fixed by a board of ex-law enforcement officials all appointed by the governor, and their desiderata of good citizenship have little to do with anything but internal order of the prison.

Texas makes sure it has a good parole statistical show by paroling people only very late in their sentence—that means there are very few parole violators and officials can say their parole workers do good work. New York's parole system is capricious and arbitrary; people are returned to prison for the silliest of reasons and without the most basic legal rights. In much of the North, prison officials encourage racial disharmony among inmates because they know if the inmates are hating and fighting one another they will have little energy left to hate and fight the prison administrators. Occasionally that backfires and the inmates get together and say, "Hey, *we're* not our enemies." California solves that problem by locking everyone up (half the inmates at San Quentin are in 24-hour lockup; 280 have been moved to special lockup cells. New York solved the problem with high-powered rifles and shotguns so eagerly triggered they gunned down hostages and inmates alike in a greedy fusillade that articulated law enforcement anxieties we can be sure no state official will ever honestly admit.

"I know of no institution," says Texas Department of Corrections Director George Beto, "unless it be organized Christianity, which has shown a greater reluctance to measure the effectiveness of its varied programs than has corrections." But almost everyone—observers, prison administrators, convicts—feel American corrections are a dismal failure; I know of no public official other than Spiro Agnew who thinks they do any real good at all. We have the longest prison sentences in the West and the greatest problem in the West with our prisoners and our ex-prisoners. Something is surely screwed up.

The problem is a well-known one in public policy: the lawmakers say they want the institution to do one thing, the people who run the institutions know that isn't what the lawmakers mean at all. The lawmakers say they want reform, but there is money only for hardware and guards; the lawmakers say the prisons should make better people, but only take notice what goes on when someone escapes or goes berserk. No warden has ever been fired because no inmate was helped in any noticeable way while under his care, but quite a few have been fired because some inmates in their care found the prison so horrid they chose to go over the wall or burn down the buildings.

People are more educated about prisons than they were three months ago: they know something about San Quentin, something about Attica, they wonder about the secrecy, the brutality, the racism, the prices paid. There are noises for legislation: hardly anyone objected to the first 28 demands of the Attica convicts, demands that would move the prison toward a condition of minimal decency; they were the same demands made by Folsom inmates two years ago, *none* of which was granted. There will be committees, lots of committees, and they will make reports that will be distributed and filed.

But we've all read those reports before and know that one function of committees and reports is to make it unnecessary to engage in other action: the investigations and the writing-up of the investigations become ends in themselves, and we are all properly decathected by that time, for we've read the reports and shaken our heads and agreed with no mean passion with the conclusions.

Meanwhile, the same wardens are there, the same walls are there, the same old guards are there. Most of the wardens came up through the ranks in this business of no lateral entry, most of the walls are superfluous and expensive, most of the guards have no training whatsoever in anything but the use of their club or rifle.

Great wrongs have occurred, but who will be punished? The guard who killed three black convicts for fighting at Soledad was not indicted, nor was there even an official statement that fighting is not necessarily an offense punishable by death; none of the state police who went berserk in Attica will be indicted, just as the guardsmen at Kent State and the police at Jackson were not indicted. Some inmates will be indicted, and a lot of inmates will have no formal charges placed against them, but will spend years before a parole hearing again has any point for them.

I remember after the Democratic Convention in Chicago in 1968: the squares were informed and outraged, the cops really *do* beat people up indiscriminately; that's not just a bunch of stories made up by niggers, freaks and dope fiends. And I remember how it faded. And I see around me how the cops still freely do just what they did in Chicago, the only difference being they are a little more free with it now because they have learned that not even the once awesome power of the press (Cronkite was enraged, NBC was saddened) brings down any real heat. No police went to jail for Chicago. That's one reason they were so free to shoot at Jackson State, Kent State, at Fred Hampton's apartment, at all those other places. The squares just shook their heads and said, "See, more of the same."

No public official in California has raised a voice in outrage at the hundreds of men locked 24 hours a day in cramped and crowded cells for no prison crime other than that the warden of San Quentin thinks they *might* be harboring political thoughts about the death of George Jackson last August.

I worry that all the present concern will dissipate, will attenuate, will dribble away in trivial cocktail conversations about "How awful it is isn't it yes it is someone ought to do something really I wonder who it will be maybe tomorrow."

I worry that prisons will continue operating as they have because after the heat dies down and the various commissions self-destruct, we will once again leave the operation of prisons to those whose job it is those who "know what they are doing." And we will help them do that job simply by not telling them they really do have to stop it now.

I think here of a priest I know in one prison who a few years ago was telling me his experiences on Death Row giving counsel and comfort to condemned men on their way out. Some of his stories were witty and entertaining and I chuckled and nodded along with everyone else. Some time later, it occurred to me that those executions probably could not have occurred without the priest's cooperation and tacit approval: his presence laid the sure hand of church and social righteousness on sending 12,000 volts of juice through some shaved and oiled poor bastard who was too dumb to cop out when he was first arrested or too poor to get a sharp lawyer. Not only did the priest literally help seat the man in the chair, but he lent the moral tone to the event that made it socially legitimate. I wonder what would have happened if the priest boycotted the execution, if he had screamed, "This is murder!" I suspect the warden would not have been so quick to push the button, the newsmen would have gone bananas. But the priest didn't do that, of course, and no one expected him to; he disapproved of executing people, but it wasn't his job to scream "This is murder!" His job was only to grease the condemned's way into the Promised Land.

Prison is perhaps necessary to protect society from the violent, but no more than 10 percent of any prison's population is really violent, and most of those people should be receiving psychiatric help (if that can be made to work) rather than simple lockup anyway. Prison is supposed to reform, but who—after all this evidence to the contrary—can suppose men are reformed by being locked for years on end in six-by-nine-foot cages in communities where homosexuality is a norm, mistrust a necessity, and hate a social commodity? What kind of foolishness informs a parole board which assumes a person who adjusts well to *that* sort of community is fit to come back outside and someone who challenges it should be welded away forever?

Confusion, violence and repression seem more and more common in prisons, and more and more inmates are responding with riots, strikes, assassinations and sabotage. The institutions are cracking at the seams and though one hopes they will crack enough to let in some light and decency, one fears they will again snap shut like a giant sea clam, suffocating in darkness everything and everyone within.

And they will blow up again. There will be more George Jacksons, men turned bitter as gall by years behind a welded door, there will be more Atticas, men spitting back in the face of almost certain death because they find that defiance preferable to the slow death of day-after-day living in brutality and squalor and lawlessness.

There is a simple economy to the social effects of the operation of public institutions: when public institutions make primary decision on the basis of internal institutional priorities their ultimate social utility decreases accordingly. What makes for good management of prisons does not necessarily make for good treatment of offenders, what makes it possible to run a prison neatly does not necessarily make it possible to send once-convicted men back into society ready to be free men.

When public institutions make their decisions without reference to the needs of the public which they presumably serve, we get a range of disasters: the killing of Fred Hampton and other Black Panthers is within that range, the development of the war in Vietnam is within that range, the harassment of the poor by welfare workers is within that range. The police make decisions on the basis of what makes sense within the police perception of the world, the military set priorities on the basis of what makes sense within the military perception of the world, the welfare worker doles out money on the basis of what makes sense in the welfare worker's perception of the world. And time and again we find ourselves with the sour feeling that the police or the military or the welfare agents have sold us out: they've worked out their own hustle, we haven't been protected or served, our money has been thrown away and our energies have been squandered.

The same thing has long gone on in prison; the only difference now is more people suddenly know about it because a lot of inmates recently refused to submit to the foolishness of their keepers. It was there all the time, that anger, that injustice, that perfectly absurd counter-productivity.

Our chickens have once again come home to roost, and once again we learn that the first thing the returning fowl does is shit all over the henhouse. Our decision is whether to get used to the stink and live with it or take on the unpleasant job of cleaning it up.

But Americans, sadly, seem able to become used to almost anything.

SCANDAL IN VIRGINIA*

When a patient in a Virginia state-prison hospital named Edward Belvin threatened to scream if he was not given medicine, he was summarily thrown into solitary confinement, and chained to the cell bars—his neck taped agains the bars—for fourteen hours. Then Belvin, a sixth-grade dropout who reportedly had attempted suicide, was left naked in his tiny cell for seventeen days. In the course of a ten-year term for robbery, a prisoner named Robert Landman was forced to spend 266 days in solitary and another 743 days locked in his regular cell—all without benefit of a hearing, apparently for nothing more than serving up legal advice to fellow inmates. Philip Lassiter, a black prisoner with a record of mental disturbance, died in solitary of sickle cell anemia, after screaming unheeded, literally night and day, for nearly a week. The brutal episodes were among dozens of cases cited by a Federal judge last week in a scathing, 74-page decision that exposed Virginia's entire correctional system as a showcase of what is wrong with American prisons today.

The ruling came on a class action filed against Virginia's top correctional officers in April of 1969 by five inmates of Richmond's old, red brick state penitentiary. Attorney Philip J. Hirschkop, who pleaded the inmates' case, promptly hailed it as "a bill of rights for inmates." And indeed, although the decision by U.S. District Judge Robert R. Merhige Jr. is still subject to appeal, it is at least a step in that direction. Merhige held that the Constitution's due-process clause applies to convicts as well as to free citizens. To insure that they get the protections it affords, the judge devised a set of minimal procedural standards and prohibitions for prison officials—and ordered that they be implemented immediately.

Merhige's directives were prompted by a 25-page compendium of alleged

*Newsweek 78(Nov. 15, 1971):39.

abuses culled from ten days of testimony by Richmond inmates. The abuses date back over a six-year period, but Merhige stressed that they represent common penal procedures, not isolated incidents. There were numerous tales of prisoners who were fed nothing but bread and water, of forced nudity, nightstick beatings and the use of chains, handcuffs, tape and even tear gas for punitive restraint—punishments, prisoners charged, that were sometimes dispensed for nothing more than attempting to communicate with their lawyers. One inmate who was sentenced to solitary confinement for "loud talking," Merhige noted, was chained to his bars for five days, and not even released to relieve himself.

The state's "segregation units"—maximum-security compounds that cut off supposedly hard-core felons from the rest of the inmates—were worse still. And prisoners were as arbitrarily assigned to segregation as they were to solitary, Merhige noted. Once inside, prisoners sometimes forfeit any time toward early release they may have accumulated through good behavior. In the worst of the units, Richmond's notorious C-Building, a walled, 100-man prison-within-a-prison dubbed "little Alcatraz," some prisoners have languished for months without a hearing—and parole, says Merhige, is "almost nonexistent."

JUNGLE LIFE*

Crime roots in many soils and is nurtured by many forces—poverty, drugs, mental aberration, perhaps even faulty chromosomes. But far and away the most fertile ground for the cultivation of criminals is the prison system.

Every year 2.5 million American men, women and children are locked up in local jails, state or federal prisons, awaiting trial for offenses ranging from shoplifting to murder, from political demonstrations to treason.

During confinement, they undergo a stunning variety of experiences. And in many cases, their ordeals depend less upon their crimes than upon their places of incarceration.

They may wait, drunk or sober, in the vomit-infested drunk-tanks in Denver. They may put in 12-hour days picking cotton behind a gunline in Mississippi.

They may be beaten with paddles in Tennessee, be thrown nude into totally dark isolation cells in Maryland, be raped by members of their sex in New Orleans or Philadelphia.

*Adapted from Nicholas Horrock, "U.S. Prison System Exemplifies Life in 'Jungle'," *Newsweek* Feature Service, Feb. 14, 1971.

They may cut the tendons of their legs as a means of protest in Kansas. Out of desperation, they may hang themselves in New York.

All this might make its grisly kind of sense if the nation's prison system accomplished what it sets out to do—to make the punishment so painful that crime will not be repeated.

But somewhere between the crime and completion of the punishment, the system goes awry. As a result, within five years after their release, 70 percent of the men who have spent time in prison will be locked up again, many for a more serious crime. In fact, according to the Presidential Commission on Law Enforcement and the Administration of Justice, the average first-time offender will become involved in at least three additional arrests.

"In many ways, our system nurtures criminals with the same care the Air Force Academy turns out second lieutenants," Jo Wallach, task force director of the Presidential Joint Commission on Correctional Manpower said. "The only difference is that most of society believes we are deterring people from crime, and some of the public even believes we are rehabilitating them."

Seldom, indeed, has so little been accomplished for so many at so huge a cost. The U.S. prison system costs taxpayers more than $1 billion every year. It employs 200,000 guards, correctional officers and custodial personnel.

Yet all the system ever has accomplished is to put the problem and the prisoners temporarily out of sight and recently even this dubious accomplishment has not been performed satisfactorily. The nation's prisons and jails are becoming a good deal more visible than they used to be.

In the first place, they are picking up a different sort of clientele. Previously, prison populations were comprised almost exclusively of the poor and uneducated. Only rarely, as in cases of "financial criminals" such as embezzlers, or occasional "crime of passion" murderers did a member of the educated middle class end up behind bars.

But the drug scene and the protest movement brought a sprinkling of new blood to the old system. Lately, the sons and daughters of the white middle class have been exposed to experiences that once were reserved for the poor. Moreover, feeling little or no guilt for the offense for which they were arrested, these new "criminals," and their families have been willing to speak up afterwards. . . .

Young women have complained bitterly of the humiliating physical searches performed by prison personnel. There have been allegations of corruption by prison officials, of inequities in the courts, of almost casual brutality by guards—slapping, pushing and the like. One of the most frequent charges is that older, bigger prisoners make homosexual rapes on new young prisoners and that the guards permit it to occur.

Society never quite has decided whether prisons are primarily for rehabilitation or for revenge.

If rehabilitation is the goal, the work barely has begun. But if the aim is to punish the criminal for his offenses against the straight, square world, to degrade him and make his life behind bars as miserable as possible, then the goal has been achieved many times over. Yet this achievement, if it is achievement is due to the men who are nominally in charge of the prisons than to the men who run them—the inmates.

"I have never understood," New York's parole board chairman, Russell G. Oswald, said, "how we believe we can take sick people, lock them up with a lot of other sick people, do nothing to cure them and then expect them to turn out well."

It has been said many times over that to live in prison is to live in a jungle. This is manifestly unfair to the measured, logical and, above all, natural world of the wild. Prison life is a perversion of the rules of nature and, predictably enough, it produces a perverted society.

In Washington's jail, for example, any young white man weighing less than 150 pounds is likely to be the unwilling host of a "blanket party." As soon as the guards leave the barrack-like dormitories, a blanket is thrown over the new arrival's head, dozens of hands pummel him and series of unseen men commit homosexual rape upon him.

The guard force is inadequate to control the situation. Usually there is one guard posted outside each 50-man dormitory.

"He's not going to enter that dorm at night even if he thinks 10 people are being murdered," Kenneth Hardy, director of Washington's Department of Corrections, said. "What's more, the victim wouldn't identify his attackers even if he could, but he usually can't. We find him beaten and bleeding on the next round of the guards and take him to the hospital."

Washington prisons, of course, have no monopoly on the gang homosexual rape. It goes on all across the country. An investigation by the Philadelphia district attorney two years ago revealed there were at least 1,000 aggressive homosexual assaults a year in the city's jails and prisons. Some even took place in the van between court and the jail buildings.

"Virtually every slightly built young man committed by the courts is sexually approached within a day or two after his admission to prison," the report said. "Many of these young men are overwhelmed and repeatedly raped by gangs of inmate aggressors. Others are compelled by the terrible threat of gang rape to seek protection by entering into a "housekeeping' arrangement with an individual tormentor."

The investigation uncovered other chilling facts. Two-thirds of the aggressors in these attacks were in jail for serious, assaultive crimes; on the other hand, the victims usually were charged with minor offenses.

Conditions are nearly as bad in women's prisons and in some there is a pattern of complicity on the part of the staff. . . .

"Nobody seemed to care about that stuff around there," a former inmate of the Washington jail said. "There was a matron who used to sit in the room where we watched television while the girls were making out, and she never did anything. She just stared."

Other forms of corruption are common in the nation's prisons. Drugs, especially, are available for a price. They come in taped to the undersides of trucks. Girls pass them to boyfriends with a kiss on visitors' day. Guards are in on the traffic.

Everyone has a deal, an angle, a gimmick. An inmate of a Maryland institution made $1,700 in three years selling Benzedrine inhalers for $3 each. He kept $1, paid $2 to the guard lieutenant who brought them in.

Food is a regular source of graft. Though inmates of most prisons are fed on budgets of 60 to 80 cents a day, even these spare rations always do not reach the prisoners. "Sandwich men" who buy or steal meat from the galley go about at night selling meat sandwiches. One man made $40 a day, splitting the take with the prisoner staffer who gave him the food.

Money buys everything, not only all types of drugs and pills, but the privilege of being moved from one cell to another to join a homosexual partner, or to get away from one. Many guards are bribable; some meet the bribe more than halfway.

"You lean on a guy a little bit . . . harass him . . . jostle him . . . write him up," a guard who was fired from a Maryland institution recounted. "Then one day you tell him, 'It doesn't have to be this way,' and the next time his wife comes to visit him, she brings $10 for you. You've got to pick a guy with a little money, that's all."

How do they get away with it all? Why isn't the public up in arms at the way its $1-billion-a-year-prison system is being run?

In part, a reason is that the public would just as soon not know. The prisons at least serve the function of burying the criminal, for the time being, and what goes on behind the walls comfortably is invisible to the average American who happens never to have gotten in trouble with the law.

But the invisibility is cultivated carefully from within by prison staffs. With considerable success, prison officials control all the information that flows in and out. Personal letters are censored, letters from unauthorized persons stopped.

In the vast majority of cases, it is impossible for a prisoner to complain to an outsider, even an elected official, about his treatment. If he smuggles such a letter out, the chances are that he will become a victim of retaliation by the staff.

. . . .

The emphasis in the U.S. prison system is almost entirely custodial. People don't get helped in jail; they just get filed away.

Two-thirds of the local jails sampled by the Presidential Commission on Crime and Delinquency had no rehabilitation program.

Though most state and federal prisons and juvenile schools do have "programs," the paucity of money and staff make them ineffective. Only 50 psychiatrists or psychologists work directly with the 220,000 adult inmates in state and federal prisons, a ratio of one counselor to 4,000 prisoners.

For a population group noted for illiteracy or little formal education, there are only 900 academic prison teachers, one for every 225 prisoners.

Job-training, by and large, is a joke. There are a few promising projects going on, computer-training in Massachusetts and furniture-making in California, but these are the rare exceptions.

Unions oppose the teaching of craft skills in prisons, employers are slow to hire ex-cons and most jail-taught skills are unusable. "Did you ever try looking for a job making license plates?" one bitter veteran of the U.S. prison system asked.

Even for juvenile offenders, where the need for education is perhaps most pressing, the programs are pathetically inadequate. In fact, juvenile prisoners generally get the worst of the bargain in almost every jail.

For example, only Mississippi and Arkansas officially permit the whipping of adult felons. But five states—Indiana, Virginia, Tennessee, Idaho and Montana—legally allow the strap or the paddle to be used on children, while outlawing the practice on adults.

This kind of arbitrary use of power pervades all penal institutions and, more than anything else, it creates a smoldering sense of injustice among the prisoners. In fact, the resentment often starts with the sentencing process.

A flurry of muggings on the outside will raise judicial concern, and sentences. Men who would have gotten five years for a crime will get 10 and the longer sentence seldom will make them more contrite.

Maryland Commissioner of Corrections Joseph Cannon said: "You can imagine how a kid feels when he comes here to do three years for car-stripping from the Eastern Shore (a rural Maryland area) and finds some guy down the line with a six-month bit for the same offense in Baltimore."

Lately, there has been some evidence of a trend toward shorter sentences. Several lengthy investigations have been made to learn how much deterrence the threat of long sentences provides. The answer seems to be: not much.

The California Assembly commissioned one such study, with special attention to the situation in Los Angeles where sentences for assaulting policemen had been increased greatly.

"After five years of increasing penalties," the report concluded, "a Los Angeles policeman was almost twice as likely to be attacked as he was before the increases."

On the general subject of longer sentences, the report also declared:

"If the assumption that severe penalties reduce crime were true, government could, though at considerable expense, control crime effectively. Unfortunately, the assumption is not correct. This expensive system does not work."

From a prisoner in San Quentin, who has spent half his 40 years behind bars, there is corroborating testimony. "Nobody stands there with a gun in his hand," he said, "and tries to remember whether armed robbery is a 5-to-15 or a 20-to-life." . . .

Prison authorities, many as slow to learn a lesson as the prisoners they supervise, have been reluctant to change their approach. For the vast majority of men behind bars, prison is a bleak, hopeless and ultimately counterproductive experience.

"I suspect," psychiatrist Karl Menninger wrote in his book, "The Crime of Punishment," "that all the crimes committed by all the jailed criminals do not equal in social damage that of the crimes committed against them."

INTRIGUE AND PERVERSION*

"After many years of degradation, humiliation and living a life of intrigue and perversion, you ask me to step from my 'den of iniquity' into your paradise and you expect me to make this transition overnight. I marvel at your naivete.

"Fate stirs the finger of fear within me. Like a wild beast I shall soon be unleashed to prey amongst you. I have survived my ordeal in this concrete and steel jungle and I am ready for the hunt."

WHERE IS THY VICTORY?**

The prison cannot gain a victory over the political prisoner because he

*From an interview with a just-released prison inmate, *New York Times,* Feb. 11, 1970.

**Adapted from Huey P. Newton, "Prison, Where is the Victory?" *The Black Panther,* Jan. 3, 1970, centerfold.

has nothing to be rehabilitated from or to. He refuses to accept the legitimacy of the system and refuses to participate. To participate is to admit that the society is legitimate because of its exploitation of the oppressed. This is the idea which the political prisoner does not accept, this is the idea for which he has been imprisoned, and this is the reason why he cannot cooperate with the system. The political prisoner will, in fact, serve his time just as will the "illegitimate capitalist." Yet the idea which motivated and sustained the political prisoner rests in the people; all the prison has is a body.

The dignity and beauty of man rests in the human spirit which makes him more than simply a physical being. This spirit must never be suppressed for exploitation by others. As long as the people recognize the beauty of their human spirits and move against suppression and exploitation, they will be carrying out one of the most beautiful ideas of all time. Because the human whole is much greater than the sum of its parts, the ideas will always be among the people. The prison cannot be victorious because walls, bars and guards cannot conquer or hold down an idea. . . .

TERMINAL DISEASE*

. . . "No one really wants to believe what goes on behind those walls that bury men, who, for various reasons are serving prison sentences, justly or unjustly. Here a revolution is being born and nurtured that defies belief. The blinded taxpayer supports a system that, if continued, as presently administered and structured, will destroy him. Of the men who leave the prisons of this country, 60 percent return; 15 percent—or more—continue a life of crime and are never caught. Why? Why do the 60 percent return? Because the men are angry, bitter, destroyed, and dehumanized. Neither within the walls of the prison nor on the outside are they given a chance to function as human beings with dignity and honor once the stigma of a prison term has been stamped upon them. Why did Mayor Lindsay of New York say the prisoners' grievances were justified? Why did he lay much of the blame on the courts of the nation? Because our system of justice has prostituted the word justice. Can anyone know what it is like to serve 10 years for a five-year sentence? A man's parole can be violated for as simple

*Wife of a Terminal Island Federal Penitentiary inmate, as quoted by Bruno St. Jon, "The Terminal Disease," *Los Angeles News Advocate*, Oct. 16, 1970:2.

a thing as a traffic ticket. If his tone of voice is irritated when replying to the traffic officer, he may be slapped into prison again. No wonder these men are angry." . . .

Americans Under Surveillance

The first article which follows seems uncannily prophetic given the late '74 and early '75 revelations about the CIA. To those in the know, the recent charges that the CIA has violated its charter by spying on Americans have a yawning "So what else is new?" quality about them. Much more serious is what may reasonably be inferred from this spying of Americans on Americans; as David McReynolds points out, it signifies a basic flaw in American society. It is not the CIA, or the FBI, or Army intelligence, or city "anti-subversive" squads that are corrupt so much as the kind of society that spawns such units. In addition, intelligence activity directed against political dissenters is corrupting in itself. In the words of a 19th century Englishman, Sir Erskine May:

> *Nothing is more revolting . . . than the espionage which forms part of the administrative system of continental despotisms. It haunts men like an evil genius, chills their gayety, restrains their wit, casts a shadow over their friendships, and blights their domestic hearth. The freedom of a country may be measured by its immunity from this baleful agency.*

THE CORRUPTION OF AMERICAN LIFE*

. . . For me, the most shocking aspect of the information we now have on the CIA is the extent to which the CIA represents the corruption of American life. A little spying between enemies is a friendly and accepted thing. But the relationship of the CIA to the NSA [National Student Association—ed.] (to pick out only one relationship among many) reveals to how profound an extent the American government has become the enemy of American values.

At the risk of being called a red-baiter for going back over old (but historically accurate) ground, let me compare the present situation to the

*Adapted from David McReynolds, *We Have Been Invaded by the 21st Century* (New York: Praeger Publishers, 1970), pp. 228-231.

REWARD
FOR INFORMATION LEADING TO THE APPREHENSION OF —

JESUS CHRIST

WANTED — FOR SEDITION, CRIMINAL ANARCHY —
VAGRANCY, AND CONSPIRING TO OVERTHROW THE
ESTABLISHED GOVERNMENT

DRESSES POORLY, SAID TO BE A CARPENTER BY TRADE, ILL —
NOURISHED, HAS VISIONARY IDEAS, ASSOCIATES WITH COMMON
WORKING PEOPLE THE UNEMPLOYED AND BUMS. ALIEN —
BELEIVED TO BE A JEW ALIAS: 'PRINCE OF PEACE, SON OF
MAN'—'LIGHT OF THE WORLD' &c &c PROFESSIONAL AGITATOR.
RED BEARD, MARKS ON HANDS AND FEET THE RESULT OF
INJURIES INFLICTED BY AN ANGRY MOB LED BY RESPECTABLE
CITIZENS AND LEGAL AUTHORITIES.

'TWAS EVER THUS

rise of McCarthyism. I have always held that the Communist Party itself helped make McCarthyism possible. During the late 1930's and throughout the 1940's, the CP gained very real influence within this nation. It held key posts in publishing houses, school systems, trade unions, and the government. Those posts were gained and that power acquired through hiding one's membership in the CP, moving up in the bureaucratic chain of command and winning power or influence through the sheer inertia of a seniority system. Various front committees were set up, enlisting, for the purpose of the letterhead, non-Communist public figures. The Communist Party did use deceit to win its moderate influence and power, and it justified that deceit by arguing that, if it were more honest, it could never have won such influence. The end justified the means.

The result, however, is that, when McCarthy emerged and made his insane accusations, they had a ring of truth. Since virtually all Communists denied ever having been Communists, the mere fact that a man insisted on his innocence might be seen as proof of his guilt. And those who might otherwise have defended the Communists in their time of troubles had been so burned and embittered at having earlier been used for political purposes with which they did not agree, and were so furious at having found their organizations subverted and their personal trust abused, that they became, too often, pathological in their anti-Communism. The secrecy of the Communists fed the paranoia of McCarthy, and, while I think that period was one of the most disgraceful in the history of our nation, the Communists must share in some part of the blame for the hysteria we term McCarthysim. Privately (of course not publicly), I think some CP leaders would now agree with me.

Yet we have done precisely this with the CIA. We have betrayed not only foreign trade-unions or foreign press-associations—which, God knows, would be evil in itself—but we have turned subversion upon ourselves, against our own citizens. I have no sympathy for the NSA leaders who sold out—but there were only a handful of those. What of the hundreds and thousands of students within NSA (or within any of the other organizations subverted by the CIA) who trusted their leadership and believed in the integrity of the policies their organizations adopted? A handful of the members of these groups will regret that no one offered them a slice of the CIA pie—but most of the members have been hurt in the terrible and dehumanizing way that we always hurt someone who trusted us and whom we then betray.

Even on a practical level, we are going to suffer. Every Peace Corps worker will now be suspect. Every dedicated archeologist working in the sands of time in Egypt or India will be looked upon as an agent. Every scholar will be doubted when he travels abroad. Every tourist will be seen as a spy. All of the positive work of American voluntary organizations working throughout the world will now be very much harder. What victories the CIA gained in the short run, it will lose in the long run, with interest.

But the price we will pay does not end there. Now that we know we have government that believes lying and deceit is not something for exceptional circumstances but simply standard operating procedure, it is a vast understatement to say our credibility has been weakened. Why, if the CIA could invade Cuba and could involve itself in the slaughter of between 300,000 and 500,000 Indonesian Communists and pro-Communists, should it not have arranged for the murder of Malcolm X? The French have been hostile to us in part because they think we plotted against de Gaulle several years ago. The French are probably right—but even if they are wrong, who would now believe any denial from the White House? There are those who believe John Kennedy's murder was the result of a plot in which the FBI and the CIA were involved. That is a fantastic, lunatic, paranoid charge. The trouble is it might also be true. And whether it is true or not true, many citizens will find it quite possible to believe that one part of the government plots the assassination of private citizens or even of public leaders: all that we have learned inclines us toward that kind of paranoid view. We have really corrupted something without which a democracy cannot endure very long—a sense of trust and good will that, to some extent, cuts across even class lines. The men who run the CIA are brilliant at tactics but very stupid in working out their long-range results.

But I return to an earlier point—I do not blame the CIA. I blame *us*—our society. We are lacking in moral fiber, as Goldwater used to tell us in 1964. That inner lack is not indicated by the amount of love-making going on among the kids, or by the fact they smoke pot, or by the fact homosexuals are more open now than they once were. The morality of a nation is not judged by how it makes love. Our corruption is shown by something quite different—our willingness to treat people as commodities that can be bought and sold. The CIA buys the NSA, and the liberals object because they feel it was either clumsily handled or unnecessary, while the conservatives object to the fact that anyone objects at all. It hasn't seemed to occur to many people that what the CIA did was morally wrong. And that those who knew about it and tolerated it or authorized it were also morally wrong.

When we talk about "morality" and the lack of it, about the "corruption of our youth," we like to take off after the queers and acid heads and pot heads and pornographers. It is painful to realize the corruption is not there at all—it was in Eisenhower and Kennedy and Stevenson and *The New York Times*. They were willing to buy off the world if they could get away with it. The CIA isn't a monster of some kind—it is just a reflection of us. We will buy off a revolution, if we can, and, if we can't, then we'll get nasty and use napalm.

The CIA is being justified on the grounds that every method that will defeat Communism is valid. But why, may I ask, were we trying to stop Communism in the first place? Was it not because Communism—particularly as we saw it under Stalin—used individual human beings as means and not as holy, unique, and absolute ends? What is the difference, really, between an American society run by the CIA and the Pentagon and one run by the Russians? (If I were given a choice, I'd opt for the former only because I am a poor student of language and don't think I could learn Russian.) It may be that, in some sense, the Ruysians or the Chinese are our enemies—in a very distant sense. But, in terms of immediate reality, it is *our* government that is subverting us. The "invasion of totalitarianism" is already well under way. Washington is the headquarters, and all of us are collaborators unless we begin to remind the government that there are some things decent and loyal Americans do not do. . . .

SURVEILLANCE AND THE DEMOCRATIC PROCESS*

The author of this selection is Frank Donner, a lawyer who directs the American Civil Liberties Union's Project on Political Surveillance at Yale Law School. In another publication he observed, "It would be difficult to overstate the threat a political surveillance system poses to the democratic process. Yet it cannot be denied that never before in American history have so many governmental agencies engaged in political surveillance, and never before have there been so many objectionable surveillance practices" (Civil Liberties, Feb 71, p. 1). *Some of these practices and agencies are described by Mr. Donner in the following paper which he originally prepared for the 1974 Chief Justice Earl Warren Conference on Advocacy—Subject: Privacy in a Free Society.*

Law enforcement and crime prevention require the investigation of suspects. This is a fact of life, and no sensible person thinks that such an investigation, properly conducted, constitutes an invasion of privacy.

However, when the state undertakes an investigation of someone because of his or her political beliefs or associations, it crosses over into a wholly different territory. The search for actual or potential enemies of the government necessarily involves enormous numbers of people, whereas

*Adapted from Frank J. Donner, "Political Intelligence: Cameras, Informers, and Files," *Civil Liberties Review* (Summer 1974):8-25.

conventional criminal investigations are usually limited to a few. Political investigations delve deep into the lives of suspects, rather than being concerned with one activity. In order to make a judgment about a subject's politics, an investigator may find it necessary to probe his habits, visitors, sex life, reading preferences, use of leisure time, views on topics of the day, lifestyle, educational background, correspondents—and on and on. Moreover, the political investigator's occupational bias is invariably negative. His attitude is: Why take chances when the safety of the government is at stake? Ironically this exaggeration is virtually "built-in," for in our democratic system only a very great "danger" can justify such extraordinary intrusions on individuals.

A conventional investigation may alienate, even dehumanize, the subject, but it does not rob him of the means to alter the policies and decisions that have victimized him. Political surveillance tampers with the very process by which political change is brought about. It is not merely that political surveillance challenges the constitutional freedom of expression, as courts are beginning to recognize; it also destroys the precondition of such freedom by inspiring widespread fear and distrust. Because it is so broad, penetrating, and hostile, its impact far exceeds its literal reach and results in pervasive self-censorship. Political surveillance thus produces the greatest return of repression for the least investment of power.

The hostility that inevitably accompanies political surveillance tends to transform it from a means to an end in itself. And the gravity of its impact leads in a vicious circle to an exaggeration of the threat that it said to justify it. The investigator, sensing the fear in those he investigates, chooses to believe that it is their political "guilt" that makes them afraid. This atmosphere generates on the one hand a dangerous aggressiveness by surveillance agents, and on the other an evasive response by their target.

During the past decade, we have seen an extraordinary growth in political surveillance on all levels of government—federal, state, and local. This increase can be understood as a response to the proliferating protest movements of the '60s: the opposition to the Vietnam War, the demands for civil rights, the youth revolt, and the activities of the New Left. Intelligence agencies and police units became suddenly and painfully aware of the inadequacy of their techniques, the limitations of their coverage, and the uselessness of their files, which were choked with the dossiers of aging or dead radicals. There was an almost inevitable overreaction and with it a swift embrace of new technologies of identification and surveillance.

Two practices, which we might call "growth areas" of surveillance, particularly came into wide use. The first is photography, which has become a powerful weapon against political demonstrations and rallies; the second is infiltration, which is characteristically used against new political organizations. Both of them stimulate a torrent of data, which is then stored in files and dossiers. Taken together, these three aspects of intelligence represent an unheralded threat to our civil liberties.

The fact that the wave of protest appears to have crested has not diminished the threat of these intelligence practices. The history of political surveillance makes it disturbingly clear that techniques for monitoring dissenters become institutionalized and survive the unrest that spawned them. A survey of government's containment and repression of the recent movements for change leaves little doubt of the emergence of a pattern that may well become the model for governmental action at a future time of social failure.

A structural change in intelligence institutions has armed U.S. surveillance practices with a new capability. For many years intelligence institutions on all government levels operated in jurisdictional duplication and conflict. About a decade ago, local and national intelligence agencies began to coalesce into an "intelligence community." For example, the young demonstrators who came to Chicago in 1968 encountered "red squad" operators from their home towns who were cooperating with their federal counterparts, as well as with secret operatives from the army and navy. The new collaboration was also clear in the FBI's counterintelligence program, or "COINTELPRO," which began in the late '60s and ended in 1971. COINTELPRO was really a collection of seven programs of disruption and demoralization of political targets. The FBI coordinated and assisted urban police units in such activities as carrying out raids and making harassing arrests.

More generally, we must recognize the extent to which our culture has made intelligence acceptable, even glamorizing it. With the help of books and films we have built a fantasy system around spies and spying. As Patrick J. McGarvey wrote in his 1973 book *The Myth and the Madness*:

> Intelligence seems to be a virility symbol for many Americans—one that immediately equates the profession with such allegedly masculine ventures as murder, coup-plotting, intrigue, and a dash of illicit love-making. Their minds somehow entangle the violence of pro football, the screen antics of James Bond, and lingering World War II memories of parachuting behind enemy lines with an exaggerated sense of "duty, honor, country."

This fantasy system which glorifies the spy also paints his antagonist as inhuman. He is not an enemy, he is the "other," the image by which we negatively define ourselves and celebrate our virtues. The antagonist is almost supernaturally crafty and seems to win every round, only to be foiled at the very end by the courage and resourcefulness of the spy-hero.

But how different are the real life Watergate spies: Liddy, Hunt, Ulasewicz, Segretti, McCord!

Watergate, however, has also shown that intelligence threatens to become a mode of governance, a way of exercising governmental power that outruns the forms of law. Some of the evolving techniques of operational intelligence need but be explored to make us aware of the dangers.

Photography as a political weapon. The sophisticated use of photography as a surveillance tool began only a little more than ten years ago. Prior to that time physical surveillance of political meetings and rallies was not uncommon. The role of the police was simply to collect literature, take notes on speeches, and check automobile license numbers. But with the eruption of ghetto unrest, peace protests, and campus activism, the picture changed.

The transformation of the intelligence role of the municipal police must be viewed in a context of mounting friction. To the policeman, public protest was an unwelcome disruption. His response to antiwar activities was particularly hostile because he saw himself as a beleagured defender of "patriotic" values. When protest became highly widespread and activist, he tended to use his authority aggressively to protect his threatened values.

The changed role of the police was flavorfully and frankly described by Inspector Harry Fox of the Philadelphia police in Senate testimony a few years ago. Inspector Fox said, "Police have now become 'watchdogs' and 'observers' of vocal, subversive and revolutionary-minded people." In Philadelphia, this function has been institutionalized in a civil disobedience unit of selected plainclothesmen.

> They cover all meetings, rallies, lectures, marches, sit-ins, lay-downs, fasts, vigils or any other type of demonstration that has ominous overtones. . . . These officers know by sight the hard-core men and women who lead and inspire demonstrations. They know their associates, family ties, techniques, and affiliations with organizations leaning toward Communism both on and off the Attorney General's list. They see them day in and day out recruiting, planning, carrying signs, and verbally assaulting the principles of our democracy. Yes, the police role has become one of . . . surveillance, taking photographs, identifying participants, and making records of the events.

The role of the policeman as an adversary of dissenters leads him into right-wing politics, and his professionalism is in turn undermined by his political values. As this process develops, the policemen is increasingly tempted to resort to harassment. His targets are quick to sense this personal quality. They feel forced either to respond in kind or to abandon their protest altogether.

In this conflict between the police and the demonstrators the camera plays an important role. Police agents in communities throughout the country nowadays systematically photograph all political and social protest activities. Any "incident" considered "controversial" is a predictable subject for the police photographer. In 1970 the photographers attached to the Philadelphia intelligence unit covered more than a thousand demonstrations. Activities in opposition to the Vietnam War were automatically considered "controversial," but not those in favor. In the South, integrationist racial protest was accorded top photographic priority. . . .

Photography has—and is intended to have—an intimidating impact on the subject. Most police functionaries will privately admit this, although their public justifications for the practice are quite different: they say they need to have a record "in case there is a disturbance," or, the photographs are just an instructional tool in lectures to policemen on "crowd control." The true purpose is exposed when it turns out, as it often does, that the police cameramen have been pretending to snap pictures long after they have run out of film. When asked about this, a member of an antisubversive unit explained, "Sometimes I go out on an assignment with an empty camera. Just taking the pictures cools the agitators." . . .

The chilling effects of informers. If photography is the hallmark of the urban red squads, the infiltration of informers is the favorite surveillance mechanism of the FBI. Surveillance agencies on every level of government use political informers, but the bureau's use of them is far more pervasive.

There are three sorts of political informers: the defector, or renegade; the "plant," who is recruited for the express purpose of infiltrating a target group; and the informer, who is "in place," i.e., already a bona fide member of a group.

The defector can supply information about the group's size, composition, and leadership, but cannot serve as a source of continuing information. He "cooperates with the FBI" first through a process of debriefing and then as a witness. But even as a witness the defector has questionable value. His bias and eagerness for revenge frequently break through his recitals on the witness stand.

The plant is the most common kind of informer, and generally the most productive. A former FBI agent, Robert Wall, described the plant's advantages to me in 1972:

> Your best bet . . . was to get somebody who was completely unconnected with the organization, preferably somebody on the college campus, some kid who was young enough to fit in the group, had time to spare and was willing to cooperate, and then put him in the group cold. . . . It was rare you got an informant who was already established in an organization because first of all you couldn't talk to him without getting the door slammed in your face . . . so you usually tried to recruit somebody fresh and new.

From the FBI's point of view, the plant has an advantage as a witness even over the "in place" informer or defector: it is easier to claim that he was motivated purely by patriotism and is untainted by feelings of guilt, revenge, or self-justification. . . .

There is no way for an informer to avoid betrayal. In order to overcome suspicion he must become friendly with his target and share the social life of his victims. His wife and children must be used to further the deception. He wins trust in order to do his targets injury. Not that men are grudging of their trust. On the contrary, we accept the stranger because trust is a human need. This vulnerability, this need to trust, prevails even when the risks are obvious. The victim is shamed by his doubts because they mock his humanity. In short, the informer preys on what is best in us.

Emerson Poe was the best friend of Scott Camil, a Florida leader of Vietnam Veterans Against the War. The two spent much time together. Camil's girl friend, Nancy McCown, visited Poe and his wife on many occasions. When Mrs. Poe had a miscarriage, Miss McCown helped with the household chores. She and Camil also visited and helped out when Poe became ill, and on one occasion helped decorate the Poe's Christmas tree. The Poes were hospitable and helpful to their friends, too. They organized a surprise birthday party for Miss McCown at their house and invited her parents. On August 17, 1973, Poe appeared as a surprise witness against Camil in a federal prosecution, and testified that his relationship to Camil was instigated by the FBI, that his friendship was simulated, and that he had been a paid informer from the beginning.

Many targets find it difficult to accept the fact that the informer is a plant rather than a defector whose initial commitment was abandoned out of weakness, fear, or pressure. This consoling, self-protective interpretation may well be an accurate version of the inner reality. The informer is rarely untouched by his intended victims or their cause. The plant gives a great deal to the target group and its members. Some of his contributions are, of course, motivated by the need to preserve his cover. But an informer rarely confines himself to the minimum required to disarm suspicion. To be sure, his contributions typically embrace such routine organizational chores as distributing leaflets, attending meetings, securing financial support, and proselytizing for new members. In addition, the spy frequently contribures some special skill or resource which increases his value to the group. He may be an expert chauffeur (like Gene Roberts in the Panther 21 case), a well-muscled bodyguard (like Robert Pierson in the Chicago conspiracy case), may enjoy a unique degree of mobility and access to others (Boyd F. Douglas, Jr., in the Harrisburg conspiracy case), know where to buy dynamite (Raymond Wood, in the Statue of Liberty case), be familiar with explosives and firearms (Tommy the Traveller), have unusual financial resources (Horace Parker in the Seattle 7 case), or know how to solve technical problems (Robert Hardy in the Camden 28 case).

Even the more passive informer typically gives more of himself than the role demands. As another ex-student informer, William T. Divale, put it to me:

> I began to like the people and to enjoy being with them. They cared about me in a way that was new to me. Besides, I learned a lot and I got turned on—at first by the program and then by the actions. When I led the campus demonstrations I did it because I wanted to. Of course, when I got home that night I wrote it up in my report. But I began to feel like a shit.

In short, many informers betray not only their targets but themselves. . . .

Where it all ends up: files and dossiers. It is the special need to feed names into the file system which makes the informer such an important intelligence source. Files are the working capital of intelligence. They offer to the agency that controls them an assurance of continuity and funding even when the political climate is unfavorable.

The mere fact that data appear in a file becomes a warrant of its truth and accuracy, however dubious it might otherwise be. Stanton Wheeler has observed in his 1969 book, *On Record*, that "a file or dossier is likely to attain a *legitimacy and authority* that is lacking in more informal types of communication. . . . We talk about the kind of record a person develops, typically meaning the sorts of formal evaluations contained in files and dossiers." The arrangement of a mass of material into subversive classifications, of events into a chronological sequence, of names by alphabetical order, can somehow surround a body of questionable data, assembled by the most arbitrary and unreliable standards, with the aura of objectivity and professionalism. The serried ranks of file cabinets join the microscope, camera, and electronic transmitter as valuable instruments of scientific investigation.

Political files reinforce and deepen the restraining effect of surveillance. Their mere existence, no matter how limited their access, inspires fear. Files "document" the intelligence professional's thesis that dissent is a form of political original sin, and that it is the vigilance of intelligence that has until now warded off the holocaust planned by the subversives. Files create a usable past; they impose on the political life of an individual a history he cannot erase; they make him a "subject" tied forever to political views and associations that he may have abandoned long since.

The informer is encouraged to give the highest priority to the identification of individuals, and not to concern himself too much with "line" or theory. As ex-agent Robert Wall put it, "The great stress with your informant is on names, especially of the leadership and then, from there, report names of individuals who are a moving force in the organization, who are the committee chairmen, who are the organizers."

Here is a description by a recently resigned FBI agent of how the informer's reports are processed for filing in individual and organizational dossiers:

> In D. C. we have an individual file and an organizational file. . . . We start out by investigating an organization; then when we had compiled a big file on the organization itself, we'd start investigating all of the officers in the organization on an individual basis and then prominent members of the organization, also on an individual basis. Each one of these people would have a separate file on them and into that file would go, first of all, all the background information we could dig up on a guy—from whatever source we could get it from. Then we'd go into all of the informant's statements that identified him at a given meeting or at a given demonstration or rally. That also would go into the reports from other agencies, that this guy had done such and such.
>
> The agent then summarized and interpreted the reports and this would mean his interpretation of everything that was said about the guy. Any subject that was going to be around or was in a prominent position, the agent would have to report on to the bureau. And he would do this by making up a report, which was supposed to be a kind of factual report, but he would take and extrapolate from all this mass of information he got from an informant a synopsis or a summary of all the activities the guy had been in.

The information collected in political surveillance frequently has little immediate value, but is considered vital for long-range purposes. It is classified as "strategic" intelligence and consists of biographical files and indices. Names are important because surveillance operations are premised on the politics of deferred reckoning. Such files are "warehoused"; that is, they are stored and kept current against a time when information about the subject's background may become valuable. It is routine for a filing system to preserve records of behavior or transactions dating back 20 or 30 years. After all, a seemingly obsolete entry dating back to the '40s might provide a vital clue to a subversive conspiracy. The best gauge of the political slant of a subject is the way the twig was bent long ago.

Intelligence files are used by the intelligence "community" to help its friends and discredit its critics. Urban red squads leak file material to friendly officials and reporters. The New York City red squad (the Bureau of Special Services or BOSS) made this a regular practice until the late '60s. At the 1963 libel trial brought by John Henry Faulk, the blacklisted news commentator, it was revealed that one of the defendants, Vincent Hartnett, had operated a highly profitable "smear and clear" service in which he investigated people in the entertainment world and used the threat of exposure to extract "investigative" fees from sponsors. When Hartnett was asked on the witness stand to reveal the source of his information, he testified that he had called BOSS Leiutenant Thomas E. Crain some 70 times, and on occasion he received information from BOSS files.

In 1970, Philadelphia's anti-subversive police chief, George Fencl, boasted to a nationwide television audience:

> We have made a record of every demonstration that we handled in the city of Philadelphia and reduced this to writing, first by report and then taking out the names of persons connected with the different movements. We have some 18,000 names and we made what we call an alphabetical file. We make a 5 by 8 card on each demonstrator. ... This card shows such information as the name, address, picture if possible, and a little rundown on the person ... which group he pickets with and so forth. Also, on the back of the card we show the different demonstrations, date, time, and location and the groups that the person has picketed with. We have some 600 different organizations that we've encountered in the Philadelphia area.

Frank L. Rizzo, first as Philadelphia police commissioner, then as mayor, used these files to silence his critics. In the course of a feud in 1967, he told members of the board of education, "I've got enough on every one of you ... to run you out of the city." When he ran for mayor in 1971 he boasted to the press that he "had something on" all of his opponents in a primary election.

FBI director J. Edgar Hoover's exploitation of files was far more ominous. The bureau's total collection (not confined to political subjects) consists of acres of files and six-and-a-half million index cards which are increasing at the rate of nine hundred thousand a year. These cards list both primary subjects of investigation and individuals who are collaterally referred to in the files. Hoover used the files to blackmail hostile legislators. According to recent verified disclosures, he even placed the bureau's investigative resources at the disposal of legislative supporters for use against political challengers. The FBI also cultivated a stable of friendly reporters to whom it regularly leaked file material damaging to its critics.
. . .

In contrast to many European countries, the United States has never in its history authorized a political police force, a special body responsible for the safety of government, independent of all other instruments of state administration and enjoying unlimited jurisdiction and autonomy. Rather,

American political intelligence is the illegitimate offspring of law enforcement. In times of stress, local and federal police units became identified with vital interests, and developed efficient techniques of entrenching themselves. Over the years, the operational intelligence modes of deception and manipulation were deployed against the political process: representative government itself became a "subject." The surviving, pervasive ambiguity in the authority to engage in intelligence reflects a barely suppressed conflict between our fears and our democratic commitment.

Once intelligence functions were institutionalized, the implementing practices—photography, informers, and files—were justified on the too-simple basis of "professionalism." After all, the intelligence functionary was the expert and knew how to accomplish his unit's "mission." The result is that agencies of government that pose an unacceptable threat to the democratic process itself have become virtually immune from accountability and correction. . . .

FIRST AMENDMENT ON TRIAL*

This story was written shortly before Roger Priest was court martialed and separated from the Navy "without honor."

"I believe that every man in uniform is a citizen first and a serviceman second, and that we must resist any attempt to isolate or separate the defenders from the defended."

—Richard M. Nixon

Roger Priest is resisting. He is resisting an attempt by the U.S. Navy to send him to jail for 39 years for the crime of printing a newspaper.

The Navy is afraid of Priest, apparently. When they first found out he was publishing a newspaper, they assigned no fewer than 25 intelligence agents to follow him. They transferred him out of a comfortable desk job at the Pentagon. They began writing down everything he said.

And they got permission from the District of Columbia Department of Sanitation to confiscate and scrutinize all of the garbage left for collection outside the apartment house where Priest lives—looking for the real dirt, no doubt.

As a result, Priest has become something of a celebrity. More has been written in the press about this tall, blond, 25-year-old Texan than about any other enlisted man in the history of the U.S. Navy. Not everyone, after all, is important enough to have his garbage examined by Naval intelligence.

*Adapted from Alan Lewis, "First Amendment on Trial," *Argus* 5 (student feature magazine, College Park campus, University of Maryland).

"During the month of May, 1969," Priest says in his quiet, rambling, down-home Southwestern drawl, "I started noticing some people following me, some pigs—that's what they are, too, they even look like pigs. They all dressed alike, looked alike with their crewcuts, a couple of them were big fat rednecks, ready to shoot anyone that's dissenting, to use any means at all to stop dissent.

"They don't care about stomping on people's Constitutional rights. I know that my mail's been tampered with, which is against the law. There were two pieces of first-class mail that they stole right out of my apartment.

"Everytime I would leave my apartment, I would be followed by these people. There would always be two agents in the car, and every car had the same kind of little radio antenna on the left rear fender, every damn one of them. One day driving across the city my roommate and I counted six different cars following us, each one with the little antenna on the fender, and two agents with crewcuts.

"And I hadn't even been charged with anything at the time."

The agents weren't trying to find something to charge him with. "They were trying to intimidate me. It wasn't surveillance. When a guy's being followed by the FBI he doesn't know he's being followed. These guys were standing outside of my apartment pointing up at my window, they would stand right in front of the building walking back and forth, and they had this little bitty wire coming down from their ears, like a hearing aid, and they would be talking into it."

Priest paused a moment to demonstrate how one surreptitiously talks into one's armpit, and then continued, more gravely. "I was really getting scared 'cause they had guns on them. I didn't know who they were. They looked too stupid to be FBI. The only thing I could figure was that they were trying to harass me into stopping the paper, to strike some fear into me.

"You don't follow a guy bumper-to-bumper if you just want to maintain surveillance. If you follow a guy bumper-to-bumper, you're trying to harass him."

CHARGE II. Violation of the Uniform Code of Military Justice Article 134.

Specification 1: In that Roger Lee Priest, journalist seaman apprentice, United States Navy, did, at Washington, D.C., on or about 1 April, 1969, with intent to interfere with, impair and influence the loyalty, morale and discipline of the military and naval forces of the United States, did cause to be printed and distributed a pamphlet entitled "OM, 1 April 1969, The

Serviceman's newsletter," which said pamphlet contained statements advising and urging insubordination, disloyalty and the refusal of duty by members of the military and naval forces of the United States.

Roger Priest wasn't always a revolutionary. He started out as an apolitical liberal, working with the student government at the University of Houston, and only very slowly underwent the long and tortuous process of radicalization that has turned so many nice young kids into effete, impudent snobs.

"How did a nice boy from Texas get into a thing like this? I joined the United States Navy."

. . . .

The process of dehumanization that is basic training started Priest's radicalization. "They just try to break a man down and build him up to their own image of what a man should be. As soon as you step out of the plane they have you standing at attention for several hours in the cold, just standing there for no reason."

"The first thing they do is give you a haircut, and I mean a real haircut, not what the Conspiracy got, they cut all your hair off. Then you're isolated from everybody. Then they start threatening you."

Protesting against what was going on was not easy, Priest remembers. "They point out to you in a very graphic fashion what happens to malcontents and resisters. They had this one company that they put troublemakers into, and they would have to wear pink hats. Everywhere that they went, they had to double-time, and they didn't do it on verbal command, they did it on the command of a whistle."

Recruits were forced to ostracize the dissidents and to ridicule them whenever possible. Tasks that would be too degrading for the worst fraternity initiation were assigned to the company of malcontents.

The San Diego Naval Recruit Station, where Priest was stationed, was right across the street from another radicalizing influence—a Marine recruit facility.

"We would watch young Marine recruits being brutalized by sergeants, and I mean brutalized, kicked and beaten right in broad daylight, in front of everyone. This wasn't in the back woods of South Carolina, this was right along a public highway. We'd see an ambulance following the recruits around the compound, and when one of those guys would straggle and fall they'd beat him and kick him, and then the ambulance would take him away, and we saw all this."

After basic training, Priest was sent to the Pentagon, where he served for a time as a public relations aide. It was there that his radicalization was completed. "You reach a point where you just can't take it anymore, where you rebel. You're backed up against the wall, and the strain is so great that you strike back. You're aware of what the consequences might be, but you do it anyway."

The breaking point for Priest was his court martial for willfully disobeying an order from a WAVE to stamp addresses on some envelopes. The whole thing, he says, was a misunderstanding, but he was busted from the rank of E-3 to E-2 and fined $75. The officer who heard his case was another WAVE and a friend of the woman whose order had been willfully disobeyed.

Reading about the Presidio affair further compounded the fracture suffered by Priest's moderation. He somehow couldn't believe that enlisted men had been sentenced to 16 years in jail for sitting down in a stockade yard and singing "America the Beautiful."

Priest's first overt act of protest was his participation in the counter-inaugural demonstrations in Washington last January, "when Nixon, his excellency, was being christened."

During the demonstrations he met Andy Stapp of the American Servicemen's Union. "I asked him what would happen if I started a newspaper. He said 'They'd probably transfer you and start processing you for a discharge or maybe they'd frame you up on some charge.'"

Despite this prognosis, Priest decided to go ahead with his newspaper. He also decided to designate the War Resister's League as the benificiary of his GI life insurance plan, an action that caused no small amount of consternation among the Navy power structure. It might start a trend, you understand, and just think what that might lead to. Having men killed in action wasn't so bad, but what would the Navy do if they had to pay the War Resisters League $10,000 per stiff? Priest had to be stopped.

An article about the *great insurance caper* appeared in the Washington Post on March 24, the same day that the first issue of OM appeared. Although Priest had religiously avoided violating Navy regulations, he was immediately removed from the Pentagon. Soon afterwards, he began being tailed by the garbage freaks from Naval intelligence. . . .

THE ARMY INVADES CIVILIAN LIFE*

The U.S. Army is collecting and computerizing information on the political activities of thousands of American civilians, a former Intelligence Corps captain has reported.

*Source: Article titled "Army Checks on Civilians, Article Claims," *Los Angeles Times*, Jan. 16, 1970; exclusive from the *Chicago Sun-Times*.

The former captain, in the Washington Monthly, reported that the Army Intelligence Command keeps watch not only on "violence-prone" groups, but also on such nonviolent organizations as the *National Assn. for the Advancement of Colored People, the American Civil Liberties Union and Women Strike for Peace.*

The article was written by Christopher H. Pyle, now a Ph.D. candidate at Columbia University, who served two years in Army Intelligence.

The Army Intelligence Command at Ft. Holabird, Md., declined immediate comment on the article.

According to Pyle, "military undercover agents have posed as press photographers covering antiwar demonstrations, as students on college campuses and as 'residents' at Resurrection City."

Daily reports on political 'incidents'—from protest speeches to major confrontations—are sent to every major troop command in the United States over a special nationwide Army wire service.

"The Army also periodically publishes an 8-by-10-inch glossy-cover paperback booklet known in intelligence circles as the 'blacklist'." Pyle siad.

"The 'blacklist' is an encyclopedia of profiles of people and organizations who, in the opinion of Intelligence Command officials who compile it, might 'cause trouble for the Army'."

The information is gathered by the CONUS (for continental United States) intelligence branch of the U.S. Army Intelligence Command, according to Pyle.

"Sometime in the near future, the Army will link its Teletype reporting system to a computerized data bank" that will be able to produce printouts in 96 categories including "personality reports" and "incident reports."

"The personality reports . . . will be used to supplement the Army's 7 million individual security clearance dossiers and to generate new files on the political activities of civilians wholly unassociated with the military," Pyle said.

The files, Pyle said, "are likely to be made available to any federal agency that issues security clearances, conducts investigations or enforces laws," including the Civil Service Commission, Secret Service and FBI.

Pyle said the Army has "long established legitimate responsibilities" requiring domestic intelligence, such as early warning on incidents likely to produce mass violence that the Army might be called in to put down.

This, he said, was the original purpose for creation of the CONUS branch in 1965, the year of the Watts riot in Los Angeles.

"In the summer of 1967, however, its scope widened to include the political beliefs and actions of individuals and organizations active in the civil rights, white supremacy, Black Power and antiwar movements.

"Today, the Army keeps files on the membership, ideology, programs and practices of virtually every activist political group in the country," said Pyle.

COURT UPHOLDS ARMY SPYING ON CIVILIANS*

Led by Chief Justice Warren E. Burger, a narrowly divided Supreme Court yesterday barred a trial of the Army's surveillance of civilians.

Burger said in the 5-4 decision that courts cannot serve "as virtually continuing monitors of the wisdom and soundness of executive action." That, he said, is a job for Congress.

The surveillance, conducted by some 1,000 agents beginning in 1965, was challenged in a suit brought by four individuals and nine groups, some of them war protesters.

Burger said they evidently wanted to use the courts to probe the Army's intelligence-gathering activities, with which they disagreed.

Instead of showing their freedom of speech had been injured or even threatened, the chief justice said, they presented allegations of a subjective nature.

Therefore, Burger said, the suit cannot be considered.

The ruling, reversing a federal appeals court here which had ordered a full-dress inquiry, was produced by the four Nixon administration appointees plus Justice Byron R. White. . . .

– – – – –

The system of *espionage* being thus established, the country will swarm with informers, spies, delators, and all that odious reptile tribe that breed in the sunshine of despotic power. . . . The hours of the most unsuspecting confidence, the intimacies of friendship, or the recesses of domestic retirement, afford no security. The companion whom you must trust, the friend in whom you must confide, . . . are all tempted to betray your imprudence or unguarded follies; to misrepresent your words; to convey them, distorted by calumny, to the secret tribunal where jealousy presides—where fear officiates as accuser, and suspicion is the only evidence that is heard.

Representative Edward Livingston,
New York, 1798—commenting on
the proposed "alien sedition" laws.**

*AP dispatch, June 27, 1972.

**Annals of the Congress of the United States, 5th Congress, Vol. 2 (Washington: Gales and Seaton, 1851), p. 2014.

Conclusion to Law and Order Selections

IS FREEDOM DYING?*

"Those, who would give up essential liberty to purchase a little temporary safety," said Benjamin Franklin, two centuries ago, "deserve neither liberty nor safety."

Today we are busy doing what Franklin warned us against. Animated by impatience, anger and fear, we are giving up essential liberties, not for safety, but for the appearance of safety. We are corroding due process and the rule of law not for Order, but for the semblance of order. We will find that when we have given up liberty, we will not have safety, and that when we have given up justice, we will not have order.

. . . .

Those in high office do not openly proclaim their disillusionment with the principles of freedom, but they confess it by their conduct, while the people acquiesce in their own disinheritance by abandoning the "eternal vigilance" that is the price of liberty.

There is nothing more ominous than this popular indifference toward the loss of liberty, unless it is the failure to understand what is at stake. Two centuries ago, Edmund Burke said of Americans that they "snuff the approach of tyranny in every tainted breeze." Now, their senses are blunted. The evidence of public-opinion polls is persuasive that a substantial part of the American people no longer know or cherish the Bill of Rights. They are, it appears, quite prepared to silence criticism of governmental policies if such criticism is thought—*by the Government*—damaging to the national interest. They are prepared to censor newspaper and television reporting if such reports are considered—*by the Government*—damaging to the national interest! As those in authority inevitably think whatever policies they pursue, whatever laws they enforce, whatever wars they fight, are in the national interest, this attitude is a formula for the ending of all criticism, which is another way of saying for the ending of democracy.

Corruption of language is often a first sign of a deeper malaise of mind and spirit, and it is ominous that invasions of liberty are carried on, today,

*Adapted from Henry Steele Commager, "Is Freedom Dying in America?" *Look* 34(July 14, 1970):16–21.

in the name of constitutionalism, and the impairment of due process, in the name of Law and Order. Here it takes the form of a challenge to the great principle of the separation of powers, and there to the equally great principle of the superiority of the civil to the military authority. Here it is the intimidation of the press and television by threats both subtle and blatant, there of resort to the odious doctrine of "intent" to punish anti-war demonstrators. Here it is the use of the dangerous weapon of censorship, overt and covert, to silence troublesome criticism, there the abuse of the power of punishment by contempt of court. The thrust is everywhere the same, and so too the animus behind it: to equate dissent with lawlessness and nonconformity with treason. The purpose of those who are prepared to sweep aside our ancient guarantees of freedom is to blot out those great problems that glare upon us from every horizon, and pretend that if we refuse to acknowledge them, they will somehow go away. It is to argue that discontent is not an honest expression of genuine grievances but of willfulness, or perversity, or perhaps of the crime of being young, and that if it can only be stifled, we can restore harmony to our distracted society.

. . . .

The philosophy behind all this, doubtless unconscious, is that government belongs to the President and the Vice President; that they are the masters, and the people, the subjects. A century ago, Walt Whitman warned of "the never-ending audacity of elected persons"; what would he say if he were living today? Do we need to proclaim once more the most elementary principle of our constitutional system: that in the United States, the people are the masters and all officials are servants—officials in the White House, in the Cabinet, in the Congress, in the state executive and legislative chambers; officials, too, in uniform, whether of the national guard or of the police?

Those who are responsible for the campaign to restrict freedom and hamstring the Bill of Rights delude themselves that if they can but have their way, they will return the country to stability and order. They are mistaken. They are mistaken not merely because they are in fact hostile to freedom, but because they don't understand the relation of freedom to the things they prize most—to security, to order, to law.

What is that relationship?

For 2,500 years, civilized men have yearned and struggled for freedom from tyranny—the tyranny of despotic government and superstition and ignorance. What explains this long devotion to the idea and practice of freedom? How does it happen that all Western societies so exalt freedom that they have come to equate it with civilization itself?

Freedom has won its exalted place in philosophy and policy quite simply because, over the centuries, we have come to see that it is a necessity; a necessity for justice, a necessity for progress, a necessity for survival.

How familiar the argument that we must learn to reconcile the rival claims of freedom and order. But they do not really need to be reconciled; they were never at odds. They are not alternatives, they are two sides to the same coin, indissolubly welded together. The community—society or nation—has an interest in the rights of the individual because without the exercise of those rights, the community itself will decay and collapse. The individual has an interest in the stability of the community of which he is a part because without security, his rights are useless. No community can long prosper without nourishing the exercise of individual liberties for, as John Stuart Mill wrote a century ago, "A State which dwarfs its men, in order that they may be more docile instruments in its hands . . . will find that with small men no great thing can really be accomplished." And no individual can fulfill his genius without supporting the just authority of the state, for in a condition of anarchy, neither dignity nor freedom can prosper.

The function of freedom is not merely to protect and exalt the individual, vital as that is to the health of society. Put quite simply, we foster freedom in order to avoid error and discover truth; so far, we have found no other way to achieve this objective. So, too, with dissent. We do not indulge dissent for sentimental reasons; we encourage it because we have learned that we cannot live without it. A nation that silences dissent, whether by force, intimidation, the withholding of information or a foggy intellectual climate, invites disaster. A nation that penalizes criticism is left with passive acquiescence in error. A nation that discourages originality is left with minds that are unimaginative and dull. And with stunted minds, as with stunted men, no great thing can be accomplished.

It is for this reason that history celebrates not the victors who successfully silenced dissent but their victims who fought to speak the truth as they saw it. It is the bust of Socrates that stands in the schoolroom, not the busts of those who condemned him to death for "corrupting the youth." It is Savonarola we honor, not the Pope who had him burned there in the great Piazza in Florence. It is Tom Paine we honor, not the English judge who outlawed him for writing *The Rights of Man*.

Our own history, too, is one of rebellion against authority. We remember Roger Williams, who championed toleration, not John Cotton, who drove him from the Bay Colony; we celebrate Thomas Jefferson, whose motto was "Rebellion to tyrants is obedience to God," not Lord North; we read Henry Thoreau on civil disobedience, rather than those messages of President Polk that earned him the title "Polk the Mendacious"; it is John Brown's soul that goes marching on, not that of the judge who condemned him to death at Charles Town.

Why is this? It is not merely because of the nobility of character of these martyrs. Some were not particularly noble. It is because we can see now that they gave their lives to defend the interests of humanity, and that they, not those who punished them, were the true benefactors of humanity.

But it is not just the past that needed freedom for critics, nonconformists and dissenters. We, too, are assailed by problems that seem insoluble; we, too, need new ideas. Happily, ours is not a closed system—not yet, anyway. We have a long history of experimentation in politics, social relations and science. We experiment in astrophysics because we want to land on the moon; we experiment in biology because we want to find the secret of life; we experiment in medicine because we want to cure cancer; and in all of these areas, and a hundred others, we make progress. If we are to survive and flourish, we must approach politics, law and social institutions in the same spirit that we approach science. We know that we have not found final truth in physics or biology. Why do we suppose that we have found final truth in politics or law? And just as scientists welcome new truth wherever they find it, even in the most disreputable places, so statesmen, jurists and educators must be prepared to welcome new ideas and new truths from whatever sources they come, however alien their appearance, however revolutionary their implications.

"There can *be* no difference anywhere," said the philosopher William James, "that doesn't make a difference elsewhere—no difference in abstract truth that doesn't express itself in a difference in concrete fact. . . ."

Let us turn then to practical and particular issues and ask, in each case, what are and will be the consequences of policies that repress freedom, discourage independence and impair justice in American society, and what are, and will be, the consequences of applying to politics and society those standards and habits of free inquiry that we apply as a matter of course to scientific inquiry?

Consider the erosion of due process of law—that complex of rules and safeguards built up over the centuries to make sure that every man will have a fair trial. Remember that it is designed not only for the protection of desperate characters charged with monstrous crimes; it is designed for every litigant. Nor is due process merely for the benefit of the accused. As Justice Robert H. Jackson said, "It is the best insurance for the Government itself against those blunders which leave lasting stains on a system of justice. . . ."

And why is it necessary to guarantee a free trial for all—for those accused of treason, for those who champion unpopular causes in a disorderly fashion, for those who assert their social and political rights against community prejudices, as well as for corporations, labor unions and churches? It is, of course, necessary so that justice will be done. Justice is the end, the aim, of government. It is implicitly the end of all governments; it is quite explicitly the end of the United States Government, for it was "in order to . . . establish justice" that the Constitution was ordained.

Trials are held not in order to obtain convictions; they are held to find justice. And over the centuries, we have learned by experience that unless we conduct trials by rule and suffuse them with the spirit of fair play, justice will not be done. The argument that the scrupulous observance of technicalities of due process slows up or frustrates speedy convictions is, of course, correct, if all you want is convictions. But why not go all the way and restore the use of torture? That got confessions and convictions! Every argument in favor of abating due process in order to get convictions applies with equal force to the use of the third degree and the restoration of torture. It is important to remember that nation after nation abandoned torture (the Americans never had it), not merely because it was barbarous, but because, though it wrung confessions from its victims, it did not get justice. It implicated the innocent with the guilty, it outraged the moral sense of the community. Due process proved both more humane and infinitely more efficient.

Or consider the problem of wiretapping. That in many cases wiretapping "works" is clear enough, but so do other things prohibited by civilized society, such as torture or the invasion of the home. But "electronic surveillance," siad Justice William J. Brennan, Jr., "strikes deeper than at the ancient feeling that a man's home is his castle; it strikes at freedom of communication, a postulate of our kind of society. . . . Freedom of speech is undermined where people fear to speak unconstrainedly in what they suppose to be the privacy of home or office."

Perhaps the most odious violation of justice is the maintenance of a double standard: one justice for blacks and another for whites, one for the rich and another for the poor, one for those who hold "radical" ideas and another for those who are conservative and respectable. Yet we have daily before our eyes just such a double standard of justice. The "Chicago Seven," who crossed state lines with "intent" to stir up a riot, have received heavy jail sentences, but no convictions have been returned against the Chicago police who participated in that riot. Black Panthers are on trial for their lives for alleged murders, but policemen involved in wantonly attacking a Black Panther headquarters and killing two blacks have been punished by demotion.

Turn to the role and function of freedom in our society—freedom of speech and of the press—and the consequences of laying restrictions upon these freedoms. The consequence is, of course, that society will be deprived of the inestimable advantage of inquiry, criticism, exposure and dissent. If the press is not permitted to perform its traditional function of presenting the whole news, the American people will go uninformed. If television is dissuaded from showing controversial films, the people will be denied the opportunity to know what is going on. If teachers and scholars are discouraged from inquiring into the truth of history or politics or anthropology, future generations may never acquire those habits of intellectual independence essential to the working of democracy. An enlightened citizenry is necessary for self-government. If facts are withheld, or distorted, how can the people be enlightened, how can self-government work?

The real question in all this is what kind of society do we want? Do we want a police society where none are free of surveillance by their government? Or do we want a society where ordinary people can go about their business without the eye of Big Brother upon them?

The Founding Fathers feared secrecy in government not merely because it was a vote of no-confidence in the intelligence and virtue of the people but on the practical ground that all governments conceal their mistakes behind the shield of secrecy; that if they are permitted to get away with this in little things, they will do it in big things—like the Bay of Pigs or the invasion of Cambodia.

And if you interfere with academic freedom in order to silence criticism, or critics, you do not rid the university of subversion. It is not ideas that are subversive, it is the lack of ideas. What you do is to silence or get rid of those men who have ideas, leaving the institution to those who have no ideas, or have not the courage to express those that they have. Are such men as these what we want to direct the education of the young and advance the cause of learning?

The conclusive argument against secrecy in scientific research is that it will in the end give us bad science. First-rate scientists will not so gravely violate their integrity as to confine their findings to one government or one society, for the first loyalty of science is to scientific truth. "The Sciences," said Edward Jenner of smallpox fame, "are never at war." We have only to consider the implications of secrecy in the realm of medicine: What would we think of doctors favoring secrecy in cancer research on the grounds of "national interest"?

The argument against proscribing books, which might normally be in our overseas libraries, because they are critical of Administration policies is not that it will hurt authors or publishers. No. It is quite simply that if the kind of people who believe in proscription are allowed to control our libraries, these will cease to be centers of learning and become the instruments of party. The argument against withholding visas from foreign scholars whose ideas may be considered subversive is not that this will inconveneince them. It is that we deny ourselves the benefit of what they have to say. Suppose President Andrew Jackson had denied entry to Alexis de Tocqueville on the ground that he was an aristocrat and might therefore be a subversive influence on our democracy? We would have lost the greatest book ever written about America.

There is one final consideration. Government, as Justice Louis D. Brandeis observed half a century ago, "is the potent, the omnipresent teacher. For good or for ill, it teaches the whole people by its example." If government tries to solve its problems by resort to large-scale violence, its citizens will assume that violence is the normal way to solve problems. If government itself violates the law, it brings the law into contempt, and breeds anarchy. If government masks its operations, foreign and domestic, in a cloak of secrecy, it encourages the creation of a closed, not an open, society. If government shows itself impatient with due process, it must expect that its people will come to scorn the slow procedures of orderly debate and negotiation and turn to the easy solutions of force. If government embraces the principle that the end justifies the means, it radiates approval of a doctrine so odious that it will in the end destroy the whole of society. If government shows, by its habitual conduct, that it rejects the claims of freedom and of justice, freedom and justice will cease to be the ends of our society.

Eighty years ago, Lord Bryce wrote of the American people that "the masses of the people are wiser, fairer and more temperate in any matter to which they can be induced to bend their minds, than most European philosophers have believed possible for the masses of the people to be."

Is this still true? If the American people can indeed be persuaded to "bend their minds" to the great questions of the preservation of freedom, it may still prove true. If they cannot, we may be witnessing, even now, a dissolution of the fabric of freedom that may portend the dissolution of the Republic.

INDECENCY AND OUR SYSTEM OF INJUSTICE*

The crime of indecency can take subtle forms:
In Minneapolis, a 29-year-old man was arrested for lying nude on the bed in his third-floor apartment while watching a football game on

Playboy 20(February 1973):44.

television. Two teenaged girls observed him from a neighboring apartment building and called the police. According to a newspaper account of the trial, the presiding judge pronounced the man guilty even before the defense presented its argument. When the public defender protested, the judge withdrew his ruling, then reissued it before the defense could give its closing argument. Again the attorney protested and was allowed to conclude his case before the defendant was convicted. Now police are looking for the man who failed to return for sentencing. One observer commented: "He may have lost faith in our system of justice."

Is "Free Enterprise" the Answer?

One frequently hears or reads the admonition that political-economic problems of society can most efficiently be solved by a "free market economy." Let the government stop interferring with business, say free enterprise advocates, and a trickle-down process will guarantee that as each serves his self-interest the general welfare will be enhanced. The trouble with such advice is that, contrary to the belief of naive editorialists and similar types, there is no truly free enterprise in America today aside from some very minor aspects of the economy such as prostitution, independent professionals, and small-time merchants and craftsmen.

All the major parts of the political-economic order are dominated by a combine of gigantic business firms working together with federal agencies to produce an economy that is controlled from top to bottom, including supplies, manufacture, demand, distribution, pricing, competition, and regulation. As Roszak has put it,

> We call it 'free enterprise.' But it is a vastly restrictive system of oligopolistic market manipulation, tied by institutionalized corrupton to the greatest munitions boondoggle in history and dedicated to infantilizing the public by turning it into a herd of compulsive consumers.*

Economist John Kenneth Galbraith has discussed at length the reasons which account for the growth of large-scale business and its collaboration with regulatory agencies. He concludes that modern industry is so complex, involving such a vast investment of resources and time, that it can no longer afford the hazards of a free market. Hence, ". . . we have an economic system which, whatever its formal ideological billing, is in substantial part a planned economy."** The accompanying seven articles and excerpts illustrate some of the important implications of the developments mentioned by Galbraith. The first three pieces, by Viorst, Green, and Schiller, describe the monopolistic tendencies of American industry; the

*Theodore Roszak, *The Making of a Counter Culture*: Reflections on the Technocratic Society and Its Youthful Opposition (Garden City, N.Y.: Anchor Books, Doubleday and Co., Inc., 1969), p. 16.

**John Kenneth Galbraith, *The New Industrial State* (Boston: Houghton Mifflin Company, 1967), p. 6.

next three pices, by *The Progressive*, Heilbroner, and Hickel, are concerned with corporate irresponsibility; and the final piece deals with some of the major problems of the economy.

MONOPOLIZE AND PROSPER*

Richard Hofstadter, the late historian, called it "one of the faded passions of American reform." John Kenneth Galbraith dismissed it as a "charade," and the *Wall Street Journal* has compared it to the majestic but impotent British monarchy. In its infancy, it was given the evocative title "trust-busting." But few trusts have been dissolved since the first antitrust act was passed in 1890, and, to this day, trust-busting remains less a genuine objective of American law, social policy, and economic organization than a facet of American mythology.

Trust-busting is a facet of the mythology that holds that business enterprises win that share of the market to which their competitive vigor, measured in terms of the price and quality of their product, entitles them. It is a facet of the mythology that holds that federal law-enforcement authorities show neither fear nor favor in making certain that this competition is preserved against the depredations of the occasional avaricious businessman. It is a facet of the mythology that holds that electoral politics effectively governs the practices of the corporate system.

In fact, the dominant sector of the American economy is characterized by minimal, or the most imperfect, competition—and is likely to remain so. Federal legal authorities do very little to enforce competition—and have never intended otherwise. Electoral politics is dependent upon the returns of the corporate system—and the relationship will not change as long as candidates need private contributions to run for office. In short, antitrust policy serves as a facade for federal officials and corporate executives to engage in collusion to create an appearance of vigilance in behalf of an economic structure that has never existed—and grows more distant from existence every day.

More distant, since the domination of the nation's productive potential by a relatively few corporations is not something that was accomplished—and finished—back in history. In 1941, two-thirds of the nation's industrial assets were held by the top 1,000 corporations. By 1971, this same

*Adapted from Milton Viorst, "Gentlemen Prefer Monopoloy," *Harper's Magazine*, 245(Nov 72):32, 34, 36, 38.

proportion was held by 200 corporations. The top 100 corporations have, in the past twenty years, doubled the percentage of their control over the nation's productive assets. What this trend proclaims is that American industrial concentration is getting more severe from day to day. If antitrust were real, this would not be happening.

In examining where trust-busting has gone astray, Ralph Nader's recent study group on antitrust enforcement tells of former Assistant Attorney General William Orrick, a lawyer of proved skill and dedication who was appointed by Robert Kennedy in 1962 to head the Justice Department's Antitrust Division. The study said:

> When Orrick attempted to learn the policy of the Antitrust Division, he found there was none. The agency was a "reactive" one, with more than 95 percent of its cases begun by a letter of complaint from outside. Little initiative investigation occurred, and there was no real planned enforcement. Seventy percent of pending matters concerned price-fixing and behavioral problems; only 30 percent dealt with structural problems like mergers and monopolization. To remedy this misemphasis, Orrick created a new Policy Planning section in the Division. He had a team probe the dozen most concentrated industries in the country, with an eye toward bringing monopolization and divestiture suits . . . But nothing happened. No big cases were brought, and the overall number of cases filed dropped precipitously . . .

It was under Orrick that a team of lawyers in the Antitrust Division took genuine aim at General Motors, the granddaddy of American trusts. General Motors produces 54 percent of the nation's cars and, unlike lesser giants, has the capacity to make decisions that determine the fate of the entire economy. Over the years the federal government has brought eighteen antitrust suits against GM, a dozen of which it actually won. But all of them dealt with peripheral activities such as bus, locomotive, and spare-parts manufacturing, and none ever went to the heart of GM's control of the auto market and its influence over the society. Until the trust busters do something about the power of GM, any other suit they bring will seem somehow unconvincing.

Indeed, the history of GM leaves little doubt that the *purpose* of its founders was not to prosper by manufacturing a better or cheaper car but to acquire a domination of the industry by the simple device of takeovers. Established in 1908, General Motors absorbed within a year Oldsmobile and Cadillac and narrowly missed out on a bid for Ford. Though there were still eighty-eight firms in the industry as late as 1921, GM acquired Chevrolet and Fisher Body a few years later, and its sales rose to 43 percent of the market. By 1935 only ten companies remained, and today there are four—the other three surviving, economists agree, largely at GM's sufferance.

The suit prepared by Orrick's lawyers alleged that GM had been formed by some forty illegal mergers, had driven out competition through the devices of planned obsolescence and exclusive dealerships, had safeguarded its flanks by depositing cash in politically influential banks throughout the country, and had raised advertising expenditures to a level that prohibited any other manufacturer from entering the market. The suit proposed that General Motors reconstitute itself into enough companies—generally held at from three to nine—to accomplish the restoration of competitive conditions in the automobile industry.

Why the government did not bring the suit to court has never been made clear. Since the suit's existence was not publicly acknowledged, the steps that led to its quashing were hardly likely to be placed in the arena of open debate. . . .

. . . as advisers responsible for the smooth flow of the economy, the President's economists said that an antitrust suit of such magnitude would disrupt the stock market, dampen the GNP, and create unemployment. Besides, they argued, it's no simple task to dismember a great corporation—and even if the trustbusters win the case, they could lose the remedy. Better, they said, to discipline GM through tax policy, licensing statutes, or stringent regulation.

In short, they declared that General Motors, whatever its record, had become such a bulwark of the American economy that the government could not risk its dismemberment. In wider terms, they were acknowledging that the competitive economy that antitrust law was designed to defend is no more than a theoretician's delusion.

The dominating trait of the American economy, then, is not competition but a tight control that is shared by no more than three or four companies over each of the major industrial markets. Besides automobiles, some of these markets are: aluminum (Alcoa, Reynolds, Kaiser); soaps (Procter & Gamble, Colgate, Lever Brothers); steel (U.S. Steel, Bethlehem, National, Republic); tires (Goodyear, Firestone, U.S. Rubber, Goodrich); copper (Kennecott, Phelps Dodge, Anaconda). Recently, a Federal Trade Commission staff report estimated that "if highly concentrated industries were deconcentrated to the point where the four largest firms control forty percent or less of an industry's sales, prices would fall by twenty-five percent or more." According to the best computations, shared monopoly currently characterizes a third of all American business and two-thirds of American manufacturing capacity. Most experts agree that the antitrust statutes are more than adequate to break up these concentrations. But the record makes clear that, despite the law, the trustbusters find no imperative in them.

. . . .

So why all the zeal on the part of the Nixon Administration—at least, prior to its celebrated change of mind—to break up ITT? One can only surmise. But it is surely a relevant consideration that ITT is not one of those sturdy, old-fashioned trusts like General Motors or Standard Oil, which are run by old-money Republician WASPs. It is a conglomerate, one of the new breed of trusts that are run mostly by fast-buck parvenus, of more recent ethnic stock, who are often Democratic.

. . . .

Ultimately, what was unusual about the ITT case was not that it was dropped but that, thanks to Jack Anderson's memos, the public acquired some glimmer of *why* it was dropped. The reasons, as the Administration contends, may have been quite legal. But, on the basis of the evidence, we know that (1) the leaders of the party in power had the option to prosecute ITT on charges of violating the antitrust laws, (2) ITT offered this party a substantial sum of money, usually put at $400,000, as a campaign contribution, and (3) the party in power agreed to an out-of-court settlement, along lines that were agreeable to ITT, in lieu of prosecution. The least we can say, lacking proof of an illegal transaction, is that a conflict-of-interest was plainly established. Indeed, the virtue of the ITT case is the clarity it brings to the normally obscure process of corporate influence on the political system. It also makes vivid the contention of Professor Galbraith that antitrust policy is nothing more than a charade.

. . . .

For antitrust enforcement runs counter to the natural inertia of the American political system. How can one expect an administration—any administration—to curb the power of the giant corporations that are its chief source of political financing? As Jay Gould, the legendary railroad magnate, charmingly phrased his philosophy of nonpartisan subornation a century ago: "I was a Republican in Republican districts, a Democrat in Democratic districts. But everywhere I was for Erie." Philip Hart of Michigan, one of the few members of the Senate committed to antitrust principles, updated Jay Gould in a recent analysis of ITT's influence. "When a corporation wants to discuss something with its political representative," he said, "you can be sure it will be heard. When a company operates in thirty states, it will be heard by thirty times as many representatives." As Hart suggests, economic exploitation is the lesser price the society pays for corporate concentration. The greater is the debilitation of the process of government. Antitrust could be an instrument of emancipation, but it will remain a facet of American mythology as long as the political parties remain in the thrall of corporate money.

THE NON-MONOPOLIST PAYS THE COST OF MONOPOLY*

Monopoly. The word has typically projected antique images on our memory screens—a combative Teddy Roosevelt, industrial tycoons, corporate empires, victimized farmers. Recent and converging events, however, have resurrected monopoly as a current problem:

. . . .

Much of the American economy can neither be characterized as monopolistic (like Xerox, Western Electric, or IBM) nor as competitive (the wheat and fashion markets). Between the two are "shared monopolies"—a form of flawed competition where only a handful of large firms produce a particular product. Shared monopolists often act as would a monopolist, with the result that prices invariably increase. For example, our steel industry, dominated by four firms controlling fifty-four percent of all shipments, periodically raises its prices despite idle capacity of about a third and despite the availability of cheaper imported steel.

Industrial economists agree that when four or fewer firms control fifty percent or more of a market, a shared monopoly results. Collective or conspiratorial behavior, not competitive, then pervades productive activity. Such industries are many and recognizable: automobiles (General Motors, Ford, Chrysler); aluminum (Alcoa, Reynolds, Kaiser); soap detergents (Procter & Gamble, Colgate and Lever Brothers); cereals (Kellogg, General Foods, General Mills, Quaker Oats); electric light bulbs (General Electric, Westinghouse, Sylvania); cigarettes (Reynolds, American, Philip Morris), and others.

The extent of shared monopolies can modestly be described as staggering. In 1959 economists Carl Kaysen and Donald Turner concluded in their now classic *Antitrust Policy* that "there are more concentrated than unconcentrated industries in manufacturing and mining, they are larger in aggregate size, and they tend to occupy a more important position in the economy." More than a decade later, two other authors on Corporate America agreed. Economics professors William Shepherd and Richard Barber have both calculated that shared monopolies control about

*Adapted from Mark J. Green, "The High Cost of Monopoly," *The Progressive* 36(March 1972):15–19.

two-thirds of all industry. These are the industries of our giant firms: General Motors has 800,000 employes worldwide and collects more in total sales (some $20 billion annually) than the budgets of all but three countries; the advertising budget of Procter & Gamble alone is *twenty times* as large as the appropriation of the Justice Department's Antitrust Division, which must monitor a trillion dollar economy; the six largest firms in *Fortune's* 500 (there are 400,000 manufacturing firms in this country) earn fully twenty-five percent of all industrial profits.

Based on *market concentration*—the share of business held by the leading firms in a particular industry—there has been a slight increase in the already high level of concentraton during the past two decades. But based on *aggregate concentration*—the ownership of all manufacturing assets by our biggest corporations—the increase has been dramatic. While the top 200 industrial firms controlled forty-seven percent of total assets in 1950, by 1965 they controlled fifty-five percent. Willard Mueller, former chief economist of the Federal Trade Commission, testified before the Senate Antitrust and Monopoly Subcommittee in November, 1969:

"You may recall that I testified before this Committee in 1966 that, should postwar trends in aggregate concentration continue, by 1975 the 200 largest manufacturing corporations would control two-thirds of all manufacturing assets. Unhappily, we have reached this level ahead of schedule. *Today the top 200 manufacturing corporations already control about two-thirds of all assets held by corporations engaged primarily in manufacturing.*" (Emphasis added.)

Also, the 100 largest corporations today have a greater share of manufacturing assets than did the 200 largest in 1950, the year Congress enacted the Celler-Kefauver Act to stop the trend toward industrial concentration. And our top 200 corporations now control the same share of assets held by the *thousand* largest in 1941, the year the landmark Temporary National Economic Committee submitted its final report to Congress recommending an "Investigation of Concentration of Economic Power." How can one comprehend power of this magnitude? Imagine a college classroom seating just 200, and there you could sit the rulers of two-thirds of American industry and more than one-third of all the world's industrial production. Pharaohs and emperors would be envious.

The disfiguring of free enterprise by monopoly imposes serious economic and social tolls. Foremost is the overpricing that occurs when one or a few firms control a market. A staff report now at the Federal Trade Commission estimates that "if highly concentrated industries were deconcentrated to the point where the four largest firms control forty percent or less of an industry's sales, *prices would fall by twenty-five percent or more.*" The examples are numerous:

¶ There were a number of competing milk firms in Minneapolis-St. Paul in the mid-Sixties, but only three big milk firms in neighboring Duluth-Superior; although costs were similar in both markets, the half-gallon wholesale price in 1967 was 33.8 cents in Minneapolis-St. Paul, forty-five cents in Duluth.

¶ While there were once as many as eighty-eight competing auto manufacturers in 1921, today the "Big Three" produce eighty-three percent of all cars sold in the United States and ninety-seven percent of all domestic models. Industrial economist Leonard Weiss, of the University of Wisconsin, has estimated that the noncompetitive state of the auto industry costs $1.6 billion per year.

¶ Federal Trade Commission studies have found that cereal prices are fifteen to twenty-five percent higher than would exist under competition because of domination of the industry by just four firms. . . .

Such overpricing leads to lost output. Monopoly misallocates resources, creating excess capacity and a smaller Gross National Product than is our national potential. Recent studies by economists William Shepherd and F. M. Scherer have tried to quantify this lost GNP, concluding that *the overall cost of monopoly and shared monopoly in terms of lost production is somewhere between $48 billion and $60 billion annually.* The tax revenues alone from this wealth could go a long way toward ending both poverty and pollution in this country.

Monopoly overcharging also results in an inequitable transfer cost. When consumers pay excessive prices for their purchases, monopoly profits then redistribute income from the consuming public to the shareholders of particular corporations. Professor Shepherd of the University of Michigan has estimated this redistribution of wealth at $23 billion annually. And "people's capitalism"—that "the people" own our corporations—is no rebuttal. Although millions own some stock, only a relative handful reap the lions's share of corporate dividends. A 1963 study, containing the most recent figures available, pointed out that 1.6 percent of the adult population of the United States owned 82.4 percent of all publicly held stock. This redistribution of wealth—exacerbating the wealth extremes of a society where the richest one percent of U.S. families receive more income than the bottom twenty percent and the top five percent more than the bottom forty percent—can eventually have serious political consequences. "A man who thinks that economics is only a matter for professors," writes author-economist Robert L. Heilbroner, "forgets that this is the science that has sent men to the barricades."

Lost output and income transfers are not the only ill effects of monopolies. Other dynamic costs are less capable of measurement but still severely damage our industrial and social health:

Inflation and Unemployment. Concentrated industries can largely shrug off the classical monetary and fiscal restraints, not reducing their high prices as consumer demand declines. In 1970, both before and after the automobile strike, General Motors announced price increases attempting to maintain their targeted twenty percent return (on net worth after taxes) rather than suffer a less than monopoly-like return. Due to such market power of big firms, we are in what economist Paul Samuelson calls a "sellers' inflation"—where higher costs are simply passed on to the consumer in the form of higher prices.

In 1969 the FTC's Bureau of Economics pointed out that "major concentrated industries, through the exercise of discretionary pricing power, contribute to both inflation and unemployment." Unemployment results since monopolies, as noted, significantly reduce our manufacturing output—which in turn reduces the number of workers who would otherwise be producing. If monopoly disruption were accountable for only twenty percent of all the unemployed, this still translates into over a million unemployed workers. And to the extent that unemployment is an official policy to combat inflation—two million people have been thrown out of work between 1969 and 1971 with this purpose in mind—a "stagflation" created by our shared monopolies dims the employment picture.

Political and Social Effects. Assuming that Corporate America has political power, what then are the costs of increasing concentration of economic power? As economic diversity decreases, the number of units contributing to the political process decreases accordingly. And as political pluralism weakens, so does democracy. James Madison argued in the Federalist Papers that political freedom requires many "factions," setting faction against faction until a political equipoise results. But as large numbers of independent firms are swallowed up, we instead race toward *America, Inc.,* in Mintz's and Cohen's phrase, "one gigantic industrial and financial complex functioning much like a separate government." . . .

Those large firms which dominate an industry, by their orchestrated power, can resist governmental and public pressure more easily than smaller firms of lesser political clout. And as big firms push out or buy out the small, the "mavericks" of industry disappear. Their disappearance reduces a source of political options since, as the number of private sources for social risk capital is reduced, the unpopular or new cause will find it that much more difficult to secure backing.

The social blights of racism and pollution have been associated with the discretionary power of monopolies freed from the spurs of competition. Economist William Shepherd studied racial patterns in white-collar jobs, concluding that firms with market power could afford the luxury of discriminating against blacks—and they did. But competitive firms, which had to hire the best employes at the going rate—whether they were black or white—were found to discriminate less. Also there is very little incentive for shared monopolists to be progressive on pollution, with their heavy investment in existing capital assets and with their ability already to exact monopoly-like returns. The *Auto-Smog Conspiracy* case provides one clear example. In this case the Justice Department charged the Big Four auto firms with illegally suppressing anti-exhaust technology and implementation.

Proponents of Big Business, on the other hand, argue that there are alternate benefits in our state of super-concentration. But on close examination, their verbal arrows become boomerangs:

Innovation. First popularized by the eminent Joseph Schumpeter, and recently adopted by John Kenneth Galbraith, the idea is that big firms can innovate better because they are able to risk the necessary large investments in research and development (R&D). "A benign providence," Galbraith has intoned, "has made the modern industry of a few large firms an almost perfect instrument for inducing technical change."

But nearly all objective evidence refutes this assertion. When you have a huge investment in present machinery, and when an unknown return is to be substituted for your sixteen to twenty percent return, there is little need to embrace new technologies. Economist Leonard Weiss, after examining many analyses of R&D expenditures, concluded: "Most studies show that within their range of observation, size adds little to research intensity and may actually detract from it in some industries." Also, it should be stressed that about two-thirds of the research done in the United States is subsidized by the Federal Government anyway—not by big private industry.

A look at the concentrated steel industry revealed that of thirteen major inventions between 1940 and 1955, none was produced by the American steel companies. A small Austrian firm, one-third the size of one U.S. Steel plant, introduced the revolutionary oxygen steelmaking process. The first American company to adopt it was McLouth Steel, which had less than one percent of industry capacity; it was ten years later when U.S. Steel and Bethlehem followed suit.

But steel has a long history of technological immobility. What of a large corporation commonly considered a major innovator, like General Electric, "where progress is our most important product"? In the household appliance field alone, the late T. K. Quinn, a former GE vice-president, credited small companies with the discovery and production of, among other items: the electric toaster, electric range, electric refrigerator, electric dryer, electric dishwasher, vacuum cleaner, clothes-washing machine, and deep freeze. Quinn concluded that "the record of the giants is one of moving in, buying out, and absorbing the smaller concerns." Nor was industrial bigness a *sine qua non* to the development of stainless steel razor blades, transistor radios, photo copying machines, and the "quick" photograph. Wilkinson, Sony, Xerox, and Polaroid were all small or unknown when they introduced these products.

Efficiencies. The reputed efficiencies of large scale operation become inefficiencies when the scale grows too large. Competition is the whip of efficiency, driving firms to produce better goods at lower costs in order to increase sales and profits. Monopoly and oligopoly, however, lead to "the quiet life," in Judge Learned Hand's phrase, a state of mind and economy where there is little pressure to seek out efficiencies. In an age which has witnessed the collapse of the Penn-Central (a firm which was the result of a merger with claimed efficiencies because of its large size), and the near collapses of Ling-Temco-Voigt (LTV) and Lockheed aircraft firms, it should be evident that being big does not mean being efficient. Robert Townsend has put it more impressionistically: "Excellence and bigness are incompatible." . . .

THE IMAGE MONOPOLISTS*

The original version of *The First Freedom* appeared in 1946, and was dedicated by its author, Morris Ernst, "To the Members of the Congress of the United States on whom we must rely to restore free enterprise in movies, radio, and press." This misplaced trust aside, the book called attention, in documented detail, to widespread monopolistic developments in the American press, radio and motion picture industries. Still, Ernst was not without hope. "I am convinced," he wrote then, that "it is not too late to stem the tide. But we must act fast and with bravery."

More than two decades later, Bryce Rucker, with Ernst's approval, has published under the same title an updated inventory of the organizational state of American mass communications. Expectations for remedial change, along with confidence in the essential health of the media, are barely visible this second time around. In an introduction to the modernized work, Ernst observes dejectedly: "The most frightening part of Professor Rucker's exploration may well be seen in the simple and dirty fact that the abandonment of the idea of competition of ideas can scarcely be debated in our culture today. It will be of interest to note," Ernst adds, "whether the Rucker facts and thesis are even given public attention in the mass media." He concludes it would be a miracle to expect such an event.

*Adapted from Herbert I. Schiller's review of Bryce W. Rucker's *The First Freedom* (Carbondale, Illinois: Southern Illinois University Press, 1968), in *The Nation* 206(June 24, 1968):835–836.

Is this despair justified? In 1946, Ernst had recommended, among other measures, that joint communications ventures be prohibited; that newspapers be divested of the ownership of radio stations; that radio stations be pried loose from broadcasting networks; that N.B.C. be liberated from RCA; that the chain ownership of radio stations, newspapers and theatres be disallowed; and that FCC control be imposed over the speculative sale of radio stations.

The latest evidence, painstakingly and impressively accumulated by Rucker, demonstrates that the trends uncovered by Ernst have become dominant and seemingly institutionalized national patterns. In a word, the movement to monopolization in the mass media has accelerated. Chains reach across the land. In 1967, newspaper combines "owned 871 of the 1,767 daily newspapers ... or 49.3 percent of the total." Chains owned the five largest general circulation dailies, and nineteen of the top twenty-five. Chains owned 31.4 percent of the commercial AM and a similar percentage of FM radio stations. Television, just appearing when Ernst made his pioneer study, but now the most influential of all the mass media, Rucker finds "virtually taken over by enterprising chain broadcasters," who now control 73.6 percent of all commercial stations.

The process of concentrated control extends in all directions. Newspapers own huge numbers of television stations. In 1967, publishers "held interests in a third of the VHF stations (156) and in 22 percent of the UHF stations (28)." Beyond this, "newspaper-television monopolies existed in 27 American cities" and varying degrees of joint media control prevail in scores of other communities. Last year, on the newspaper front alone, there were competing dailies in only sixty-four of America's 1,547 daily newspaper cities. In several states, no competing papers exist in any localities.

. . . .

Bryce Rucker systematically examines the entire image-making apparatus (with the exception of motion pictures) and finds it interconnected at almost every vital point. Two international news services, AP and UPI, themselves the instruments of tightly held interests, provide the world view of most Americans, since these services, with few exceptions, are the main sources of international news for the nation's press and broadcasters.

The communications technostructures prefer to minimize their economic impulses and to emphasize a posture of public spiritedness, but profit seeking is their driving force. In a thirteen-year period, from 1954 to 1966, "4,369 broadcasting stations as well as 538 television stations, changed hands at a total cost of $1,536,014,367." This mountain of capital gains, incidentally, derives from the assignment of licenses, granted by the FCC to private broadcasters on a temporary basis, for the use of public property—the radio spectrum.

This should suggest that the mass media are more than the well-paid servants of commerce, though they are certainly that. In structure, operation and motivation, the business of communications is distinguishable from other corporate business only in its claim of special constitutional privilege. It utilizes technology to reinforce market position, and Rucker details any number of anticompetitive practices including price fixing, kickbacks and pools.

. . . .

. . . What is more, the media's conditions do not reflect malfunctioning in vestigial economic activities. Monopoly, profit maximization and a public-be-damned stance are located in the most dynamic, modernized and "cleanest" industries. These constitute the central nervous system of the social order. They provide the national image of what is normal, what is orderly, what is preferable, and what is just. But these perspectives are the carefully tooled products of business structures heavily concentrated, self-serving, and as indifferent to the public interest as any 19th-century trust. Moreover, the doctored outputs of the American mass media are penetrating international markets and have created a monumental problem for those concerned with safeguarding national cultural sovereignties.

Is the present course reversible? Ernst, nearly a quarter of a century ago, appealed to Congress. Rucker, more realistically, notes that "Approximately twenty-five congressmen or members of their family own interests in radio and television properties. ... Less well known, but even more serious, probably half of the senators and representatives through their law firms represent broadcasters ... (and) what should we call the free radio and television time given to two-thirds of the members of Congress by their local stations?" Not surprisingly, Congress is quick to censure even the mildest efforts of that notorious paper tiger regulator, the FCC, when it moves to remind broadcasters of their public responsibilities.

THE DOLLAR PATRIOTS*

America's superpatriots, whether engaged in politics, industry, or the work of old line veterans' organizations, always stand ready to denounce

*Adapted from *The Progressive* 35(December 1971):7-8.

anti-war protest as a betrayal of "the boys who are out there fighting for our country."

But the jingoists rarely, if ever, condemn those who are to blame when the military-industrial complex turns out arms, military aircraft, and other equipment whose faulty construction endangers the lives of those same "boys out there." Thus we did not expect, nor did we hear, cries of outrage from the superpatriots over recent revelations involving the Air Force's C-5A cargo plane, and the alleged deceit practiced by the Colt Industries Firearms Group in turning out the M-16, the basic combat weapon of U.S. armed forces.

The Air Force discovered that seven of its sixty huge C-5A planes have engine mountings which probably were cracked even before they left the factory. The C-5A fleet was grounded after an engine on one of them broke loose from the wing and crashed on the runway when the pilot applied full power. An Air Force investigation disclosed that cracks in the pylons that hold the engine to the wing had caused the break in the plane whose staggering cost overruns were brought to public attention months ago by Senator William Proxmire, Wisconsin Democrat.

Lockheed Aircraft Corporation of Marietta, Georgia, builds the huge plane but the pylons are supplied by a subcontractor, Rohr Corporation of Chula Vista, California. The Air Force, after checking the fleet, released twenty-three of the planes as safe to fly. The C-5A—the world's largest and highest-priced plane—originally was expected to cost $28 million each; they now cost nearly $60 million apiece. The planned fleet of eighty-one planes will cost $4.9 billion—if there are no additional cost overruns. Air Force Secretary Robert C. Seamans told Congress that Lockheed has been directed to review Rohr's manufacturing and quality control procedures—an elementary safeguard that should have been standard practice from the outset.

The Lockheed and Air Force record on the mammoth plane has been so shocking that Senator Proxmire has demanded that the C-5A program "be stopped with completion of the planes on the assembly line." According to a Pentagon report, he said, only forty of the sixty planes delivered "are needed to do the job."

Proxmire pointed out that the Air Force said nothing when the engine fell off one of the planes, but the story got out anyway. When a landing gear malfunctioned, the Air Force was silent again until the Senator announced the incident.

"These accidents," he said, "occurred after the General Accounting Office released a study showing major deficiencies in the C-5A's landing gear, wings, and sophisticated electronics equipment. Testimony before my committee had disclosed C-5As being produced with missing parts."

As for Colt, now the sole supplier of the M-16 rifle, that arms firm was charged by the Connecticut Citizen Action Group, established by Ralph Nader, with deliberately hiding defects in the manufacture of the weapon. Colt's employees, the Nader group charged in a twenty-one page report, have been ordered over the past several years "to conceal defects, to switch defective parts out of sight of Government inspectors, and to straighten crooked barrels by 'whacking' them on the floor." The report was based on interviews with seven present and four former employees of Colt at the Hartford plant; five of those interviewed made their statements under oath. In endurance test firings of M-16s selected at random, the report charged, employees were under "standing orders" from management to replace weakened parts of the rifles with new parts while Colt's "quality control technicians would distract Government inspectors."

Colt has categorically denied "the implications of the allegations," and the Nader Action Group has called for an investigation by the Department of Justice and Congress. Senator Abraham A. Ribicoff, Connecticut Democrat, has requested the Senate Armed Services Committee to give the charges immediate attention.

Even the enormous cost of the C-5A fleet still may not buy safety for its crews and does not provide genuine security for the nation. A faulty M-16 rifle could fail an infantryman in combat. Will the superpatriots and their organizations now demand that military suppliers begin thinking less of corporate profits and more about "the boys out there"? We doubt it—on the basis of bitter experience.

CORPORATE ATROCITIES*

In this piece, social scientist Robert Heilbroner sums up his reaction to a series of studies indicating that many American businessmen will stop at nothing, including literal murder, in their insatiable search for additional profits.

By a curious coincidence, I first read the chapters of this book, many of them still in rough draft, during the very week that Lieutenant Calley was found guilty of shooting twenty-two South Vietnamese civilians, and the

*Adapted from Robert L. Heilbroner, in Robert L. Heilbroner, et al, *In the Name of Profit* (Garden City, N.Y.: Doubleday and Company, Inc., 1972), pp. 223–225.

thought that ran through my head was whether there was not an unhappy similarity between the events described in these pages and those for which that pathetic murderous young officer was tried.

For like My Lai, the incidents in this book are atrocities. Moreover, in one case as in the other, the atrocities are not merely hideous exceptions but, rather, discovered cases of a continuing pattern of misbehavior. Behind My Lai lay the unpublicized shelling of hamlets and hospitals, the "surgical" bombings from 50,000 feet, the search-and-destroy missions. Behind the incidents in this book lie the stream of petty wrongdoing over which the Better Business Bureau casts its ineffective eye, and the larger cases of more or less deliberately perpetrated harm that a careful reader can unearth, almost any day, in the back pages of *The New York Times*.

I do not wish to push the analogy too far. Yet, consider the case of Libby, McNeil & Libby, a major foodpacker that found itself hampered by the imposition of a ban on cyclamates issued by the Food and Drug Administration in 1969. Over the next sixteen months, Libby sold some 300,000 cases of cyclamate-sweetened fruit to customers in West Germany, Spain and elsewhere. "Fortunately," the *Wall Street Journal* quotes James Nadler, Libby's vice-president for international business, "the older civilizations of the world are more deliberate about judging momentary fads that are popular in the U.S. from time to time."[1] The momentary fad to which he was referring was the upshot of nineteen years of increasingly alarming laboratory findings concerning the effects of cyclamates on chick embryos—effects that produced grotesque malformations similar to those induced by thalidomide.[2]

What we have there is a business version of the principle behind the Vietnam War—the imposition of casualties on other peoples in the name of some tenet, such as freedom or profits, as the case may be. Not that Libby is the only adherent to this principle. The *Journal* article goes on to report that Parke, Davis & Co. sells its Chloromycetin to foreign nations without some of the warnings concerning dangerous side effects that it is forced to display here, and with a much wider range of recommended applications than it is allowed to mention here. The same double standard is true for Merck & Co.'s antirheumatic drug Indocin, sold abroad under much less cautious description than at home.

If these practices are not atrocities, I do not know what an atrocity is. . . .

REFERENCES

[1] *The Wall Street Journal*, Feb. 11, 1971.
[2] James Turner, *The Chemical Feast* (New York, 1970), p. 12.

FREE ENTERPRISE SLAVERY*

The author, former governor of Alaska, was Secretary of the Interior during the first Nixon administration until he was forced out because of his zeal in protecting the environment.

We are supposed to be a country of great freedom. But the coal miner is not a free man. One out of six miners is going to be killed or injured this year. Someone has got to protect that man. Often today he is in slavery, like the slaves in Biblical times. But to our discredit and shame he is a slave within a free enterprise system.

After John L. Lewis passed his peak, the United Mine Workers Union lost its militancy and cast its lot with industry during the serious depression coal experienced in the early 1950's. Possibly because he was old and tired, possibly because he felt deep coal mining could no longer compete with other sources of energy, Lewis more or less acquiesced in the scuttling of two-thirds of his own union. You can do something for the miner's children, but it is difficult to retrain a coal miner past the age of fifty to do another kind of useful work.

The remaining miners are a captive labor force. There is no place for them to go, physically and literally, except down into the mine. If they refuse to go into the mine, they cannot get unemployment compensation. But what good is it if a man earns a dollar for bread when simultaneously his mind, heart and soul are being destroyed?

Most of the mine owners do not live in New York or Washington. They live in the mountains themselves, in the "hollers" of the Bluefields and the Beckleys. This comes the closest to a plantation society that we have today in this country. The Depression of the 1930's put an end to such mastership in most of America, but mastership has persisted in the coal industry. This situation bothered me so much at the time that I pursued the problem after I was out of office. It was several months before I was able to document anything resembling the facts.

One of the travesties in the Bureau of Mines has to do with the safety records of large companies, which play games with statistics. A common gimmick is to keep a man on the payroll and not list him as injured if his layoff is a week or less. Industry has been keeping these statistics with one hand and reaching around and patting itself on the back with the other

*From Walter J. Hickel, *Who Owns America?* (Englewood Cliffs, New Jersey: Prentice-Hall, Inc., 1971), pp. 134-135.

hand, telling itself what a great safety record it has. What's more, the Bureau of Mines accident report was tabulated the same way.

This is an example of the "buddy system" in which certain bureaus of the Department long ago became involved. For more than 100 years, these bureaus were actually in a silent partnership with the industries they were supposed to police. It is a shameful picture, and such an unnecessary one. What was once a great labor union and what could be a great industry are cooperating to maintain what is essentially a slavery system in the name of free enterprise. . . .

PERMANENT INFLATION*

A hypothetical question: What would happen if Adam Smith, president of the Super-Gimmick Manufacturing Co., called in the leaders of the union in his plant and said, "For the past twenty years every contract we have negotiated has given a substantial increase to all members of the union. During the past few years these raises have been bigger than ever. They have, in fact, considerably exceeded all the savings we have been able to make by installing more efficient machinery and developing new processes. As a result, we have had to push up the prices of all Super-Gimmick products—and naturally, our sales have been falling off, in spite of our best advertising efforts.

"As you gentlemen know, the company lost money last year, and this year our losses seem likely to be even greater. The banks are reluctant to lend us any more money so long as we are running in the red. When we open our next contract negotiation, therefore, I am going to have to ask the union not to demand a further wage increase. Indeed, with utmost reluctance I must ask you to accept a temporary pay cut—not a big one, just about half of your last raise—until we can get the firm back on solid ground."

Recently I sketched out this little scenario for a friend of mine who has spent most of his working life as an arbitrator of labor disputes.

"What would happen?" he said. "That's easy. Adam Smith would have a strike on his hands. Even if the union leaders agreed to his proposition, the rank and file would override them. Besides, Smith would be accused of refusing to bargain in good faith—and the National Labor Relations Board almost certainly would uphold the charge.

*Adapted from John Fischer, "Nixonomics: Well, You Can't Have Everything," *Harper's Magazine* 243(November 1971):10, 12, 14, 16-17, 20-23.

"What you don't seem to understand is that wage negotiations these days are strictly a one-directional business—always up."

I remember that remark every time . . . official optimists in Washington proclaim their determination to keep inflation, somehow, under control. I would like to believe them, but skepticism keeps seeping in. For I am beginning to suspect that we may have reached a point in history where no administration, Republican or Democratic, is actually capable of stopping inflation, no matter how firm its intentions.

The unions don't deserve all the blame. Shares of it also rest on the increasingly rigid structure of American business, and on the new facts of our political life. "Blame," in fact, may not be an appropriate word. Perhaps it would be more accurate to say that the character of our whole society has changed so drastically during the past decade or two that it no longer responds to the so-called laws of economics. Neither the classic nor the Keynesian remedies seem to work anymore. . . .

The reason for this glum foreboding is that the competitive free enterprise system apparently has gone dead on us—not everywhere, but in nearly all the places that matter most. Nobody planned it that way. Certainly it did not succumb to any of those sinister leftist plots that haunt the dreams of the John Birch Society. It just got nibbled away by thousands of separate decisions, public and private, most of which seemed good ideas at the time. I am not sure that its demise is altogether a bad thing. The point is that we knew how to make the old system work, after a fashion, but we have not yet learned how to operate the cumbersome, stiff-jointed political economy—neither capitalist nor socialist—that has grown up in its place.

Under the old system, the cure for inflation was unpleasant but simple. The government merely had to raise taxes and interest rates, restrict bank credit, and cut its own spending, thus reducing the supply of money in circulation. Industry then found it could no longer borrow to build new factories, so the construction trades and machine tool makers had to close down. (Traditionally, that was the first sign of a turn in the economic tide.) Their unemployed workers stopped buying everything, except groceries, and some of them actually went hungry. With sales falling, other businesses soon had to lay off help, cut wages, and pare down prices and profit margins in a desperate effort to hold on to their share of the dwindling market. A good many of them went broke. Their inventories, thrown on the market at bankruptcy rates, pushed prices down still further. When enough people—say 10 percent of the labor force—were out of work, you could be sure that the surge of inflation would be broken.

To reverse the process, as John Maynard Keynes taught us, the government could simply spend more money than it collected in taxes, simultaneously cutting interest rates and loosening up the supply of credit.

In theory, the resulting budget deficit would be balanced off with a surplus when business picked up again. And, also according to Keynesian theory, the government should be able to "fine tune" the economy by delicate adjustment of its fiscal and monetary levers, so that the up and down swings would be relatively small, prices would remain fairly steady, and nobody would need to be out of work for a very long time.

But now, alas, we are discovering that some of the levers no longer move—and that we, the voters, will not permit any President to yank the others hard enough to have much effect.

For one thing, the government now finds it practically impossible to make really big cuts in the federal budget. Too many costs are fixed: interest on the public debt, veterans' pensions, Social Security, a military establishment that evidently can't be shrunk much even in peacetime. Other items, such as farm subsidies, make no economic sense but are deemed politically untouchable.

Moreover, Washington no longer controls the dominating share of public spending. State and city budgets have been swelling like a bloated hippopotamus for a long time now, and the federal government has no way to cinch them in. Their inflationary pressure largely offsets any feasible cuts in federal spending.

The biggest change of all, however, is in public feeling, as demonstrated by our voting behavior. We no longer will tolerate the old, painful remedies for inflation. We simply will not stand for a 10 percent rate of unemployment, or even 5 percent for very long.

Neither will we tolerate the suffering that hammered down wages and prices in the bad old days. When a man loses his job today, he doesn't go hungry. He goes on relief. He is under no compulsion, then, to take any job he can get at any wage. In like fashion, we will not permit any really Draconian reduction in those humanitarian services—welfare, Medicare, education—that account for such a large share of public spending. Presumably this means that we have become a more kindly people; but such generous impulses are of no help in curbing inflation.

We are seldom willing to pay for our generosity either. At this moment my own state of Connecticut offers a spectacular example of public irrationality, of an electorate that seems determined to give away its cake and keep it too.

The state has been running in the red for quite a while and last year the voters finally got concerned enough to elect a Republican governor, Thomas J. Meskill, who was pledged to reform the tax system and pay off the accumulated deficit. And he actually did try. After months of fussing, he finally got the legislature to pass, and he signed, an income tax that would do the job.

Did the poeple of Connecticut celebrate this act of statesmanship with fireworks and dancing in the streets? Well, not exactly. Instead they boiled up the most fearsome display of spontaneous wrath in living memory. The legislators, scared out of their wits, if any, hastily reassembled to replace the income tax with something more palatable. The result was a gimcrack package of special levies, including a 6.5 percent sales tax, the highest in the country. It will not produce the needed revenues. It bears hardest on those least able to pay. The governor denounced it as a "miserable failure." But, presumably in desperation, he signed it.

Then, when he began to cut back by about $84 million on spending for education, welfare, and aid to the cities, the populace—this time led by a posse of mayors—threw another tantrum. Their message was perfectly clear: they won't stand for any paring of public services, but they can't abide enough taxes to foot the bill. What they really want, in short, is more inflation.

Most Presidents at most times are, alas, in a fix quite similar to Governor Meskill's. The same message comes though, loud and menacing, in most other state legislatures, and in Congress as well. As a result, a balanced budget has become something of a curiosity, like a businessman without credit cards. That is why only one half of the Keynesian theory really works: it is easy for a government to pile up a debt in hard times, but almost impossible for it to pay off the debt when the economy swings up.

. . . .

A people unwilling to govern its own impulses, even when they are contradictory, isn't likely to discipline its labor unions. Especially when the unions have some justification for their intrasigent behavior, and also the political muscle to get away with it.

Their justification is that competition has gone out of fashion, for all practical purposes, in many industries dominated by a few big companies. The oligopolies can "administer" their prices pretty much as they please, regardless of the state of the market or government monetary pressure. The public agencies set up to regulate them often behave like collaborators rather than watchdogs. Now, too, inefficient corporations are largely sheltered from the risks that beset old-fashioned capitalism. Witness the case of Lockheed. When inept management led it to the verge of bankruptcy, the government bailed it out—in spite of the fact that the public interest would have been best served by letting the firm go out of business. Since the country is over-supplied with aerospace manufacturing capacity, the resources lavished on Lockheed obviously could be better employed elsewhere.

Under these circumstances, the unions naturally feel that they too deserve some protection from the rigors of competition. And as we all know, they have got it. A half-century of special-interest legislation has granted them exemption from antitrust laws and court injunctions and has given them a protective agency of their own, the National Labor Relations Board.

. . . .

In theory, the President and Congress could cut the unions down to size, by repealing all or most of the special legislation that protects them. Merely denying welfare payments to strikers and assessing heavy fines for wildcat and illegal strikes would help a lot—if public officials had the guts to enforce such rules. I can't see any of this happening, however, any more than I can imagine the government breaking up the 500 biggest corporations into thousands of independent, fiercely competitive little firms. Neither is politically feasible.

. . . .

Consequently the real question, it seems to me, is not whether we are going to have more inflation, but how much and how fast. If the unions are willing to pay *some* attention to the guidelines, if jawboning and parameters and the Administration's pleas for self-restraint manage to hold the rate of inflation to something like 3 or 4 percent a year, then the economy probably can continue to function indefinitely. Not very efficiently and not at all fairly, but probably without a major disaster.

Even such a relatively modest rate of inflation is unfair, because the cost falls most heavily on those least able to stand it. Just as inflation helps organized labor (so long as wages go up faster than prices), it hurts unorganized labor, including migrant workers, the marginal farmers of the South and Appalachia, the unskilled, and the blacks who are denied union membership. It also penalizes old people living on pension, savings, and Social Security, since they have no way to raise their incomes in step with the cost of living.

Inflation is inefficient, because it discourages saving and distorts the direction of investment. During a period of continuous inflation, a mortgage is a spendid deal for the borrower, because he can pay it off in dollars worth, say, fifty cents. For the same reason, it is a lousy deal for the lender. Under such circumstances only fools (and apparently they are still plentiful) will invest their savings in mortgages or saving accounts or building and loan associations—the chief sources of investment for the housing the country so urgently needs. Home building will attract savings only if interest rates are permitted to rise to something like 8 percent—normal interest, plus a premium large enough to cover inflation. And rates that high in themselves discourage home building, and also add to the already running inflationary pressures. Similarly, the prudent investor will avoid other fixed-income investments, such as U.S. savings bonds, municipal bonds (which finance the rebuilding of our cities), and industrial bonds (which partly finance the growth we need to put the unemployed back to work).

Instead the canny man will put his savings into the speculative rather than traditionally sound investments. Sure, if he buys stock in a football team or a beach resort or a highly experimental electronics company, he may lose everything; but at least he has a chance of making a killing too. Whereas if he leaves his money in a building and loan association, it is sure to be eroded away, year by year, by the inflationary tide. His other choice is to forget about savings altogether and spend every dime as soon as he lays his hands on it.

Either choice, obviously, is bad for the country as a whole. For a high rate of savings, directed to meet real needs, is the indispensable foundation of a healthy economy. It is also the only source of money for such things as hospitals, universities, and cleaning up our environment.

That kind of situation, however, is probably the best we can hope for in the foreseeable future. Things could get a lot worse.

If inflation should ever get entirely out of hand— . . . and wages and prices begin to soar at the rate of 20 percent or more a year—then we are in for real trouble. That kind of runaway inflation is the most destructive of all social solvents, short of war. It destroys the middle class, the bedrock of social stability. It makes any rational planning for the future impossible. It makes political extremists out of people who have lost both their savings and their hopes, and it encourages politicians with foam on their lips to promise some sort of certainty at any cost. Usually it leads to a breakdown of the existing social system and the advent of some variety of authoritarian government. We have seen it happen in Germany and Russia after World War I, and in much of Latin America and Africa today. And even a dictatorial regime can't always succeed in halting runaway prices, as the current plight of Yugoslavia and Brazil testifies.

The moral, I guess, is that you can't have everything.

You can't have full employment without some inflation. You can't have a completely stable economy and a completely democratic society, including free labor unions and a free market, at the same time. You can't have even a moderate inflation, together with a just and efficient economic system. You can't have balanced budgets and a happy electorate. Yet you can risk unbridled inflation only at the hazard of social disaster; for that kind of inflation really *does* hurt everybody, including the unions—always the first institution to be smashed by an authoritarian government, of the left or the right.

The most we can do, in all likelihood, is to muddle along with a series of compromises that are disagreeable but not quite intolerable: a little inflation, a little unemployment, a moderate restraint on the freedom of action of both unions and business, a somewhat misguided pattern of savings and investment, a measure of continuing injustice to the poor, the old, the unskilled, and the black. . . .

DETROIT TODAY; TOMORROW THE NATION*

Beginning early in 1974, and continuing into 1975, the "permanent inflation" described in the preceding article by John Fischer has been accompanied by a recession that has sometimes threatened to develop into a full-fledged depression. The negative effects of these contradictory economic trends—inflation coupled with recession—have hit Detroit, Michigan particularly hard. The latest available figures (in January 1975) show that the unemployment rate in Detroit's inner city is over 30%. Detroit's plight has general significance because what happens in Motor City has so often been a harbinger of what is later going to happen in the nation as a whole. And, says journalist William Stevens, ". . . in this time of steadily worsening recession, the message from Detroit grows more unsettling all the time." The news from Washington is even more unsettling—when the Federal government attempts to stop recessionary trends, it fuels inflation; and when it attempts to stop inflation, it generates unemployment. Either condition, if allowed to become severe enough, has the revolutionary potential mentioned in this article by William Stevens.

. . . A fearful uncertainty grips much of the city. Automobile production is at a 23-year low for December, and there are virtually no signs of upturn. Unemployment in the metropolitan area is expected to surpass 10 percent for December. Things are not yet catastrophic, but some persons including the Mayor, detect a potential for serious social dislocation, even strife, should the recession continue far into 1975.

To get a sense of what is happening, one must go behind doors. This is an interior city. . . .

*Adapted from William K. Stevens, "Detroit in Recession Reflects Fear and Strength," *The New York Times*, 30 Dec 74, pp. 25Cff.

Often it is focused in bars. There are thousands of them around the city—almost always plain and unpretentious on the outside, frequently colorful and sometimes lavish on the inside. Much of neighborhood life is centered there, as it is in recreational pursuits such as softball and bowling. It is impossible to imagine Detroit without them, and the better-known ones attract a clientele from all across the city.

One such place is Watts's Club Mozambique on the northwest side. Crowds, predominately black, flock there to hear live jazz. Members of the Detroit Pistons are regular patrons, as are some politicians and many, many auto workers who have grown accustomed to living well during the good times of the last decade.

Cornelius Watts, owner of the club, has offered free admission to laid-off auto workers. Some have shown up, but the business generally is way down.

Oliver Dickerson was there the other night, though. He is a 35-year-old Chrysler worker, one of the hundreds of thousands of blacks who make up about half of the city's population of 1.5 million, and a member of what is perhaps the most affluent black community in the country. Atlanta may have a greater number of upper-middle-class blacks, but Detroit probably has proportionately more who have become solidly fixed in the lower-and middle-middle classes.

Mr. Dickerson is also one of some 50,000 Detroit-area auto workers who were laid off this week. . . .

"What's happening now is going to hurt years from now," he said. "In the past, you could get a job in Detroit when you couldn't get one anywhere else. You could get ahead here. Every day, people have been coming up into the middle class and straining to stay there. Now you're on the verge of going back into the hole."

Edward Petrey, a 32-year-old former Kentuckian, represents another side of Detroit, the white Appalachian people who trekked north to Detroit City to seek a better life, much as did the blacks. Mr. Petrey came here in 1963, and has lived a generally comfortable existence in an unassuming one-story shingled house in the suburb of Hazel Park.

He works for a company that builds spot-welding machinery for the Ford Motor Company. Sixty of the 135 workers at the small plant had been laid off, and they get no S.U.B. [Supplemental Unemployment Benefit—Ed.] pay. Mr. Petrey's hours have been cut to 32 a week, and he is expecting to be laid off any day. The cut in hours, plus inflationary pressures, "are dribblin' me down a little bit at a time," he said.

He has had to cut down on buying and "quit goin' South so many times to replenish his spirit.

"That's hurt more than anything," Mr. Petrey said the other day. If things get worse, he said, he will likely have to leave Detroit and go back to Kentucky permanently.

There are those as Oliver Dickerson said, who are worse off. There are the poor, the chronically unemployed and the unemployable.

There are estimated 105,000 persons in danger of malnutrition among Detroit's population, and they are flocking to food-handout centers.

Some of them have been observed in restaurants near the Fisher and General Motors Buildings in midtown. They buy a cup of coffee, wait for a diner to finish eating and leave, then slide into the booth and finish what is left. . . .

The familiar Detroit, the Detroit of legend, emerged largely in the nineteen-forties and fifties. It was the image of a roistering, hell-for-leather town, a working man's town of fascinating ethnic variety; a town short on what are known in gourmet circles as "good restaurants," but a place where the preparation of a hamburger has been elevated to high art. It was a place rich in out-of-the-way ethnic restaurants which were hard to find but offered Old-World delicacies well worth the search. It was a beer-and-pretzels sports town, the town of the Tigers of Hank Greenberg and Al Kaline, the Lions of Bobby Layne and the Red Wings of Gordy Howe.

The image took on new, and ultimately dominant, dimensions when the blacks and the hillbillies streamed north during and after World War II. By the nineteen-sixties, Detroit City was also Motown, Soul City, the Detroit of Diana Ross and Stevie Wonder and the black pop-music explosion.

Other explosions, too. The riot of 1967, when black frustration made Detroit symbolic of a riotous era in urban America.

Detroit had fancied itself as a leader of the governmental effort to solve the urban crisis. The riot burst that bubble, and with it went the optimism about restructuring urban society. Agencies designed to help the poor turned into calcified bureaucracies, and the Federal Government's plans to buy and re-sell inner-city housing backfired and led to the abandonment and destruction of whole neighborhoods.

It seemed that the harder men tried, the worse things got.

During the nineteen-fifties and sixties, the government built freeways, and the white middle class—thereby guaranteed easy access to downtown jobs without being chained to the city itself—moved out in increasing numbers. Black and white became more polarized than ever. Whites, displaying the same xenophobia that had been directed at other immigrants in times past, began blaming "them," the blacks, for the deterioration of the city.

The city did become physically obsolete, and efforts to renew it lagged continually. The influence of the burgeoning post-war generation flooded every aspect of city life. Crime soon became largely the province of the young and it soared. Detroit had become "murder city," with the greatest number of homicides per capita of the nation's 25 largest cities. Whites recoiled at the thought of going downtown at night. . . .

Yet with it all, the city retained some graces and advantages simply by virtue of being a big city. There is the Detroit Symphony—a fine orchestra, although like most, it does not make money—and dozens of art galleries along with a number of theater and dance companies. . . .

Most of all, one major positive fact has gone largely unappreciated: In Detroit City, as elsewhere, masses of rural migrants—with an individual lifetime in many cases—achieved a successful middle-class lifestyle. They have homes and cars of their own, and leisure time to spend using boats, snowmobiles and even vacation retreats.

A 1969 study of 18 major urban areas showed that in terms of money income per person, adjusted for cost-of-living differences, Detroiters were wealthiest with $4,724. The New York area ranked fourth with $4,513; the 18-area average was $4,195.

But now, as Mayor Young asserts, much of it could turn out to have been illusory. Masses who had come to think of themselves as middle-class or who have never known hard times, people like Oliver Dickerson, are suddenly encountering at least a measure of the reality that once faced their fathers.

"Now that the wrinkles have come back in their bellies," the Mayor said the other day, "they're startin' to think of themselves as workers again."

In the view of the Mayor and others, there is a danger here: some laid-off auto workers, products of the inner city, have, at times, lived on the edge of crime. Pushed too far, it is reasoned, they will turn to it to make ends meet. "It's generally accepted that a bad economy has a tremendous impact on the crime problem," according to Police Chief Philip G. Tannian.

But more deeply, it is being suggested that a more general revolutionary atmosphere might develop if the recession is too severe and too long. Expectations among workers have been heightened, it is said. They have not just tasted the good life, but drunk deeply of it. There is the precedent, and the legacy, of the student and black rebellions of the nineteen-sixties. People in general are more sophisticated and less docile than they were during the Depresssion. It is a major concern among Detroiters who think about such things. . . .

Is "Withdrawal" the Answer?

A number of people conclude that the only way to handle serious problems is to retreat from them into some other order of reality. The retreat takes a number of forms: drugs, religion, rural communes, racial enclaves, etc. As these illustrative articles suggest, such escapes from reality seldom if ever constitute a viable means to rectify wrong. They work, in given instances, for brief periods. But in most cases they are soon revealed as superficial answers to problems which can be solved, if at all, only by a fundamental alteration of our entire social system.

THE NEEDLE OF DEATH*

Here we have the story of an eighteen year old British youth who is a legal addict—that is, he is "certified" and receives his drugs by prescription. Even so, his life, what there is of it, is an unending series of horrors. As bad as it is, the story would be far worse if told about the average American addict who must obtain his supplies at the highly inflated prices typical of illegal transactions.

... He never regulates his fixes by hour or minute, by office workers' hasty looking at the time for tea break. Usually the mood, sleep and no sleep for nights before, arguments with another addict, lack of money, worry over the coming night's sleep, combine to a confusion which his inadequacy cannot resolve without another fix—that can't be yet—there is little left.

He walks across Leicester Square, drawing the two bottles to the top of his pocket, cradling them in his hand, tapping, shaking with his fingers, checking, calculating that he has as much heroin and cocaine as he thought. Sometimes he has pulled out bottles of the day before, month before, and they lie there empty and clouded by the dusty remains of the cocaine, misted on the moist glass, useless, unattainable even with hot water, and at first his stomach has turned because there was nothing left, he thought,

*Adapted from Paul Hunter, *Needle of Death* (London: Studio Vista Limited, 1967), pp. 7-15.

until he saw a bottle with some heroin and a little cocaine and his step
picked up as he walked on with more confidence.

. . . .

All the heroin, all the cocaine is used to move through an ordinary day
provided nothing traumatic happens (like a dropped dustbin lid which will
leave him shaking for half an hour), when no discomfort is produced
because of what someone says or doesn't say but indicates by attitude—
worse than someone being plain angry because with unspoken attitudes
there is no comeback and it all builds up inside him so that he weeps at
the least excuse—but doesn't want sympathy—embarrassed because he's
afraid of embarrassing the person sitting next to him—so more tears stream
down his face because he can't say to someone that he's never seen before
that he's sad or something, because that doesn't mean anything anyway
and it would worry this person, who looks pretty worried anyway, even
more and it's then he knows that he is going to have to fix pretty soon if
he's not going to cry until midnight feeling silly because he doesn't know
why he's crying and he doesn't want people to look at him as they do.

He stands up wearily and walks out into the open. . . .

The rain seems to be everywhere—under his skin—and he turns into
Charing Cross Road to pause in a book shop for a while and look through
the magazines produced by hippies for hippies who are happy and know all
about being *avant-garde*—they seem dull as ever and anyway he's already
seen them; rain can be put up with for a while so long as there's a fix at
the end; he's begun to shake just a little which means that if he tries to
space out the fix any more he'll vomit. Rather than that he walks on
through the rain, making for the room, thinking of the fix, moving swiftly
through the crowds who are shopping, going home from work, browsing,
waiting or just hurrying to shelter from the rain and the cold, their minds
preoccupied, thinking of many things; he thinks simply of one thing and
walks.

> 'Drug addiction is a state, a periodic or chronic intoxication produced
> by the repeated consumption of a drug (natural or synthetic). Its
> characteristics include (1) an overpowering desire or need (com-
> pulsion) to continue taking the drug and to obtain it by any means;
> (2) a tendency to increase the dose; (3) a psychic (psychological) and
> generally a physical dependence on the effects of the drug; (4)
> detrimental effect on the individual and on society.'
> *World Health Organization Commission on Addiction-producing Drugs.*

Hands still in his pockets, his fingers tightly clenching his works; checking the top of his bottle (once it came off, cocaine spilled into his pocket

lining and he cried all day), feeling for a syringe, digging into another pocket for a needle that is sharp, he settles into his stride, glances into a shop window and is knocked into the gutter by a bowler-hatted man strutting paunchily past. Recovering, he turns and stares angrily at the receding figure, eyes following it angrily, as it disappears into the tube station oblivious of an 18-year-old, body tensing with fury, mouth tightly clenched. He turns, and carries on walking across the road, trying not to be angry, trying to be calm because if he's tense when it comes to the fix he won't be able to concentrate and, because his hand continues to shake, the heroin will pass into his system subcutaneously instead of intravenously; it's the difference between a skinpop and a mainline; or between the heroin and cocaine passing into the tissues just beneath the skin, being absorbed slowly, less effectively than the mainline, where the heroin and cocaine passing directly into his vein flow through his blood stream, through his heart to his brain.

Each day his prescription gives him two grains of heroin, two grains of cocaine. Each day twelve small white pills, a little bottle of white powder. Each of the twelve tiny jacks is one-sixth of a grain of heroin—relatively a small dose, but even so there were months in hospital with doctors, psychiatrists, nurses and psychologists all trying to cure him of his addiction and, helplessly, within a few days of leaving them he was walking the same streets, staring without interest at the same scenes, regularly fixing a dose of heroin to tolerate existence ... to tolerate something. Crossing the road he swings open the door and starts to climb the stairs hoping to find somebody, realising by the dead silence above him that no one is there and he will fix alone.

> 'a person who, not requiring the continued use of the drug for the relief of the symptoms of an organic disease, has acquired an overpowering desire for its continuance, and withdrawal of the drug leads to definite symptoms of mental or physical distress or disorder.'
> *Departmental Commission on Morphine and Heroin Addiction*

As he opens the door and glances round he remembers sharply, for no apparent reason, an addict, dead of an overdose, found sitting on a lavatory seat with the syringe still in his arm and how the lavatory cleaner who found him was frightened and angry because he hadn't seen that sort of thing before and *if they're going to do that why don't they go somewhere else dirty bastards?* Forgetting almost before remembering he turns to a table at the centre of the room, taking off his jacket, glancing at his T-shirt (borrowed from someone who had got hold of it in Sweden); looking round he sees a glass and fills it with water.

. . . .

(In a toilet he would climb on to the lavatory bowl and take water from the cistern.) Sterile water, syringes and needles are rarely, if ever prescribed by the doctor—an ampoule of sterile water at 8d—a disposable syringe 8d to 1s 4d—needles between 2d and 4d. Each injection takes money that could have been spent on food. He may take 8 injections a day.

> '[The addict] is liable to infection by a dirty needle, is an easy victim of all kinds of diseases through general physical debility ... the death rate in the young age groups under consideration was over twenty times the expected mortality rate.'
>
> *A. Kaldegg*, New Society, *2 February 1967*

It can't be his left arm which is covered with sores and scabs and more sores, and a cocaine abscess painfully oozes a trickle of fluid. When abscesses are on both arms it is almost impossible to put in a needle without it hurting like hell, and even when he's free sometimes of abscesses some veins just don't seem to exist. They're difficult to hit through overuse with the wrong needles.

He takes the syringe and lays it on the table. He takes the needle from its protective foil and fits it into the barrel of the syringe. Inserting the needle into the water he pulls back on the plunger; drawing water bubbling back into the barrel. There is an air leak and he has some vaseline with which to run the plunger and make it slide against the barrel walls more smoothly; if he cannot fix, this is the worst happening in the world because it is all there but you can't do anything with it.

He examines his arm.

On some veins there are hundreds of little red pinpricks, minutely neatly spaced along their length. They itch. Although the veins on the back of his hand are quite distinct, they are lousy for fixing because they puff up and itch more insistently than on any other part of the body. Taking his belt from round his trousers he extends his right arm and with his left wraps it round the top of his arm, clenching his fist, bending and straightening his arm, trying to push blood into tired veins, waiting for a minute or two, peering to find a blue ridge which could turn out a good fix. Like some connoisseur he raises his arm for the light to play on it and runs his fingers softly up and down, pausing at different points, listening with his touch, trying to find a mark which will feel fresh; and then he must remember if it was good last time. His mind drifts over the last ten or so fixes, evaluating each qualitatively, dismissing the poor fixes, moving on until he touches the point where he made a really good fix, transferring his fingers to that part of his arm until he feels the mark, senses the vein. Taking the three remaining jacks left he drops them into the syringe and then shakes in the rest of the cocaine from the flat end of his nail clippers and gently shakes the barrel, tapping it to get rid of air bubbles, waiting until both are in solution, patiently holding back quite deliberately. He holds the syringe between two fingers, raises it towards the light and then brings it gently towards the surface of his skin. He passes the needle through his skin very, very slowly as with some delicate tapestry. The skin clings to the needle; the needle slides on terribly slowly until it is buried to its hilt. Then transferring his grip, leaving the syringe hanging free, hanging by the needle, he moves his hand until he can draw the plunger of the barrel from the syringe, looking for blood. Sometimes blood spurts into the syringe obediently and immediately. This time there is no blood. He pulls out the needle about half an inch from his arm and pushes it again trying to break into the side of the vein, his lips pursed. Again he transfers his grip.

Again there is no blood.

Swearing he kicks his left foot a little and pulls the needle from his arm. Blood trickles towards his elbow. He holds the syringe up against the light and squeezes it a little, watching for the minute spurt of liquid that will mean that the needle is not blocked. In his determination to find a vein as quickly as possible his grip loosens on the barrel and it drops, spilling tiny pools of clear liquid on the table top. Swearing again, he carefully aims the needle at the pools and tries to salvage what he can. The ritual begins again. The needle moves in and out trying to find a vein. No pain registers on his face. His fingers move swiftly again and he draws back the plunger.

Nothing.

NOTHING.

Moving his fingers toward the hilt of the needle he angles it once more, digging deeper.

Longingly.

Impatiently now.

And then it's ... *there*—a tiny trace of blood which looks almost lost, oozing quietly, waving up the centre of the barrel until it loses its momentum, unfolding, breaking until it is diffused and is diluted by the heroin and cocaine.

This moment is beautiful and cherished and he sits more squarely on the chair. Adjusting the needle a little, more blood spurts, a deeper colour now, into the syringe. Placing a finger on the plunger he pushes it slowly and firmly into the barrel until he knows the content of the syringe is within his vein, leaving the syringe dangling in his arm he whips off the belt.

Heroin is running free, he knows it was a mainline, words mean nothing now.

It explodes and for a few seconds clouds his mind dreamily. His face relaxes and his eyes close gently, an almost imperceptible smile on his face as if someone had complimented him on his clothes, though he wouldn't have minded if they hadn't said anything anyway. Then minutes spent flushing blood into his arm and out again watching it absent-mindedly, playing and picking at blood clots, and where his arm had been itching picking the scabs with his needle and watching the blood spread down.

There is nothing else to do.

The heroin is deep within him.

He feels good with himself.

> 'the depressant actions include analgesia (relief of pain), sedation (freedom from anxiety), muscular relaxation, decreased motor activity, hypnosis (drowsiness and lethargy) and euphoria (a sense of well-being).'
>
> *D. P. Ausubel*

The heroin absorbs him, mind and body, his very self, his feelings, his perception, his love and anxiety melt and transform themselves into a certainty, a unity, where total frustration becomes a beautiful acceptable oneness.

. . . .

Sometimes he fixes in a night club, crouched over the lavatory and afterwards stands with his eyes closed, all going on about him—people dancing and his own feelings, his very self melt, fuse and drift at one. He is a communion of the within and the without and it is inexpressibly what only he can know. Nothing is positive—nothing is negative. Every complicaton becomes a single warmth; to talk about it is a hang-up. He pays little attention to those standing near him and turns to the juke box and the all-absorbing, magnetically drawing, sound of the record. The feeling is him. His body starts to relax, waving forwards from the waist downwards; it has found a meaning and rhythm within the record that is his, uniquely his. No one knows the beauty, the pleasant goodness of being there just at that second. It is unique, the past, the present, the future, are not only unproblematical, they are harmonized, merging with ease, peace and happiness at the being, that is so undeniable it's as fragile and vulnerable as the brain tissues and soft bone that lie beneath the soft skin of a minute-old baby.

Then it's gone, almost before he knew it was there, and he realises as a thousand times before the inevitable transience of the needle relationship.

. . . .

TODAY'S EXORCISTS*

Your editor is perhaps immodest to include an adaptation of another one of his own writings; the piece is, in addition, dated in that it deals with a phase of the Vietnam war. But on the other hand the implication of the piece is timeless and universal—namely, that large-scale organized religion almost always functions such that the established distribution of privilege is justified, sanctified, and protected from any implication that the powers from on high would disapprove of it.

Early this year, at a large Methodist church in Phoenix, Arizona, I underwent one of the most shattering experiences of my career: in the middle of a speech I had been invited to give at a meeting of the official board I was interrupted and—amid cires of "commie," "red tactics," "get him out of here"—I was ejected from the building.

The invitation to speak had come from the church's social concerns committee, whose members, having concluded that United States military activity in Vietnam is unjustified, wished to circulate "Negotiation Now!" petitions among the membership. They asked the minister so to inform the congregation from the pulpit; he replied that he wanted to find out the board's reaction first. Therefore the social concerns committee asked for and was granted a block of time at the next meeting of the board. To support their position, they asked me to come and explain why I am opposed to our presence in Vietnam. I agreed to the arrangements and appeared as scheduled.

There were perhaps 50 people in the chapel—board members and representatives of various committees scheduled to make reports. I was introduced with a brief explanation of why the social concerns committee wanted me to speak to the board.

My first point—first because it seems to me to be the most basic—was that it is erroneous to assert that our fundamental enemy is communism; rather, our most dangerous enemy is hunger, disease, poverty, inherited privilege—the conditions that lead people to turn to extreme "isms" as a possible answer to their problems. It is naive and simplistic to say, therefore, that the enemy is communism; communism is a consequence, not primarily a cause. To support this point I quoted Senator George McGovern, veteran of 35 combat missions as a pilot in World War II and a Methodist layman:

*Adapted from Thomas Ford Hoult, "Exorcism, Middle Class Church Style," *The Christian Century* 85(March 6, 1968):294-295.

THE MINISTER *Who Proves to the Rich Supporters of His Church That a Camel Can Go Through the Eye of a Needle*

A country that builds a government responsive to the needs of the citizenry—that faces up to the internal problems of misrule, injustice and human misery, need have little fear of falling victim to a "war of liberation." A government that ignores these fundamental concerns of its people, as the dictators of South Vietnam have done, is headed for trouble and does not deserve to be saved—indeed, it probably cannot be saved—by American soldiers.

At that point an elderly member of the board rose to protest: "I object to this defense of communism." There was a dead silence while my reply was awaited.

"I am not defending communism," I said. "I am trying to indicate that support for the war rests on some misleading ideas about the nature of the problems we face."

The man was not satisfied: "It sounds like defense of communism to me and I won't listen to any more. I call on the board to stop this right now!"

The moderator asked the social concerns committee chairman to clarify the situation. She repeated her opening remarks: "We feel negotiation is called for and we wanted the board to know why. The speaker is trying to tell you why."

"Well," said the moderator, "we have a lot of important business to attend to. How much more time did you plan to take?"

"We were given 45 minutes," she answered.

"I've heard more than enough," said the original objector. "I'm leaving until this nonsense is stopped." Whereupon he marched out of the room.

Another man rose to give a short but impassioned speech to the effect that the Methodist Church should never support one side of a controversial issue. His contention aroused enthusiastic applause.

The moderator asked the social concerns chairman why both sides of the issue were not being presented. "Because we wanted to indicate *our* reasons for favoring negotiation, not the opposite." she answered.

Numerous mutterings and patently impolite comments began to surface. "None of his business," said one man. "Get him out of here," said a young woman. I remained at the podium, listening, waiting, thinking.

The minister rose to explain that he had thought I was going to talk about "Negotiation Now!"—not about the war—and that he wanted to find out the sense of the board before the petitions were presented to the membership.

The moderator then announced that since it was his understanding that the board would not stop the circulation of the petitions, there was no reason to consider the war any further. The chairman of the social concerns committee agreed, whereupon the moderator indicated that I should leave the room.

"I would like to ask your permission to say one more thing," I said to the moderator. Receiving no response from him, I went on:

> This morning some students asked me if it was proper for the American Sociological Association to go on record as favoring our withdrawal from Vietnam. The students expressed their opinion that a *scientific* organization should remain neutral. My response was that in political affairs there is no such thing as a "neutral" position. To quote Gandhi: "Politics enmeshes us as with a serpent's coils from which there is no escape." If you assess any action in terms of its consequences, the result of a so-called nonposition is to support the status quo. Therefore, if you do not take a stand against the war in Vietnam, the consequence of your action is support for it. This church, if it does not collectively take a stand against the war, is backing it.

Members of the audience responded with answers whose gist was "We *want* to support the war!" Facial expressions and voice tones indicated total hostility to any thoughtful consideration of the issues involved. It would be easy, and it is tempting, to judge that such belligerence was sparked by a very few "minutemen" types. But not one person rose to say as much as "Let us at least observe the norms of elementary politeness to a guest." Not one!

Disheartened, dismayed, I concluded: "It seems incredible to me that you people feel you represent the Prince of Peace." The response to this admittedly overly provocative observation was such as to lead me to toss out another: "I fear that if Jesus walked in these doors, you will tell him to leave because of his long hair and bare feet."

"That remark is a commie tactic," said a woman board member. "That's a red smear."

I made my way out—dazed, profoundly disturbed. I was accompanied by eight or ten people who offered apologies for the "misunderstanding," for the mass impoliteness. "For Methodism," said one man. A woman observed: "Our tactics were all wrong. We were trying an educational approach with a board that doesn't know the meaning of education."

I had no legitimate grounds for feeling righteous, but I asked, "How can you stand it?"

"It's hard, but we want to keep trying," said one of the men.

"I admire your persistence," I said. "But I think it is utterly realistic to observe that you're probably faced with a hopeless task."

Later, with the help of my colleagues at the university, I tried to account for two things: What explains the board's extreme reaction to my really very mild observations about communism? And why should I feel so completely shattered by the experience?

We concluded that the answer to the first question is similar to the one Arnold Toynbee finally worked out when he was puzzled as to why American audiences become so glum when he describes the deep and unbridgeable gulf between China and Russia:

> Why should Americans be displeased at a major change in the international situation that is manifestly to the advantage of the United States? Finally, it occurred to me that this political advantage . . . is less precious, for some Americans . . . than a psychological asset that China has deprived them of by the same act. China has exploded the myth of "monolithic world communism." But perhaps this myth, dreamed by Lenin, answered to some American need.

This "need" is the belief that the United States has the cherished role of St. George fighting the dragon, of the Archangel Michael contending with the devil. But if there is no international communist conspiracy, where then is the devil?

This is what I did to the board: I took away their devil. In effect, the board members probably said to themselves something that could be paraphrased thus: "If the enemy is not that handy, foreign phenomenon—communism—but is instead hunger, disease and hopelessness, then my wonderful, upper middle class, white, privileged world is really threatened. No! It's too horrible! I can't look! Out, damned spot!" and I—or rather my notions about what the enemy actually is—was the spot, and had to go.

As for my extreme reaction, I supsect my young son put his finger on the cause. When I described the incident to the family, he said, "It's scary." That's it—it's a frightening thought that the board members of that big Methodist church in Phoenix, Arizona, are probably representative of a multitude of middle class churches across the land. And, in turn, such official boards are made up of the very people who constitute the power structure of the nation. They make the decisions—in the newspapers, the large corporations, the law firms, the government offices which control our destiny—and they use organized religion as a sanction for their special privileges and a cover for their cruelty and greed. To the degree that this is true, it is sobering indeed to realize that we are at the mercy of people who are possessed by the sense of desperation that has led others like them to do just what I said the poor finally do—turn to some extreme "ism" as an answer to their feelings of helplessness in the face of danger. That the board members, in their fear, turn to the far right whereas the hungry turn far left, seems of little consequence. For in the end the general result in both cases is the same—repression, abrogation of civil liberties, monolithic rule from the top. . . .

THE ZEN CHILD*

Their bellies bloated, their legs badly bowed, the two little boys made a pathetic sight as they slumped frog-like and lethargic on their haunches throughout the examination at Children's Hospital in San Francisco. One was 2½, the other 1½; neither could walk or crawl; the older child had a vocabulary of two words and weighed 16 pounds, the younger just managed to tip the scales at 11 pounds; their hair was coarse and brittle, and they were extremely cranky.

Horrified, pediatrician Dr. Josette Mondanaro and her colleagues made bone development tests of the children. Normally, a child's "bone age" should be within two months of his actual age, but in the tests the 2½-year-old showed a bone age of six months, and the 1½-year-old registered three months. Diagnosis showed that both little boys were suffering from severe cases of rickets and scurvy—and that they had been living for months on the Zen macrobiotic diet of their hippie parents.

Zen macrobiotics, a concept of spiritual and physical enrichment through a diet based ultimately on brown rice, is the brainchild of the late George Ohsawa, a Japanese-born, Paris-based philosopher who died six years ago. Though disavowed by genuine Zen Buddhists, the macrobiotic diet has attained at least 10,000 dedicated adherents across the U.S., many of them hippies and other young dropouts. The diet has come under heavy attack from doctors and nutritionists and has caused at least one death plus an untold number of cases of scurvy, rickets, anemia and other forms of advanced malnutrition. Now pediatricians are becoming concerned over growing evidence that the risks posed by the fad are being passed on by the hippie generation to their children—with more serious results.

Ideal: A quick look at the Ohsawa regimen provides reason for the concern. Adherents of Zen macrobiotics progress from diet—3, consisting of a fairly well-balanced mix of meats, vegetables and fruits, to +7, an "ideal" diet consisting entirely of grains and a drastically limited intake of liquids and salt.

The results of such a diet when consumed regularly by a child can be frightening, though the number of children harmed in this fashion is probably quite low. Dr. Cyril Ramer, a San Francisco pediatrician with a large practice among members of the hip culture, told *Newsweek*'s Elizabeth Coleman about a 1½-year-old she saw: "In one year, the baby had gained half a pound. It couldn't walk, couldn't crawl, couldn't speak."

In the case of Mondanaro's two small boy patients, the parents had

Newsweek 80 (Sept. 18, 1972):71.

switched to Zen macrobiotics as a way of kicking the drug habit, and were raising their sons largely on rice, soy products, seaweed and Chinese cabbage. "As they became older," says Mondanaro, "the children became fussy eaters, so their diet became even more restricted." Ironically enough, the parents brought their youngsters to Mondanaro not because they were concerned about the state of their health—but to show the doctor how well the Zen macrobiotic diet worked. Concerned friends had tricked the parents into visiting the clinic with their children by telling them that Mondanaro was "interested in Zen macrobiotics."

Mondanaro patiently told the parents that the children must have more calcium, protein, and vitamin C in their diets. The parents refused to abandon macrobiotics altogether, but they finally agreed to give their sons oranges, meat, fish, eggs and dairy products. After six months, the children no longer show the painful, fragile bones of rickets, nor the skin eruptions of scurvy. The eldest is now starting to walk. Even so, the future for the youngsters is not promising.

What worries Mondanaro and other pediatricians who have observed the children of macrobiotic devotees is the possible long-term effects of nutritional deprivation on the growing child. Young adults, they note, have a lifetime of good nutrition behind them so that they can go on deprivation diets; if they are careful and plan their diets so as to include all the proper nutrients, macrobiotics is quite safe. But children are different. "If you starve a child in the first year, when it triples in weight and doubles its length," says Ramer, "you not only cut down on the size of cells, but the number of them. A child can never totally recover from that." Of particular concern is the effect of malnutrition on the developing brain and central nervous system; malnourished children often lag intellectually. Adherents of the macrobiotic fad, says San Francisco pediatrician Dr. John Bolton, like to claim that the small size of their youngsters proves that nutrients are going to the brain rather than the body and profess themselves pleased that theirs are not typical "overfed" American babies. "But that," says Bolton, "is hogwash."

Abuse: Mondanaro says that most of the patients insist on blaming their children's diseases on the inferiority of the body, rather than the inadequacies of the macrobiotic diet. "That they can ignore the obvious says a lot about the people who are into the diet," she notes. "They are fanatics." Bolton says many such parents disappear into the hippie underground when a doctor diagnoses malnutrition in one of their children. The answer, he insists, is to report the parents to the authorities and perhaps make their children wards of the state. "This," says Bolton, "should be in the same category as child abuse."

TECHNOLOGY DEFENDED*

In contemplating the sorry state of the world today, some observers such as the distinguished philosopher and theologian Jacques Ellul, have come to believe that our troubles are due primarily to science and technology. Man, they imply, should never have begun the exploration of the laws governing the material universe. Once formulated, these laws, proceeding on a momentum of their own, will imprison him. "Enclosed within his artificial creation," syas Ellul, "man finds that there is no exit, that he cannot pierce the shell of technology to find again the ancient milieu to which he was adapted for hundreds of thousands of years." This would seem to indicate that we did better in the Stone Age.

The Nobel Prize physicist Max Born comes close to agreeing with this view. "I am haunted by the idea." he declares, "that the break in human civilization caused by the discovery of the scientific method may be irreparable."

The philosophy of retreat to a simpler era may have had some validity 200 years ago when Rousseau was celebrating the virtues of Cro-Magnon man, but too much water has gone through the turbines. The growth curves of science and technology have profoundly changed the cultural habits of the West and have made deep inroads on the East—witness Japan.

I believe that the way to come to terms with technology today is, first, to understand it and, then, to encourage its good effects on the human condition and at the same time try to discourage its bad effects. I cannot follow the mystique that technology has laws of its own, over and beyond human intervention.

Is it possible to conceive of a civilized society in the 1970s without electric power, motor vehicles, railroads, airplanes, telephones, television, elevators, flush toilets, central heating, airconditioning, antibiotics, vaccines, and antiseptics?

. . . .

The necessity for caution in evaluation is apparent in the case of the internal combustion engine—probably the most popular piece of technology ever invented. The automobile has markedly improved the human condition by providing greater mobility and convenience, while degrading it with air pollution. How long before the liabilities overwhelm the assets? Even if the technicians devise a pollution-free engine, the miseries and tragedies of

*Adapted from Stuart Chase, "Two Cheers for Technology," *Saturday Review* 54(Feb. 20, 1971):20–21, 76–77.

highway accidents and traffic jams remain, indeed expand with population and affluence.

Where does the balance of a given technology lie now? Where will it be a decade hence? How does the balance shift from area to area—high-energy cultures, low-energy cultures, big city, open country? Under intensive analysis, the balance shifts with time, and with place, for nearly every item under consideration.

There are three major threats to mankind today, all due primarily to technology: 1) the arms race in nuclear weapons, which, if continued, can only end in World War III; 2) the accelerating destruction of the environment; and 3) the population explosion. For easy reference, I once called these threats "bombs, bulldozers, and babies." The effect of technology is obvious enough in the first two, but the third requires a moment's thought. Modern medicine in its control of epidemics, for instance, has enormously reduced death rates all over the world, in low-energy societies as well as high. Birth control, however, has not kept pace with death control, and through the widening gap population pours. At the present rate of growth, there will be twice as many people in the world by the year 2000. But again we must be careful of an "all good" or "all bad" evaluation. Modern medicine in one sense is a great boon, but death control without a compensating birth control is the unquestioned reason for the population explosion that is rapidly becoming a menace to the human condition.

Again, nuclear weapons, by a curious logical paradox, could conceivably become mankind's greatest asset. Robert Oppenheimer once called the atomic bomb "a great peril and a great hope," by which he meant that it made large-scale wars unwinnable—an exercise in mutual suicide. But as diplomacy now stands, the arms race is more of a liability than an asset—particularly when biological and chemical weapons are brought into the equation. I am unaware of anything that can be said in favor of these despicable technologies.

The destruction of the environment, which is now on an exponential curve, also seems to be an unmitigated liability to the human condition. There is, however, a small offset. Many of the destructive forces cross national boundaries—industrial smog, oil spills, fallout, pollution of rivers that flow through two or more sovereign states. Only international cooperation can cope with these diasasters, and so the demand for a stronger world organization is increased.

Bombs, bulldozers, and babies may be the major threats to the human condition today, but they are by no means the only ones for which technology is responsible. Noise pollution, for instance, is an extension of air pollution. Anyone living near a jetport—or even trying to do so—suffers, as does anyone whose home is near a highway infested with heavy-duty trucks. The decibed count goes steadily up in high-energy societies, and more and more people suffer from defective hearing. But we really haven't heard anything yet. Wait until the SSTs smash their fifty-mile corridors of sonic boom from coast to coast, along with smashed windows, crockery, and nervous systems.

As agriculture is mechanized by the automated cotton picker and other labor-saving devices, displaced farm workers—black, brown, yellow and white—lose their livelihoods and descend on the cities, where the ghettos, already overburdened, try to accommodate them. See Harlem in New York, "La Perla" in San Juan, the vast shacktowns of Caracas—see them and weep for the human condition.

As the sharecroppers move in at least in America—the middle class moves out en masse to the suburbs, where the open land is geometrically sliced into subdivisions. The lowing of cattle gives way to the grunt of the bulldozer, and the station wagons pile up at the supermarket. "Spread city," or megalopolis, is rapidly becoming a forbidding place in which to live, for rich as well as poor. Last year, when S. J. Perelman left New York City for good, he exclaimed: "Plants can live on carbon dioxide, but I can't."

The international trade in non-nuclear weapons—jet fighters, tanks, machine guns—is now estimated at $5 billion a year. Every mini-nation in Africa and Asia seems ready to mortgage its future in order to be immediately outfitted with lethal weapons. The big nations, the sellers, in this profitable trade are always glad to clear their stocks of old models.

The crime rate is greatly aided by the getaway car, and civilian terror and confusion are aided by anonymous telephone warnings of bombs about to be exploded. The hijacking of airliners, and the consequent holding of passengers as hostages, is something quite new in political terrorism. Its only offset is another demonstration that, in an age of high technology, this is one world or none.

Certainly, there are additional liabilities, but those that I have indicated are a representative lot—perhaps the most serious ones. Let us turn now to the assets. What has technology done for the good life?

The human condition in high-energy societies has been improved by better diets, health care, education, and scientific knowledge of vitamins. Young people are now taller, stronger, and better favored than their parents or grandparents, This is markedly true in Japan. In America, some 40 percent of all youngsters of college age are in college. When I was a young man, the figure was below 5 percent.

People in high-energy cultures live longer, are more literate, and enjoy more travel and recreation than the generation that preceded them, while the ratio of poor people to total population has declined drastically. No society in history has ever remotely approached the standard of living enjoyed in the United States, defined in either dollars or materials consumed. No society has ever been so well nourished, so well bathed, so well doctored. No civilized society, furthermore, has ever worked such short hours to produce and distribute the necessities of life.

Two dark spots in this otherwise bright picture must be noted.

America's affluent society does not adequately care for its old people. The elderly have a sharply declining place in the family compared with the grandparents of a simpler age. The average "home for the aged" can hardly be called an asset to the human condition.

And secondly, this affluent society is built on an exceedingly shaky foundation of natural resources. Here we connect with the liability of a degenerating environment. The United States with only some 6 percent of the world's population uses up some 40 percent of the world's annual production of raw materials. If all the world enjoyed American affluence, there would be about twelve times the current demand for raw materials— an impossible drain on the resources of this planet.

Here is an equation that must be faced, probably before the twentieth century has run its course. If the so-called hungry world of Asia, Africa, and Latin America is significantly to increase its living standards, America and other high-energy societies must decrease their consumption of raw materials. This does not mean that the latter must retreat to the economy of scarcity, but it does mean an economy programmed for a great reduction in waste, for recycling used materials, for the elimination of planned obsolescence.

If the technology of production is really to serve the human condition, it might well have as its goal the concept of "perpetual yield." The lumber barons of the nineteenth century in America operated on a "cut out and get out" program that promised to destroy the forests of the continent. Beginning in Maine, they slashed through New York, Michigan, Wisconsin, Minnesota, and on to the West Coast, leaving behind a desolation where the very soil was burned away. Then came a miracle. The lumber industry, at least some of the larger companies, realized that they were sawing off the limb on which they sat. They halted their wholesale policy of slash and burn, adopted "selective cutting" to keep the forests healthy and planted millions of young trees. They shifted to a perpetual-yield basis, whereby a forest would be cut no faster than its annual growth.

Is this not a sound goal for all economic growth? *Keep the natural resources of the planet on a perpetual-yield basis.* The calculations will change, of course, as technology improves the yield. A fine example is the growing possibility, through intensive research and development, for employing thermonuclear *fusion* as the world's chief energy source. There is very little danger of radiation, and the hydrogen of the seven oceans will form the raw material for the process—good for thousands of years. Coal, oil, natural gas, and hydroelectric developments will no longer be prime sources. Fusion power—probably employing lasers—can be a great asset of technology, indeed, and might be operational within a generation. The rapidly developing new methods for recycling wastes of all kinds, solid and liquid, would also form an important part of the perpetual-yield concept.

Labor-saving devices in the field have just about abolished the institution of slavery all over the world, while in the home they have liberated women from a load of grinding toil, at least in high-energy societies.

Technology is now making it possible to mine the ocean and is thus opening a vast treasure chest. It has been proposed that the United Nations receive a royalty from these riches as they are developed. No nation, no corporation, no person owns the open oceans and its floor; it belongs to all mankind—with decent respect, of course, to all forms of life within it, and the ecosystems that govern it. Intelligently planned and carefully exploited, it may well be that the raw materials and foodstuffs of the oceans can markedly increase the concept of perpetual yield, and permit a higher ceiling for living standards all round.

It is not difficult to make a terrifying indictment of technology. It is not difficult to make a heartening list of benefits. The problem is so complex on one level, and yet, in essence, so simple. Granting the available resources of this planet, how many human beings and their fellow creatures can be supported at a level that makes life worth the living? A dependable evaluation is very difficult. We can be sure, however, that nothing is to be gained by following the prophets of doom back to the Stone Age.

I'VE HARDLY BEGUN TO FIGHT*

This and the next piece were written by a black American who was director of the U.S. Office of Information during part of the Lyndon Johnson administration; he is now a prize-winning columnist.

At a recent meeting of the Louisiana Education Association, a group of black professional educators, an incredible little vignette was played out.

The group was meeting in New Orleans to talk about ways to curb or halt the massive firings and demotions of black teachers and principals

*Carl T. Rowan, syndicated columnist, March 3, 1970.

which are taking place in numerous school districts that are forced to implement court-ordered desegregation plans.

Despite an obvious vested interest in keeping their jobs, these black educators were unwilling to attack integration or the courts whose desegregation orders had fanned the anger that cost them their livelihood. To do that would be to betray the black children whom they had seen cheated and stunted during years of Jim Crow schooling.

* * * *

Then into this gathering walked Roy Innis, national leader of the Committee on Racial Equality, both of which used to be in the militant front lines of the struggle against Jim Crow.

Innis told these black educators that he was on a little tour conferring with governors and other white politicians in Southern states, trying to get their backing for what he calls "a practical new alternative to desegration."

What Innis, a black man, offered was a form of educational apartheid. Atlanta, for example, would cease to be one school district, or one political entity, in which the courts could require the pairing of schools to break up segreation. Innis would split Atlanta into two separate school districts, one predominantly black, the other predominantly white.

Innis reasons that to the extent that members of one race lived in the other district, there would be desegregation, but that the fundamental result would be separation. He theorizes that whites will love this because "they don't want Mary Jane in the same classroom as a black boy" and that black parents will accept it because it would give them total control of black schools.

* * * *

Most of those troubled black educators went home from that New Orleans meeting confused, dismayed, and just plain angry that in so short a time the educational picture had deteriorated from one of bright hope to chaos.

Innis's bumbling efforts at hanky-panky with segregationist governors is symbolic of the confusion and thrashing about that has led so many people of all races to cry, "Integration is dead."

Blacks who once got their heads split open as they defied Jim Crow in grubby sandwich shops and grimy bus depots are suddenly throwing their hands up in surrender, convinced that the white man will never let blacks into his schools, neighborhoods, churches, and other institutions.

White liberals who once faced social ostracism and economic reprisals rather than abandon the ideal of racial equality are also bowing to what they think is a hopeless situation.

Perhaps intergration is dead. If so, much of the idealism, the mortality, the hope of America died with it.

Well, they needn't save me a place at the mourner's bench.

Let those who will proclaim doomsday, but I say NO!

We black people face a few years of tough sledding. But it is the lesson of history, not sentimentality, that tells me that I cannot give up on integration.

"Improve ghetto schools!" I support that out of knowledge that there is no alternative for the next several years. But I do not accept it as a substitute for integration, for I know that there is no such thing as "separate but equal" school systems.

The snowplow, the garbage truck, the fire engine, and the money will always arrive first in the neighborhoods where people have economic and political clout. Any poor, inarticulate, powerless black guy who sits in the slums expecting the state to make his schools equal to those in the affluent white neighborhoods is a 10 times bigger fool than the man who thinks school integration is feasible.

Show me a society where apartheid marks the relationship between a majority and a minority, and I'll show you a minority that is getting short shrift on every count.

* * * *

Let those who will surrender in the fight against Jim Crow. As for me, I've hardly begun to fight. If they ban busing in favor of "neighborhood schools," then I'm what's coming to their neighborhoods.

Integration won't be dead till I am, and I expect to leave a bit of progeny behind that will not give up the fight.

Fifteen years ago the segregationists seemed utterly defeated. But they never gave up the fight. And they had a choice, indeed a wiser and nobler one than the course they chose.

But black people have no sane choice other than to continue to struggle for first-class citizenship within the larger society. To those who turn tail and embrace defeat and despair, I say: Shame! Shame! Shame!

HAIR AIN'T WHERE IT'S AT*

White readers ... can move on to the crossword puzzle, or the bridge column, or the sports pages. I want to rap a bit with my black readers today.

*Carl T. Rowan, Feb. 4, 1973.

And if what I say angers a few brothers and sisters, so be it. But it's time blacks—especially young blacks—stopped deluding themselves into believing that the sheepish following of stupid fads is "black solidarity."

* * * *

It is time to stop swallowing this malarkey that styling your hair in 30 nappy plaits, with enough head skin showing to cane-bottom granny's rocker, is the epitome of "pride in racial heritage."

That folderol over "ancient African hairstyles" gave me a special pain in the scalp because I read it just after reading a very troubling article by a black senior at Harvard.

* * * *

This young man, Sylvester Monroe, wrote in the Saturday Review of Education about what has happened as black students have let their search for "blackness" and "pride" carry them to a separatism that shuts them off from the intellectual strength of Harvard.

So true. A lot of young people think they are snowing Whitey. They go through his university, take his degree, without submitting to the rigors of his academic procedures. They get away with it because Whitey can't cope with "black solidarity."

But these young blacks are snowing themselves. Sometimes destroying themselves. Not many are as honest as Monroe, who admits he is nervous as hell about leaving Harvard to compete in a "complex, demanding white world." Monroe fears that he has screwed himself by spending three years at Harvard in "an isolated black vacuum."

* * * *

Let's face reality; we don't have enough firepower to take this country; we don't have enough manpower to dominate it; we don't have enough dollar-power to buy it. And we'll be short of all these "powers" until we develop a lot more brainpower.

So, in the name of the souls of black folk, let's say to hell with this nonsense about hair. Let's face up to some tests of manhood and womanhood that are truly relevant or black uplift.

Is Welfare the Answer?

A standard answer to such mass problems as poverty and deprivation is "welfare"—i.e., grants in aid to help families meet their basic needs. But everyone now agrees that the welfare programs that have evolved have been inadequate, demeaning to the recipients, and not conducive to the growth of creative independence. But what can be done about it? The author of the first selection asserts, "Welfare won't work, but what will?" As indicated by the federal government report on income transfer programs, it is both simplistic and meaningless to say to the poor, "If you don't work, you won't eat." In the first place, about 80% of those on welfare *cannot* work: dependent children, the aged, the disabled, etc. Further, as Massachusetts congressman Michael Harrington has put it, to demand that the poor act just like everyone else is as sensible as asking a one-legged man to run like a normal man should. In a multitude of cases, the poor have been reared so that steady work becomes a psychic as well as a physical impossibility.

WELFARE WON'T WORK, BUT WHAT WILL?*

Mrs. Jeannie Lopez is a thirty-four-year-old divorced mother of six children who lives in Kansas City, Kansas. Like many fellow welfare clients, she has other problems besides being poor. Her basic problem, though, still is money. This is not surprising, considering that Kansas, at best, has paid its welfare families on an average of $988 a year less than the official minimum for survival set by the U.S. Office of Economic Opportunity. But last fall the situation of Mrs. Lopez and of other welfare recipients in Kansas became even more critical. The state legislature voted to cut monthly welfare allotments by 20 percent, which meant that Mrs. Lopez was reduced to $317 a month with which to feed, clothe, and house her family. This spring, after months of lobbying by welfare rights groups, some of the cuts were restored. But Mrs. Lopez no longer receives state reimbursement for what Kansas considers "extras," for example, money

*Adapted from Bruce Porter, "Welfare Won't Work, But What Will?" *Saturday Review* 55(June 3, 1972):48-52.

spent on school books (she is attending a local community college in hopes of someday becoming a social worker) or the $15 it costs in car fare each month to get herself and her children to and from their medical appointments—for the battery of ailments that afflicts the Lopez family. Mrs. Lopez has become deeply disheartened by the turn of events. "We've got the distinct impression," she says, "that what they are saying to us is, 'Just go over in the corner and lie down and die.' "

Not die, exactly. The Kansas legislature would be just as happy if Mrs. Lopez and every other welfare mother and child in the state simply packed up and moved somewhere else. Given the realities of welfare in 1972, however, there are precious few places left for them to go. The idea of welfare has never quite jibed with the puritan ethic in the United States, but today the welfare system is going through the most abrupt and massive turnaround since the system began thirty-seven years ago. It is as if the country had suddenly forsworn all the liberal shibboleths of the last decade—especially the ones about the "deserving poor." People now, more than ever, seem to perceive welfare clients, not simply as a class of unworthies, but as ones whose poverty status poses almost a moral affront to the American way of life. "Welfare people," says George Sternlieb, director of the Center for Urban Policy Research of Rutgers University in New Jersey, "are now the closest thing to untouchables that this country has got."

The initial sign that welfare was under the gun came with the cutbacks in state and municipal welfare budgets. Since 1970 some two dozen states have reduced their outlays for recipients—to the point where forty-two states now give people less than what the states themselves certify is needed for survival.

. . . .

The ultimate sign, however, that antiwelfarism is no temporary aberration has surfaced in New York, the bastion of liberal welfare policies and the home of the largest municipal welfare system in the nation. About a year ago Mayor John Lindsay became convinced that reform was needed in the city's ungainly department of welfare, with its sprawling $3 billion budget, 1.3 million welfare clients (nearly one-tenth the national welfare load), and 30,000 employees—and he made a fateful decision to do something about it. The changes that have been made since are significant, not only because of what they reflect about the national disenchantment with welfare and how it has intensified, but because they may be pointing the way to a major philosophical overhaul, growing out of that disenchantment, of the whole concept of welfare administration. . . .

Placed in charge of the whole operation was a thirty-two-year-old, nervously energetic graduate of the Harvard Business School named Arthur Spiegel. Spiegel had made a name for himself a couple of years ago as a quick-witted program manager in the city's Housing and Development Administration. He left government service for a while to go into a private industry, and when Mayor Lindsay's recruiters set out to persuade him to return, they found him busy peddling second-home developments in Pennsylvania's Pocono Mountains. Around the department Spiegel is known as a "character." Staff members like to call him "crazy" in the sense of being a mad genius. He never sits still. Talking to people in his office, he prowls the carpet restlessly, his shirttail hanging out of his pants and his hand darting up compulsively to fiddle with a cowlick at the back of his head. He talks constantly in profanity, as if to emphasize that at last welfare problems are being examined in a hard-nosed fashion, and his words are jettisoned in rapid and sometimes disjointed bursts. In a place as ingrained and oldline as the welfare department, Spiegel comes as a dash of ice-cold water.

His mission, as he sees it, is not only to begin undoing the tangle that has developed over a long period of administrative neglect but to create a whole new welfare environment in New York City that might become a model for the rest of the country. "What welfare has done," he says, "is it has eliminated a sense of consequence in people. They're taught that nothing will happen when they do something wrong. Take rent. The client finds an apartment and the welfare department pays, within reason, whatever it costs. Then, say, you don't pay your rent and you get evicted. The welfare department pays your back rent, or it moves you and pays your moving costs and it puts you up at a hotel while you're finding an apartment. Then it pays the security to the landlord.

"Well, we're going to stop doing all that. We're going to stop paying moving costs. Rent will be a fixed rate, and the client will have to haggle like everyone else. If the landlord wants security, then the client can borrow it from the department and pay it back over a long period of time. If the client can't manage, then we'll treat him differently. He'll get government chits if he can't handle money, a two-party check. Treat him like a child. We've got to start creating a sense of consequence, the same sense that the rest of society operates under. We've got to try to simulate the real financial world here, because on welfare the real world just doesn't exist."

It is still too early to tell whether this philosophical redirection will have any lasting effect on the welfare rolls, but the structure and tenor of the department itself have already begun to change significantly. When John Alexander came over from his job as director of management engineering at

Allied Chemical, for instance, not only was he appalled at what he considered gross inefficiency—it was taking 100 department bureaucrats, he estimates, to do the work of sixty-five or seventy-five employees in private industry—he was also disturbed by the amount of money that was wasted. As of January the backlog of unaccomplished work had reached 160,000 "units"—a welfare case, for example, that should be closed but remains open or a client's budget that was set too high or too low and remains unchanged—and was costing the city at least $2 million more each month than it would have if the units were attended to promptly.

. . . .

The reason behind the new moves, however, has less to do with the problems of welfare than with its politics. And no one is more responsible for creating the politics than those who are now complaining most bitterly about Spiegel's hard, businesslike reforms—the welfare rights groups that drove the welfare system to its presently tottering state.

Pushed forward by the rights groups—antipoverty workers, poverty-war lawyers, and welfare clients themselves—New York's relief rolls grew phenomenally in the 1960s. Whereas during the previous decade the number of people on welfare actually decreased (340,000 in 1950, against only 323,000 in 1960), the figures in the 1960s proceeded to triple and now in the early part of the 1970s are almost four times what they were a decade ago. Almost as many people were added to the welfare rolls in 1969 alone as accounted for the whole welfare load in 1960. As of March of 1972 the number of recipients had reached 1.3 million, which means that one out of every six persons who live in the city is on welfare. But what strained the system and bothered the politicians even more was that the costs were rising faster than the people. In 1965 the city was spending $272 million; today, seven years later, the amount is $1.3 billion, or nearly five times as much.

However, in the viewpont of Frances Fox Piven and Richard Cloward, the two teachers at Columbia's School of Social Work who helped start the welfare rights movement back in 1964-65, this was all part of a grand national strategy. In the 1950s, they had reasoned, welfare all around the country was so tightly run and so discriminatory against blacks and members of other minority groups that thousands of eligibles were being kept off the rolls. By gathering up these hordes and thrusting them against the various municipal welfare departments, they thought, the movement could make the system groan and finally collapse. At that point cities and states would be so incapable of patching things up they would have to beseech the federal government for help; whereupon, the government would respond with reform. The first part of the plan, of course, worked beautifully. It was in the second part that the trouble started. "They wanted to break the system," says Sternlieb. "Well, it broke all right, but it broke the wrong way."

The basic error of the welfare rightists was that they kept on talking about "welfare reform" without saying exactly what it was supposed to mean. Consequently, everyone could agree that the system was terrible, but each had his own idea as to what to do about it. For Cloward and Piven, reform never really went beyond just getting more and more people on welfare. "Thousands of people are getting it who weren't before," said Piven. "Thousands of mothers can send their kids to school with new clothes. They can get furniture, buy food. Poor people are getting money—that's real reform."

Some liberals, though, who had applauded the Cloward-Piven strategy as a way to achieve some kind of lasting change in the system began feeling betrayed. For, after years of holding the gates against welfare repression, after years of defending the system against cutbacks by conservative state legislatures, the liberals awoke to discover that their partners in the reform movement had succeeded only in bankrupting the system out from under them. The Left had created such a shambles of welfare that it became no longer politically defensible, and hence it was vulnerable to forays from the antiwelfare politicians of the Right.

This has been the pattern nationwide but nowhere more evident or more disruptive than in New York. When in the 1960s the city's welfare system began to open up its rolls, for example, it found that it could not do so in an orderly fashion. Something that started out as a controlled loosening of the system in response to the newly found eligible poor turned into something that looked like a free-for-all raid on the public treasury. First off, there was the problem of caseworkers who, through sympathy for their clients' plight, would instruct them in how to milk the system. In the late 1960s, for instance, there was such a thing as the "special grant."—money a caseworker could get for his client for such things as linoleum, window gates, and furniture. In theory the purpose of granting the money was to bring a client's household up to a "minimum standard of decency." In practice it was used for just about everything else. The client who was shrewd enough to get a special grant or had a "kind" enough caseworker used it to supplement her or his meager allowance for children's clothes or to put better food on the table or give the family a rare movie treat. All of these were worthy expenditures, but none of them had anything to do with what the client was legally entitled to. For caseworkers, giving out special grants became a way to reward good clients and to make cantankerous ones subservient. It made case workers feel good, it became a liberal badge of honor, and it was an easy way to get back at the Establishment.

The special grants also proved to be a main organizing tool for the welfare rights movement of New York. With some organization members walking out of centers with $800, $900, as much as $1,000 in their pockets, it became quickly apparent to nonmembers that the movement might gain them immediate benefits. Not surprisingly, within one year the money spent on special grants in New York nearly tripled. Also it should have come as no surprise that, faced with such a massive and sudden drain on the system, the state legislature promptly responded by rescinding the special grants altogether, leaving future welfare clients worse off than the ones who had come before them.

What made the general problem of fraud even worse was the department's refusal to admit to it. For years the conventional wisdom among liberals held that chiselers accounted for only 3 or 4 percent of the rolls. Now, however, studies in New York are turning up a much higher rate— possibly 10 to 15 percent. And when Sternlieb did a welfare-housing survey for the Ford Foundation recently, his researchers found no one living at the addresses given for ten out of fifty randomly selected welfare recipients, even though relief checks were being sent out every two weeks and were being cashed. When the department uncovered such cases on its own, however, the statistics did not go in the "fraud" column but in one headed "whereabouts unknown."

Then, with the department growing so rapidly, the bureaucrats found they simply could not push the paper around fast enough to keep up with the new welfare clients. It would take six months, for instance, to discover that a client had been sent duplicate checks in the mail and had cashed both of them, thus ending up with twice as much money as he should. In addition, the tangle of paper was so bad that, once the department discovered the mistake, it rarely got around to collecting the money owed by the client. The amount involved was piddling in the ten-figure budgeting of New York's welfare system—about $6 million a year—but it provided antiwelfare legislators in the state capital with still another knout with which to wallop welfare.

Even more embarrassing was the problem of drug addicts. Addicts were put on welfare a year-and-a-half ago on the theory that disabled people should have public support, while trying to cure themselves in drug treatment programs. The problem was that the city's methadone program, the one DSS seemed to favor, had a waiting list six months long. In its place some addicts would simply invent programs of their own, so they could say to the department that they were undergoing rehabilitation. The most notorious non-program was the Ajax Treatment Program in Brooklyn, which amounted to a shooting gallery where addicts would pool their welfare checks and go out and buy heroin.

It was only a matter of time before such goings-on came under serious attack. And that assault began last spring when New York Governor Nelson Rockefeller came up with his own ideas for welfare reform and sent them rolling through the Albany legislature. Not only did the state cut grants 10 percent across the board, but it passed a miniature Talmadge Amendment that required every able-bodied recipient, including welfare mothers with school-aged children, to sign up at the employment office or lose their checks. Then Rockefeller added a little fillip of his own. Any reliefer who couldn't find work in the private economy, read the new law, would have to work off his (or her) welfare check by doing labor for the city—a concept of dealing with poverty that went into vogue in London during the days when they had workhouses for the poor and a man named Charles Dickens to write about them.

For the city's welfare department, Rockefeller's welfare laws spelled the final collapse. Faced with the gigantic job of setting up the work program, registering all the clients, and complying with the various ins and outs of the legislation, the city had no choice but a complete and massive overhaul of its welfare system. "The state law blew the fuses," says Spiegel. "The department was in such a goddamned mess, it just couldn't cope anymore. Something really major had to be done."

In another sense, though, the state work law was only an excuse for revamping the system. The real reason goes much deeper, for what seems to have happened in the beginning of the 1970s is that all around the country many liberal urban economists and sociologists plainly and simply started to question whether welfare is really good for people. While few of the negatives can be proved conclusively, the answers they are getting do not seem very encouraging. For instance, until 1960 the graph for U.S. welfare rolls and the one showing the unemployment rate would rise and fall together. After 1960 the correlation was shattered, and while unemployment fell, welfare took off like a bird. Coincidentally, during the same period welfare payments rose at a rate that was 60 percent faster than the one for wages, whereas before 1960 the rates had been substantially the same. These statistics, of course, don't really prove that welfare encourages worklessness. Still it couldn't be argued that welfare was exactly encouraging people to go out and get jobs.

Urbanologists have been having similar qualms over the effect of welfare on the family structure—particularly in view of the alarming proportion of fatherless families, not only among blacks but increasingly of late among Puerto Ricans as well. But the ultimate complaint by liberals is that welfare doesn't even provide much welfare, and under the present political realities its chance of ever providing anyone with decent income is pretty slim.

All of this is leading to a growing consensus from both Left and Right that welfare has been distorted out of anything resembling its original purpose. As Assistant City Budget Director Jonathan Weiner notes: "The welfare system was designed originally to deal with widows and cripples and the elderly, and it is now taking care of a whole class of people, which is a dramatic and quantum jump. No longer is welfare some desperate, last-chance thing. It is something that is just *there*. For the blacks it's become one way to escape intolerable conditions. Other groups didn't have the option of welfare when they came to the city, and they saved up for a whole generation and deprived themselves of everything, and they got their kids out. There are some economists who feel that just because it was *there* as an alternative, welfare may have retarded a whole generation of blacks. And it's now time to think of other alternatives."

Ironically, one of the brightest alternatives in the country could eventually emerge from the regressive legislation passed by New York State. As it is now, the work-relief program imposed by Albany has accomplished little that was hoped for it. Barely 10 percent of the 50,000 reliefers statewide who registered at state employment offices have managed to find jobs.

But while the private job market can find no room for welfare people who want to work, the public job market has never had enough workers to do the things that need to be done. And with some major revisions and a lot of help from the federal government, the new work program could be the start of real welfare change. Such a change would amount to no less than a massive and permanent public works program that not only would act to abolish welfare as people now know it but would put tens of thousands of people to work improving the deteriorating conditions in the city. "On the one hand, you've got people living in crummy conditions, in bad housing, filthy alleys," says Paul Elston, the thirty-one-year-old director of the city's work-relief program. "On the other, you've got a large reservoir of people on welfare who are paid to do nothing. It's absolutely insane. Why can't you get them together and begin doing something about these problems?"

Municipal hospitals could easily absorb 10,000 more workers; the private hospitals, another 20,000. Ten thousand could be employed as classroom aides in the school system and 5,000 more in day care centers. When the city runs out of jobs, more could be found, say, in improving the environment. Elston has already begun looking into reclamation projects for bottles and cans. He talks of having welfare clients gather up all the used paper in New York. He has even investigated the possibility of shipping it to Europe, where there is a strong market for recycled paper. When the mind conjures up all the jobs that could be done, the vistas become downright limitless. Welfare would once again be reserved for the maimed, the halt, and the blind. Then the public service jobs could be a way out of poverty for the blacks and Puerto Ricans as once the needle trades were for the Jews. "What you end up doing," says Elston, "is subsidizing any kind of business or service you think is socially useful but not economically self-sustaining. All you're talking about is utilizing the public income to allow people to work and live decently."

As Spiegel sees it, welfare now has no other choice than to become "workfare," because under its current onus the system faces nothing but cutbacks and more repression. "What we want to do is to integrate welfare people into the rest of society." And in their heart of hearts, thinks Spiegel, his critics want the same thing he does. "If you really listen to what these welfare rights guys are saying when they get through all the bullshit—what they're saying is, 'Abolish welfare.' and that's what we're really trying to do."

Abolishing welfare and putting welfare recipients to work, even at public jobs, is easier said than done, however. Some 10,000 New York City welfare recipients are now employed at "jobs" in the parks, sanitation, and other public works. Most work one day a week, and they get no training; and instead of a living wage—say, $6,000 a year for a family of four—they get no paycheck at all. They stand out as reliefers, and in most cases the work they do isn't very productive. "It's a case," says former Welfare Commissioner Mitchell Ginsberg, "where, instead of having two men provide toilet paper for the ladies' room, there's now three, and the third guy in on welfare. I believe people are better off working, but they need something to work at. Most work relief turns out to be make-work or no work at all. It's self-defeating because welfare people know it's a sham and so do all the other workers. It only reinforces their own sense of failure."

Then there is the fact that many welfare people aren't healthy enough to work. In the course of one survey, the Brookings Institute of Long Island found that only 40 percent of the AFDC mothers interviewed were free of some basic sort of health complaint. And when the city looked into its Home Relief rolls to find employables for the state program last year, it found that only 20 percent were even remotely healthy enough to work—and this meant registering hapless derelicts off the Bowery and spindly, fifty-five-year-old railroad pension widows whose normal habitats are the seedy, single-room-occupancy hotels along upper Broadway.

If none of these problems proves fatal to "workfare," the state of the national economy may. Already the unemployment rate for the regular work force in urban areas stands at about 7 percent without competition from welfare recipients for jobs. And what decent-paying public service jobs might be created by government would likely be filled long before they went to reliefers—if they are created at all. Only a few months before he delivered his paean to work at the signing of the Talmadge Amendment, President Nixon vetoed a $2-billion public works program precisely because it would have created permanent jobs rather then temporary ones.

. . . .

One thing is becoming increasingly clear as the nation gropes to reform and rationalize its welfare system—that the private economy in this country has lost its capacity to employ all those who want to be employed by it. Without some kind of institutionalized, decent-paying public job alternatives, no welfare legislaton, no matter how liberal or regressive, is going to do the job that lawmakers assign to it. "With welfare," says George Sternlieb of Rutgers, "what you're dealing with are people who have simply fallen out of the employment market. No one really needs them. No one wants them. The question then is, Do you slow down the production machine and put them to work, even though it would be inefficient? Do you do what we're doing at the moment, which is just paying people to stay away? Or do you do the third choice, which is taxing the private economy to put these people to work in the public area?"

These are questions that officials have just begun to grapple with in New York City, that sooner or later will confront every city in the country. The answers are emerging slowly and often painfully, but they would appear to be pointing toward abolishing welfare, as Arthur Spiegel put it, in favor of some means of providing work for everyone.

As with many beginnings, this current tendency suffers from dire inadequacies, mainly ones that involve lack of training, meaningless jobs, and wages that, if they exist at all, are exceedingly meager. Still, trying to deal with the problem by simply tightening up on welfare and lashing back at recipients—as much of the nation appears inclined to do—is hardly any answer at all. It is a little like outlawing poverty and then expecting the poor suddenly to vanish. The price of doing nothing, on the other hand, is to stick with the present welfare system, and no one is inclined to do that anymore.

— — — — —

"Mr. Donovan, my husband's back from jail so the welfare cut out my ADC because I got a unreported male in the house. Does that mean my kids can't eat because their Daddy's home?"*

*From Ben H. Bagdikian, *In the Midst of Plenty*: The Poor in America (Boston: Beacon Press, 1964), p. 11.

TAXING THE POOR THROUGH INCOME TRANSFERS*

... What is especially disturbing to many taxpayers are ... taxes that pay the costs of welfare. These same taxpayers may not realize that the incentive and equity problems they face under the tax system are minor compared to the nightmarish set of rules imposed on many recipients of public aid. In fact, the harried taxpayer would find a great many similarities between the impact of taxes and the impact of Government income transfer programs.

Public income transfers are Government payments or benefits provided to persons other than as compensation for goods and services rendered. Such public transfer programs as public assistance, food stamps, public housing, unemployment insurance, and social security redistribute the incomes generated in the market place, often to the nonworking part of the population. As with taxes, these public transfers influence incentives to work, to change income sources, and to shift expenditure patterns. It is natural that taxes and transfers produce similar effects since transfers are essentially negative taxes and taxes are negative transfers. Receiving a transfer payment from the Government can be viewed as paying a negative tax. A rise in a positive tax payment or a fall in a negative tax payment looks the same to the individual and to the Government. In both cases the income to the individual falls and the resources of the Government rise. To illustrate the similarity more vividly, consider a social security recipient who increases his earnings by $1. The Government will receive about 20 cents from the increase in personal income and social security tax payments and possibly 50 cents from a decrease in social security payments. To the recipient the two kinds of cash losses look the same. His lower social security payment is as much a tax as is his explicit income and payroll tax payment.

Public transfers can be much more discouraging than taxes. Nowhere is this more evident than in the case of work incentives. In contrast to the rhetoric of Government officials exhorting recipients to work for their income, the Government itself imposes the largest barrier to work. Program design is such that earnings may be worth very little to many recipients. Some welfare mothers gain only 33 cents in total net income for each added dollar earned over wide ranges of income, while the unemployment insurance claimant may forfeit a dollar of benefits for each dollar earned.

*Adapted from Studies in Public Welfare, Paper No. 4, *Income Transfer Programs: How They Tax the Poor*. A Volume of Studies Prepared for the Use of the Subcommittee on Fiscal Policy of the Joint Economic Committee, Congress of the United States (Washington: U.S. Government Printing Office, 1972), pp. vi-vii.

A $2.40-per-hour job is worth only 80 cents per hour to a welfare recipient if his benefits are reduced by $1.60. Instead of feeling resentment against those recipients who do not work, the taxpayer who has examined these program rules might be surprised at the large number of recipients who do work despite significant disincentives to work.

Taxpayers facing tax rates in the neighborhood of 50 to 75 percent often find ways of shifting their income in such a way as to avoid taxes. Transfer programs encourage recipients to try the same thing. Unfortunately, the only way for recipients to shift their income and avoid benefit reductions is to misreport income. Instead of working at a job covered by social security and reporting his earnings to the Government, the recipient might take work which pays in cash. A job paid in cash turns out to be worth much more than its actual wage rate. It may be a job in an illicit occupation. Thus, it becomes more attractive financially to take an illicit job paying $1.50 per hour than to take and report the income from a legitimate job paying $2.40 per hour.

Encouragement of some uses of income over others is another feature common to both the tax system and the transfer system. What differs is the kind of activity that is encouraged and discouraged. Taxes often encourage socially desirable behavior, such as becoming a homeowner and cutting back on smoking and drinking, while transfers often penalize the virtuous, such as those who save and who economize on rent. The low-income person who saves in a bank account may find himself ineligible for welfare benefits while another person with the same income is in no such trouble because he bought a new television set with his spare cash. The welfare mother who moves in with her mother to save on rent and to send her children to camp may find that her rent savings simply reduce her welfare grant and do not provide the money for camp. . . .

BLAME THE VICTIM*

Harvard social scientist Daniel Patrick Moynihan, recently a Nixon-appointed ambassador, authored a report that is a classic of the "Blame the victim" type. Note that although the report, as described by Jencks, is seemingly compassionate, it subtly changes from a sympathetic depiction of history to a blaming description of what prevails today. In effect, Moynihan said, it is not the system that has led to black degredation; it is

*Adapted from Christopher Jencks, "The Moynihan Report," *New York Review of Books* 5(Oct. 14, 1965):39.

black culture *that produces inadequate black families. With such research as their "authority," tight-fisted politicians and administrators justify welfare program alterations that have the effect of further demeaning recipients.*

After six months of private circulation among government officials and a steadily widening circle of increasingly loose-mouthed journalists, the controversial "Moynihan Report" on the Negro family has been released to the public . . .

Moynihan's thesis can be summarized as follows: 1. American slavery was the worst version of slavery in human history. 2. The legacy of Negro slavery in America was twofold: segregation and discrimination against Negroes by whites and establishment of an American Negro culture which disqualifies many of its participants for life in modern America even when the terms of competition are fair and opportunities open. 3. The central defect of American Negro life is the "matrifocal" family, in which the male is a transient who provides neither a regular income, consistent discipline and direction, nor an example to his sons of what they might hope to become as adults. 4. The psychological, social, and economic problems generated by matriarchy are getting worse, not better. Despite all the recent civil rights and poverty legislation, the chasm separating lower-class Negroes from the mainstream of American life is growing wider and deeper. Only a minority is acquiring the more patriarchal, middle-class family style, and only a minority shows signs of participating in the middle class's increasing affluence. 5. The establishment of a "stable" (i.e., more or less "patri-focal") Negro family structure should therefore be made a national goal, and national policy in many different fields should be adjusted to promote this goal.

Moynihan's analysis is in the conservative tradition that guided the drafting of the poverty program (in whose formulation he participated during the winter of 1963-4). The guiding assumption is that social pathology is caused less by basic defects in the social system than by defects in particular individuals and groups which prevent their adjusting to the system. The prescription is therefore to change the deviants, not the system.

. . . years ago the children of the poor were to be helped to escape from the "culture of poverty" by more intensive schooling, induction into the Job Corps, provision of more guidance and counselling, and so forth. Now the lower-class Negro family is to be made more like the middle-class white family—though by means which Moynihan does not specify.

Needless to say, this approach has met with enthusiastic support from those middle-class Americans who feel that if "they" were just more like "us," everything would be all right. (Many successful Negroes hold this view, and some of them are active in the civil rights movement.)

Is Revolution the Answer?

Almost from the beginning of recorded history, a basic problem for people at large has been their exploitation at the hands of the powerful. And periodically, the exploited rise up in revolt, hoping thus to throw off the chains that bind them. Occasionally they succeed; surely the Cuban masses are better off under the rule of their communist bureaucracy than they were with the Batista government. But such a result is atypical. In most cases, revolution—as distinguished from wars of national liberation, which frequently succeed—simply substitutes one set of exploiters for another. As a British miner put it after the mines were nationalized, "There's still the bloody boss." Or, as historian Crane Brinton found, the characteristic last step in the revolutionary process is "return to most of the . . . interactions in the old network."*

Despite the disappointing results usually obtained from revolutionary tactics, thoughtful people find that they are justifiable, and perhaps unavoidable, when three conditions prevail: a) the established order is truly intolerable, b) all peaceful attempts to initiate change have failed, and c) there is widespread commitment to fundamental change. These three controlling conditions are necessary because revolution is an incredibly serious step; whether or not it succeeds, the terrorism it generates is bound to shatter almost all close relationships. And if it is successful, it must be accompanied by ceaseless organizational effort to achieve even minimal results; if unsuccessful, its proponents are written off as traitors.

The accompanying illustrative pieces are meant to throw light on 1) the limitations of revolution as an answer to social problems, and 2) revolution's inevitability when conditions are ripe. One of the major difficulties with revolution is that its advocates are so often either thoughtless vandals or true-believer types whose prime interest is to see that non-believers suffer, burn, swing, or otherwise succumb to the untender mercies of "the saved." It is equally clear that some revolutionists are deeply committed to the highest humanitarian standards; but even they, under the stress of counter-revolutionary terror, can become bestial.

– – – – –

*Crane Brinton, *Anatomy of Revolution*, rev. and enlarged ed. (New York: Vintage Books, a division of Random House, Inc., 1965), p. 258.

There is probably no greater mark of economic illiteracy than the failure to realize that we must live in a world of imperfect men, imperfect markets, and imperfect information, no matter what economic or political system we have.

The only responsible approach to social problems is that which tries to find the overall least-cost system, not that which blindly seeks an unattainable ideal.

The demand for perfection has, throughout history, led to much greater evil than our current reformers can complain about.

attributed to Prof. Henry G. Manne

— — — — —

AN AMERICAN TERRORIST*

Seeking to interview a "terrorist," the author placed an ad in an underground newspaper. A youth responded by phone and agreed to a rendezvous on a lonely stretch of beach. Because of the conditions of the encounter, the youth's statements could not be checked, but some of them were later verified by independent sources. In any event, the normally skeptical reporter became convinced that the youth was a genuine specimen of what he claimed to be.

"We'll blow up the whole f----- world if it comes down to it. And if our people start getting hassled and busted, we'll shoot police cruisers full of holes and kill every pig on the street."

The hard words sounded incongruous coming from the diminutive, red-haired kid in blue jeans and mustard-colored windbreaker who had approached me across the sunny Venice beach, glancing furtively over his shoulder to make sure that "the pig" wasn't lurking nearby.

He said his name was Larry. Period. He had lustrous brown eyes and softly freckled cheeks, and he wore his hair short. The haircut, he says, is camouflage. He belongs to a 50-member, all-white, all-male revolutionary terrorist gang, he says, and the short hair keeps him and other members of his group from attracting the attention of "the pig."

Over the course of the next week, in a series of interviews that totaled perhaps 24 hours, "Larry" revealed himself to be politically naive and a

*Karl Fleming, " 'We'll Blow Up the World'," *Newsweek* 76(Oct. 12, 1970):49–50, 55.

mere foot soldier in his bitter, rebellious band—a spear carrier not privy to political strategy and top-priority secrets. Nevertheless, the information he had absorbed provided a rare glimpse of the operations and violent schemes of what appears to be a widespread if haphazardly organized network of underground guerrilla bands.

Larry's own group has no name—for security reasons. Its members range in age from 18 to 23 and one-third of them—like Larry himself—are Vietnam veterans. Using his Army training as a demolitions expert, Larry has, he says, taught other revolutionaries how to use explosives, has gone on weekend shooting maneuvers with his group and has helped pinpoint potential targets such as power plants and armaments factories. He won't talk about whether he has personally blown anything up. "You don't want to hear about that," he says.

But he does offer a rationale of sorts for his group's activities. "The main reason for blowing up what we have so far," he says, "is just to let the people know we are here." Similarly, he wanted to tell his story to me, he says, so that "the people" can be won over to the coming revolution. "The people have to be told that we're not really a bunch of Communist murderers in disguise," says Larry. "We want change now. And nothing is at our disposal but violence. We can't even demonstrate without getting clubbed and tear-gassed. Well, if we can't live in peace, then the rich can't live in peace. There will be all-out war within a year. And when the pig picks up arms this time, he won't get rocks and bottles back—he'll get rifle rounds."

Larry's concept of the brave new world that would follow the revolution amounts to little more than rudimentary anarchism. "Our idea is that a person ought to be able to do anything he wants to do—smoke dope or make love on the beach—as long as he doesn't hurt anybody else," he says. "There is a lot of talk going on among all the groups about what kind of government we would have. It wouldn't be one man. Maybe a group of 100. It would be something like a democracy, but more free than one. Private-enterprise capitalism would be out. People wouldn't have to 'rip off' [steal] anymore. They would have what they need."

Larry is 19 and a high-school dropout, the son of a Midwest steel-worker. During his year in Vietnam he mastered lessons that would be valuable when he turned revolutionary. In "Nam," Larry learned, for example, how to extract a pound of C4 plastic explosive from a Claymore mine and ship it back to the U.S., and how to construct a bomb and place it against a building so that the charge will do the most damage. And his opportunity to rebel came soon enough. Always a malcontent, Larry finally refused to fight any more after he had killed three Viet Cong. He recalled his feelings during our conversations: "Man, they've got VC who'll stand in a field and shoot at jets with rifles. They must believe strong in something. I can't kill people like that. I had just as soon kill Americans."

He talked that way in Vietnam, too—and attracted the attention of a member of the White Panthers, a Stateside revolutionary group. The White Panther, Larry says, "asked me if I wanted to join a group when I got home and fight against the U.S. I said sure, I could dig it." The recruiter gave Larry some phone numbers in Arizona, California, Montana, Ohio, Kentucky and Tennessee. After getting his undesirable discharge, Larry says, he used the numbers to make contact with his Los Angeles group....

Larry's organization meets weekly, each time in a different place. The meetings last two to three hours. Attendance three times a month is mandatory. Members split up into five-man squads and train in demolition, street fighting, booby trapping, bomb setting, sniping, night marching and foraging. If there is a particularly dangerous mission to do, the members cut cards or draw straws. No more than ten people go on a job, so as not to jeopardize the whole organization....

The members work at "straight" jobs, some as electricians, telephone repairmen, truck drivers and laborers. The "main man" is a waiter, Larry believes. But, typically, he isn't sure....

Larry says he has personally visited five revolutionary bomber groups. From conversations, he deduces the total number of such organizations in the U.S. to be as high as twenty. "Some of them are crazy and blow stuff up just to hear the noise," he says. "But some of them are really mellow, like the dudes who got the Shaker Heights [Ohio] police station. Man, that was a good demolition job."...

His organization, he says, has 30 weapons, including an M-1 rifle, a shotgun, a .357 Magnum, a .30-06 rifle and a Browning automatic. On weekends, the members take their weapons and travel in several vehicles to camps where they train within a five-hour drive of Los Angeles. On three weekend trips, Larry says he tutored other members in demolition and had target practice with the M-1. He says they have 100 cases—2,500 sticks—of dynamite hidden away, but not at the camps. To get dynamite, he says, you have to steal it, or "dress up like a super-farmer and go into some little country town and buy it for blowing up stumps."

Before joining the California group several months ago, Larry says he visited a secret guerrilla camp so high in the Colorado mountains that it is obscured most of the year by clouds. His tale of the camp plays like a vignette from one of Jean Luc Godard's more imaginative revolutionary fantasies—but Larry insists it is all true.

He got in touch with the mountain guerrillas, he says, by using another telephone number given him in Vietman. After reaching a contact in Flagstaff, Arizona, he says, he was told to travel to a certain intersection, where he was met by a guide who emerged from a clump of trees. They hiked six hours before reaching the camp, a strung-out array of sleeping bags and tents pitched beneath pine trees. Larry estimates that there were fully 1,000 people in the camp—most of them, he says he was told, were college students there for summer training. The guerrillas, he says, practiced firing and demolition and even staged mock battles. Their rations included rabbit and venison cooked on skewers over open fires, fish and a few staples. Provisions were bought in several different towns, Larry says, to avoid arousing suspicion.

About 100 guerrillas stay all year, he reports, burying their firewood in snow banks, cooking surreptitiously—living sparely so as to escape detection. Whatever money they needed was brought in by student sympathizers. Most of the members of the permanent guerrilla group, Larry gathered, were wanted by the police.

He stayed, he says, only a day, although he was asked by the leader, "a Castro-looking dude smoking a cigar," to remain as a demolition teacher. But he couldn't stand the cold, and for that reason also passed up a similar camp in Montana and chose California instead. From talking to the mountain rebels, Larry says he concluded that there are as many as ten such camps at various spots around the country.

I told Larry that some people simply wouldn't believe him, so he grudgingly agreed to submit to a lie detector test if I wanted it. To try to corroborate and flesh out the story, I asked him to arrange for me to meet other members of his group. But fearing identification, they refused. However, I did get Larry to carry a tape recorder to last week's meeting, and to invite the unidentified leader to say anything he wished. Larry returned with this terse, harsh-voiced message on the tape:

"What we're doing, we're making things so f------ uncomfortable people can't brush us off like fleas. We want freedom and peace, not half-truths and bull----. Small group? Man, others are everywhere. Watch out, maybe your best friend is out to overthrow a government. Naw, man, we're not f------ followers of some Communist organization. Man, you want a message for the people: do what you believe in, but don't believe in something you're going to hate. Freedom and peace shall follow."

Next day, Larry telephoned to say the organization was now fearful that he had become a security risk and had ordered him into temporary exile. He said he was splitting—he didn't say to where.

BRINGING THE COUNTRY TO ITS KNEES*

The author was of course one of America's most famous prison inmates;

*Adapted from George Jackson, *Blood in My Eye* (New York: Random House, Inc., 1972), pp. 1, 6-10, 30-34, 41, 59.

he is now dead as a result of a prison shooting incident. It was in an attempt to arrange conditions so that George's release could be bartered that his young brother Jonathan invaded a court room and, together with Ruchell Magee and others, attempted to shoot their way to freedom. Several, including Jonathan and the judge, died in the attempt. Professor Angela Davis was indicted for conspiring with Jonathan, but was acquitted. Aspects of Ruchell Magee's case are, at this writing, still in litigation.

We must accept the eventuality of bringing the U.S.A. to its knees; accept the closing off of critical sections of the city with barbed wire, armored pig carriers crisscrossing the streets, soldiers everywhere, tommy guns pointed at stomach level, smoke curling black against the daylight sky, the smell of cordite, house-to-house searchers, doors being kicked in, the commonness of death.

. . . .

Revolution within a modern industrial capitalist society can only mean the overthrow of all existing property relations and the destruction of all institutions that directly or indirectly support existing property relations. It must include the total suppression of all classes and individuals who endorse the present state of property relations or who stand to gain from it. Anything less than this is reform.

Government and the infrastructure of the enemy capitalist state must be destroyed to get at the heart of the problem: property relations. Otherwise there is no revolution. Reshuffle the governmental personnel and forms, without changing property relations and economic institutions, and you have produced simply another reform stage in the old bourgeois revolution. The power to alter the present imbalances, to remedy the critical defects of an advanced industrial state ordered on an antiquated set of greed-confused motives, rests with control over production and distribution of wealth. If the 1 percent who presently control the wealth of the society maintain their control after any reordering of the state, the changes cannot be said to be revolutionary.

. . . .

Revolutionary change means the seizure of all that is held by the 1 percent, and the transference of these holdings into the hands of the remaining 99 percent. If the 1 percent are simply displaced by another 1 percent, revolutionary change has not taken place. A social revolution after the fact of the modern corporate capitalist state can only mean the breakup of that state and a completely new form of economics and culture. As slaves, we understand that ownership and the mechanics of distribution must be reversed. The problems of the Black Colony and the Brown Colony, those of the entire 99 percent who are being manipulated, can never be redressed as long as the necessary resources for their solution are the personal property of an extraneous minority motivated solely by the need for its own survival. And that extraneous minority will never consider the proper solutions.

. . . .

The principal reservoir of revolutionary potential in Amerika lies in wait inside the Black Colony. Its sheer numerical strength, its desperate historical relation to the violence of the productive system, and the fact of its present status in the creation of wealth force the black stratum at the base of the whole class structure into the forefront of any revolutionary scheme. Thirty percent of all industrial workers are black. Close to 40 percent of all industrial support roles are filled by blacks. Blacks are still doing the work of the greatest slave state in history. The terms of our servitude are all that have been altered.

. . . .

Revolution builds in stages; it isn't cool or romantic; it's bold and vicious; it's stalking and being stalked—the opposition rising above our level of violence to repress us, and our forces learning how to counter this repression and again pulling ourselves above their level of violence. That process repeats itself again and again until finally the level is reached where the real power of the people is felt and the ruling class is suppressed. The power of the people lies in its greater potential violence. . . .

We are at an impasse now, because the next level of revolutionary consciousness and activity cannot be reached without calling down on the nation a corresponding and perhaps overreactionary repression. And it's not the people who dread this next level of commitment. They don't understand the significance of it as yet. The dread, the fear, rests with some of the old-guard elements. I refer you again to Mao: "When revolution fails . . . it's the fault of the vanguard party."

Some of the fear is an honest fear that revolution will be repressed entirely. These thinkers have historical references that roll them back to Europe to the time of Hitler's Germany and Italy in the twenties and thirties. But I say that can never happen here. That was too long ago, too far away, and none of those European countries had thirty million irate niggers on their hands.

. . . .

The reality of power's automatic defense reflexes makes it possible for us to measure our own effectiveness. Their efforts to seriously repress us indicate that we have reached people—that we are finally in the fight. And we cannot ever be truly repressed. There is quite simply no way for an established government to defeat an internal, determined, aggressive enemy. Especially in an urban society. The mechanics, logic, and logistics of urban people's guerrilla warfare cannot be defeated.

In the opening stages of such a conflict, before a unified left can be established, before most people have accepted the inevitability of war, before we are able militarily to organize massive violence, we must depend on limited, selective violence tied to an exact political purpose. In the early service of the people there must be totally committed, professional revolutionaries who understand that all human life is meaningless if it is not accompanied by the controls that determine its quality. I am one of these. My life has absolutely no value. I'm the man under hatches, the desperate one. We will make the revolution. Nothing can stop us, we are not intimidated by the specter of repression—we're already repressed. The Black Legion* and their terror leaves us cold, unafraid. We will meet it with a counter-terror. We'll never, never allow ourselves to be immobilized by a tactic that actually works better for us. The lynch-murder of a friend—it makes me angry, not afraid. I'm the next man that must be lynched! My forefather trembled when his brother was lynched, but *my* brother's immolation means war to the death, war to the utmost, war to the knife!!

Violence is not supposed to work in Amerika. For no one, that is, except the "omnipotent administrator." But this has yet to be proved to my satisfaction since I know that a bomb is a bomb is a bomb; it twists steel, shatters concrete and dismembers men everywhere else in the world. Why not those made in Amerika? A bullet fired from an assault rifle in the hands of a Vietnamese liberation fighter will kill a pig in Vietnam. Why won't it kill a pig in the place where pigs are made?

. . . .

If we accept revolution, we must accept all that it implies: repression, counter-terrorism, days filled with work, nervous strain, prison, funerals.

. . . .

The enemy culture, the established government, exists first of all because of its ability to govern, to maintain enough order to ensure that a cycle of sorts exists between the various levels and elements of the society.

*An armed anti-labor terrorist group active in the thirties, reputedly financed by sections of the automotive industry.—Ed.

"Law and Order" is their objective. Ours is "Perfect Disorder." Our aim is to stop the life cycle of the enemy culture and replace it with our own revolutionary culture. This can be done only by creating perfect disorder within the cycle of the enemy culture's life process and leaving a power vacuum to be filled by our building revolutionary culture.

. . . .

"POWER TO THE PEOPLE" AND TYRANNY*

Some of the banners raised by the antiwar demonstrators ... proclaimed: "All Power to the People." While I agree with the aims of the demonstrators, I fear that their slogan is mindless and menacing to the future of democracy.

Power is dangerous in anybody's hands; it is most dangerous in the hands of a mob—and a mob is what "people" become when they are not constrained by law.

Our Constitution wisely separates and divides powers, so that even the majority itself cannot ride roughshod over a minority without abusing and distorting our Constitutional safeguards.

If the demonstrators' slogan were to become a reality, they would be the first to suffer under it. There is good reason to believe that most of the "people" in the U.S. today are hostile, or at least indifferent to, the Bill of Rights.

Given full power, these people would treat the demonstrators far more severely than even the Nixon administration has.

* * *

Many, if not most, people do not believe in democracy for others; and most contemporary Americans would not sign the Declaration of Independence if it were offered them today; it is too "revolutionary."

In point of fact, the founders of this country wisely turned down "all power" for ourselves, knowing how quickly and easily such uncontrolled power could be turned into a tyranny of the mass, which is the worst tyranny of all.

Those who claim to speak for "the people" usually express and embody the most irrational elements in our nature—a Hitler or a Stalin can then perpetrate the bloodiest of injustices under the cover of representing "the people," when what they really represent is our appetite for vengeance and our search for scapegoats.

* * *

*Adapted from Sidney J. Harris, syndicated columnist, Oct. 16, 1971.

Ironically, if the people were given power right now, their first act would be to crush the kind of dissent manifested by the demonstrators.

It is only the law—fragile and perverted though it may have become—that prevents them from exercising such despotism against minority groups. "All power" granted to the majority would be the death of democratic dissent.

This country was established to avoid the excesses of an elite on the one hand and the mass on the other.

If we are ruled by an elite, the way to reform it is by fairer use of the law, not by tearing down the institutions and processes that alone make democracy possible.

In so doing, the apostles of "power to the people" merely pave the way for a dictatorship under which they will be first to go.

ON EXTREME COMMITMENT*

Any realistic appraisal of the process of political change in America must recognise that violence, extremism, and the resort to extra-legal and extra-parliamentary tactics, are a major part of the story. Reliance on extremist tactics may be related to two aspects of American culture: the emphasis on the attainment of ends, on one hand, and the strong hold of religious moralism, on the other.

The strong emphasis on an "open society," on achievement, on "getting ahead," has been linked by many analysts of American society (especially the sociologist Robert Merton) with making it an "ends-oriented" culture as distinct from a "means-oriented" one. In the former type winning is what counts, not how one wins. Conversely, social systems with a more rigid status-system, with a greater emphasis on the norms of aristocracy or élitism, are more likely to be concerned with appropriate means; the norms place greater stress on conforming to the proper code of behaviour. The comment by the famed American baseball manager, Leo Durocher, that "nice guys finish last," may be counter-posed against the old Olympic motto that "it matters not who wins the game, it matters how you play." The latter, of course, is the aristocratic code of ruling class which "won" some generations back, and which, in effect, is seeking to prevent the "outs" from pressing too hard to replace it. The differences between an achievement- and "ends-oriented" society and an élitist- and "means-

*Adapted from Seymour Martin Lipset, "On the Politics of Conscience & Extreme Commitment," *Encounter* 31(Aug 68):66–71.

oriented" one are subtle, and hard to demonstrate in any rigorous fashion, but they are real and determine, in my view, many aspects of life, including the crime rate and general willingness to rely on militant political tactics. American extremism may be seen as another example of the propensity to seek to attain ends by any means, whether legitimate or not.

Moralism is also a source of extremism. Americans tend to be a moralistic people, an orientation which they inherit from their Protestant sectarian past. This is the one country in the world dominated by the religious traditions of Protestant "dissent," Methodists, Baptists, and the other numerous sects. The teachings of these denominations have called on men to follow their conscience, in ways that the denominations that have evolved from state churches (Catholic, Lutheran, Anglican, and Orthodox Christian) have not. The American Protestant religious ethos is basically Arminian. It assumes, in practice, if not in theology, the perfectibility of man, his obligation to avoid sin; while the churches accept the inherent weakness of man, his inability to escape sinning and error, the need for the church to be forgiving and protecting.

The American, therefore, as political and religious man, has been a utopian moralist who presses hard to attain and institutionalise virtue, or to destroy evil men and wicked institutions and practices. Almost from the beginning of the Republic, one finds a plethora of "do-good" reform organisations seeking to foster Peace, protect the Sabbath, reduce or eliminate the use of alcoholic beverages, wipe out the corrupt irreligious institution of Free Masonry, destroy the influence of the Papists, and Slavery, eliminate Corruption, extend the blessings of Education, etc., etc.

The strength of such moralistic pressures can be best seen in the widespread opposition to almost every war in which the United States has participated, with the possible exception of World War II. Conscientious objection to participation in "unjust wars" has been more common in the United States than in any other country in the world. Large numbers of people refused to go along with the War of 1812, with the Mexican War, with the Civil War, with World War I, and with the Korean War. They took it as self-evident that they must obey their conscience rather than the dictates of their country's rulers. And the same moralistic element which has fostered resistance to each war has led some Americans to press hard for those political changes which are in line with their conscience. Such extreme behaviour by moralistic reformers has made the task of running this country extremely difficult. Those in authority have often found themselves in the position of President Johnson, denounced as wicked men who sponsor evil and corrupt policies. Consensus politics has never been an effective answer to moralistic politics. As a result, the moralistic reformers have often obtained their objectives, by winning the agreement of the moderate majority. Outraged by their tactics, the moderates have often given in either because they came to feel that the activists are "basically in the right," or in order to keep the peace, to reduce divisiveness and restore the broken consensus.

Extremism in act, if not in objective, is (to paraphrase Rap Brown) "as American as cherry pie." The contemporary reliance on civil disobedience tactics by elements in the Civil Rights and anti-war movements clearly places a severe strain on the operation of a democratic system, but the American system has survived such efforts in the past. There is, in my view, little reason to fear or hope that the current unrest will topple the established order.

It is important to recognise, moreover, that those who have engaged in civil disobedience and confrontation tactics have not always achieved their objectives. By resorting to such tactics, they run the risk of turning many moderates against them, of creating a "backlash" which strengthens their opponents, and not only defeats them, but helps to reverse social trends which they favour. Inherently, civil disobedience weakens the respect for the rule of law which guarantees the rights of all minorities, of all whose opinions or traits are considered obnoxious by the majority. Hence, the use of civil disobedience as a political tactic is only justified as an extreme last-ditch measure, to be employed when there are no other means available to realise certain moral values. Indiscriminate use of confrontationist tactics can only result in the undermining of the rule of law and the encouragement to all groups (including the military) to take the law and general power into their hands whenever they feel frustrated politically.

WORKING–CLASS AUTHORITARIANISM*

The gradual realization that extremist and intolerant movements in modern society are more likely to be based on the lower classes than on the middle and upper classes has posed a tragic dilemma for those intellectuals of the democratic left who once believed the proletariat necessarily to be a force for liberty, racial equality, and social progress. The Socialist Italian novelist Ignazio Silone has asserted that "the myth of the liberating power of the proletariat has dissolved along with that other myth of progress. The recent examples of the Nazi labor unions, like those of

*Seymour Martin Lipset, *Political Man*, The Social Bases of Politics (Garden City, N.Y.: Anchor Books, Doubleday and Co., Inc., 1963), pp. 87–90.[1]

Salazar and Peron ... have at last convinced of this even those who were reluctant to admit it on the sole grounds of the totalitarian degeneration of Communism."[2]

Dramatic demonstrations of this point have been given recently by the southern workers' support of White Citizens' Councils and segregation in the United States and by the active participation of many British workers in the 1958 race riots in England. A "Short Talk with a Fascist Beast" (an eighteen-year-old casual laborer who took part in the beating of Negroes in London), which appeared in the left socialist *New Statesman*, portrays graphically the ideological syndrome which sometimes culminates in such behavior. "Len's" perspective is offered in detail as a prelude to an analytical survey of the authoritarian elements of the lower-class situation in modern society.

'That's why I'm with the Fascists,' he says. 'They're against the blacks. That Salmon, he's a Communist. The Labour Party is Communist too. Like the unions.' His mother and father, he says, are strick Labour supporters. Is he against the Labour Party? 'Nah, I'm for them. They're for y'know—us. I'm for the unions too.' Even though they were dominated by Communists? 'Sure,' he says. 'I like the Communist Party. It's powerful, like.' How can he be for the Communists when the fascists hate them?

Len says, 'Well, y'know, I'm for the fascists when they're against the nigs. But the fascists is really for the rich people y'know, like the Tories. All for the guv'nors, people like that. But the Communists are very powerful.' I told him the Communist Party of Britain was quite small.

'But,' he says, 'they got Russia behind them.' His voice was full of marvel. 'I admire Russia. Y'know, the people. They're peaceful. They're strong. When they say they'll do a thing, they do it. Not like us. Makes you think: they got a weapon over there can wipe us all out, with one wave of a general's arm. Destroy us completely and totally. Honest, those Russians. When they say they'll do a thing, they do it. Like in Hungary. I pity those people, the Hungarians. But did you see the Russians went in and stopped them. Tanks. Not like us in Cyprus. Our soldiers got shot in the back and what do we do? The Communists is for the small man.'[3]

Such strikingly visible demonstrations of working-class ethnic prejudice and support for totalitarian political movements have been paralleled in studies of public opinion, religion, family patterns, and personality structure. Many of these studies suggest that the lower-class way of life produces individuals with rigid and intolerant approaches to politics.

At first glance the facts of political history may seem to contradict this. Since their beginnings in the nineteenth century, workers' organizations and parties have been a major force in extending political democracy, and in waging progressive political and economic battles. Before 1914, the classic division between the working-class left parties and the economically privileged right was not based solely upon such issues as redistribution of income, status, and educational opportunities, but also rested upon civil liberties and international policy. The workers, judged by the policies of their parties, were often the backbone of the fight for greater political democracy, religious freedom, minority rights, and international peace, while the parties backed by the conservative middle and upper classes in much of Europe tended to favor more extremist political forms, to resist the extension of the suffrage, to back the established church, and to support jingoistic foreign policies.

Events since 1914 have gradually eroded these patterns. In some nations working-class groups have proved to be the most nationalistic sector of the population. In some they have been in the forefront of the struggle against equal rights for minority groups, and have sought to limit immigration or to impose racial standards in countries with open immigration. The conclusion of the anti-fascist era and the emergence of the cold war have shown that the struggle for freedom is not a simple variant of the economic class struggle. The threat to freedom posed by the Communist movement is as great as that once posed by Fascism and Nazism, and Communism, in all countries where it is strong, is supported mainly by the lower levels of the working class, or the rural population.[4] No other party has been as thoroughly and completely the party of the working class and the poor. Socialist parties, past and present, secured much more support from the middle classes than the Communists have.

Some socialists and liberals have suggested that this proves nothing about authoritarian tendencies in the working class, since the Communist party often masquerades as a party seeking to fulfill the classic Western-democratic ideals of liberty, equality, and fraternity. They argue that most Communist supporters, particularly the less educated, are deceived into thinking that the Communists are simply more militant and efficient socialists. I would suggest, however, the alternative hypothesis that, rather than being a source of strain, the intransigent and intolerant aspects of Communist ideology attract members from that large stratum with low incomes, low-status occupations, and low education, which in modern industrial societies has meant largely, though not exclusively, the working class.

The social situation of the lower strata, particularly in poorer countries with low levels of education, predisposes them to view politics as black and white, good and evil. Consequently, other things being equal, they should be more likely than other strata to prefer extremist movements which suggest easy and quick solutions to social problems and have a rigid outlook. . . .

REFERENCES

[1] An early version of this chapter was written for a conference on "The Future of Liberty" sponsored by the Congress for Cultural Freedom in Milan, Italy, in September 1955.

[2] "The Choice of Comrades," *Encounter*, 3 (December 1954), p. 25. Arnold A. Rogow writing in the Socialist magazine *Dissent* even suggests that "the liberal and radical approach has always lacked a popular base, that in essence, the liberal tradition has been a confined minority, perhaps elitist, tradition." "The Revolt Against Social Equality," *Dissent*, 4 (1957), p. 370.

[3] Clancy Sigal in the *New Statesmen*, October 4, 1958, p. 440.

[4] The sources of variation in Communist strength from country to country have already been discussed in Chap. 2, in relation to the level and speed of economic development.

EXPRESSIVE VIOLENCE*

Although race riots have for the moment gone "out of style," it is most unwise to forget that they were, in effect, agonized cries from the hearts of beleagured people. The lot of these people has not changed significantly since the 1960's, hence it is only realistic to expect that they will rise up again—and again and again, until we make sufficient fundamental changes to undermine the riot-generating conditions.

Enraged by long-standing grievances and the persistent failure of authorities to act, a surly crowd gathers in the streets. Armed soldiers seek to disperse the clots of people. Someone throws a stone. Panicky, the custodians of order nervously finger their weapons. A shot is fired. Suddenly a black man clutches his breast and falls to the street dead. The uprising begins.

Watts 1965? Hough 1966? Detroit 1967? No, the above scene took place in Boston in 1770. The angry crowd was protesting the unwillingness of the Crown to allow them to share in determining their own political destiny. The gendarmes were British soldiers. The black man was Crispus Attucks.

Violence has "worked" in American history. Every fourth grader knows that America won its independence through a violent revolution, wrenched the West from the Indians by brute force, preserved the Union in a bloody

*Harvey Cox, "The Riots: No Winners—Only Losers," *Christianity and Crisis* 27(Aug. 7, 1967):181-182.

Civil War, became a world power through two destructive world wars and is now protecting the luckless people of Vietnam by incinerating their tiny country with napalm and high explosives. After all this, to scold the inmates of our black ghettos for resorting to violence when singing, marching, praying and picketing have failed seems at best a trifle hypocritical.

Violence has also "worked" elsewhere. Our pious insistence that "violence never accomplished anything" sounds a bit silly when we remember the raucous gaggle of furious fishwives who trooped through Paris to Versailles to ignite the French Revolution. And what about the impact of the ragged crowd that stormed the Winter Palace in St. Petersburg in October 1917? The fact is that urban violence *has* accomplished things in the past.

Yes, but will it "work" today? The question sounds insane to ghetto residents. They know that the violence of slavetraders, slumlords and bigotry has "worked" all too well over the centuries to keep them down. And they know that this type of violence still has them in its clutches. Black unemployment is still 250 percent greater than white unemployment. Among youth, it is eight times as high.

But isn't progress being made? Aren't Negroes "moving too fast"? One statistic speaks volumes. Infant mortality among blacks was 66 percent higher than among whites in 1950; today it is 90 percent higher. Ghetto youngsters don't read government statistics, but eight out of ten Negro young men in Hough are out of work. They know it hurts and humiliates. Let us not ask these violated young men whether violence works. It has worked on them and they know it. Besides, the outbreaks in today's black ghettos are not calibrated on a cost-effectiveness computer. Heaving a molotov cocktail is not really a way of accomplishing something; it is a way of *expressing* something: fury, frustration, hatred. For the black youth who smashes Whitey's car window, the act works if his rage cannot be misunderstood.

Today's ghetto violence is not a tool. It is a scream. Why else should it seem so strategically misdirected? The revolutionary crowds in Paris and Moscow did not smash into liquor stores and haberdasheries. They broke into palaces and seized the organs of government. Harassing firemen has never won a revolution. Even if white merchants finally flee the Harlems they have bled for so long, the result will not be epochal. The Negro merchants who move in will soon discover that power over the ghetto has little to do with who sells the transistors. The real power belongs to people whose offices and homes lie miles away from the devastation.

Expressive violence may provide the brutalized victims of racism some fleeting or symptomatic relief. It will touch the root of oppression, how-ever, only if it becomes organized and tactically focused. This is the real spectre that should haunt us—not the sportive and inchoate violence of Newark, but the recognition that a very small number of desperate people with only a few weapons and just a smidgin of tactical imagination could cripple and strangle a whole metropolitan area. And when cities stop functioning, the nation expires.

Let us not waste another breath trying to convince the children of Crispus Attucks that violence never works. But it always evokes counterviolence, and frequently the pain and bitterness it produces cancel out anything it gains. Is there another way? There is. But in recalling it we realize we may already be too late. Not to admit this grim possibility would be idle. Still, it may not be too late. No one really knows.

If white America hears the scream and foregoes giving unsought advice to Negroes, there are things that could still be done. We *could* quintuple the poverty budget and put it directly into the hands of black neighbor-hood groups rather than sifting it through the sticky tentacles of city hall poverty offices. We *could* embark on a massive program of low cost housing, with the construction jobs and the control of the projects firmly in the hands of ghetto residents themselves. We *could* redirect the billions we compulsively throw at Vietnam into rebuilding the rat-infested centers of our cities. We *could* begin paying at least as much for education as we do for booze. We *could* place police, welfare and health services under the direction of the people they are supposed to serve.

We *could* refocus our energy and imagination into one last effort to save ourselves from the furies. The trouble is that disparate groups of people have always opposed any real national program of this type, any re-direction of our wealth into the starving public sector. Now, however, such groups think they have a sure-fire clincher for their argument. Much of such a national effort would benefit Negroes, and they obviously just don't deserve anything. Racism has now nudged us to the edge of catastrophe. At the same time it prevents our taking the steps that are needed to save ourselves. It is racism that is our real national enemy. It will certainly destroy us all, and soon, unless we destroy it.

We *could*. But will we? King George III refused to believe the reports from Boston. An eight-year war ensued. A national guardsman described the Newark uprising as "just like a war between two nations." Maybe he was wrong, maybe just premature. That war has not quite begun, not yet. If it does, God help us. We will assuredly disembowel ourselves as a nation and, just as in a hydrogen war, there will be no winners, white or black. Only losers.

WHO'S AFRAID OF REVOLUTION*

A group of protestors gathers in the streets to decry government policies—they are angry, they are loud and abusive, they are demanding disobedience. Facing them is a unit of militia, their rifles loaded, their bayonets fixed, their young faces betraying their fright and inexperience. The situation grows more tense, more heated, more dangerous.

Suddenly, somehow, a guardsman fires into the crowd. Claiming later that he had been fired upon first although there was no proof, and immediately, the rest of the detachment fires—point blank, into the mass of protestors, killing a few and wounding several more. Later, the funeral of these dissidents becomes an occasion for great and widespread demonstration against the Establishment.

Kent State, 1970?
No, Boston, 1770.

Almost two hundred years to the day. The Boston Massacre it was called although only three (only?) actually died that day, one less than at Kent. (Two more died later of their wounds.) But its effect on the stormy events of the 1770's was incalculable.

In 1773 an act of outright civil disobedience and vandalism occurred, one which could rival if not surpass the sacking of our draft board offices today. Ships in Boston Harbor were boarded and their cargoes of tea dropped into the sea. This act, and the subsequent repressions inflicted by the Establishment, were directly responsible for the outbreak of the armed rebellion that became the American Revolution.

An American can dispute the values and/or dangers of civil disobedience, but if he is historically informed he cannot possibly label such protest as un-American. Our nation, like it or not, was founded on it. Violence, rebellion and treason. Pretty words? No. American? Definitely!

— — — — —

"If the politicians of the old China had been upright and honest, China would not have taken the course she did, and a New China might not have been born."

Attributed to Chou En-lai

*Peter Stone, "Afraid of Revolution?" *New York Times*, Oct. 3, 1970. *Mr. Stone is the librettist of the musical "1776."*

IN PRAISE OF SUSTAINED OUTRAGE, UNADJUSTMENT, AND MADNESS*

Is it true what they keep telling us—the end is coming? "The Western civilization that we know is almost certain to disintegrate," says Henry Kissinger, urging reforms. Gunnar Myrdal says he's "very scared at what's happening now. The trend at present is leading to hell." The President of France believes that "all . . . curves are leading us to disaster." Even among the less mighty, the future is getting a bad press. After talking with some students recently about possibilities for social reform, one said to me: "You don't understand. I just read a book by a scientist who said humanity has only 30 years to go before we're all annihilated. We've destroyed the environment, we're overpopulating and life will be insupportable."

If all this is true—that we sit now in death row, awaiting the chaplain to escort us the last mile—why is there such calm? People continue to visit the shops, talk with neighbors, commute to work and pay their bills. Few grumble, few shake their shoulders to throw off the weight of gloom. The calmness is reassuring—at least until it is examined. But when it is—when questions are asked and garbled non-answers are given—the calmness becomes more frightening than the predictions of doom. It suggests that large numbers of citizens, in the face of such immense disasters as famine, pollution, inflation and recession, choose to adjust to them rather than offer some measure of resistance. Adjustment to the abnormal becomes a greater threat than the abnormalcies themselves.

Most of us not only have become passive bystanders to the large deteriorations—starvation in Africa and India, abuse of the American land by the strip miners, government corruption or the white-collar crime wave—but we are inert about many of the deteriorations in our personal lives, the one place presumably where people are not caged in powerlessness. Our annual dental bill is about $5 billion. Some 90 million citizens have had at least eighteen teeth filled, pulled or decayed, with 56 million teeth yanked annually. Yet, amid these oral sensations, annual soft-drink sales are $6 billion, per capita consumption of sugar is 120 pounds. Is it wild to take these facts and conclude that we are a nation of rotting teeth because we are adjusted to living with vast amounts of useless sugar? Even without "wild" thinking, we know that 57,000 deaths a year are attributed to lung cancer from cigarettes. The packs warn of the danger, yet sales are higher than ever.

*Adapted from Colman McCarthy, "Adjusting to the Abnormal," *Newsweek* 85 (13 Jan 75):11.

If there is little concern among so many citizens about saving their own teeth and lungs, how can a population be aroused to saving distant countries from starvation? The latter is seen as an abstraction, an issue to be debated at conferences by the experts, not a calamity personally endured. What Bernanos wrote in "Tradition of Freedom" appears to be true: "The horrors we have seen, the still greater horrors which we shall presently see, are not signs that rebels, insubordinate, untamable men, are increasing in constant numbers, but rather that there is a constant increase, a stupendously rapid increase, in the number of obedient, docile men."

In seeking cures for the epidemic of adjustment, a childish wishfulness often appears in many otherwise intelligent people: if only someone would rise from among us who could free our country from this bondage! Naturally, the politicians play to this hunger, each claiming to be the shepherd who can find green pastures again. But they can't. Mass movements don't work, whether people are asked to follow along as good sheep or good Germans. Something is subtracted from the sum of the person's individuality and emotions. An equation is created: adjust to the subhuman and you may become subhuman.

For a common example, cities are so clogged with cars that the pressure of traffic easily induces many usually mild people into savage aggression. It is common to see motorists blaring their horns when the light turns green. When traffic moves, the horn blower is now viciously cutting you off to get into your lane because it looks faster—but never is—and he gives you the finger on passing back to his lane. These scenes from the daily urban-scape are brush strokes of hatred. Yet an hour later, who is home playing gently with his kids, talking calmly with his wife, his face serene with no twitching of traffic-jam hate? The same person. Now he's changed into a lamb again. He was a downtown savage for 45 minutes, but what is that?

Because adjustment is made in small fits—we snip our values into tame sizes and heap the rest into a pile, leaving our integrity clothed only in shreds—we see each yielding as inconsequential. If disaster came in killer doses we would fight it. But when the adjustment is only some minor irk, why resist? This is why so many of those who do resist are seen as strange. The person who refuses to adjust to the abnormal is made to seem odd, becoming a public nuisance who won't get in line to enroll quietly in his local behavior-modification center.

What the nonadjusted citizen has, and uses fully, is a capacity for sustained outrage. It is often said about these forbidding times that because so many abuses, scandals, tragedies, gyps, deceits and disasters pound upon our consciousness—a Roman sacking of the mind—who can keep up with them all, let along stay angry or shocked? Any cupful of outrage a person might have is soon spilled.

There is no easy or pat answer to that, except to pay homage to those citizens who keep alive in themselves a sense of defiance or resistance, whether it is only ice cream laced with additives that they refuse to accept as normal, or large contemporary horrors like the Pentagon's profligacy, those corporations that are unaccountable, or dirty drinking water, now that the Mississippi may be a river of cancer. To refuse to accept these events as normal is to verify Pascal's thought: not to be mad would be another form of madness. . . .

PART 4

What Can be Done?

A CONCLUDING ESSAY BY THOMAS FORD HOULT

I. Counsel of despair vs. counsel of hope. The foregoing, considered in toto, is obviously a depressing collection. But it is deliberately so to make the point as powerfully as it can be made that this country, along with others, is seriously troubled. The problems are such that if they are not adequately handled, and soon, it will be too late—too late politically and too late ecologically.

The question then arises, what can we do? Where do we go from here? In considering such questions, several cautions are in order. First, it is quite useless to say despairingly that the situation is so bad nothing can be done. Those taking such a tack all but guarantee that disaster will indeed prevail. In contrast, there is something to be said for one Puritan value: *Never* say die. This particularly applies to the United States. The very fact that it has ideals which can be contrasted with realities is ground for hope. Such ideals are working material out of which a better future can be forged. As David McReynolds has phrased it (1970:232)*—and I share his orientation in every way—:

> We can take hope from one thing. While all men can be corrupted,
> they have also the power of their own salvation. The whore can stop

*In this final part—Part IV—of the present volume, full citation information is shown in the alphabetical listing which follows the last page.

553

whoring. The thief can reform. So long as a man is alive, he is never finally and truly lost. There is always the chance that he will find himself before his death and, thus, die as a man. A society such as ours is so terribly powerful that it can probably long survive its no less terrible corruption. But I frankly do not care whether such a society—corrupt and powerful—lives or dies. My loyalty is to the ideals of the past and the dreams of the future. I want us to be honest not because we would be more powerful (we would not) nor because we would endure longer, but because we would feel like men and women—like human beings—for however long such an experiment in decency might last.

One version of the "nothing can be done" syndrome is the idea that elite control is so well-established it is not really possible to make needed changes. But specially privileged and seemingly all-powerful elites have always dominated social systems; despite this, vast changes have occurred. Slavery and serfdom were abolished, universal political emancipation has been adopted in many Western nations, the idea of collective responsibility for social welfare has been widely accepted, cruel treatment of prisoners is at least cause for scandal—these and related steps toward a more humane social order have been achieved in the face of rigid opposition by power-elites. Such elites, thus, do not control *everything*; occasionally they even fail to dominate some of their own elements. Furthermore, in complex societies there are competing elites so that control from the top is sometimes incomplete and ineffective. And, as Lipset has pointed out (in Michels, 1962:35), "'... power is only one of several cognate factors in the determination of social events."

The analyses of pseudo-realists must be cast aside along with the despair which says there is no hope. Pseudo-realists are well represented by social scientists who concentrate their total energy on showing why things must be as they are. But there are no great accomplishments by those who center on what "has to be." Heights are achieved by those who, seeing accurately what is *and not liking it,* focus on *what can be.* The watchword for such people is that today's reality is NOT tomorrow's necessity.

Along with rejecting despair and pseudo-realistic analyses, it is wise to avoid over-confidence that there is an easy solution to political-economic problems and crises. In truth, there is no Gordian knot to cut. There is a *knot,* yes, but it is vastly complicated and rock hard. It cannot be cut; it must, with infinite patience, be untangled. The untangling calls for detailed plans and technical knowledge which are beyond the scope of the present work. However, it is possible to indicate some general aspects of what we must avoid and what we must do if we are to have the slightest chance of building a humanistically just society. The things I indicate are based on personal evaluations and should not be presumed to represent "sociological principles"; however, I am reasonably certain that a large majority of sociologists, including even the most technically-oriented, would agree with the general thrust of my conclusions.

II. More than justice needed. In the preceding paragraph I used the phrase *"humanistically* just society." The good society cannot be built from justice alone; justice must be tempered with a humanistic concern for all societal participants, for we are all unwitting products of the forces that have shaped us. If justice were the only ingredient in making the good society, then it could be achieved easily: just line up exploiters and cheaters and shoot them down. That would be "poetic justice." But it would also establish jungle principles such that revengeful exploited and cheated would soon suffer again, more terribly than ever. David McReynolds (1970:200-201) has made the point with his usual grace:

> Justice is a term as elusive as guilt and responsibility. Justice can never be fully achieved, and, if we make justice our sole objective, "untainted" by any cowardly and bourgeois ideas of compassion, it is certain that massive injustice will follow from our actions. The Russian Communists sought justice, not mercy, and we do not yet know how many died as a result; we only know the number of murdered seems to be greater than the number of Jews killed by Hitler. Justice is not revenge, with which it is usually confused. Justice is a concept that applies to the living and, particularly, to the innocent. The search for revenge defeats the search for justice. Let us suppose that, "to secure justice," I go and shoot a cop. What have that cop's wife and children done to me that I have the right to inflict on them widowhood and fatherlessness? Why must they suffer? Justice is oriented to the future, not to the past. Our job is not half so much "bringing the cops to justice" as it is to "let justice roll down like the waters"—that is, to house the homeless, clothe the naked, feed the hungry, provide work for the jobless. To create a just society is not a matter of shooting some people and jailing others—it is a matter, rather, of recognizing that we are, collectively, victims of a situation or a system, and to seek our universal liberation.

III. Organize. McReynolds quite rightly suggests the need for fundamental change in the system. How can this be achieved? The answer is deceptively simple: *Organize.* As the late Saul Alinsky indicated in his *Reveille for Radicals* (1969), "people's organizations" can accomplish remarkable results even under the most depressing circumstances. Black Americans, when mobilized during the early 1960's, *organized* marches and demonstrations and brought about a permanent reshuffle in the political balance of power in the Deep South; auto workers were hapless victims of their employers until they *organized*; teachers, *organized*, are beginning to exercize some control over their economic destiny.

Along with organization, Sidney Slomich suggests, is the need for speaking out, for protesting, so that the military-industrial monster which sits on the nation's chest can be thrown off:

> The hope of this nation, that of any nation, is its people. You are that hope. The entire system of expertise and secrecy designed to prevent the people of this country from determining their own destinies is basically a fake. Over the last twenty years I have had continuous Top Secret clearances from the Army, State, CIA, Defense, ACDA—sometimes from more than one. I never learned one thing of value. Everything valuable that I have learned, know, said, perceived, or written has come from an open, scholarly unclassified source or from newspapers, journals, or my own observations. All these sources are open to you.
>
> There is no silent majority. Man is a speaking animal. There is only a silenced majority, a repressed, clamped-down, and frightened majority. You. You have been frightened, you have been silenced.
>
> Look, these war rooms paneled in walnut, those massive files, those contracts for millions of dollars worth of death and death-research, those fancy desks and chairs, all the paraphernalia of power, bases, buildings, bombs, and all the rest, they are all yours. They belong to you. Take them back, make a human use of them, make this your society, as it is your life. Everything you do, everything you can do, to please yourself and build your life is more beautiful and more real than the fakery, abstraction, obsession, and desire for death that rules this country today. That's the only secret worth knowing. Once you know it you can take back this nation—with difficulty.
>
> Once you know it you will. And then we'll speak not of the American Nightmare, but the American Dream... (Slomich, 1971:284-285).

Organization and a willingness to speak out are obviously not sufficient. Organize to what purpose? Speak out on what subjects? In my view, the answers to these questions must be *political*. That is, I believe that the only way the major problems of the nation and the world will be solved is with the ultimate power which can be achieved through political action alone. But I do not mean to imply that our problems are such that dictatorship is called for. Indeed, it seems to me the very opposite is what is needed. We need, that is, to engage in appropriate organized political action so that pseudo-democracy, with its manipulated majority, can be replaced by the genuine article. A truly representative democracy has the nine virtues delineated by Mannheim (1950:149-154), including integrative power, cooperative endeavor, public accountability, and flexibility. In addition, only in a genuine democracy can there be any hope of creating and preserving those two basic essentials of the good life, *liberty* and *equality*. They certainly cannot be achieved with three commonly prevailing political-economic orientations: the far left which stresses equality at the expense of liberty; centrism, which extols liberty over equality; and right extremism which doesn't provide for either.

IV. Radical-liberalism. A fourth political-economic orientation, the radical-liberal—as described by the late Arnold Kaufman (1968)—is in my opinion "the only way to go." It is the political path to the humanistically just society because it combines the best of socialism and liberalism; it therefore stresses both equality and liberty. And it has other virtues. It is leftist enough to genuinely reorder priorities and redistribute power and privilege so that a multitude of outsiders (blacks, underclass whites, migrants, browns, reds) and fringe-clingers (the vast majority of ethnics) can become full-fledged insiders. But at the same time, it is not so far to the left that it is likely to illustrate the principle that political-economic extremes tend to breed their opposite; indeed, it is centrist enough so that the political party adopting it as a philosophy would find it easier to do precisely what a party must do if it would become a thriving majority— namely, hold together a wide range of disparate interests rather than puristically driving them out. These virtues promise more than a large coalition of the disadvantaged; they also attract genuine liberals and even the conservative-minded and highly-privileged who are sufficiently aware— the Kennedys, for example. It is only superficially paradoxical for wealthy people to be radically liberal; the knowledgeable, privileged or not, know the society must be altered fundamentally lest Armageddon prevail. If the radically liberal millionaire is asked "But will you be satisfied in having a lot less?" he might well answer, "I'd better be; having *less* is better than having nothing at all."

But even the most efficacious political-economic orientation will not suffice if it is applied "here" but "not there." Neither liberty nor equality is divisible. "Liberty is the only thing you cannot have unless you are willing to give it to others," WIlliam Allen White observed; and, "the wretched of the earth" will destroy it if their condition is not radically altered. Hence the nation-state, as a totally independent political entity, can no longer be tolerated. It is not just that if we don't make it one world, there will be no world to make—though that is starkly true. It is this, also:

> . . . the present-day agency of despotism on the world level is the western nation-state, which has ceased to be an instrument of human betterment and has become instead its obstacle. As a result, the

nation-state is destined to suffer the fate that was finally administered to the oppressive feudal estate of the middle ages (Wheeler, 1971:280).

Another thing that must be done is to supplant most of the remaining remnants of large-scale free enterprise with essentially nonprofit cooperative enterprise. It is simply impossible to manifest ethical or ecologically sane behavior within the framework of an economic system which makes survival dependent upon competitive aggression: ". . . unfettered liberty and self-reliance, sometimes justified with a sprinkling of religion, simply do not fit the new one-world pattern, no matter how sincerely older America would like to believe they do" (Tobin, 1972). Free enterprise in medical care illustrates the problem. In the "free market" involving illness and medicine, the former has been forced out of the market in the sense that the great majority simply cannot now afford a serious illness. It is true of course that American medical care includes very sophisticated hardware and specialized knowledge, but these benefit only the privileged few. The masses simply suffer or die young.

Another sacred cow that must be disavowed is *growth*, except for that which takes the form of improving the environment. We cannot deal adequately with this subject here—it is discussed at length in the environmental section of Part II. It will suffice at the moment to indicate that since the biosphere in which we live is a closed system, we must to a large degree become zero-growth advocates if animate life is to continue. But here we run into one of those knotty complications; zero-growth threatens to prevent satisfying the desires of those who have long been exploited and who desperately want to begin living the good life (materially speaking). There is only one solution to this dilemma. The *haves* must begin sharing with the *have-nots* even though it would be vastly complicated to implement such a sharing program (Heilbroner, 1970:281). As Paul Ehrlich has put it, "The way to responsibility is for the developed nations to limit their population size and redistribute technology and resources" (*Environmental Action*, 8 July 72:12).

V. Democratic socialism. It may seem strange that I, being obviously antagonistic to arbitrary authority—as suggested by a multitude of the selections included in Part I of the present work—should opt for the modicum of socialism implied by radical-liberalism. Socialism, many assume, means the growth of government bureaucracy and this is a frightening prospect. But, as Bensman and Vidich point out (1971:26-27), bureaucratization is already a threat to individual freedom, perhaps the major threat, in non-socialist as well as in socialist nations. *More* threatening, however, is the present system which threatens to evolve rather rapidly into a garrison state, rightist if not leftist. Further, I know of no way other than socialism to achieve the widespread relative equality that is an essential part of the truly just society. As James Baldwin has expressed it (1972:175), "The necessity for formal socialism is based on the observation that the world's present economic arrangements doom most of the world to misery. . . ." This does not imply that socialism, in itself, is a talisman. It would be "illusory and irrelevant" to draw such a conclusion, sociologist Robert Nisbet rightly observes. But he adds (1953:281)—conservative though he is— ". . . all States in the future will be able to demonstrate, and will *have* to demonstrate, attributes of socialism."

So, albeit trepidatiously, I am willing to gamble that we can develop a form of socialism wherein democratically chosen government officials would be responsive to the citizenry. To make them so responsive, there would need to be an organizational setup something like the federal system originally suggested for the United States. That is, the totality of units would have to be decentralized in important respects, yet united on a world scale. In Wheeler's terms (1971:287), the world that is needed, the only one that will work, ". . . will be larger on the outside and smaller on the inside. It will involve the entire world but it will be made up of man-sized autonomous communities possessing their own individual integrity." Elements of such self-governing units have appeared in Yugoslavia, where the self-management movement (i.e., worker-controlled industry) has been well established (Adizes, 1971; Broekmeyer, 1970; Kolaja, 1966). Wheeler (1971:274) is optimistic about the possibilities for developing many more relatively independent community units: ". . . cybernated societies will possess the option of designing small, economically autonomous communities that can be organized on the basis of cultural amenities rather than commercial values."

The importance of decentralization is widely recognized. Years ago, in his *The Quest for Community* (1953:esp. Ch. 11 and Conclusion), Nisbet made a prophetic call for a decentralized socio-economic system. More recently, Professor Nisbet described a later version of the book (1962) as ". . . an unabashed plea for *division of power, decentralization, social pluralism,* and *multiplication* of more or less *autonomous groups and associations* in the social order" (Horowitz, 1969:204; italics in original).*

---

*It is sadly ironic to note that despite his plea for decentralization, divided power, and local autonomy, Professor Nisbet joined with a few other social scientists in calling for the 1972 re-election of a national administration that spent four years accumulating and exercising more centralized power than had ever before in the country's history been gathered into so few hands.

Political scientist Murray Levin has issued a related plea; he says it is not enough to understand the limitations of classic, dead-center liberalism— "The alternative of a humane and decentralized and participatory socialism must be offered" (1971:285). Social critic Michael Novak (1972:239-243) also sees the desirability of developing autonomous communities; but he feels that the advantage of such autonomy would be negated if the communities were permitted to grow much larger than 100,000 residents. Places larger than this generate bureaucracies of such size and complexity that it is difficult to pinpoint responsibility for the public welfare. The advantage of community autonomy itself, from Novak's point of view, would be that people who wanted to maintain a particular life style could find a suitable setting. Novak would therefore provide places where white supremicists could live out their fantasies, or where black nationalists could express theirs. He speculates that there might even be cities of sin, or WASP havens ("the cleanest city of the land"). The possibilities are endless. Why not a city for Elks, all with white horns? And maybe even some for those who still believe in the dream of the fully integrated community made up of a kaleidoscopic mix, all parts of which respect all others.

Decentralized or not, in my view socialism would become a Frankensteinian monster if it were not restricted primarily to the heights of industry. That is, it would apply in the fullest sense only to those aspects of the economic order that are so pervasive they have become the tail wagging the dog: the automobile industry, chemistry, steel, pharmaceuticals, banking, petroleum, and the like. The future is going to be collective whether we want it that way or not. But the cure will be worse than the disease if we do not make it a sane collectivism, a controlled collectivism, a humanizing collectivism. If we don't make it such, then it will surely become a Stalinized system where a new elite, with the ultimate power given it by modern technology, will achieve near-permanent dominance.

VI. The GAI. The most important aspect of genuine socialism (i.e., socialism for all, not just for the rich) is its equalitarian stress. This is vital because there is no meaningful liberty for the poor; there is only ugly constraint. As it has been said, the rich and the poor are equally free to sleep under bridges; but such "freedom" is a matter of necessity for the poor. The rich have a number of options, including more comfortable places to sleep. Increasing options for the poor boils down to improving their economic status. But how can this be done without lessening the option potential of the rich? The answer is that it can't, despite Abraham Lincoln's much cited observation that justice is not served if the rich are "robbed" so that the poor may be helped. That might have been true in Lincoln's day, but in a *closed* system—which is what we now have due to ecological conditions—additional freedoms for one set of units usually cannot be achieved without reducing related freedoms of other units. This applies to all aspects of life. Securing the freedom of theater patrons from the panic that might ensue if individuals could shout "fire" at any time, puts a damper on the freedom of potential shouters; but scarcely any would argue it is inequitable to restrict freedom in this manner. The widely accepted principle is this: To obtain equity for many, it is sometimes essential to place reasonable restrictions on selected freedoms of a few.

The restricted-freedom principle would necessarily be applied to the economic realm in the humanistically just society; only thus could substance be given to the basic humanistic value that all individuals should have the opportunity to develop their full potential, short of harming others. The practical result would be to reduce quite sharply the present gross differential between the options open to rich and poor; and it would mean that individuals could not be permitted to accumulate private property in amounts sufficient to give them unwarranted power over others. But, as suggested in the foregoing introduction to Part II, the just society does not require that everyone must be absolutely equal in economic status. Achieving such an absolute—presuming it were desirable, which is highly questionable—would destroy that other necessary ingredient of justice, *liberty*; it would require total control over conception and over all educational experiences so that none would become "more equal" than others. On the other hand, it is unjust to make people suffer grievously because factors over which they have no control—inadequate parents, for example—render them unable to cope effectively.

So the problem to be solved is this: without unduly interfering with liberty, the gap between the fortunate and the unfortunate must be bridged, establishing a greater measure of equality. This goal can be reached most efficaciously by guaranteeing that all families, in one way or another, will have at least a *minimum* annual income which can be supplemented by working. I stress the word "minimum" because workers who would supply the surplus needed to support the income maintenance program—and the program should be supported by surplus lest inflation result—would surely overthrow a system which did not give the more productive at least a modicum of special advantage or extra reward (see Yuchtman, 1972:588-589).

A guaranteed annual income would at one sweep do away with the inadequate welfare system that is so universally condemned. At the same time, it would probably create a conviction on the part of the multitude that they too have a stake in the society and its preservation. These two potential benefits of the GAI have been enough to sway a number of skeptics. But they do not convince everyone. Those who have a shallow knowledge of England's Speenhamland Law are particularly negative. This law took its name from the Berkshire town in which it was first adopted in 1795. It provided that subsidies in aid of wages should be granted in accordance with a scale that was correlated with the price of bread. A similar plan was soon adopted in many other areas, finally covering much of the rural part of the country. After several decades, it was clear that "the rates" scheme (the popular designation) was seriously defective. Instead of subsidizing wages, it tended to displace them; and it changed "respectable poor" into groveling paupers. Therefore, the Speenhamland laws were preciptiously repealed in 1835.

On its face, the Speenhamland experiment appears similar to modern proposals for a guaranteed annual income. But the knowledgeable know the two phenomena are only superficially alike. Their most basic difference is that they have dissimilar roots. The Speenhamland laws were prompted by covetousness on the part of employers, not by any abstract ideas of justice or because of pressure from the poor. As Polanyi describes the situation (1944:Ch. 8), the allowance system was intended to make it unnecessary for rural squires to have to pay wages realistically competing with those being offered by developing town industries. The allowances, thus, were:

> ... a device contrived by squirearchy to meet a situation in which physical mobility could no longer be denied to labor, while the squire wished to avoid such unsettlement of local conditions, including higher wages, as was involved in the acceptance of a free national labor market (Polanyi, 1944:89).

Once the laws were adopted, the squires were motivated to pay lower and lower wages because they knew that no matter how little they paid, the rates subsidy would maintain worker income at the established minimum. Workers, in turn, knowing that they would not be paid more no matter how hard they worked, were not motivated to exert effort on behalf of employers. Indeed, many of them, since they made no more working than not, simply stopped work. The final result was naturally chaos and scandal.

One of the most serious deficiencies of the plan was that it was everywhere accompanied by what were known as Anti-Combination laws. These prohibited workers from organizing for collective bargaining. But for these anti-union laws, Polanyi argues (1944:81), ". . . Speenhamland might have had the effect of raising wages instead of depressing them as it actually did." Wages were finally depressed below subsistence levels since there were no minimum wage laws. Thus, ever more were forced on the rates and worker demoralization became ubiquitous. But the demoralization was not necessarily due to not working in itself; there is evidence that the demoralization was associated with lack of opportunity. One of the evidences for this is that in any given area, there was a direct correlation between the number on the rates and the speed with which the commons —land traditionally open for all to use for grazing and gardening—were enclosed for exclusive use by local gentry (Polanyi, 1944:93).

None of the conditions which undermined the effective working of the Speenhamland laws prevails in America today. Still, there are many who argue that a guaranteed annual income plan will fail. Some say we could not afford such a plan. They are misled on two grounds: they demean our truly incredible productive capacity; and they forget that a government, with power potential for controlling prices and wages, can "afford" many things impossible for private enterprise. And then there are those who claim to be concerned that a guaranteed income would undermine character. This is a suspicious claim; it smacks of prejudice against the poor. As Robert Theobald has put it (1970:107-108),

> The poverty in the Western world can only be explained by a failure of conscience, by an unfounded and heartless belief that the poor only have themselves to blame for their situation. The minimum step which we must take if we are to eliminate the poverty which exists in the United States is to introduce the guaranteed income.

Why don't those who profess worry about the supposed character-destroying potential of guaranteed income also worry about wealthy parents who assure their children a comfortable place in life? It is significant that few such children are ruined by knowing they will not want.

There are also the Puritan-minded who fret about idleness. However, it cannot be assumed that most Americans would be satisfied with meeting their needs minimally. Certainly, vast numbers—including poor families which have already, as part of an experiment, had their incomes supplemented for several years (Gallagher, 1972)—are not so satisfied at the present time. However, given the ecological state of the world and the constantly decreasing demands for industrial workers, it would actually be a gain if many people chose to live their lives in "decent poverty," sculpting, dabbling in music, writing poetry, or just sitting. They might bring a measure of relaxation, maybe even of beauty, to a world sorely in need of such things. "The lilies of the field, they toil not, neither do they spin," yet they grace us with their delicate nature and the gods favor them with the basic essentials needed for an adequate life.

REFERENCES Cited in Part IV

Adizes, Ichak
    1971 Industrial Democracy: Yugoslave Style; the effect of decentraliza-
        tion on organizational behavior. New York: Free Press.
Alinsky, Saul D.
    1969 Reveille for Radicals. New York: Vintage Books.
Baldwin, James
    1972 No Name in the Street. New York: Dial Press.
Broekmeyer, J.M., editor
    1970 Yugoslav Workers' Selfmanagement: proceedings of a symposium
        held in Amsterdam, 7-9 January, 1970. Dordrecht-Holland: D.
        Reidel Publishing Company.
Gallagher, Robert S.
    1972 "Interim report on the outcome of the guaranteed income."
        Saturday Review 55(1 July):5-7.
Horowitz, Irving Louis, editor
    1969 Sociological Self-Images: a collective portrait. Berkeley, California.
        Sage Publications.
Kaufman, Arnold S.
    1968 The Radical Liberal: new man in American politics. New York:
        Atherton Press.
Kolaja, Jiri
    1966 Workers' Councils: The Yugoslav Experience. New York: Frederick
        A. Praeger, Publishers.
Levin, Murray B.
    1971 Political Hysteria in America; the democratic capacity for repres-
        sion. New York: Basic Books, Inc.
Mannheim, Karl
    1950 Freedom, Power, and Democratic Planning. New York: Oxford
        University Press.
McReynolds, David
    1970 We Have Been Invaded by the 21st Century. New York: Praeger Pub-
        lishers.
Michels, Robert
    1962 [c1915] Political Parties: a sociological study of the oligarchical
        tendencies of modern democracy. Translated by Eden and Ceder
        Paul. New York: Collier Books.
Nisbet, Robert
    1953 The Quest for Community. New York: Oxford University Press.
    1962 Community and Power. New York: Oxford University Press.

Novak, Michael
1972 The Rise of the Unmeltable Ethnics: politics and culture in the seventies. New York: The Macmillan Co.
Polanyi, Karl
1944 The Great Transformation. New York: Rinehart & Company, Inc.
Slomich, Sidney J.
1971 The American Nightmare. New York: The Macmillan Company.
Theobald, Robert
1970 An Alternative Future for America II. Chicago: The Swallow Press, Inc.
Tobin, Richard L.
1972 "The Puritan ethic today." Saturday Review 55(1 Jan):16.
Wheeler, Harvey
1971 The Politics of Revolution. Berkeley, California: The Glendessary Press, Inc.
Yuchtman, Ephraim
1972 "Reward distribution and work-role attractiveness in the kibbutz— reflections on equity theory." American Sociological Review 37(Oct):581-595.

Subject Index

Name Index

Acknowledgements

The compiler-editor of this volume expresses his
gratitude to the authors and publishers of
works from which selections have been reprinted
or adapted.

●Morris Ginsberg, *On Justice in Society*, Cornell University Press.
●Sidney Lens, *The Forging of the American Empire*, Thomas Y. Crowell Company.
●Pierre Van Paassen, *Days of Our Years*, rev. ed., Garden City Publishing Co.
●*The Arizona Republic*, (Editorial).
●Robert Jay Lifton, *Death in Life*: Survivors of Hiroshima, Random House, Inc.
●*Sane World*.
●Fred Warner Neal, "Government by Myth," *The Center Magazine*.
●Arthur Hoppe, *The Scottsdale (Arizona) Daily Progress*.
●Theo Sommer, "An Erosion of Mutual Trust," *Saturday Review*.
●Gloria Emerson, "Each Day is a Separate Ordeal," *Saturday Review*.
●Oriana Fallaci, *Nothing, and So Be It:* A Personal Search for Meaning in War, Doubleday & Co., Inc.
●Rev. Alfred M. Smith, Bulletin, Scottsdale (Arizona) United Methodist Church.
●Robert Jay Lifton, "Beyond Atrocity," *Saturday Review*.
●Shana Alexander, "Prisoners of Peace," *Newsweek*.
●Richard J. Barnet, *The Economy of Death*, Atheneum.
●Sidney J. Slomich, *The American Nightmare*, The Macmillan Company.
●Daniel S. Greenberg, "Test-Tube Warfare, The Fake Renunciation," *World*.
●Leo Sartori, "The Myth of MIRV," *Saturday Review*.
●Herman Kahn, *On Thermonuclear War*, 2nd ed., Princeton University Press.
●E. Digby Baltzell, *The Protestant Establishment*: Aristocracy and Caste in America, Random House, Inc.
●*Time*.
●Joseph Wechsberg, editor, *The Murderers Among Us*: The Simon Wiesenthal Memoirs, McGraw-Hill Book Company.
●Thomas Land, "20 Minutes Per Murder," *The New Leader*.
●Solomon Northup, *Twelve Years A Slave*: Edited by Sue Eaken and Joseph Logsdon, Louisiana State University Press.

579

●Ida B. Wells-Barnett, *On Lynchings*: Southern Horrors; A Red Record; Mob Rule in New Orleans, Arno Press and *The New York Times*.

●Walter White, *Rope and Faggot*, Arno Press and The New York Times.

●Anna Arnold Hedgeman, *The Trumpet Sounds*: A Memoir of Negro Leadership, Holt, Rinehart and Winston.

●Testimony by the late Jackie Robinson at a Congressional hearing, Source: *Human Resources Development*, Part I, U.S. Government Printing Office.

●David Hilliard, "If You Want Peace, You've Got to Fight for It," *The Black Panther*.

●"The Negro in America, What Must Be Done," *Newsweek*.

●Dick Gregory, *The Shadow That Scares Me*, Pocket Books.

●Kenneth B. Clark, *The Negro Protest*: James Baldwin, Malcolm X, Martin Luther King talk with Kenneth B. Clark, Beacon Press.

●Irving Howe, "Picking Up the Pieces," *Dissent*.

●William Taylor, "School Desegregation: a New Time of Crisis," *ADA World*.

●Hubert G. Locke, *The Care and Feeding of White Liberals*: The American Tragedy and the Liberal Dilemma, Newman Press.

●Roger Wilkins, Boston *Globe*.

●John Schoonbeck, "Why Did Walter Die?" *Time*.

●Edgar S. Cahn, editor; Jerry J. Berman, W. Dayton Coles, Jr., Nancy Esposito, F. Browning Pipestem, Associate Editors, *Our Brother's Keeper*, The Indian in White America, New Community Press, Inc.

●Dee Brown, *Bury My Heart at Wounded Knee*: An Indian History of the American West, Bantam Books.

●U.S. Commission on Civil Rights, *Stranger in One's Land*, U.S. Government Printing Office.

●Kathy Mulherin, "Chicanos Turn to Brown Power: 'Five Years behind the blacks, but we'll catch up very fast,' " *National Catholic Reporter*.

●Maisie and Richard Conrat, *Executive Order 9066*: The Internment of 110,000 Japanese Americans, California Historical Society.

●Audrie Girdner and Anne Loftis, *The Great Betrayal*: The Evacuation of the Japanese-Americans During World War II, The Macmillan Co.

●Thomas S. Szasz, *The Manufacture of Madness*: A Comparative Study of the Inquisition and the Mental Health Movement, Harper and Row.

●Robert B. Edgerton, *The Cloak of Competence*, Stigma in the Lives of the Mentally Retarded, University of California Press.

●Studs Terkel, *Working*: People Talk About What They Do All Day and How They Feel About What They Do, Pantheon Books.

●Sheilah Drummond, "Hairy Legs Freak Fishy Liberal," *Berkeley Tribe*.

●Linda Hess's review of Joel Fort, *The Pleasure Seekers*, The Drug Crisis, Youth and Society, *Saturday Review*.

●Don Duncan, with J. A. C. Dunn, "Notes Toward a Definition of the Uniform Code of Military Justice, as Particularly Applied to the Person of Captain Howard Levy," *Ramparts*.

●Simone de Beauvoir, *The Coming of Age*, translated by Patrick O'Brian, G. P. Putnam's Sons.

●*Barbara Isenberg, "To Be Old and Poor is to be Alone, Afraid, Ill-Fed and Unknown," The Wall Street Journal.*

●Moriz Dreyfus, "Other Side of the Coin: What Became of That Pension?" *The Arizona Republic.*

●Sharon R. Curtin, *Nobody Ever Died of Old Age*, Little, Brown and Co.

●*Los Angles Times.*

●Philip Stern and George de Vincent, *The Shame of a Nation*, Ivan Obolensky, Inc.

●*Washington Post* Service.

●Walter J. Hickel, *Who Owns America?* Prentice-Hall, Inc.

●Arthur R. Simon, *Faces of Poverty*, Concordia Publishing House.

●Peter Schuck, "Tied to the Sugar Lands," *Saturday Review.*

●Robert Coles, *Still Hungry in America*, World Publishing Co.

●Dale Wright, *They Harvest Despair*: The Migrant Farm Worker, Beacon Press.

●Ben H. Bagdikian, *In the Midst of Plenty*: The Poor in America, Beacon Press.

●Sylvia Porter, syndicated columnist.

●Erwin Knoll, "It's Only Money," *The Progressive.*

●Michael M. Schneider, "Middle America: Study in Frustration," *The Center Magazine.*

●Lester C. Thurow and Robert E. B. Lucas, *The American Distribution of Income*: A Structural Problem; A Study Prepared for the Use of the Joint Economic Committee, Congress of the United States, U.S. Government Printing Office.

●Gabriel Kolko, *Wealth and Power in America*: An Analysis of Social Class and Income Distribution, Praeger Publishers.

●Abraham Ribicoff, "The Alienation of the American Worker," *Saturday Review.*

●Abbie Hoffman, "The Doctor Revolt," *Win.*

●John Wilkinson, "This Whole Medical Matter," *Center Report.*

●Select Committee on Human Needs, U.S. Senate, The Food Gap: poverty and malnutrition in the United States, U.S. Government Printing Office.

●*The Washington Post* Service.

●Harrison Wellford, *Sowing the Wind*, A Report from Ralph Nader's Center for Study of Responsive Law, Grossman Publishers, Inc.

●*Consumer Reports.*

●Mark Reader, "Life in Death: On Surmounting the Environmental Crisis," unpublished paper.

●Alton Blakeslee, "Of Cats and Rats, Roaches and Such," AP Science dispatch.

●A. V. Krebs, "Corporate Farms: The Grass Isn't Always Greener," *Environmental Action.*

●Stewart Udall and Jeff Stansbury, "Beryllium Disease is Death Sentence for Factory Workers," *The Arizona Republic.*
●David Lyle, "The Human Race Has, Maybe, Thirty-Five Years Left," *Esquire.*
●Nancy D. Joyner, "Bucharest—1974," *AAUW Journal.*
●Ben Funk, "Ocala Forest, Once Inspiring, Is a Dump," AP dispatch.
●David Nevin, " 'These Murdered Old Mountains,' " *Life.*
●Wayne Gard, "How They Killed the Buffalo," *American Heritage.*
●Paul R. Ehrlich and John P. Holdren, "The Heat Barrier," *Saturday Review.*
●Senator Mike Gravel, "Moratorium Politics: Finding the Critical Mass," *Environmental Action.*
●Lenore Marshall, "The Nuclear Sword of Damocles," *The Living Wilderness.*
●*Washington Star* Service.
●Robert Brigham, "Crisis at Sea: The Threat of No More Fish," *Life.*
●"Escambia Bay, in Its Dying Agony, is a Victim of Pollution," AP dispatch.
●James Bishop Jr., "The Polluter's Wedge: Give Out Jobs, Pay Taxes . . . and Don't Forget to Lobby," *Newsweek* Feature Service.
●Amitai Etzioni, "On Incrementing a Hurricane," *Science.*
●Paul Ehrlich, "Eco-Catastrophe!" *Ramparts.*
●Mary Jo Bane and Christopher Jencks, "The Schools and Equal Opportunity," *Saturday Review of Education.*
●Marc Libarle and Tom Seligson, editors, *The High School Revolutionaries*, Random House, Inc.
●Thomas Ford Hoult, "Don't Worry, Only the Worst Become Administrators," *Changing Education.*
●John Holt, "School is Bad for Children," *The Saturday Evening Post.*
●Morris J. Starsky, "Campus Struggles and the Coming American Revolution," paper presented to the Southwestern Socialist Conference, Los Angeles, California.
●Blanche D. Blank, "Degrees: Who Needs Them?" *AAUP Bulletin.*
●Colin Greer, "Public Schools: The Myth of the Melting Pot," *Saturday Review.*
●Hubert G. Locke, *The Care and Feeding of White Liberals*: The American Tragedy and the Liberal Dilemma, Newman Press.
●Garry Wills, "Working Within the System Won't Change Anything," *The Center Magazine.*
●Simon Winchester, "Needed: A Captain of the Ship," *The Guardian.*
●Joseph Morgenstern, "Death of a Citizen," *Newsweek.*
●Goldie Holt, *Civil Liberties.*
●John Hersey, *The Algiers Motel Incident*, Alfred Knopf.
●Jerome H. Skolnick, "Black Separatism," *Chicago Today.*
●Eric Crist, *Civil Liberties.*
●Walter Lowenfels, *The Writing on the Wall*, Doubleday and Co.

●Daniel Berrigan, *The Trial of the Catonsville Nine*, Beacon Press.
●*Time.*
●Letter to the editor by Larry Darrel, *The New Leader.*
●Hallowell Bowser, "The Gentle Gendarmes," *Saturday Review.*
●"Up Against That Wall, Punk, or I'll Cripple You," *New Times.*
●Tom Hayden, *Rebellion in Newark*, Random House, Inc.
●*New York Times* Service dispatch.
●Howard James, *Crisis in the Courts*, David McKay Company, Inc.
●Edward P. Morgan's Introduction to Frances Strauss, *"Where Did the Justice Go?"*, Gambit Incorporated.
●Michael Tigar and Madeleine Levy, "An Eight-Point Indictment of the Grand Jury System," *Center Report.*
●Charles R. Garry, "Who's An Officer of the Court?" *Trial.*
●Peter Schrag, "The Law-and-Order Issue," *Saturday Review.*
●John Kincaid, "Do Not Probe Your Secret Government," *Sane World.*
●Tom Wicker, "American Justice," *The New York Times.*
●Danny Lyon, *Conversations with the Dead*: Photographs of Prison Life With the Letters and Drawings of Billy McCune #122054, Holt, Rinehart and Winston.
●Bruce Jackson, "Beyond Attica," *Transaction.*
●*Newsweek.*
●Nicholas Horrock, "U.S. Prison System Exemplifies Life in 'Jungle'," *Newsweek* Feature Service.
●Interview with a just-released prison inmate, *New York Times*, Feb. 11, 1970.
●Huey P. Newton, "Prison, Where is the Victory?" *The Black Panther.*
●Bruno St. Jon, "The Terminal Disease," *Los Angeles News Advocate.*
●David McReynolds, *We Have Been Invaded by the 21st Century*, Praeger Publishers.
●Frank J. Donner, "Political Intelligence: Cameras, Informers, and Files," *Civil Liberties Review.*
●Alan Lewis, "First Amendment on Trial," *Argus.*
●"Army Checks on Civilians, Article Claims," *Chicago Sun-Times.*
●AP dispatch.
●*Annals of the Congress of the United States*, 5th Congress, Vol. 2, Gales and Seaton.
●Henry Steele Commager, "Is Freedom Dying in America?" *Look.*
●*Playboy.*
●Theodore Roszak, *The Making of a Counter Culture*: Reflections on the Technocratic Society and Its Youthful Opposition, Anchor Books, Doubleday and Co., Inc.
●John Kenneth Galbraith, *The New Industrial State*, Houghton Mifflin Company.
●Milton Viorst, "Gentlemen Prefer Monopoly," *Harper's Magazine.*
●Mark J. Green, "The High Cost of Monopoly," *The Progressive.*

●Herbert I. Schiller's review of Bryce W. Rucker's *The First Freedom*, *The Nation*.

●*The Progressive*.

●Robert L. Heilbroner, *In the Name of Profit*, Doubleday and Company, Inc.

●Walter J. Hickel, *Who Owns America?* Prentice-Hall, Inc.

●John Fischer, "Nixonomics: Well, You Can't Have Everything," *Harper's Magazine*.

●William K. Stevens, "Detroit in Recession Reflects Fear and Strength," *The New York Times*.

●Paul Hunter, *Needle of Death*, Studio Vista Limited.

●Thomas Ford Hoult, "Exorcism, Middle Class Church Style," *The Christian Century*.

●*Newsweek*.

●Stuart Chase, "Two Cheers for Technology," *Saturday Review*.

●Carl T. Rowan, syndicated columnist.

●Bruce Porter, "Welfare Won't Work, But What Will?" *Saturday Review*.

●Studies in Public Welfare, Paper No. 4, *Income Transfer Programs: How They Tax the Poor*, U.S. Government Printing Office.

●Christopher Jencks, "The Moynihan Report," *New York Review of Books*.

●Crane Brinton, *Anatomy of Revolution*, rev. and enlarged ed., Vintage Books.

●Karl Fleming, " 'We'll Blow Up the World'," *Newsweek*.

●George Jackson, *Blood in My Eye*, Random House, Inc.

●Sidney J. Harris, syndicated columnist.

●Seymour Martin Lipset, "On the Politics of Conscience & Extreme Commitment," *Encounter*.

●Seymour Martin Lipset, *Political Man*: The Social Bases of Politics, Anchor Books, Doubleday and Co., Inc.

●Harvey Cox, "The Riots: No Winners—Only Losers," *Christianity and Crisis*.

●Peter Stone, "Afraid of Revolution?" *New York Times*.

●Colman McCarthy, "Adjusting to the Abnormal," *Newsweek*.